ORION BLUE BOOK

VINTAGE GUITARS
&
COLLECTIBLES
2006

FIRST QUARTER
WINTER EDITION

ORION RESEARCH CORPORATION
14555 N. Scottsdale Rd. Suite 330
Scottsdale, Arizona 85254
voice: 480.951.1114   fax: 480.951.1117
email: sales@orionbluebook.com
web site: www.orionbluebook.com

2006 Winter Edition

Roger Rohrs
Publisher

ORION'S PUBLISHER, ROGER ROHRS

Listed in Who's Who in American Colleges and Universities, Mr. Rohrs graduated from Polytechnic State University in San Luis Obispo, California. He received a B.A. in Business with a concentration in Marketing in 1969. Following graduation, Mr. Rohrs served as an Army officer in Vietnam where he received an Air Combat Medal and Purple Heart.

Mr. Rohrs returned to California to resume his business career with Warehouse Sound Company and a chain of retail stereo stores named Stereo West. These two businesses evolved from a stereo store Mr. Rohrs and two partners had begun during their college years. The annual sales volume of these businesses reached eight million dollars within four years of operation.

The original Orion Blue Book began in 1973 during Mr. Rohrs' ownership of the stereo retail stores. Seeing a need for his salespeople to have a uniform reference for pricing used equipment, Mr. Rohrs compiled the Orion Trade-In Guide. It also served as a training guide for new salespeople who were unfamiliar with product lines and retail pricing.

In 1977, Mr. Rohrs cofounded Nautilus Recordings. Nautilus Recordings became well known as a producer and distributor of audiophile recordings.

In 1979, Mr. Rohrs exchanged his interest in Nautilus Recordings for exclusive ownership of the Orion Trade-In Guide. Since then, he and his wife, Marty Rohrs, who is responsible for Orion's Public Relations have developed this single book into a product line containing eleven separate Blue Books: Audio, Camera, Car Stereo, Computer, Copier, Guitars and Musical Instruments, Gun, Power Tool, Professional Sound, Video and Television, and Vintage Guitar and Collectibles. Marty also developed an integral part of our research-The Board of Advisor Program.

In addition to the above business ventures, Mr. Rohrs has owned restaurants, a retail clothing store, and a graphic arts and printing establishment. He is a licensed California Real Estate Broker and business consultant. In 1995, Mr. Rohrs saw that the Internet was fast becoming the marketplace of the world. Early that year, Orion became Internet certified, and now Mr. Rohrs consults with businesses on providing an Internet presence.

ISBN 0-932089-66-6(ANNUAL)
ISBN 0-932089-50-X (Winter)
ISSN 1056-8581
Copyright © 1990-2006 Orion Research Corporation   **2006 Winter Edition**
First Printing January 2006

CONTENTS

Save $20 on your next Orion Blue Book Purchase.

PROFIT

Accept only those products which will yield a profit margin within a reasonable time in your region. The prices within the Orion Blue Book reflect a national average price that a dealer will be able to obtain within 30 days. Dealers often make more profit on used equipment than on the sale of new equipment. If you over-allow on trade-ins, your ability to resell the product at a profitable price is diminished.

> CAUTION: Fluctuations in the value of the dollar against foreign currencies have an impact on the value of imported equipment. Values are based on the exchange rate of 2005.

REGIONAL PRICING

Evaluate your local or regional demand for certain product lines or even individual products within the line. The values in the Orion Blue Book are based on national averages determined by dealer surveys.

TEST

All equipment should be carefully tested before allowing a trade-in. Scrutinize all mechanical equipment. The color and paint should be original as well as the pickup. It is advisable to play the guitar and listen for good sound quality. You should also check amplifiers for damaged speakers etc.

COSMETIC CONDITION

Consideration of the unit's cosmetic condition is a good indication of the kind of care the unit has received. Scratches and dents would be more reflective of condition than the age of the product. If any items are missing you should deduct a reasonable amount from the determined value. Any modifications will also have an effect on its value.

PRODUCT REQUEST FILE

Keep a current file list of those products not in your used department which customers are requesting. Ask the customer for the price range they are willing to pay. This will help you determine local demand.

DISPLAY

Make the Orion Blue Book accessible to your customers. Some dealers chain the book to the counter. The customer can then determine the used value of the products without taking the salesperson away from another customer.

ADVERTISING   The Orion Blue Book has been used as a promotional tool by many dealers. Advertisements are placed offering 150% of the Orion Blue Book's "average" trade-in value for a specific product line. For example: "this week only, trade in your AMPEG products and receive 150% of the Orion Blue Book's average price."

YOUR STORE NAME

TRADE-IN DAYS
150% TRADE-IN VALUE TOWARDS PURCHASE

Get 150% of the Orion Blue Book used average trade-in value on your Ampeg equipment towards the purchase of Ampeg equipment. Your store reserves the right to inspect and refuse certain trades.

CAUTION: Be sure to qualify which manufacturers' products you want. In failing to specify, you will wind up paying too much for products you don't want and will have trouble reselling them. For this promotion, use quality lines which you carry in your store. It is also advisable to limit your promotion to a specific time period.

Free Radio Time: Radio talk shows always need interesting, knowledgeable guests. Many dealers contact local radio stations and volunteer to be on a talk show. Listeners are invited to call in and find out the value of their used equipment from an expert, the dealer. By using the Blue Books, the dealer can send any of his salespeople to offer this service to the radio listeners, you are not only receiving free advertising, you are demonstrating that you are an expert in your area.

SURVEY PARTICIPATION   Orion has an active dealer survey program. By completing the survey, which is located in the back of the book, you will receive a $20 coupon towards the purchase of an Orion Blue Book.

TYPE	YR	MFG	MODEL	SELL EXC	SELL AVG	BUY EXC	BUY AVG
MIC	57-64	AKG	**C-12 TUBE MULTI-PATTERN**	5685	**4860**	4285	3690
GTAMP	60	FENDER	**CONCERT/4x10"/BRN**	1500	**1290**	1130	975
ELGUIT	62	GIBSON	**SUPER 400 CES/SUNBURST/POINTED CUT**	11370	**9470**	8200	5080
GUITAR	59	MARTIN	**D-28E/FLATTOP/2 PU** SERIAL #165577-171047	3150	**2710**	2375	2045
ELGUIT	59	RICKENBAC	**4000 BASS/AUTUMN GLO**	1830	**1575**	1370	1180
BANJO	11	VEGA	**FAIRBANKS WHYTE LADY #2/OPEN BACK**	1780	**1530**	1340	1155
SYNTH	78-82	YAMAHA	**CS-80 ANALOG**	630	**550**	480	415

TYPE	Category of unit: Banjo, Electric Guitar, Guitar, Guitar Amp, Mandolin, Mandola, Microphone, Power Amplifier, Preamplifier, Receiver, Steel Guitar, Synthesizer, Test Equipment, Tuner, and Ukulele.
YR	Year the unit was released for sale.
MFG	Manufacturer of unit. The full name of each manufacturer appears before each grouping.
MODEL	Identification of product by model number and/or name.
SELL EXC	The selling price if all original parts and in excellent condition.
SELL AVG	The selling price if all original parts and in average condition.
BUY EXC	Price paid to the customer if the unit is in excellent working order and appearance. All original with no modifications.
BUY AVG	Average price paid to the customer for a product. Might show some wear.

SAVE $20.00 ON YOUR NEXT ORDER
FILL OUT THE SURVEY IN THE BACK OF THE BOOK

ANT	ANTIGUA
BDY	BODY
BLK	BLACK
BLND	BLOND
B&S	BACK & SIDES
B&W	BLACK & WHITE
BR/BRN	BROWN
BRD	BURGUNDY
CAB	CABINET
CH	CHANNEL
CHY	CHERRY
CNDY	CANDY
CONCRT	CONCERT
CON	CONTROL
CRE	CREAM
CRLY	CURLY
CUT/CA	CUTAWAY
DAK	DAKOTA
DK	DARK
DBL	DOUBLE
EBO	EBONY
EFFECTS	EFFECTS
ELGUIT	ELECTRIC GUITAR
ES	ELECTRIC SPANISH
FGRBD	FINGERBOARD
FLM	FLAME
GLD	GOLD
GR/GRN	GREEN
GTAMP	GUITAR AMPLIFIER
GUITAR	ACOUSTIC GUITAR
HMBKR	HUMBUCKER
HB	HUMBUCKING
HRDWARE/HDWA	HARDWARE
JEN	JENSEN
MAHG/MHGY	MAHOGANY
MANDOL	MANDOLINS
MANDOLA	MANDOLA
MIC	MICROPHONE
MID	MID-RANGE
MPL	MAPLE
NA/NAT	NATURAL
NK/NCK	NECK
NAR	NARROW
NP	NAMEPLATE
OP-BK	OPEN BACK
PRE	PREAMPLIFIER
PU	PICKUP
PWR	POWER AMPLIFIER
R&W	RED & WHITE
RCV	RECEIVER
REG	REGULATOR
RESON	RESONATOR
REV	REVERB
RND	ROUND
RSWD	ROSEWOOD
SGL	SINGLE
SHLDR	SHOULDER
SG	SOLID GUITAR
SLD	SOLID
SLVR	SILVER
SM	SMALL
SMK	SMOKE
SPKR/SPKRS	SPEAKER
SPRU	SPRUCE
SQ	SQUARE
STDBY	STANDBY
STGUIT	STEEL GUITAR
STRG	STRING
SUBST/SBRST/SB	SUNBURST
SW	SWITCHMASTER
SWTCH	SWITCH
SYNTH	SYNTHESIZER
T	THIN BODY
TBL	TURNTABLE
TH	THIN HOLLOWBODY
TENN	TENNESSEAN
TEST	TEST EQUIPMENT
TNR	TUNER
TRAN	TRANSPARENT
TREM	TREMOLO
TW	TWEED
TX	TOLEX
UKE	UKULELE
UPRIGHT	UPRIGHT BASS
VI/VIB	VIBRATO
WAL	WALNUT
WHT	WHITE

BOARD OF ADVISORS

Orion Research Corporation is proud to introduce our Board of Advisors. During the past year, these Board members have completed an extensive review of data projected for this years edition of the Orion Blue Book. The Board has been a valued addition to the existing Dealer Survey Program in providing the most accurate pricing possible. Our thanks to these board members for sharing their time and expertise.

History of AKG and Neumann Microphone Consultants

Christina Burkhardt
AKG Acoustics
Lembockgasse 21-25
PO Box 158
A-1230
Vienna, Austria

Kevin Madden
AKG Acoustics
1449 Donelson Pike suite #12
Nashville, TN 37217-2640
(615) 360-0499
fax (615) 360-0275

Karl Winkler
Sennheiser / Neumann Electronics
1 Enterprise Drive
Old Lyme, CT 06371
(860) 434-9190
fax (860) 434-9022

Hirsh Gardner
Daddy's Used Gear By Mail
165 Massachusetts Avenue
Boston, MA 02215
(617) 247-0909
email: hag111@aol.com
-Drummer with MCA, Electra Recording Artist "New England".
-Record Producer: winner of the "Boston-Phoenix Best Poll" producer of the year.
-Sales Rep Daddy's since 1990, winner of "Used Gear Salesman of The Year" award 1992-1996
-Employee of the The Year 1992

Combining his expert knowledge of vintage recording equipment studio gear, his years of recording and touring experience, five years of being the top salesman at Daddy's Junky Music, Hirsh brings a wealth of knowledge and experience to his customers.

Daddy's has 19 retail stores and is celebrating its 30th anniversary this year.

Mario Campa
Toys From The Attic
203 Mamaroneck Ave.
White Plains, NY 10601
voice: 914.421.0069
fax: 914.328.3852
email: info@tfta.com
url: www.tfta.com

John and Mario first met in college in 1981 in front of a stereo. Their mutual love of guitar and music secured what has been a long standing friendship which in 1995 developed into a business known as **Toys From The Attic**. Their unique and diverse approach, half of the business specializing in high-end musical instruments and the other half high-end audio, has been very well received. It truly shows their love and dedication to music. Their strict grading policies and dedication to customer satisfaction have been their keys to success.

Both sides of the business specialize in pre-owned gear, as well as several new lines specially selected for their extraordinary quality and value. All pre-owned items are tested and serviced when necessary. High quality repair services remains another of their specialities.

Every item is sold with a money back guarantee and their showroom is a must see when traveling in the Northeast.

They are members of the Academy for the Advancement of High-End Audio and the Mail Order Merchants Association.

Clay Harrel
url: clay.by.net
email: hag111@adl.com
Clay is a private guitar collector. He buys guitars made from 1920 to 1970 by Gibson, Fender, Martin, Gretsch, Epiphone, National, Dobro, and Rickenbacker.

Fletcher
Mercenary Audio
131 Morse St.
Foxboro, MA 02035
(508) 543-0069
fax (508) 543-9670
url: www.mecenary.com
Fletcher, as he is known in the industry, brings 24 years of professional audio experience to **Mercenary Audio**. Starting in 1973, as a live sound mixer for local New York bands, Fletcher combined his technical and business abilities by opening a sound reinforcement company in 1975. Fletcher is a graduate of Emerson College with a BS degree in Mass Communications.

His hands on live audio and recording experience ranges from several years as a program producer for radio stations WLIR in New York, WERS and WCOZ in Boston, to national tours with nationally known recording artists. Fletcher also has practical business experience in the industry, having been the studio manager for World Class Studio for Normandy Sound.

Since the opening of **Mercenary Audio** in 1989, Fletcher has continued to work as a recording engineer/producer on current projects with artists such as Benn Orr of the Cars, Peter Wolf of the J. Geils Band, and local artist Black Number Line. He feels it is vitally important that he and his staff continue in the recording field, in order to keep abreast of the technology and intelligently share this information with Mercenary's clients. This is the key to keeping Mercenary separate and above its competitors.

Tim Becker
Martin Music
910 N. 21st Street
Newark, OH 43055
(740) 366-2344
fax (740) 366-2345
Tim is the owner of **Martin Music**, founded in 1948. He was a 15 year employee of Coyle Music. As a clarinet, guitar and sax player he collects band instruments, especially clarinets.

Tim is also a Music Business Historian and Member of A.M.I.S.; he is a professional appraisor and buyer of guitars, pianos, and band instruments.

HISTORY OF VINTAGE AKG MICROPHONES

Courtesy of Christina Burkhardt
AKG – Vienna, Austria

1946   AKG DYN Series – including Dyn 60, Dyn 60G, Dyn 60K, Dyn 60K-Studio, etc. All parts are hand made. Annual output 500 to 600 units.

1947   First AKG condenser Tube Microphone. The capsule is a predecessor of the CK12. The diaphragm is made from Styroflex foil, gold sputtered by Goerz.

1950   AKG starts designing the world's first high quality dynamic microphone, the D12 with its "mass-loaded tube".

1951   Dual-diaphragm microphone is developed and called the "C2". About 500 units are made.

1953   Breakthrough of the D12, a large-diaphragm mic that not only provides the first true cardioid polar pattern but introduces engineering innovations such as the mass-loaded tube and "deep-drawn" diaphragm. Film sound engineers too praise the directivity and remarkable low susceptibility to wind noise. The same year also sees the birth of another legendary AKG product: the C12, the first remote controlled multipattern capacitor microphone. The C12 was originally made in runs of 50 units per month and became an international best-seller.

1954   Under water loudspeakers and microphones (Dyn 120 UWS) are developed, the latter derived from the Dyn 60K. The specifications are impressive: Watertight down to 330 ft. at a diving rate of 25 ft./minute: frequency range 30 to 20,000 Hz; sensitivity 0.2 M/Ybar; seawater-proof, chrome plated brass case; weight 15 lbs.; size: 9.8 x 5.5 dia. in. The total output of 20 units was sold to scientists and port authorities. Hans Hass uses a Dyn 120 UWS in shooting his first underwater sound movie, "Abenteuer im Roten Meer" (Adventures in the Red Sea) which won first prize at the "Biennale" biannual film festival at Venice, Italy.

1955   The first postwar Salzburg Festival uses AKG microphones. A unidirectional microphone is specifically designed for Herbert von Karajan. Unlike in his later years, Karajan rejected all audio equipment. When he conducted a performance, he allowed no microphones to be visible to the audience. So AKG had to design a special shotgun microphone that could be set up far from the musicians, in the wings or in the orchestra pit.
D36: The world's first dynamic microphone with remotely selectable polar patterns.
C28: A small-diaphragm condenser microphone.

1956   D11: Unidirectional dynamic microphone for amateur tape recordists.
Introduction of professional cardioid microphones with adjustable rear sound entries for reduced proximity effect. (D24, D19)
Introduction of the Dyn 200 Series of dynamic microphones including gooseneck models and M410, M411 OEM microphones for Telefunken. The east bloc business grows significantly.

1957   The "sheet metal capsule", a dynamic capsule in a tight sheet-metal case, is developed and used over the following years in many AKG microphones including the D9, D11, and D14 as well as OEM microphones for Saba, Korting, Telefunken, Stuzzi, and Eumig.

1958   D15: First dynamic reporters' microphone with a tight unidirectional pattern.
D25: Shock mounted, unidirectional dynamic microphone for use on a fishpole in radio, TV, and film work.
D30: First dynamic studio microphone with four selectable polar patterns.

1959   D45—as D30, except with shock mount and remotely selectable polar patterns.

1960   AKG designs and manufactures for Telefunken, the ELA M250 and ELA M251, two extremely rare thus much sought-after collector's items.
Rerun of the C12 and several other versions for Telefunken and Siemens using the then advanced GE 6072 double triode.
Design of the first professional small-diaphragm condenser microphone with miniature tube (Nuvistor), the AKG C60.

HISTORY OF VINTAGE AKG MICROPHONES
continued

1960/61   The c26 and c30 capacitor microphones are developed further into the c60 with Nuvistor miniature tube (the name is derived from "nueva vista" – a new vision).

1962   A v-shaped dual microphone for interviewing (ENG) use is built and later continued by another company that even applies for a patent assigned by one Mr. Hagopian.
The C12A Nuvistor condenser microphone is developed as a predecessor of today's C414.

1963   The DX11 reverb microphone is a innovative idea which, however, is not accepted by the market. This is one of the few flops in AKG's history of success.

1964   The "CMS" modular capacitor microphone system with the C451 with FET preamp and CK1, CK2, etc. is developed and later becomes famous all over the world. After initial problems have been solved, it strengthens AKG's monopoly with BBX. The capsules originally had embossed metal diaphragms that were susceptible to humidity and therefore later replaced with plastic diaphragms.

1970   The C412, a solid-state version of the C12A with three polar patterns and a preattenuation pad selectable on the microphone is designed.

1971   A high quality electret capsule for use in a new, professional small cassette recorder from UHER is developed (OEM order).
The C412 is further improved and renamed C414.

1972   The C24 is relaunched as the C24-cb large-diaphragm stereo capacitor microphone with separately, remotely selectable polar patterns for each channel.

1973   The first production runs of electret microphones are made.
The first AKG dummy head microphone, made by AKG Munich, is used for head related stereo (binaural) recording.

1975   The D140 is a small, top quality dynamic studio microphone with virtually no competition at the time.

1977   C414 EB: First C414 version with improved circuitry and integrated XLR connector.
The C303 line level microphone with built-in compressor and headphone monitor amplifier for the newly created ORF regional TV stations is designed and made in small runs
The C414 is retouched again, specifically the housing, and fitted with an XLR connector. The designation is changed to C414EB.

1978   The first true vocal microphone line is developed. Originally planned as "Alpha", "Beta", and "Gamma", they are later renamed D310, D320, and D330. The first endorsement contracts are concluded with Jon Hiseman, Roger Whittaker, and other artists.

1979   C422 eb: Large diaphragm stereo condenser microphone with advanced solid-state electronics.

1983   New CMS system comprising a C460 electronic preamp and CK61, CK62, and CK63 capsules also includes remote capsules CK1X, CK2X that can be connected to the preamp with cables up to 200 ft. long.
The AKG Tube: Black market prices for C12 microphones skyrocket. Responding to the market situation, AKG makes the first rerun of a large-diaphragm tube microphone using the same 6072 tube as the original C12.

HISTORY OF VINTAGE NEUMANN MICROPHONES

Courtesy of Karl Winkler, Neumann, USA

U 47 (Large diaphragm tube mic made from 1949 through 1965. Features two polar patterns – cardioid and omni. Uses VF14 tube.)

M 49 (Large diaphragm tube mic made from 1951 through 1974. Features remote controlled variable polar patterns. Uses AC701k tube.)

M 50 (Small diaphragm tube mic made from 1951 through 1971. Omni polar pattern only with capsule mounted in sphere. Uses AC701k tube.)

KM 53 (Small diaphragm tube mic made from 1953 through 1968. Omni polar pattern only. Uses AC701k tube.)

KM 54 (Small diaphragm tube mic made from 1953 through 1969. Cardioid polar pattern only. Uses AC701k tube.)

KM 56 (Small diaphragm tube mic made from 1955 through 1970. Three polar patterns – omni, cardioid and figure 8. Uses AC701k tube.)

U 48 (Large diaphragm tube mic made from 1957 through 1965. Features two polar patterns – figure 8 and omni. Uses VF14 tube.)

SM 2 (Small diaphragm stereo tube mic made from 1957 through 1966. Features remote polar pattern control. Uses two AC701k tubes.)

KM 253 (Small diaphragm tube mic made from 1960 through 1967. Omni polar pattern only, connectors with high RF immunity for broadcast environment. Uses AC701k tube.)

KM 253 (Small diaphragm tube mic made from 1960 through 1969. Cardioid polar pattern only, connectors with high RF immunity for broadcast environment. Uses AC701k tube.)

U 67 (Large diaphragm tube mic made from 1960 through 1971 with "revival issue" of 400 units in 1992. Features three polar patterns – cardioid, omni and figure 8 high pass filter and 14-dB pad. Uses EF86 tube.)

M 249 (Large diaphragm tube mic made from 1960 through 1969. Features remote controlled variable polar patterns and connectors with high immunity to RF for broadcast environment. Uses AC701k tube.)

M 250 (Small diaphragm tube mic made from 1960 through 1969. Omni polar pattern only with capsule mounted in sphere; utilizes connectors with high immunity to RF for broadcast environment. Uses AC701k tube.)

KM 256 (Small diaphragm tube mic made from 1961 through 1970. Features three polar patterns – cardioid, omni and figure 8. Connectors with high immunity to RF used for broadcast environment. Uses AC701k tube.)

SM 23 (Small diaphragm stereo tube mic made from 1961 through 1966. Features remote polar pattern control. Uses two AC701k tubes.)

M 269 (Large diaphragm tube mic made from 1962 through 1973. Features three polar patterns – cardioid, omni and figure 8, high pass filter and 14-dB pad. Uses AC701k tube to be compatible with broadcast facility power supplies.)

SM 69 (Large diaphragm stereo tube mic made from 1964 through 1973. Features remote control of polar patterns. Uses two AC701k tubes.)

HISTORY OF VINTAGE NEUMANN MICROPHONES

continued

KM 63   (Small diaphragm tube mic made from 1964 through 1971. Omni polar pattern only. Uses AC701k tube.)

KM 64   (Small diaphragm tube mic made from 1964 through 1971. Cardioid polar pattern only. Uses AC701 tube.)

KM 65   (Small diaphragm tube mic made from 1964 through 1971. Cardioid polar pattern only with bass rolloff. Uses AC701k tube.)

U 64   (Small diaphragm tube mic made from 1964 through 1971. Cardioid polar pattern only. Uses 7586 nuvistor.)

KM 66   (Small diaphragm tube mic made in 1966 only. Three polar patterns – omni, cardioid, figure 8. Uses AC701k tube.)

KM 83   (Small diaphragm FET mic made from 1966 through 1988. Omni polar pattern only. Phantom 48V powered.)

KM 84   (Small diaphragm FET mic made from 1966 through 1988. Cardioid polar pattern only. Phantom 48V powered.)

KM 85   (Small diaphragm FET mic made from 1966 through 1988. Cardioid polar pattern with bass rolloff. Phantom 48V powered.)

U 87   (Large diaphragm FET mic made from 1967 through 1986. Three polar patterns – cardioid, omni and figure 8. Phantom 48V powered plus optional internal battery.)

KM 86   (Small diaphragm FET mic made from 1968 through 1986. Three polar patterns – cardioid, omni and figure 8 plus high pass filter and pad switch. Phantom 48V powered.)

U 47   (Large diaphragm FET mic made from 1969 through 1986. Cardioid polar pattern only. Includes high pass filter and pad switch. Phantom 48v powered.)

KM 88   (Small diaphragm FET mic made from 1968 through 1986. Three polar patterns - cardioid, omni and figure 8 plus high pass filter and pad switch. Phantom 48V powered.)

SM 69   (Large diaphragm stereo mic made from 1969 through present. Features remote control of polar patterns. Requires external pattern switch/power supply unit.)

KMS 85   (Small diaphragm vocalist mic made from 1971 to ?? [probably mid 1970s]. Cardioid pattern only. Phantom 48V powered.)

KU 80   (Artificial head mic made from 1973 to ?? [probably late 1970s]. Two omni microphones installed in simulated ears. Phantom 48V powered.)

A Few Words About Vintage Guitars
by Clay Harrell

What is a Vintage Guitar?

"Vintage" is a term that has acquired a new meaning apart from its original usage. The term is a combination of Vint (of the vine) and Age (time of creation). This term is used in the wine industry to indicate a wine's harvest date. The use of "vintage" has been modified by collectors to mean old, such as a "vintage car" or "vintage clothing". This extension of the meaning is used in guitar terminology to mean "an original, older guitar."

The most collectible guitars are those made from the mid 1920's to 1969. Guitars made prior to the mid 1920's are generally too primitive in design to have collectible value (of course there are some exceptions, but 99% of the time this holds true). Guitars after 1969, even though they may be over 25 years old, generally have no collectibility. All the major guitar manufacturers were in dire straits during the 1970's. They were either bought out by larger conglomerates looking to make guitars as quickly as possible, and/or their quality and choice of materials had become substandard.

Many people ask if their new guitar will be valuable in the future. Frankly, no one knows. But my off-the-cuff response would be, "no". The materials, environment and society of pre-1970 was much different, thus producing different instruments which I feel can not be duplicated today. However all the major guitar manufacturers are certainly trying to recapture the past with their "vintage reissue" guitars. But just remember, when you are buying a new guitar and the dealer says, "you know some day this will be a very collectible guitar", don't believe it. He doesn't have a crystal ball.

What makes a guitar collectible/valuable?

As with baseball cards, Barbie dolls, and other collectibles, condition is very important. Instruments in "mint" condition are always worth more than instruments in excellent condition. Also, we need to explain the term "mint", as it is constantly misrepresented. "Mint" means in the same condition as if you purchased the item new today. There is no such thing as "mint for its age". Either an item is mint (brand new condition) or it's not.

Guitars must also meet several other criteria to be collectible. One of the most important aspects is originality. Any modifications, replaced parts or repairs, no matter how practical, will decrease the value of an instrument. Even replacing the original case or re-fretting the guitar (the equivalent to replacing a car's tires) will decrease its value. Originality is even more important to a guitar's collectibility than condition. For example, a "beat-up" original finish guitar will always be worth more than a perfectly refinished one. Even if the new finish is done professionally and looks perfect, it will be worth approximately half the price of an original finish guitar or maybe even less.

Another thing that effects value is demand. The Fender electric mandolin, although very rare, is not worth very much. The reason is demand, or "who wants it?". If the instrument has limited popularity, for whatever reason, it will appeal to a limited crowd. Hence, it will not be worth as much as a popular instrument that has greater demand.

To some extent, rarity has only limited connection to value. For example, the Fender Telecaster is collectible and valuable, even though Fender made tens of thousands of them from 1950 to 1965 (Fender's most collectible era). The reason again is demand. Although the Telecaster is not rare compared to their electric mandolin, it is a very popular guitar today (the key word here is **today**). Hence, it is worth considerably more than the electric mandolin since it appeals to more people.

To summarize, for an instrument to be valuable there must be:
>   -Originality (stock, unmodified, no repairs).
>   -Condition. The better the condition, the more valuable it is.
>   -Demand for the model and year.

Without the above three items you merely have a used guitar, not a vintage guitar.

Clay Harrell is a private guitar collector. He buys guitars made from 1920 to 1970 by Gibson, Fender, Martin, Gretsch, Epiphone, National, Dobro, and Rickenbacker. His Internet web site is **http://clay.by.net**. He can be reached by e-mail at **harrelc@aa.wl.com**

ALEMBIC, INC.
3005 WILJAN COURT
SANTA ROSA, CA 95407-5702
(707) 523-2611
Fax (707) 523-2935

ALTEC LANSING
C/O ELECTRO-VOICE
BURNSVILLE, MN 55337
(952) 884-4051
Fax (952) 884-0043

AMPEG
SEE ST. LOUIS MUSIC INC.

DOBRO
SEE GIBSON GUITAR CORP.

D'AQUISTO
20 E. INDUSTRY CT.
DEER PARK, NY 11729
(516)586-4426
Fax (516)586-4472

EPIPHONE COMPANY
645 MASSMAN DR.
NASHVILLE, TN 37210
(615) 871-4500
Fax (615) 872-7768

FENDER MUSICAL INST.
8860 E. CHAPARREL RD. STE 100
SCOTTSDALE, AZ 85250
(480)596-9690
Fax (480) 596-1384

GIBSON GUITAR CORP.
309 PLUS PARK BLVD.
NASHVILLE, TN 37217
(615) 871-4500
Fax (615) 884-7219

GOYA
SEE MARTIN GUITAR CO.

GRETSCH
P.O. BOX 2468
SAVANNAH, GA 31402
(912) 748-7070
Fax (912) 748-6005

GUILD MUSIC CORP.
SEE FENDER MUSICAL INST.

HIWATT AMPLIFICATION
8163 LANKERSHIM BLVD.
NORTH HOLLYWOOD, CA 91605
(818) 764-8383
Fax (818) 764-0080

HOFNER
SEE THE MUSIC GROUP

IBANEZ
1726 WINCHESTER RD
BENSALEM, PA 19020
(215) 638-8670
Fax (215) 245-8583

KAY GUITAR COMPANY
C/O ASIAN-AMER. MFG.
17091 DAILMLER ST
IRVINE, CA 92614
(949) 752-0050
Fax (949) 752-0056

MARANTZ AMERICA, INC.
1100 MAPLEWOOD DRIVE
ITASCA, IL 60143
(630) 741-0300
Fax (630) 741-0301

MARSHALL AMPS
316 SERVICE RD.
MELVILLE, NY 11747

MARTIN GUITAR CO.
P.O. BOX 329
NAZARETH, PA 18064
(610) 759-2837
Fax (610) 759-5757

McINTOSH LAB., INC.
2 CHAMBERS STREET
BINGHAMTON, NY 13903-2699
(307) 723-3512
Fax (607) 724-0549

MUSICMAN/ERNIE BALL
151 SUBURBAN ROAD
SAN LOUIS OBISPO, CA 93401
(800) 544-7726
Fax (805) 544-7275

NATIONAL RESO-PHONIC GUITARS
871 C VIA ESTEBAN
SAN LUIS OBISPO, CA. 93401
(805) 546-8442
Fax (805) 546-8430

OVATION INSTRUMENTS
C/O KAMAN MUSIC CORP.
20 OLD WINDSOR ROAD
BLOOMFIELD, CT 06002-0507
(860) 509-8888
Fax (860) 509-8890

RAMIREZ
C/O DAVID PERRY GUITAR IMPORTS
PO BOX 188
LEESBURG, VA 20175
(800) 593-1331
Fax (703) 771-8170

RECORDING KING
SEE GIBSON GUITAR CORP

B.C. RICH INT'L, INC.
4940 DELHI PIKE
CINCINNATI, OH 45238
(513) 451-5000
Fax (513) 347-2298

RCA
10330 N. MERIDIAN STREET
INDIANAPOLIS, IN 46290
(317) 587-4832

RICKENBACKER INT'L
3895 S. MAIN STREET
SANTA ANA, CA 92707-5710
(714) 545-5574
Fax (714) 754-0135

ROLAND
5100 S. EASTERN AVENUE
LOS ANGELES, CA 90040
(323) 890-3700
Fax (323) 890-3701

SENNHEISER ELECTRONICS CORP.
1 ENTERPRISE DRIVE
OLD LYME, CT 06371
(860) 434-9190
Fax (860) 434-1759

ST. LOUIS MUSIC, INC.
1400 FERGUSON AVE.
ST. LOUIS, MO 63133
(314) 727-4512
Fax (314) 727-8929

THE MUSIC GROUP
10949 PENDLETON STREET
SUN VALLEY, CA 91352
(818) 252-6305
Fax (818) 252-6351

VOX AMPLIFIERS
316 S. SERVICE RD.
MELVILLE, NY 11747
(516) 333-9100

WASHBURN INT'L
444 E. COURTLAND ST
MUNDELEIN, IL 60060
(847) 949-0444
Fax (847) 949-8444

YAMAHA CORP OF AMER.
6600 ORANGETHORPE AVE.
BUENA PARK, CA 90620
(714) 522-9011

2006 ORDER FORM
ORION BLUE BOOKS

	TOTAL

2006 AUDIO

70,321 products from over 1,400 manufacturers. Hardbound, listing the following: Cassettes, 4&8-track Cartridges, CD players, Digital Audio Tape Players, Equalizers, Integrated and Power Amplifiers, Preamplifiers, Speakers, Receivers, Reel-to-Reels, Signal Processors, Systems, Turntables, and more. ....**$225 per book** _____

2006 CAMERA

24,983 products from over 400 manufacturers. Hardbound, listing the following: 35mm Cameras, Medium Format, Press View, Instamatic, Disk, TLR & Self Processing Cameras, Lenses, Back, Bellows, Viewfinders, Enlargers, Exposure Meters, Slide Projectors & Viewers, Movie Cameras, Projectors, and more. ....**$155 per book** _____

2006 CAR STEREO

49,488 products from over 200 manufacturers. Hardbound, listing the following: Cassette Receivers, CD Players, Digital Audio Tape Players, Equalizers, Power Amplifiers, Speakers, and more. ....**$155 per book** _____

2006 COMPUTER (Quarterly)

63,553 hardware products from over 1000 manufacturers. Hardbound, listing the following: Systems, Fax Machines, Monitors, Printers, Plotters, Scanners, Modems, Disk Drives, Tape Backups, Terminals, and more. ....**$155 per book** _____
....**$620 annual subscription** _____

2006 COPIER

3,852 Copiers, Typewriters and Duplicators are listed in this softbound volume. ....**$59 per book** _____

2006 GUITARS & MUSICAL INSTRUMENTS

82,834 products from over 450 manufacturers. Hardbound, listing the following: Guitars, Guitar Amps, Tuners, Drums, Cymbals, Banjos, Brass Winds, Wood Winds, Cellos, Harps, Dulcimers, Keyboards, Keyboard Amps, Mandolins, Marimbas, Synthesizers, Violins, Xylophones, and more.**$225 per book** _____

	TOTAL

24th Issue GUN & SCOPES

19,543 products from over 300 manufacturers. Softbound, listing the following: Handguns, Rifles, Shotguns, and Black Powder Firearms. ....**$45 per book** _____

2006 POWER TOOL (APRIL)

20,134 products from over 120 manufacturers. Hardbound, listing the following: Compressors, Pumps, Generators, Saws, including Circular, Reciprocal, Sabre, etc., Power Screwdrivers, Demolition Tools, Planers, Chisels, Scalers, Boring Drills, Nailers, and more. ....**$94 per book** _____

2006 PROFESSIONAL SOUND

51,964 products from over 350 manufacturers. Hardbound, listing the following: Monitors, MIDIs, Microphones, Equalizers, Enclosures, Mixers, Reel-to-Reels, Signal Processors, Wireless Systems, Crossover networks, Integrated and Power Amplifiers, Raw Speaker Components, PA Systems, and more. ....**$155 per book** _____

2006 VIDEO & TELEVISION

45,210 products from over 200 manufacturers. Hardbound, listing the following: TVs, VCRs, Camcorders, Laser Videodisc Players, B&W Cameras, Color Video Cameras, Broadcast Cameras, Electronic Still Video Cameras, Lenses, Umatic Recorder/Players, electronic games, more. **$155 per book** _____

2006 VINTAGE GUITARS & COLLECTIBLES (Quarterly)

11,513 Vintage Guitars listed in this quarterly hardbound volume. Also available on an annual subscription of 4 issues. ....**$54 per book** _____
....**$216 annual subscription** _____

CALL FOR CD PRICES

☐ **BOOK**   ☐ **WEB**

Name: _____   Method of Payment: ☐ Enclosed check   ☐ C.O.D.   ☐ Credit Card

Shipping Address (no P.O. Boxes): Street _____

City _____   State _____   Zip _____   Phone _____

If paying by Credit Card: ☐ American Express   ☐ Discover   ☐ Mastercard   ☐ Visa

Name on Card: _____   Card Number: _____

Expiration Date: _____   Signature: _____

SATISFACTION GUARANTEED

You will receive a full refund (less shipping) if the Orion Blue Book is returned within 20 days.

Orion Research Corporation

14555 N. Scottsdale Rd. #330
Scottsdale, AZ 85254-3487
voice: (480) 951-1114 fax: (480) 951-1117
email: sales@orionbluebook.com

ORDER HOTLINE
1-800-844-0759

FAX HOTLINE
1-800-375-1315

Subtotal _____
Less Survey Discount _____
Sales Tax (7.2% Arizona only) _____
Shipping & Handling (**$10.00 per book**) _____
COD (USA ONLY) $7.50 per order _____
Total _____

DATING YOUR GUITAR

Date your guitar! That's right, find out when your guitar was made.

ALEMBIC

The first 2 numbers of the serial number correspond to the year it was built. There may also be present a letter code designating a certain model. The latter digits indicate the individual instrument and its place in production.

AMERICAN ARCHTOPS

The digits after the dash in the serial number are the year that the guitar was made in.

TOM ANDERSON

The neck plate of each guitar has the date it was completed along with the letters A,N or P which stands for a.m., noon or p.m.

ARPEGGIO KORINA

The first 2 numbers (they will have a space between them) are the year of manufacture, then a 0, then the production number for that year.

BENEDETTO

Benedetto archtops have a 4 or 5 digit serial number ..the last 2 digits in the # are the year in which the instrument was made .. the digits in front of the last 2 are the instruments place in production...

G. S. BRANDT

The year is on the label inside of the guitar - you can also use a mirror to read the inside of the top of the guitar which is signed and dated...

BREEDLOVE

On the label, inside of the guitar - the first two numbers of the serial number is the year the instrument was made.

BUSCARINO

The last two digits of the serial number is the year in which the guitar was made in.

M. CAMPELLONE

The first three digits of the serial number are the sequence of production - the next two are the month - the last two are the year in which the guitar was made.

CARVIN

From 1964 thru 1968 Carvin Guitars DO NOT HAVE serial numbers...then in 1970 they started off with number 5000...

Year Serial #
1970 5000
1980-1983 11,000 - 13,000
1983-1984 13,001 - 15,000
1985-1986 17,000 - 20,000
1988-1989 22,000 - 25,000
1989-1991 26,000 - 33,000
1992-???? 35,000- ????

CITRON

The first two digits of the serial number is the month in which the guitar was made...the second two digits are the year in which the guitar was made.

COLLINGS

The date is on the label on the inside of the guitar.

COMINS

The date is on the label on the inside of the guitar.

CHARLES COTE' BASSES

Before 1995 Charles Cote' Basses Do Not Have Serial Numbers...starting in 1995 each bass has a 5 digit serial # ..the first 2 #'s are the year in which it was manufactured .. the last three #'s are the sequence in manufacturing of that year.

DANELECTRO

Most Danelectro serial #'s have 4 digits .. the first 2 are the week of completion. The last digit is the year.

D'ANGELICO

John D'Angelico built 1,164 guitars, all by hand .. the first few had no serial #'s.

Year - Serial #

1932- 1005-1097	1934	1936- 1105-1235	1937 - 1234-1317
1938 - 1318-1385	1939 - 1388-1456	1940 - 1457-1508	1941 - 1509-1562
1942 – 1563-1621	1943 – 1922-1658	1944 – 1659-1681	1945 – 1982-1702
1946 – 1703-1740	1947 – 1738-1781	1948 – 1782-1804	1949 – 1805-1831
1950 – 1832-1855	1951 – 1886-1908	1952 – 1886-1908	1953 – 1909-1936
1954 – 1933-1962	1955 – 1989-2017	1956 – 1989-2017	1957 – 2018-2040
1958 – 2041-2067	1959 – 2068-2098	1960 – 2099-2122	1961-64 – 2123-2164
1965-66 – 2212-2214			

D'AQUISTO

Year - Serial #

1965 - 1001-1005	1966 - 1006-1014	1967 - 1015-1022	1968 - 1023-1029
1969 - 1030-1036	1970 - 1037-1043	1971 - 1044-1050	1972 - 1051-1063
1973 - 1064-1073	1974 - 1074-1084	1975 - 1085-1094	1976 - 1095-1102
1977 - 1103-1112	1978 - 1113-1125	1979 - 1126-1133	1980 - 1134-1142
1981 - 1143-1151	1982 - 1152-1160	1983 - 1161-1164	1984 - 1166-1175
1985 - 1176-1183	1986 - 1185-1192	1987 - 1193-1202	1988 - 1201-1210
1989 - 1211-1217	1990 - 1218-1228		

DEAN

Dean guitars made in the USA have a 7 digit serial number .. the first 2 numbers are the year of manufacture ..the remaining numbers are the production numbers. ..this does not apply to Dean imported guitars (no year in the serial number..consult an expert or call Dean for the year of manufacture).

DOBRO / REGAL

Year - Serial #
1928 - 900-1700
1929 - 1800-2000
1930-1931 - 3000
1932-1933 - 5000-5500
1934-1936 - 5700-7600
1937 - 8000-9000

B prefix on most 1931-1932 Cyclops models. Regal (OMI - 1970 on) .. 1970-1979 "D" or "B" followed by 3 or 4 digits (ranking) & last number (year) .. "B" = Metal .. "D"= Wood

1980-1987 the number before the letter is the year. 1988 on the last 2 numbers are the year.

EISELE

Get a mirror and look at the underside of the top of the guitar for the date.

ENGLISH

The date is on the label on the inside of the guitar.

EPIPHONE

Epiphone started in 1928 making banjos and was family owned for years .. then it was sold to C.G.Conn company .. then back to the original family .. then were made by Gibson Guitar ...and were American made until approx. 1970 ..then production was moved to Japan and later Korea.

Year - Serial #

1930-1932 - 10,000 series	1932 - 5000	1933 - 6000	1934 - 7000
1935 - 8000-9000	1936 - 10,000	1937 - 11,000	1938 - 12,000
1939-1940 - 13,000	1941-1942 - 14,000	1943 - 18,000	1944 - 19,000; 51,000-52,000
1945 - 52,000-54,000	1946 - 54,000-55,000	1947 - 56,000	1948 - 57,000
1949 - 58,000	1950 - 59,000	1951 and some 1930's - 60,000-63,000	1952 - 64,000
1953 - 64,000-66,000	1954 - 68,000	1955-1957 - 69,000	

EPIPHONE MADE BY GIBSON 1958-1961

Year - Serial #
1958 - A-1000
1959 - A-2000
1960-1961 - A3000/A4000

FENDER

Year - Serial #

1950-1954 - Up to 6,000	1954-1956 - Up to 10,000- 4 or 5 digits (inc 0 or – prefix)	1955-1956 - 10,000 -" " " "	1957 - 10,000-20,000-5 or 6 digits (inc 0 or – prefix)
1958 - 20,000-30,000 -" "	1959 - 30,000-40,000	1960 - 40,000-50,000	1961 - 50.000-70,000
1962 - 60,000-90,000	1963 - 80,000-90,000	1963 - Up to L10,000 L + 5 digits...(beginning of the infamous "L" Series)	1963 - L10,000-L20,000
1964 - L20,000-L50,000	1965 - L50,000-L90,000	1965 - 100,000	1966-1967 - 100,000- 200,000
1968 - 200,000	1969-1970 - 200,000- 300,000	1971-1972 - 300,000	1973 - 300,000-500,000
1974-1975 - 400,000-500,000	1976 - 500,000-700,000	1976 - 76 or S6 + 5 digits	1977 - S7 or S8 + 5 digits
1978 - S7, S8 or S9 + 5 digits	1979 - S9 or E0 + 5 digits	1980-1981 - S9, E0 or E1 + 5 digits	1982 - E1,E2 or E3 + 5 digits
1983 - E2 or E3 + 5 digits	1984 - E3 or E4 + 5 digits	1987 - E4 + 5 digits	1988 - E4 or E8 + 5 digits
1989 - E4 or E8 + 5 digits	1990 - E8 or N9 + 5 digits	1990 - N0 + 5 digits	1991 - N1 + 5/6 digits
1992 - N2 + 5/6 digits			

FROGGY BOTTOM

The month and year that the guitar was made will be on the label on the inside of the guitar.

G & L

"G" is for Guitar..."B" is for Bass..."BC" is for Broadcaster.

Year - Serial #

1980 - G000530 -B000518	1981 - G003122 -B001917
1982 - G009886 -B008525	1983 - G011654 -B010382
1984 - G013272 -B014266	1985 - G014690 -B016018
1986 - G017325 -B017691	1987 - G020241 -B018063
1988 - G023725 -B019627	1989 - G024983 -B020106
1990 - G026344 -B021788	1991 - G027163 -B023013
1992 - G029962 -B024288	

GIBSON

Year - Serial #

1903 - 1500	1904 - 2500	1905 - 3500	1906 - 5500
1907 - 8300	1908 - 9700	1909 - 10,100	1910 - 10,600
1911 - 10,850	1912 - 13,350	1913 - 16,100	1914 - 20,150
1915 - 25,150	1916 - 32,000	1917 - 39,500	1918 - 47,900
1919 - 53,800	1920 - 63,650	1921 - 69,300	1922 - 71,400
1923 - 74,900	1924 - 81,200	1925 - 82,700	1926 - 83,600
1927 - 85,400	1928 - 87,300	1929 - 89,750	1930 - 90,200
1931 - 90,450	1932 - 90,700	1933 - 91,400	1934 - 92,300
1935 - 92,800	1936 - 94,100	1937 - 95,200	1938 - 95,750
1939 - 96,050	1940 - 96,600	1941 - 97,400	1942 - 97,700
1943 - 97,850	1944 - 98,250	1945 - 98,650	1946 - 99,300
1947 - 99,999			

(A-Series from 1947-1961)

Year - Serial #

1947 - A1304	1948 - A2665
1949 - A4413	1950 - A6597
1951 - A9419	1952 - A12,462
1953 - A16,101	1954 - A18,667
1955 - A21,909	1956 - A24,755
1957 - A26,819	1958 - A28,880
1959 - A32,284	1960 - A35,645
1961 - A36,147	

EPIPHONE A-SERIES ..1958-1961 (see section of the Dating Service)

Year - Serial #
1958 - A1000
1959 - A2000
1960-1961 - A3000-A4222

GIBSON-SERIAL #'s 1961-1969...(various models)

Year - Serial #

1961 - 100-42,440	1962 - 42,441-61,180
1963 - 61,450-64,222	1964 - 64,240-70,501
1962 - 71,180-96,600	1963 - 96,601-99,999
1967 - 000001-099999	1963-1967 -100,000-106,099
1963 - 106,100-106,899	1963-1967 -109,000-1,099,999
1963 - 110,000-111,549	1963-1967 - 111,550-115,799
1963 - 115,800-118,299	1963-1967 - 118,300-120,999
1963 - 121,000-139,999	

Gibsons 1960-1975 serial numbers overlap depending on the various models ..it is best to contact an expert or
Gibson with the model, color and serial # for accurate dating .. a
simi-coherent serial# system returns in 1975 but still has a lot of overlapping depending
on the year and the model.

GIBSON SERIAL NUMBERS 1975-1977... (1975 still has many overlaps)

Year - Serial # Prefix
1975 - 99
1976 - 00
1977 - 06

GIBSON SERIAL NUMBERS 1977 TO NOW
8 digit number : ydddynnn

yy (1st. & 5th. digit)= year of manufacture
dd. (digits 2-4)= day of year
nnn (digits 6-8)=daily # rank

Some Heritage and Vintage reissue have the vintage style serial number.

GOODALL

Look on the label inside of the sound hole for the date the guitar was made.

GRETSCH

Years 1965-1972 = the first 1 or 2 numbers = the month (1-12)...the next number = the last number of the year...the rest of the numbers are the instruments number.

Years 1973-1981 = 1 or 2 numbers before the hyphen = the month (1-12)...the first number after the hyphen = the last number of the year ... the rest of the numbers are the instruments number.

Syncromatic Serial Numbers ... 1940-1949 = 007 - 900

Year - Serial #

1949-1950 - 3000	1951 - 4000-5000
1952 - 5000-8000	1953 - 9000-12,000
1954 - 12,000-16,000	1955 - 17,000-21,000
1957 - 22,000-26,000	1958 - 27,000-30,000
1959 - 30,000-34,000	1960 - 34,000-39,000
1961 - 39,000-45,000	1962 - 46,000-52,000
1963 - 53,000-63,000	1964 - 63,000-77,000
1964-early 1965 - 77,000-84,000	

GUILD

Year - Serial #

1952 - 350	1953 - 840
1954 - 1526	1955 - 2468
1956 - 3830	1957 - 5712
1958 - 8348	1959 - 12035
1960 - 14713	1961 - 18419
1962 - 22722	1963 - 28943
1964 - 38636	

From 1965 thru 1969 Guild Guitars had different serial numbers for different models of instruments...then in 1970 they changed back to the original system or serial numbers.

Year - Serial #

1970 - 50978	1971 - 61463
1972 - 75602	1973 - 95496
1974 - 112803	1975 - 130304
1976 - 149625	1977 - 169867
1978 - 195067	

1979 - 211877... up until 9-30-79...then they changed back to a different series of serial numbers per model again.

HOLLENBECK

Read the label on the inside of the guitar for the date.

IBANEZ

In dating Ibanez guitars made before 1987 .. the first letter is the month (A is Jan., B is Feb, C is March..etc) the next two numbers are the year .. the next four numbers are the production number that month (they only produced 9999 pieces each month)..(example) ...C760287 = March 1976 the 287th. piece made.

In dating Ibanez guitars made after 1987 .. the letter is now the factory designation .. the first number is the year built ... the next five numbers are the production number of the piece for the year ..(example) .. F700015 = the 15th. guitar made in 1987.

LACEY

The date that the guitar was made will be on the truss rod cover.

LANGEJANS

The date that the guitar was made is on the label inside of the sound hole.

BILL LAWRENCE

The first two numbers of the serial number are the year that the guitar was made in - then a letter for the month (A=Jan., B=Feb., C=March, etc) then comes the guitars place in production.

C. F. MARTIN

Year - Serial #

1898 - 8343	1899 - 8716	1900 - 9125	1901 - 9310
1902 - 9528	1903 - 9810	1904 - 9988	1905 - 10,120
1906 - 10,329	1907 - 10,727	1908 - 10,883	1909 - 11,018
1910 - 11,203	1911 - 11,413	1912 - 11,565	1913 - 11,821
1914 - 12,047	1915 - 12,209	1916 - 12,390	1917 - 12,988
1918 - 13,450	1919 - 14,512	1920 - 15,848	1921 - 16,758
1922 - 17,839	1923 - 19,891	1924 - 22,008	1925 - 24,116
1926 - 28,689	1927 - 34,435	1928 - 37,568	1929 - 40,843
1930 - 45,317	1931 - 49,589	1932 - 52,590	1933 - 55,084
1934 - 58,679	1935 - 61,947	1936 - 65,176	1937 - 68,865
1938 - 71,667	1939 - 74,061	1940 - 76,734	1941 - 80,013
1942 - 83,107	1943 - 86,724	1944 - 90,149	1945 - 93,623
1946 - 98,158	1947 - 103,468	1948 - 108,269	1949 - 112,961
1950 - 117,961	1951 - 122,799	1952 - 128,436	1953 - 134,501
1954 - 141,345	1955 - 147,328	1956 - 152,775	1957 - 159,061
1958 - 165,576	1959 - 171,047	1960 - 175,689	1961 - 181,297
1962 - 187,384	1963 - 193,327	1964 - 199,626	1965 - 207,030
1966 - 217,215	1967 - 230,095	1968 - 241,925	1969 - 256,003
1970 - 271,633	1971 - 294,270	1972 - 313,302	1973 - 333,873
1974 - 353,387	1975 - 371,828	1976 - 388,800	1977 - 399,625
1978 - 407,800	1979 - 419,900	1980 - 430,300	1981 - 436,474
1982 - 439,627	1983 - 446,101	1984 - 453,300	1985 - 460,575
1986 - 468,175	1987 - 476,216	1988 - 483,952	1989 - 493,279
1990 - 503,309	1991 - 512,487	1992 - 522,655	1993 - 535,223
1994 - 551,696	1995 - 570,434		

McCOLLUM

Look at the inside of the top for the date of the guitar with a mirror.

McKERRIHAN ARCHTOPS

Look on the inside of the guitar ...it will be signed and dated ...on solid bodys look under the neck pickup.

MEGAS

The date is on the label inside of the guitar.

MORTORO

The last two numbers in the serial number are the year of the guitar- unless the guitar is a 7 or 8 string in which case there will be an extra number on the end of the serial number (the second and third numbers from the end of the serial number would be the year of the guitar if its a 7 or 8 string).

PSR/PAUL REED SMITH

The first digit of the serial number is the last digit of the year in which the guitar was made.

RAREBIRD

Beginning in 1976, some of the early models have an eagle on the headstock with a 6 digit serial number that stands for the "Day-Month-Year" of the instrument (DDMMYY).

In 1988 they switched to a 4 digit serial number .. the first 2 numbers are the sequence in production the last 2 numbers are the year of manufacture.

RIBBECKE

Look on the label for the date + the first two digits of the serial number are usually the year.

RICKENBACKER

Serial numbers 1960 - 1986 = the year is the first letter, the month is the second letter...

Serial numbers 1986-1995 = the year is the number after the letter..the letter is the month ...

Year - Letter

1961 -A	1962 -B
1963 -C	1964 -D
1965 -E	1966 -F
1967 -G	1968 -H
1969 –I	1970 -J
1971 -K	1972 -L
1973 -M	1974 -N
1975 -O	1976 -P
1977 -Q	1978 –R
1979 -S	1980 -T
1981 -U	1982 -V
1983 -W	1984 -X
1985 -Y	1986 –Z

Month - Code

Jan- A	Feb- B
Mar.- C	April- D
May- E	June- F
July- G	Aug- H
Sept- I	Oct- J
Nov- K	Dec- L

Year - Number
1987- 0
1988 -1
1989 -2
1990 -3
1991 -4
1992 -5
1993 -6
1994 -7

SADOWSKI

Inside of the control panel is the date in which the guitar was made.

SHANTI

Use a mirror to read just behind the last tone bar on the inside of the top of the instrument which is signed and dated.

STROMBERG

The Strombergs (Charles and Elmer) made approximately 640 instruments up until 1955 when they both died. They used their business cards as labels in the guitars, the telephone number on the card helps to determine the approximate year the instrument was made.

Year - Phone # on the Card
1920-1927...Bowdoin 1728R or 1728M
1927-1929...Bowdoin 6559W or 1242W
1929-1932...Bowdoin 1878R
1932-1945...CA 3174
1949-1955...CA 7-3174

TAYLOR

Starting in 1974 ...the first two digits in the serial number is the year that the instrument was manufactured.

RICK TURNER

The first two digits in the serial number is the year in which the guitar was made.

WASHBURN

George Washburn started making guitars in 1864 .. the company has changed hands many times since then ..Washburn guitars had a fire sometime in the 1920's that destroyed everything, including all records and paperwork that they had prior to the day of the fire ... then the same thing happened again in the 1950's !!

From 1988 on ... on some models (but not all) - the first two digits of the serial number is the year the guitar was made.

On all limited editions ..the year will be in the "Model Name" of the guitar ... (example) ..."D-95 LTD" = 1995 ..."D-92LTD" = 1992 ...etc...

XOTIC

The first digit of the serial number is the year in which the guitar was made.

Our sincere thanks to John at Ducks Deluxe who provided all the information for dating your guitars. For further information, please e-mail ducks@ducksdeluxe.com or go to their web-site, www.ducksdeluxe.com.

TYPE	YR	MFG	PRICES--BASED ON 100% ORIGINAL MODEL	SELL EXC	SELL AVG	BUY EXC	BUY AVG
			ABBOTT MUSICAL INSTRUMENTS				
MANDOLIN	33	ABBOTT	**MODEL 1** FLATBACK	602	**462**	408	360
MANDOL	34	ABBOTT	**MODEL F** ARCHED	598	**459**	405	357
UKULELE	27	ABBOTT	**SILVER DOLLAR**	448	**344**	304	268
UKE	28	ABBOTT	**SILVER DOLLAR**	577	**443**	392	345
UKE	29	ABBOTT	**SILVER DOLLAR**	590	**453**	400	353
			ACOUSTIC				
ELEC. GUITAR & BASS	72	ACOUSTIC	**BLACK WIDOW** BLACK, SOLID BODY	1,216	**933**	825	727
ELGUIT	73	ACOUSTIC	**BLACK WIDOW** BLACK, ROSEWOOD, 24-FRET, 2 HB	1,336	**1,025**	906	799
ELGUIT	74	ACOUSTIC	**BLACK WIDOW** BLACK, 20-FRET, 1 HB	607	**466**	411	363
ELGUIT	75	ACOUSTIC	**BLACK WIDOW** BLACK, SOLID BODY	620	**476**	421	371
GUITAR AMP	71	ACOUSTIC	**134 LEAD** 4x10" SPEAKERS	520	**399**	353	311
GTAMP	71	ACOUSTIC	**135 LEAD** 12" SPEAKER	383	**294**	259	229
GTAMP	71	ACOUSTIC	**360**	319	**245**	216	190
GTAMP	74	ACOUSTIC	**370 BASS** 200 WATT, 406 CABINET, EQ	703	**540**	477	420
			ACRO				
PRE	58	ACRO	**20/20 TUBE STEREO** 18 WATT	422	**324**	286	252
PRE	58	ACRO	**S-1001 TUBE**	323	**248**	219	193
PRE	57	ACRO	**UL-II TUBE MONO** 60 WATT	579	**444**	392	346
			ACUSTA				
SPKR	04	ACUSTA	**CVM-3 KIT** WALNUT 15" SUBWOOFER, 80 WATTS	796	**611**	540	476
			AKG ACOUSTICS				
ELEC. GUITAR & BASS	67	AKG	**ES-335** BURGUNDY MIST	5,178	**3,976**	3,514	3,098
MIC	57-64	AKG	**C-12** TUBE, MULTI-PATTERN	7,209	**5,535**	4,892	4,312
MIC	64-73	AKG	**C-12A** TUBE, MULTI-PATTERN	1,552	**1,191**	1,053	928
MIC	64	AKG	**C-12VR** TUBE, MONO CONDENSER	3,556	**2,730**	2,413	2,127
MIC	59-78	AKG	**C-24** MULTI-PATTERN CONDENSER	8,867	**6,808**	6,016	5,304
MIC	55	AKG	**C-28** SMALL DIAPHRAGM CONDENSER	2,917	**2,240**	1,979	1,745
MIC	65-67	AKG	**C-60** TUBE, CONDENSER	1,027	**788**	696	614
MIC	65	AKG	**C-61** TUBE	1,408	**1,081**	956	842
MIC	88	AKG	**C-401B** FIGURE 8, MICRO CONDENSER	176	**135**	120	105
MIC	70	AKG	**C-412** SOLID STATE	1,830	**1,405**	1,241	1,094
MIC	82	AKG	**C-414E1** MULTI-PATTERN, REMOTE	971	**745**	658	580
MIC	68	AKG	**C-414EB** CONDENSER	1,356	**1,041**	920	811
MIC	77-82	AKG	**C-414EB** MULTI-PATTERN CONDENSER	1,443	**1,108**	979	863
MIC	74	AKG	**C-414ULS**	1,210	**929**	821	724
MIC	64	AKG	**C-451** MODULAR CAPACITOR, FET	717	**551**	487	429
MIC	68	AKG	**C-451E** NICKEL CARDIOID COMBO	624	**479**	424	373
MIC	77	AKG	**C-452EB** BLACK, COMBO CONDENSER	310	**238**	210	185
MIC	78	AKG	**CK-1S** CARDIOID NICKEL CAPSULE	262	**201**	177	156
MIC	84	AKG	**CK-2X** OMNI BLACK CAPSULE	417	**320**	283	249
MIC	78	AKG	**CK-22** OMNI BLACK CAPSULE	439	**337**	297	262
MIC	98	AKG	**CK-31 DISCREET CARDIOID CAPSULE**	144	**110**	98	86
MIC	98	AKG	**CK-32 DISCREET OMNI**	144	**110**	98	86
MIC	98	AKG	**CK-33 HYPERCARDIOID CAPSULE**	231	**178**	157	138
MIC	64	AKG	**D-12E** CARDIOID DYNAMIC	584	**448**	396	349

TYPE	YR	MFG	PRICES--BASED ON 100% ORIGINAL MODEL	SELL EXC	SELL AVG	BUY EXC	BUY AVG

ALAMO

TYPE	YR	MFG	MODEL	SELL EXC	SELL AVG	BUY EXC	BUY AVG
ELEC. GUITAR & BASS	61	ALAMO	**FIESTA**	355	**272**	240	212
ELGUIT	63	ALAMO	**TITAN MARK I SPANISH**	472	**362**	320	282
GUITAR AMP	62	ALAMO	**CAPRI MODEL 2560**	328	**251**	222	196
GTAMP	65	ALAMO	**MONTCLAIR REVERB** 1x12" SPEAKER	412	**316**	279	246
GTAMP	64	ALAMO	**PARAGON PIGGYBACK BASS** 1x15" SPEAKER	580	**445**	393	347

ALEMBIC, INC

TYPE	YR	MFG	MODEL	SELL EXC	SELL AVG	BUY EXC	BUY AVG
ELEC. GUITAR & BASS	79	ALEMBIC	**PICCOLO BASS**	1,330	**1,021**	902	795
ELGUIT	71	ALEMBIC	**SERIES 1 BASS**	3,045	**2,338**	2,066	1,821
ELGUIT	74	ALEMBIC	**SERIES 1 BASS**	3,347	**2,570**	2,271	2,002
ELGUIT	74	ALEMBIC	**STANLEY CLARKE BASS**	1,835	**1,409**	1,245	1,098

ALTEC LANSING TECHNOLOGIES, INC.

TYPE	YR	MFG	MODEL	SELL EXC	SELL AVG	BUY EXC	BUY AVG
ENCL	62	ALTEC	**609**	271	**208**	183	162
ENCL	78	ALTEC	**612 CABINET ONLY**	439	**337**	297	262
MIC	47	ALTEC	**21B ANTIQUE CONDENSER** "COKE BOTTLE"	883	**678**	599	528
MIC	39-60	ALTEC	**639A or B "BIRD CAGE" DYNAMIC** RIBBON	2,065	**1,585**	1,401	1,235
MIC	56	ALTEC	**660A DYNAMIC**	603	**463**	409	361
PRE	55	ALTEC	**1588B**	418	**321**	284	250
PRE	62	ALTEC	**A-333A MONO** 2x6L6G TUBES	280	**215**	190	167
PRE	62	ALTEC	**A-433A**	170	**130**	115	101
PWR	73-78	ALTEC	**340A**	351	**270**	238	210
PWR	62	ALTEC	**A-127B** 2x6L6G TUBES	480	**368**	326	287
PWR	62	ALTEC	**A-287F** 2x845 or 284 TUBES, 75 WATT	1,355	**1,040**	919	810
PWR	62	ALTEC	**A-287W** 2x805 TUBES	1,235	**948**	838	739
PWR	62	ALTEC	**A-340A** 35 WATT	245	**188**	166	146
PWR	62	ALTEC	**A-350A** 2x6550 TUBES, 40 WATT	368	**282**	250	220
PWR	62	ALTEC	**A-1530A** 70 WATT	748	**574**	507	447
RAW	62	ALTEC	**288A/B/C** DRIVER, 24, 20, 16 OHMS	264	**202**	179	158
RAW	62	ALTEC	**290A/B/C** DRIVER	230	**177**	156	138
RAW	74-79	ALTEC	**406-8C PAIR**	607	**466**	411	363
RAW	62	ALTEC	**515** 15", 16 0HM	133	**102**	90	79
RAW	62	ALTEC	**515B** 15", 16 OHM	192	**147**	130	115
RAW	62	ALTEC	**600B** 12" CONE	91	**70**	62	54
RAW	73	ALTEC	**601A/B** 12" CONE	246	**189**	167	147
RAW	73-78	ALTEC	**601C/D** 12" CONE	184	**141**	125	110
RAW	73-78	ALTEC	**602A/B/C/D** 14" CONE	245	**188**	166	146
RAW	73-78	ALTEC	**603A/B** 15" CONE	98	**75**	66	58
RAW	62	ALTEC	**603B** 15" CONE	147	**113**	100	88
RAW	48-53	ALTEC	**604** 15" CONE, COAXIAL HORN TWEETER, CROSSOVER	253	**194**	171	151
RAW	53	ALTEC	**604B** 15", CROSSOVER	502	**386**	341	300
RAW	65	ALTEC	**604B** CROSSOVER	431	**331**	292	257
RAW	65-70	ALTEC	**604C/D** 15" CONE, CROSSOVER	383	**294**	259	229
RAW	53-58	ALTEC	**604E** 15" CONE, CROSSOVER	462	**355**	313	276
RAW	55-60	ALTEC	**605A** 15" CONE, CROSSOVER	533	**409**	361	318
RAW	62	ALTEC	**605A** 15" CONE, CROSSOVER	399	**307**	271	239
RAW	60-65	ALTEC	**605B** 15" CONE, CROSSOVER	293	**225**	199	175
RAW	62	ALTEC	**606A**	163	**125**	110	97
RAW	62	ALTEC	**606A** 15" CONE	314	**241**	213	188
RAW	62	ALTEC	**606B** 12" CONE	238	**183**	161	142

TYPE	YR	MFG	PRICES--BASED ON 100% ORIGINAL MODEL	SELL EXC	SELL AVG	BUY EXC	BUY AVG
RAW	73	ALTEC	**682A**	124	**95**	84	74
RAW	74	ALTEC	**683A**	118	**91**	80	71
RAW	62	ALTEC	**702A** DRIVER	397	**305**	269	237
RAW	62	ALTEC	**720A** DRIVER	332	**255**	225	198
RAW	62	ALTEC	**728B** 12" CONE	734	**564**	498	439
RAW	60	ALTEC	**755C 12" PAIR**	563	**432**	382	337
RAW	74-79	ALTEC	**802A/B/C/D** DRIVER	250	**192**	170	150
RAW	74	ALTEC	**802B** DRIVER	303	**233**	205	181
RAW	60	ALTEC	**803B 15" PAIR**	399	**307**	271	239
RAW	73	ALTEC	**805** 15" CONE	116	**89**	79	69
RAW	76-81	ALTEC	**806A** DRIVER	332	**255**	225	198
RAW	73-78	ALTEC	**811B** HIGH FREQUENCY HORN	377	**289**	256	225
RAW	60	ALTEC	**3000B HORN TWEETER**	383	**294**	259	229
RAW	62	ALTEC	**A-31 HORN** HAS 720A DRIVER	853	**655**	579	510
RAW	62	ALTEC	**H-803** 2x4" CELLS	175	**135**	119	105
RAW	62	ALTEC	**H-805** 2x4" CELLS	250	**192**	170	150
RAW	62	ALTEC	**H-1003** 2x5" CELLS	252	**193**	171	150
RAW	62	ALTEC	**H-1803** 3x6" CELLS	337	**258**	228	201
SPKR	62	ALTEC	**607** 15" or 12", MAHOGANY or WALNUT	281	**215**	190	168
SPKR	62	ALTEC	**608A** 15", ALDER or WALNUT	327	**251**	221	195
SPKR	62	ALTEC	**609B** 12" 412A	283	**217**	192	169
SPKR	62	ALTEC	**609CC** 8" 408A	287	**221**	195	172
SPKR	62	ALTEC	**815** 288C 1505, 2x515	869	**667**	589	519
SPKR	74-79	ALTEC	**819AI STONEHENGE PAIR**	857	**658**	582	513
SPKR	47	ALTEC	**820A** 802B, H802, 2x803A, H-800D	733	**563**	497	438
SPKR	74	ALTEC	**820C** 802B, H-811. 2x803A, N-800D	725	**557**	492	434
SPKR	62	ALTEC	**824A** 12", 412A, 3000A	230	**177**	156	138
SPKR	62	ALTEC	**826A** ICONIC 801A, H-811A, 803A	459	**352**	311	274
SPKR	62-65	ALTEC	**830A LAGUNA PAIR**	1,870	**1,436**	1,269	1,118
SPKR	64-69	ALTEC	**831A CAPISTRANO PAIR**	1,218	**935**	826	728
SPKR	64-69	ALTEC	**836A LIDO PAIR**	431	**331**	292	257
SPKR	64-69	ALTEC	**837A AVALON PAIR**	648	**497**	440	387
SPKR	74-79	ALTEC	**843A MALIBU PAIR**	1,286	**988**	873	769
SPKR	73-78	ALTEC	**873A BARCELONA PAIR**	2,311	**1,775**	1,568	1,382
SPKR	79-81	ALTEC	**893C PAIR**	311	**239**	211	186
SPKR	76	ALTEC	**A-7 UTILITY VOICE OF THE THEATER**	384	**294**	260	229
SPKR	77-82	ALTEC	**SANTANA II PAIR**	927	**712**	629	554

ALVAREZ/ALVAREZ YAIRI

TYPE	YR	MFG	MODEL	SELL EXC	SELL AVG	BUY EXC	BUY AVG
GUITAR (ACOUSTIC)	75	ALVAREZ	**ARTIST** SUNBURST, FLATTOP ACOUSTIC	598	**459**	405	357
GUITAR	76	ALVAREZ	**CX-120** ROSEWOOD, BUTTERFLY TUNERS	592	**454**	402	354
GUITAR	70	ALVAREZ	**CY-140 CLASSICAL** CEDAR TOP, JACARANDA BACK/SIDES	743	**571**	504	444
GUITAR	85	ALVAREZ	**DY-51 DREADNOUGHT** NATURAL	650	**499**	441	389
GUITAR	80	ALVAREZ	**DY-58** FLAT TOP, 9-STRINGS, DOUBLES ON THE THREE HIGH STRINGS	712	**546**	483	426
GUITAR	82	ALVAREZ	**DY-60**	688	**528**	467	412
GUITAR	77	ALVAREZ	**DY-77** NATURAL	947	**727**	642	566
GUITAR	80	ALVAREZ	**DY-80 CANYON CREEK** 12-STRING, FLAMED CORAL ROSEWOOD BODY	710	**545**	481	424
GUITAR	70	ALVAREZ	**DY-90 DREADNOUGHT** ROSEWOOD BACK/SIDES	1,064	**817**	722	636
GUITAR	77	ALVAREZ	**MODEL 5056** ROSEWOOD, "TREE OF LIFE" INLAY	1,036	**795**	703	619
GUITAR	89	ALVAREZ	**MODEL 5063**	570	**437**	386	341

TYPE	YR	MFG	PRICES--BASED ON 100% ORIGINAL MODEL	SELL EXC	SELL AVG	BUY EXC	BUY AVG
GUITAR	89	ALVAREZ	**MODEL 5414** 12-STRING	608	**466**	412	363
STEEL GUITAR	60	ALVAREZ	**MODEL 5010** KOA	605	**465**	411	362

AMPEG by ST LOUIS MUSIC, INC

TYPE	YR	MFG	MODEL	SELL EXC	SELL AVG	BUY EXC	BUY AVG
ELEC. GUITAR & BASS	60	AMPEG	**AEB-1 BASS** SOLID BODY	1,223	**939**	829	731
ELGUIT	65	AMPEG	**AEB-1 BASS** SOLID BODY	1,034	**794**	702	619
ELGUIT	66	AMPEG	**AEB-1 BASS** SUNBURST	673	**516**	456	402
ELGUIT	67	AMPEG	**AEB-1 BASS**	669	**514**	454	400
ELGUIT	62	AMPEG	**ASB BASS** SOLID BODY, HORNS	834	**640**	566	499
ELGUIT	68	AMPEG	**ASB BASS** SOLID BODY, HORNS	796	**611**	540	476
ELGUIT	67	AMPEG	**ASB-1 DEVIL BASS** FIREBURST, LONG HORN	3,343	**2,567**	2,268	1,999
ELGUIT	67	AMPEG	**AUB-1 BASS** FRETLESS	1,317	**1,011**	893	787
ELGUIT	68	AMPEG	**AUB-1 BASS** FRETLESS	1,288	**989**	874	770
ELGUIT	69	AMPEG	**AUB-1 BASS** FRETLESS	1,246	**957**	845	745
ELGUIT	63	AMPEG	**AUSB** FRETLESS, HORNS	1,000	**767**	678	598
ELGUIT	63	AMPEG	**BABY BASS** RED BODY/NECK	3,571	**2,742**	2,423	2,136
ELGUIT	64	AMPEG	**BABY BASS** CREAM, WHITE NECK	3,307	**2,539**	2,244	1,978
ELGUIT	65	AMPEG	**BABY BASS** RED BODY/NECK	3,169	**2,433**	2,150	1,896
ELGUIT	66	AMPEG	**BABY BASS** SUNBURST	2,245	**1,724**	1,523	1,343
ELGUIT	68	AMPEG	**BABY BASS** SUNBURST	2,188	**1,680**	1,485	1,309
ELGUIT	68	AMPEG	**BABY BASS** RED BODY/NECK	3,045	**2,338**	2,066	1,821
ELGUIT	60	AMPEG	**BABY BASS 4** FIBERGLASS	1,790	**1,375**	1,215	1,071
ELGUIT	62	AMPEG	**BABY BASS 4** FIBERGLASS	1,981	**1,521**	1,344	1,185
ELGUIT	68	AMPEG	**BABY BASS 4** WHITE, FIBERGLASS	2,017	**1,548**	1,368	1,206
ELGUIT	69	AMPEG	**BABY BASS 4** BLACK, FIBERGLASS	1,047	**804**	710	626
ELGUIT	70	AMPEG	**BABY BASS 4** SUNBURST, FIBERGLASS	1,311	**1,007**	889	784
ELGUIT	65	AMPEG	**BABY BASS 5** SUNBURST, 5-STRING	978	**751**	664	585
ELGUIT	69	AMPEG	**DAN ARMSTRONG LUCITE**	1,990	**1,528**	1,350	1,190
ELGUIT	70	AMPEG	**DAN ARMSTRONG LUCITE** RT PU	1,886	**1,448**	1,279	1,128
ELGUIT	71	AMPEG	**DAN ARMSTRONG LUCITE**	1,865	**1,432**	1,266	1,116
ELGUIT	69	AMPEG	**LONG HORN BASS** RED & BLACK SUNBURST	673	**516**	456	402
ELGUIT	60	AMPEG	**SCROLL BASS** RED SUNBURST, LEFT-HANDED	897	**688**	608	536
ELGUIT	66	AMPEG	**SCROLL BASS**	871	**669**	591	521
ELGUIT	63	AMPEG	**SONIC SIX by BURNS** CHERRY, SOLID BODY, TREMOLO, 2 PU's	474	**364**	322	284
ELGUIT	67	AMPEG	**SSB BASS** SMALL SOLID BODY	480	**368**	326	287
ELGUIT	66	AMPEG	**SSUB-1 BASS** FRETLESS	441	**338**	299	263
ELGUIT	72	AMPEG	**SUPER STUD** SOLID BODY	367	**282**	249	219
ELGUIT	63	AMPEG	**THINLINE by BURNS** DOUBLE CUTAWAY, 2 PU's	611	**469**	414	365
ELGUIT	64	AMPEG	**THINLINE by BURNS** SEMI-HOLLOW BODY, TWO F-HOLES, DOUBLE CUTAWAY, TREMOLO	582	**447**	395	348
ELGUIT	63	AMPEG	**WILD DOG by BURNES** SUNBURST, TREMOLO, 3 PU's	635	**487**	430	379
ELGUIT	63	AMPEG	**WILD DOG DELUXE by BURNS** SUNBURST, SOLID BODY, BOUND NECK, TREMOLO	715	**549**	485	428
ELGUIT	64	AMPEG	**WILD DOG DELUXE by BURNS** SUNBURST, SOLID BODY, BOUND NECK, TREMOLO	692	**531**	469	414
GUITAR AMP	57	AMPEG	**5-18D** BLUE SPECKLE, P12N SPEAKER	441	**338**	299	263
GTAMP	66	AMPEG	**B-15N BASS** BLACK TOLEX FLIPTOP	590	**453**	400	353
GTAMP	70	AMPEG	**B-15N BASS**	582	**447**	395	348

TYPE	YR	MFG	MODEL	SELL EXC	SELL AVG	BUY EXC	BUY AVG
			PRICES--BASED ON 100% ORIGINAL				
GTAMP	73	AMPEG	**B-15N BASS** BLACK TOLEX FLIPTOP	562	**431**	381	336
GTAMP	75	AMPEG	**B-15N BASS** BLACK TOLEX FLIPTOP	473	**363**	321	283
GTAMP	69	AMPEG	**B-18 BASS** FLIPTOP	549	**422**	373	328
GTAMP	69	AMPEG	**B-25 TUBE** RED-BLACK PAISLEY	552	**423**	374	330
GTAMP	70	AMPEG	**B-25 TUBE** 2-CHANNEL, 50 WATT	552	**423**	374	330
GTAMP	63	AMPEG	**ECHO TWIN** 2x12" SPEAKERS	278	**214**	189	166
GTAMP	64	AMPEG	**ECHO TWIN SUPER ET-2**	445	**342**	302	266
GTAMP	70	AMPEG	**G-110** 10" SPEAKER, REVERB, TREMOLO	145	**111**	98	87
GTAMP	64	AMPEG	**GEMINI I** BLUE, 12" SPEAKER	321	**246**	218	192
GTAMP	65	AMPEG	**GEMINI I** 12" SPEAKER	303	**233**	205	181
GTAMP	69	AMPEG	**GEMINI I** 12" SPEAKER	325	**250**	221	194
GTAMP	63	AMPEG	**GEMINI II** TUBE, TREMOLO, VIBRATO	682	**523**	462	408
GTAMP	66	AMPEG	**GEMINI II** 15" COMBO	623	**479**	423	373
GTAMP	58	AMPEG	**JET 12** GREY SPARKLE	266	**204**	180	159
GTAMP	60	AMPEG	**JET 12** COPPER, 1x12"	257	**197**	174	154
GTAMP	63	AMPEG	**JET 12**	226	**173**	153	135
GTAMP	64	AMPEG	**JET 12** GREY TOLEX	224	**172**	152	134
GTAMP	65	AMPEG	**JET 12** BLUE DIAMOND	204	**157**	139	122
GTAMP	66	AMPEG	**JET 12** GREY	193	**148**	131	115
GTAMP	68	AMPEG	**JET 12** BLUE, 1x12"	181	**139**	123	108
GTAMP	52	AMPEG	**M-12** 1x12" JENSEN, 2-CHANNEL & VIB	343	**264**	233	205
GTAMP	60	AMPEG	**M-12** 1x12" JENSEN, P12-R SPEAKER	288	**221**	196	172
GTAMP	63	AMPEG	**M-15** 15" SPEAKER, 2-CHANNEL, VIBRATO	250	**192**	170	150
GTAMP	58	AMPEG	**PORTAFLEX BASS** 35 WATT COMBO	464	**356**	315	278
GTAMP	60	AMPEG	**PORTAFLEX B-12** 12" JBL	560	**430**	380	335
GTAMP	65	AMPEG	**PORTAFLEX B-12**	490	**376**	332	293
GTAMP	67	AMPEG	**PORTAFLEX B-12XT**	547	**420**	371	327
GTAMP	64	AMPEG	**PORTAFLEX B-15** 15" SPEAKER	571	**438**	387	341
GTAMP	65	AMPEG	**PORTAFLEX B-15 BASS**	544	**417**	369	325
GTAMP	69	AMPEG	**PORTAFLEX SB-12**	281	**215**	190	168
GTAMP	61	AMPEG	**REVERBEROCKET**	607	**466**	411	363
GTAMP	62	AMPEG	**REVERBEROCKET**	516	**396**	350	308
GTAMP	64	AMPEG	**REVERBEROCKET** BLUE DIAMOND	502	**386**	341	300
GTAMP	66	AMPEG	**REVERBEROCKET**	470	**361**	319	281
GTAMP	68	AMPEG	**REVERBEROCKET**	442	**339**	300	264
GTAMP	67	AMPEG	**REVERBEROCKET II**	451	**346**	306	270
GTAMP	69	AMPEG	**REVERBEROCKET II**	490	**376**	332	293
GTAMP	70	AMPEG	**REVERBEROCKET II**	481	**369**	326	288
GTAMP	72	AMPEG	**REVERBEROCKET II**	330	**253**	224	197
GTAMP	60	AMPEG	**STEREO 435-S** 2x12" SPEAKERS	353	**271**	240	211
GTAMP	58	AMPEG	**STEREO TWIN** 2x12" SPEAKERS, VIBRATO	356	**273**	241	213
GTAMP	69	AMPEG	**SVT** HEAD CABINET	697	**535**	473	417
GTAMP	69	AMPEG	**SVT BASS**	694	**533**	471	415
GTAMP	72	AMPEG	**SVT BASS** 8x10" CABINET	696	**534**	472	416
GTAMP	79	AMPEG	**SVT BASS**	658	**505**	446	393
GTAMP	74	AMPEG	**V-2** 4x12" CABINET	448	**344**	304	268
GTAMP	72	AMPEG	**V-4** STACK (2)4x12" CABINETS	827	**635**	561	495
GTAMP	74	AMPEG	**V-4** STACK (2)4x12" CABINETS	825	**633**	560	493
GTAMP	76	AMPEG	**VT-22**	564	**433**	383	337

TYPE	YR	MFG	PRICES--BASED ON 100% ORIGINAL MODEL	SELL EXC	SELL AVG	BUY EXC	BUY AVG
GTAMP	74	AMPEG	VT-40 4x10" SPEAKERS, COMBO	355	272	240	212
GTAMP	76	AMPEG	VT-40 4x10" SPEAKERS, COMBO	351	270	238	210
SIGNAL PROCESSOR	81	AMPEG	A-1 DISTORTION	178	136	120	106
SGNPRO	81	AMPEG	A-2 COMPRESSOR	171	131	116	102
SGNPRO	81	AMPEG	A-3 OVERDRIVE	175	135	119	105
SGNPRO	81	AMPEG	A-4 PHASER	176	135	120	105
UPRIG	59	AMPEG	UPRIGHT BASS FIBERGLASS	1,312	1,007	890	785
UPRIGHT	60	AMPEG	UPRIGHT BABY BASS SUNBURST	1,893	1,454	1,285	1,132
UPRIGHT	63	AMPEG	UPRIGHT BABY BASS WHITE	2,057	1,579	1,396	1,230
UPRIGHT	65	AMPEG	UPRIGHT BABY BASS SUNBURST	1,330	1,021	902	795
UPRIGHT	70	AMPEG	UPRIGHT BABY BASS BROWN SUNBURST	1,496	1,148	1,015	895

ARGONE

TYPE	YR	MFG	MODEL				
MIC	48	ARGONE	AR-57 CAPSULE CHROME	257	197	174	154

ARP INSTRUMENTS

TYPE	YR	MFG	MODEL				
SYNTHESIZER	79	ARP	1623 SEQUENCER	388	298	263	232
SYNTH	80	ARP	2353 SOLUS ANALOG	563	432	382	337
SYNTH	70	ARP	2500 MODULAR	1,724	1,324	1,170	1,031
SYNTH	71	ARP	2600	3,293	2,529	2,235	1,970
SYNTH	71	ARP	2601 KEYBOARD ANALOG	2,172	1,668	1,474	1,299
SYNTH	72	ARP	2823 ODYSSEY ANALOG	703	540	477	420
SYNTH	76	ARP	AVATAR	434	333	294	259
SYNTH	70	ARP	AXXE I ANALOG	726	558	493	434
SYNTH	75	ARP	AXXE I	638	490	433	381
SYNTH	78	ARP	QUADRA	957	735	649	572

AUDIO DS

TYPE	YR	MFG	MODEL				
EQUAL	04	AUDIO DS	E-900-RS SWEEP 4-BAND STEREO	1,286	988	873	769
SIGNAL PROCESSOR	04	AUDIO DS	F-769X-RS BROADCAST LIMITER	1,301	999	883	778
SGNPRO	04	AUDIO DS	PANSCAN AUTOMATIC PANNER	1,059	813	718	633

AUDIO RESEARCH CORPORATION

TYPE	YR	MFG	MODEL				
PRE	69	AUDIORES	SP-2 TUBE	358	275	243	214
XOVER	72	AUDIORES	EC-2 TUBE	706	542	479	422

B & O

TYPE	YR	MFG	MODEL				
MIC	55	B & O	FENTONE BI-DIRECTIONAL RIBBON	1,273	977	864	761

B & W

TYPE	YR	MFG	MODEL				
SPKR	04	B & W	DM--602 S2 7" BASS	551	423	373	329

BACON & DAY

TYPE	YR	MFG	MODEL				
BANJO	20	BACON	A-1 TENOR	816	626	554	488
BANJO	25	BACON	A-1 SUPER TENOR	1,542	1,184	1,046	922
BANJO	30	BACON	BELMONT 5-STRING, RESONATOR	1,284	986	871	768
BANJO	58	BACON	BELMONT 5-STRING	925	710	627	553
BANJO	64	BACON	BELMONT 5-STRING, RESONATOR	1,321	1,014	896	790
BANJO	22	BACON	BLUE BELL TENOR, RESONATOR	1,477	1,134	1,002	883
BANJO	21	BACON	BLUE BELL BANJO-MANDOLIN OPEN BACK	753	578	511	450
BANJO	20	BACON	BLUE RIBBON TENOR, OPEN BACK	995	764	675	595
BANJO	20	BACON	BLUE RIBBON STYLE A, SUPER 5-STRING	1,329	1,020	902	795
BANJO	24	BACON	CELLO BANJO	6,354	4,879	4,312	3,801
BANJO	38	BACON	CELLO BANJO	2,427	1,863	1,646	1,451
BANJO	40	BACON	CELLO BANJO 4-STRING, F-HOLE FLANGE	2,196	1,686	1,490	1,313
BANJO	15	BACON	FF PROFESSIONAL #1	3,557	2,731	2,413	2,127

TYPE	YR	MFG	PRICES--BASED ON 100% ORIGINAL MODEL	SELL EXC	SELL AVG	BUY EXC	BUY AVG
BANJO	25	BACON	**MONTANA SILVER BELL #1 SPECIAL**	3,259	**2,502**	2,211	1,949
BANJO	26	BACON	**MONTANA SILVER BELL #1 SPECIAL**	3,258	**2,501**	2,210	1,949
BANJO	28	BACON	**MONTANA SILVER BELL #1 SPECIAL** PLECTRUM	3,248	**2,494**	2,204	1,943
BANJO	28	BACON	**MONTANA SILVER BELL #1 SPECIAL**	3,253	**2,498**	2,207	1,946
BANJO	29	BACON	**MONTANA SILVER BELL #1 SPECIAL** TENOR	3,241	**2,488**	2,199	1,938
BANJO	30	BACON	**MONTANA SILVER BELL #1 SPECIAL**	3,240	**2,487**	2,198	1,938
BANJO	30	BACON	**MONTANA SILVER BELL #3** TENOR	3,942	**3,027**	2,675	2,358
BANJO	40	BACON	**NE PLUS ULTRA SILVER BELL** TENOR	4,777	**3,668**	3,242	2,858
BANJO	46	BACON	**NE PLUS ULTRA SILVER BELL** TENOR	5,509	**4,230**	3,738	3,295
BANJO	60	BACON	**NE PLUS ULTRA SILVER BELL** PLECTRUM	3,373	**2,590**	2,289	2,018
BANJO	72	BACON	**ODE STYLE 25R** MAHOGANY RIM/RESONATOR	728	**559**	494	435
BANJO	20	BACON	**PEERLESS MANDOLIN-BANJO**	939	**721**	637	562
BANJO	25	BACON	**PEERLESS MANDOLIN-BANJO** PLECTRUM	747	**573**	506	446
BANJO	26	BACON	**PEERLESS MANDOLIN-BANJO** PLECTRUM	719	**552**	487	430
BANJO	27	BACON	**PEERLESS MANDOLIN-BANJO** PLECTRUM	819	**629**	556	490
BANJO	30	BACON	**PEERLESS MANDOLIN-BANJO**	764	**587**	519	457
BANJO	36	BACON	**RHYTHM KING** TENOR, 19-FRET	801	**615**	544	479
BANJO	28	BACON	**SENORITA** TENOR, RESONATOR	1,380	**1,060**	937	826
BANJO	30	BACON	**SENORITA** TENOR, SUNBURST	1,354	**1,039**	918	810
BANJO	35	BACON	**SENORITA** TENOR, SUNBURST	1,331	**1,022**	903	796
BANJO	40	BACON	**SENORITA** TENOR, 19-FRET	1,396	**1,072**	947	835
BANJO	41	BACON	**SENORITA** TENOR, 19-FRET	1,384	**1,062**	939	828
BANJO	48	BACON	**SENORITA** 5-STRING RESONATOR	1,321	**1,014**	896	790
BANJO	50	BACON	**SENORITA** PLECTRUM	1,040	**798**	706	622
BANJO	22	BACON	**SILVER BELL 1** TENOR	2,890	**2,219**	1,961	1,729
BANJO	23	BACON	**SILVER BELL 1** TENOR	2,410	**1,850**	1,635	1,441
BANJO	24	BACON	**SILVER BELL 1** PLECTRUM	2,294	**1,762**	1,557	1,372
BANJO	24	BACON	**SILVER BELL 1** TENOR	2,912	**2,236**	1,976	1,742
BANJO	25	BACON	**SILVER BELL 1** TENOR	2,364	**1,815**	1,604	1,414
BANJO	26	BACON	**SILVER BELL 1** TENOR	2,343	**1,799**	1,589	1,401
BANJO	27	BACON	**SILVER BELL 1** TENOR	2,311	**1,775**	1,568	1,382
BANJO	27	BACON	**SILVER BELL 1** PLECTRUM, F-HOLE	2,880	**2,211**	1,954	1,723
BANJO	28	BACON	**SILVER BELL 1** TENOR	2,279	**1,750**	1,546	1,363
BANJO	29	BACON	**SILVER BELL 1** TENOR	2,158	**1,657**	1,464	1,291
BANJO	30	BACON	**SILVER BELL 1** TENOR, F-HOLE FLANGE	2,271	**1,744**	1,541	1,358
BANJO	34	BACON	**SILVER BELL 1** TENOR, F-HOLE FLANGE	1,705	**1,309**	1,157	1,020
BANJO	37	BACON	**SILVER BELL 1** TENOR	1,749	**1,343**	1,187	1,046
BANJO	24	BACON	**SILVER BELL 2** TENOR	3,579	**2,748**	2,428	2,141
BANJO	28	BACON	**SILVER BELL 2** TENOR	3,553	**2,728**	2,411	2,125
BANJO	36	BACON	**SILVER BELL 2** TENOR	3,250	**2,495**	2,205	1,944
BANJO	25	BACON	**SILVER BELL 3** TENOR	5,751	**4,416**	3,902	3,440
BANJO	26	BACON	**SILVER BELL 3** TENOR	5,615	**4,312**	3,810	3,359
BANJO	28	BACON	**SILVER BELL 3** TENOR	5,477	**4,206**	3,717	3,276
BANJO	30	BACON	**SILVER BELL SERENADER** TENOR	1,484	**1,139**	1,007	887

TYPE	YR	MFG	PRICES--BASED ON 100% ORIGINAL MODEL	SELL EXC	SELL AVG	BUY EXC	BUY AVG
BANJO	32	BACON	**SILVER BELL SERENADER** TENOR, F-HOLE	1,492	**1,146**	1,013	893
BANJO	55	BACON	**SILVER BELL SERENADER** PLECTRUM	1,321	**1,014**	896	790
BANJO	30	BACON	**SPECIAL I** TENOR, WALNUT NECK, RESONATOR	1,285	**987**	872	769
BANJO	33	BACON	**SPECIAL I** TENOR, RESONATOR	1,234	**947**	837	738
BANJO	38	BACON	**SPECIAL I** TENOR, CLOVER LEAF FLANGES	1,291	**991**	876	772
BANJO	67	BACON	**SPECIAL I** TENOR, WALNUT NECK	725	**557**	492	434
BANJO	30	BACON	**SPECIAL II** TENOR	763	**586**	518	456
BANJO	33	BACON	**STYLE 0** TENOR, TULIP FLANGE, 17-FRET	788	**605**	535	471
BANJO	30	BACON	**STYLE 1** PLECTRUM, ROSEWOOD	3,668	**2,816**	2,489	2,194
BANJO	29	BACON	**STYLE 2** TENOR	2,296	**1,763**	1,558	1,373
BANJO	20	BACON	**STYLE C MANDOLIN-BANJO**	660	**507**	448	395
BANJO	22	BACON	**STYLE C MANDOLIN-BANJO**	618	**474**	419	369
BANJO	24	BACON	**STYLE C MANDOLIN-BANJO**	583	**448**	395	349
BANJO	25	BACON	**STYLE C MANDOLIN-BANJO**	572	**439**	388	342
BANJO	28	BACON	**SULTANA 1 SILVER BELL** TENOR	4,067	**3,123**	2,760	2,433
BANJO	30	BACON	**SULTANA 1 SILVER BELL** TENOR	4,062	**3,119**	2,756	2,430
BANJO	35	BACON	**SULTANA 1 SILVER BELL** TENOR	4,058	**3,116**	2,754	2,428
BANJO	40	BACON	**SULTANA 1 SILVER BELL** TENOR	3,894	**2,990**	2,642	2,329
BANJO	30	BACON	**SULTANA 3 SILVER BELL** PLECTRUM	4,902	**3,764**	3,326	2,932
BANJO	38	BACON	**SULTANA 7 SILVER BELL** TENOR	7,532	**5,783**	5,111	4,505
BANJO	25	BACON	**SUPER A** TENOR	1,260	**967**	855	753
BANJO	20	BACON	**SUPER A-1** TENOR, SNAP-IN RESONATOR	762	**585**	517	456
BANJO	39	BACON	**SUPERTONE** 5-STRING	972	**746**	659	581
BANJO	40	BACON	**SYMPHONIE** TENOR, PERALOID FINGERBOARD	3,008	**2,309**	2,041	1,799
BANJO	24	BACON	**TENOR LUTE** 4-STRING	1,768	**1,357**	1,200	1,057
GUITAR (ACOUSTIC)	38	BACON	**RAMONA** ARCHTOP	773	**594**	525	462
GUITAR	40	BACON	**RAMONA** ARCHTOP	695	**534**	471	416
GUITAR	40	BACON	**SENORITA** SUNBURST, MAHOGANY BACK/SIDES	1,433	**1,100**	972	857
STEEL GUITAR	50	BACON	**BELMONT** 5-STRING	517	**397**	351	309

BALDWIN

TYPE	YR	MFG	MODEL	SELL EXC	SELL AVG	BUY EXC	BUY AVG
BANJO	70	BALDWIN	**2SR ELECTRIC** 5-STRING	642	**493**	436	384
BANJO	73	BALDWIN	**ODE STYLE B** DOT FINGERBOARD INLAY	1,439	**1,105**	976	860
BANJO	74	BALDWIN	**ODE STYLE B** DOT FINGERBOARD INLAY	1,423	**1,093**	965	851
BANJO	70	BALDWIN	**ODE STYLE C**	1,436	**1,103**	975	859
BANJO	75	BALDWIN	**ODE STYLE C**	1,690	**1,297**	1,146	1,011
BANJO	79	BALDWIN	**ODE STYLE C** 5-STRING, NICKEL HARDWARE	1,796	**1,379**	1,219	1,074
BANJO	76	BALDWIN	**ODE STYLE D** 5-STRING, GOLD HARDWARE	1,442	**1,107**	978	862
BANJO	77	BALDWIN	**ODE STYLE D** 5-STRING, GOLD HARDWARE	1,445	**1,110**	981	864
BANJO	60	BALDWIN	**RB-175** 5-STRING, LONG NECK, OPEN BACK	1,002	**769**	680	599
BANJO	65	BALDWIN	**RB-175** 5-STRING, LONG NECK, OPEN BACK	822	**631**	557	491
ELEC. GUITAR & BASS	69	BALDWIN	**706** DOUBLE CUTAWAY, SEMI-HOLLOW BODY, 2 F-HOLES, 2 PU's	675	**518**	458	404
ELGUIT	68	BALDWIN	**706V** DOUBLE CUTAWAY, SEMI-HOLLOW BODY, VIBRATO, 2 F-HOLES, 2 PU's	1,487	**1,142**	1,009	889
ELGUIT	67	BALDWIN	**712R** 12-STRING, DOUBLE CUTAWAY, SEMI-HOLLOW BODY, 2 PU's	675	**518**	458	404
ELGUIT	66	BALDWIN	**BABY BISON** BLACK	785	**602**	532	469
ELGUIT	66	BALDWIN	**BABY BISON** SUNBURST	929	**713**	630	556

TYPE	YR	MFG	PRICES--BASED ON 100% ORIGINAL MODEL	SELL EXC	SELL AVG	BUY EXC	BUY AVG
ELGUIT	67	BALDWIN	**BABY BISON** CHERRY	971	**745**	658	580
ELGUIT	67	BALDWIN	**BABY BISON** TRANSPARENT RED	975	**749**	661	583
ELGUIT	68	BALDWIN	**BABY BISON** NATURAL	954	**732**	647	570
ELGUIT	68	BALDWIN	**BABY BISON** SUNBURST	972	**746**	659	581
ELGUIT	69	BALDWIN	**BABY BISON** CHERRY	968	**743**	657	579
ELGUIT	64	BALDWIN	**BISON** BLACK	818	**628**	555	489
ELGUIT	65	BALDWIN	**BISON** BLACK	1,046	**803**	709	625
ELGUIT	68	BALDWIN	**BISON** BLACK	1,490	**1,144**	1,011	891
ELGUIT	69	BALDWIN	**BISON** JAZZ WHITE	1,622	**1,246**	1,101	970
ELGUIT	65	BALDWIN	**DOUBLE SIX** SUNBURST, 12-STRING	1,348	**1,035**	915	806
ELGUIT	67	BALDWIN	**DOUBLE SIX** GREEN SUNBURST, 12-STRING	855	**657**	580	511
ELGUIT	67	BALDWIN	**DOUBLE SIX** BLACK, 12-STRING	1,043	**801**	708	624
ELGUIT	70	BALDWIN	**DOUBLE SIX** SUNBURST, 12-STRING	930	**714**	631	556
ELGUIT	67	BALDWIN	**GB-66 DELUXE** SUNBURST, DOUBLE CUT, 2 PU's	658	**505**	446	393
ELGUIT	68	BALDWIN	**HANK MARVIN** WHITE	2,355	**1,808**	1,598	1,409
ELGUIT	65	BALDWIN	**JAZZ SPLIT SOUND** OFFSET DOUBLE CUTAWAY, SOLIDBODY, TREMOLO, 3 PU's	715	**549**	485	428
ELGUIT	66	BALDWIN	**MARVIN** OFFSET DOUBLE CUTAWAY, SOLIDBODY, TREMOLO, 3 PU's	722	**554**	490	432
ELGUIT	65	BALDWIN	**VIBRASLIM** DOUBLE CUTAWAY, SEMI-HOLLOW BODY, TREMOLO, 2 PU's	1,234	**947**	837	738
ELGUIT	66	BALDWIN	**VIBRASLIM** SUNBURST	673	**516**	456	402
ELGUIT	68	BALDWIN	**VIBRASLIM** THIN HOLLOW BODY, 2 PU's	865	**664**	587	517
ELGUIT	65	BALDWIN	**VIRGINIAN** NATURAL	791	**608**	537	473
ELGUIT	66	BALDWIN	**VIRGINIAN** NATURAL	753	**578**	511	450
ELGUIT	67	BALDWIN	**VIRGINIAN** NATURAL	674	**517**	457	403
ELGUIT	68	BALDWIN	**VIRGINIAN** NATURAL	672	**516**	456	402
ELGUIT	69	BALDWIN	**VIRGINIAN** NATURAL	652	**501**	443	390
ELGUIT	70	BALDWIN	**VIRGINIAN** NATURAL	650	**499**	441	389

BEHR

BANJO	04	BEHR	**T1951** TUBE ULTRA Q	240	**184**	163	144
SIGNAL PROCESSOR	04	BEHR	**MX 882** ULTRALINK PRO, 8-CHANNEL	129	**99**	88	77
XOVER	04	BEHR	**CX2300** SUPER-X	127	**98**	86	76

BENEDETTO GUITARS by FENDER MUSICAL INSTRUMENTS

GUITAR (ACOUSTIC)	80	BENEDETTO	**FRATELLO** ARCHTOP, MAPLE BACK/SIDES, INLAYS, GOLD TUNERS	9,908	**7,608**	6,723	5,927
GUITAR	93	BENEDETTO	**LA VENEZIA** ARCHTOP, EUROPEAN WOODS, BLACK TUNERS	11,589	**8,899**	7,864	6,933

BEYER

MIC	89	BEYER	**M-500STG HYPERCARDIOID DYNAMIC**	628	**482**	426	375
MIC	89	BEYER	**M-500TG HYPERCARDIOID DYNAMIC**	628	**482**	426	375

BIGSBY

ELEC. GUITAR & BASS	48	BIGSBY	**SOLID BODY** SINGLE PU	11,696	**8,980**	7,936	6,996
ELGUIT	50	BIGSBY	**SOLID BODY** DOUBLE PU	25,337	**19,455**	17,193	15,157
ELGUIT	52	BIGSBY	**SOLID BODY** DOUBLE PU	25,268	**19,402**	17,146	15,115

BOSS

SIGNAL PROCESSOR	81	BOSS	**SG-1** SLOW GEAR	162	**124**	110	97
SGNPRO	83	BOSS	**VB-2** VIBRATO	184	**141**	125	110

TYPE		YR	MFG	MODEL	SELL EXC	SELL AVG	BUY EXC	BUY AVG
				PRICES--BASED ON 100% ORIGINAL				
				BROCINER				
PRE		04	BROCINER	MARK 10	145	111	98	87
PWR		04	BROCINER	MARK 30C	168	129	114	100
				BROOK				
BANJO		04	BROOK	7	163	125	110	97
PWR		04	BROOK	10C	162	124	110	97
	PWR	04	BROOK	12A	264	202	179	158
				BRUNO				
GUITAR (ACOUSTIC)		24	BRUNO	HARP GUITAR 12-STRING+4-STRING BASS, MAHOGANY/SPRUCE TOP	2,077	1,595	1,409	1,242
MANDOLIN		24	BRUNO	BANJO-MANDOLIN 10", OPEN BACK	539	414	366	322
	MANDOL	22	BRUNO	BOWL BACK BRAZILIAN ROSEWOOD	792	608	538	474
UKULELE		20	BRUNO	SOPRANO CURLY KOA, SOUND HOLE INLAY	539	414	366	322
				BUCHLA				
SYNTHESIZER		80	BUCHLA	100 MODULAR	1,932	1,483	1,311	1,155
	SYNTH	80	BUCHLA	TOUCHE'	1,906	1,463	1,293	1,140
				BURNS/BALDWIN				
ELEC. GUITAR & BASS		67	BURNS	FLYTE	645	495	437	385
	ELGUIT	74	BURNS	FLYTE	673	516	456	402
	ELGUIT	62	BURNS	JAZZ SUNBURST, SPLIT-SOUND	792	608	538	474
	ELGUIT	64	BURNS	JAZZ SUNBURST, SPLIT-SOUND	692	531	469	414
	ELGUIT	65	BURNS	JAZZ SUNBURST, SPLIT-SOUND	685	526	465	410
	ELGUIT	66	BURNS	JAZZ SUNBURST, SPLIT-SOUND	651	500	442	389
	ELGUIT	67	BURNS	JAZZ SUNBURST, SPLIT-SOUND	631	485	428	377
	ELGUIT	68	BURNS	JAZZ SUNBURST, SPLIT-SOUND	619	475	420	370
	ELGUIT	69	BURNS	JAZZ SUNBURST, SPLIT-SOUND	652	501	443	390
	ELGUIT	64	BURNS	MARVIN	948	728	643	567
	ELGUIT	65	BURNS	NU-SONIC WHITE, TREMOLO	593	455	402	355
	ELGUIT	66	BURNS	NU-SONIC WHITE	586	450	398	351
	ELGUIT	68	BURNS	NU-SONIC BASS BLACK, 2 PU's	604	464	410	361
	ELGUIT	68	BURNS	SINGLE 6 SEMI-HOLLOW, VIBRATO, 2 PU's	603	463	409	361
	ELGUIT	63	BURNS	SPLITSONIC RED SUNBURST, 3 PU's	948	728	643	567
	ELGUIT	64	BURNS	SPLITSONIC RED SUNBURST, 3 PU's	945	725	641	565
	ELGUIT	67	BURNS	SPLITSONIC RED SUNBURST, 3 PU's	770	591	522	460
				CARVIN				
ELEC. GUITAR & BASS		72	CARVIN	DBS-98B NATURAL, DOUBLE NECK, 3 PU's, SERIAL #5000-9999	554	425	376	331
GUITAR AMP		79	CARVIN	VT-112 TUBE, 1x12" SPEAKER	228	175	155	136
	GTAMP	78	CARVIN	VT-1500 TUBE AMP HEAD, CABINET	196	150	133	117
				CHAMBERLIN				
SYNTHESIZER		61	CHAMBER	CHAMBERLIN	3,635	2,791	2,466	2,174
				CHURCH/MGM				
MIC		52	CHURCH	CHURCH MIKE TUBE NEUMANN CAPSULE	9,356	7,184	6,349	5,597
				CLASSIC GUITAR, LTD.				
ELEC. GUITAR & BASS		62	CLASSIC	GONZALES BASS	826	634	560	494
GUITAR (ACOUSTIC)		64	CLASSIC	ESTRALITA ARCHTOP	399	307	271	239
	GUITAR	55	CLASSIC	GONZALES FLATTOP	642	493	436	384
	GUITAR	66	CLASSIC	LATINO FLATTOP	1,531	1,175	1,038	915
				COLE				
BANJO		81	COLE	ECLIPSE 1881, 5-STRING, OPEN BACK	2,250	1,727	1,526	1,346

TYPE	YR	MFG	PRICES--BASED ON 100% ORIGINAL MODEL	SELL EXC	SELL AVG	BUY EXC	BUY AVG
			## COLEY				
MANDOLIN	75	COLEY	**COLEMAN MANDOLIN**	2,287	**1,756**	1,551	1,368
			## CORAL by DANELECTRO				
ELEC. GUITAR & BASS	67	CORAL	**COMBO** SUNBURST, ARCHTOP, ROUND HOLE	534	**410**	362	319
ELGUIT	60	CORAL	**FIREFLY**	610	**468**	414	365
ELGUIT	65	CORAL	**FIREFLY**	596	**458**	405	357
ELGUIT	68	CORAL	**FIREFLY** TWIN PU's	511	**393**	347	306
ELGUIT	67	CORAL	**FIREFLY BASS** HOLLOW BODY	673	**516**	456	402
ELGUIT	67	CORAL	**FIREFLY-12** 12-STRING, HOLLOW BODY	658	**505**	446	393
ELGUIT	60	CORAL	**HORNET** RED, 2 PU's	580	**445**	393	347
ELGUIT	67	CORAL	**SCORPION-12** SUNBURST	668	**513**	453	399
ELGUIT	64	CORAL	**SITAR** 13-STRING	1,704	**1,308**	1,156	1,019
ELGUIT	64	CORAL	**SITAR** 19-STRING, 3 PU's	1,886	**1,448**	1,279	1,128
ELGUIT	65	CORAL	**SITAR** 19-STRING, 3 PU's	2,064	**1,584**	1,400	1,234
ELGUIT	67	CORAL	**SITAR** 6-STRING, GOURD SHAPED, 1 PU	1,279	**982**	867	765
ELGUIT	67	CORAL	**SITAR** 13-STRING	1,714	**1,316**	1,163	1,025
ELGUIT	67	CORAL	**SITAR** 19-STRING, 3 PU's	1,888	**1,449**	1,281	1,129
ELGUIT	68	CORAL	**SITAR** 13-STRING	1,765	**1,355**	1,197	1,055
ELGUIT	68	CORAL	**SITAR** 19-STRING, 3 PU's	2,184	**1,677**	1,482	1,306
GUITAR (ACOUSTIC)	68	CORAL	**LONG-HORN** HOLLOW BODY	1,696	**1,302**	1,151	1,015
			## CORT GUITARS by WESTHEIMER CORP				
ELEC. GUITAR & BASS	98	CORT	**CURBOW RETRO** GREG CURBOW DESIGNED	511	**393**	347	306
			## CRAFTSMEN				
PWR	50	CRAFT	**C-500** TUBE MONO CLASS A TRIODE, 12 WATTS	282	**216**	191	168
PWR	50	CRAFT	**C-500 TUBE** MONO, CLASS A TRIODE	443	**340**	300	265
PWR	73	CRAFT	**C-500 WILLIAMSON AMP** 12 WATT	510	**392**	346	305
			## CRUMAR				
SYNTHESIZER	80	CRUMAR	**BIT ONE**	611	**469**	414	365
			## DAN ARMSTRONG				
EFFECTS	76	DAN ARMST	**GREEN RINGER**	483	**371**	328	289
EFFECTS	77	DAN ARMST	**RED RINGER**	443	**340**	300	265
ELEC. GUITAR & BASS	75	DAN ARMST	**DAN ARMSTRONG LUCITE BASS**	2,186	**1,678**	1,483	1,307
			## DANELECTRO, SEE ALSO CORAL, SILVERTONE				
ELEC. GUITAR & BASS	56	DANELECTR	**BASS** 4-STRING, SINGLE CUTAWAY	945	**725**	641	565
ELGUIT	57	DANELECTR	**BASS** BRONZE, 6-STRING, SINGLE CUTAWAY	1,283	**985**	870	767
ELGUIT	58	DANELECTR	**BASS** BRONZE, 6-STRING	1,271	**976**	862	760
ELGUIT	59	DANELECTR	**BASS** 6-STRING	1,263	**970**	857	755
ELGUIT	60	DANELECTR	**BASS** BLACK, 6-STRING	1,256	**964**	852	751
ELGUIT	60	DANELECTR	**BASS** BRONZE, 6-STRING	1,261	**968**	855	754
ELGUIT	60	DANELECTR	**BELLZOUKI 12**	1,441	**1,106**	978	862
ELGUIT	61	DANELECTR	**BELLZOUKI 12** 1 PU	1,226	**941**	832	733
ELGUIT	63	DANELECTR	**BELLZOUKI 12**	1,348	**1,035**	915	806
ELGUIT	65	DANELECTR	**BELLZOUKI 12** SUNBURST, 1 PU	1,318	**1,012**	894	788
ELGUIT	66	DANELECTR	**BELLZOUKI 12** 2 PU's	1,010	**775**	685	604
ELGUIT	67	DANELECTR	**BELLZOUKI 12** HORN BODY SHAPE, 2 PU's	1,310	**1,006**	889	783
ELGUIT	68	DANELECTR	**COBRA XII** 12-STRING	607	**466**	411	363

TYPE	YR	MFG	MODEL	SELL EXC	SELL AVG	BUY EXC	BUY AVG
			PRICES--BASED ON 100% ORIGINAL				
ELGUIT	58	DANELECTR	**CONVERTIBLE** DOUBLE CUTAWAY	651	**500**	442	389
ELGUIT	59	DANELECTR	**CONVERTIBLE** DOUBLE CUTAWAY, THIN BODY	728	**559**	494	435
ELGUIT	60	DANELECTR	**CONVERTIBLE** DOUBLE CUTAWAY, HOLLOW BODY	838	**644**	569	501
ELGUIT	62	DANELECTR	**CONVERTIBLE** 1 PU	686	**527**	465	410
ELGUIT	67	DANELECTR	**CONVERTIBLE**	611	**469**	414	365
ELGUIT	68	DANELECTR	**CONVERTIBLE** DOUBLE CUTAWAY	601	**461**	408	359
ELGUIT	67	DANELECTR	**CORAL HORNET 2** 2 PU's	661	**508**	449	395
ELGUIT	68	DANELECTR	**CORAL HORNET 2** 2 PU's	749	**575**	508	448
ELGUIT	69	DANELECTR	**CORAL HORNET 2** 2 PU's	720	**552**	488	430
ELGUIT	67	DANELECTR	**DRAGON** WALNUT, SINGLE CUTAWAY, ARCHTOP	611	**469**	414	365
ELGUIT	60	DANELECTR	**GUITARALIN LONG-HORN**	1,818	**1,396**	1,234	1,088
ELGUIT	61	DANELECTR	**GUITARALIN LONG-HORN**	1,379	**1,059**	936	825
ELGUIT	63	DANELECTR	**GUITARALIN LONG-HORN**	1,609	**1,235**	1,092	962
ELGUIT	71	DANELECTR	**LANCER XII** 12-STRING	551	**423**	373	329
ELGUIT	59	DANELECTR	**LONG-HORN BASS** SUNBURST, 6-STRING	1,453	**1,116**	986	869
ELGUIT	60	DANELECTR	**LONG-HORN BASS** SUNBURST, 6-STRING	1,389	**1,067**	943	831
ELGUIT	62	DANELECTR	**LONG-HORN BASS** BRONZE SUNBURST, 4-STRING	1,331	**1,022**	903	796
ELGUIT	63	DANELECTR	**LONG-HORN BASS** 6-STRING	1,304	**1,001**	885	780
ELGUIT	64	DANELECTR	**LONG-HORN BASS** SUNBURST, 4-STRING	1,052	**808**	714	629
ELGUIT	65	DANELECTR	**LONG-HORN BASS** SUNBURST, 6-STRING	1,276	**980**	866	763
ELGUIT	56	DANELECTR	**MODEL C** SINGLE CUTAWAY	584	**448**	396	349
ELGUIT	57	DANELECTR	**PRO 1** BROWN	724	**556**	491	433
ELGUIT	60	DANELECTR	**PRO 1**	665	**510**	451	397
ELGUIT	63	DANELECTR	**PRO 1** BROWN	566	**435**	384	339
ELGUIT	64	DANELECTR	**PRO 1**	694	**533**	471	415
ELGUIT	58	DANELECTR	**SHORT-HORN** BLACK, 1 PU	711	**546**	482	425
ELGUIT	60	DANELECTR	**SHORT-HORN** BRONZE, 1 PU	696	**534**	472	416
ELGUIT	60	DANELECTR	**SHORT-HORN** DOUBLE NECK	1,744	**1,339**	1,184	1,043
ELGUIT	61	DANELECTR	**SHORT-HORN** JIMMY PAGE BLACK	1,216	**933**	825	727
ELGUIT	61	DANELECTR	**SHORT-HORN** DOUBLE NECK	1,669	**1,282**	1,133	998
ELGUIT	62	DANELECTR	**SHORT-HORN** BLOND, CONVERTIBLE	678	**521**	460	406
ELGUIT	62	DANELECTR	**SHORT-HORN** DOUBLE NECK	1,669	**1,282**	1,133	998
ELGUIT	63	DANELECTR	**SHORT-HORN** BLACK, 1 PU	617	**473**	418	369
ELGUIT	63	DANELECTR	**SHORT-HORN** JIMMY PAGE BLACK	1,289	**989**	874	771
ELGUIT	64	DANELECTR	**SHORT-HORN** BLOND, CONVERTIBLE	688	**528**	467	412
ELGUIT	65	DANELECTR	**SHORT-HORN** BLACK, 2 PU's	736	**565**	500	440
ELGUIT	66	DANELECTR	**SHORT-HORN** BLACK, VIBRATO, 1 PU	628	**482**	426	375
ELGUIT	60	DANELECTR	**SHORT-HORN BASS** COPPER, 6-STRING	812	**623**	551	485
ELGUIT	62	DANELECTR	**SHORT-HORN BASS** BRONZE, 4-STRING	788	**605**	535	471
ELGUIT	63	DANELECTR	**SHORT-HORN BASS** DOUBLE NECK	1,677	**1,288**	1,138	1,003
ELGUIT	64	DANELECTR	**SHORT-HORN BASS** 15-FRET	617	**473**	418	369
ELGUIT	65	DANELECTR	**SHORT-HORN BASS** BRONZE, 6-STRING	736	**565**	500	440
ELGUIT	66	DANELECTR	**SHORT-HORN BASS** BRONZE, 6-STRING	695	**534**	471	416
ELGUIT	63	DANELECTR	**SHORT-HORN DELUXE** DARK WALNUT, 3 PU's	762	**585**	517	456

TYPE	YR	MFG	PRICES--BASED ON 100% ORIGINAL MODEL	SELL EXC	SELL AVG	BUY EXC	BUY AVG
ELGUIT	58	DANELECTR	SILVERTONE BLACK, WHITE SIDES, 2 PU's	555	426	376	332
ELGUIT	58	DANELECTR	SILVERTONE BLACK & WHITE, SINGLE CUTAWAY	580	445	393	347
ELGUIT	59	DANELECTR	SILVERTONE BROWN, WHITE SIDES, 1 PU	627	481	425	375
ELGUIT	60	DANELECTR	SILVERTONE RED & BLACK SUNBURST	545	418	370	326
ELGUIT	60	DANELECTR	SILVERTONE RED & WHITE	563	432	382	337
ELGUIT	60	DANELECTR	SILVERTONE BLACK, 1 PU	580	445	393	347
ELGUIT	60	DANELECTR	SILVERTONE RED & BLACK SUNBURST, 2 PU's	652	501	443	390
ELGUIT	61	DANELECTR	SILVERTONE BROWN, SINGLE CUTAWAY, 1 PU	555	426	376	332
ELGUIT	62	DANELECTR	SILVERTONE 2 PU's	518	398	351	310
ELGUIT	62	DANELECTR	SILVERTONE 1 PU	555	426	376	332
ELGUIT	64	DANELECTR	SILVERTONE BLACK SPARKLE, 1 PU	555	426	376	332
ELGUIT	65	DANELECTR	SILVERTONE RED & BLACK SUNBURST, DOUBLE CUTAWAY	555	426	376	332
ELGUIT	67	DANELECTR	SILVERTONE BLACK & WHITE, BUILT IN AMP, SINGLE LIPSTICK PU	573	440	389	343
ELGUIT	60	DANELECTR	SILVERTONE BASS 6-STRING	724	556	491	433
ELGUIT	67	DANELECTR	SLIMLINE SL 2V VIBROLA, 2 PU's	516	396	350	308
ELGUIT	67	DANELECTR	SLIMLINE SL 3N GATOR FINISH, 3 PU's	520	399	353	311
ELGUIT	67	DANELECTR	SLIMLINE SL12N 12-STRING	553	424	375	330
ELGUIT	60	DANELECTR	STANDARD BLACK, DOUBLE CUTAWAY, 2 PU's	1,214	932	823	726
ELGUIT	63	DANELECTR	STANDARD DOUBLE CUTAWAY, 1 PU	647	497	439	387
ELGUIT	56	DANELECTR	U-1 BRONZE, SINGLE CUTAWAY	728	559	494	435
ELGUIT	57	DANELECTR	U-1 COPPER, 1 PU	678	521	460	406
ELGUIT	58	DANELECTR	U-1 COPPER, 1 PU	693	532	470	414
ELGUIT	59	DANELECTR	U-1 COPPER, 1 PU	712	546	483	426
ELGUIT	60	DANELECTR	U-1 1 PU	697	535	473	417
ELGUIT	61	DANELECTR	U-1 1 PU	604	464	410	361
ELGUIT	62	DANELECTR	U-1 1 PU	548	421	372	328
ELGUIT	57	DANELECTR	U-2 BLACK, SINGLE CUTAWAY, 2 PU's	831	638	563	497
ELGUIT	59	DANELECTR	U-2 2 PU's	820	630	557	491
ELGUIT	65	DANELECTR	U-2 2 PU's	880	675	597	526
ELGUIT	58	DANELECTR	U-3 BLACK, 3 PU's	925	710	627	553
ELGUIT	58	DANELECTR	UB-2 SINGLE CUTAWAY, 6-STRING, 2 PU's	1,034	794	702	619
GUITAR AMP	60	DANELECTR	CADET	257	197	174	154
GTAMP	55	DANELECTR	CADET 120 1x6" GEFCO SPEAKER	430	330	291	257
GTAMP	59	DANELECTR	CENTURION 275	517	397	351	309
GTAMP	60	DANELECTR	CENTURION 275	682	523	462	408
GTAMP	63	DANELECTR	DM-10 BLUE, 1x8" JENSEN	196	150	133	117
GTAMP	66	DANELECTR	DM-10 1x8" SPEAKER, VIBRATO, TUBE	358	275	243	214
GTAMP	64	DANELECTR	DM-25 35 WATT	495	380	335	296
GTAMP	65	DANELECTR	DM-25 REVERB, TREMOLO	480	368	326	287
GTAMP	57	DANELECTR	LEADER DELUXE SIZE 12" SPEAKER	240	184	163	144
GTAMP	65	DANELECTR	REVERB UNIT	369	283	250	221
GTAMP	60	DANELECTR	SILVERTONE 2x12" SPEAKERS, TREMOLO, REVERB	589	452	399	352
GTAMP	50	DANELECTR	SPECIAL BROWN, SINGLE CHANNEL, 12" SPEAKER AND VIBRATO	257	197	174	154
GTAMP	50	DANELECTR	VIBRATO AMP BROWN TOLEX, 12 WATTS TUBE POWER, 1x10" SPEAKER	670	515	455	401

TYPE	YR	MFG	PRICES--BASED ON 100% ORIGINAL MODEL	SELL EXC	SELL AVG	BUY EXC	BUY AVG
GUITAR (ACOUSTIC)	45	DANELECTR	**SILVERTONE** SUNBURST, ARCHTOP, MAPLE BACK/SIDES	586	**450**	398	351
GUITAR	54	DANELECTR	**SILVERTONE** SUNBURST, ARCHTOP, SINGLE CUTAWAY	572	**439**	388	342
GUITAR	67	DANELECTR	**TEARDROP** SUNBURST, SPRUCE, SEMI-HOLLOW	465	**357**	316	278

D'ANGELICO

TYPE	YR	MFG	MODEL	SELL EXC	SELL AVG	BUY EXC	BUY AVG
GUITAR (ACOUSTIC)	51	DANGELICO	**"SPECIAL"** BLOND, NON-CUTAWAY, 17 1/2", SERIAL # 1856-1885	18,266	**14,025**	12,394	10,927
GUITAR	36	DANGELICO	**EXCEL** SUNBURST, EARLY STYLE STRAIGHT "F" HOLES, SERIAL # 1105-1235	17,661	**13,561**	11,984	10,565
GUITAR	37	DANGELICO	**EXCEL** SUNBURST, SERIAL # 1236-1317	17,508	**13,444**	11,881	10,474
GUITAR	37	DANGELICO	**EXCEL** BLOND, ARCHTOP, SERIAL # 1236-1317	24,945	**19,154**	16,927	14,922
GUITAR	39	DANGELICO	**EXCEL** SUNBURST, NON-CUTAWAY, SERIAL # 1318-1385	27,891	**21,416**	18,926	16,685
GUITAR	40	DANGELICO	**EXCEL** SUNBURST, SERIAL # 1457-1508	18,015	**13,833**	12,224	10,776
GUITAR	43	DANGELICO	**EXCEL** SUNBURST, CURLY MAPLE, SERIAL # 1622-1658	16,429	**12,615**	11,148	9,828
GUITAR	45	DANGELICO	**EXCEL** SUNBURST, SPRUCE, EBONY BOARD, SERIAL # 1682-1702	25,365	**19,477**	17,212	15,174
GUITAR	47	DANGELICO	**EXCEL** SUNBURST, NON-CUTAWAY, SERIAL # 1738-1781	20,440	**15,695**	13,870	12,227
GUITAR	50	DANGELICO	**EXCEL** BLOND, FULL BODY, SERIAL # 1832-1855	32,781	**25,171**	22,244	19,610
GUITAR	50	DANGELICO	**EXCEL** SUNBURST, CUTAWAY, SERIAL # 1832-1855	52,150	**40,044**	35,387	31,197
GUITAR	50	DANGELICO	**EXCEL** BLOND, CUTAWAY, SERIAL; # 1832-1855	57,738	**44,334**	39,179	34,539
GUITAR	52	DANGELICO	**EXCEL** BLOND, NON-CUTAWAY, SERIAL # 1886-1908	21,980	**16,877**	14,915	13,148
GUITAR	52	DANGELICO	**EXCEL** NATURAL, JAZZ, LEFT-HANDED, SERIAL # 1886-1908	35,445	**27,217**	24,052	21,204
GUITAR	53	DANGELICO	**EXCEL** BLOND, CUTAWAY, SERIAL # 1909-1936	41,968	**32,225**	28,478	25,106
GUITAR	56	DANGELICO	**EXCEL** NATURAL, CUTAWAY, SERIAL # 1989-2017	67,049	**51,484**	45,498	40,110
GUITAR	56	DANGELICO	**EXCEL** SUNBURST, FULL BODY, SERIAL # 1989-2017	70,304	**53,983**	47,706	42,057
GUITAR	57	DANGELICO	**EXCEL** BLOND, CUTAWAY, SERIAL # 2018-2040	41,969	**32,226**	28,479	25,106
GUITAR	59	DANGELICO	**EXCEL** NON-CUTAWAY, SERIAL # 2068-2098	26,726	**20,522**	18,135	15,988
GUITAR	59	DANGELICO	**EXCEL** SUNBURST, CUTAWAY, SERIAL # 2068-2098	48,330	**37,110**	32,795	28,911
GUITAR	59	DANGELICO	**EXCEL** BLOND, CUTAWAY, SERIAL # 2068-2098	48,876	**37,530**	33,166	29,238
GUITAR	59	DANGELICO	**EXCEL** NY SUNBURST, CUTAWAY, SERIAL # 2068-2098	55,093	**42,304**	37,385	32,957
GUITAR	60	DANGELICO	**EXCEL** FLAME MAPLE, SERIAL # 2099-2122	23,257	**17,858**	15,782	13,913
GUITAR	60	DANGELICO	**EXCEL** NATURAL, CUTAWAY, SERIAL # 2099-2122	59,599	**45,764**	40,442	35,653
GUITAR	60	DANGELICO	**EXCEL** SUNBURST, CUTAWAY, SERIAL # 2099-2122	101,185	**77,695**	68,661	60,530
GUITAR	61	DANGELICO	**EXCEL** NY BLOND, CUTAWAY, SERIAL # 2123-2164	67,962	**52,185**	46,117	40,656
GUITAR	63	DANGELICO	**EXCEL** BLOND, CUTAWAY, LEFT-HANDED, SERIAL # 2123-2164	55,929	**42,945**	37,952	33,457
GUITAR	60	DANGELICO	**EXCEL SPECIAL** BLOND, 2 PU's, SERIAL # 2099-2122	35,000	**26,875**	23,750	20,937
GUITAR	46	DANGELICO	**EXCEL TENOR** BLOND, FULL BODY, SERIAL # 1703-1740	24,718	**18,980**	16,773	14,786
GUITAR	52	DANGELICO	**MEL BAY** BLOND, FULL BODY, SERIAL # 1886-1908	31,299	**24,033**	21,238	18,723
GUITAR	38	DANGELICO	**NEW YORKER** SUNBURST, SERIAL # 1318-1385	38,897	**29,867**	26,394	23,269
GUITAR	38	DANGELICO	**NEW YORKER** SUNBURST, STRAIGHT F-HOLE, SERIAL # 1318-1385	63,286	**48,595**	42,944	37,859
GUITAR	39	DANGELICO	**NEW YORKER** SUNBURST, NON-CUTAWAY, SERIAL # 1388-1456	24,424	**18,754**	16,574	14,611
GUITAR	39	DANGELICO	**NEW YORKER** BLOND, NON-CUTAWAY, SERIAL # 1388-1456	61,383	**47,134**	41,653	36,720
GUITAR	43	DANGELICO	**NEW YORKER** BLOND, CUTAWAY, 18", SERIAL # 1622-1658	112,489	**86,375**	76,332	67,292
GUITAR	47	DANGELICO	**NEW YORKER** BLOND, CUTAWAY, SERIAL # 1738-1781	111,269	**85,439**	75,504	66,563
GUITAR	48	DANGELICO	**NEW YORKER** SUNBURST, CUTAWAY, SERIAL # 1782-1804	87,890	**67,487**	59,640	52,577
GUITAR	50	DANGELICO	**NEW YORKER** NATURAL, SERIAL # 1832-1855	84,322	**64,747**	57,218	50,442

2006 WINTER VINTAGE GUITARS & COLLECTIBLES BLUE BOOK — DAQUISTO

TYPE	YR	MFG	MODEL	SELL EXC	SELL AVG	BUY EXC	BUY AVG
GUITAR	51	DANGELICO	NEW YORKER — BLOND, CUTAWAY, SERIAL # 1856-1885	87,594	67,259	59,438	52,400
GUITAR	53	DANGELICO	NEW YORKER — BLOND, CUTAWAY, SERIAL # 1909-1936	84,392	64,801	57,266	50,484
GUITAR	54	DANGELICO	NEW YORKER — SUNBURST, FULL BODY, SERIAL # 1933-1962	86,813	66,660	58,909	51,933
GUITAR	54	DANGELICO	NEW YORKER — BLOND, CUTAWAY, SERIAL # 1933-1962	117,087	89,906	79,451	70,043
GUITAR	55	DANGELICO	NEW YORKER — SUNBURST, CUTAWAY, SERIAL # 1961-1988	72,236	55,467	49,017	43,212
GUITAR	56	DANGELICO	NEW YORKER — BLOND, CUTAWAY, SERIAL # 1989-2017	73,232	56,231	49,693	43,808
GUITAR	57	DANGELICO	NEW YORKER — SUNBURST, CUTAWAY, SERIAL # 2018-2040	93,304	71,644	63,314	55,816
GUITAR	58	DANGELICO	NEW YORKER — NATURAL, CUTAWAY, SERIAL # 2041-2067	118,049	90,644	80,104	70,618
GUITAR	59	DANGELICO	NEW YORKER — SUNBURST, NON-CUTAWAY, SERIAL # 2068-2098	70,741	54,319	48,003	42,318
GUITAR	62	DANGELICO	NEW YORKER — BLOND, CUTAWAY, SERIAL # 2123-2164	50,469	38,753	34,247	30,191
GUITAR	63	DANGELICO	NEW YORKER — NATURAL, CUTAWAY, INLAY, SERIAL # 2123-2164	108,449	83,273	73,590	64,876
GUITAR	64	DANGELICO	NEW YORKER — BLOND, CUTAWAY, SERIAL # 2123-2164	50,469	38,753	34,247	30,191
GUITAR	49	DANGELICO	NEW YORKER DELUXE — BLOND, CUTAWAY, 17", SERIAL # 1805-1831	84,938	65,220	57,636	50,811
GUITAR	60	DANGELICO	NEW YORKER SPECIAL — SUNBURST, SERIAL # 2099-2122	35,063	26,924	23,793	20,975
GUITAR	64	DANGELICO	NEW YORKER SPECIAL — SUNBURST, SERIAL # 2123-2164	77,857	59,783	52,832	46,575
GUITAR	33	DANGELICO	SELMER CUSTOM — CUTAWAY, 16", SERIAL # 1005-1097	19,068	14,641	12,939	11,406
GUITAR	36	DANGELICO	STYLE A — SUNBURST, SERIAL # 1105-1235	12,010	9,222	8,150	7,185
GUITAR	37	DANGELICO	STYLE A — SUNBURST, SERIAL # 1234-1317	11,997	9,212	8,141	7,177
GUITAR	39	DANGELICO	STYLE A — SUNBURST, ARCHTOP, SERIAL # 1388-1456	11,867	9,112	8,052	7,099
GUITAR	42	DANGELICO	STYLE A — SUNBURST, SERIAL # 1563-1621	10,622	8,156	7,207	6,354
GUITAR	39	DANGELICO	STYLE A-1 — SUNBURST, SERIAL # 1388-1456	11,384	8,741	7,725	6,810
GUITAR	40	DANGELICO	STYLE A-1 — SUNBURST, SERIAL # 1457-1508	12,214	9,379	8,288	7,307
GUITAR	42	DANGELICO	STYLE A-1 — SUNBURST, SERIAL # 1563-1621	12,556	9,641	8,520	7,511
GUITAR	49	DANGELICO	STYLE A-1 — SUNBURST, SERIAL # 1805-1831	11,528	8,851	7,822	6,896
GUITAR	36	DANGELICO	STYLE B — SERIAL # 1105-1235	20,498	15,739	13,909	12,262
GUITAR	38	DANGELICO	STYLE B — BLOND, SERIAL # 1318-1385	16,640	12,777	11,292	9,954
GUITAR	38	DANGELICO	STYLE B — SUNBURST, SERIAL # 1318-1385	18,976	14,570	12,876	11,351
GUITAR	42	DANGELICO	STYLE B — SUNBURST, SERIAL # 1563-1621	17,034	13,079	11,558	10,190
MANDOLIN	42	DANGELICO	A-STYLE PLAIN — SERIAL # 1563-1621	13,338	10,241	9,050	7,979
MANDOL	39	DANGELICO	DELUXE 2-POINT — SERIAL # 1388-1456	8,758	6,725	5,943	5,239

D'AQUISTO

TYPE	YR	MFG	MODEL	SELL EXC	SELL AVG	BUY EXC	BUY AVG
ELEC. GUITAR & BASS	78	DAQUISTO	EXCEL SOLIDBODY — SUNBURST, SERIAL # 1113-1125	21,148	16,239	14,351	12,651
ELGUIT	88	DAQUISTO	EXCEL SOLIDBODY — SUNBURST, MAPLE TOP, 2 PU's, SERIAL # 1201-1210	18,957	14,556	12,863	11,340
GUITAR (ACOUSTIC)	78	DAQUISTO	10-STRING SPECIAL — HONEY SUNBURST, MARK LEAF CASE, SERIAL # 1113-1125	62,310	47,845	42,281	37,274
GUITAR	68	DAQUISTO	EXCEL — SUNBURST, CUTAWAY, SERIAL # 1023-1029	51,227	39,335	34,761	30,645
GUITAR	78	DAQUISTO	EXCEL DELUXE — BLOND, SERIAL # 1113-1125	46,223	35,493	31,365	27,651
GUITAR	66	DAQUISTO	NEW YORKER — SUNBURST, CUTAWAY, 18", SERIAL # 1006-1014	90,105	69,187	61,142	53,902
GUITAR	69	DAQUISTO	NEW YORKER — SUNBURST, CUTAWAY, SERIAL # 1030-1036	67,458	51,798	45,775	40,354
GUITAR	77	DAQUISTO	NEW YORKER — VIOLIN FINISH, CUTAWAY, SERIAL # 1103-1112	67,802	52,062	46,008	40,560
GUITAR	77	DAQUISTO	NEW YORKER — CARVED EBONY, VIOLIN FINISH, 17", ARCHTOP, SERIAL # 1103-1112	75,696	58,123	51,365	45,282
GUITAR	81	DAQUISTO	NEW YORKER — SUNBURST, CUTAWAY, SERIAL # 1143-1151	32,963	25,311	22,368	19,719
GUITAR	85	DAQUISTO	NEW YORKER — SUNBURST, SERIAL # 1176-1183	65,664	50,420	44,558	39,281

TYPE	YR	MFG	PRICES--BASED ON 100% ORIGINAL MODEL	SELL EXC	SELL AVG	BUY EXC	BUY AVG
GUITAR	87	DAQUISTO	**NEW YORKER** BLOND, CUTAWAY, SERIAL # 1193-1202	59,336	**45,561**	40,264	35,495
GUITAR	66	DAQUISTO	**NEW YORKER DELUXE** BLOND, SERIAL # 1006-1014	86,243	**66,222**	58,522	51,592
GUITAR	70	DAQUISTO	**NEW YORKER DELUXE** SUNBURST, SERIAL # 1037-1043	81,460	**62,550**	55,277	48,731
GUITAR	72	DAQUISTO	**NEW YORKER DELUXE** SUNBURST, SERIAL # 1051-1063	80,066	**61,479**	54,330	47,896
GUITAR	72	DAQUISTO	**NEW YORKER DELUXE** BLOND, SERIAL # 1051-1063	89,288	**68,560**	60,588	53,413
GUITAR	75	DAQUISTO	**NEW YORKER DELUXE** SUNBURST, SERIAL # 1085-1094	80,521	**61,828**	54,639	48,168
GUITAR	78	DAQUISTO	**NEW YORKER DELUXE** SUNBURST, SERIAL # 1113-1125	76,565	**58,791**	51,955	45,802
GUITAR	76	DAQUISTO	**NEW YORKER SPECIAL** VIOLIN FINISH, SERIAL # 1095-1102	66,591	**51,133**	45,187	39,836
GUITAR	78	DAQUISTO	**NEW YORKER SPECIAL** SUNBURST, SERIAL # 1113-1125	60,020	**46,087**	40,728	35,905
GUITAR	79	DAQUISTO	**SOLID BODY** 7-STRING, SERIAL # 1126-1133	46,150	**35,437**	31,316	27,608
GUITAR	80	DAQUISTO	**SOLID BODY** 7-STRING, SERIAL # 1134-1142	42,062	**32,298**	28,542	25,162
MANDOLIN	72	DAQUISTO	**MANDOLIN ASYMMETRICAL** 2-POINT BODY	18,723	**14,376**	12,704	11,200

DAY SEQUERRA

TUNER	73	DAY	**MODEL 1 FM TUNER**	4,753	**3,649**	3,225	2,843

DBX

SIGNAL PROCESSOR	98	DBX	**120XP** SUBHARMONIC SYNTHESIZER	380	**292**	258	227
SGNPRO	77	DBX	**161** MONO COMPRESSOR/LIMITER	611	**469**	414	365
SGNPRO	77	DBX	**162** STEREO COMPRESSOR/LIMITER	1,246	**957**	845	745
SGNPRO	81	DBX	**902** DE-ESSER MODULE 4/F-900	434	**333**	294	259

DEARMOND

EFFECTS	77	DEARMOND	**THUNDERBOLT B** 5 OCTAVE WAH	248	**190**	168	148
EFFECTS	76	DEARMOND	**VOLUME PEDAL 1602**	179	**137**	121	107
EFFECTS	78	DEARMOND	**VOLUME PEDAL 1602**	168	**129**	114	100

DELVECCHIO DINAMICO

BANJO	68	DELVECCHI	**DINAMICO**	728	**559**	494	435
BANJO	75	DELVECCHI	**DINAMICO**	664	**509**	450	397
UKULELE	55	DELVECCHI	**DINAMICO** RESONATOR	673	**516**	456	402
UKE	60	DELVECCHI	**DINAMICO**	761	**584**	516	455

DOBRO, SEE ALSO MOSRITE, REGAL

GUITAR (ACOUSTIC)	35	DOBRO	**14 METAL BODY** SQUARE NECK, 14-FRET, SERIAL # 5700-7600	1,527	**1,173**	1,036	913
GUITAR	37	DOBRO	**14 STEEL BODY** VIOLIN EDGE, SERIAL # 8000-9000	1,519	**1,167**	1,031	909
GUITAR	36	DOBRO	**15 METAL BODY** VIOLIN EDGE, NICKLE-PLATED, SERIAL # 5700-7600	2,960	**2,272**	2,008	1,770
GUITAR	37	DOBRO	**15 METAL BODY** VIOLIN EDGE, NICKLE-PLATED, SERIAL # 8000-9000	2,940	**2,257**	1,995	1,758
GUITAR	35	DOBRO	**16 METAL BODY** VIOLIN EDGE, ENGRAVED, NICKLE-PLATED, SERIAL # 5700-7600	3,206	**2,462**	2,175	1,918
GUITAR	30	DOBRO	**19** SERIAL # 3000-	1,512	**1,161**	1,026	904
GUITAR	36	DOBRO	**19** SERIAL # 5700-7600	1,425	**1,094**	967	852
GUITAR	37	DOBRO	**19** SERIAL # 8000-9000	1,527	**1,173**	1,036	913
GUITAR	28	DOBRO	**27** DARK WALNUT, ROUND NECK, SERIAL # 900-1700	3,207	**2,463**	2,176	1,918
GUITAR	28	DOBRO	**27** ROUND NECK, 12-FRET, SERIAL # 900-1700	3,317	**2,547**	2,251	1,984
GUITAR	29	DOBRO	**27** ROUND NECK, 12-FRET, SLOT HEAD, SERIAL # 1800-2000	2,904	**2,229**	1,970	1,737
GUITAR	29	DOBRO	**27** BROWN SUNBURST, ROUND NECK, SERIAL # 1800-2000	3,037	**2,332**	2,061	1,817
GUITAR	29	DOBRO	**27** WALNUT, ROUND NECK, SERIAL # 1800-2000	3,180	**2,442**	2,158	1,902
GUITAR	30	DOBRO	**27** BROWN FINISH, SQUARE NECK, SERIAL # 3000-	2,117	**1,626**	1,437	1,266
GUITAR	32	DOBRO	**27** SQUARE NECK, SERIAL # 5000-5500	1,915	**1,470**	1,299	1,145
GUITAR	34	DOBRO	**27** SUNBURST, ROUND NECK, SERIAL # 5700-7600	2,080	**1,597**	1,412	1,244

TYPE	YR	MFG	PRICES--BASED ON 100% ORIGINAL MODEL	SELL EXC	SELL AVG	BUY EXC	BUY AVG
GUITAR	35	DOBRO	**27** ROUND NECK, 14-FRET, SERIAL # 5700-7600	1,514	1,162	1,027	905
GUITAR	35	DOBRO	**27** SUNBURST, SQUARE NECK, SERIAL # 5700-7600	2,061	1,583	1,399	1,233
GUITAR	36	DOBRO	**27** SUNBURST, RESONATOR, SERIAL # 5700-7600	2,008	1,541	1,362	1,201
GUITAR	37	DOBRO	**27** SUNBURST, ROUND NECK, HAWAIIAN, SERIAL # 8000-9000	1,439	1,105	976	860
GUITAR	40	DOBRO	**27** SUNBURST, SQUARE NECK	2,388	1,834	1,621	1,429
GUITAR	70	DOBRO	**27** SUNBURST, SQUARE NECK	3,709	2,848	2,517	2,219
GUITAR	29	DOBRO	**27 G** DARK WALNUT, SERIAL # 1800-2000	1,967	1,511	1,335	1,177
GUITAR	30	DOBRO	**27 G** HARDWOOD BODY, SERIAL # 3000-	1,963	1,507	1,332	1,174
GUITAR	32	DOBRO	**27 G** SUNBURST, WHITE BINDING TOP, SERIAL # 5000-5500	1,924	1,477	1,305	1,151
GUITAR	36	DOBRO	**27 G** SUNBURST, ROUND NECK, RESONATOR, SERIAL # 5700-7600	1,513	1,161	1,026	905
GUITAR	30	DOBRO	**27.50 REGAL TENOR** SERIAL # 3000-	999	767	677	597
GUITAR	36	DOBRO	**30** SUNBURST, ROUND NECK, 12-FRET, SERIAL # 5700-7600	1,365	1,048	926	816
GUITAR	30	DOBRO	**32** SUNBURST, ROUND NECK, SERIAL # 3000-	2,959	2,272	2,007	1,770
GUITAR	37	DOBRO	**32** METAL BODY, VIOLIN EDGE, SERIAL # 8000-9000	1,068	820	725	639
GUITAR	38	DOBRO	**32** SUNBURST, ROUND NECK, 14-FRET	1,417	1,088	962	848
GUITAR	76	DOBRO	**33** ROUND NECK	994	763	674	594
GUITAR	70	DOBRO	**33D**	1,244	955	844	744
GUITAR	71	DOBRO	**33D** ROUND NECK	1,254	963	851	750
GUITAR	75	DOBRO	**33D** ROUND NECK	1,052	808	714	629
GUITAR	75	DOBRO	**33H**	1,525	1,171	1,035	912
GUITAR	30	DOBRO	**36** ROUND NECK, SERIAL # 3000-	2,061	1,583	1,399	1,233
GUITAR	75	DOBRO	**36S** 8-STRING	975	749	661	583
GUITAR	30	DOBRO	**37** SERIAL # 3000-	3,336	2,561	2,264	1,995
GUITAR	30	DOBRO	**37** MAHOGANY, SERIAL # 3000-	3,367	2,586	2,285	2,014
GUITAR	30	DOBRO	**37** MAHOGANY, SQUARE NECK, SERIAL # 3000-	3,539	2,717	2,401	2,117
GUITAR	31	DOBRO	**37** MAHOGANY, ROUND NECK, RESONATOR, SERIAL # 3000-	3,463	2,659	2,349	2,071
GUITAR	32	DOBRO	**37** SUNBURST, SQUARE NECK,14-FRET, SERIAL # 5000-5500	2,943	2,260	1,997	1,760
GUITAR	32	DOBRO	**37** RESONATOR, SERIAL # 5000-5500	3,400	2,610	2,307	2,034
GUITAR	33	DOBRO	**37** SUNBURST, SQUARE NECK, SERIAL # 5000-5500	3,025	2,322	2,052	1,809
GUITAR	34	DOBRO	**37** SUNBURST, SQUARE NECK, SERIAL # 5700-7600	2,878	2,210	1,953	1,721
GUITAR	35	DOBRO	**37** SUNBURST, SQUARE NECK, 12-FRET, SERIAL # 5700-7600	2,399	1,842	1,627	1,435
GUITAR	36	DOBRO	**37** SUNBURST, SQUARE NECK, SERIAL # 5700-7600	2,393	1,837	1,624	1,431
GUITAR	37	DOBRO	**37** MAHOGANY, ROUND NECK, SERIAL # 8000-9000	2,018	1,549	1,369	1,207
GUITAR	37	DOBRO	**37** SUNBURST, SQUARE NECK, SERIAL # 8000-9000	2,073	1,591	1,406	1,240
GUITAR	38	DOBRO	**37** SUNBURST, SQUARE NECK	2,018	1,549	1,369	1,207
GUITAR	39	DOBRO	**37** SUNBURST, SQUARE NECK	2,050	1,574	1,391	1,226
GUITAR	40	DOBRO	**37** SUNBURST, SQUARE NECK, 12-FRET	1,802	1,383	1,222	1,078
GUITAR	28	DOBRO	**37G** MAHOGANY, ROUND NECK, SERIAL # 900-1700	2,279	1,750	1,546	1,363
GUITAR	30	DOBRO	**37G** SQUARE NECK, SERIAL # 3000-	1,671	1,283	1,133	999
GUITAR	33	DOBRO	**37G** MAHOGANY, ROUND NECK, SERIAL # 5000-5500	2,167	1,664	1,470	1,296
GUITAR	34	DOBRO	**37G** SQUARE NECK, SERIAL # 5700-7600	2,447	1,879	1,660	1,463
GUITAR	33	DOBRO	**45** SPRUCE TOP, MAHOGANY BODY, F-HOLES, SERIAL # 5000-5500	2,123	1,630	1,440	1,270
GUITAR	35	DOBRO	**45G** SPRUCE TOP, SQUARE NECK, SERIAL # 5700-7600	2,082	1,598	1,412	1,245

TYPE	YR	MFG	PRICES--BASED ON 100% ORIGINAL MODEL	SELL EXC	SELL AVG	BUY EXC	BUY AVG
GUITAR	36	DOBRO	**45G** BLOND, SERIAL # 5700-7600	1,831	**1,406**	1,242	1,095
GUITAR	38	DOBRO	**46** METAL BODY, VIOLIN EDGE, ALUMALITE	1,640	**1,259**	1,113	981
GUITAR	39	DOBRO	**46** ROUND NECK, 14-FRET, ALUMALITE	1,543	**1,185**	1,047	923
GUITAR	40	DOBRO	**46** ROUND NECK	1,579	**1,212**	1,071	944
GUITAR	40	DOBRO	**47** REGAL ROUND	1,967	**1,511**	1,335	1,177
GUITAR	37	DOBRO	**55** SUNBURST, 12-FRET, DOT INLAY, SERIAL # 8000-9000	1,361	**1,045**	924	814
GUITAR	35	DOBRO	**60** SERIAL # 5700-7600	2,440	**1,873**	1,656	1,459
GUITAR	36	DOBRO	**60** SERIAL # 5700-7600	2,113	**1,597**	1,408	1,168
GUITAR	70	DOBRO	**60D** NATURAL, SQUARE NECK, RESONATOR	1,253	**962**	850	749
GUITAR	75	DOBRO	**60D** SUNBURST, ROUND NECK	739	**567**	501	442
GUITAR	75	DOBRO	**60D** NATURAL, SQUARE NECK, RESONATOR	1,028	**789**	697	615
GUITAR	77	DOBRO	**60D** SUNBURST, SQUARE NECK	954	**732**	647	570
GUITAR	78	DOBRO	**60D** BROWN SUNBURST, SQUARE NECK	796	**611**	540	476
GUITAR	80	DOBRO	**60D** SUNBURST, SQUARE NECK	733	**563**	497	438
GUITAR	76	DOBRO	**60DN** NATURAL, MAPLE, SQUARE NECK, SERIAL #D11296	816	**617**	544	451
GUITAR	78	DOBRO	**60DN** NATURAL, SQUARE NECK	794	**609**	538	475
GUITAR	75	DOBRO	**60S** SUNBURST	926	**711**	628	554
GUITAR	38	DOBRO	**62** VIOLIN EDGE, SPANISH DANCE	1,342	**1,031**	911	803
GUITAR	28	DOBRO	**65** RESONATOR, SANDBLASTED PATTERN, SERIAL # 900-1700	3,326	**2,554**	2,257	1,989
GUITAR	29	DOBRO	**65** ROUND NECK, SERIAL # 1800-2000	2,998	**2,302**	2,034	1,793
GUITAR	30	DOBRO	**66** WOOD BODY, SERIAL # 3000-	2,402	**1,844**	1,630	1,437
GUITAR	33	DOBRO	**65** FRENCH SCROLL PATTERN, SERIAL # 5000-5500	3,300	**2,534**	2,239	1,974
GUITAR	40	DOBRO	**65** LATTICE TOP DESIGN	3,433	**2,636**	2,330	2,054
GUITAR	29	DOBRO	**65 TENOR** SERIAL # 1800-2000	2,886	**2,216**	1,958	1,726
GUITAR	78	DOBRO	**66** SUNBURST	926	**711**	628	554
GUITAR	70	DOBRO	**90** METAL BODY, SQUARE NECK, SERIAL #B285 9	833	**639**	565	498
GUITAR	28	DOBRO	**100** DELUXE WALNUT, ROUND NECK, SERIAL # 900-1700	6,969	**5,351**	4,729	4,169
GUITAR	32	DOBRO	**125** ROUND NECK, HEART INLAY, SERIAL # 5000-5500	3,557	**2,731**	2,413	2,127
GUITAR	29	DOBRO	**126T** WALNUT, SERIAL # 1800-2000	2,468	**1,895**	1,675	1,476
GUITAR	28	DOBRO	**156** ROUND NECK, SERIAL # 900-1700	17,786	**13,657**	12,069	10,640
GUITAR	35	DOBRO	**ANGELUS HAWAIIAN STYLE** SERIAL # 5700-7600	1,348	**1,035**	915	806
GUITAR	36	DOBRO	**ANGELUS HAWAIIAN STYLE** SERIAL # 5700-7600	1,041	**799**	706	623
GUITAR	37	DOBRO	**ANGELUS HAWAIIAN STYLE** SERIAL # 8000-9000	983	**755**	667	588
GUITAR	56	DOBRO	**BABY BASS** COPPER FLAKE ZORKO	2,126	**1,633**	1,443	1,272
GUITAR	35	DOBRO	**DOBRO JR** FLATTOP, SERIAL # 5700-7600	759	**583**	515	454
GUITAR	68	DOBRO	**HOUND DOG** SUNBURST, RESONATOR	693	**532**	470	414
GUITAR	30	DOBRO	**MAGNATONE CYCLOPS** RESONATOR, SERIAL # 3000-	1,514	**1,162**	1,027	905
GUITAR	31	DOBRO	**MAGNATONE CYCLOPS** ROUND NECK, SERIAL # 3000-	1,721	**1,321**	1,168	1,029
GUITAR	30	DOBRO	**PROFESSIONAL M-15 REGAL** NICKEL BODY, SERIAL # 3000-	3,300	**2,534**	2,239	1,974
GUITAR	74	DOBRO	**RESONATOR** ROSEWOOD, SQUARE NECK	3,556	**2,730**	2,413	2,127
GUITAR	76	DOBRO	**RESONATOR** SUNBURST, ROUND NECK	1,789	**1,374**	1,214	1,070
GUITAR	79	DOBRO	**RESONATOR** GOLD-PLATED, SQUARE NECK	985	**756**	668	589

TYPE	YR	MFG	PRICES--BASED ON 100% ORIGINAL MODEL	SELL EXC	SELL AVG	BUY EXC	BUY AVG
MANDOLIN	29	DOBRO	**MANDOLIN** WALNUT NECK/SIDES, INLAY	3,487	**2,678**	2,366	2,086
MANDOL	34	DOBRO	**MANDOLIN** SUNBURST, F-HOLES	1,319	**1,013**	895	789
MANDOL	35	DOBRO	**MANDOLIN** WOOD BODY	1,542	**1,184**	1,046	922
MANDOL	68	DOBRO	**RESONATOR** WOOD BODY	922	**708**	626	552
STEEL GUITAR	39	DOBRO	**METAL** 6-STRING	1,893	**1,454**	1,285	1,132
UKULELE	31	DOBRO	**CYCLOPS** ROSEWOOD, ROUND NECK	3,099	**2,379**	2,102	1,853
UKE	31	DOBRO	**CYCLOPS** EBONY, FRENCH SCROLL	3,831	**2,942**	2,599	2,292
UKE	37	DOBRO	**CYCLOPS** WOOD BODY, SQUARE HEAD SLOTS	2,026	**1,555**	1,374	1,212
UKE	32	DOBRO	**DOUBLE CYCLOPS** ROSEWOOD TOP/FINGERBOARD	1,543	**1,185**	1,047	923
UKE	32	DOBRO	**DOUBLE CYCLOPS** SQUARE NECK	2,054	**1,577**	1,393	1,228
UKE	33	DOBRO	**F-HOLES** WOOD BODY, INLAYS	1,927	**1,480**	1,307	1,153

DYNACO ELECTRONICS

TYPE	YR	MFG	MODEL	SELL EXC	SELL AVG	BUY EXC	BUY AVG
PRE	64	DYNACO	**PAS-1**	221	**170**	150	132
PRE	64-69	DYNACO	**PAS-2 KIT**	260	**200**	177	156
PRE	64-69	DYNACO	**PAS-2A ASSEMBLED**	278	**214**	189	166
PRE	64-69	DYNACO	**PAS-3 KIT**	249	**191**	169	149
PRE	64-60	DYNACO	**PAS-3A ASSEMBLED**	278	**214**	189	166
PRE	69	DYNACO	**PAS-3X KIT**	275	**211**	186	164
PRE	69-74	DYNACO	**PAS-3X/A ASSEMBLED**	266	**204**	180	159
PWR	54-60	DYNACO	**MARK II** 50 WATT	327	**251**	221	195
PWR	64-69	DYNACO	**MARK III KIT** MONO, TUBE, AMP, 60 WATTS, PAIR	784	**602**	532	469
PWR	64-69	DYNACO	**MARK IIIA ASSEMBLED** MONO, 60 WATT	685	**526**	465	410
PWR	64-69	DYNACO	**MARK IV KIT** 40 WATT	434	**333**	294	259
PWR	78	DYNACO	**MARK VI KIT** 100 WATTS	281	**215**	190	100
PWR	64	DYNACO	**ST-70**	554	**425**	376	331
PWR	64-69	DYNACO	**STEREO 35** 17 WATT	443	**340**	300	265
PWR	64-69	DYNACO	**STEREO 70 ASSEMBLED** 35 WATT	601	**461**	408	359
PWR	72-77	DYNACO	**STEREO 70 ASSEMBLED** 35 WATT	554	**425**	376	331
TUNER	64-69	DYNACO	**FM-3 ASSEMBLED**	170	**130**	115	101
TUNER	73	DYNACO	**FM-3 KIT**	316	**243**	215	189
TUNER	64	DYNACO	**FM-3A ASSEMBLED**	219	**168**	148	131

EARTHWOOD BASS by ERNIE BALL

TYPE	YR	MFG	MODEL	SELL EXC	SELL AVG	BUY EXC	BUY AVG
GUITAR AMP	77	EARTH	**MV-10**	281	**215**	190	168
GUITAR (ACOUSTIC)	75	EARTH	**EARTHWOOD BASS**	861	**661**	584	515
GUITAR	76	EARTH	**EARTHWOOD BASS E**	1,267	**973**	860	758

EAW

TYPE	YR	MFG	MODEL	SELL EXC	SELL AVG	BUY EXC	BUY AVG
SPKR	04	EAW	**KF 695ISR** 2" EXIT HF	1,289	**989**	874	771

EICO

TYPE	YR	MFG	MODEL	SELL EXC	SELL AVG	BUY EXC	BUY AVG
PWR	59	EICO	**HF-20 MONO TUBE**	136	**104**	92	81
PWR	58	EICO	**HF-20 KIT**	221	**170**	150	132
PWR	60	EICO	**HF-30** MONO TUBE	221	**170**	150	132
PWR	60-78	EICO	**HF-50 KIT**	258	**198**	175	154
PWR	60-78	EICO	**HF-60 KIT**	499	**383**	338	298
PWR	60	EICO	**HF-81** INTEGRATED STEREO TUBE	738	**566**	500	441
PWR	60	EICO	**HF-85 ASSEMBLED** TUBE	201	**154**	136	120
PWR	61-63	EICO	**HF-86 KIT** STEREO TUBE	321	**246**	218	192
PWR	61-63	EICO	**HF-87 KIT** STEREO TUBE	554	**425**	376	331
PWR	60	EICO	**HF-89 ASSEMBLED** TUBE	588	**451**	399	351
PWR	60	EICO	**HF-89 KIT** TUBE	784	**602**	532	469

EKO, MADE IN ITALY

TYPE	YR	MFG	MODEL	SELL EXC	SELL AVG	BUY EXC	BUY AVG
ELEC. GUITAR & BASS	63	EKO	**500-4V**	620	**476**	421	371

TYPE	YR	MFG	PRICES--BASED ON 100% ORIGINAL MODEL	SELL EXC	SELL AVG	BUY EXC	BUY AVG
ELGUIT	64	EKO	**700 4V**	694	**533**	471	415
ELGUIT	69	EKO	**955/2 VIOLIN BASS**	535	**411**	363	320
ELGUIT	67	EKO	**995 VIOLIN BASS** 2 PU's	631	**485**	428	377
ELGUIT	67	EKO	**BARRACUDA**	535	**411**	363	320
ELGUIT	71	EKO	**BARRACUDA**	571	**438**	387	341
ELGUIT	75	EKO	**BARRACUDA**	432	**331**	293	258
ELGUIT	66	EKO	**COBRA**	567	**436**	385	339
ELGUIT	69	EKO	**COBRA**	573	**440**	389	343
ELGUIT	69	EKO	**COBRA BASS II**	459	**352**	311	274
ELGUIT	75	EKO	**COBRA BASS II**	543	**417**	368	324
ELGUIT	67	EKO	**COBRA XII** 12-STRING	481	**369**	326	288
ELGUIT	64	EKO	**CONDOR**	551	**423**	373	329
ELGUIT	68	EKO	**CONDOR** 3 PU's	426	**327**	289	255
ELGUIT	68	EKO	**CONDOR BASS** 2 PU's	512	**393**	348	306
ELGUIT	64	EKO	**CRESTLINE** RED SPARKLE	658	**505**	446	393
ELGUIT	65	EKO	**DRAGON**	590	**453**	400	353
ELGUIT	67	EKO	**DRAGON**	611	**469**	414	365
ELGUIT	67	EKO	**FLORENTINE** DOUBLE CUTAWAY	607	**466**	411	363
ELGUIT	68	EKO	**KADETT** ORANGE, DOUBLE CUTAWAY, SOLID, 3 PU's	598	**459**	405	357
ELGUIT	70	EKO	**KADETT** SOLID BODY	609	**467**	413	364
ELGUIT	67	EKO	**KADETT XII**	607	**466**	411	363
ELGUIT	68	EKO	**KADETT XII**	594	**456**	403	355
ELGUIT	67	EKO	**LANCER**	642	**493**	436	384
ELGUIT	71	EKO	**LARK I** SUNBURST	469	**360**	318	280
ELGUIT	70	EKO	**LARK II** SUNBURST	526	**404**	357	314
ELGUIT	76	EKO	**MANTA** 2 PU's	529	**406**	359	316
ELGUIT	67	EKO	**ROK** ROCKET SHAPED	602	**462**	408	360
ELGUIT	70	EKO	**ROK IV** A.K.A. ROCKET	677	**520**	459	405
ELGUIT	67	EKO	**ROK VI**	668	**513**	453	399
ELGUIT	70	EKO	**ROK XII** 12-STRING	655	**503**	444	391
ELGUIT	64	EKO	**TONEMASTER** SQUARE NECK, LAP GUITAR	686	**527**	465	410
ELGUIT	76	EKO	**X 27** SOLID BODY, 2 PU's	470	**361**	319	281
GUITAR (ACOUSTIC)	71	EKO	**CLASSICAL** SPANISH ROSEWOOD	495	**380**	335	296
GUITAR	64	EKO	**EL DORADO 1101** 12-STRING	724	**556**	491	433
GUITAR	64	EKO	**EL DORADO 1102** 6-STRING	523	**401**	354	312
GUITAR	60	EKO	**RANCHERO FOLK BASS** NATURAL	364	**279**	247	217
GUITAR	66	EKO	**RANGER IV DREADNOUGHT** MAHOGANY BODY	534	**410**	362	319
GUITAR	70	EKO	**RANGER XII** 12-STRING	491	**377**	333	294

ELECTRO HARMONIX

TYPE	YR	MFG	MODEL	SELL EXC	SELL AVG	BUY EXC	BUY AVG
EFFECTS	78	ELECHARM	**10-BAND GRAPHIC EQUALIZER**	97	**74**	66	58
EFFECTS	79	ELECHARM	**16 SECOND DELAY FRONT CONTROLLER**	278	**214**	189	166
EFFECTS	74	ELECHARM	**BAD STONE PHASER** 2 KNOBS	138	**106**	94	83
EFFECTS	77	ELECHARM	**BAD STONE PHASER** 3 KNOBS	110	**85**	75	66
EFFECTS	79	ELECHARM	**BIG MUFF**	160	**122**	108	95
EFFECTS	74	ELECHARM	**BIG MUFF II**	150	**115**	101	89
EFFECTS	71	ELECHARM	**BIG MUFF FUZZ DELUXE** BLACK, GRAPHICS	235	**180**	159	140
EFFECTS	75	ELECHARM	**BIG MUFF FUZZ DELUXE** COMPRESSOR	157	**121**	107	94
EFFECTS	72	ELECHARM	**BLACK FINGER SUSTAINER**	161	**123**	109	96
EFFECTS	78	ELECHARM	**CLONE THEORY**	228	**175**	155	136
EFFECTS	74	ELECHARM	**CRYING TONE WAH WAH**	101	**78**	69	60
EFFECTS	78	ELECHARM	**DELUXE ELECTRIC MISTRESS**	256	**196**	174	153
EFFECTS	79	ELECHARM	**DELUXE MEMORY MAN**	266	**204**	180	159
EFFECTS	76	ELECHARM	**DR. Q FOLLOWER**	163	**125**	110	97
EFFECTS	78	ELECHARM	**ECHO FLANGER**	108	**83**	73	64

TYPE	YR	MFG	PRICES--BASED ON 100% ORIGINAL MODEL	SELL EXC	SELL AVG	BUY EXC	BUY AVG
EFFECTS	76	ELECHARM	ELECTRIC MISTRESS	160	122	108	95
EFFECTS	74	ELECHARM	FREQUENCY ANALYZER	512	393	348	306
EFFECTS	79	ELECHARM	FULL DOUBLE TRACKER SILVER, ANALOG	319	245	216	190
EFFECTS	76	ELECHARM	GOLDEN THROAT TALK BOX	159	122	107	95
EFFECTS	75	ELECHARM	HOT TUBES	202	155	137	121
EFFECTS	76	ELECHARM	HOT TUBES OVERDRIVE	206	158	139	123
EFFECTS	77	ELECHARM	INSTANT REPLAY	588	451	399	351
EFFECTS	76	ELECHARM	LITTLE BIG MUFF FUZZ	163	125	110	97
EFFECTS	74	ELECHARM	LPB-2 POWER BOOSTER	170	130	115	101
EFFECTS	77	ELECHARM	MEMORY MAN DELAY	163	125	110	97
EFFECTS	74	ELECHARM	MOLE BASS BOOSTER	136	104	92	81
EFFECTS	76	ELECHARM	OCTAVE MULTIPLEXER	421	323	285	251
EFFECTS	80	ELECHARM	POLY PHASE	240	184	163	144
EFFECTS	76	ELECHARM	QUEEN TRIGGERED WAH	294	226	199	176
EFFECTS	73	ELECHARM	SCREAMING BIRD	171	131	116	102
EFFECTS	72	ELECHARM	SCREAMING TREE	336	258	228	201
EFFECTS	76	ELECHARM	SCREAMING TREE TREBLE BOOST	252	193	171	150
EFFECTS	77	ELECHARM	SILENCER NOISE GATE	136	104	92	81
EFFECTS	78	ELECHARM	SLAP BACK ECHO	155	119	105	93
EFFECTS	75	ELECHARM	SMALL STONE CHORUS	187	143	126	111
EFFECTS	75	ELECHARM	SMALL STONE PHASER	168	129	114	100
EFFECTS	78	ELECHARM	SOUL PREACHER COMPRESSOR	96	73	65	57
EFFECTS	78	ELECHARM	SPACE DRUM	221	170	150	132
EFFECTS	77	ELECHARM	SWITCHABLE A/B BOX	87	67	59	52
EFFECTS	77	ELECHARM	SWITCHBLADE	138	106	94	83
EFFECTS	78	ELECHARM	TALKING PEDAL	309	237	209	184
EFFECTS	80	ELECHARM	VOCORDER (RACK)	840	645	570	502
EFFECTS	78	ELECHARM	Y-TRIGGER FILTER SWEEP	258	198	175	154
EFFECTS	77	ELECHARM	ZIPPER ENVELOPE FOLLOWER	180	138	122	107

ELECTRA

TYPE	YR	MFG	MODEL	SELL EXC	SELL AVG	BUY EXC	BUY AVG
ELEC. GUITAR & BASS	76	ELECTRA	ELVIN BISHOP	749	575	508	448
ELGUIT	77	ELECTRA	ELVIN BISHOP	708	544	481	424
ELGUIT	78	ELECTRA	MPC OUTLAW BACK HOLE EFFECTS	535	411	363	320
ELGUIT	77	ELECTRA	MPC OUTLAW BASS BACK HOLE EFFECTS	498	382	338	298
ELGUIT	72	ELECTRA	ROCK	459	352	311	274
ELGUIT	71	ELECTRA	ROCK LES PAUL COPY	496	380	336	296
ELGUIT	75	ELECTRA	SUPER ROCK LES PAUL COPY	488	374	331	292

ELECTRO I

TYPE	YR	MFG	MODEL	SELL EXC	SELL AVG	BUY EXC	BUY AVG
PWR	63	ELECTRO I	DUAL-100 TUBE 2 CHASSIS, 100 WATTS	2,240	1,720	1,520	1,340
PWR	68	ELECTRO I	M-60 MONO TUBE	542	416	367	324
PWR	68	ELECTRO I	M-60 MONO TUBE	433	332	294	259
PWR	64	ELECTRO I	ST-70 C-1	427	328	290	255
PWR	65	ELECTRO I	ST-70 C-2	452	347	307	270
XOVER	69	ELECTRO I	PC-1	101	78	69	60

ELECTRO VOICE

TYPE	YR	MFG	MODEL	SELL EXC	SELL AVG	BUY EXC	BUY AVG
MIC	61	ELECTRO V	950 CARDAX "MERCURY MIC"	162	124	110	97
RAW	60-77	ELECTRO V	15W 15" PAIR	250	192	170	150
RAW	60-77	ELECTRO V	18W/K	336	258	228	201
RAW	60	ELECTRO V	BB MID HORN & XOVER PAIR	388	298	263	232
RAW	60	ELECTRO V	BB-1 HORN TWEETER & XOVER PAIR	250	192	170	150
RAW	60	ELECTRO V	BB-2 HORN TWEETER & XOVER PAIR	250	192	170	150
RAW	60	ELECTRO V	BB-5 HORN TWEETER & XOVER PAIR	253	194	171	151
RAW	60	ELECTRO V	HF-1 HORN TWEETER & XOVER PAIR	253	194	171	151
RAW	60	ELECTRO V	LS-15 15" PAIR	253	194	171	151
RAW	68	ELECTRO V	LT-8 8" PAIR	253	194	171	151
RAW	68	ELECTRO V	LT-12 12" PAIR	253	194	171	151
RAW	60	ELECTRO V	MF-1 MID HORN & XOVER PAIR	253	194	171	151
RAW	60	ELECTRO V	SP-8B 8" PAIR	253	194	171	151
RAW	74	ELECTRO V	ST-350 HORN TWEETER PAIR	253	194	171	151
RAW	60	ELECTRO V	T-10A HORN MID RANGE DRVR PAIR	253	194	171	151
RAW	60	ELECTRO V	T-35 HORN TWEETER PAIR	169	129	114	101
RAW	60	ELECTRO V	T-250 HORN MID RANGE DRVR PAIR	253	194	171	151
RAW	60	ELECTRO V	T-350 HORN TWEETER PAIR	250	192	170	150
XOVER	60	ELECTRO V	X-8 PAIR	992	761	673	593
XOVER	60	ELECTRO V	X-325 PAIR	991	761	672	592

EMP

TYPE	YR	MFG	MODEL	SELL EXC	SELL AVG	BUY EXC	BUY AVG
SPKR	68	EMP	9000-M GRENADIER	1,245	956	845	745

TYPE	YR	MFG	PRICES--BASED ON 100% ORIGINAL MODEL	SELL EXC	SELL AVG	BUY EXC	BUY AVG
			ELECTRONIC MUSIC STUDIOS OF AMERICA				
SYNTHESIZER	73	EMSA	**SYNTHI A**	1,431	**1,099**	971	856
SYNTH	74	EMSA	**SYNTHI AKS**	1,544	**1,185**	1,048	923
SYNTH	72	EMSA	**VCS3 MK II**	893	**686**	606	534
SYNTH	71	EMSA	**VCS3 THE "PUTNEY"**	1,457	**1,118**	988	871
			EPIPHONE by EPIPHONE PRE-1957				
BANJO	28	EPI	**ARTIST PLECTRUM**	2,272	**1,744**	1,542	1,359
BANJO	28	EPI	**ARTIST TENOR**	3,151	**2,420**	2,138	1,885
BANJO	30	EPI	**ARTIST TENOR** SERIAL # 10000-	3,142	**2,413**	2,132	1,880
BANJO	28	EPI	**CONCERT SPECIAL RECORDING TENOR**	2,467	**1,894**	1,674	1,476
BANJO	29	EPI	**CONCERT SPECIAL RECORDING TENOR**	2,261	**1,736**	1,534	1,352
BANJO	30	EPI	**CONCERT SPECIAL RECORDING TENOR** SERIAL # 10000-	3,301	**2,535**	2,240	1,975
BANJO	28	EPI	**DELUXE RECORDING TENOR**	6,190	**4,753**	4,200	3,703
BANJO	40	EPI	**ELECTAR** SUNBURST, NO SOUND HOLE, 1 PU, SERIAL # 13000-	1,037	**796**	703	620
BANJO	28	EPI	**POT** GOLD-PLATED ENGRAVED HARDWARE	1,211	**930**	822	724
BANJO	30	EPI	**RIALTO PLECTRUM** WALNUT NECK, RESONATOR, SERIAL # 10000-	816	**626**	554	488
BANJO	28	EPI	**STYLE B TENOR**	3,060	**2,350**	2,077	1,831
ELEC. GUITAR & BASS	39	EPI	**CENTURY** WALNUT, NON-CUTAWAY, 1 PU, SERIAL # 13000-	1,451	**1,114**	984	868
ELGUIT	52	EPI	**CENTURY** MAHOGANY, NON-CUTAWAY, 1 PU, SERIAL # 64000-	881	**676**	598	527
ELGUIT	53	EPI	**CENTURY** MAHOGANY, NON-CUTAWAY, 1 PU, SERIAL # 64000-66000	881	**676**	598	527
ELGUIT	54	EPI	**CENTURY** MAHOGANY, NON-CUTAWAY, 1 PU, SERIAL # 68000-	881	**676**	598	527
ELGUIT	53	EPI	**ELECTROMATIC** NATURAL, SERIAL # 64000-66000	2,877	**2,209**	1,952	1,721
ELGUIT	38	EPI	**EMPEROR** NATURAL, ARCHTOP, SERIAL # 12000-	3,161	**2,427**	2,145	1,891
ELGUIT	38	EPI	**EMPEROR** NATURAL, FLAME BACK/SIDES, SERIAL # 12000-	3,169	**2,433**	2,150	1,896
ELGUIT	39	EPI	**EMPEROR** SUNBURST, SERIAL # 13000-	3,494	**2,683**	2,371	2,090
ELGUIT	40	EPI	**EMPEROR** BLOND, NON-CUTAWAY, ARCHTOP, SERIAL # 13000-	2,385	**1,831**	1,618	1,427
ELGUIT	41	EPI	**EMPEROR** BLOND, SERIAL # 14000-	2,364	**1,815**	1,604	1,414
ELGUIT	42	EPI	**EMPEROR** SUNBURST, SERIAL # 14000-	1,591	**1,222**	1,079	952
ELGUIT	43	EPI	**EMPEROR** NATURAL, SERIAL # 18000-	1,533	**1,177**	1,040	917
ELGUIT	43	EPI	**EMPEROR** SUNBURST, SERIAL # 18000-	1,536	**1,179**	1,042	919
ELGUIT	45	EPI	**EMPEROR** NATURAL, NON-CUTAWAY, SERIAL # 52000-54000	1,450	**1,113**	984	867
ELGUIT	45	EPI	**EMPEROR** SUNBURST, NEW YORK ARCHTOP. SERIAL # 52000-54000	1,551	**1,191**	1,052	927
ELGUIT	46	EPI	**EMPEROR** NATURAL, NON-CUTAWAY, SERIAL # 54000-55000	1,538	**1,181**	1,044	920
ELGUIT	46	EPI	**EMPEROR** SUNBURST, SERIAL # 54000-55000	1,542	**1,184**	1,046	922
ELGUIT	47	EPI	**EMPEROR** SUNBURST, ERIAL # 56000-	3,370	**2,587**	2,286	2,016
ELGUIT	48	EPI	**EMPEROR** BLOND, NEW YORK ARCHTOP, SERIAL # 57000-	3,006	**2,308**	2,039	1,798
ELGUIT	49	EPI	**EMPEROR** NATURAL, NON-CUTAWAY, SERIAL # 58000-	3,377	**2,593**	2,292	2,020
ELGUIT	50	EPI	**EMPEROR** NATURAL, ARCHTOP, CUTAWAY, SERIAL # 59000-	3,365	**2,584**	2,283	2,013
ELGUIT	50	EPI	**EMPEROR** SUNBURST. ARCHTOP CUTAWAY, SERIAL # 59000-	3,367	**2,586**	2,285	2,014
ELGUIT	51	EPI	**EMPEROR** NATURAL, NON-CUTAWAY, SERIAL # 60000-63000	3,377	**2,593**	2,292	2,020
ELGUIT	51	EPI	**EMPEROR** SUNBURST, CUTAWAY, SERIAL # 60000-63000	3,805	**2,922**	2,582	2,276
ELGUIT	51	EPI	**EMPEROR** NATURAL, VARITONE, SERIAL # 60000-63000	3,878	**2,978**	2,631	2,320
ELGUIT	54	EPI	**EMPEROR** NEW YORK ARCHTOP, SERIAL # 68000-	3,728	**2,862**	2,530	2,230
ELGUIT	54	EPI	**EMPEROR** SUNBURST, SERIAL # 68000-	3,971	**3,049**	2,694	2,375
ELGUIT	54	EPI	**EMPEROR** NATURAL, ARCHTOP, CUTAWAY, SERIAL # 68000-	6,007	**4,613**	4,076	3,593
ELGUIT	55	EPI	**EMPEROR** NATURAL, SERIAL # 69000-	3,230	**2,480**	2,191	1,932

TYPE	YR	MFG	PRICES--BASED ON 100% ORIGINAL MODEL	SELL EXC	SELL AVG	BUY EXC	BUY AVG
ELGUIT	55	EPI	**EMPEROR** SUNBURST, SERIAL # 69000-	5,246	**4,028**	3,559	3,138
ELGUIT	49	EPI	**EMPEROR REGENT** NEW YORK ARCHTOP, SERIAL # 58000-	2,321	**1,782**	1,575	1,388
ELGUIT	50	EPI	**EMPEROR REGENT** NATURAL, CUTAWAY, QUILTED MAPLE, SERIAL # 59000-	3,879	**2,979**	2,632	2,320
ELGUIT	51	EPI	**EMPEROR REGENT** BLOND, FLAME MAPLE, SERIAL # 60000-63000	3,875	**2,975**	2,629	2,318
ELGUIT	51	EPI	**EMPEROR REGENT** NATURAL, CUTAWAY, ARCHTOP, SERIAL # 60000-63000	3,877	**2,977**	2,631	2,319
ELGUIT	53	EPI	**EMPEROR REGENT** BLOND, CUTAWAY, SERIAL # 64000-66000	3,864	**2,967**	2,622	2,311
ELGUIT	55	EPI	**HARRY VOLPE** SUNBURST, DOT INLAY, NON-CUTAWAY, SERIAL # 69000-	2,403	**1,845**	1,630	1,437
ELGUIT	39	EPI	**ZEPHYR** SERIAL # 13000-	1,380	**1,060**	937	826
ELGUIT	40	EPI	**ZEPHYR** BLOND, SERIAL # 13000-	1,982	**1,522**	1,345	1,185
ELGUIT	42	EPI	**ZEPHYR** BLOND, SERIAL # 14000-	1,803	**1,384**	1,223	1,078
ELGUIT	43	EPI	**ZEPHYR** BLOND	1,799	**1,382**	1,221	1,076
ELGUIT	44	EPI	**ZEPHYR** BLOND	1,831	**1,406**	1,242	1,095
ELGUIT	49	EPI	**ZEPHYR** SUNBURST	2,065	**1,585**	1,401	1,235
ELGUIT	51	EPI	**ZEPHYR** SUNBURST	2,226	**1,709**	1,510	1,331
ELGUIT	54	EPI	**ZEPHYR** SUNBURST, CUTAWAY	1,880	**1,443**	1,276	1,124
ELGUIT	41	EPI	**ZEPHYR DELUXE** BLOND	3,971	**3,049**	2,694	2,375
ELGUIT	42	EPI	**ZEPHYR DELUXE** BLOND	3,847	**2,954**	2,610	2,301
ELGUIT	45	EPI	**ZEPHYR DELUXE** BLOND	3,878	**2,978**	2,631	2,320
ELGUIT	51	EPI	**ZEPHYR DELUXE** BLOND	3,872	**2,973**	2,628	2,316
ELGUIT	41	EPI	**ZEPHYR DELUXE REGENT** SUNBURST	4,047	**3,108**	2,746	2,421
ELGUIT	42	EPI	**ZEPHYR DELUXE REGENT** NATURAL	4,065	**3,121**	2,758	2,432
ELGUIT	46	EPI	**ZEPHYR DELUXE REGENT** SUNBURST	4,174	**3,205**	2,832	2,497
ELGUIT	48	EPI	**ZEPHYR DELUXE REGENT** NATURAL	4,102	**3,150**	2,783	2,454
ELGUIT	49	EPI	**ZEPHYR DELUXE REGENT** NATURAL	3,449	**2,648**	2,340	2,063
ELGUIT	49	EPI	**ZEPHYR DELUXE REGENT** SUNBURST	4,063	**3,120**	2,757	2,430
ELGUIT	50	EPI	**ZEPHYR DELUXE REGENT** SUNBURST	3,360	**2,580**	2,280	2,010
ELGUIT	50	EPI	**ZEPHYR DELUXE REGENT** NATURAL	3,422	**2,628**	2,322	2,047
ELGUIT	51	EPI	**ZEPHYR DELUXE REGENT** SUNBURST	3,232	**2,481**	2,193	1,933
ELGUIT	51	EPI	**ZEPHYR DELUXE REGENT** NATURAL	3,298	**2,532**	2,238	1,973
ELGUIT	52	EPI	**ZEPHYR DELUXE REGENT** NATURAL	3,360	**2,580**	2,280	2,010
ELGUIT	52	EPI	**ZEPHYR DELUXE REGENT** BLOND	3,960	**3,040**	2,687	2,369
ELGUIT	53	EPI	**ZEPHYR DELUXE REGENT** SUNBURST	3,857	**2,961**	2,617	2,307
ELGUIT	53	EPI	**ZEPHYR DELUXE REGENT** NATURAL	3,876	**2,976**	2,630	2,318
ELGUIT	54	EPI	**ZEPHYR DELUXE REGENT** SUNBURST	3,853	**2,959**	2,615	2,305
ELGUIT	51	EPI	**ZEPHYR EMPEROR REGENT** BLOND, 3 PU's, SERIAL #61688	5,613	**4,310**	3,809	3,358
ELGUIT	52	EPI	**ZEPHYR EMPEROR REGENT** SUNBURST, 3 PU's	5,383	**4,134**	3,653	3,220
ELGUIT	53	EPI	**ZEPHYR EMPEROR REGENT** SUNBURST, 3 PU's	5,137	**3,944**	3,486	3,073
ELGUIT	53	EPI	**ZEPHYR EMPEROR REGENT** BLOND	5,237	**4,021**	3,553	3,132
ELGUIT	54	EPI	**ZEPHYR EMPEROR REGENT** BLOND	5,404	**4,149**	3,667	3,232
ELGUIT	51	EPI	**ZEPHYR REGENT** SUNBURST	2,227	**1,710**	1,511	1,332
ELGUIT	52	EPI	**ZEPHYR REGENT** SUNBURST, NEW YORK ARCHTOP	2,274	**1,746**	1,543	1,360
ELGUIT	53	EPI	**ZEPHYR REGENT** SUNBURST	3,006	**2,308**	2,039	1,798

TYPE	YR	MFG	PRICES--BASED ON 100% ORIGINAL MODEL	SELL EXC	SELL AVG	BUY EXC	BUY AVG
ELGUIT	54	EPI	**ZEPHYR REGENT** SUNBURST, CUTAWAY, 1-DeARMOND PU	2,962	**2,274**	2,010	1,772
ELGUIT	49	EPI	**ZEPHYR TENOR** NATURAL, NON-CUTAWAY, 1-17" WIDE PICKUP (RARE MODEL)	1,910	**1,467**	1,296	1,143
GUITAR (ACOUSTIC)	33	EPI	**BEVERLY** DARK BROWN, FLATTOP	626	**480**	424	374
GUITAR	32	EPI	**BLACKSTONE** SUNBURST	1,296	**995**	880	775
GUITAR	33	EPI	**BLACKSTONE** SUNBURST	1,728	**1,326**	1,172	1,033
GUITAR	34	EPI	**BLACKSTONE** SUNBURST	1,662	**1,276**	1,127	994
GUITAR	35	EPI	**BLACKSTONE** SUNBURST	1,258	**966**	854	753
GUITAR	38	EPI	**BLACKSTONE** SUNBURST	1,406	**1,080**	954	841
GUITAR	41	EPI	**BLACKSTONE** SUNBURST	1,263	**970**	857	755
GUITAR	42	EPI	**BLACKSTONE** SUNBURST, LEFT-HANDED	1,282	**984**	870	767
GUITAR	43	EPI	**BLACKSTONE** BLOND	1,328	**1,019**	901	794
GUITAR	45	EPI	**BLACKSTONE** BLOND	1,363	**1,046**	924	815
GUITAR	46	EPI	**BLACKSTONE** SUNBURST	1,335	**1,025**	905	798
GUITAR	48	EPI	**BLACKSTONE** SUNBURST	1,246	**957**	845	745
GUITAR	49	EPI	**BLACKSTONE** SUNBURST	1,303	**1,001**	884	779
GUITAR	32	EPI	**BROADWAY** SUNBURST	3,712	**2,850**	2,519	2,221
GUITAR	34	EPI	**BROADWAY** SUNBURST	3,674	**2,821**	2,493	2,198
GUITAR	35	EPI	**BROADWAY** SUNBURST	2,998	**2,302**	2,034	1,793
GUITAR	36	EPI	**BROADWAY** NATURAL	2,959	**2,272**	2,007	1,770
GUITAR	37	EPI	**BROADWAY** NATURAL	2,878	**2,210**	1,953	1,721
GUITAR	37	EPI	**BROADWAY** SUNBURST	3,646	**2,800**	2,474	2,181
GUITAR	39	EPI	**BROADWAY** TENOR, SUNBURST	1,294	**994**	878	774
GUITAR	44	EPI	**BROADWAY** NATURAL	2,343	**1,799**	1,589	1,401
GUITAR	45	EPI	**BROADWAY** NATURAL	2,270	**1,743**	1,540	1,358
GUITAR	46	EPI	**BROADWAY** NATURAL	2,236	**1,717**	1,517	1,337
GUITAR	46	EPI	**BROADWAY** SUNBURST	2,241	**1,720**	1,520	1,340
GUITAR	48	EPI	**BROADWAY** SUNBURST	2,168	**1,664**	1,471	1,297
GUITAR	49	EPI	**BROADWAY** NATURAL	2,108	**1,619**	1,431	1,261
GUITAR	50	EPI	**BROADWAY** TENOR, SUNBURST	1,201	**922**	815	718
GUITAR	50	EPI	**BROADWAY** NATURAL	2,077	**1,595**	1,409	1,242
GUITAR	51	EPI	**BROADWAY** SUNBURST	2,993	**2,298**	2,031	1,790
GUITAR	53	EPI	**BROADWAY** SUNBURST	2,989	**2,295**	2,028	1,788
GUITAR	50	EPI	**BROADWAY REGENT** SUNBURST	2,394	**1,838**	1,624	1,432
GUITAR	51	EPI	**BROADWAY REGENT** SUNBURST	2,377	**1,825**	1,613	1,422
GUITAR	55	EPI	**BROADWAY REGENT** SUNBURST	2,424	**1,861**	1,645	1,450
GUITAR	51	EPI	**BYRON** SUNBURST	949	**729**	644	568
GUITAR	55	EPI	**BYRON** SUNBURST	823	**632**	558	492
GUITAR	41	EPI	**CORONET** ARCHTOP, HOLLOW BODY	1,014	**779**	688	607
GUITAR	35	EPI	**DELUXE** SUNBURST, ARCHTOP	3,557	**2,731**	2,413	2,127
GUITAR	38	EPI	**DELUXE** SUNBURST, ARCHTOP	3,380	**2,595**	2,293	2,022
GUITAR	39	EPI	**DELUXE** SUNBURST, ARCHTOP	4,468	**3,431**	3,032	2,673
GUITAR	42	EPI	**DELUXE** BLOND	4,480	**3,440**	3,040	2,680

TYPE	YR	MFG	PRICES--BASED ON 100% ORIGINAL MODEL	SELL EXC	SELL AVG	BUY EXC	BUY AVG
GUITAR	43	EPI	**DELUXE** NATURAL	3,298	**2,532**	2,238	1,973
GUITAR	46	EPI	**DELUXE** SUNBURST, ARCHTOP	5,339	**4,099**	3,622	3,193
GUITAR	48	EPI	**DELUXE** NEW YORK ARCHTOP	3,063	**2,352**	2,078	1,832
GUITAR	50	EPI	**DELUXE** BLOND	3,060	**2,350**	2,077	1,831
GUITAR	51	EPI	**DELUXE** SUNBURST, ARCHTOP	3,407	**2,616**	2,311	2,038
GUITAR	51	EPI	**DELUXE** NATURAL, CUTAWAY	4,026	**3,091**	2,732	2,408
GUITAR	52	EPI	**DELUXE** SUNBURST	3,044	**2,337**	2,065	1,821
GUITAR	53	EPI	**DELUXE** SUNBURST	3,060	**2,350**	2,077	1,831
GUITAR	55	EPI	**DELUXE** NATURAL	3,052	**2,343**	2,071	1,825
GUITAR	55	EPI	**DELUXE** SUNBURST, ARCHTOP	3,433	**2,636**	2,330	2,054
GUITAR	55	EPI	**DELUXE** NATURAL, CUTAWAY	3,933	**3,020**	2,669	2,353
GUITAR	50	EPI	**DEVON** SUNBURST, NEW YORK ARCHTOP	3,246	**2,493**	2,203	1,942
GUITAR	50	EPI	**DEVON** BLOND, NEW YORK ARCHTOP	3,342	**2,566**	2,267	1,999
GUITAR	51	EPI	**DEVON** OVAL FINGERBOARD INLAY	3,394	**2,606**	2,303	2,030
GUITAR	53	EPI	**DEVON** SUNBURST, NEW YORK ARCHTOP	2,358	**1,811**	1,600	1,411
GUITAR	54	EPI	**DEVON** SUNBURST	1,276	**980**	866	763
GUITAR	55	EPI	**DEVON** SUNBURST, NEW YORK ARCHTOP, OVAL FINGERBOARD INLAY	1,970	**1,512**	1,336	1,178
GUITAR	50	EPI	**DOUBLE ARCHTOP** F-HOLE	833	**639**	565	498
GUITAR	38	EPI	**ELECTAR** FLATTOP, F-HOLE	865	**664**	587	517
GUITAR	36	EPI	**ELECTAR SPANISH** BLOND	2,055	**1,578**	1,394	1,229
GUITAR	37	EPI	**ELECTAR SPANISH** ELECTRIC ARCHTOP	893	**686**	606	534
GUITAR	39	EPI	**EMPEROR** SUNBURST, ARCHTOP	6,620	**5,083**	4,492	3,960
GUITAR	40	EPI	**EMPEROR** SUNBURST	5,200	**3,992**	3,528	3,110
GUITAR	51	EPI	**EMPEROR** NATURAL, ARCHTOP	5,139	**3,946**	3,487	3,074
GUITAR	54	EPI	**EMPEROR** NATURAL, CUTAWAY, ARCHTOP	6,274	**4,817**	4,257	3,753
GUITAR	54	EPI	**EMPEROR** NATURAL, CUTAWAY, ARCHTOP, NEW YORK PU's	6,506	**4,995**	4,414	3,892
GUITAR	52	EPI	**ESTRELLA** BLOND, SPRUCE TOP	1,206	**926**	818	721
GUITAR	44	EPI	**FT- 30** MAHOGANY BROWN	892	**685**	605	533
GUITAR	44	EPI	**FT- 45** NATURAL	1,578	**1,211**	1,070	944
GUITAR	45	EPI	**FT- 75** NEW YORK FLATTOP	1,338	**1,027**	908	800
GUITAR	44	EPI	**FT- 79 TEXAN** MAPLE BACK/SIDES, FLATTOP	3,417	**2,623**	2,318	2,044
GUITAR	48	EPI	**FT- 79 TEXAN** MAPLE BACK/SIDES, FLATTOP	1,870	**1,436**	1,269	1,118
GUITAR	49	EPI	**FT- 79 TEXAN** MAPLE BACK/SIDES, FLATTOP	3,255	**2,500**	2,209	1,947
GUITAR	53	EPI	**FT- 79 TEXAN** MAPLE BACK/SIDES, FLATTOP	1,649	**1,266**	1,119	986
GUITAR	44	EPI	**FT-110** NATURAL	1,843	**1,415**	1,250	1,102
GUITAR	50	EPI	**FT-110** FLATTOP	2,466	**1,893**	1,673	1,475
GUITAR	51	EPI	**FT-110** FLATTOP	2,400	**1,842**	1,628	1,435
GUITAR	52	EPI	**FT-110** FLATTOP	2,179	**1,673**	1,478	1,303
GUITAR	53	EPI	**FT-110** FLATTOP	2,162	**1,660**	1,467	1,293
GUITAR	52	EPI	**FT-210 DELUXE** CUTAWAY, NEW YORK FLATTOP	3,439	**2,641**	2,333	2,057
GUITAR	38	EPI	**MADRID** SUNBURST, NEW YORK FLATTOP	2,296	**1,763**	1,558	1,373
GUITAR	39	EPI	**MADRID** SUNBURST, NEW YORK FLATTOP	2,292	**1,760**	1,555	1,371

TYPE	YR	MFG	PRICES--BASED ON 100% ORIGINAL MODEL	SELL EXC	SELL AVG	BUY EXC	BUY AVG
GUITAR	36	EPI	**NAVARRE** HAWAIIAN, MASTERBUILT LABEL	1,495	**1,130**	997	826
GUITAR	38	EPI	**NAVARRE** SUNBURST, NEW YORK FLATTOP	1,318	**996**	879	728
GUITAR	32	EPI	**OLYMPIC** MAHOGANY, ARCHTOP	962	**738**	652	575
GUITAR	33	EPI	**OLYMPIC** SUNBURST, ARCHTOP	1,256	**964**	852	751
GUITAR	35	EPI	**OLYMPIC** MAHOGANY, ARCHTOP	1,235	**948**	838	739
GUITAR	39	EPI	**OLYMPIC** SUNBURST, ARCHTOP	1,209	**928**	820	723
GUITAR	40	EPI	**OLYMPIC** SUNBURST, ARCHTOP	967	**743**	656	578
GUITAR	41	EPI	**OLYMPIC** SUNBURST, ARCHTOP	910	**699**	617	544
GUITAR	43	EPI	**OLYMPIC** TENOR, SUNBURST, ARCHTOP	857	**658**	582	513
GUITAR	44	EPI	**OLYMPIC** SUNBURST, ARCHTOP	791	**608**	537	473
GUITAR	27	EPI	**RECORDING A** NEW YORK FLATTOP	1,460	**1,103**	973	807
GUITAR	28	EPI	**RECORDING A** NEW YORK FLATTOP	1,713	**1,315**	1,162	1,025
GUITAR	24	EPI	**RECORDING D** NEW YORK ARCHTOP	1,925	**1,478**	1,306	1,151
GUITAR	27	EPI	**RECORDING D** NEW YORK ARCHTOP	1,477	**1,116**	984	816
GUITAR	28	EPI	**RECORDING D** NEW YORK ARCHTOP	1,622	**1,246**	1,101	970
GUITAR	28	EPI	**RECORDING E** SUNBURST	4,017	**3,084**	2,726	2,403
GUITAR	44	EPI	**RITZ** NATURAL, TORTOISE SHELL BINDING	956	**734**	649	572
GUITAR	33	EPI	**ROYAL MASTERBILT** SUNBURST, MAHOGANY BACK/SIDES	1,262	**969**	856	755
GUITAR	34	EPI	**ROYAL MASTERBILT** SUNBURST, WALNUT BACK/SIDES	883	**678**	599	528
GUITAR	34	EPI	**SPARTAN** SUNBURST	1,335	**1,025**	905	798
GUITAR	35	EPI	**SPARTAN** SUNBURST	1,064	**817**	722	636
GUITAR	38	EPI	**SPARTAN** SUNBURST	1,266	**972**	859	757
GUITAR	44	EPI	**SPARTAN** SUNBURST, ARCHTOP, WALNUT BACK/SIDES,GREACIAN COLUMN INLAY	1,348	**1,035**	915	806
GUITAR	45	EPI	**SPARTAN** SUNBURST, NEW YORK ARCHTOP	1,044	**802**	709	625
GUITAR	47	EPI	**SPARTAN** BLOND	1,044	**802**	709	625
GUITAR	33	EPI	**TRIUMPH** SUNBURST, NON-CUTAWAY	3,431	**2,635**	2,328	2,052
GUITAR	34	EPI	**TRIUMPH** SUNBURST, NON-CUTAWAY	3,375	**2,592**	2,290	2,019
GUITAR	35	EPI	**TRIUMPH** SUNBURST, NON-CUTAWAY	3,258	**2,501**	2,210	1,949
GUITAR	38	EPI	**TRIUMPH** SUNBURST, NON-CUTAWAY	3,505	**2,691**	2,378	2,097
GUITAR	41	EPI	**TRIUMPH** SUNBURST, NON-CUTAWAY	3,262	**2,505**	2,213	1,951
GUITAR	43	EPI	**TRIUMPH** SUNBURST, NON-CUTAWAY	3,103	**2,383**	2,105	1,856
GUITAR	44	EPI	**TRIUMPH** SUNBURST, NON-CUTAWAY	3,016	**2,315**	2,046	1,804
GUITAR	45	EPI	**TRIUMPH** SUNBURST, NON-CUTAWAY	2,888	**2,217**	1,960	1,727
GUITAR	46	EPI	**TRIUMPH** SUNBURST, NON-CUTAWAY	2,382	**1,829**	1,616	1,425
GUITAR	46	EPI	**TRIUMPH** NATURAL BLOND, NON-CUTAWAY	3,454	**2,652**	2,343	2,066
GUITAR	47	EPI	**TRIUMPH** SUNBURST, NON-CUTAWAY	2,332	**1,791**	1,583	1,395
GUITAR	47	EPI	**TRIUMPH** NATURAL BLOND, NON-CUTAWAY	3,383	**2,598**	2,295	2,024
GUITAR	48	EPI	**TRIUMPH** SUNBURST, NON-CUTAWAY	2,260	**1,735**	1,533	1,352
GUITAR	49	EPI	**TRIUMPH** NATURAL BLOND, NON-CUTAWAY	3,170	**2,434**	2,151	1,896
GUITAR	51	EPI	**TRIUMPH** SUNBURST, NON-CUTAWAY	2,164	**1,662**	1,469	1,295
GUITAR	53	EPI	**TRIUMPH** SUNBURST, NON-CUTAWAY	2,947	**2,263**	2,000	1,763
GUITAR	55	EPI	**TRIUMPH** TENOR, NATURAL BLOND	1,258	**966**	854	753

TYPE	YR	MFG	PRICES--BASED ON 100% ORIGINAL MODEL	SELL EXC	SELL AVG	BUY EXC	BUY AVG
GUITAR	50	EPI	TRIUMPH REGENT NATURAL BLOND, CUTAWAY	3,581	2,750	2,430	2,142
GUITAR	51	EPI	TRIUMPH REGENT SUNBURST, CUTAWAY	3,528	2,709	2,394	2,110
GUITAR	51	EPI	TRIUMPH REGENT NATURAL BLOND, CUTAWAY	3,543	2,721	2,404	2,119
GUITAR	52	EPI	TRIUMPH REGENT NATURAL BLOND, CUTAWAY	3,515	2,699	2,385	2,103
GUITAR	53	EPI	TRIUMPH REGENT SUNBURST, CUTAWAY	3,828	2,939	2,597	2,290
GUITAR	30	EPI	ZENITH SUNBURST	1,283	985	870	767
GUITAR	32	EPI	ZENITH SUNBURST	1,255	964	851	751
GUITAR	33	EPI	ZENITH SUNBURST	1,338	1,027	908	800
GUITAR	34	EPI	ZENITH SUNBURST	1,301	999	883	778
GUITAR	35	EPI	ZENITH SUNBURST	1,280	982	868	765
GUITAR	36	EPI	ZENITH SUNBURST, LEFT-HANDED	1,223	939	829	731
GUITAR	36	EPI	ZENITH SUNBURST	1,262	969	856	755
GUITAR	37	EPI	ZENITH SUNBURST	1,234	947	837	738
GUITAR	42	EPI	ZENITH SUNBURST	1,008	774	684	603
GUITAR	43	EPI	ZENITH SUNBURST	1,011	776	686	605
GUITAR	44	EPI	ZENITH SUNBURST	987	758	670	590
GUITAR	47	EPI	ZENITH SUNBURST	954	732	647	570
GUITAR	48	EPI	ZENITH SUNBURST	940	722	638	562
GUITAR	49	EPI	ZENITH SUNBURST	920	706	624	550
GUITAR	50	EPI	ZENITH SUNBURST	901	692	611	539
GUITAR	51	EPI	ZENITH SUNBURST	887	681	601	530
GUITAR	52	EPI	ZENITH SUNBURST	876	673	595	524
GUITAR	53	EPI	ZENITH SUNBURST	856	657	581	512
MANDOLIN	35	EPI	ADELPHI SUNBURST, F-HOLES	1,284	986	871	768
MANDOL	39	EPI	ADELPHI SUNBURST, F-HOLES	1,330	1,021	902	795
MANDOL	44	EPI	ADELPHI SUNBURST, F-HOLES	1,261	968	855	754
MANDOL	45	EPI	ADELPHI SUNBURST, F-HOLES	1,352	1,038	918	809
MANDOL	47	EPI	ADELPHI SUNBURST, F-HOLES	1,201	922	815	718
MANDOL	44	EPI	RIVOLI SUNBURST, A STYLE	1,338	1,027	908	800
MANDOL	51	EPI	RIVOLI SUNBURST, OVAL SOUND HOLE	761	584	516	455
MANDOL	34	EPI	STRAND SUNBURST, MASTERBUILT PEGHEAD	1,863	1,431	1,264	1,114
MANDOL	44	EPI	STRAND SUNBURST, CENTER-DIP PEGHEAD	1,023	786	694	612
STEEL GUITAR	40	EPI	CENTURY LAP STEEL BLACK, 6-STRING	650	499	441	389
STGUIT	51	EPI	CENTURY LAP STEEL SUNBURST	685	526	465	410
STGUIT	52	EPI	CENTURY LAP STEEL BLACK	757	581	513	452
STGUIT	41	EPI	CORONET BLACK, 6-STRING, BLADE PU	901	692	611	539
STGUIT	37	EPI	ELECTAR C SUNBURST	789	606	535	472
STGUIT	37	EPI	ELECTAR M BLACK	777	596	527	464
STGUIT	38	EPI	ELECTAR M BLUE ART DECO	663	509	449	396
STGUIT	39	EPI	ELECTAR M BLACK	770	591	522	460
STGUIT	43	EPI	ELECTAR ZEPHYR LAP STEEL 8-STRING	750	576	509	448
UKULELE	50	EPI	BARITONE	430	330	291	257

Copyright 2006 - Orion Research Corp., Scottsdale, AZ (480) 951-1114
FAX (480) 951-1117 - e-mail: sales@orionbluebook.com

TYPE	YR	MFG	PRICES--BASED ON 100% ORIGINAL MODEL	SELL EXC	SELL AVG	BUY EXC	BUY AVG
			EPIPHONE				
BANJO	68	EPIPHONE	**ARTIST TENOR**	1,067	**819**	724	638
BANJO	63	EPIPHONE	**CAMPUS LONGNECK**	697	**535**	473	417
BANJO	64	EPIPHONE	**LONG NECK PETE SEEGER STYLE** 5-STRING	733	**563**	497	438
BANJO	65	EPIPHONE	**LONG NECK POT** 5-STRING	794	**609**	538	475
BANJO	67	EPIPHONE	**MINISTREL**	922	**708**	626	552
BANJO	65	EPIPHONE	**MINISTREL** FLAT HEAD MASTERTONE STYLE TONE RING	697	**535**	473	417
BANJO	65	EPIPHONE	**MINISTREL**	1,037	**796**	703	620
BANJO	67	EPIPHONE	**MINISTREL** EB-88 1 PIECE FLANGE, SERIAL #056285	1,341	**1,030**	910	802
ELEC. GUITAR & BASS	58	EPIPHONE	**BROADWAY** NATURAL, 1 ROUNDED CUTAWAY	1,430	**1,098**	970	855
ELGUIT	59	EPIPHONE	**BROADWAY** SUNBURST, 1 ROUNDED CUTAWAY	1,346	**1,033**	913	805
ELGUIT	61	EPIPHONE	**BROADWAY** BLOND, 1 ROUNDED CUTAWAY	948	**728**	643	567
ELGUIT	63	EPIPHONE	**BROADWAY** NATURAL; 1 ROUNDED CUTAWAY	893	**686**	606	534
ELGUIT	63	EPIPHONE	**BROADWAY** SUNBURST, 1 ROUNDED CUTAWAY	1,019	**782**	691	609
ELGUIT	64	EPIPHONE	**BROADWAY** SUNBURST, 1 ROUNDED CUTAWAY	1,010	**775**	685	604
ELGUIT	65	EPIPHONE	**BROADWAY** SUNBURST, 1 ROUNDED CUTAWAY	889	**682**	603	531
ELGUIT	65	EPIPHONE	**BROADWAY** BLOND, HOLLOW BODY	1,031	**792**	699	617
ELGUIT	66	EPIPHONE	**BROADWAY** SUNBURST, 1 ROUNDED CUTAWAY	1,043	**801**	708	624
ELGUIT	66	EPIPHONE	**BROADWAY** BLOND, HOLLOW BODY	1,202	**923**	816	719
ELGUIT	67	EPIPHONE	**BROADWAY** SUNBURST, 1 ROUNDED CUTAWAY	834	**640**	566	499
ELGUIT	67	EPIPHONE	**BROADWAY** CHERRY, HOLLOW BODY	1,002	**769**	680	599
ELGUIT	68	EPIPHONE	**BROADWAY** SUNBURST, HOLLOW BODY	666	**511**	452	398
ELGUIT	68	EPIPHONE	**BROADWAY** NATURAL, 1 ROUNDED CUTAWAY	694	**533**	471	415
ELGUIT	69	EPIPHONE	**BROADWAY** SUNBURST, 1 ROUNDED CUTAWAY	658	**505**	446	393
ELGUIT	69	EPIPHONE	**BROADWAY** SUNBURST	1,015	**780**	689	607
ELGUIT	67	EPIPHONE	**CAIOLA CUSTOM** YELLOW SUNBURST	1,657	**1,272**	1,124	991
ELGUIT	68	EPIPHONE	**CAIOLA CUSTOM** WALNUT, 2 MINI HUMBUCKERS	1,700	**1,305**	1,153	1,017
ELGUIT	68	EPIPHONE	**CAIOLA CUSTOM** CHERRY, 2 MINI HUMBUCKERS	1,704	**1,308**	1,156	1,019
ELGUIT	69	EPIPHONE	**CAIOLA CUSTOM** WALNUT, 2 MINI HUMBUCKERS	1,643	**1,261**	1,114	982
ELGUIT	64	EPIPHONE	**CAIOLA ROYAL** TAN, 2 MINI HUMBUCKERS	1,276	**980**	866	763
ELGUIT	65	EPIPHONE	**CAIOLA ROYAL** TAN, 2 MINI HUMBUCKERS	1,321	**1,014**	896	790
ELGUIT	65	EPIPHONE	**CAIOLA STANDARD** WALNUT, 2 MINI HUMBUCKERS	1,314	**1,009**	892	786
ELGUIT	65	EPIPHONE	**CAIOLA STANDARD** SUNBURST, 2 P-90's	1,319	**1,013**	895	789
ELGUIT	66	EPIPHONE	**CAIOLA STANDARD** CHERRY, 2 P-90's	1,317	**1,011**	893	787
ELGUIT	67	EPIPHONE	**CAIOLA STANDARD** SUNBURST, 2 P-90's	1,310	**1,006**	889	783
ELGUIT	67	EPIPHONE	**CAIOLA STANDARD** CHERRY, 2 P-90's	1,313	**1,008**	891	785
ELGUIT	68	EPIPHONE	**CAIOLA STANDARD** SUNBURST, 2 P-90's	1,406	**1,080**	954	841
ELGUIT	69	EPIPHONE	**CAIOLA STANDARD** CHERRY, 2 P-90's	855	**657**	580	511
ELGUIT	61	EPIPHONE	**CASINO** SUNBURST, DOUBLE CUTAWAY, 2 PU's, NON-VIB	1,310	**1,006**	889	783
ELGUIT	62	EPIPHONE	**CASINO** SUNBURST, DOUBLE CUTAWAY, 1 PU	779	**598**	528	466
ELGUIT	63	EPIPHONE	**CASINO** SUNBURST, DOUBLE CUTAWAY, 1 PU, VIBRATO	724	**556**	491	433
ELGUIT	63	EPIPHONE	**CASINO** SUNBURST, DOUBLE CUTAWAY, 1 PU, LEFT-HANDED	769	**590**	522	460
ELGUIT	64	EPIPHONE	**CASINO** CHERRY, DOUBLE CUTAWAY, 1 PU	679	**522**	461	406
ELGUIT	65	EPIPHONE	**CASINO** CHERRY, DOUBLE CUTAWAY, 2 PU's	1,638	**1,258**	1,111	980

TYPE	YR	MFG	PRICES--BASED ON 100% ORIGINAL MODEL	SELL EXC	SELL AVG	BUY EXC	BUY AVG
ELGUIT	65	EPIPHONE	**CASINO** SUNBURST, DOUBLE CUTAWAY, 2 PU's	1,638	**1,258**	1,111	980
ELGUIT	66	EPIPHONE	**CASINO** SUNBURST, DOUBLE CUTAWAY, 1 PU, VIBRATO	788	**605**	535	471
ELGUIT	66	EPIPHONE	**CASINO** SUNBURST, DOUBLE CUTAWAY, 2 PU's	1,638	**1,258**	1,111	980
ELGUIT	67	EPIPHONE	**CASINO** CHERRY, DOUBLE CUTAWAY, 1 PU, VIBRATO	660	**507**	448	395
ELGUIT	67	EPIPHONE	**CASINO** SUNBURST, DOUBLE CUTAWAY, 1 PU	680	**522**	462	407
ELGUIT	67	EPIPHONE	**CASINO** SUNBURST, DOUBLE CUTAWAY, 2 PU's	1,528	**1,173**	1,037	914
ELGUIT	68	EPIPHONE	**CASINO** SUNBURST, 1 PU	660	**507**	448	395
ELGUIT	68	EPIPHONE	**CASINO** SUNBURST, DOUBLE CUTAWAY, 2 PU's	980	**752**	665	586
ELGUIT	68	EPIPHONE	**CASINO** CHERRY, 2 PU's	980	**752**	665	586
ELGUIT	69	EPIPHONE	**CASINO** CHERRY, DOUBLE CUTAWAY, 1 PU, VIBRATO	673	**516**	456	402
ELGUIT	58	EPIPHONE	**CENTURY** SUNBURST, NON-CUTAWAY, 1 PU	948	**728**	643	567
ELGUIT	59	EPIPHONE	**CENTURY** SUNBURST, NON-CUTAWAY, 1 PU	948	**728**	643	567
ELGUIT	60	EPIPHONE	**CENTURY** SUNBURST, NON-CUTAWAY, 1 PU	889	**682**	603	531
ELGUIT	60	EPIPHONE	**CENTURY** BURGUNDY, NON-CUTAWAY, 1 PU	946	**726**	642	566
ELGUIT	61	EPIPHONE	**CENTURY** BURGUNDY, NON-CUTAWAY, 1 PU	945	**725**	641	565
ELGUIT	64	EPIPHONE	**CENTURY** BURGUNDY	885	**680**	601	529
ELGUIT	65	EPIPHONE	**CENTURY** BURGUNDY, NON-CUTAWAY, 1 PU	889	**682**	603	531
ELGUIT	66	EPIPHONE	**CENTURY** SUNBURST, NON-CUTAWAY, 1 PU	829	**637**	563	496
ELGUIT	68	EPIPHONE	**CENTURY** SUNBURST, NON-CUTAWAY, 1 PU	825	**633**	560	493
ELGUIT	58	EPIPHONE	**CORONET** SUNBURST, 1 PU	552	**423**	374	330
ELGUIT	59	EPIPHONE	**CORONET** BLACK, 1 PU	542	**416**	367	324
ELGUIT	61	EPIPHONE	**CORONET** CHERRY, 1 PU	577	**443**	392	345
ELGUIT	62	EPIPHONE	**CORONET** CHERRY, 1 PU	538	**413**	365	322
ELGUIT	63	EPIPHONE	**CORONET** GREEN, 1 PU	511	**393**	347	306
ELGUIT	63	EPIPHONE	**CORONET** CHERRY, 1 PU	516	**396**	350	308
ELGUIT	64	EPIPHONE	**CORONET** CHERRY, 1 PU	474	**364**	322	284
ELGUIT	65	EPIPHONE	**CORONET** CHERRY, 1 PU	443	**340**	300	265
ELGUIT	65	EPIPHONE	**CORONET** TRANSPARENT GREEN, 1 PU	445	**342**	302	266
ELGUIT	66	EPIPHONE	**CORONET** CHERRY, 1 PU	423	**325**	287	253
ELGUIT	61	EPIPHONE	**CRESTWOOD CUSTOM** WHITE, 2 MINI HUMBUCKERS	739	**567**	501	442
ELGUIT	65	EPIPHONE	**CRESTWOOD CUSTOM** RED, 2 MINI HUMBUCKERS, VIB	948	**728**	643	567
ELGUIT	67	EPIPHONE	**CRESTWOOD CUSTOM** WHITE, 2 MINI HUMBUCKERS, VIB	1,321	**1,014**	896	790
ELGUIT	68	EPIPHONE	**CRESTWOOD CUSTOM** RED, 2 MINI HUMBUCKERS, VIB	889	**682**	603	531
ELGUIT	63	EPIPHONE	**CRESTWOOD DELUXE** RED, 3 MINI HUMBUCKERS, VIB	1,008	**774**	684	603
ELGUIT	65	EPIPHONE	**CRESTWOOD DELUXE** RED, 3 MINI HUMBUCKERS, VIB	857	**658**	582	513
ELGUIT	65	EPIPHONE	**CRESTWOOD DELUXE** WHITE, 3 MINI HUMBUCKERS, VIB	1,363	**1,046**	924	815
ELGUIT	66	EPIPHONE	**CRESTWOOD DELUXE** RED, 3 MINI HUMBUCKERS, VIB	1,321	**1,014**	896	790
ELGUIT	59	EPIPHONE	**DELUXE CUTAWAY MODEL A-212** SUNBURST	7,547	**5,795**	5,121	4,515
ELGUIT	50	EPIPHONE	**DELUXE REGENT** SUNBURST, NEW YORK ARCHTOP	1,338	**1,027**	908	800
ELGUIT	66	EPIPHONE	**DWIGHT** CHERRY, SOLID BODY, 1 PU	741	**569**	503	443
ELGUIT	67	EPIPHONE	**DWIGHT** CHERRY, SOLID BODY, 1 PU	728	**559**	494	435
ELGUIT	64	EPIPHONE	**EMBASSY DELUXE BASS** RED, SOLID BODY	1,378	**1,058**	935	824

TYPE	YR	MFG	PRICES--BASED ON 100% ORIGINAL MODEL	SELL EXC	SELL AVG	BUY EXC	BUY AVG
ELGUIT	65	EPIPHONE	**EMBASSY DELUXE BASS** RED, SOLID BODY	911	700	618	545
ELGUIT	68	EPIPHONE	**EMBASSY DELUXE BASS** RED, SOLID BODY	969	744	658	580
ELGUIT	61	EPIPHONE	**EMPEROR** NATURAL	2,014	1,547	1,367	1,205
ELGUIT	62	EPIPHONE	**EMPEROR** SUNBURST	1,893	1,454	1,285	1,132
ELGUIT	63	EPIPHONE	**EMPEROR** CURLY MAPLE, 18 1/2" WIDE	1,376	1,056	934	823
ELGUIT	64	EPIPHONE	**EMPEROR** SUNBURST	1,977	1,518	1,342	1,183
ELGUIT	78	EPIPHONE	**EMPEROR JAZZ BOX** BLOND,SPRUCE TOP,FLAMED MAPLE GACK/SIDES/NECK,HB's	635	487	430	379
ELGUIT	68	EPIPHONE	**ENTRADA EC-90**	353	266	235	195
ELGUIT	60	EPIPHONE	**GRANADA** SUNBURST, DOT INLAY, NON-CUTAWAY	656	503	445	392
ELGUIT	64	EPIPHONE	**GRANADA** SUNBURST, DOT INLAY, NON-CUTAWAY	652	501	443	390
ELGUIT	65	EPIPHONE	**GRANADA** SUNBURST, VINE INLAY	650	499	441	389
ELGUIT	67	EPIPHONE	**GRANADA** SUNBURST, DOT INLAY, CUTAWAY	598	459	405	357
ELGUIT	68	EPIPHONE	**GRANADA** SUNBURST, DOT INLAY, CUTAWAY	593	455	402	355
ELGUIT	64	EPIPHONE	**HOWARD ROBERTS** SUNBURST, HOLLOW	2,976	2,285	2,020	1,780
ELGUIT	65	EPIPHONE	**HOWARD ROBERTS** SUNBURST	2,969	2,279	2,014	1,776
ELGUIT	65	EPIPHONE	**HOWARD ROBERTS** BLOND, HOLLOW	3,328	2,555	2,258	1,991
ELGUIT	66	EPIPHONE	**HOWARD ROBERTS** WALNUT, HOLLOW	2,973	2,283	2,017	1,778
ELGUIT	68	EPIPHONE	**HOWARD ROBERTS** NATURAL	2,968	2,279	2,014	1,775
ELGUIT	68	EPIPHONE	**HOWARD ROBERTS**	2,968	2,279	2,014	1,775
ELGUIT	65	EPIPHONE	**HOWARD ROBERTS CUSTOM** BLACK, TUN-O-MAT	3,328	2,555	2,258	1,991
ELGUIT	67	EPIPHONE	**HOWARD ROBERTS SE** SUNBURST, HOLLOW	2,982	2,290	2,023	1,784
ELGUIT	61	EPIPHONE	**NEWPORT BASS** SOLID CHERRY, 1 PU	846	650	574	506
ELGUIT	62	EPIPHONE	**NEWPORT BASS** SOLID CHERRY, 1 PU	603	463	409	361
ELGUIT	63	EPIPHONE	**NEWPORT BASS** SOLID CHERRY, 1 PU	603	463	409	361
ELGUIT	63	EPIPHONE	**NEWPORT BASS** 2 PU's	665	510	451	397
ELGUIT	63	EPIPHONE	**NEWPORT BASS** CHERRY, 2 PU's	686	527	465	410
ELGUIT	65	EPIPHONE	**NEWPORT BASS** SOLID CHERRY, 1 PU,BAT WING HEADSTOCK	604	464	410	361
ELGUIT	67	EPIPHONE	**NEWPORT BASS** SOLID CHERRY, 1 PU	738	566	500	441
ELGUIT	68	EPIPHONE	**NEWPORT BASS** SOLID CHERRY, 1 PU	803	616	544	480
ELGUIT	60	EPIPHONE	**OLYMPIC** SUNBURST, 1 PU, SINGLE CUTAWAY	697	535	473	417
ELGUIT	61	EPIPHONE	**OLYMPIC** SUNBURST, 1 PU, SINGLE CUTAWAY	650	499	441	389
ELGUIT	62	EPIPHONE	**OLYMPIC** SUNBURST, 1 PU, 3/4 SCALE	638	490	433	381
ELGUIT	64	EPIPHONE	**OLYMPIC** SUNBURST, 1 PU, DOUBLE CUTAWAY	611	469	414	365
ELGUIT	65	EPIPHONE	**OLYMPIC** INVERNESS GREEN, 2 PU's	567	436	385	339
ELGUIT	65	EPIPHONE	**OLYMPIC** CHERRY, 1 PU	571	438	387	341
ELGUIT	65	EPIPHONE	**OLYMPIC** CALIFORNIA CORAL, 1 PU	585	449	397	350
ELGUIT	65	EPIPHONE	**OLYMPIC** SUNBURST, 1 PU	604	464	410	361
ELGUIT	65	EPIPHONE	**OLYMPIC** CHERRY, 2 PU's	673	516	456	402
ELGUIT	66	EPIPHONE	**OLYMPIC** SUNBURST, 1 PU, VIBRATO	656	503	445	392
ELGUIT	67	EPIPHONE	**OLYMPIC** CHERRY, 1 PU	673	516	456	402
ELGUIT	68	EPIPHONE	**OLYMPIC** CHERRY, BATWING	604	464	410	361
ELGUIT	68	EPIPHONE	**OLYMPIC** SUNBURST, 1 PU, BATWING PEGHEAD	647	497	439	387
ELGUIT	69	EPIPHONE	**OLYMPIC** CHERRY, 1 PU, VIBRATO	611	469	414	365

TYPE	YR	MFG	PRICES--BASED ON 100% ORIGINAL MODEL	SELL EXC	SELL AVG	BUY EXC	BUY AVG
ELGUIT	60	EPIPHONE	**OLYMPIC 3/4** SUNBURST, SINGLE CUTAWAY	703	**540**	477	420
ELGUIT	60	EPIPHONE	**OLYMPIC DOUBLE** SINGLE CUTAWAY	693	**532**	470	414
ELGUIT	64	EPIPHONE	**OLYMPIC DOUBLE** SUNBURST, 2 PU's	664	**509**	450	397
ELGUIT	65	EPIPHONE	**OLYMPIC DOUBLE** SUNBURST, 2 PU's	660	**507**	448	395
ELGUIT	65	EPIPHONE	**OLYMPIC DOUBLE** CHERRY, 2 PU's	664	**509**	450	397
ELGUIT	66	EPIPHONE	**OLYMPIC DOUBLE** CHERRY, 2 PU's	656	**503**	445	392
ELGUIT	67	EPIPHONE	**OLYMPIC DOUBLE** SPARKLING BURGUNDY	663	**509**	449	396
ELGUIT	68	EPIPHONE	**OLYMPIC DOUBLE** CHERRY	657	**504**	446	393
ELGUIT	69	EPIPHONE	**OLYMPIC DOUBLE** DOUBLE CUTAWAY	647	**497**	439	387
ELGUIT	62	EPIPHONE	**OLYMPIC SPECIAL** SUNBURST	685	**526**	465	410
ELGUIT	63	EPIPHONE	**OLYMPIC SPECIAL** SUNBURST	682	**523**	462	408
ELGUIT	64	EPIPHONE	**OLYMPIC SPECIAL** SUNBURST, DOUBLE CUTAWAY	675	**518**	458	404
ELGUIT	65	EPIPHONE	**OLYMPIC SPECIAL** SUNBURST, DOUBLE CUTAWAY	665	**510**	451	397
ELGUIT	67	EPIPHONE	**OLYMPIC SPECIAL** SUNBURST	663	**509**	449	396
ELGUIT	62	EPIPHONE	**PROFESSIONAL** CHERRY, 1 PU	1,276	**980**	866	763
ELGUIT	65	EPIPHONE	**PROFESSIONAL** CHERRY	1,323	**1,016**	898	791
ELGUIT	63	EPIPHONE	**PROFESSIONAL THIN** SUNBURST, DOUBLE CUTAWAY	1,273	**977**	864	761
ELGUIT	65	EPIPHONE	**PROFESSIONAL THIN** CHERRY, DOUBLE CUTAWAY	1,321	**1,014**	896	790
ELGUIT	62	EPIPHONE	**RIVIERA**	2,968	**2,279**	2,014	1,775
ELGUIT	65	EPIPHONE	**RIVIERA** CHERRY, 12-STRING, FREQUENSATOR	2,298	**1,764**	1,559	1,374
ELGUIT	66	EPIPHONE	**RIVIERA** CHERRY, 12-STRING, FREQUENSATOR	2,296	**1,763**	1,558	1,373
ELGUIT	67	EPIPHONE	**RIVIERA** CHERRY, 12-STRING, FREQUENSATOR	2,169	**1,665**	1,472	1,297
ELGUIT	68	EPIPHONE	**RIVIERA** CHERRY, 12-STRING, FREQUENSATOR	2,040	**1,566**	1,384	1,220
ELGUIT	62	EPIPHONE	**RIVIERA THIN** TAN, FREQUENSATOR	689	**529**	468	412
ELGUIT	62	EPIPHONE	**RIVIERA THIN** SUNBURST, FREQUENSATOR	715	**549**	485	428
ELGUIT	63	EPIPHONE	**RIVIERA THIN** CHERRY, FREQUENSATOR	700	**537**	475	418
ELGUIT	64	EPIPHONE	**RIVIERA THIN** CHERRY, FREQUENSATOR	692	**531**	469	414
ELGUIT	65	EPIPHONE	**RIVIERA THIN** SUNBURST, FREQUENSATOR	669	**514**	454	400
ELGUIT	66	EPIPHONE	**RIVIERA THIN** CHERRY, FREQUENSATOR	663	**509**	449	396
ELGUIT	66	EPIPHONE	**RIVIERA THIN** SUNBURST, FREQUENSATOR	665	**510**	451	397
ELGUIT	67	EPIPHONE	**RIVIERA THIN** GREEN, FREQUENSATOR	645	**495**	437	385
ELGUIT	67	EPIPHONE	**RIVIERA THIN** SUNBURST, FREQUENSATOR	670	**515**	455	401
ELGUIT	67	EPIPHONE	**RIVIERA THIN** CHERRY, FREQUENSATOR	673	**516**	456	402
ELGUIT	68	EPIPHONE	**RIVIERA THIN** SUNBURST, FREQUENSATOR	649	**498**	440	388
ELGUIT	68	EPIPHONE	**RIVIERA THIN** CHERRY, FREQUENSATOR	652	**501**	443	390
ELGUIT	64	EPIPHONE	**RIVIERA THIN ROYAL** TAN, FREQUENSATOR	692	**531**	469	414
ELGUIT	64	EPIPHONE	**RIVOLI BASS** SUNBURST, SYMETR, DOUBLE CUTAWAY, 1 PU	1,303	**1,001**	884	779
ELGUIT	65	EPIPHONE	**RIVOLI BASS** SUNBURST, SYMETR, DOUBLE CUTAWAY, 1 PU	956	**734**	649	572
ELGUIT	67	EPIPHONE	**RIVOLI BASS** SUNBURST, SYMETR, DOUBLE CUTAWAY, 1 PU	1,211	**930**	822	724
ELGUIT	67	EPIPHONE	**RIVOLI BASS** NATURAL, SYMETR, DOUBLE CUTAWAY, 1 PU	1,214	**932**	823	726
ELGUIT	68	EPIPHONE	**RIVOLI BASS** SUNBURST, SYMETR, DOUBLE CUTAWAY, 1 PU	906	**695**	614	542
ELGUIT	58	EPIPHONE	**SHERATON** NATURAL, 3 PU's	9,105	**6,991**	6,178	5,447

TYPE	YR	MFG	PRICES--BASED ON 100% ORIGINAL MODEL	SELL EXC	SELL AVG	BUY EXC	BUY AVG
ELGUIT	58	EPIPHONE	SHERATON NATURAL, 2 NEW YORK PU's	9,114	6,998	6,184	5,452
ELGUIT	61	EPIPHONE	SHERATON SUNBURST	7,890	6,058	5,354	4,720
ELGUIT	61	EPIPHONE	SHERATON NATURAL, 3 PU's	8,498	6,525	5,766	5,083
ELGUIT	63	EPIPHONE	SHERATON SUNBURST	7,894	6,062	5,357	4,722
ELGUIT	64	EPIPHONE	SHERATON SUNBURST	7,890	6,058	5,354	4,720
ELGUIT	64	EPIPHONE	SHERATON NATURAL	8,498	6,525	5,766	5,083
ELGUIT	65	EPIPHONE	SHERATON GOLD-NATURAL, VIBRATO	7,648	5,872	5,190	4,575
ELGUIT	66	EPIPHONE	SHERATON CHERRY	7,890	6,058	5,354	4,720
ELGUIT	66	EPIPHONE	SHERATON NATURAL	8,498	6,525	5,766	5,083
ELGUIT	67	EPIPHONE	SHERATON SUNBURST	7,588	5,826	5,149	4,539
ELGUIT	67	EPIPHONE	SHERATON CHERRY	7,590	5,828	5,150	4,540
ELGUIT	67	EPIPHONE	SHERATON NATURAL	7,890	6,058	5,354	4,720
ELGUIT	68	EPIPHONE	SHERATON SUNBURST	7,588	5,826	5,149	4,539
ELGUIT	62	EPIPHONE	SORRENTO 2 PU's	1,046	803	709	625
ELGUIT	63	EPIPHONE	SORRENTO SUNBURST, 2 PU, SMALL HEADSTOCK	2,990	2,296	2,029	1,788
ELGUIT	61	EPIPHONE	SORRENTO THIN SUNBURST	908	697	616	543
ELGUIT	62	EPIPHONE	SORRENTO THIN	899	690	610	538
ELGUIT	64	EPIPHONE	SORRENTO THIN	889	682	603	531
ELGUIT	65	EPIPHONE	SORRENTO THIN SUNBURST, 1 PU	855	657	580	511
ELGUIT	65	EPIPHONE	SORRENTO THIN NATURAL	859	659	582	513
ELGUIT	66	EPIPHONE	SORRENTO THIN SUNBURST	846	650	574	506
ELGUIT	67	EPIPHONE	SORRENTO THIN SUNBURST	838	644	569	501
ELGUIT	60	EPIPHONE	WILSHIRE SUNBURST	1,845	1,417	1,252	1,104
ELGUIT	61	EPIPHONE	WILSHIRE CHERRY	1,264	970	858	756
ELGUIT	62	EPIPHONE	WILSHIRE CHERRY	1,019	782	691	609
ELGUIT	63	EPIPHONE	WILSHIRE CHERRY	1,000	767	678	598
ELGUIT	63	EPIPHONE	WILSHIRE SUNBURST, 12-STRING	1,358	1,043	921	812
ELGUIT	64	EPIPHONE	WILSHIRE CHERRY	973	747	660	582
ELGUIT	65	EPIPHONE	WILSHIRE CHERRY	2,402	1,844	1,630	1,437
ELGUIT	66	EPIPHONE	WILSHIRE SUNBURST, 12-STRING	847	651	575	507
ELGUIT	66	EPIPHONE	WILSHIRE CHERRY, BATWING PEGHEAD	878	674	595	525
ELGUIT	67	EPIPHONE	WILSHIRE CHERRY	872	669	592	521
ELGUIT	68	EPIPHONE	WILSHIRE PACIFIC BLUE METALLIC	889	682	603	531
ELGUIT	68	EPIPHONE	WILSHIRE CHERRY, 12-STRING	1,069	821	725	639
ELGUIT	60	EPIPHONE	WINDSOR SUNBURST	1,225	940	831	732
ELGUIT	61	EPIPHONE	WINDSOR NATURAL	1,219	936	827	729
ELGUIT	60	EPIPHONE	ZEPHYR THINLINE	2,185	1,677	1,482	1,307
ELGUIT	65	EPIPHONE	ZEPHYR EMPEROR REGENT NATURAL, 3 ON-OFF TOGGLES	2,185	1,677	1,482	1,307
ELGUIT	58	EPIPHONE	ZEPHYR REGENT SUNBURST	2,293	1,761	1,556	1,372
ELGUIT	58	EPIPHONE	ZEPHYR THIN SUNBURST, CUTAWAY, 2 PU's	3,804	2,921	2,581	2,275
ELGUIT	59	EPIPHONE	ZEPHYR THIN SUNBURST, CUTAWAY, 2 PU's	2,293	1,761	1,556	1,372
ELGUIT	60	EPIPHONE	ZEPHYR THIN SUNBURST, CUTAWAY, 2 PU's	2,293	1,761	1,556	1,372
ELGUIT	61	EPIPHONE	ZEPHYR THIN NATURAL, CUTAWAY, 2 PU's	2,293	1,761	1,556	1,372

TYPE	YR	MFG	PRICES--BASED ON 100% ORIGINAL MODEL	SELL EXC	SELL AVG	BUY EXC	BUY AVG
ELGUIT	61	EPIPHONE	**ZEPHYR THIN** SUNBURST, CUTAWAY, 2 PU's	2,293	1,761	1,556	1,372
GUITAR AMP	62	EPIPHONE	**CENTURY** 15" JENSEN	652	501	443	390
GTAMP	62	EPIPHONE	**DEVON** 10" SPEAKER	534	410	362	319
GTAMP	74	EPIPHONE	**E-65** 1x10", 5 WATT	152	116	103	91
GTAMP	65	EPIPHONE	**GA-50**	405	311	275	242
GTAMP	63	EPIPHONE	**GALAXY** GREY, 1x10" JENSEN, REV TREM	416	319	282	249
GTAMP	65	EPIPHONE	**JMF H-25 HEAD**	399	307	271	239
GTAMP	66	EPIPHONE	**MAXIMA** 100 WATTS, 2 SPEAKER BOTTOMS,2x10" SPEAKERS IN EACH BOTTOM	281	215	190	168
GTAMP	62	EPIPHONE	**PACEMAKER**	319	245	216	190
GTAMP	64	EPIPHONE	**PACEMAKER**	288	221	196	172
GTAMP	65	EPIPHONE	**PACEMAKER** 1x8" SPEAKER	239	184	162	143
GTAMP	65	EPIPHONE	**PACEMAKER EA-50** 12 WATTS, 1x10 CTS SPEAKER, GRAY TOLEX	511	393	347	306
GTAMP	61	EPIPHONE	**PROFESSIONAL** CHERRY	833	639	565	498
GTAMP	60	EPIPHONE	**ZEPHYR**	353	271	240	211
GTAMP	61	EPIPHONE	**ZEPHYR** EA-15RV	692	531	469	414
GUITAR (ACOUSTIC)	66	EPIPHONE	**BARCELONA CLASSICAL** MAPLE BACK/SIDES	544	417	369	325
GUITAR	62	EPIPHONE	**BARD FT-112** NATURAL, 12-STRING, MAHOGANY	991	761	672	592
GUITAR	63	EPIPHONE	**BARD FT-112** NATURAL, 12-STRING, MAHOGANY	880	675	597	526
GUITAR	64	EPIPHONE	**BARD FT-112** NATURAL, 12-STRING	792	608	538	474
GUITAR	64	EPIPHONE	**BARD FT-112** NATURAL, 12-STRING, MAHOGANY	876	673	595	524
GUITAR	65	EPIPHONE	**BARD FT-112** NATURAL, 12-STRING	779	598	528	466
GUITAR	65	EPIPHONE	**BARD FT-112** NATURAL, 12-STRING, MAHOGANY	835	641	566	499
GUITAR	66	EPIPHONE	**BARD FT-112** NATURAL, 12-STRING, MAHOGANY	841	645	570	503
GUITAR	67	EPIPHONE	**BARD FT-112** NATURAL, 12-STRING	769	590	522	460
GUITAR	67	EPIPHONE	**BARD FT-112** NATURAL, 12-STRING, MAHOGANY	837	643	568	501
GUITAR	67	EPIPHONE	**BARD FT-112** SUNBURST, 12-STRING	852	654	578	509
GUITAR	61	EPIPHONE	**CABALLERO FT- 30** MAHOGANY, FLATTOP	554	425	376	331
GUITAR	63	EPIPHONE	**CABALLERO FT- 30** MAHOGANY, FLATTOP	554	425	376	331
GUITAR	64	EPIPHONE	**CABALLERO FT- 30** MAHOGANY, FLATTOP	554	425	376	331
GUITAR	65	EPIPHONE	**CABALLERO FT- 30** TENOR, MAHOGANY, FLATTOP	554	425	376	331
GUITAR	66	EPIPHONE	**CABALLERO FT- 30** MAHOGANY, FLATTOP	554	425	376	331
GUITAR	67	EPIPHONE	**CABALLERO FT- 30** MAHOGANY, FLATTOP	554	425	376	331
GUITAR	68	EPIPHONE	**CABALLERO FT- 30** MAHOGANY, FLATTOP	554	425	376	331
GUITAR	72	EPIPHONE	**CABALLERO FT- 30** MAHOGANY, FLATTOP	554	425	376	331
GUITAR	58	EPIPHONE	**CORTEZ FT- 45**	1,627	1,249	1,104	973
GUITAR	61	EPIPHONE	**CORTEZ FT- 45** SUNBURST, FLATTOP	1,341	1,030	910	802
GUITAR	64	EPIPHONE	**CORTEZ FT- 45** SUNBURST, FLATTOP	1,048	804	711	627
GUITAR	66	EPIPHONE	**CORTEZ FT- 45** SUNBURST, FLATTOP	983	755	667	588
GUITAR	67	EPIPHONE	**CORTEZ FT- 45**	980	752	665	586
GUITAR	65	EPIPHONE	**CORTEZ FT- 45N** NATURAL, FLATTOP	1,053	809	715	630
GUITAR	66	EPIPHONE	**CORTEZ FT- 45N** NATURAL, FLATTOP	1,052	808	714	629
GUITAR	67	EPIPHONE	**CORTEZ FT- 45N** BLOND, FLATTOP	1,048	804	711	627
GUITAR	68	EPIPHONE	**CORTEZ FT- 45N** BLOND, FLATTOP	1,046	803	709	625
GUITAR	59	EPIPHONE	**DELUXE REGENT** SUNBURST, ARCHTOP	5,045	3,874	3,423	3,018
GUITAR	63	EPIPHONE	**ELDORADO FT- 90** BLOND	1,627	1,249	1,104	973

TYPE	YR	MFG	PRICES--BASED ON 100% ORIGINAL MODEL	SELL EXC	SELL AVG	BUY EXC	BUY AVG
GUITAR	65	EPIPHONE	**ELDORADO FT- 90** CHERRY SUNBURST	1,341	**1,030**	910	802
GUITAR	65	EPIPHONE	**ELDORADO FT- 90** NATURAL, SERIAL #541164	1,627	**1,249**	1,104	973
GUITAR	66	EPIPHONE	**ELDORADO FT- 90** CHERRY SUNBURST	1,341	**1,030**	910	802
GUITAR	68	EPIPHONE	**ELDORADO FT- 90** SUNBURST	1,243	**954**	843	743
GUITAR	69	EPIPHONE	**ELDORADO FT- 90** SUNBURST	1,048	**804**	711	627
GUITAR	68	EPIPHONE	**ELDORADO FT- 90N** BLOND	1,341	**1,030**	910	802
GUITAR	59	EPIPHONE	**EMPEROR** SUNBURST, THINLINE	3,767	**2,893**	2,556	2,253
GUITAR	63	EPIPHONE	**EMPEROR** NATURAL, CURLY MAPLE	3,787	**2,908**	2,570	2,265
GUITAR	68	EPIPHONE	**EMPEROR A-112** SUNBURST	1,582	**1,215**	1,073	946
GUITAR	63	EPIPHONE	**EMPEROR A-112N** BLOND	3,683	**2,828**	2,499	2,203
GUITAR	59	EPIPHONE	**EMPEROR E-112T** SUNBURST	5,934	**4,557**	4,027	3,550
GUITAR	65	EPIPHONE	**EMPEROR E-112T** BLOND	3,722	**2,858**	2,526	2,227
GUITAR	66	EPIPHONE	**EMPEROR E-112T** SUNBURST	3,946	**3,030**	2,678	2,361
GUITAR	59	EPIPHONE	**EXCELLENTE FT-120** ROSEWOOD, FLATTOP	2,185	**1,677**	1,482	1,307
GUITAR	64	EPIPHONE	**EXCELLENTE FT-120** ROSEWOOD, FLATTOP	2,293	**1,761**	1,556	1,372
GUITAR	66	EPIPHONE	**EXCELLENTE FT-120** ROSEWOOD, FLATTOP	1,966	**1,510**	1,334	1,176
GUITAR	68	EPIPHONE	**EXCELLENTE FT-120** ROSEWOOD, FLATTOP	1,311	**1,007**	889	784
GUITAR	63	EPIPHONE	**EXCELLENTE FT-350**	3,304	**2,537**	2,242	1,976
GUITAR	66	EPIPHONE	**F- 20NT** NATURAL, MAHOGANY BACK/SIDES	499	**383**	338	298
GUITAR	64	EPIPHONE	**F- 25** WHITE PICKGUARDS, FLATTOP	704	**540**	478	421
GUITAR	64	EPIPHONE	**F- 25** SPRUCE TOP, MAHOGANY BACK/SIDES	708	**544**	481	424
GUITAR	64	EPIPHONE	**F- 25** NATURAL, FLATTOP	728	**559**	494	435
GUITAR	67	EPIPHONE	**F- 25** SPRUCE TOP, MAHOGANY BACK/SIDES	665	**510**	451	397
GUITAR	66	EPIPHONE	**F- 25 000 SIZE** NATURAL, SPRUCE TOP	510	**392**	346	305
GUITAR	68	EPIPHONE	**FOLKSTER FT- 95** FLATTOP	515	**389**	343	284
GUITAR	63	EPIPHONE	**FRONTIER FT-110** NATURAL	724	**556**	491	433
GUITAR	64	EPIPHONE	**FRONTIER FT-110** NATURAL	722	**554**	490	432
GUITAR	65	EPIPHONE	**FRONTIER FT-110** NATURAL	697	**535**	473	417
GUITAR	66	EPIPHONE	**FRONTIER FT-110** SUNBURST	693	**532**	470	414
GUITAR	66	EPIPHONE	**FRONTIER FT-110** NATURAL	695	**534**	471	416
GUITAR	67	EPIPHONE	**FRONTIER FT-110** SUNBURST	666	**511**	452	398
GUITAR	68	EPIPHONE	**FRONTIER FT-110** NATURAL	723	**555**	490	432
GUITAR	68	EPIPHONE	**FRONTIER FT-110** SUNBURST	731	**561**	496	437
GUITAR	64	EPIPHONE	**FT- 28** TENOR, MAHOGANY	695	**534**	471	416
GUITAR	70	EPIPHONE	**FT-165** ROSEWOOD BACK/SIDES, 12-STRING	598	**459**	405	357
GUITAR	64	EPIPHONE	**HOWARD ROBERTS**	3,149	**2,418**	2,137	1,884
GUITAR	66	EPIPHONE	**HOWARD ROBERTS STANDARD** SUNBURST	2,141	**1,644**	1,453	1,281
GUITAR	65	EPIPHONE	**MADRID EC-30 CLASSICAL**	598	**459**	405	357
GUITAR	66	EPIPHONE	**NEWPORT BASS** SOLID CHERRY, 1 PU	820	**630**	557	491
GUITAR	64	EPIPHONE	**SERENADER** NATURAL	792	**608**	538	474
GUITAR	63	EPIPHONE	**SERENADER FT- 85** 12-STRING, FLATTOP	759	**583**	515	454
GUITAR	64	EPIPHONE	**SERENADER FT- 85** 12-STRING, FLATTOP	722	**554**	490	432
GUITAR	67	EPIPHONE	**SERENADER FT- 85** 12-STRING, FLATTOP	696	**534**	472	416

TYPE	YR	MFG	PRICES--BASED ON 100% ORIGINAL MODEL	SELL EXC	SELL AVG	BUY EXC	BUY AVG
GUITAR	67	EPIPHONE	**SEVILLE**	592	**454**	402	354
GUITAR	63	EPIPHONE	**SORRENTO E452 THIN** SUNBURST, CUTAWAY, 1 PU	1,242	**953**	842	743
GUITAR	63	EPIPHONE	**SORRENTO E452 THIN** NATURAL, CUATAWY, 1 PU	1,248	**958**	847	747
GUITAR	64	EPIPHONE	**SORRENTO E452 THIN** NATURAL, CUTAWAY, 2 PU's	1,288	**989**	874	770
GUITAR	66	EPIPHONE	**SORRENTO E452 THIN** SUNBURST, CUTAWAY, 1 PU	1,219	**936**	827	729
GUITAR	67	EPIPHONE	**SORRENTO E452 THIN** SUNBURST, CUTAWAY, 2 PU's	1,056	**810**	716	631
GUITAR	68	EPIPHONE	**SORRENTO E452 THIN** SUNBURST, CUTAWAY, 2 PU's	1,025	**787**	696	613
GUITAR	58	EPIPHONE	**TEXAN FT-79** NATURAL	2,185	**1,677**	1,482	1,307
GUITAR	63	EPIPHONE	**TEXAN FT-79** NATURAL	2,185	**1,677**	1,482	1,307
GUITAR	64	EPIPHONE	**TEXAN FT-79** SUNBURST	2,130	**1,635**	1,445	1,274
GUITAR	66	EPIPHONE	**TEXAN FT-79** SUNBURST	2,339	**1,768**	1,559	1,293
GUITAR	67	EPIPHONE	**TEXAN FT-79** SUNBURST	2,130	**1,635**	1,445	1,274
GUITAR	68	EPIPHONE	**TEXAN FT-79** SUNBURST	1,855	**1,425**	1,259	1,110
GUITAR	69	EPIPHONE	**TEXAN FT-79**	1,638	**1,258**	1,111	980
GUITAR	60	EPIPHONE	**TEXAN FT-79N** NATURAL BLOND	2,467	**1,894**	1,674	1,476
GUITAR	62	EPIPHONE	**TEXAN FT-79N** NATURAL BLOND	1,915	**1,470**	1,299	1,145
GUITAR	64	EPIPHONE	**TEXAN FT-79N** NATURAL BLOND	1,899	**1,458**	1,288	1,136
GUITAR	65	EPIPHONE	**TEXAN FT-79N** NATURAL BLOND	1,787	**1,372**	1,212	1,069
GUITAR	67	EPIPHONE	**TEXAN FT-79N** NATURAL BLOND	1,781	**1,368**	1,209	1,065
GUITAR	69	EPIPHONE	**TEXAN FT-79N** NATURAL BLOND	1,942	**1,491**	1,317	1,161
GUITAR	63	EPIPHONE	**TEXAN JOHN LENNON** SUNBURST	3,757	**2,885**	2,549	2,247
GUITAR	64	EPIPHONE	**TEXAN JOHN LENNON** SUNBURST	3,757	**2,885**	2,549	2,247
GUITAR	66	EPIPHONE	**TEXAS** SUNBURST	3,589	**2,756**	2,435	2,147
GUITAR	67	EPIPHONE	**TRIUMPH** SUNBURST, CUTAWAY	1,935	**1,486**	1,313	1,157
GUITAR	59	EPIPHONE	**TRIUMPH REGENT** SUNBURST, CUTAWAY	3,170	**2,434**	2,151	1,896
GUITAR	60	EPIPHONE	**TRIUMPH REGENT** SUNBURST, CUTAWAY	3,063	**2,352**	2,078	1,832
GUITAR	61	EPIPHONE	**TRIUMPH REGENT** NATURAL BLOND, CUTAWAY	1,905	**1,462**	1,292	1,139
GUITAR	63	EPIPHONE	**TRIUMPH REGENT** SUNBURST, CUTAWAY	2,307	**1,771**	1,565	1,380
GUITAR	64	EPIPHONE	**TRIUMPH REGENT** SUNBURST, CUTAWAY	2,289	**1,757**	1,553	1,369
GUITAR	65	EPIPHONE	**TRIUMPH REGENT** SUNBURST, CUTAWAY, SERIAL #407167	1,834	**1,408**	1,244	1,097
GUITAR	66	EPIPHONE	**TRIUMPH REGENT** SUNBURST, LEFT-HANDED	3,132	**2,405**	2,125	1,873
GUITAR	67	EPIPHONE	**TRIUMPH REGENT** NATURAL BLOND, CUTAWAY	1,747	**1,321**	1,165	966
GUITAR	67	EPIPHONE	**TRIUMPH REGENT** SUNBURST, OVAL HOLE, (RARE) FLOATING JOHNNY SMITH TYPE PU	3,132	**2,405**	2,125	1,873
GUITAR	68	EPIPHONE	**TRIUMPH REGENT** SUNBURST, CUTAWAY	3,121	**2,396**	2,118	1,867
GUITAR	58	EPIPHONE	**ZENITH** SUNBURST	1,271	**976**	862	760
GUITAR	62	EPIPHONE	**ZENITH** SUNBURST	1,311	**1,007**	889	784
GUITAR	64	EPIPHONE	**ZENITH** SUNBURST	852	**654**	578	509
GUITAR	66	EPIPHONE	**ZENITH** SUNBURST	887	**681**	601	530
GUITAR	67	EPIPHONE	**ZENITH** SUNBURST	872	**669**	592	521
MANDOLIN	70	EPIPHONE	**A-5 COPY FLORENTINE** CUTAWAY, MADE IN JAPAN	832	**638**	564	497
MANDOL	66	EPIPHONE	**VENETIAN ELECTRIC by GIBSON** HIGHLY FIGURED CURLY MAPLE,1 P-90 SINGLE COIL PU	726	**558**	493	434
STEEL GUITAR	64	EPIPHONE	**TROUBADOUR** FLATTOP	887	**681**	601	530
STGUIT	66	EPIPHONE	**TROUBADOUR** FLATTOP	778	**597**	528	465

TYPE	YR	MFG	PRICES--BASED ON 100% ORIGINAL MODEL	SELL EXC	SELL AVG	BUY EXC	BUY AVG
STGUIT	67	EPIPHONE	TROUBADOUR FLATTOP	688	528	467	412

EVEN

TYPE	YR	MFG	MODEL	SELL EXC	SELL AVG	BUY EXC	BUY AVG
BANJO	79	EVEN	2830 OMNIPRESSOR	1,294	994	878	774
BANJO	n/a	EVEN	H-3000/HS-395 ULTRA HARMONIZER	1,601	1,229	1,086	958
BANJO	89	EVEN	OMNIPRESSOR	1,043	801	708	624

FAIRCHILD

TYPE	YR	MFG	MODEL	SELL EXC	SELL AVG	BUY EXC	BUY AVG
PWR	62-69	FAIRCHILD	255 TUBE MONO	308	236	209	184
PWR	59-77	FAIRCHILD	260 TUBE MONO	240	184	163	144
PWR	59	FAIRCHILD	275 TUBE MONO	716	550	486	428
PWR	61	FAIRCHILD	HF-87 KIT STEREO, TUBE, 35 WATTS	287	221	195	172
SIGNAL PROCESSOR	61	FAIRCHILD	660 MONO LIMITER	162	124	110	97
SGNPRO	61	FAIRCHILD	661TL NOISE GATE	773	594	525	462
SGNPRO	61	FAIRCHILD	663 COMPRESSOR	773	594	525	462
SGNPRO	61	FAIRCHILD	666 MONO COMPRESSOR	8,346	6,408	5,663	4,992
SGNPRO	58	FAIRCHILD	670 STEREO LIMITER	16,280	12,500	11,047	9,739

FAIRLIGHT INSTRUMENTS

TYPE	YR	MFG	MODEL	SELL EXC	SELL AVG	BUY EXC	BUY AVG
SYNTHESIZER	80	FAIRLI	FAIRLIGHT CMI	1,955	1,501	1,326	1,169

FARFISA

TYPE	YR	MFG	MODEL	SELL EXC	SELL AVG	BUY EXC	BUY AVG
SYNTHESIZER	67	FARFISA	COMPACT DELUXE	779	598	528	466
SYNTH	66	FARFISA	VIP-233 DOUBLE KEYBOARD	478	367	324	286

FAVILLA BROTHERS

TYPE	YR	MFG	MODEL	SELL EXC	SELL AVG	BUY EXC	BUY AVG
GUITAR (ACOUSTIC)	31	FAVILLA	6/8 NEW YORK DOUBLE NECK	2,924	2,245	1,984	1,749
GUITAR	29	FAVILLA	00 NEW YORK FLATTOP	2,264	1,738	1,536	1,354
GUITAR	34	FAVILLA	DETROIT FLATTOP	1,992	1,529	1,352	1,191
GUITAR	38	FAVILLA	DETROIT ARCHTOP, 16"	2,349	1,804	1,594	1,405
UKULELE	55	FAVILLA	BARITONE	552	423	374	330

FENDER MUSICAL CORP.

TYPE	YR	MFG	MODEL	SELL EXC	SELL AVG	BUY EXC	BUY AVG
BANJO	70	FENDER	ALLEGRO TENOR	778	597	528	465
BANJO	71	FENDER	ALLEGRO 5-STRING	704	540	478	421
BANJO	68	FENDER	ARTIST PLECTRUM	708	544	481	424
BANJO	68	FENDER	ARTIST TENOR	747	573	506	446
BANJO	70	FENDER	ARTIST TENOR	708	544	481	424
BANJO	70	FENDER	ARTIST DELUXE	1,460	1,121	991	873
BANJO	70	FENDER	CONCERT TONE	1,444	1,109	980	864
BANJO	74	FENDER	CONCERT TONE PLECTRUM	1,229	944	834	735
BANJO	74	FENDER	CONCERT TONE TENOR	1,303	1,001	884	779
BANJO	82	FENDER	LEO 5-STRING, CLEAR HEAD, RESONATOR	1,034	794	702	619
EFFECTS	70	FENDER	DIMENSION IV SOUND EXPANDER	163	125	110	97
EFFECTS	64	FENDER	ELECTRONIC ECHO CHAMBER TAPE ECHO	512	393	348	306
EFFECTS	65	FENDER	FE-1000 ELECTRONIC ECHO CHAMBER	720	552	488	430
EFFECTS	76	FENDER	FUZZ-WAH	181	139	123	108
EFFECTS	64	FENDER	REVERB TANK TUBE, BLACK, WHITE KNOBS	924	709	627	552
EFFECTS	68	FENDER	VOLUME PEDAL CHROME	187	143	126	111
ELEC. GUITAR & BASS	65	FENDER	BASS V SUNBURST, 5-STRING	1,674	1,285	1,136	1,001
ELGUIT	65	FENDER	BASS V LAKE PLACID BLUE, 5-STRING	2,246	1,725	1,524	1,344
ELGUIT	66	FENDER	BASS V SUNBURST, 5-STRING	1,691	1,298	1,147	1,011
ELGUIT	66	FENDER	BASS V CANDY APPLE RED, 5-STRING	2,196	1,686	1,490	1,313
ELGUIT	66	FENDER	BASS V OCEAN TURQUOISE, 5-STRING	3,336	2,561	2,264	1,995
ELGUIT	67	FENDER	BASS V LAKE PLACID BLUE, 5-STRING	1,694	1,301	1,149	1,013

TYPE	YR	MFG	PRICES--BASED ON 100% ORIGINAL MODEL	SELL EXC	SELL AVG	BUY EXC	BUY AVG
ELGUIT	68	FENDER	**BASS V** SUNBURST, 5-STRING	1,559	**1,197**	1,057	932
ELGUIT	69	FENDER	**BASS V** SUNBURST, 5-STRING	1,556	**1,195**	1,056	931
ELGUIT	70	FENDER	**BASS V** SUNBURST, 5-STRING	1,448	**1,111**	982	866
ELGUIT	71	FENDER	**BASS V** SUNBURST, 5-STRING	1,626	**1,248**	1,103	972
ELGUIT	62	FENDER	**BASS VI** 3-TONE SUNBURST, 6-STRING, 3 PU's, TREM, CLAY DOTS	3,706	**2,845**	2,514	2,217
ELGUIT	63	FENDER	**BASS VI** SUNBURST, 6-STRING	2,999	**2,303**	2,035	1,794
ELGUIT	63	FENDER	**BASS VI** LAKE PLACID BLUE, 6-STRING	4,164	**3,197**	2,825	2,491
ELGUIT	63	FENDER	**BASS VI** BLACK, 6-STRING	4,175	**3,206**	2,833	2,497
ELGUIT	63	FENDER	**BASS VI** CANDY RED, GREEN GUARD 7/10	6,445	**4,949**	4,373	3,855
ELGUIT	64	FENDER	**BASS VI** SUNBURST, 6-STRING	2,999	**2,303**	2,035	1,794
ELGUIT	64	FENDER	**BASS VI** LAKE PLACID BLUE, 6-STRING	3,977	**3,053**	2,698	2,379
ELGUIT	65	FENDER	**BASS VI** SUNBURST, 6-STRING	3,084	**2,368**	2,093	1,845
ELGUIT	65	FENDER	**BASS VI** LAKE PLACID BLUE, 6-STRING	3,857	**2,961**	2,617	2,307
ELGUIT	66	FENDER	**BASS VI** SUNBURST, 6-STRING	3,327	**2,555**	2,257	1,990
ELGUIT	67	FENDER	**BASS VI** SUNBURST, 6-STRING	2,320	**1,781**	1,574	1,388
ELGUIT	68	FENDER	**BASS VI** SUNBRUST, 6-STRING	2,284	**1,754**	1,550	1,366
ELGUIT	70	FENDER	**BASS VI** SUNBURST, 6-STRING	2,115	**1,624**	1,435	1,265
ELGUIT	73	FENDER	**BASS VI** SUNBURST, 6-STRING	1,900	**1,459**	1,289	1,136
ELGUIT	50	FENDER	**BROADCASTER**	38,207	**29,338**	25,926	22,856
ELGUIT	51	FENDER	**BROADCASTER**	24,151	**18,545**	16,388	14,447
ELGUIT	67	FENDER	**BRONCO** RED, 1 PU, 24" SCALE, SLAB SOLIDBODY	631	**485**	428	377
ELGUIT	68	FENDER	**BRONCO** RED, 1 PU, 24" SCALE, SLAB SOLIDBODY, TREMOLO, SERIAL #206453	631	**485**	428	377
ELGUIT	69	FENDER	**BRONCO** RED, 1 PU, 24" SCALE, SLAB SOLIDBODY, TREMOLO	631	**485**	428	377
ELGUIT	70	FENDER	**BRONCO** RED, SLAB SOLIDBODY, 1 PU, TREMOLO	596	**458**	405	357
ELGUIT	71	FENDER	**BRONCO** RED, 1 PU, 24" SCALE, SLAB SOLIDBODY, TREMOLO	596	**458**	405	357
ELGUIT	72	FENDER	**BRONCO** RED, 1 PU, 24" SCALE, SLAB SOLIDBODY, TREMOLO	596	**458**	405	357
ELGUIT	73	FENDER	**BRONCO** RED, 1 PU, 24" SCALE, SLAB SOLIDBODY, TREMOLO, SERIAL #376380	596	**458**	405	357
ELGUIT	74	FENDER	**BRONCO** RED, 1 PU, 24" SCALE, SLAB SOLIDBODY, TREMOLO	596	**458**	405	357
ELGUIT	75	FENDER	**BRONCO** RED, 1 PU, 24" SCALE, SLAB SOLIDBODY, TREMOLO	596	**458**	405	357
ELGUIT	76	FENDER	**BRONCO** RED, 1 PU, 24" SCALE	537	**412**	364	321
ELGUIT	77	FENDER	**BRONCO** RED, 1 PU, 24" SCALE	537	**412**	364	321
ELGUIT	78	FENDER	**BRONCO** RED, 1 PU, 24" SCALE	537	**412**	364	321
ELGUIT	81	FENDER	**BULLET**	287	**221**	195	172
ELGUIT	66	FENDER	**CORONADO BASS** LAKE PLACID BLUE	1,357	**1,042**	921	812
ELGUIT	66	FENDER	**CORONADO I** CHERRY RED, 1 PU, DOUBLE CUT, TREMOLO, DOT INLAY	738	**566**	500	441
ELGUIT	66	FENDER	**CORONADO I** ORANGE CUSTOM COLOR, 1 PU, DOUBLE CUT, TREMOLO, DOT INLAY	948	**728**	643	567
ELGUIT	66	FENDER	**CORONADO I** BLUE CUSTOM COLOR, DOUBLE CUT, 1 PU, TREMOLO	1,053	**809**	715	630
ELGUIT	66	FENDER	**CORONADO I** WHITE, UNFADED, 1 PU, DOUBLE CUT, TREMOLO, DOT INLAY	1,053	**809**	715	630
ELGUIT	67	FENDER	**CORONADO I** SUNBURST, 1 PU, TREMOLO, SERIAL #200865	738	**566**	500	441
ELGUIT	67	FENDER	**CORONADO I** ORANGE CUSTOM COLOR, 1 PU, DOUBLE CUT, TREMOLO, DOT INLAY	948	**728**	643	567
ELGUIT	67	FENDER	**CORONADO I** BLUE CUSTOM COLOR, DOUBLE CUT, 1 PU, TREMOLO	1,053	**809**	715	630
ELGUIT	67	FENDER	**CORONADO I** WHITE, UNFADED, 1 PU, DOUBLE CUT, TREMOLO, DOT INLAY	1,053	**809**	715	630
ELGUIT	68	FENDER	**CORONADO I** SUNBURST, 1 PU, SERIAL #622740	669	**514**	454	400

TYPE	YR	MFG	PRICES--BASED ON 100% ORIGINAL MODEL	SELL EXC	SELL AVG	BUY EXC	BUY AVG
ELGUIT	69	FENDER	CORONADO I SUNBURST	648	**497**	440	387
ELGUIT	70	FENDER	CORONADO I SUNBURST, 1 PU, DOUBLE CUT,TREMOLO,DOT INLAY,STRING BOUND	631	**485**	428	377
ELGUIT	66	FENDER	CORONADO I BASS SUNBURST, 1 PU	599	**460**	406	358
ELGUIT	68	FENDER	CORONADO I BASS SUNBURST	623	**479**	423	373
ELGUIT	68	FENDER	CORONADO I BASS WHITE, 1 PU	623	**479**	423	373
ELGUIT	65	FENDER	CORONADO II SUNBURST. 2 PU's	685	**526**	465	410
ELGUIT	66-67	FENDER	CORONADO II SUNBURST, 2 PU's, SERIAL #500641	658	**505**	446	393
ELGUIT	66	FENDER	CORONADO II TRANSPARENT ORANGE	663	**509**	449	396
ELGUIT	66-67	FENDER	CORONADO II CHERRY RED, 2 PU's	666	**511**	452	398
ELGUIT	67	FENDER	CORONADO II CHERRY RED, 2 PU's, SERIAL #180882-201286	611	**469**	414	365
ELGUIT	67-68	FENDER	CORONADO II ANTIGUA, 2 PU's	631	**485**	428	377
ELGUIT	67	FENDER	CORONADO II SUNBURST, 2 PU's, SERIAL #180882-201286	640	**491**	434	383
ELGUIT	67	FENDER	CORONADO II WILDWOOD GOLD, 2 PU's, SERIAL #180882-201286	1,068	**820**	725	639
ELGUIT	68	FENDER	CORONADO II ANTIGUA, 2 PU's, SERIAL #503008	590	**453**	400	353
ELGUIT	68	FENDER	CORONADO II SUNBURST, 2 PU's, SERIAL #503008	607	**466**	411	363
ELGUIT	68	FENDER	CORONADO II LAKE PLACID BLUE	692	**531**	469	414
ELGUIT	68	FENDER	CORONADO II ORANGE	762	**585**	517	456
ELGUIT	68	FENDER	CORONADO II CHERRY RED	803	**616**	544	480
ELGUIT	68	FENDER	CORONADO II WILDWOOD	963	**739**	653	576
ELGUIT	69	FENDER	CORONADO II ANTIGUA, 2 PU's	855	**657**	580	511
ELGUIT	69	FENDER	CORONADO II SUNBURST, 2 PU's	855	**657**	580	511
ELGUIT	70	FENDER	CORONADO II ANTIGUA, 2 PU's	848	**651**	576	507
ELGUIT	71	FENDER	CORONADO II ANTIGUA, 2 PU's	846	**650**	574	506
ELGUIT	73	FENDER	CORONADO II SUNBURST, 2 PU's	841	**645**	570	503
ELGUIT	74	FENDER	CORONADO II CHERRY RED, 2 PU's	835	**641**	566	499
ELGUIT	67	FENDER	CORONADO II BASS SUNBURST, 2 PU's	611	**469**	414	365
ELGUIT	68	FENDER	CORONADO II BASS SUNBURST, 2 PU's	666	**511**	452	398
ELGUIT	69	FENDER	CORONADO II BASS SUNBURST, 2 PU's	602	**462**	408	360
ELGUIT	71	FENDER	CORONADO II BASS ANTIGUA	582	**447**	395	348
ELGUIT	66-67	FENDER	CORONADO XII SUNBURST, 12-STRING	668	**513**	453	399
ELGUIT	67	FENDER	CORONADO XII SUNBURST, 12-STRING	670	**515**	455	401
ELGUIT	67	FENDER	CORONADO XII	725	**557**	492	434
ELGUIT	67	FENDER	CORONADO XII ORANGE, 12-STRING	932	**716**	633	558
ELGUIT	68	FENDER	CORONADO XII WILDWOOD GOLD, 12-STRING	706	**542**	479	422
ELGUIT	68	FENDER	CORONADO XII RAINBOW GOLD	953	**731**	646	570
ELGUIT	69	FENDER	CORONADO XII SUNBURST, 12-STRING	595	**457**	404	356
ELGUIT	69	FENDER	CORONADO XII ANTIGUA, 12-STRING	871	**669**	591	521
ELGUIT	84-94	FENDER	D'AQUISTO ELITE	1,626	**1,248**	1,103	972
ELGUIT	84	FENDER	D'AQUISTO STANDARD	1,476	**1,133**	1,001	883
ELGUIT	66	FENDER	DUO SONIC II LIGHT BLUE, KLUSON TUNERS, WHITE PICKGRD	1,008	**774**	684	603
ELGUIT	58	FENDER	DUO-SONIC DESERT SAND, ANODIZED PICKGUARD	1,262	**969**	856	755
ELGUIT	62	FENDER	DUO-SONIC SUNBURST	758	**582**	514	453
ELGUIT	57	FENDER	DUO-SONIC 3/4 TAN, SERIAL #19459-21921	805	**618**	546	481

TYPE	YR	MFG	PRICES--BASED ON 100% ORIGINAL MODEL	SELL EXC	SELL AVG	BUY EXC	BUY AVG
ELGUIT	58	FENDER	**DUO-SONIC 3/4** TAN, SERIAL #15642-28853	949	**729**	644	568
ELGUIT	59	FENDER	**DUO-SONIC 3/4** TAN, SERIAL #31988-91408	650	**499**	441	389
ELGUIT	60	FENDER	**DUO-SONIC 3/4** SUNBURST, SERIAL #44142-58544	673	**516**	456	402
ELGUIT	60	FENDER	**DUO-SONIC 3/4** TAN, SERIAL #44142-58544	730	**560**	495	436
ELGUIT	61	FENDER	**DUO-SONIC 3/4** SUNBURST	682	**523**	462	408
ELGUIT	62	FENDER	**DUO-SONIC 3/4** SUNBURST, SERIAL #77201-87360	467	**358**	316	279
ELGUIT	63	FENDER	**DUO-SONIC 3/4** WHITE, SERIAL #89686-99155/L14848	455	**350**	309	272
ELGUIT	63	FENDER	**DUO-SONIC 3/4** SUNBURST	464	**356**	315	278
ELGUIT	64	FENDER	**DUO-SONIC 3/4** TAN, SERIAL #L27092-L54517	658	**505**	446	393
ELGUIT	65	FENDER	**DUO-SONIC 3/4** TAN, SERIAL #119359/L74879-L86654	628	**482**	426	375
ELGUIT	66	FENDER	**DUO-SONIC 3/4** RED, SERIAL #105288-148942	452	**347**	307	270
ELGUIT	69	FENDER	**DUO-SONIC 3/4** SUNBURST	604	**464**	410	361
ELGUIT	69	FENDER	**DUO-SONIC 3/4** TAN, SERIAL #44142-58544	605	**465**	411	362
ELGUIT	64	FENDER	**DUO-SONIC II** RED, 24", SERIAL #L5225-L55651	619	**475**	420	370
ELGUIT	64	FENDER	**DUO-SONIC II** WHITE	683	**524**	463	408
ELGUIT	65-69	FENDER	**DUO-SONIC II** WHITE	620	**476**	421	371
ELGUIT	65-69	FENDER	**DUO-SONIC II** RED, 24"	647	**497**	439	387
ELGUIT	66	FENDER	**DUO-SONIC II** WHITE, 24", SERIAL #105579-133083	581	**446**	394	347
ELGUIT	66	FENDER	**DUO-SONIC II** RED, 24", SERIAL #105579-133083	582	**447**	395	348
ELGUIT	65	FENDER	**ELECTRIC XII** SUNBURST,12-STRING,SPLIT PU's	2,113	**1,622**	1,434	1,264
ELGUIT	65	FENDER	**ELECTRIC XII** BLACK, 12-STRING,	3,006	**2,308**	2,039	1,798
ELGUIT	65	FENDER	**ELECTRIC XII** CANDY APPLE RED	3,006	**2,308**	2,039	1,798
ELGUIT	65	FENDER	**ELECTRIC XII** LAKE PLACID BLUE	3,006	**2,308**	2,039	1,798
ELGUIT	65	FENDER	**ELECTRIC XII** OLYMPIC WHITE	3,006	**2,308**	2,039	1,798
ELGUIT	65	FENDER	**ELECTRIC XII** SHERWOOD GREEN	3,309	**2,541**	2,245	1,979
ELGUIT	65	FENDER	**ELECTRIC XII** SURF GREEN	3,309	**2,541**	2,245	1,979
ELGUIT	65	FENDER	**ELECTRIC XII** BLUE ICE	3,416	**2,623**	2,318	2,043
ELGUIT	65	FENDER	**ELECTRIC XII** FIREMIST GOLD	3,416	**2,623**	2,318	2,043
ELGUIT	65	FENDER	**ELECTRIC XII** OCEAN TURQUOISE	3,551	**2,727**	2,409	2,124
ELGUIT	65	FENDER	**ELECTRIC XII** SHORELINE GOLD	3,551	**2,727**	2,409	2,124
ELGUIT	65	FENDER	**ELECTRIC XII** SONIC BLUE	3,551	**2,727**	2,409	2,124
ELGUIT	66	FENDER	**ELECTRIC XII** SUNBURST BLOCK (LATE 66)	1,761	**1,352**	1,195	1,053
ELGUIT	66	FENDER	**ELECTRIC XII** SUNBURST, DOT INLAY, UNBOUND	1,879	**1,443**	1,275	1,124
ELGUIT	66	FENDER	**ELECTRIC XII** LAKE PLACID BLUE, 12-STRING	2,348	**1,803**	1,593	1,404
ELGUIT	66	FENDER	**ELECTRIC XII** OLYMPIC WHITE, 12-STRING, SPLIT PU's	2,348	**1,803**	1,593	1,404
ELGUIT	66	FENDER	**ELECTRIC XII** BLACK	2,348	**1,803**	1,593	1,404
ELGUIT	66	FENDER	**ELECTRIC XII** CANDY APPLE RED	2,429	**1,865**	1,648	1,453
ELGUIT	66	FENDER	**ELECTRIC XII** FIESTA RED, 12-STRING, SPLIT PU's	2,466	**1,893**	1,673	1,475
ELGUIT	66	FENDER	**ELECTRIC XII** DAKOTA RED	2,466	**1,893**	1,673	1,475
ELGUIT	66	FENDER	**ELECTRIC XII** DAPHINE BLUE	2,466	**1,893**	1,673	1,475
ELGUIT	66	FENDER	**ELECTRIC XII** BLUE ICE	3,142	**2,413**	2,132	1,880
ELGUIT	66	FENDER	**ELECTRIC XII** BURGANDY MIST	3,142	**2,413**	2,132	1,880

TYPE	YR	MFG	PRICES--BASED ON 100% ORIGINAL MODEL	SELL EXC	SELL AVG	BUY EXC	BUY AVG
ELGUIT	66	FENDER	**ELECTRIC XII** CHARCOAL FROST	3,142	**2,413**	2,132	1,880
ELGUIT	66	FENDER	**ELECTRIC XII** FIREMIST GOLD	3,142	**2,413**	2,132	1,880
ELGUIT	66	FENDER	**ELECTRIC XII** FIREMIST SILVER	3,142	**2,413**	2,132	1,880
ELGUIT	66	FENDER	**ELECTRIC XII** FOAM GREEN	3,142	**2,413**	2,132	1,880
ELGUIT	66	FENDER	**ELECTRIC XII** INCA SILVER	3,142	**2,413**	2,132	1,880
ELGUIT	66	FENDER	**ELECTRIC XII** OCEAN TURQUOISE	3,142	**2,413**	2,132	1,880
ELGUIT	66	FENDER	**ELECTRIC XII** SONIC BLUE	3,279	**2,518**	2,225	1,961
ELGUIT	66	FENDER	**ELECTRIC XII** SHERWOOD GREEN	3,416	**2,623**	2,318	2,043
ELGUIT	66	FENDER	**ELECTRIC XII** SURF GREEN	3,416	**2,623**	2,318	2,043
ELGUIT	66	FENDER	**ELECTRIC XII** TEAL GREEN	3,416	**2,623**	2,318	2,043
ELGUIT	66	FENDER	**ELECTRIC XII** SHORELINE GOLD, 12-STRING	3,459	**2,656**	2,347	2,069
ELGUIT	67	FENDER	**ELECTRIC XII** SUNBURST BLOCK	1,761	**1,352**	1,195	1,053
ELGUIT	67	FENDER	**ELECTRIC XII** LAKE PLACID BLUE	2,231	**1,713**	1,513	1,334
ELGUIT	68	FENDER	**ELECTRIC XII** SUNBURST	1,644	**1,262**	1,115	983
ELGUIT	69	FENDER	**ELECTRIC XII** SUNBURST, 12-STRING, SPLIT PU's	1,826	**1,402**	1,239	1,092
ELGUIT	69	FENDER	**ELECTRIC XII** CANDY APPLE RED	2,113	**1,622**	1,434	1,264
ELGUIT	51	FENDER	**ESQUIRE** BLOND, BLACK PICKGUARD, SINGLE CUT, 1 PU, ASH BODY	13,763	**10,568**	9,339	8,233
ELGUIT	52	FENDER	**ESQUIRE** BLOND, BLACK PICKGUARD, 1 PU, SINGLE CUT, ASH BODY, MAPLE NECK	12,512	**9,607**	8,490	7,485
ELGUIT	53	FENDER	**ESQUIRE** BLOND, BLACK PICKGUARD, 1 PU, SINGLE CUT, ASH BODY	12,512	**9,607**	8,490	7,485
ELGUIT	54	FENDER	**ESQUIRE** BLOND, WHITE PICKGUARD, SINGLE CUT, 1 PU, ASH BODY	10,418	**7,999**	7,069	6,232
ELGUIT	54	FENDER	**ESQUIRE** BLOND, BLACK PICKGUARD, 1 PU, SINGLE CUT, ASH BODY	12,512	**9,607**	8,490	7,485
ELGUIT	55	FENDER	**ESQUIRE** BLOND, WHITE PICKGUARD, SINGLE CUT, 1 PU, ASH BODY	10,418	**7,999**	7,069	6,232
ELGUIT	56	FENDER	**ESQUIRE** TWEED, MAPLE NECK	8,391	**6,443**	5,693	5,019
ELGUIT	56	FENDER	**ESQUIRE** BLOND, WHITE PICKGUARD, SINGLE CUT, 1 PU, ASH BODY	8,580	**6,588**	5,822	5,132
ELGUIT	57	FENDER	**ESQUIRE** BLOND, WHITE PICKGUARD, 1 PU, SINGLE CUT, ASH BODY	8,580	**6,588**	5,822	5,132
ELGUIT	58	FENDER	**ESQUIRE** BLOND, WHITE PICKGUARD, 1 PU, SINGLE CUT, ASH BODY	8,580	**6,588**	5,822	5,132
ELGUIT	59	FENDER	**ESQUIRE** BLOND, WHITE PICKGUARD, MAPLE BOARD, 1 PU, SINGLE CUT	6,464	**4,963**	4,386	3,867
ELGUIT	59	FENDER	**ESQUIRE** BLOND, WHITE PICKGUARD, SLAB BOARD, 1 PU, SINGLE CUT	7,231	**5,553**	4,907	4,326
ELGUIT	60	FENDER	**ESQUIRE** BLOND, WHITE PICKGUARD, SINGLE CUT, 1 PU, ASH BODY	6,390	**4,907**	4,336	3,823
ELGUIT	60	FENDER	**ESQUIRE** SUNBURST, WHITE PICKGUARD, 1 PU, SINGLE CUT, ASH BODY	7,844	**6,023**	5,323	4,692
ELGUIT	61	FENDER	**ESQUIRE** BLOND, WHITE PICKGUARD, 1 PU, SINGLE CUT, ASH BODY	6,864	**5,270**	4,658	4,106
ELGUIT	61	FENDER	**ESQUIRE** SUNBURST, WHITE PICKGUARD, 1 PU, SINGLE CUT, ASH BODY	7,722	**5,929**	5,240	4,619
ELGUIT	62	FENDER	**ESQUIRE** BLOND, WHITE PICKGUARD, 1 PU, SINGLE CUT, ASH BODY	6,619	**5,082**	4,491	3,959
ELGUIT	63	FENDER	**ESQUIRE** BLOND, WHITE PICKGUARD, 1 PU, SINGLE CUT, ASH BODY	6,128	**4,705**	4,158	3,666
ELGUIT	63	FENDER	**ESQUIRE** SUNBURST, WHITE PICKGUARD, 1 PU, SINGLE CUT, ASH BODY	6,373	**4,894**	4,325	3,812
ELGUIT	63	FENDER	**ESQUIRE** CANDY APPLE RED, WHITE PICKGUARD, SINGLE CUT, 1 PU	7,967	**6,118**	5,406	4,766
ELGUIT	63	FENDER	**ESQUIRE** LAKE PLACID BLUE, WHITE PICKGUARD, SINGLE CUT, 1 PU	8,335	**6,400**	5,655	4,986
ELGUIT	63	FENDER	**ESQUIRE** OLYMPIC WHITE, WHITE PICKGUARD, SINGLE CUT, 1 PU	8,335	**6,400**	5,655	4,986
ELGUIT	64	FENDER	**ESQUIRE** BLOND, WHITE PICKGUARD, 1 PU, SINGLE CUT, ASH BODY	7,109	**5,459**	4,824	4,253
ELGUIT	65	FENDER	**ESQUIRE** BLOND, WHITE PICKGUARD, 1 PU, SINGLE CUT, ASH BODY	5,638	**4,329**	3,825	3,372
ELGUIT	65	FENDER	**ESQUIRE** LAKE PLACID BLUE, WHITE PICKGUARD, 1 PU, SINGLE CUT	6,864	**5,270**	4,658	4,106
ELGUIT	66	FENDER	**ESQUIRE** BLOND, WHITE PICKGUARD, 1 PU, SINGLE CUT, ASH BODY	6,006	**4,612**	4,075	3,593

TYPE	YR	MFG	PRICES--BASED ON 100% ORIGINAL MODEL	SELL EXC	SELL AVG	BUY EXC	BUY AVG
ELGUIT	66	FENDER	ESQUIRE OLYMPIC WHITE, WHITE PICKGUARD, 1 PU, SINGLE CUT, ASH BODY	6,496	4,988	4,408	3,886
ELGUIT	67	FENDER	ESQUIRE BLOND, WHITE PICKGUARD, 1 PU, SINGLE CUT, ASH BODY	4,412	3,388	2,994	2,639
ELGUIT	67	FENDER	ESQUIRE OLYMPIC WHITE, WHITE PICKGUARD, 1 PU, SINGLE CUT, ASH BODY	6,128	4,705	4,158	3,666
ELGUIT	67	FENDER	ESQUIRE LAKE PLACID BLUE, WHITE PICKGUARD, 1 PU, SINGLE CUT	6,250	4,799	4,241	3,739
ELGUIT	67	FENDER	ESQUIRE ICE BLUE METALLIC, WHITE PICKGUARD, 1 PU, SINGLE CUT	7,109	5,459	4,824	4,253
ELGUIT	68	FENDER	ESQUIRE BLOND, WHITE PICKGUARD, 1 PU, SINGLE CUT, ASH BODY	4,045	3,106	2,745	2,420
ELGUIT	68	FENDER	ESQUIRE SUNBURST, WHITE PICKGUARD, 1 PU, SINGLE CUT, ASH BODY	4,400	3,378	2,986	2,632
ELGUIT	69	FENDER	ESQUIRE BLOND, WHITE PICKGUARD, 1 PU, SINGLE CUT, ASH BODY	3,676	2,823	2,495	2,199
ELGUIT	69	FENDER	ESQUIRE SUNBURST, WHITE PICKGUARD, 1 PU, SINGLE CUT, ASH BODY	3,676	2,823	2,495	2,199
ELGUIT	70	FENDER	ESQUIRE BLOND, WHITE PICKGUARD, 1 PU, SINGLE CUT, ASH BODY	3,309	2,541	2,245	1,979
ELGUIT	35	FENDER	ESQUIRE BLOND, 1 PU	5,308	4,076	3,602	3,175
ELGUIT	59	FENDER	ESQUIRE CUSTOM BOUND ALDER SUNBURST BODY, WHITE PICKGUARD, 1 PU	15,014	11,529	10,188	8,982
ELGUIT	60	FENDER	ESQUIRE CUSTOM BOUND ALDER SUNBURST BODY, WHITE PICKGUARD, 1 PU	14,890	11,433	10,104	8,907
ELGUIT	61	FENDER	ESQUIRE CUSTOM BOUND ALDER SUNBURST BODY,SLAB BOARD,WHITE PICKGUARD	12,387	9,511	8,405	7,410
ELGUIT	62	FENDER	ESQUIRE CUSTOM BOUND ALDER SUNBURST BODY,CURVE BOARD,WHITE PICKGUARD	10,786	8,282	7,319	6,452
ELGUIT	62	FENDER	ESQUIRE CUSTOM BOUND ALDER SUNBURST BODY,SLAB BOARD,WHITE PICKGUARD	12,387	9,511	8,405	7,410
ELGUIT	63	FENDER	ESQUIRE CUSTOM BOUND ALDER SUNBURST BODY,CURVE BOARD,WHITE PICKGUARD	12,262	9,416	8,321	7,335
ELGUIT	64	FENDER	ESQUIRE CUSTOM BOUND ALDER SUNBURST BODY,CURVE BOARD,WHITE PICKGUARD	12,262	9,416	8,321	7,335
ELGUIT	65	FENDER	ESQUIRE CUSTOM BOUND ALDER SUNBURST BODY,RSWD FNGRBRD,WHITE PICKGUARD	6,496	4,988	4,408	3,886
ELGUIT	66	FENDER	ESQUIRE CUSTOM BOUND ALDER SUNBURST BODY,RSWD FNGRBRD,WHITE PICKGUARD	6,496	4,988	4,408	3,886
ELGUIT	67	FENDER	ESQUIRE CUSTOM BOUND ALDER SUNBURST BODY, RSWD BRD, WHITE PICKGUARD	6,496	4,988	4,408	3,886
ELGUIT	68	FENDER	ESQUIRE CUSTOM BOUND ALDER SUNBURST BODY,RSWD FNGRBRD,WHITE PICKGUARD	6,006	4,612	4,075	3,593
ELGUIT	69	FENDER	ESQUIRE CUSTOM BOUND ALDER SUNBURST BODY,RSWD FNGRBRD,WHITE PICKGUARD	5,883	4,517	3,992	3,519
ELGUIT	70	FENDER	ESQUIRE CUSTOM BOUND ALDER SUNBURST BODY,RSWD FNGRBRD,WHITE PICKGUARD	5,883	4,517	3,992	3,519
ELGUIT	65	FENDER	ESQUIRE CUSTOM LT SUNBURST, ROSEWOOD BOARD, LEFT-HANDED	7,769	5,965	5,272	4,647
ELGUIT	65	FENDER	ESQUIRE CUSTOM LT SUNBURST, LEFT-HANDED	9,346	7,176	6,342	5,591
ELGUIT	61	FENDER	JAGUAR SUNBURST	7,866	6,040	5,338	4,706
ELGUIT	62	FENDER	JAGUAR SUNBURST, SLABOARD	2,240	1,720	1,520	1,340
ELGUIT	62	FENDER	JAGUAR SUNBURST, GREEN GUARD, CLAY DOTS	3,006	2,308	2,039	1,798
ELGUIT	62	FENDER	JAGUAR BLACK	3,800	2,917	2,578	2,273
ELGUIT	62	FENDER	JAGUAR LAKE PLACID BLUE	3,922	3,011	2,661	2,346
ELGUIT	62	FENDER	JAGUAR OLYMPIC WHITE	3,922	3,011	2,661	2,346
ELGUIT	62	FENDER	JAGUAR DAPHNE BLUE	4,534	3,482	3,077	2,712
ELGUIT	62	FENDER	JAGUAR FIESTA RED	4,534	3,482	3,077	2,712
ELGUIT	62	FENDER	JAGUAR CANDY APPLE RED	7,869	6,042	5,339	4,707
ELGUIT	63	FENDER	JAGUAR SUNBURST, SERIAL #20631-158483/L01083-L35810	2,466	1,893	1,673	1,475
ELGUIT	63	FENDER	JAGUAR BLACK	3,676	2,823	2,495	2,199
ELGUIT	63	FENDER	JAGUAR CANDY APPLE RED	3,676	2,823	2,495	2,199
ELGUIT	63	FENDER	JAGUAR OLYMPIC WHITE, SERIAL #20631-158483/L01083-L35810	3,676	2,823	2,495	2,199
ELGUIT	63	FENDER	JAGUAR FIESTA RED, SERIAL #20631-158483/L01083-L35810	4,289	3,293	2,910	2,566
ELGUIT	63	FENDER	JAGUAR SEE-THRU BLOND, ASH	7,868	6,041	5,339	4,706
ELGUIT	64	FENDER	JAGUAR SUNBURST, SERIAL #103717/L18181-L64673	2,348	1,803	1,593	1,404

2006 WINTER VINTAGE GUITARS & COLLECTIBLES BLUE BOOK

FENDER

TYPE	YR	MFG	MODEL	SELL EXC	SELL AVG	BUY EXC	BUY AVG
			PRICES--BASED ON 100% ORIGINAL				
ELGUIT	64	FENDER	**JAGUAR** CANDY APPLE RED, SERIAL #1037171/L18181-L64673	3,554	2,729	2,412	2,126
ELGUIT	64	FENDER	**JAGUAR** LAKE PLACID BLUE, SERIAL #103717/L18181-L64673	3,554	2,729	2,412	2,126
ELGUIT	64	FENDER	**JAGUAR** OLYMPIC WHITE	3,554	2,729	2,412	2,126
ELGUIT	64	FENDER	**JAGUAR** CANDY APPLE RED, LEFT-HANDED	7,870	6,043	5,340	4,708
ELGUIT	65	FENDER	**JAGUAR** SUNBURST	2,231	1,713	1,513	1,334
ELGUIT	65	FENDER	**JAGUAR** BLACK	3,416	2,623	2,318	2,043
ELGUIT	65	FENDER	**JAGUAR** CANDY APPLE RED, SERIAL #89376-209297/L16891-L97962	3,551	2,727	2,409	2,124
ELGUIT	65	FENDER	**JAGUAR** LAKE PLACID BLUE	3,551	2,727	2,409	2,124
ELGUIT	65	FENDER	**JAGUAR** OLYMPIC WHITE, SERIAL #89376-209297/L16891-L97962	3,551	2,727	2,409	2,124
ELGUIT	65	FENDER	**JAGUAR** SHORE LINE GOLD, GOLD HARDWARE	3,800	2,917	2,578	2,273
ELGUIT	65	FENDER	**JAGUAR** SONIC BLUE GREEN GUARD	3,800	2,917	2,578	2,273
ELGUIT	65	FENDER	**JAGUAR** FIREMIST GOLD	3,800	2,917	2,578	2,273
ELGUIT	66	FENDER	**JAGUAR** SUNBURST	1,420	1,090	963	849
ELGUIT	66	FENDER	**JAGUAR** BLACK, DOT INLAY, BINDING	1,562	1,199	1,060	934
ELGUIT	66	FENDER	**JAGUAR** OLYMPIC WHITE, DOT INLAY, SERIAL #113301-240568/L27443-L892	1,696	1,302	1,151	1,015
ELGUIT	66	FENDER	**JAGUAR** CANDY APPLE RED, DOT INLAY, SERIAL #113301-240568/L27443-L8	1,772	1,361	1,203	1,060
ELGUIT	66	FENDER	**JAGUAR** LAKE PLACID BLUE, DOT INLAY	2,027	1,556	1,375	1,212
ELGUIT	66	FENDER	**JAGUAR** SUNBURST, LEFT-HANDED, SERIAL #113301-240568/L27443-L89246	2,197	1,687	1,491	1,314
ELGUIT	66	FENDER	**JAGUAR** FIESTA RED, DOT INLAY, SERIAL #113301-240568/L27443-L89246	3,036	2,331	2,060	1,816
ELGUIT	67	FENDER	**JAGUAR** SUNBURST, SERIAL #22074-705980/L62623	1,384	1,062	939	828
ELGUIT	67	FENDER	**JAGUAR** BLACK, SERIAL #22074-705980/L62623	1,496	1,148	1,015	895
ELGUIT	67	FENDER	**JAGUAR** LAKE PLACID BLUE	1,986	1,525	1,348	1,188
ELGUIT	68	FENDER	**JAGUAR** SUNBURST, SERIAL #214627-237386	1,340	1,029	909	801
ELGUIT	68	FENDER	**JAGUAR** LAKE PLACID BLUE, SERIAL #214627-237386	1,844	1,416	1,251	1,103
ELGUIT	68	FENDER	**JAGUAR** TEAL GREEN METALLIC	2,083	1,599	1,413	1,246
ELGUIT	68	FENDER	**JAGUAR** OLYMPIC WHITE	2,404	1,846	1,631	1,438
ELGUIT	69	FENDER	**JAGUAR** SUNBURST	1,341	1,030	910	802
ELGUIT	69	FENDER	**JAGUAR** OLYMPIC WHITE	1,555	1,194	1,055	930
ELGUIT	69	FENDER	**JAGUAR** SUNBURST, LEFT-HANDED	2,341	1,798	1,589	1,400
ELGUIT	71-75	FENDER	**JAGUAR** SUNBURST	1,361	1,045	924	814
ELGUIT	71	FENDER	**JAGUAR** LAKE PLACID BLUE	1,498	1,150	1,016	896
ELGUIT	71	FENDER	**JAGUAR** BLACK	1,547	1,188	1,050	925
ELGUIT	73	FENDER	**JAGUAR** SUNBURST	1,291	991	876	772
ELGUIT	74	FENDER	**JAGUAR** SUNBURST	1,284	986	871	768
ELGUIT	60	FENDER	**JAZZ BASS** SUNBURST, STACK KNOB, SERIAL #44043-66626	12,352	9,484	8,382	7,389
ELGUIT	60	FENDER	**JAZZ BASS** WHITE, STACK KNOB, SERIAL #44043-66626	13,183	10,123	8,945	7,886
ELGUIT	61	FENDER	**JAZZ BASS** SUNBURST, CONCENTRIC KNOB, SERIAL #56017-74757	11,502	8,832	7,805	6,880
ELGUIT	61	FENDER	**JAZZ BASS** FIESTA RED, CONCENTRIC KN, SERIAL #56017-74757	12,801	9,829	8,686	7,658
ELGUIT	62	FENDER	**JAZZ BASS** OLYMPIC WHITE, 3 KNOBS, SERIAL #75765-95570/L49923	7,059	5,420	4,790	4,223
ELGUIT	62	FENDER	**JAZZ BASS** SUNBURST, SERIAL #75765-95570/L49923	8,116	6,232	5,507	4,855
ELGUIT	62	FENDER	**JAZZ BASS** FIESTA RED, CONCENTRIC KN	9,933	7,627	6,740	5,942
ELGUIT	63	FENDER	**JAZZ BASS** SUNBURST, SERIAL #57263-97989/L01885-L59792	6,801	5,222	4,615	4,068

TYPE	YR	MFG	MODEL	SELL EXC	SELL AVG	BUY EXC	BUY AVG
			PRICES--BASED ON 100% ORIGINAL				
ELGUIT	63	FENDER	**JAZZ BASS** OLYMPIC WHITE, SERIAL #57263-97989/L01885-L59792	8,148	**6,256**	5,529	4,874
ELGUIT	63	FENDER	**JAZZ BASS** CORAL PINK, MATCHING HEADSTOCK, 3 KNOB	10,027	**7,699**	6,804	5,998
ELGUIT	64	FENDER	**JAZZ BASS** SUNBURST, SERIAL #L16100-L85607	5,981	**4,593**	4,059	3,578
ELGUIT	64	FENDER	**JAZZ BASS** LAKE PLACID BLUE, SERIAL #L16100-L85607	6,357	**4,881**	4,313	3,802
ELGUIT	64	FENDER	**JAZZ BASS** SUNBURST, LEFT-HANDED, SERIAL #L16100-L85607	7,267	**5,580**	4,931	4,347
ELGUIT	65	FENDER	**JAZZ BASS** SUNBURST, SERIAL #91213-129012/L05549-L99849	5,679	**4,361**	3,853	3,397
ELGUIT	65	FENDER	**JAZZ BASS** OLYMPIC WHITE, SERIAL #11746-117472/L05549-L99849	6,799	**5,221**	4,613	4,067
ELGUIT	65	FENDER	**JAZZ BASS** BLACK	7,169	**5,504**	4,864	4,288
ELGUIT	65	FENDER	**JAZZ BASS** FIESTA RED, SERIAL #91213-129012/L05549-L99849	7,271	**5,583**	4,933	4,349
ELGUIT	65	FENDER	**JAZZ BASS** LAKE PLACID BLUE	7,435	**5,709**	5,045	4,448
ELGUIT	65	FENDER	**JAZZ BASS** SONIC BLUE, MATCHING HEADSTOCK	7,921	**6,082**	5,375	4,738
ELGUIT	66	FENDER	**JAZZ BASS** SUNBURST, SERIAL #12050-210867/L09298-L66240	3,500	**2,687**	2,375	2,093
ELGUIT	66	FENDER	**JAZZ BASS** OLYMPIC WHITE	3,772	**2,896**	2,559	2,256
ELGUIT	66	FENDER	**JAZZ BASS** CANDY APPLE RED	3,948	**3,031**	2,679	2,361
ELGUIT	66	FENDER	**JAZZ BASS** BLACK, DOT INLAY	4,957	**3,806**	3,363	2,965
ELGUIT	66	FENDER	**JAZZ BASS** OCEAN TURQUOISE, DOT INLAY	7,119	**5,467**	4,831	4,259
ELGUIT	67	FENDER	**JAZZ BASS** SUNBURST, SERIAL #200294-219686	2,910	**2,235**	1,975	1,741
ELGUIT	68	FENDER	**JAZZ BASS** SUNBURST, SERIAL #18565-249563	2,420	**1,858**	1,642	1,447
ELGUIT	68	FENDER	**JAZZ BASS** FIREMIST SILVER, SERIAL #185656-249563	3,588	**2,755**	2,435	2,146
ELGUIT	68	FENDER	**JAZZ BASS** 3-TONE SUNBURST,ROSEWOOD BOARD	3,601	**2,765**	2,444	2,154
ELGUIT	69	FENDER	**JAZZ BASS** CANDY APPLE RED, 4-BOLT, SERIAL #224160-282725	2,088	**1,603**	1,417	1,249
ELGUIT	69	FENDER	**JAZZ BASS** SUNBURST, SERIAL #224160-282725	2,190	**1,682**	1,486	1,310
ELGUIT	69	FENDER	**JAZZ BASS** LAKE PLACID BLUE	5,241	**4,024**	3,556	3,135
ELGUIT	70	FENDER	**JAZZ BASS** BLACK, 4-BOLT NECK, SERIAL #295831-599166	1,872	**1,437**	1,270	1,120
ELGUIT	70	FENDER	**JAZZ BASS** OLYMPIC WHITE	1,900	**1,459**	1,289	1,136
ELGUIT	70	FENDER	**JAZZ BASS** SUNBURST	3,208	**2,463**	2,177	1,919
ELGUIT	71	FENDER	**JAZZ BASS** SUNBURST, MAPLE NECK	2,632	**2,021**	1,786	1,574
ELGUIT	71	FENDER	**JAZZ BASS** BLACK, WHITE PICKGUARD, RSWD FRTBRD, MED FRETS	3,749	**2,879**	2,544	2,243
ELGUIT	72	FENDER	**JAZZ BASS** SUNBURST, SERIAL #271353-403365	1,663	**1,277**	1,128	994
ELGUIT	72	FENDER	**JAZZ BASS** BLACK	2,159	**1,658**	1,465	1,291
ELGUIT	73	FENDER	**JAZZ BASS** BROWN, MAPLE FINGERBOARD	1,256	**964**	852	751
ELGUIT	73	FENDER	**JAZZ BASS** BLACK, MAPLE NECK	1,410	**1,082**	956	843
ELGUIT	73	FENDER	**JAZZ BASS** BLOND, SERIAL #387485-551463	1,469	**1,128**	997	879
ELGUIT	73	FENDER	**JAZZ BASS** NATURAL, MAPLE NECK, SERIAL #387485-551463	1,639	**1,259**	1,112	980
ELGUIT	73	FENDER	**JAZZ BASS** SUNBURST	1,761	**1,352**	1,195	1,053
ELGUIT	74	FENDER	**JAZZ BASS** BROWN, MAPLE NECK, SERIAL #547912-647445	1,244	**955**	844	744
ELGUIT	74	FENDER	**JAZZ BASS** BLACK, MAPLE NECK, SERIAL #547912-647445	1,383	**1,062**	938	827
ELGUIT	74	FENDER	**JAZZ BASS** BLOND	1,456	**1,118**	988	871
ELGUIT	74	FENDER	**JAZZ BASS** NATURAL, SERIAL #547912-647445	1,981	**1,521**	1,344	1,185
ELGUIT	74	FENDER	**JAZZ BASS** SUNBURST	2,591	**1,990**	1,758	1,550
ELGUIT	75	FENDER	**JAZZ BASS** BLACK, SERIAL #614166-688002	1,281	**983**	869	766
ELGUIT	75	FENDER	**JAZZ BASS** BLOND, PEARLOID INLAYS, MARCUS MILLER STYLE	1,430	**1,098**	970	855

TYPE	YR	MFG	PRICES--BASED ON 100% ORIGINAL MODEL	SELL EXC	SELL AVG	BUY EXC	BUY AVG
ELGUIT	75	FENDER	**JAZZ BASS** NATURAL, SERIAL #614166-688002	1,564	**1,201**	1,061	935
ELGUIT	75	FENDER	**JAZZ BASS** SUNBURST, MAPLE NECK, SERIAL #353388-371828	2,213	**1,699**	1,501	1,323
ELGUIT	76	FENDER	**JAZZ BASS** OLYMPIC WHITE, MAPLE NECK	1,221	**938**	829	730
ELGUIT	76	FENDER	**JAZZ BASS** NATURAL	1,433	**1,100**	972	857
ELGUIT	77	FENDER	**JAZZ BASS** BLACK, MAPLE NECK	1,061	**815**	720	635
ELGUIT	77	FENDER	**JAZZ BASS** BROWN, MAPLE NECK	1,232	**946**	836	737
ELGUIT	77	FENDER	**JAZZ BASS** SUNBURST, MAPLE NECK	1,248	**958**	847	747
ELGUIT	77	FENDER	**JAZZ BASS** WHITE, MAPLE NECK	1,320	**1,013**	896	789
ELGUIT	77	FENDER	**JAZZ BASS** NATURAL, MAPLE NECK	1,442	**1,107**	978	862
ELGUIT	78	FENDER	**JAZZ BASS** WINE RED, SLAB FRETBOARD	1,052	**808**	714	629
ELGUIT	78	FENDER	**JAZZ BASS** OLYMPIC WHITE	1,219	**936**	827	729
ELGUIT	78	FENDER	**JAZZ BASS** BLACK, MAPLE NECK	1,223	**939**	829	731
ELGUIT	78	FENDER	**JAZZ BASS** NATURAL, MAPLE NECK, SERIAL #S731966	1,264	**970**	858	756
ELGUIT	78	FENDER	**JAZZ BASS** SUNBURST, MAPLE NECK, SERIAL #S731966	1,265	**971**	858	757
ELGUIT	78	FENDER	**JAZZ BASS** BROWN, MAPLE NECK, SERIAL #S731966	1,340	**1,029**	909	801
ELGUIT	78	FENDER	**JAZZ BASS** ANTIGUA, SERIAL #S731966	1,345	**1,032**	912	804
ELGUIT	80	FENDER	**JAZZ BASS** ANTIGUA	1,305	**1,002**	886	781
ELGUIT	84	FENDER	**JAZZ BASS** BLACK	841	**645**	570	503
ELGUIT	58	FENDER	**JAZZMASTER** SUNBURST, SERIAL #31474-40403	3,799	**2,917**	2,577	2,272
ELGUIT	58	FENDER	**JAZZMASTER** SAN MARINO BLUE	7,040	**5,405**	4,777	4,211
ELGUIT	59	FENDER	**JAZZMASTER** SUNBURST, ANODIZED PICKGUARD, SERIAL #31734-101396	3,412	**2,620**	2,315	2,041
ELGUIT	59	FENDER	**JAZZMASTER** BLOND, GOLD HARDWARE	5,016	**3,851**	3,404	3,000
ELGUIT	60	FENDER	**JAZZMASTER** OLYMPIC WHITE	3,286	**2,523**	2,229	1,965
ELGUIT	60	FENDER	**JAZZMASTER** SUNBURST	3,596	**2,761**	2,440	2,151
ELGUIT	60	FENDER	**JAZZMASTER** BLOND SEE-THROUGH	3,614	**2,775**	2,452	2,162
ELGUIT	61	FENDER	**JAZZMASTER** NATURAL	1,898	**1,457**	1,288	1,135
ELGUIT	61	FENDER	**JAZZMASTER** SUNBURST, SERIAL #56090-70445	2,132	**1,637**	1,447	1,275
ELGUIT	61	FENDER	**JAZZMASTER** BLOND, LEFT-HANDED	3,886	**2,984**	2,637	2,324
ELGUIT	62	FENDER	**JAZZMASTER** SUNBURST, SERIAL #70860-96846/L05540-L27818	2,130	**1,635**	1,445	1,274
ELGUIT	62	FENDER	**JAZZMASTER** OLYMPIC WHITE, SERIAL #70860-96846/L05540-L27818	3,001	**2,304**	2,036	1,795
ELGUIT	62	FENDER	**JAZZMASTER** FIESTA RED, SERIAL #70860-96846/L05540-L27818	3,615	**2,776**	2,453	2,162
ELGUIT	62	FENDER	**JAZZMASTER** BURGUNDY MIST	3,903	**2,997**	2,648	2,334
ELGUIT	63	FENDER	**JAZZMASTER** OLYMPIC WHITE	3,050	**2,342**	2,070	1,825
ELGUIT	63	FENDER	**JAZZMASTER** CANDY APPLE RED	3,091	**2,373**	2,097	1,849
ELGUIT	63	FENDER	**JAZZMASTER** BLONDE, SERIAL #66908-121637/L00446-L38685	3,099	**2,379**	2,102	1,853
ELGUIT	63	FENDER	**JAZZMASTER** SUNBURST, SERIAL #66908-121637/L00446-L38685	3,187	**2,447**	2,162	1,906
ELGUIT	63	FENDER	**JAZZMASTER** LAKE PLACID BLUE, SERIAL #66908-121637/L00446-L38685	3,482	**2,673**	2,362	2,083
ELGUIT	64	FENDER	**JAZZMASTER** OLYMPIC WHITE, SERIAL #L07397-L68238	2,459	**1,888**	1,668	1,471
ELGUIT	64	FENDER	**JAZZMASTER** SUNBURST, SERIAL #L07397-L68238	2,984	**2,291**	2,025	1,785
ELGUIT	64	FENDER	**JAZZMASTER** CANDY APPLE RED	3,192	**2,451**	2,166	1,909
ELGUIT	64	FENDER	**JAZZMASTER** DAKOTA RED	3,325	**2,553**	2,256	1,989
ELGUIT	64	FENDER	**JAZZMASTER** LAKE PLACID BLUE, SERIAL #L07397-L68238	3,489	**2,679**	2,368	2,087

TYPE	YR	MFG	PRICES--BASED ON 100% ORIGINAL MODEL	SELL EXC	SELL AVG	BUY EXC	BUY AVG
ELGUIT	64	FENDER	**JAZZMASTER** SONIC BLUE, SERIAL #L07397-L68238	3,769	**2,894**	2,558	2,255
ELGUIT	64	FENDER	**JAZZMASTER** BURGUNDY MIST, SERIAL #L07397-L68238	4,362	**3,349**	2,960	2,609
ELGUIT	65	FENDER	**JAZZMASTER** OLYMPIC WHITE, SERIAL #38862-145681/L06727-L99227	2,287	**1,756**	1,551	1,368
ELGUIT	65	FENDER	**JAZZMASTER** CANDY APPLE RED, SERIAL #38862-145681/L06727-L99227	2,320	**1,781**	1,574	1,388
ELGUIT	65	FENDER	**JAZZMASTER** SUNBURST, BOUND FRETBRD WITH DOTS, TORTOISE PICKGUARD	2,352	**1,806**	1,596	1,407
ELGUIT	65	FENDER	**JAZZMASTER** SONIC BLUE	3,053	**2,344**	2,071	1,826
ELGUIT	65	FENDER	**JAZZMASTER** OLYMPIC WHITE, LEFT-HANDED, SERIAL #38862-145681/L06727-L99	3,332	**2,558**	2,261	1,993
ELGUIT	65	FENDER	**JAZZMASTER** BLOND, SERIAL #38862-145681/L06727-L99227	3,418	**2,624**	2,319	2,044
ELGUIT	65	FENDER	**JAZZMASTER** LAKE PLACID BLUE	3,535	**2,715**	2,399	2,115
ELGUIT	65	FENDER	**JAZZMASTER** FIREMIST GOLD	4,007	**3,077**	2,719	2,397
ELGUIT	66	FENDER	**JAZZMASTER** SUNBURST, DOT INLAY, SERIAL #119049-501282	2,037	**1,564**	1,382	1,218
ELGUIT	66	FENDER	**JAZZMASTER** CANDY APPLE RED, DOT INLAY, SERIAL #119049-501282	2,281	**1,751**	1,548	1,364
ELGUIT	66	FENDER	**JAZZMASTER** LAKE PLACID BLUE, DOT INLAY	2,442	**1,875**	1,657	1,461
ELGUIT	66	FENDER	**JAZZMASTER** BLACK, ORIGINAL CUSTOM COLOR	4,945	**3,797**	3,356	2,958
ELGUIT	67	FENDER	**JAZZMASTER** SUNBURST, BLOCK INLAY, SERIAL #149078-502479	1,820	**1,397**	1,235	1,088
ELGUIT	68	FENDER	**JAZZMASTER** SUNBURST, SERIAL #185186	1,772	**1,361**	1,203	1,060
ELGUIT	69	FENDER	**JAZZMASTER** SUNBURST, BOUND ROSEWOOD BOARD, BLOCK INLAY	1,236	**949**	839	739
ELGUIT	70	FENDER	**JAZZMASTER** SUNBURST	950	**730**	645	568
ELGUIT	71- 75	FENDER	**JAZZMASTER** SUNBURST	947	**727**	642	566
ELGUIT	72	FENDER	**JAZZMASTER** SUNBURST	871	**669**	591	521
ELGUIT	72	FENDER	**JAZZMASTER** CANDY APPLE RED, SERIAL #391167	1,454	**1,117**	987	870
ELGUIT	74	FENDER	**JAZZMASTER** SUNBURST	663	**509**	449	396
ELGUIT	76- 82	FENDER	**JAZZMASTER** SUNBURST	661	**508**	449	395
ELGUIT	77	FENDER	**JAZZMASTER** SUNBURST	658	**505**	446	393
ELGUIT	78	FENDER	**JAZZMASTER** SUNBURST	657	**504**	446	393
ELGUIT	80	FENDER	**JAZZMASTER** SUNBURST	636	**488**	431	380
ELGUIT	79	FENDER	**LEAD I**	431	**331**	292	257
ELGUIT	81	FENDER	**LEAD I**	424	**325**	288	253
ELGUIT	68	FENDER	**LTD** HOLLOW BODY, QUILTED MAPLE	3,347	**2,570**	2,271	2,002
ELGUIT	70	FENDER	**LTD** HOLLOW BODY, QUILTED MAPLE	2,347	**1,802**	1,592	1,404
ELGUIT	71	FENDER	**LTD** HOLLOW BODY, QUILTED MAPLE	2,220	**1,705**	1,507	1,328
ELGUIT	57	FENDER	**MANDO ELECTRIC** BLOND	3,353	**2,574**	2,275	2,005
ELGUIT	58	FENDER	**MANDO ELECTRIC** SUNBURST 3-TONE	2,406	**1,848**	1,633	1,439
ELGUIT	65	FENDER	**MARAUDER** SUNBURST	9,014	**6,922**	6,117	5,392
ELGUIT	66	FENDER	**MARAUDER** SUNBURST	8,889	**6,825**	6,032	5,317
ELGUIT	70	FENDER	**MAVERICK** SUNBURST	1,285	**987**	872	769
ELGUIT	71	FENDER	**MAVERICK** SUNBURST	1,069	**821**	725	639
ELGUIT	68- 75	FENDER	**MONTEGO I** SUNBURST, HOLLOW BODY, 1 PU	1,519	**1,167**	1,031	909
ELGUIT	71	FENDER	**MONTEGO I** SUNBURST, HOLLOW BODY, 1 PU	1,345	**1,032**	912	804
ELGUIT	75	FENDER	**MONTEGO I** SUNBURST	1,069	**821**	725	639
ELGUIT	69	FENDER	**MONTEGO II** SUNBURST, HOLLOW BODY, 2 PU's	1,750	**1,344**	1,187	1,047
ELGUIT	71	FENDER	**MONTEGO II** SUNBURST, HOLLOW BODY, 2 PU's	1,594	**1,224**	1,082	954
ELGUIT	75	FENDER	**MONTEGO II** SUNBURST	1,398	**1,074**	949	836

TYPE	YR	MFG	PRICES--BASED ON 100% ORIGINAL MODEL	SELL EXC	SELL AVG	BUY EXC	BUY AVG
ELGUIT	69	FENDER	**MUSICLANDER** LAKE PLACID BLUE	1,373	**1,054**	931	821
ELGUIT	69	FENDER	**MUSICLANDER SWINGER**	954	**732**	647	570
ELGUIT	70	FENDER	**MUSICLANDER SWINGER** SERIAL #255017-272793	950	**730**	645	568
ELGUIT	71	FENDER	**MUSICLANDER SWINGER** SERIAL #256809-271956	948	**728**	643	567
ELGUIT	57	FENDER	**MUSICMASTER** BLOND, SERIAL #12717-22598/-18916- -22214	714	**548**	484	427
ELGUIT	57	FENDER	**MUSICMASTER** TAN	719	**552**	487	430
ELGUIT	58	FENDER	**MUSICMASTER** TAN	716	**550**	486	428
ELGUIT	58	FENDER	**MUSICMASTER** BLOND	722	**554**	490	432
ELGUIT	59	FENDER	**MUSICMASTER** BLOND, SERIAL #31563-022878/-23611	710	**545**	481	424
ELGUIT	60- 64	FENDER	**MUSICMASTER** BLOND, SERIAL #42216-58644	649	**498**	440	388
ELGUIT	61	FENDER	**MUSICMASTER** SUNBURST	617	**473**	418	369
ELGUIT	62	FENDER	**MUSICMASTER** SUNBURST	612	**470**	415	366
ELGUIT	62	FENDER	**MUSICMASTER** WHITE, SERIAL #73457-92718/L08931	612	**470**	415	366
ELGUIT	63	FENDER	**MUSICMASTER** WHITE, SERIAL #15682-98685/L00186-L24179	577	**443**	392	345
ELGUIT	63	FENDER	**MUSICMASTER** SUNBURST. SERIAL #15682-98685/L00186-L24179	582	**447**	395	348
ELGUIT	65	FENDER	**MUSICMASTER** BLUE	509	**391**	345	304
ELGUIT	65	FENDER	**MUSICMASTER** RED	509	**391**	345	304
ELGUIT	65	FENDER	**MUSICMASTER** WHITE	516	**396**	350	308
ELGUIT	66	FENDER	**MUSICMASTER** RED, SERIAL #158057-160133	508	**390**	345	304
ELGUIT	66	FENDER	**MUSICMASTER** BLUE	511	**393**	347	306
ELGUIT	67	FENDER	**MUSICMASTER** WHITE, SERIAL #203956	509	**391**	345	304
ELGUIT	68	FENDER	**MUSICMASTER** WHITE	507	**389**	344	303
ELGUIT	68	FENDER	**MUSICMASTER** RED	508	**390**	345	304
ELGUIT	69	FENDER	**MUSICMASTER** SONIC BLUE, SOLID BODY	509	**391**	345	304
ELGUIT	69	FENDER	**MUSICMASTER** RED, SERIAL #271329-296111	511	**393**	347	306
ELGUIT	70- 74	FENDER	**MUSICMASTER** RED, BLUE OR WHITE	455	**350**	309	272
ELGUIT	71	FENDER	**MUSICMASTER** WHITE	453	**348**	307	271
ELGUIT	71	FENDER	**MUSICMASTER** BLUE-GREEN	458	**351**	310	274
ELGUIT	73	FENDER	**MUSICMASTER** BLUE	452	**347**	307	270
ELGUIT	73	FENDER	**MUSICMASTER** WHITE	452	**347**	307	270
ELGUIT	74	FENDER	**MUSICMASTER** CREAM	398	**306**	270	238
ELGUIT	74	FENDER	**MUSICMASTER** RED	451	**346**	306	270
ELGUIT	75	FENDER	**MUSICMASTER** BLUE	372	**286**	253	223
ELGUIT	75- 80	FENDER	**MUSICMASTER** BLACK OR WHITE	381	**293**	259	228
ELGUIT	75	FENDER	**MUSICMASTER** RED	396	**304**	269	237
ELGUIT	78	FENDER	**MUSICMASTER** WHITE	380	**292**	258	227
ELGUIT	67	FENDER	**MUSICMASTER BASS** RED	571	**438**	387	341
ELGUIT	70	FENDER	**MUSICMASTER BASS** SONIC BLUE	562	**431**	381	336
ELGUIT	70	FENDER	**MUSICMASTER BASS** SONIC BLUE	567	**436**	385	339
ELGUIT	71	FENDER	**MUSICMASTER BASS** WHITE	561	**430**	380	335
ELGUIT	73	FENDER	**MUSICMASTER BASS** RED	555	**426**	376	332
ELGUIT	78	FENDER	**MUSICMASTER BASS** BLACK	452	**347**	307	270

TYPE	YR	MFG	PRICES--BASED ON 100% ORIGINAL MODEL	SELL EXC	SELL AVG	BUY EXC	BUY AVG
ELGUIT	78	FENDER	**MUSICMASTER BASS** WHITE, BLACK PICKGUARD, RSWD FRTBRD,1 SINGLE COIL PU	664	**509**	450	397
ELGUIT	65	FENDER	**MUSICMASTER II** RED	509	**391**	345	304
ELGUIT	65	FENDER	**MUSICMASTER II** DAPHNE BLUE	598	**459**	405	357
ELGUIT	66	FENDER	**MUSICMASTER II** WHITE, SERIAL #118372-203501	505	**387**	342	302
ELGUIT	67	FENDER	**MUSICMASTER II** RED	586	**450**	398	351
ELGUIT	67	FENDER	**MUSICMASTER II** LONG SCALE	607	**466**	411	363
ELGUIT	64- 65	FENDER	**MUSTANG** WHITE, SERIAL #L41937-L63050	704	**540**	478	421
ELGUIT	65	FENDER	**MUSTANG** WHITE	682	**523**	462	408
ELGUIT	65	FENDER	**MUSTANG** DAKOTA RED	846	**650**	574	506
ELGUIT	65	FENDER	**MUSTANG** SONIC BLUE, SERIAL #102526-124001/L23537-L99089	936	**718**	635	560
ELGUIT	66- 69	FENDER	**MUSTANG** BLUE, SERIAL #105853-501486	657	**504**	446	393
ELGUIT	66- 69	FENDER	**MUSTANG** RED, SERIAL #105853-501486	657	**504**	446	393
ELGUIT	66- 69	FENDER	**MUSTANG** WHITE	658	**505**	446	393
ELGUIT	67	FENDER	**MUSTANG** WHITE	649	**498**	440	388
ELGUIT	67	FENDER	**MUSTANG** RED, SERIAL #175239-208631	650	**499**	441	389
ELGUIT	67	FENDER	**MUSTANG** COMP YELLOW, RACING STRIPES	762	**585**	517	456
ELGUIT	67	FENDER	**MUSTANG** BLUE, LEFT-HANDED	1,451	**1,114**	984	868
ELGUIT	68	FENDER	**MUSTANG** WHITE	647	**497**	439	387
ELGUIT	68	FENDER	**MUSTANG** BLUE	658	**505**	446	393
ELGUIT	68	FENDER	**MUSTANG** RED	731	**561**	496	437
ELGUIT	69	FENDER	**MUSTANG** COMP RED, RACING STRIPES, SERIAL #269928	674	**517**	457	403
ELGUIT	69	FENDER	**MUSTANG** RED	712	**546**	483	426
ELGUIT	70- 79	FENDER	**MUSTANG** COMP RED, RACING STRIPES	648	**497**	440	387
ELGUIT	70- 79	FENDER	**MUSTANG** BLACK, SERIAL #301922	719	**552**	487	430
ELGUIT	70- 79	FENDER	**MUSTANG** BLUE, SERIAL #301922	810	**622**	550	485
ELGUIT	71	FENDER	**MUSTANG** COMP CANDY APPLE RED	650	**499**	441	389
ELGUIT	71	FENDER	**MUSTANG** SUNBURST, SERIAL #317526-335966	655	**503**	444	391
ELGUIT	71	FENDER	**MUSTANG** WHITE, SERIAL #317799-588161	673	**516**	456	402
ELGUIT	71	FENDER	**MUSTANG** CANDY APPLE RED, STRIPES	810	**622**	550	485
ELGUIT	71	FENDER	**MUSTANG** COMP RED, RACING STRIPES	834	**640**	566	499
ELGUIT	71	FENDER	**MUSTANG** COMP YELLOW, RACING STRIPES	834	**640**	566	499
ELGUIT	72	FENDER	**MUSTANG** CANDY APPLE RED	598	**459**	405	357
ELGUIT	72	FENDER	**MUSTANG** COMP BLUE, RACING STRIPES, SERIAL #359003-360239	601	**461**	408	359
ELGUIT	72	FENDER	**MUSTANG** COMP RED, RACING STRIPES, SERIAL #359003-360239	604	**464**	410	361
ELGUIT	72	FENDER	**MUSTANG** SUNBURST	650	**499**	441	389
ELGUIT	72	FENDER	**MUSTANG** SUNBURST, LEFT-HANDED	663	**509**	449	396
ELGUIT	72	FENDER	**MUSTANG** YELLOW, SERIAL #359003-360239	669	**514**	454	400
ELGUIT	72	FENDER	**MUSTANG** BLUE, SERIAL #359003-360239	739	**567**	501	442
ELGUIT	73	FENDER	**MUSTANG** SUNBURST, LEFTHANDED	595	**457**	404	356
ELGUIT	73	FENDER	**MUSTANG** RED, SERIAL #411526	616	**473**	418	368
ELGUIT	73	FENDER	**MUSTANG** WHITE	618	**474**	419	369
ELGUIT	73	FENDER	**MUSTANG** SUNBURST, SERIAL #411526	619	**475**	420	370

TYPE	YR	MFG	MODEL	SELL EXC	SELL AVG	BUY EXC	BUY AVG
			PRICES--BASED ON 100% ORIGINAL				
ELGUIT	73	FENDER	**MUSTANG** BLACK	623	**479**	423	373
ELGUIT	73	FENDER	**MUSTANG** COMP LAKE PLACID BLUE	726	**558**	493	434
ELGUIT	74	FENDER	**MUSTANG** SUNBURST	605	**465**	411	362
ELGUIT	74	FENDER	**MUSTANG** RED	610	**468**	414	365
ELGUIT	74	FENDER	**MUSTANG** BLUE	616	**473**	418	368
ELGUIT	75	FENDER	**MUSTANG** BLACK	565	**434**	383	338
ELGUIT	75	FENDER	**MUSTANG** WHITE	568	**436**	386	340
ELGUIT	75	FENDER	**MUSTANG** SUNBURST	571	**438**	387	341
ELGUIT	75	FENDER	**MUSTANG** BROWN	669	**514**	454	400
ELGUIT	76	FENDER	**MUSTANG** WHITE, LEFT-HANDED	554	**425**	376	331
ELGUIT	76	FENDER	**MUSTANG** SUNBURST	556	**427**	377	332
ELGUIT	76	FENDER	**MUSTANG** NATURAL	560	**430**	380	335
ELGUIT	76	FENDER	**MUSTANG** BLUE	674	**517**	457	403
ELGUIT	76	FENDER	**MUSTANG** SEA FOAM GREEN	688	**528**	467	412
ELGUIT	77	FENDER	**MUSTANG** BLACK	562	**431**	381	336
ELGUIT	77	FENDER	**MUSTANG** WHITE	565	**434**	383	338
ELGUIT	77	FENDER	**MUSTANG** SUNBURST	758	**582**	514	453
ELGUIT	77	FENDER	**MUSTANG** CHERRY	761	**584**	516	455
ELGUIT	78	FENDER	**MUSTANG** RED	448	**344**	304	268
ELGUIT	78	FENDER	**MUSTANG** BROWN	452	**347**	307	270
ELGUIT	78	FENDER	**MUSTANG** ANTIGUA	565	**434**	383	338
ELGUIT	78	FENDER	**MUSTANG** NATURAL	666	**511**	452	398
ELGUIT	78	FENDER	**MUSTANG** BLUE	742	**570**	503	444
ELGUIT	79	FENDER	**MUSTANG** BROWN	484	**372**	329	290
ELGUIT	79	FENDER	**MUSTANG** ANTIGUA	621	**477**	421	371
ELGUIT	81	FENDER	**MUSTANG** RED	481	**369**	326	288
ELGUIT	67	FENDER	**MUSTANG BASS** NATURAL	842	**646**	571	503
ELGUIT	71	FENDER	**MUSTANG BASS** COMPETITION RED	749	**575**	508	448
ELGUIT	76	FENDER	**MUSTANG BASS** SUNBURST	695	**534**	471	416
ELGUIT	52	FENDER	**PRECISION BASS** BUTTERSCOTCH, SLAB BODY	7,450	**5,720**	5,055	4,456
ELGUIT	52	FENDER	**PRECISION BASS** BLOND, SLAB BODY ONLY, SERIAL #299-1351	8,800	**6,757**	5,972	5,264
ELGUIT	53	FENDER	**PRECISION BASS** BUTTERSCOTCH	7,161	**5,498**	4,859	4,283
ELGUIT	53	FENDER	**PRECISION BASS** BLOND, SERIAL #0608-1632	8,748	**6,717**	5,936	5,233
ELGUIT	54	FENDER	**PRECISION BASS** BUTTERSCOTCH, SLAB BODY	6,840	**5,252**	4,642	4,092
ELGUIT	54	FENDER	**PRECISION BASS** SUNBURST	6,866	**5,272**	4,659	4,107
ELGUIT	54	FENDER	**PRECISION BASS** BLOND	8,793	**6,751**	5,966	5,260
ELGUIT	55	FENDER	**PRECISION BASS** SUNBURST	6,556	**5,034**	4,449	3,922
ELGUIT	55	FENDER	**PRECISION BASS** BLOND, SERIAL #0534-11255	7,754	**5,954**	5,262	4,639
ELGUIT	56	FENDER	**PRECISION BASS** SUNBURST	7,742	**5,945**	5,253	4,631
ELGUIT	56	FENDER	**PRECISION BASS** SUNBURST 2-TONE, SERIAL #1341-75820/CONTOURED BODY	8,802	**6,758**	5,972	5,265
ELGUIT	57	FENDER	**PRECISION BASS** SUNBURST 2-TONE, SPLIT PICKUPS/ANODIZED GUARD	9,046	**6,946**	6,138	5,411
ELGUIT	58	FENDER	**PRECISION BASS** OLYMPIC WHITE	5,138	**3,945**	3,486	3,073

TYPE	YR	MFG	MODEL	SELL EXC	SELL AVG	BUY EXC	BUY AVG
			PRICES--BASED ON 100% ORIGINAL				
ELGUIT	58	FENDER	**PRECISION BASS** SUNBURST	6,450	4,952	4,376	3,858
ELGUIT	58	FENDER	**PRECISION BASS** SUNBURST 3-TONE, SERIAL #26150-028058/-24233, SPLIT PICKUPS	6,577	5,050	4,463	3,934
ELGUIT	58	FENDER	**PRECISION BASS** BLOND, SERIAL #26150-028058/-24233	6,961	5,345	4,724	4,164
ELGUIT	59	FENDER	**PRECISION BASS** OLYMPIC WHITE, SLAB BOARD	6,200	4,760	4,207	3,709
ELGUIT	59	FENDER	**PRECISION BASS** SUNBURST 3-TONE, SERIAL #32573-95325	6,582	5,054	4,466	3,937
ELGUIT	59	FENDER	**PRECISION BASS** SUNBURST, ROSEWOOD SLAB BOARD	7,045	5,410	4,781	4,214
ELGUIT	60	FENDER	**PRECISION BASS** OLYMPIC WHITE	4,760	3,655	3,230	2,847
ELGUIT	60	FENDER	**PRECISION BASS** SUNBURST	5,658	4,344	3,839	3,384
ELGUIT	60	FENDER	**PRECISION BASS** BLONDE SEE-THRU	6,205	4,765	4,211	3,712
ELGUIT	61	FENDER	**PRECISION BASS** OLYMPIC WHITE	5,551	4,263	3,767	3,321
ELGUIT	62	FENDER	**PRECISION BASS** SEA FOAM GREEN, SERIAL #70856-306266/L00938	4,406	3,383	2,989	2,635
ELGUIT	62	FENDER	**PRECISION BASS** SUNBURST, SERIAL #70856-306266/L00938	5,341	4,101	3,624	3,195
ELGUIT	63	FENDER	**PRECISION BASS** CANDY APPLE RED	5,510	4,231	3,739	3,296
ELGUIT	63	FENDER	**PRECISION BASS** SUNBURST	5,611	4,308	3,807	3,356
ELGUIT	63	FENDER	**PRECISION BASS** OLYMPIC WHITE, SERIAL #22520-98462/L0827-L00387	5,789	4,445	3,928	3,463
ELGUIT	64	FENDER	**PRECISION BASS** SUNBURST 3-TONE, SERIAL #34654-76736/L01734-L85182	3,483	2,674	2,363	2,083
ELGUIT	64	FENDER	**PRECISION BASS** OLYMPIC WHITE, SERIAL #34854-76736/L01734-L85182	4,046	3,107	2,745	2,420
ELGUIT	64	FENDER	**PRECISION BASS** CANDY APPLE RED	5,096	3,913	3,458	3,048
ELGUIT	64	FENDER	**PRECISION BASS** SHORELINE GOLD, LEFT-HANDED	5,493	4,218	3,727	3,286
ELGUIT	64	FENDER	**PRECISION BASS** SUNBURST	6,081	4,669	4,126	3,638
ELGUIT	64	FENDER	**PRECISION BASS** LAKE PLACID BLUE	6,156	4,727	4,177	3,682
ELGUIT	64	FENDER	**PRECISION BASS** BURGUNDY MIST, SERIAL #34654-76736/L01734-L85182	6,162	4,731	4,181	3,686
ELGUIT	65	FENDER	**PRECISION BASS** SUNBURST	3,842	2,950	2,607	2,298
ELGUIT	65	FENDER	**PRECISION BASS** OLYMPIC WHITE	4,049	3,109	2,748	2,422
ELGUIT	65	FENDER	**PRECISION BASS** CANDY APPLE RED, SERIAL #100339-176651/L32519-L99751	4,874	3,742	3,307	2,915
ELGUIT	65	FENDER	**PRECISION BASS** SHERWOOD GREEN, SERIAL #100339-176651/L32519-L99751	4,883	3,749	3,313	2,921
ELGUIT	65	FENDER	**PRECISION BASS** LAKE PLACID BLUE	5,072	3,894	3,442	3,034
ELGUIT	65	FENDER	**PRECISION BASS** BLOND SEE-THRU	5,492	4,217	3,727	3,285
ELGUIT	65	FENDER	**PRECISION BASS** BLACK	5,522	4,240	3,747	3,303
ELGUIT	66	FENDER	**PRECISION BASS** SUNBURST, SERIAL #73159-247551	3,417	2,623	2,318	2,044
ELGUIT	66	FENDER	**PRECISION BASS** OLYMPIC WHITE	3,560	2,733	2,416	2,129
ELGUIT	66	FENDER	**PRECISION BASS** LAKE PLACID BLUE, SERIAL #73159-247551	4,056	3,114	2,752	2,426
ELGUIT	66	FENDER	**PRECISION BASS** CANDY APPLE RED, SERIAL #73159-247551	4,389	3,370	2,978	2,625
ELGUIT	66	FENDER	**PRECISION BASS** INCA SILVER	6,000	4,607	4,072	3,589
ELGUIT	67	FENDER	**PRECISION BASS** CANDY APPLE RED, SERIAL #187113-303652	3,291	2,527	2,233	1,969
ELGUIT	68	FENDER	**PRECISION BASS** SUNBURST	1,674	1,285	1,136	1,001
ELGUIT	69	FENDER	**PRECISION BASS** SUNBURST, SERIAL #228425-635656	1,769	1,358	1,200	1,058
ELGUIT	69	FENDER	**PRECISION BASS** OLYMPIC WHITE, FIGURED BIRDS EYE NECK, ROSWD FRTBRD	2,084	1,600	1,414	1,246
ELGUIT	70	FENDER	**PRECISION BASS** SUNBURST, FRETLESS, SERIAL #292195-322961	1,478	1,135	1,003	884
ELGUIT	70	FENDER	**PRECISION BASS** OLYMPIC WHITE, SERIAL #292195-322961	1,831	1,406	1,242	1,095
ELGUIT	71	FENDER	**PRECISION BASS** SUNBURST	1,352	1,038	918	809
ELGUIT	71	FENDER	**PRECISION BASS** OLYMPIC WHITE	1,728	1,326	1,172	1,033

TYPE	YR	MFG	PRICES--BASED ON 100% ORIGINAL MODEL	SELL EXC	SELL AVG	BUY EXC	BUY AVG
ELGUIT	72	FENDER	**PRECISION BASS** RED, FRETLESS, SERIAL #315451-390396	1,273	**977**	864	761
ELGUIT	72	FENDER	**PRECISION BASS** BLOND, FRETLESS, ROSEWOOD	1,302	**1,000**	883	779
ELGUIT	72	FENDER	**PRECISION BASS** SUNBURST, FRETLESS	1,337	**1,026**	907	799
ELGUIT	72	FENDER	**PRECISION BASS** SUNBURST	1,620	**1,244**	1,099	969
ELGUIT	72	FENDER	**PRECISION BASS** CANDY APPLE RED	1,678	**1,289**	1,139	1,004
ELGUIT	73	FENDER	**PRECISION BASS** SUNBURST, MAPLE NECK	1,048	**804**	711	627
ELGUIT	73	FENDER	**PRECISION BASS** SUNBURST, FRETLESS	1,225	**940**	831	732
ELGUIT	73	FENDER	**PRECISION BASS** BLACK, MAPLE NECK	1,295	**995**	879	775
ELGUIT	73	FENDER	**PRECISION BASS** CREAM	1,319	**1,013**	895	789
ELGUIT	73	FENDER	**PRECISION BASS** OLYMPIC WHITE	1,336	**1,025**	906	799
ELGUIT	73	FENDER	**PRECISION BASS** NATURAL, MAPLE NECK	1,348	**1,035**	915	806
ELGUIT	74	FENDER	**PRECISION BASS** BROWN	766	**588**	519	458
ELGUIT	74	FENDER	**PRECISION BASS** NATURAL, MAPLE NECK	777	**596**	527	464
ELGUIT	74	FENDER	**PRECISION BASS** NATURAL, LEFT-HANDED	791	**608**	537	473
ELGUIT	74	FENDER	**PRECISION BASS** ROSEWOOD, FRETLESS	808	**620**	548	483
ELGUIT	74	FENDER	**PRECISION BASS** SUNBURST	835	**641**	566	499
ELGUIT	74	FENDER	**PRECISION BASS** BLACK, MAPLE BOARD, SERIAL #402899-7652691	859	**659**	582	513
ELGUIT	74	FENDER	**PRECISION BASS** NATURAL, FRETLESS, SERIAL #402899-7652691	1,011	**776**	686	605
ELGUIT	74	FENDER	**PRECISION BASS** SUNBURST, FRETLESS, SERIAL #402899-580000	1,052	**808**	714	629
ELGUIT	74	FENDER	**PRECISION BASS** OLYMPIC WHITE	1,439	**1,105**	976	860
ELGUIT	74	FENDER	**PRECISION BASS** LAKE PLACID BLUE, ROSEWOOD	1,448	**1,111**	982	866
ELGUIT	74	FENDER	**PRECISION BASS** LEFT-HANDED, SUNBURST, NATURAL	1,898	**1,457**	1,288	1,135
ELGUIT	75	FENDER	**PRECISION BASS** BROWN, MAPLE NECK, SERIAL #619243	742	**570**	503	444
ELGUIT	75	FENDER	**PRECISION BASS** SUNBURST, SERIAL #608195-650392	779	**598**	528	466
ELGUIT	75	FENDER	**PRECISION BASS** NATURAL, MAPLE NECK, SERIAL #608195-650392	841	**645**	570	503
ELGUIT	75	FENDER	**PRECISION BASS** NATURAL, MAPLE NECK, LEFT-HANDED	848	**651**	576	507
ELGUIT	75	FENDER	**PRECISION BASS** SUNBURST, LEFT-HANDED	893	**686**	606	534
ELGUIT	75	FENDER	**PRECISION BASS** BLACK, MAPLE NECK	947	**727**	642	566
ELGUIT	75	FENDER	**PRECISION BASS** SUNBURST, FRETLESS, SERIAL #608195-650392	954	**732**	647	570
ELGUIT	75	FENDER	**PRECISION BASS** BLOND, SERIAL #608195-650392	956	**734**	649	572
ELGUIT	76	FENDER	**PRECISION BASS** NATURAL, SERIAL #588481-7651858/S870439	846	**650**	574	506
ELGUIT	76	FENDER	**PRECISION BASS** SUNBURST, MAPLE NECK, SERIAL #588481-7651858	848	**651**	576	507
ELGUIT	76	FENDER	**PRECISION BASS** OLYMPIC WHITE, SERIAL #588481-7651858/S870439	969	**744**	658	580
ELGUIT	76	FENDER	**PRECISION BASS** BLACK, MAPLE NECK, SERIAL #588481-7651858/S870439	977	**750**	663	584
ELGUIT	76	FENDER	**PRECISION BASS** CANDY APPLE RED	1,043	**801**	708	624
ELGUIT	76	FENDER	**PRECISION BASS** BLACK, LEFT-HANDED, SERIAL #588481-7651858/S870439	1,064	**817**	722	636
ELGUIT	76	FENDER	**PRECISION BASS** FRETLESS MAPLE NECK	1,069	**821**	725	639
ELGUIT	77	FENDER	**PRECISION BASS** NATURAL, MAPLE NECK, SERIAL #45606	842	**646**	571	503
ELGUIT	77	FENDER	**PRECISION BASS** SUNBURST, MAPLE NECK	873	**670**	592	522
ELGUIT	77	FENDER	**PRECISION BASS** NATURAL, FRETLESS, ROSEWOOD	978	**751**	664	585
ELGUIT	77	FENDER	**PRECISION BASS** BLACK, MAPLE NECK	992	**761**	673	593
ELGUIT	78	FENDER	**PRECISION BASS** SUNBURST, MAPLE NECK, SERIAL #S745231-S868960	846	**650**	574	506

TYPE	YR	MFG	PRICES--BASED ON 100% ORIGINAL MODEL	SELL EXC	SELL AVG	BUY EXC	BUY AVG
ELGUIT	78	FENDER	**PRECISION BASS** CHERRY TRANSPARENT	848	**651**	576	507
ELGUIT	78	FENDER	**PRECISION BASS** NATURAL, SERIAL #S745231-S868960	889	**682**	603	531
ELGUIT	78	FENDER	**PRECISION BASS** ANTIGUA, MAPLE NECK, SERIAL #S745231-S868960	892	**685**	605	533
ELGUIT	78	FENDER	**PRECISION BASS** SUNBURST, LEFT-HANDED, SERIAL #S745231-S868960	939	**721**	637	562
ELGUIT	78	FENDER	**PRECISION BASS** OLYMPIC WHITE	949	**729**	644	568
ELGUIT	78	FENDER	**PRECISION BASS** BLACK, MAPLE NECK, SERIAL #S745231-S868960	956	**734**	649	572
ELGUIT	78	FENDER	**PRECISION BASS** BLACK, LEFT-HANDED	964	**740**	654	576
ELGUIT	78	FENDER	**PRECISION BASS** NATURAL, FRETLESS	975	**749**	661	583
ELGUIT	79	FENDER	**PRECISION BASS** NATURAL	750	**576**	509	448
ELGUIT	79	FENDER	**PRECISION BASS** SAPPHIRE BLUE	753	**578**	511	450
ELGUIT	79	FENDER	**PRECISION BASS** SUNBURST	854	**656**	579	511
ELGUIT	79	FENDER	**PRECISION BASS** OLYMPIC WHITE, ROSEWOOD, SERIAL #S792565-S904744	1,061	**815**	720	635
ELGUIT	79	FENDER	**PRECISION BASS** BLACK, MAPLE NECK	1,293	**993**	877	773
ELGUIT	87	FENDER	**PRECISION BASS '57 REISSUE** SUNBURST	789	**606**	535	472
ELGUIT	83	FENDER	**PRECISION BASS ELITE II** PEWTER METALLIC	661	**508**	449	395
ELGUIT	80	FENDER	**PRECISION BASS SPECIAL**	635	**487**	430	379
ELGUIT	80	FENDER	**PRECISION BASS SPECIAL** BLUE METALLIC	781	**600**	530	467
ELGUIT	81	FENDER	**PRECISION BASS SPECIAL** RED, ACTIVE ELECTRONICS	633	**486**	430	379
ELGUIT	82	FENDER	**PRECISION BASS SPECIAL** CANDY APPLE RED	781	**600**	530	467
ELGUIT	80	FENDER	**SQUIER BULLET** SUNBURST, MAPLE	269	**207**	183	161
ELGUIT	75	FENDER	**STARCASTER** SUNBURST, HOLLOW BODY, 2 PU's	1,253	**962**	850	749
ELGUIT	76	FENDER	**STARCASTER** SUNBURST, HOLLOW BODY, 2 PU's	1,053	**809**	715	630
ELGUIT	76	FENDER	**STARCASTER** BLOND, HOLLOW BODY, 2 PU's	1,303	**1,001**	884	779
ELGUIT	77	FENDER	**STARCASTER** BLACK, HOLLOW BODY, 2 PU's, SERIAL #S709138	1,295	**995**	879	775
ELGUIT	77	FENDER	**STARCASTER** NATURAL, HOLLOW BODY, 2 PU's	1,333	**1,024**	905	797
ELGUIT	77	FENDER	**STARCASTER** WHITE, HOLLOW BODY, 2 PU's, SERIAL #S709138	1,346	**1,033**	913	805
ELGUIT	54	FENDER	**STRATOCASTER** SUNBURST 2-TONE, SERIAL #19-09599	26,033	**19,989**	17,665	15,573
ELGUIT	54	FENDER	**STRATOCASTER** SUNBURST, NON-TREMOLO/TWO-TONE	26,508	**20,354**	17,987	15,857
ELGUIT	54	FENDER	**STRATOCASTER** BLOND, GOLD HARDWARE, SERIAL #19-09599	29,949	**22,997**	20,323	17,916
ELGUIT	54	FENDER	**STRATOCASTER** SHORELINE GOLD	58,727	**45,094**	39,850	35,131
ELGUIT	55	FENDER	**STRATOCASTER** SUNBURST 2-TONE, SERIAL #0962-10910	30,733	**23,599**	20,855	18,385
ELGUIT	55	FENDER	**STRATOCASTER** SUNBURST 2-TONE, SERIAL #0962-10910 LEFT-HANDED	31,021	**23,820**	21,050	18,557
ELGUIT	55	FENDER	**STRATOCASTER** SUNBURST	35,972	**27,621**	24,409	21,519
ELGUIT	56	FENDER	**STRATOCASTER** SUNBURST	22,226	**17,066**	15,082	13,296
ELGUIT	56	FENDER	**STRATOCASTER** CANDY APPLE RED	23,451	**18,007**	15,913	14,029
ELGUIT	56	FENDER	**STRATOCASTER** SUNBURST 2-TONE, SERIAL #0999-29629	29,413	**22,585**	19,959	17,595
ELGUIT	57	FENDER	**STRATOCASTER** SUNBURST	16,484	**12,657**	11,185	9,861
ELGUIT	57	FENDER	**STRATOCASTER** SHELL PINK	18,079	**13,882**	12,267	10,815
ELGUIT	57	FENDER	**STRATOCASTER** DAKOTA RED, SERIAL #7019-027770 NON-TREMOLO	26,186	**20,107**	17,769	15,665
ELGUIT	57	FENDER	**STRATOCASTER** SUNBURST 2-TONE, SERIAL #7019-02770/L16720-L25700	32,729	**25,131**	22,209	19,579
ELGUIT	57	FENDER	**STRATOCASTER** SUNBURST 2-TONE, TREMOLO	36,036	**27,670**	24,453	21,557
ELGUIT	57	FENDER	**STRATOCASTER** BLOND, GOLD HARDWARE, "MARY KAYE"	40,979	**31,466**	27,807	24,514

TYPE	YR	MFG	PRICES--BASED ON 100% ORIGINAL MODEL	SELL EXC	SELL AVG	BUY EXC	BUY AVG
ELGUIT	57	FENDER	**STRATOCASTER** SHORELINE GOLD, SERIAL #7019-027770/L16720-L25700	42,767	**32,839**	29,020	25,583
ELGUIT	58	FENDER	**STRATOCASTER** SUNBURST, NON-TREMOLO	13,087	**10,049**	8,880	7,828
ELGUIT	58	FENDER	**STRATOCASTER** SUNBURST, HARD-TAIL	13,371	**10,267**	9,073	7,999
ELGUIT	58	FENDER	**STRATOCASTER** SUNBURST, LEFT-HANDED	18,085	**13,887**	12,272	10,819
ELGUIT	58	FENDER	**STRATOCASTER** BLACK, SERIAL #7954-028255/-21257- -223972	22,398	**17,199**	15,199	13,399
ELGUIT	58	FENDER	**STRATOCASTER** SUNBURST 2-TONE	24,092	**18,499**	16,348	14,412
ELGUIT	58	FENDER	**STRATOCASTER** SUNBURST 3-TONE, SERIAL #7954-028255/-21257- -223972	24,715	**18,977**	16,770	14,784
ELGUIT	58	FENDER	**STRATOCASTER** BLOND, GOLD HARDWARE, SERIAL #7954-028255/-21257- 223972	35,157	**26,996**	23,857	21,031
ELGUIT	59	FENDER	**STRATOCASTER** SUNBURST 3-TONE	17,517	**13,451**	11,887	10,479
ELGUIT	59	FENDER	**STRATOCASTER** SUNBURST 2-TONE, SERIAL #29178-027343/-19655	23,550	**18,083**	15,980	14,088
ELGUIT	59	FENDER	**STRATOCASTER** BLOND, GOLD HARDWARE, "MARY KAYE"	32,188	**24,716**	21,842	19,255
ELGUIT	60	FENDER	**STRATOCASTER** SUNBURST, 2.5-TONE	14,292	**10,974**	9,698	8,549
ELGUIT	60	FENDER	**STRATOCASTER** BLACK	14,565	**11,184**	9,883	8,713
ELGUIT	60	FENDER	**STRATOCASTER** SUNBURST 2-TONE, SERIAL #44221-64087	14,616	**11,223**	9,918	8,743
ELGUIT	60	FENDER	**STRATOCASTER** LEFT HANDED, 2.5-TONE	14,639	**11,241**	9,933	8,757
ELGUIT	60	FENDER	**STRATOCASTER** SUNBURST, NON-TREMOLO	17,136	**13,158**	11,628	10,251
ELGUIT	60	FENDER	**STRATOCASTER** SUNBURST, 3-TONE	17,505	**13,441**	11,878	10,472
ELGUIT	60	FENDER	**STRATOCASTER** CANDY APPLE RED METALLIC, SERIAL #44221-64087	18,735	**14,386**	12,713	11,207
ELGUIT	60	FENDER	**STRATOCASTER** OLYMPIC WHITE, SERIAL #44221-64087	18,742	**14,391**	12,717	11,211
ELGUIT	60	FENDER	**STRATOCASTER** BLOND, GOLD HARDWARE	19,625	**15,069**	13,317	11,740
ELGUIT	60	FENDER	**STRATOCASTER** FIESTA RED	19,813	**15,214**	13,445	11,852
ELGUIT	60	FENDER	**STRATOCASTER** SURF GREEN, SERIAL #44221-64087	19,915	**15,292**	13,514	11,913
ELGUIT	60	FENDER	**STRATOCASTER** DAKOTA RED	20,590	**15,810**	13,971	12,317
ELGUIT	60	FENDER	**STRATOCASTER** SHORELINE GOLD, LEFT-HANDED, SERIAL #44221-64087	22,655	**17,396**	15,373	13,552
ELGUIT	60	FENDER	**STRATOCASTER** DAPHNE BLUE, NON-TREMOLO	23,884	**18,339**	16,207	14,287
ELGUIT	60	FENDER	**STRATOCASTER** BURGUNDY MIST, SERIAL #44254-	25,384	**19,491**	17,225	15,185
ELGUIT	61	FENDER	**STRATOCASTER** SUNBURST, SERIAL #52034-92689	13,656	**10,485**	9,266	8,169
ELGUIT	61	FENDER	**STRATOCASTER** SUNBURST, LEFT-HANDED	14,801	**11,365**	10,044	8,854
ELGUIT	61	FENDER	**STRATOCASTER** OLYMPIC WHITE	15,501	**11,903**	10,519	9,273
ELGUIT	61	FENDER	**STRATOCASTER** BLOND SEE-THRU	17,224	**13,225**	11,688	10,303
ELGUIT	61	FENDER	**STRATOCASTER** FIESTA RED	19,412	**14,906**	13,173	11,613
ELGUIT	61	FENDER	**STRATOCASTER** SHERWOOD GREEN METALLIC, SLAB ROSEWOOD BOARD	25,006	**19,201**	16,968	14,959
ELGUIT	62	FENDER	**STRATOCASTER** SUNBURST, SERIAL #55045-97560/L00543-L19427	9,550	**7,333**	6,480	5,713
ELGUIT	62	FENDER	**STRATOCASTER** OLYMPIC WHITE, SERIAL #55045-97560/L00543-L19427	13,611	**10,451**	9,236	8,142
ELGUIT	62	FENDER	**STRATOCASTER** SONIC BLUE	13,923	**10,691**	9,448	8,329
ELGUIT	62	FENDER	**STRATOCASTER** FIESTA RED	17,932	**13,769**	12,168	10,727
ELGUIT	62	FENDER	**STRATOCASTER** LAKE PLACID BLUE	20,044	**15,391**	13,601	11,990
ELGUIT	62	FENDER	**STRATOCASTER** BURGUNDY MIST, SERIAL #55045-97560/L00543-L19427	21,026	**16,145**	14,268	12,578
ELGUIT	62	FENDER	**STRATOCASTER** SHORELINE GOLD, SERIAL #55045-97560/L00543-L19427	21,336	**16,383**	14,478	12,763
ELGUIT	63	FENDER	**STRATOCASTER** FIESTA RED, LEFT-HANDED	10,214	**7,843**	6,931	6,110
ELGUIT	63	FENDER	**STRATOCASTER** SUNBURST 3-TONE	11,474	**8,810**	7,786	6,864
ELGUIT	63	FENDER	**STRATOCASTER** SUNBURST,ROSEWD FNGRBRD,SERIAL #29582-007020/L00201-L43141	12,213	**9,378**	8,287	7,306

TYPE	YR	MFG	PRICES--BASED ON 100% ORIGINAL MODEL	SELL EXC	SELL AVG	BUY EXC	BUY AVG
ELGUIT	63	FENDER	**STRATOCASTER** OLYMPIC WHITE, SERIAL #29582-007020/L00201-L43141	12,629	**9,697**	8,569	7,554
ELGUIT	63	FENDER	**STRATOCASTER** CANDY APPLE RED, SERIAL #29582-007020/L00201-L43141	12,686	**9,741**	8,608	7,589
ELGUIT	63	FENDER	**STRATOCASTER** FIESTA RED, SERIAL #29582-007020/L00201-L43141	14,101	**10,828**	9,569	8,435
ELGUIT	63	FENDER	**STRATOCASTER** BLOND, GOLD HARDWARE, "MARY KAYE"	20,020	**15,372**	13,585	11,976
ELGUIT	63	FENDER	**STRATOCASTER** SEA FOAM GREEN	22,454	**17,242**	15,237	13,432
ELGUIT	64	FENDER	**STRATOCASTER** SUNBURST, SERIAL #27180-190815/L04974-L87120	8,611	**6,612**	5,843	5,151
ELGUIT	64	FENDER	**STRATOCASTER** CANDY APPLE RED, SERIAL #27180-190815/L04974-L87120	10,297	**7,906**	6,987	6,159
ELGUIT	64	FENDER	**STRATOCASTER** RED, LEFT-HANDED, SERIAL #27180-190815/L04974-L87120	11,150	**8,562**	7,566	6,670
ELGUIT	64	FENDER	**STRATOCASTER** OLYMPIC WHITE, SERIAL #27180-190815/L04974-L87120	11,421	**8,770**	7,750	6,832
ELGUIT	64	FENDER	**STRATOCASTER** SALMON PINK	11,827	**9,081**	8,025	7,075
ELGUIT	64	FENDER	**STRATOCASTER** CANDY APPLE RED, LEFT-HANDED	11,829	**9,083**	8,027	7,076
ELGUIT	64	FENDER	**STRATOCASTER** LAKE PLACID BLUE	12,593	**9,669**	8,545	7,533
ELGUIT	64	FENDER	**STRATOCASTER** SHORELINE GOLD, SERIAL #27180-190815/L04974-L87120	16,144	**12,396**	10,955	9,658
ELGUIT	64	FENDER	**STRATOCASTER** BURGUNDY MIST, SERIAL #27180-190815/L04974-L87120	16,400	**12,592**	11,128	9,810
ELGUIT	65	FENDER	**STRATOCASTER** SUNBURST, LEFT-HANDED, SERIAL #26704-139227/L26114-L99809	9,140	**7,018**	6,202	5,467
ELGUIT	65	FENDER	**STRATOCASTER** SUNBURST, SERIAL #26704-139227/L26114-L99809	9,327	**7,162**	6,329	5,579
ELGUIT	65	FENDER	**STRATOCASTER** CANDY APPLE RED, SERIAL #26704-139227/L26114-L99809	11,709	**8,991**	7,945	7,004
ELGUIT	65	FENDER	**STRATOCASTER** LAKE PLACID BLUE, SERIAL #26704-139227/L26114-L99809	11,876	**9,119**	8,059	7,104
ELGUIT	65	FENDER	**STRATOCASTER** OLYMPIC WHITE	11,960	**9,183**	8,116	7,154
ELGUIT	65	FENDER	**STRATOCASTER** SONIC BLUE, SERIAL #26704-139227/L26114-L99809	12,285	**9,433**	8,336	7,349
ELGUIT	65	FENDER	**STRATOCASTER** DAPHNE BLUE	12,314	**9,455**	8,356	7,366
ELGUIT	65	FENDER	**STRATOCASTER** CHARCOAL FROST	12,958	**9,950**	8,793	7,751
ELGUIT	65	FENDER	**STRATOCASTER** BLACK	13,046	**10,018**	8,853	7,804
ELGUIT	65	FENDER	**STRATOCASTER** BURGUNDY/BLUE SPARKLE	13,161	**10,105**	8,930	7,873
ELGUIT	65	FENDER	**STRATOCASTER** BLUE ICE METALLIC	15,874	**12,189**	10,772	9,496
ELGUIT	65	FENDER	**STRATOCASTER** FIREMIST GOLD	16,945	**13,011**	11,498	10,137
ELGUIT	65	FENDER	**STRATOCASTER** SEA FOAM GREEN, SERIAL #26704-139227/L26114-L99809	17,831	**13,692**	12,099	10,667
ELGUIT	66	FENDER	**STRATOCASTER** SUNBURST 3-TONE	5,215	**4,005**	3,539	3,120
ELGUIT	66	FENDER	**STRATOCASTER** SUNBURST, ROSEWOOD FINGERBOARD	6,014	**4,618**	4,081	3,597
ELGUIT	66	FENDER	**STRATOCASTER** BLOND, SERIAL #112115-361639	7,116	**5,464**	4,829	4,257
ELGUIT	66	FENDER	**STRATOCASTER** CANDY APPLE RED, SERIAL #112115-361639	8,378	**6,433**	5,685	5,012
ELGUIT	66	FENDER	**STRATOCASTER** OLYMPIC WHITE	8,849	**6,794**	6,004	5,293
ELGUIT	66	FENDER	**STRATOCASTER** SONIC BLUE	9,536	**7,322**	6,471	5,705
ELGUIT	66	FENDER	**STRATOCASTER** BLACK, SERIAL #112115-361639	9,561	**7,341**	6,488	5,719
ELGUIT	66	FENDER	**STRATOCASTER** INCA SILVER	13,133	**10,084**	8,911	7,856
ELGUIT	67	FENDER	**STRATOCASTER** SUNBURST, MAPLE CAP, SERIAL #182354-239316	8,407	**6,456**	5,705	5,029
ELGUIT	67	FENDER	**STRATOCASTER** OLYMPIC WHITE, MAPLE CAP	8,896	**6,830**	6,036	5,321
ELGUIT	67	FENDER	**STRATOCASTER** LAKE PLACID BLUE	11,788	**9,051**	7,999	7,051
ELGUIT	67	FENDER	**STRATOCASTER** INCA SILVER, SERIAL #182354-239316	12,395	**9,517**	8,410	7,414
ELGUIT	68	FENDER	**STRATOCASTER** SUNBURST, NON-TREMOLO	6,044	**4,641**	4,101	3,615
ELGUIT	68	FENDER	**STRATOCASTER** SUNBURST, ROSEWOOD CAP	6,356	**4,880**	4,313	3,802
ELGUIT	68	FENDER	**STRATOCASTER** BLACK, MAPLE CAP ONLY	8,406	**6,455**	5,704	5,029

TYPE	YR	MFG	PRICES--BASED ON 100% ORIGINAL MODEL	SELL EXC	SELL AVG	BUY EXC	BUY AVG
ELGUIT	68	FENDER	**STRATOCASTER** OLYMPIC WHITE, MAPLE CAP	8,533	**6,552**	5,790	5,104
ELGUIT	69	FENDER	**STRATOCASTER** SUNBURST, ROSEWOOD CAP, SERIAL #167362-356440	4,453	**3,419**	3,021	2,663
ELGUIT	69	FENDER	**STRATOCASTER** SUNBURST, LEFT-HANDED, SERIAL #167362-356440	4,851	**3,725**	3,292	2,902
ELGUIT	69	FENDER	**STRATOCASTER** BLOND	6,033	**4,632**	4,094	3,609
ELGUIT	69	FENDER	**STRATOCASTER** OLYMPIC WHITE, MAPLE CAP	6,195	**4,757**	4,204	3,706
ELGUIT	70	FENDER	**STRATOCASTER** SUNBURST, NON-TREMOLO	3,149	**2,418**	2,137	1,884
ELGUIT	70	FENDER	**STRATOCASTER** SUNBURST, TREMOLO	3,580	**2,749**	2,429	2,141
ELGUIT	70	FENDER	**STRATOCASTER** CANDY APPLE RED	7,197	**5,526**	4,883	4,305
ELGUIT	70	FENDER	**STRATOCASTER** LAKE PLACID BLUE	7,474	**5,739**	5,072	4,471
ELGUIT	71	FENDER	**STRATOCASTER** OLYMPIC WHITE, SERIAL #66767-581817	3,588	**2,755**	2,435	2,146
ELGUIT	71	FENDER	**STRATOCASTER** SUNBURST	3,604	**2,767**	2,445	2,156
ELGUIT	71	FENDER	**STRATOCASTER** SUNBURST, LEFT-HANDED	4,456	**3,421**	3,024	2,665
ELGUIT	72	FENDER	**STRATOCASTER** NATURAL, TREMOLO	2,363	**1,814**	1,603	1,413
ELGUIT	72	FENDER	**STRATOCASTER** BLOND	2,466	**1,893**	1,673	1,475
ELGUIT	72	FENDER	**STRATOCASTER** OLYMPIC WHITE	2,466	**1,893**	1,673	1,475
ELGUIT	72	FENDER	**STRATOCASTER** SUNBURST, NON-TREMOLO	3,028	**2,325**	2,055	1,811
ELGUIT	72	FENDER	**STRATOCASTER** BLACK, LEFT-HANDED	3,360	**2,580**	2,280	2,010
ELGUIT	72	FENDER	**STRATOCASTER** BLACK, TREMOLO, 4 BOLT, SERIAL #000001-712344	3,588	**2,755**	2,435	2,146
ELGUIT	72	FENDER	**STRATOCASTER** DAKOTA RED	3,598	**2,763**	2,441	2,152
ELGUIT	73	FENDER	**STRATOCASTER** BLACK, TREMOLO, 3 BOLT	1,879	**1,443**	1,275	1,124
ELGUIT	73	FENDER	**STRATOCASTER** SUNBURST, SERIAL #358820-552416/S777565	1,973	**1,515**	1,339	1,180
ELGUIT	73	FENDER	**STRATOCASTER** NATURAL, SERIAL #358820-552416/S777565	1,989	**1,527**	1,349	1,189
ELGUIT	73	FENDER	**STRATOCASTER** BROWN, TREMOLO	2,042	**1,568**	1,386	1,222
ELGUIT	73	FENDER	**STRATOCASTER** BLOND	2,047	**1,572**	1,389	1,224
ELGUIT	73	FENDER	**STRATOCASTER** OLYMPIC WHITE	2,348	**1,803**	1,593	1,404
ELGUIT	73	FENDER	**STRATOCASTER** CANDY APPLE RED, SERIAL #358820-552416/S777565	2,466	**1,893**	1,673	1,475
ELGUIT	73	FENDER	**STRATOCASTER** LAKE PLACID BLUE	2,466	**1,893**	1,673	1,475
ELGUIT	73	FENDER	**STRATOCASTER** WALNUT, LEFT-HANDED	3,301	**2,535**	2,240	1,975
ELGUIT	74	FENDER	**STRATOCASTER** NATURAL, NON-TREMOLO	1,398	**1,074**	949	836
ELGUIT	74	FENDER	**STRATOCASTER** SUNBURST	1,439	**1,105**	976	860
ELGUIT	74	FENDER	**STRATOCASTER** BROWN, HARD-TAIL	1,526	**1,172**	1,035	913
ELGUIT	74	FENDER	**STRATOCASTER** BLACK, HARD-TAIL	1,543	**1,185**	1,047	923
ELGUIT	74	FENDER	**STRATOCASTER** NATURAL, TREMOLO	1,761	**1,352**	1,195	1,053
ELGUIT	74	FENDER	**STRATOCASTER** BLOND	1,811	**1,390**	1,228	1,083
ELGUIT	74	FENDER	**STRATOCASTER** OLYMPIC WHITE	1,879	**1,443**	1,275	1,124
ELGUIT	74	FENDER	**STRATOCASTER** SUNBURST, LEFT-HANDED	2,051	**1,575**	1,392	1,227
ELGUIT	74	FENDER	**STRATOCASTER** NATURAL, LEFT-HANDED	2,257	**1,733**	1,532	1,350
ELGUIT	74	FENDER	**STRATOCASTER** CANDY RED, ROSEWOOD NECK	3,130	**2,403**	2,124	1,872
ELGUIT	74	FENDER	**STRATOCASTER** OLYMPIC WHITE, LEFT-HANDED	3,319	**2,549**	2,252	1,985
ELGUIT	75	FENDER	**STRATOCASTER** SUNBURST, SERIAL #562789-717257	1,351	**1,038**	917	808
ELGUIT	75	FENDER	**STRATOCASTER** SUNBURST, NON-TREMOLO, SERIAL #562789-717257	1,378	**1,058**	935	824
ELGUIT	75	FENDER	**STRATOCASTER** BLACK, TREMOLO, SERIAL #562789-717257	1,386	**1,064**	940	829

TYPE	YR	MFG	PRICES--BASED ON 100% ORIGINAL MODEL	SELL EXC	SELL AVG	BUY EXC	BUY AVG
ELGUIT	75	FENDER	**STRATOCASTER** SUNBURST, LEFT-HANDED	1,391	**1,068**	943	832
ELGUIT	75	FENDER	**STRATOCASTER** BROWN	1,505	**1,155**	1,021	900
ELGUIT	75	FENDER	**STRATOCASTER** CREAM	1,528	**1,173**	1,037	914
ELGUIT	75	FENDER	**STRATOCASTER** NATURAL	1,555	**1,194**	1,055	930
ELGUIT	75	FENDER	**STRATOCASTER** OLYMPIC WHITE	1,761	**1,352**	1,195	1,053
ELGUIT	76	FENDER	**STRATOCASTER** SUNBURST, SERIAL #7679077	1,064	**817**	722	636
ELGUIT	76	FENDER	**STRATOCASTER** BLACK	1,199	**921**	813	717
ELGUIT	76	FENDER	**STRATOCASTER** NATURAL, SERIAL #554808-7667908/S767274-S769905	1,266	**972**	859	757
ELGUIT	76	FENDER	**STRATOCASTER** WHITE, LEFT-HANDED, SERIAL #554808-7667908/S767274-S769905	1,267	**973**	860	758
ELGUIT	76	FENDER	**STRATOCASTER** NATURAL, NON-TREMOLO	1,291	**991**	876	772
ELGUIT	76	FENDER	**STRATOCASTER** SUNBURST, LEFT-HANDED	1,378	**1,058**	935	824
ELGUIT	77	FENDER	**STRATOCASTER** SUNBURST, NON-TREMOLO	948	**728**	643	567
ELGUIT	77	FENDER	**STRATOCASTER** NATURAL, SERIAL #5778859/S770029-S775989	990	**760**	671	592
ELGUIT	77	FENDER	**STRATOCASTER** BROWN, HARDTAIL	1,069	**821**	725	639
ELGUIT	77	FENDER	**STRATOCASTER** SUNBURST	1,301	**999**	883	778
ELGUIT	77	FENDER	**STRATOCASTER** BLACK, SERIAL #5778859/S770029-S775989	1,357	**1,042**	921	812
ELGUIT	77	FENDER	**STRATOCASTER** BLOND	1,408	**1,081**	956	842
ELGUIT	77	FENDER	**STRATOCASTER** NATURAL, LEFT-HANDED	1,672	**1,283**	1,134	1,000
ELGUIT	77	FENDER	**STRATOCASTER** OLYMPIC WHITE	1,680	**1,290**	1,140	1,005
ELGUIT	77	FENDER	**STRATOCASTER** BLACK, LEFT-HANDED	1,691	**1,298**	1,147	1,011
ELGUIT	77	FENDER	**STRATOCASTER** SHELL PINK	10,417	**7,998**	7,068	6,231
ELGUIT	78	FENDER	**STRATOCASTER** ANTIGUA, SERIAL #5942888/S766838-S940993	993	**762**	674	594
ELGUIT	78	FENDER	**STRATOCASTER** SUNBURST, NON-TREMOLO	1,008	**774**	684	603
ELGUIT	78	FENDER	**STRATOCASTER** SUNBURST	1,029	**790**	698	615
ELGUIT	78	FENDER	**STRATOCASTER** CREAM, SERIAL #5942888/S766838-S940993	1,210	**929**	821	724
ELGUIT	78	FENDER	**STRATOCASTER** NATURAL	1,246	**957**	845	745
ELGUIT	78	FENDER	**STRATOCASTER** BROWN	1,251	**960**	848	748
ELGUIT	78	FENDER	**STRATOCASTER** BLOND	1,288	**989**	874	770
ELGUIT	78	FENDER	**STRATOCASTER** BLACK	1,498	**1,150**	1,016	896
ELGUIT	78	FENDER	**STRATOCASTER** BLOND, LEFT-HANDED	1,560	**1,197**	1,058	933
ELGUIT	78	FENDER	**STRATOCASTER** BLACK, LEFT-HANDED, TREMOLO, MAPLE NECK	1,587	**1,218**	1,076	949
ELGUIT	79	FENDER	**STRATOCASTER** CREAM, SERIAL #250025-900301/S360837-S938786	778	**597**	528	465
ELGUIT	79	FENDER	**STRATOCASTER** BROWN, SERIAL #250025-900301/S360837-S938786 NON-TREMOLO	845	**649**	573	505
ELGUIT	79	FENDER	**STRATOCASTER** SUNBURST, NON-TREMOLO	847	**651**	575	507
ELGUIT	79	FENDER	**STRATOCASTER** SEAFOAM GREEN, MAPLE NECK	868	**666**	589	519
ELGUIT	79	FENDER	**STRATOCASTER** NATURAL, NON-TREMOLO	883	**678**	599	528
ELGUIT	79	FENDER	**STRATOCASTER** ORANGE, SERIAL #S980453	896	**688**	608	536
ELGUIT	79	FENDER	**STRATOCASTER** ANTIGUA, NON-TREMOLO, SERIAL #250025-900301/S360837-S938786	899	**690**	610	538
ELGUIT	79	FENDER	**STRATOCASTER** WALNUT, SERIAL #250025-900301/S360837-S938786	901	**692**	611	539
ELGUIT	79	FENDER	**STRATOCASTER** SUNBURST, SERIAL #250025-900301/S360837-S938786	927	**712**	629	554
ELGUIT	79	FENDER	**STRATOCASTER** RED, SERIAL #S938786	968	**743**	657	579
ELGUIT	79	FENDER	**STRATOCASTER** NATURAL, HARD-TAIL	969	**744**	658	580

TYPE	YR	MFG	PRICES--BASED ON 100% ORIGINAL MODEL	SELL EXC	SELL AVG	BUY EXC	BUY AVG
ELGUIT	79	FENDER	**STRATOCASTER** ANTIGUA, SERIAL #250025-900301/S360837-S938786	971	**745**	658	580
ELGUIT	79	FENDER	**STRATOCASTER** MAUI BLUE, MAPLE NECK	1,006	**773**	683	602
ELGUIT	79	FENDER	**STRATOCASTER** WHITE, SERIAL #250025-900301/S360837-S938786	1,010	**775**	685	604
ELGUIT	79	FENDER	**STRATOCASTER** BLACK, NON-TREMOLO, SERIAL #250025-900301/S360837-S938786	1,046	**803**	709	625
ELGUIT	79	FENDER	**STRATOCASTER** BLOND, SERIAL #250025-900301/S360837-S938786	1,056	**810**	716	631
ELGUIT	79	FENDER	**STRATOCASTER** BLACK, SERIAL #250025-900301/S360837-S938786	1,070	**822**	726	640
ELGUIT	79	FENDER	**STRATOCASTER** BLACK, LEFT-HANDED	1,239	**952**	841	741
ELGUIT	79	FENDER	**STRATOCASTER** CANDY APPLE RED	1,341	**1,030**	910	802
ELGUIT	79	FENDER	**STRATOCASTER** OLYMPIC WHITE	1,369	**1,051**	929	819
ELGUIT	79	FENDER	**STRATOCASTER** SILVER ANN	2,010	**1,543**	1,364	1,202
ELGUIT	80	FENDER	**STRATOCASTER** BLACK, SERIAL #5869789	631	**485**	428	377
ELGUIT	80	FENDER	**STRATOCASTER** CANDY APPLE RED	680	**522**	462	407
ELGUIT	80	FENDER	**STRATOCASTER** BLACK, LEFT-HANDED	687	**528**	466	411
ELGUIT	81	FENDER	**STRATOCASTER** WALNUT	680	**522**	462	407
ELGUIT	81	FENDER	**STRATOCASTER** SHORELINE GOLD, GOLD HARDWARE	1,688	**1,296**	1,146	1,010
ELGUIT	82	FENDER	**STRATOCASTER** BLACK	629	**483**	427	376
ELGUIT	82	FENDER	**STRATOCASTER** RED 2-TONE	631	**485**	428	377
ELGUIT	83	FENDER	**STRATOCASTER** BLACK, LEFT-HANDED	628	**482**	426	375
ELGUIT	83	FENDER	**STRATOCASTER** BLACK	638	**490**	433	381
ELGUIT	84	FENDER	**STRATOCASTER** BOWLING BALL BLUE, RED or YELLOW	1,842	**1,414**	1,250	1,102
ELGUIT	88	FENDER	**STRATOCASTER** PAISLEY	841	**645**	570	503
ELGUIT	80	FENDER	**STRATOCASTER "THE STRAT"**	781	**600**	530	467
ELGUIT	82	FENDER	**STRATOCASTER '62 REISSUE** FIESTA RED	756	**580**	513	452
ELGUIT	83	FENDER	**STRATOCASTER '62 REISSUE** SUNBURST	758	**582**	514	453
ELGUIT	86	FENDER	**STRATOCASTER '62 REISSUE** LAKE PLACID BLUE	753	**578**	511	450
ELGUIT	79	FENDER	**STRATOCASTER 25th ANNIVERSARY** SILVER METALLIC, MAPLE 4-BOLT NECK	751	**577**	509	449
ELGUIT	89	FENDER	**STRATOCASTER 35th ANNIVERSARY** SUNBURST	1,862	**1,430**	1,263	1,114
ELGUIT	78	FENDER	**STRATOCASTER ANNIVERSARY** WHITE, SERIAL #5942888/S766838-S940993	1,298	**996**	880	776
ELGUIT	79	FENDER	**STRATOCASTER ANNIVERSARY** SILVER, SERIAL #250025-258078/S51853	1,037	**796**	703	620
ELGUIT	79	FENDER	**STRATOCASTER ANNIVERSARY IV** IVORY	1,901	**1,460**	1,290	1,137
ELGUIT	69	FENDER	**STRATOCASTER CUSTOM VINTAGE** 3-TONE BURST, PEARLOID PICKGUARD, TREMOLO, MAPLE NECK	1,210	**929**	821	724
ELGUIT	88	FENDER	**STRATOCASTER DELUXE PLUS**	764	**587**	519	457
ELGUIT	83	FENDER	**STRATOCASTER ELITE** NATURAL	944	**724**	640	564
ELGUIT	83	FENDER	**STRATOCASTER ELITE** ROSEWOOD or MAPLE	948	**728**	643	567
ELGUIT	83	FENDER	**STRATOCASTER GOLD ELITE**	917	**704**	622	548
ELGUIT	81	FENDER	**STRATOCASTER SMITH**	930	**714**	631	556
ELGUIT	88	FENDER	**STRATOCASTER YNGWIE MALMSTEEN**	1,070	**822**	726	640
ELGUIT	51	FENDER	**TELECASTER** BUTTERSCOTCH	18,873	**14,491**	12,806	11,290
ELGUIT	51	FENDER	**TELECASTER** NO-CASTER, SERIAL #0585-2752	26,188	**20,109**	17,771	15,666
ELGUIT	52	FENDER	**TELECASTER** BLOND, SERIAL #0293-5221	14,346	**11,015**	9,734	8,582
ELGUIT	52	FENDER	**TELECASTER** BUTTERSCOTCH	15,211	**11,680**	10,322	9,099
ELGUIT	53	FENDER	**TELECASTER** BLOND	13,395	**10,285**	9,089	8,013
ELGUIT	53	FENDER	**TELECASTER** BUTTERSCOTCH	15,867	**12,183**	10,766	9,491
ELGUIT	54	FENDER	**TELECASTER** BLOND, WHITE PICKGUARD, SERIAL #0502-11035	12,908	**9,911**	8,759	7,721

TYPE	YR	MFG	PRICES--BASED ON 100% ORIGINAL MODEL	SELL EXC	SELL AVG	BUY EXC	BUY AVG
ELGUIT	54	FENDER	**TELECASTER** BUTTERSCOTCH	13,343	**10,246**	9,054	7,982
ELGUIT	54	FENDER	**TELECASTER** WHITE PICKGUARD, SERIAL #0502-11035	13,398	**10,288**	9,091	8,015
ELGUIT	54	FENDER	**TELECASTER** BLOND	13,896	**10,670**	9,430	8,313
ELGUIT	54	FENDER	**TELECASTER** BLOND, LEFT-HANDED	13,978	**10,733**	9,485	8,362
ELGUIT	55	FENDER	**TELECASTER** BLOND, SERIAL #0617-28705	5,738	**4,406**	3,894	3,433
ELGUIT	55	FENDER	**TELECASTER** WHITE PICKGUARD, SERIAL #7045-12842/-21616	10,253	**7,873**	6,957	6,133
ELGUIT	56	FENDER	**TELECASTER** BLOND	8,197	**6,294**	5,562	4,903
ELGUIT	56	FENDER	**TELECASTER** BLOND, REPRO TUNERS	8,766	**6,731**	5,948	5,244
ELGUIT	56	FENDER	**TELECASTER** WHITE PICKGUARD, SERIAL #2431-16492/-11406	10,289	**7,900**	6,982	6,155
ELGUIT	56	FENDER	**TELECASTER** FLAME MAPLE NECK, SERIAL #2431-16492/-11406	11,775	**9,042**	7,990	7,044
ELGUIT	57	FENDER	**TELECASTER** BLOND, SERIAL #18817-023394/-17815- -20077	9,097	**6,985**	6,173	5,442
ELGUIT	57	FENDER	**TELECASTER** V-NECK, SERIAL #18817-023394/-17815- -20077	9,597	**7,369**	6,512	5,741
ELGUIT	57	FENDER	**TELECASTER** BLOND, MAPLE NECK	10,906	**8,374**	7,400	6,524
ELGUIT	57	FENDER	**TELECASTER** NATURAL	11,878	**9,121**	8,060	7,106
ELGUIT	57	FENDER	**TELECASTER** FIESTA RED	14,726	**11,308**	9,993	8,809
ELGUIT	57	FENDER	**TELECASTER** DAKOTA RED, MAPLE NECK	19,975	**15,338**	13,554	11,949
ELGUIT	58	FENDER	**TELECASTER** SUNBURST, SERIAL #28721-027722/-24785	7,925	**6,085**	5,377	4,740
ELGUIT	58	FENDER	**TELECASTER** BLOND	8,197	**6,294**	5,562	4,903
ELGUIT	59	FENDER	**TELECASTER** MAPLE NECK, SERIAL #37659	8,102	**6,221**	5,497	4,846
ELGUIT	59	FENDER	**TELECASTER** BLOND, MAPLE NECK	9,857	**7,568**	6,688	5,896
ELGUIT	60	FENDER	**TELECASTER** BLOND	7,882	**6,052**	5,348	4,715
ELGUIT	60	FENDER	**TELECASTER** SONIC BLUE	13,003	**9,984**	8,823	7,778
ELGUIT	61	FENDER	**TELECASTER** BLOND, SERIAL #59330-72711	9,159	**7,033**	6,215	5,479
ELGUIT	62	FENDER	**TELECASTER** BLOND	8,994	**6,906**	6,103	5,380
ELGUIT	62	FENDER	**TELECASTER** FIESTA RED	10,259	**7,877**	6,961	6,137
ELGUIT	63	FENDER	**TELECASTER** BLOND, SERIAL #83717/L10439-L43106	7,184	**5,516**	4,875	4,298
ELGUIT	63	FENDER	**TELECASTER** SONIC BLUE	9,561	**7,341**	6,488	5,719
ELGUIT	63	FENDER	**TELECASTER** BLACK, SERIAL #83717/L10439-L43106	9,987	**7,668**	6,776	5,974
ELGUIT	63	FENDER	**TELECASTER** FIESTA RED, CURVED ROSEWOOD FRETBOARD	11,514	**8,841**	7,813	6,888
ELGUIT	64	FENDER	**TELECASTER** SUNBURST, CLAY DOTS	6,994	**5,370**	4,746	4,184
ELGUIT	65	FENDER	**TELECASTER** POST-CBS, SERIAL #103997-158977/L69635-L78135	5,147	**3,952**	3,492	3,079
ELGUIT	65	FENDER	**TELECASTER** BLOND	6,110	**4,692**	4,146	3,655
ELGUIT	65	FENDER	**TELECASTER** CANDY APPLE RED	7,921	**6,082**	5,375	4,738
ELGUIT	66	FENDER	**TELECASTER** BLOND, SERIAL #112172-293692	3,617	**2,777**	2,454	2,164
ELGUIT	66	FENDER	**TELECASTER** MAHOGANY, SERIAL #112172-293692	3,627	**2,785**	2,461	2,170
ELGUIT	66	FENDER	**TELECASTER** SUNBURST, SERIAL #112172-293692	3,852	**2,958**	2,614	2,304
ELGUIT	66	FENDER	**TELECASTER** BUTTERSCOTCH, SERIAL #142069	5,045	**3,874**	3,423	3,018
ELGUIT	66	FENDER	**TELECASTER** MAPLE NECK, BIGSBY	5,604	**4,303**	3,803	3,352
ELGUIT	67	FENDER	**TELECASTER** BLOND, ROSEWOOD BOARD, SERIAL #115560-3156657	3,262	**2,505**	2,213	1,951
ELGUIT	67	FENDER	**TELECASTER** NATURAL	3,274	**2,514**	2,222	1,959
ELGUIT	67	FENDER	**TELECASTER** NATURAL, LEFT-HANDED, ROSEWOOD BOARD, SERIAL #115560-315665	3,298	**2,532**	2,238	1,973
ELGUIT	67	FENDER	**TELECASTER** MAPLE NECK, SERIAL #115560-3156657	3,300	**2,534**	2,239	1,974

TYPE	YR	MFG	PRICES--BASED ON 100% ORIGINAL MODEL	SELL EXC	SELL AVG	BUY EXC	BUY AVG
ELGUIT	67	FENDER	TELECASTER CREAM, BIGSBY	3,346	2,569	2,270	2,001
ELGUIT	67	FENDER	TELECASTER BLOND, SERIAL #115560-3156657	3,489	2,679	2,368	2,087
ELGUIT	67	FENDER	TELECASTER CANDY APPLE RED	3,932	3,019	2,668	2,352
ELGUIT	67	FENDER	TELECASTER DAKOTA RED, ROSEWOOD SLAB BOARD	12,719	9,767	8,631	7,609
ELGUIT	68	FENDER	TELECASTER BLOND, SERIAL #125316-397081	3,320	2,549	2,253	1,986
ELGUIT	68	FENDER	TELECASTER BLOND, ROSEWOOD BOARD, SERIAL #125316-397081	3,354	2,575	2,276	2,006
ELGUIT	68	FENDER	TELECASTER BLOND, MAPLE NECK	3,370	2,587	2,286	2,016
ELGUIT	68	FENDER	TELECASTER WHITE, ROSEWOOD FRETBOARD	3,430	2,634	2,327	2,052
ELGUIT	68	FENDER	TELECASTER MAPLE FINGERBOARD, SERIAL #125316-397081	3,494	2,683	2,371	2,090
ELGUIT	68	FENDER	TELECASTER BLACK, SERIAL #125316-397081	3,545	2,722	2,406	2,121
ELGUIT	68	FENDER	TELECASTER CANDY APPLE RED, MAPLE NECK	5,069	3,892	3,439	3,032
ELGUIT	68	FENDER	TELECASTER LAKE PLACID BLUE, SERIAL #125316-397081	5,827	4,474	3,954	3,486
ELGUIT	68	FENDER	TELECASTER PAISLEY, SERIAL #125316-397081	6,593	5,062	4,474	3,944
ELGUIT	68	FENDER	TELECASTER ROSEWOOD BODY	6,681	5,130	4,534	3,997
ELGUIT	68	FENDER	TELECASTER FLORAL, SERIAL #125316-397081	6,933	5,324	4,705	4,147
ELGUIT	69	FENDER	TELECASTER BLOND	2,287	1,756	1,551	1,368
ELGUIT	69	FENDER	TELECASTER CREAM, ROSEWOOD BOARD, SERIAL #219796-286616	2,368	1,818	1,607	1,417
ELGUIT	69	FENDER	TELECASTER MAPLE NECK, BIGSBY	2,401	1,843	1,629	1,436
ELGUIT	69	FENDER	TELECASTER BLOND, ROSEWOOD BOARD, SERIAL #219796-286616	2,433	1,868	1,651	1,455
ELGUIT	69	FENDER	TELECASTER SUNBURST	3,321	2,550	2,254	1,987
ELGUIT	69	FENDER	TELECASTER PAISLEY	5,617	4,313	3,812	3,360
ELGUIT	69	FENDER	TELECASTER ROSEWOOD BODY	7,818	6,003	5,305	4,677
ELGUIT	70	FENDER	TELECASTER BLOND, SERIAL #206276-615270	2,016	1,548	1,368	1,206
ELGUIT	70	FENDER	TELECASTER CREAM, SERIAL #206276-615270	2,143	1,646	1,454	1,282
ELGUIT	70	FENDER	TELECASTER BLOND, MAPLE NECK, SERIAL #206276-615270	2,879	2,211	1,953	1,722
ELGUIT	70	FENDER	TELECASTER BLOND, SINGLE STRING TREE, ROSEWOOD NECK	3,584	2,752	2,432	2,144
ELGUIT	70	FENDER	TELECASTER CANDY APPLE RED	4,826	3,705	3,274	2,887
ELGUIT	70	FENDER	TELECASTER ROSEWOOD	5,825	4,472	3,952	3,484
ELGUIT	71	FENDER	TELECASTER CREAM	1,503	1,154	1,019	899
ELGUIT	71	FENDER	TELECASTER SUNBURST, MAPLE NECK	1,611	1,237	1,093	964
ELGUIT	71	FENDER	TELECASTER BLACK	1,684	1,293	1,143	1,007
ELGUIT	71	FENDER	TELECASTER BLOND, MAPLE NECK, SERIAL #32501-509993	1,802	1,383	1,222	1,078
ELGUIT	71	FENDER	TELECASTER BLOND, ROSEWOOD NECK	1,803	1,384	1,223	1,078
ELGUIT	71	FENDER	TELECASTER BLOND	2,035	1,562	1,380	1,217
ELGUIT	71	FENDER	TELECASTER LAKE PLACID BLUE, SERIAL #32501-509993	3,085	2,369	2,093	1,845
ELGUIT	71	FENDER	TELECASTER CANDY APPLE RED, MAPLE NECK	3,093	2,375	2,099	1,850
ELGUIT	71	FENDER	TELECASTER ROSEWOOD BODY, SERIAL #32501-509993	6,826	5,241	4,632	4,083
ELGUIT	72	FENDER	TELECASTER BROWN	1,253	962	850	749
ELGUIT	72	FENDER	TELECASTER NATURAL, SERIAL #56115-539372/S723141	1,563	1,200	1,060	935
ELGUIT	72	FENDER	TELECASTER SUNBURST, MAPLE NECK, SERIAL #56115-539372/S723141	1,602	1,230	1,087	958
ELGUIT	72	FENDER	TELECASTER BLACK, SERIAL #56115-539372/S723141	1,627	1,249	1,104	973
ELGUIT	72	FENDER	TELECASTER BLOND, MAPLE NECK	1,790	1,375	1,215	1,071

TYPE	YR	MFG	PRICES--BASED ON 100% ORIGINAL MODEL	SELL EXC	SELL AVG	BUY EXC	BUY AVG
ELGUIT	72	FENDER	**TELECASTER** LAKE PLACID BLUE, SERIAL #56115-539372/S723141	3,297	**2,531**	2,237	1,972
ELGUIT	72	FENDER	**TELECASTER** ROSEWOOD BODY, SERIAL #56115	7,190	**5,521**	4,879	4,301
ELGUIT	73	FENDER	**TELECASTER** BLACK	1,620	**1,244**	1,099	969
ELGUIT	73	FENDER	**TELECASTER** BLOND, MAPLE NECK	1,714	**1,316**	1,163	1,025
ELGUIT	73	FENDER	**TELECASTER** BLOND, LEFT-HANDED	1,815	**1,394**	1,231	1,086
ELGUIT	73	FENDER	**TELECASTER** BROWN w/BIGSBY	1,899	**1,458**	1,288	1,136
ELGUIT	74	FENDER	**TELECASTER** NATURAL	984	**755**	668	588
ELGUIT	74	FENDER	**TELECASTER** SUNBURST, MAPLE NECK	1,301	**999**	883	778
ELGUIT	74	FENDER	**TELECASTER** BLOND, MAPLE NECK	1,385	**1,063**	940	828
ELGUIT	74	FENDER	**TELECASTER** BLOND, SERIAL #60443-580031/S702161	1,396	**1,072**	947	835
ELGUIT	74	FENDER	**TELECASTER** BLACK	1,451	**1,114**	984	868
ELGUIT	74	FENDER	**TELECASTER** CANDY APPLE RED, MAPLE NECK	2,040	**1,566**	1,384	1,220
ELGUIT	75	FENDER	**TELECASTER** SUNBURST, MAPLE NECK	1,021	**784**	693	611
ELGUIT	75	FENDER	**TELECASTER** BLOND	1,374	**1,055**	932	822
ELGUIT	75	FENDER	**TELECASTER** CREAM, MAPLE NECK, SERIAL #606109-655092	1,380	**1,060**	937	826
ELGUIT	75	FENDER	**TELECASTER** BLACK	1,410	**1,082**	956	843
ELGUIT	75	FENDER	**TELECASTER** BLOND, MAPLE NECK	1,699	**1,304**	1,152	1,016
ELGUIT	76	FENDER	**TELECASTER** BLOND, MAPLE NECK	1,071	**823**	727	641
ELGUIT	76	FENDER	**TELECASTER** CREAM, BLACK PICKGUARD	1,221	**938**	829	730
ELGUIT	76	FENDER	**TELECASTER** CREAM, MAPLE NECK	1,235	**948**	838	739
ELGUIT	76	FENDER	**TELECASTER** CREAM, WHITE PICKGUARD	1,235	**948**	838	739
ELGUIT	77	FENDER	**TELECASTER** BLOND	1,019	**782**	691	609
ELGUIT	77	FENDER	**TELECASTER** NATURAL, LEFT-HANDED, MAPLE NECK	1,273	**977**	864	761
ELGUIT	78	FENDER	**TELECASTER** WINE, MAPLE NECK	884	**679**	600	529
ELGUIT	78	FENDER	**TELECASTER** SUNBURST, LEFT-HANDED	903	**694**	613	540
ELGUIT	78	FENDER	**TELECASTER** BLOND, LEFT-HANDED	990	**760**	671	592
ELGUIT	78	FENDER	**TELECASTER** SUNBURST, ROSEWOOD	1,027	**788**	696	614
ELGUIT	78	FENDER	**TELECASTER** BLACK	1,043	**801**	708	624
ELGUIT	78	FENDER	**TELECASTER** ANTIGUA	1,053	**809**	715	630
ELGUIT	78	FENDER	**TELECASTER** NATURAL, ROSEWOOD BOARD	1,226	**941**	832	733
ELGUIT	78	FENDER	**TELECASTER** BLOND, MAPLE NECK, SERIAL #S806520-S846983	1,321	**1,014**	896	790
ELGUIT	78	FENDER	**TELECASTER** OLYMPIC WHITE	1,333	**1,024**	905	797
ELGUIT	78	FENDER	**TELECASTER** BLOND, ROSEWOOD NECK	2,010	**1,543**	1,364	1,202
ELGUIT	78	FENDER	**TELECASTER** WHITE, ROSEWOOD NECK	2,010	**1,543**	1,364	1,202
ELGUIT	82	FENDER	**TELECASTER** BLACK AND GOLD	941	**723**	639	563
ELGUIT	84	FENDER	**TELECASTER**	588	**451**	399	351
ELGUIT	88	FENDER	**TELECASTER 40th ANNIVERSARY**	1,070	**822**	726	640
ELGUIT	68	FENDER	**TELECASTER BASS** BLOND, MAPLE NECK	2,677	**2,056**	1,817	1,601
ELGUIT	68	FENDER	**TELECASTER BASS** PINK PAISLEY, SERIAL #139157-289309	3,797	**2,916**	2,577	2,271
ELGUIT	68	FENDER	**TELECASTER BASS** FLORAL	4,875	**3,743**	3,308	2,916
ELGUIT	69	FENDER	**TELECASTER BASS** BLOND, SERIAL #228951-271946	1,654	**1,270**	1,122	989
ELGUIT	69	FENDER	**TELECASTER BASS** FLORAL, SERIAL #228951-271946	3,604	**2,767**	2,445	2,156
ELGUIT	69	FENDER	**TELECASTER BASS** PINK PAISLEY, SERIAL #228951-271946	3,669	**2,817**	2,489	2,194

TYPE	YR	MFG	PRICES--BASED ON 100% ORIGINAL MODEL	SELL EXC	SELL AVG	BUY EXC	BUY AVG
ELGUIT	70	FENDER	**TELECASTER BASS** BLOND, MAPLE NECK	1,475	**1,132**	1,000	882
ELGUIT	70	FENDER	**TELECASTER BASS** PINK PAISLEY	4,836	**3,713**	3,281	2,893
ELGUIT	72	FENDER	**TELECASTER BASS** BROWN STAIN, SERIAL #351991	862	**662**	585	515
ELGUIT	72	FENDER	**TELECASTER BASS** NATURAL, SERIAL #351436-402487	938	**720**	636	561
ELGUIT	72	FENDER	**TELECASTER BASS** CREAM, SERIAL #351436-402487	972	**746**	659	581
ELGUIT	72	FENDER	**TELECASTER BASS** BLOND, MAPLE NECK, SERIAL #351436-402487	1,336	**1,025**	906	799
ELGUIT	73	FENDER	**TELECASTER BASS** CREAM	934	**717**	633	558
ELGUIT	73	FENDER	**TELECASTER BASS** BLOND, SERIAL #400779-402188	997	**766**	677	596
ELGUIT	73	FENDER	**TELECASTER BASS** NATURAL	1,342	**1,031**	911	803
ELGUIT	74	FENDER	**TELECASTER BASS** BLOND	1,226	**941**	832	733
ELGUIT	75	FENDER	**TELECASTER BASS** BLOND, MAPLE NECK	1,021	**784**	693	611
ELGUIT	77	FENDER	**TELECASTER BASS** BLACK	880	**675**	597	526
ELGUIT	78	FENDER	**TELECASTER BASS** SUNBURST	855	**657**	580	511
ELGUIT	78	FENDER	**TELECASTER BASS** ANTIGUA, MAPLE BOARD	897	**688**	608	536
ELGUIT	59	FENDER	**TELECASTER CUSTOM** SUNBURST	12,045	**9,249**	8,173	7,205
ELGUIT	60	FENDER	**TELECASTER CUSTOM** SUNBURST, 2-TONE, SERIAL #44282-57746	12,947	**9,941**	8,785	7,745
ELGUIT	60	FENDER	**TELECASTER CUSTOM** SUNBURST	14,613	**11,221**	9,916	8,742
ELGUIT	61	FENDER	**TELECASTER CUSTOM** SUNBURST, SERIAL #63204	13,806	**10,601**	9,368	8,259
ELGUIT	62	FENDER	**TELECASTER CUSTOM** SUNBURST, SERIAL #94745/L01635-L13181	11,213	**8,610**	7,609	6,708
ELGUIT	62	FENDER	**TELECASTER CUSTOM** RED, SERIAL #76816-85944	12,819	**9,843**	8,698	7,668
ELGUIT	63	FENDER	**TELECASTER CUSTOM** SUNBURST, SERIAL #97069-99304/L15823-L63644	9,101	**6,988**	6,175	5,444
ELGUIT	63	FENDER	**TELECASTER CUSTOM** ROSEWOOD, SERIAL #L16550-L42308	10,066	**7,729**	6,830	6,021
ELGUIT	64	FENDER	**TELECASTER CUSTOM** BLACK, SERIAL #L50451-L69740	19,066	**14,640**	12,938	11,406
ELGUIT	66	FENDER	**TELECASTER CUSTOM** SUNBURST, ROSEWOOD BOARD	7,294	**5,601**	4,949	4,363
ELGUIT	67	FENDER	**TELECASTER CUSTOM** SUNBURST, SERIAL #208410	5,253	**4,034**	3,565	3,142
ELGUIT	68	FENDER	**TELECASTER CUSTOM** WHITE, BLACK BINDING	3,663	**2,813**	2,485	2,191
ELGUIT	68	FENDER	**TELECASTER CUSTOM** SUNBURST	6,017	**4,620**	4,083	3,599
ELGUIT	68	FENDER	**TELECASTER CUSTOM** CANDY APPLE RED	11,644	**8,941**	7,901	6,965
ELGUIT	69	FENDER	**TELECASTER CUSTOM** CANDY APPLE RED	4,269	**3,278**	2,897	2,554
ELGUIT	69	FENDER	**TELECASTER CUSTOM** SUNBURST, ROSEWOOD NECK	8,730	**6,703**	5,924	5,222
ELGUIT	70	FENDER	**TELECASTER CUSTOM** SUNBURST	3,318	**2,548**	2,251	1,985
ELGUIT	71	FENDER	**TELECASTER CUSTOM** SUNBURST, ROSEWOOD	3,545	**2,722**	2,406	2,121
ELGUIT	72	FENDER	**TELECASTER CUSTOM** BLACK, 2nd EDITION	1,221	**938**	829	730
ELGUIT	72	FENDER	**TELECASTER CUSTOM** SUNBURST	1,223	**939**	829	731
ELGUIT	72	FENDER	**TELECASTER CUSTOM** WHITE	1,244	**955**	844	744
ELGUIT	72	FENDER	**TELECASTER CUSTOM** SUNBURST, 2nd EDITION	1,340	**1,029**	909	801
ELGUIT	72	FENDER	**TELECASTER CUSTOM** BLACK, WHITE BINDING, SERIAL #356969-419864	4,140	**3,179**	2,809	2,476
ELGUIT	72	FENDER	**TELECASTER CUSTOM** MAPLE NECK, SERIAL #356969-419864	4,361	**3,348**	2,959	2,608
ELGUIT	73	FENDER	**TELECASTER CUSTOM** BLOND, MAPLE NECK, SERIAL #417124-517644	1,243	**954**	843	743
ELGUIT	73	FENDER	**TELECASTER CUSTOM** BLACK	1,244	**955**	844	744
ELGUIT	73	FENDER	**TELECASTER CUSTOM** SUNBURST	1,246	**957**	845	745
ELGUIT	74	FENDER	**TELECASTER CUSTOM** WALNUT	1,014	**779**	688	607

TYPE	YR	MFG	PRICES--BASED ON 100% ORIGINAL MODEL	SELL EXC	SELL AVG	BUY EXC	BUY AVG
ELGUIT	74	FENDER	**TELECASTER CUSTOM** SUNBURST, SERIAL #554139	1,022	**785**	693	611
ELGUIT	74	FENDER	**TELECASTER CUSTOM** BLACK, MAPLE FINGERBOARD	1,271	**976**	862	760
ELGUIT	74	FENDER	**TELECASTER CUSTOM** BROWN	1,302	**1,000**	883	779
ELGUIT	74	FENDER	**TELECASTER CUSTOM** NATURAL, MAPLE	1,303	**1,001**	884	779
ELGUIT	74	FENDER	**TELECASTER CUSTOM** BLOND, SERIAL #576865	1,304	**1,001**	885	780
ELGUIT	75	FENDER	**TELECASTER CUSTOM** SUNBURST	906	**695**	614	542
ELGUIT	75	FENDER	**TELECASTER CUSTOM** NATURAL, MAPLE NECK	947	**727**	642	566
ELGUIT	75	FENDER	**TELECASTER CUSTOM** WALNUT	997	**766**	677	596
ELGUIT	75	FENDER	**TELECASTER CUSTOM** BLACK, SERIAL #555119	1,243	**954**	843	743
ELGUIT	75	FENDER	**TELECASTER CUSTOM** BLOND, ROSEWOOD BOARD, SERIAL #555119	1,691	**1,298**	1,147	1,011
ELGUIT	76	FENDER	**TELECASTER CUSTOM** BROWN	944	**724**	640	564
ELGUIT	76	FENDER	**TELECASTER CUSTOM** SUNBURST, ROSEWOOD	977	**750**	663	584
ELGUIT	76	FENDER	**TELECASTER CUSTOM** BLACK	1,033	**793**	701	618
ELGUIT	77	FENDER	**TELECASTER CUSTOM** SUNBURST, SERIAL #S712043	960	**737**	652	574
ELGUIT	77	FENDER	**TELECASTER CUSTOM** BLACK	1,013	**778**	687	606
ELGUIT	77	FENDER	**TELECASTER CUSTOM** FIESTA RED	1,243	**954**	843	743
ELGUIT	78	FENDER	**TELECASTER CUSTOM** BROWN	897	**688**	608	536
ELGUIT	78	FENDER	**TELECASTER CUSTOM** NATURAL	986	**757**	669	590
ELGUIT	78	FENDER	**TELECASTER CUSTOM** WINE	1,047	**804**	710	626
ELGUIT	72	FENDER	**TELECASTER DELUXE**	963	**739**	653	576
ELGUIT	73	FENDER	**TELECASTER DELUXE** SUNBURST, SERIAL #516776-672663	946	**726**	642	566
ELGUIT	73	FENDER	**TELECASTER DELUXE** NATURAL, 2 HUMBUCKER PU's	1,022	**785**	693	611
ELGUIT	74	FENDER	**TELECASTER DELUXE** BROWN, 2 PU's	900	**691**	611	538
ELGUIT	74	FENDER	**TELECASTER DELUXE** BLACK, MAPLE NECK, SERIAL #568350	1,000	**767**	678	598
ELGUIT	75	FENDER	**TELECASTER DELUXE** BROWN, MAPLE NECK, SERIAL #656632	856	**657**	581	512
ELGUIT	75	FENDER	**TELECASTER DELUXE** BLACK, SERIAL #656632	876	**673**	595	524
ELGUIT	75	FENDER	**TELECASTER DELUXE** NATURAL	889	**682**	603	531
ELGUIT	76	FENDER	**TELECASTER DELUXE** BROWN, MAPLE BOARD	977	**750**	663	584
ELGUIT	76	FENDER	**TELECASTER DELUXE** BLACK	997	**766**	677	596
ELGUIT	76	FENDER	**TELECASTER DELUXE** BLOND, MAPLE NECK	1,005	**772**	682	601
ELGUIT	77	FENDER	**TELECASTER DELUXE** NATURAL	964	**740**	654	576
ELGUIT	77	FENDER	**TELECASTER DELUXE** BLACK, MAPLE NECK	997	**766**	677	596
ELGUIT	77	FENDER	**TELECASTER DELUXE** BLOND, MAPLE NECK	1,028	**789**	697	615
ELGUIT	78	FENDER	**TELECASTER DELUXE** NATURAL	971	**745**	658	580
ELGUIT	78	FENDER	**TELECASTER DELUXE** WHITE	984	**755**	668	588
ELGUIT	78	FENDER	**TELECASTER DELUXE** ANTIGUA	1,047	**804**	710	626
ELGUIT	79	FENDER	**TELECASTER DELUXE**	866	**665**	588	518
ELGUIT	83	FENDER	**TELECASTER ELITE** ROSEWOOD or MAPLE	738	**566**	500	441
ELGUIT	83	FENDER	**TELECASTER ELITE** WALNUT	1,053	**809**	715	630
ELGUIT	83	FENDER	**TELECASTER ELITE GOLD** ROSEWOOD or MAPLE	948	**728**	643	567
ELGUIT	83	FENDER	**TELECASTER ELITE LEFT-HANDED**	948	**728**	643	567
ELGUIT	67	FENDER	**TELECASTER THINLINE** SUNBURST	4,292	**3,296**	2,913	2,568
ELGUIT	68	FENDER	**TELECASTER THINLINE** SUNBURST	3,022	**2,321**	2,051	1,808

TYPE	YR	MFG	PRICES--BASED ON 100% ORIGINAL MODEL	SELL EXC	SELL AVG	BUY EXC	BUY AVG
ELGUIT	68	FENDER	**TELECASTER THINLINE** NATURAL	3,477	**2,670**	2,359	2,080
ELGUIT	68	FENDER	**TELECASTER THINLINE** MAHOGANY, MAPLE	3,512	**2,696**	2,383	2,101
ELGUIT	68	FENDER	**TELECASTER THINLINE** ASH, TELE PU, SERIAL #125316-397081	4,431	**3,403**	3,007	2,651
ELGUIT	69	FENDER	**TELECASTER THINLINE** SUNBURST, SERIAL #219796-286616	3,510	**2,695**	2,381	2,099
ELGUIT	69	FENDER	**TELECASTER THINLINE** MAHOGANY, SERIAL #219796-286616	3,587	**2,754**	2,434	2,146
ELGUIT	69	FENDER	**TELECASTER THINLINE** NATURAL, SERIAL #219796-286616	4,002	**3,073**	2,716	2,394
ELGUIT	69	FENDER	**TELECASTER THINLINE** CANDY APPLE RED	4,111	**3,157**	2,789	2,459
ELGUIT	69	FENDER	**TELECASTER THINLINE** BLACK PEARL	4,166	**3,199**	2,827	2,492
ELGUIT	69	FENDER	**TELECASTER THINLINE** OCEAN TURQUOISE	4,970	**3,816**	3,372	2,973
ELGUIT	69	FENDER	**TELECASTER THINLINE** CANARY YELLOW	9,296	**7,138**	6,308	5,561
ELGUIT	70	FENDER	**TELECASTER THINLINE** SUNBURST, SERIAL #206276-615270	1,456	**1,118**	988	871
ELGUIT	70	FENDER	**TELECASTER THINLINE** SILVER SPARKLE, SERIAL #206276-615270	2,437	**1,871**	1,653	1,457
ELGUIT	70	FENDER	**TELECASTER THINLINE** NATURAL	3,048	**2,340**	2,068	1,823
ELGUIT	71	FENDER	**TELECASTER THINLINE** NATURAL, HOLLOW BODY	1,450	**1,113**	984	867
ELGUIT	71	FENDER	**TELECASTER THINLINE** MAHOGANY	1,454	**1,117**	987	870
ELGUIT	71	FENDER	**TELECASTER THINLINE** BLACK, SERIAL #32501-509993	1,459	**1,120**	990	873
ELGUIT	71	FENDER	**TELECASTER THINLINE** OLYMPIC WHITE, SERIAL #32501-509993	3,549	**2,725**	2,408	2,123
ELGUIT	71	FENDER	**TELECASTER THINLINE** SALMON PINK	3,911	**3,003**	2,653	2,339
ELGUIT	72	FENDER	**TELECASTER THINLINE** BLACK, MAPLE FRET	1,448	**1,111**	982	866
ELGUIT	72	FENDER	**TELECASTER THINLINE** MAHOGANY, SERIAL #56115-539372/S723141	1,450	**1,113**	984	867
ELGUIT	72	FENDER	**TELECASTER THINLINE** WHITE	1,453	**1,116**	986	869
ELGUIT	72	FENDER	**TELECASTER THINLINE** BLOND	1,454	**1,117**	987	870
ELGUIT	72	FENDER	**TELECASTER THINLINE** SUNBURST, SERIAL #56115-539372/S723141	1,505	**1,155**	1,021	900
ELGUIT	72	FENDER	**TELECASTER THINLINE** NATURAL ASH, SERIAL #56115-539372/S723141	1,812	**1,391**	1,229	1,084
ELGUIT	73	FENDER	**TELECASTER THINLINE** NATURAL ASH, SERIAL #316015-527527	1,454	**1,117**	987	870
ELGUIT	73	FENDER	**TELECASTER THINLINE** SUNBURST	1,454	**1,117**	987	870
ELGUIT	74	FENDER	**TELECASTER THINLINE** BLACK	1,424	**1,093**	966	852
ELGUIT	74	FENDER	**TELECASTER THINLINE** ASH	1,454	**1,117**	987	870
ELGUIT	74	FENDER	**TELECASTER THINLINE** BROWN, SERIAL #60443-580031/S702161	1,454	**1,117**	987	870
ELGUIT	74	FENDER	**TELECASTER THINLINE** SUNBURST, SERIAL #60443-580031/S702161	1,458	**1,119**	989	872
ELGUIT	74	FENDER	**TELECASTER THINLINE** WHITE	4,026	**3,091**	2,732	2,408
ELGUIT	75	FENDER	**TELECASTER THINLINE** BROWN, SERIAL #606109-655092	1,507	**1,157**	1,022	901
ELGUIT	75	FENDER	**TELECASTER THINLINE** NATURAL, SERIAL #606109-655092	1,535	**1,179**	1,041	918
ELGUIT	76	FENDER	**TELECASTER THINLINE** NATURAL	1,410	**1,082**	956	843
ELGUIT	77	FENDER	**TELECASTER THINLINE** MOCCA	1,391	**1,068**	943	832
ELGUIT	77	FENDER	**TELECASTER THINLINE** BLACK	1,403	**1,077**	952	839
ELGUIT	78	FENDER	**TELECASTER THINLINE** SUNBURST, LEFT-HANDED, SERIAL #S806520-S846983	1,554	**1,193**	1,054	929
GUITAR AMP	54	FENDER	**BANDMASTER** TWEED, 1x15"	3,791	**2,911**	2,572	2,267
GTAMP	56	FENDER	**BANDMASTER** TWEED, 3x10"	3,676	**2,823**	2,495	2,199
GTAMP	58	FENDER	**BANDMASTER** TWEED, NARROW PANEL, 3x10"	3,736	**2,868**	2,535	2,235
GTAMP	59	FENDER	**BANDMASTER** TWEED, 3x10	4,884	**3,750**	3,314	2,921
GTAMP	59	FENDER	**BANDMASTER** TWEED, 3x10"	5,559	**4,269**	3,772	3,325

TYPE	YR	MFG	PRICES--BASED ON 100% ORIGINAL MODEL	SELL EXC	SELL AVG	BUY EXC	BUY AVG
GTAMP	62	FENDER	**BANDMASTER** WHITE, HEAD ONLY	710	**545**	481	424
GTAMP	62	FENDER	**BANDMASTER** BLOND-WHEAT, 2x12" CAB	896	**688**	608	536
GTAMP	63	FENDER	**BANDMASTER** SMOOTH WHITE, 40 WATTS, STANDARD WHITE KNOB CONTROL LAYOUT	1,258	**966**	854	753
GTAMP	63	FENDER	**BANDMASTER** WHITE TOLEX, BLACK FACE, 2x12" CABINET	1,644	**1,262**	1,115	983
GTAMP	64	FENDER	**BANDMASTER** BLACK FACE, 2x12"	881	**676**	598	527
GTAMP	64	FENDER	**BANDMASTER** WHITE, HEAD AND CABINET	887	**681**	601	530
GTAMP	64	FENDER	**BANDMASTER** TAN GRILL, WHITE TOLEX, HEAD AND CABINET	1,393	**1,069**	945	833
GTAMP	65	FENDER	**BANDMASTER** BLACK, HEAD ONLY	677	**520**	459	405
GTAMP	65	FENDER	**BANDMASTER** BLACK, PRE-CBS ELECTRIC	865	**664**	587	517
GTAMP	65	FENDER	**BANDMASTER** HEAD AND BOTTOM	869	**667**	589	519
GTAMP	66	FENDER	**BANDMASTER** HEAD ONLY	655	**503**	444	391
GTAMP	67	FENDER	**BANDMASTER** BLACK TOLEX, 40 WATT TUBE HEAD,TREMOLO	835	**641**	566	499
GTAMP	68	FENDER	**BANDMASTER** SILVER FACE, REVERB, HEAD	613	**471**	416	367
GTAMP	68	FENDER	**BANDMASTER** BLACK FACE, 2x12"	650	**499**	441	389
GTAMP	69	FENDER	**BANDMASTER** SILVER FAVE, HEAD ONLY	554	**425**	376	331
GTAMP	71	FENDER	**BANDMASTER** REVERB	584	**448**	396	349
GTAMP	72	FENDER	**BANDMASTER** REVERB, HEAD ONLY	564	**433**	383	337
GTAMP	75	FENDER	**BANDMASTER** REVERB, 2x12"	616	**473**	418	368
GTAMP	79	FENDER	**BANDMASTER** SILVER, REVERB, HEAD ONLY	535	**411**	363	320
GTAMP	80	FENDER	**BANDMASTER** SILVER FACE, REVERB	507	**389**	344	303
GTAMP	52	FENDER	**BASSMAN** TWEED, 1x15"	3,671	**2,819**	2,491	2,196
GTAMP	53	FENDER	**BASSMAN** TWEED, 1x15"	2,210	**1,697**	1,500	1,322
GTAMP	54	FENDER	**BASSMAN** TWEED, 1x15"	3,022	**2,321**	2,051	1,808
GTAMP	55	FENDER	**BASSMAN** TWEED, 4x10"	4,292	**3,296**	2,913	2,568
GTAMP	55	FENDER	**BASSMAN** TWEED, 4x10"	4,827	**3,706**	3,275	2,887
GTAMP	56	FENDER	**BASSMAN** TWEED, 2-INPUT, 4x10"	4,020	**3,087**	2,728	2,405
GTAMP	57	FENDER	**BASSMAN** TWEED	4,138	**3,177**	2,808	2,475
GTAMP	57	FENDER	**BASSMAN** TWEED	4,198	**3,224**	2,849	2,511
GTAMP	58	FENDER	**BASSMAN** TWEED, 4x10"	5,427	**4,167**	3,682	3,246
GTAMP	58	FENDER	**BASSMAN** MID RANGE CONTROL, 4-INPUT, 4x10"	5,638	**4,329**	3,825	3,372
GTAMP	59	FENDER	**BASSMAN** TWEED, MID CONTROL	6,643	**5,101**	4,508	3,974
GTAMP	61	FENDER	**BASSMAN** WHITE TOLEX TOP/BOTTOM, 2x12"	1,641	**1,260**	1,114	982
GTAMP	62	FENDER	**BASSMAN** WHITE, HEAD	1,333	**1,024**	905	797
GTAMP	62	FENDER	**BASSMAN** TOP/BOTTOM, 2x12"	1,338	**1,027**	908	800
GTAMP	63	FENDER	**BASSMAN** BLOND TOP/BOTTOM, 2x12"	1,305	**1,002**	886	781
GTAMP	64	FENDER	**BASSMAN** CABINET	692	**531**	469	414
GTAMP	64	FENDER	**BASSMAN** BLACK FACE, HEAD	717	**551**	487	429
GTAMP	64	FENDER	**BASSMAN** WHITE TOLEX, GOLD GRILL CLOTH	1,064	**817**	722	636
GTAMP	65	FENDER	**BASSMAN** BLACK TOLEX, BLACK FACE, 2x12"	889	**682**	603	531
GTAMP	68	FENDER	**BASSMAN** SILVER FACE, HEAD ONLY	785	**602**	532	469
GTAMP	69	FENDER	**BASSMAN** SILVER, HEAD	893	**686**	606	534
GTAMP	69	FENDER	**BASSMAN** TOP/BOTTOM, 2x15"	1,245	**956**	845	745

TYPE	YR	MFG	PRICES--BASED ON 100% ORIGINAL MODEL	SELL EXC	SELL AVG	BUY EXC	BUY AVG
GTAMP	70	FENDER	**BASSMAN** HEAD	673	**516**	456	402
GTAMP	70	FENDER	**BASSMAN** SILVER FACE, 2x15"	736	**565**	500	440
GTAMP	70	FENDER	**BASSMAN** SILVER PANEL, 4x10"	764	**587**	519	457
GTAMP	72	FENDER	**BASSMAN** 2x15"	571	**438**	387	341
GTAMP	73	FENDER	**BASSMAN** SILVER FACE, HEAD	574	**441**	389	343
GTAMP	74	FENDER	**BASSMAN** SILVER FACE, 4x10"	565	**434**	383	338
GTAMP	72	FENDER	**BASSMAN 10** 4x10" SPEAKERS	693	**532**	470	414
GTAMP	75	FENDER	**BASSMAN 10**	633	**486**	430	379
GTAMP	81	FENDER	**BASSMAN 10** 4x10" SPEAKERS	591	**454**	401	353
GTAMP	70	FENDER	**BASSMAN 50** BLACK TOLEX, 2x15" SPEAKER CONFIGURATION	398	**306**	270	238
GTAMP	70	FENDER	**BASSMAN 50** SILVER FACE, 2x15" SPEAKERS	704	**540**	478	421
GTAMP	73	FENDER	**BASSMAN 50** 2x12" SPEAKERS	633	**486**	430	379
GTAMP	76	FENDER	**BASSMAN 50** 2x15" SPEAKERS	697	**535**	473	417
GTAMP	73	FENDER	**BASSMAN 100** 2x15" CABINET	638	**490**	433	381
GTAMP	73	FENDER	**BASSMAN 100** 4x12"	688	**528**	467	412
GTAMP	77	FENDER	**BASSMAN 100**	645	**495**	437	385
GTAMP	78	FENDER	**BASSMAN 100** 2x15" CABINET	567	**436**	385	339
GTAMP	80	FENDER	**BASSMAN 100** 4x10"	610	**468**	414	365
GTAMP	68	FENDER	**BRONCO** 8" SPEAKER	322	**247**	218	192
GTAMP	69	FENDER	**BRONCO**	319	**245**	216	190
GTAMP	70	FENDER	**BRONCO** 8" SPEAKER	314	**241**	213	188
GTAMP	53	FENDER	**CHAMP** TWEED	919	**706**	623	550
GTAMP	55	FENDER	**CHAMP** TWEED	924	**709**	627	552
GTAMP	56	FENDER	**CHAMP** 6" SPEAKER	874	**671**	593	523
GTAMP	57	FENDER	**CHAMP** TWEED	968	**743**	657	579
GTAMP	58	FENDER	**CHAMP** 8" SPEAKER	936	**718**	635	560
GTAMP	59	FENDER	**CHAMP** TWEED	944	**724**	640	564
GTAMP	59	FENDER	**CHAMP** 8" SPEAKER	1,010	**775**	685	604
GTAMP	61	FENDER	**CHAMP** 6" SPEAKER	879	**664**	586	486
GTAMP	62	FENDER	**CHAMP** TWEED	745	**572**	506	446
GTAMP	63	FENDER	**CHAMP** 6" SPEAKER	766	**588**	519	458
GTAMP	63	FENDER	**CHAMP** TWEED, BLACK CABINET, 8" SPEAKER	815	**626**	553	487
GTAMP	63	FENDER	**CHAMP** TWEED	965	**741**	655	577
GTAMP	64	FENDER	**CHAMP** BLACK FACE	678	**521**	460	406
GTAMP	65	FENDER	**CHAMP** BLACK FACE, SCRIPT NAME PLATE	601	**461**	408	359
GTAMP	66	FENDER	**CHAMP** BLACK FACE, SCRIPT NAME PLATE	538	**413**	365	322
GTAMP	67	FENDER	**CHAMP** BLACK TOLEX, T WATTS, 1x8" JENSEN REISSUE SPEAKER	626	**480**	424	374
GTAMP	68	FENDER	**CHAMP** SILVER FACE, 8" SPEAKER	442	**339**	300	264
GTAMP	70	FENDER	**CHAMP** SILVER FACE	432	**331**	293	258
GTAMP	74	FENDER	**CHAMP** SILVER FACE	417	**320**	283	249
GTAMP	75	FENDER	**CHAMP** SILVER FACE	432	**331**	293	258
GTAMP	76	FENDER	**CHAMP** SILVER FACE	443	**340**	300	265
GTAMP	78	FENDER	**CHAMP** 8" SPEAKER	206	**158**	139	123

TYPE	YR	MFG	PRICES--BASED ON 100% ORIGINAL MODEL	SELL EXC	SELL AVG	BUY EXC	BUY AVG
GTAMP	79	FENDER	CHAMP SILVER FACE	509	391	345	304
GTAMP	49	FENDER	CHAMP 600 LEATHERETTE 2-TONE	2,095	1,609	1,421	1,253
GTAMP	50	FENDER	CHAMP 600 BROWN	1,011	776	686	605
GTAMP	51	FENDER	CHAMP 600	1,286	988	873	769
GTAMP	52	FENDER	CHAMP 600 BROWN AND WHITE 2-TONE	1,064	817	722	636
GTAMP	48	FENDER	CHAMP 800 GREY TWEED	1,435	1,102	974	858
GTAMP	60	FENDER	CONCERT BROWN, 4x10"	2,004	1,539	1,360	1,199
GTAMP	62	FENDER	CONCERT BROWN, 4x10"	1,743	1,339	1,183	1,043
GTAMP	63	FENDER	CONCERT BROWN, 4x10"	1,358	1,043	921	812
GTAMP	64	FENDER	CONCERT BLACK TOLEX, 4x10"	1,424	1,093	966	852
GTAMP	68	FENDER	D-120 JBL SPEAKER ONLY	240	184	163	144
GTAMP	49	FENDER	DELUXE TWEED, TV FRONT	2,026	1,555	1,374	1,212
GTAMP	51	FENDER	DELUXE	1,967	1,511	1,335	1,177
GTAMP	51	FENDER	DELUXE TV FRONT, 12" SPEAKER	2,004	1,539	1,360	1,199
GTAMP	52	FENDER	DELUXE WIDE BODY, NO TUBES, JENSEN	1,753	1,346	1,190	1,049
GTAMP	52	FENDER	DELUXE TWEED, TV MODEL	1,973	1,515	1,339	1,180
GTAMP	52	FENDER	DELUXE TWEED	2,213	1,699	1,501	1,323
GTAMP	53	FENDER	DELUXE WIDE PANEL, NO TUBES, JENSEN	1,675	1,286	1,136	1,002
GTAMP	53	FENDER	DELUXE TWEED	1,796	1,379	1,219	1,074
GTAMP	53	FENDER	DELUXE TWEED, TV FRONT	1,832	1,406	1,243	1,096
GTAMP	54	FENDER	DELUXE TWEED	2,014	1,547	1,367	1,205
GTAMP	55	FENDER	DELUXE TWEED, JENSEN ALNICO	1,719	1,320	1,166	1,028
GTAMP	56	FENDER	DELUXE TWEED	1,862	1,430	1,263	1,114
GTAMP	57	FENDER	DELUXE	1,935	1,486	1,313	1,157
GTAMP	58	FENDER	DELUXE	2,122	1,629	1,440	1,269
GTAMP	58	FENDER	DELUXE TWEED	2,393	1,837	1,624	1,431
GTAMP	59	FENDER	DELUXE TWEED	2,215	1,701	1,503	1,325
GTAMP	60	FENDER	DELUXE TWEED, 12" JENSEN	1,753	1,346	1,190	1,049
GTAMP	61	FENDER	DELUXE BROWN TOLEX	1,350	1,037	916	808
GTAMP	62	FENDER	DELUXE BROWN TOLEX	1,393	1,069	945	833
GTAMP	63	FENDER	DELUXE BROWN TOLEX	2,072	1,591	1,406	1,239
GTAMP	63	FENDER	DELUXE BLACK FACE, REVERB	7,486	5,748	5,079	4,478
GTAMP	64	FENDER	DELUXE OXFORD, REVERB	1,830	1,405	1,241	1,094
GTAMP	64	FENDER	DELUXE BLACK TOLEX	1,872	1,437	1,270	1,120
GTAMP	65	FENDER	DELUXE BLACK TOLEX	1,545	1,186	1,048	924
GTAMP	65	FENDER	DELUXE BLACK FACE, REVERB, NAME PLATE	7,482	5,745	5,077	4,476
GTAMP	66	FENDER	DELUXE BLACK FACE, REVERB, NAME PLATE	7,478	5,742	5,074	4,473
GTAMP	67	FENDER	DELUXE BLACK FACE, REVERB, NAME PLATE	7,473	5,738	5,071	4,470
GTAMP	68	FENDER	DELUXE SILVER FACE, REVERB	464	356	315	278
GTAMP	71	FENDER	DELUXE REVERB	460	353	312	275
GTAMP	72	FENDER	DELUXE SILVER FACE, REVERB, 12" JENSEN	458	351	310	274
GTAMP	73	FENDER	DELUXE SILVER FACE, REVERB	452	347	307	270
GTAMP	74	FENDER	DELUXE SILVER FACE, REVERB	451	346	306	270
GTAMP	75	FENDER	DELUXE REVERB	448	344	304	268

TYPE	YR	MFG	PRICES--BASED ON 100% ORIGINAL MODEL	SELL EXC	SELL AVG	BUY EXC	BUY AVG
GTAMP	75	FENDER	**DELUXE** SILVER FACE	655	**503**	444	391
GTAMP	77	FENDER	**DELUXE** REVERB	442	**339**	300	264
GTAMP	78	FENDER	**DELUXE** REVERB	437	**336**	297	261
GTAMP	68	FENDER	**DIMENSION IV** VIBRATO ECHO	540	**415**	367	323
GTAMP	46	FENDER	**DUAL PROFESSIONAL** 2x10" DUAL 616's	4,475	**3,436**	3,036	2,677
GTAMP	63	FENDER	**DUAL SHOWMAN** WHITE, 2x12" JBL's	3,025	**2,322**	2,052	1,809
GTAMP	64	FENDER	**DUAL SHOWMAN** BLACK	3,036	**2,331**	2,060	1,816
GTAMP	67	FENDER	**DUAL SHOWMAN** BLACK FACE, HEAD	1,338	**1,027**	908	800
GTAMP	68	FENDER	**DUAL SHOWMAN** SILVER FACE, CABINET, FENDER SPEAKERS	950	**730**	645	568
GTAMP	69	FENDER	**DUAL SHOWMAN** SILVER FACE, HEAD	554	**425**	376	331
GTAMP	69	FENDER	**DUAL SHOWMAN** SILVER FACE, 2x15" CABINET	1,557	**1,196**	1,057	931
GTAMP	74	FENDER	**DUAL SHOWMAN** 2 D-130F SPEAKERS AND CABINET	687	**528**	466	411
GTAMP	56	FENDER	**HARVARD** 10" SPEAKER	1,420	**1,090**	963	849
GTAMP	56	FENDER	**HARVARD** TWEED, 1x18", 10 WATTS	1,472	**1,130**	999	881
GTAMP	57	FENDER	**HARVARD** TWEED, 1x18"	1,246	**957**	845	745
GTAMP	58	FENDER	**HARVARD** TWEED, 1x12"	1,258	**966**	854	753
GTAMP	59	FENDER	**HARVARD** TWEED, 1x10"	1,249	**959**	848	747
GTAMP	60	FENDER	**HARVARD** TWEED, 1x10"	1,248	**958**	847	747
GTAMP	79	FENDER	**HARVARD** SOLID STATE	439	**337**	297	262
GTAMP	70	FENDER	**LIBRA 105** WALL, SOLID STATE	670	**515**	455	401
GTAMP	47	FENDER	**MODEL 26** 6" SPEAKER	3,129	**2,402**	2,123	1,871
GTAMP	47	FENDER	**MODEL 26** 15" SPEAKER	3,246	**2,493**	2,203	1,942
GTAMP	47	FENDER	**MODEL 26** 2 6V6 TUBES, 6", 8", 10" SPEAKERS	3,878	**2,978**	2,631	2,320
GTAMP	76	FENDER	**MODEL G-105** 2x12" SPEAKERS, SOLID STATE	439	**337**	297	262
GTAMP	70	FENDER	**MUSICMASTER BASS** SILVER FACE, 1x12"	416	**319**	282	249
GTAMP	76	FENDER	**MUSICMASTER BASS** 1x12", 12 WATTS	398	**306**	270	238
GTAMP	82	FENDER	**MUSICMASTER BASS**	369	**283**	250	221
GTAMP	49	FENDER	**PRINCETON** TWEED	1,787	**1,372**	1,212	1,069
GTAMP	49	FENDER	**PRINCETON** TWEED, TV FRONT	1,867	**1,433**	1,266	1,116
GTAMP	50	FENDER	**PRINCETON** TWEED, TV FRONT	1,564	**1,201**	1,061	935
GTAMP	51	FENDER	**PRINCETON** TWEED, TV FRONT	1,601	**1,229**	1,086	958
GTAMP	52	FENDER	**PRINCETON** TWEED	1,489	**1,143**	1,010	891
GTAMP	53	FENDER	**PRINCETON** TWEED	1,433	**1,100**	972	857
GTAMP	54	FENDER	**PRINCETON** TWEED, 8" SPEAKER	1,601	**1,229**	1,086	958
GTAMP	56	FENDER	**PRINCETON** TWEED, 8" SPEAKER	1,507	**1,157**	1,022	901
GTAMP	57	FENDER	**PRINCETON** TWEED	1,460	**1,121**	991	873
GTAMP	58	FENDER	**PRINCETON** TWEED	1,415	**1,087**	960	846
GTAMP	59	FENDER	**PRINCETON** TWEED	1,477	**1,134**	1,002	883
GTAMP	59	FENDER	**PRINCETON**	1,507	**1,157**	1,022	901
GTAMP	60	FENDER	**PRINCETON** TWEED	1,460	**1,121**	991	873
GTAMP	61	FENDER	**PRINCETON** BROWN TOLEX	992	**761**	673	593
GTAMP	62	FENDER	**PRINCETON** BROWN TOLEX	1,228	**943**	833	734
GTAMP	63	FENDER	**PRINCETON** BROWN TOLEX	703	**540**	477	420

TYPE	YR	MFG	MODEL — PRICES--BASED ON 100% ORIGINAL	SELL EXC	SELL AVG	BUY EXC	BUY AVG
GTAMP	63	FENDER	PRINCETON — BLACK	716	**550**	486	428
GTAMP	64	FENDER	PRINCETON — BLACK TOLEX, REVERB	692	**531**	469	414
GTAMP	64	FENDER	PRINCETON — BROWN TOLEX	747	**573**	506	446
GTAMP	64	FENDER	PRINCETON — REVERB	1,031	**792**	699	617
GTAMP	65	FENDER	PRINCETON — BLACK FACE, REVERB, 1x10"	838	**644**	569	501
GTAMP	65	FENDER	PRINCETON — BLACK TOLEX, REVERB	906	**695**	614	542
GTAMP	65	FENDER	PRINCETON — BLACK TOLEX, REVERB	1,236	**949**	839	739
GTAMP	66	FENDER	PRINCETON — OXFORD	645	**495**	437	385
GTAMP	66	FENDER	PRINCETON — BLACK FACE	689	**529**	468	412
GTAMP	66	FENDER	PRINCETON — BLACK TOLEX, REVERB	1,022	**785**	693	611
GTAMP	66	FENDER	PRINCETON — BLACK FACE, REVERB	1,046	**803**	709	625
GTAMP	67	FENDER	PRINCETON — BLACK FACE, REVERB	826	**634**	560	494
GTAMP	67	FENDER	PRINCETON — REVERB, SCRIPT NAME PLATE	876	**673**	595	524
GTAMP	68	FENDER	PRINCETON — SILVER FACE, REVERB	697	**535**	473	417
GTAMP	69	FENDER	PRINCETON — REVERB	639	**491**	433	382
GTAMP	69	FENDER	PRINCETON — SILVER FACE, REVERB	682	**523**	462	408
GTAMP	70	FENDER	PRINCETON — SILVER FACE, REVERB	663	**509**	449	396
GTAMP	70	FENDER	PRINCETON — REVERB	673	**516**	456	402
GTAMP	71	FENDER	PRINCETON — REVERB	624	**479**	424	373
GTAMP	74	FENDER	PRINCETON — REVERB	588	**451**	399	351
GTAMP	74	FENDER	PRINCETON — SILVER FACE	600	**460**	407	359
GTAMP	76	FENDER	PRINCETON — REVERB	589	**452**	399	352
GTAMP	77	FENDER	PRINCETON — REVERB	535	**411**	363	320
GTAMP	48	FENDER	PRO — TWEED, TV FRONT	1,723	**1,323**	1,169	1,031
GTAMP	49	FENDER	PRO — TWEED, TV FRONT	2,126	**1,633**	1,443	1,272
GTAMP	50	FENDER	PRO — TWEED, TV FRONT	1,828	**1,404**	1,241	1,094
GTAMP	53	FENDER	PRO — TWEED, TV FRONT	1,892	**1,453**	1,284	1,132
GTAMP	54	FENDER	PRO — TWEED, NARROW PANEL	2,464	**1,892**	1,672	1,474
GTAMP	55	FENDER	PRO — TWEED, NARROW PANEL	2,103	**1,615**	1,427	1,258
GTAMP	60	FENDER	PRO — BROWN TOLEX	1,606	**1,233**	1,089	960
GTAMP	61	FENDER	PRO — BROWN TOLEX, 1x15" JENSEN	1,261	**968**	855	754
GTAMP	62	FENDER	PRO — BROWN TOLEX	1,321	**1,014**	896	790
GTAMP	63	FENDER	PRO — BROWN TOLEX, 1x15" JENSEN	1,252	**961**	849	749
GTAMP	64	FENDER	PRO — BLACK TOLEX, 1x15" JENSEN	1,019	**782**	691	609
GTAMP	65	FENDER	PRO — BLACK FACE, REVERB	1,697	**1,303**	1,152	1,015
GTAMP	66	FENDER	PRO — BLACK, REVERB, SCRIPT NAME PLATE, 2x12"	1,634	**1,254**	1,108	977
GTAMP	67	FENDER	PRO — BLACK, REVERB, SCRIPT NAME PLATE, 2x12"	1,494	**1,147**	1,013	893
GTAMP	67	FENDER	PRO — BLACK FACE, REVERB	1,565	**1,202**	1,062	936
GTAMP	68	FENDER	PRO — SILVER FACE, REVERB, 2x12"	1,255	**964**	851	751
GTAMP	69	FENDER	PRO — SILVER FACE, REVERB	1,252	**961**	849	749
GTAMP	70	FENDER	PRO — REVERB, 10.5" DEEP	985	**756**	668	589
GTAMP	71	FENDER	PRO — SILVER FACE, REVERB	924	**709**	627	552

TYPE	YR	MFG	PRICES--BASED ON 100% ORIGINAL MODEL	SELL EXC	SELL AVG	BUY EXC	BUY AVG
GTAMP	72	FENDER	**PRO** SILVER FACE, REVERB	902	**693**	612	540
GTAMP	72	FENDER	**PRO** REVERB, 2x12"	929	**713**	630	556
GTAMP	73	FENDER	**PRO** SILVER FACE, REVERB	819	**629**	556	490
GTAMP	74	FENDER	**PRO** REVERB, 2x12"	870	**668**	590	520
GTAMP	76	FENDER	**PRO** SILVER FACE, REVERB	673	**516**	456	402
GTAMP	82	FENDER	**PRO** BLACK FACE, REVERB	612	**470**	415	366
GTAMP	72	FENDER	**QUAD** REVERB	610	**468**	414	365
GTAMP	79	FENDER	**QUAD** REVERB, 4x12", 100 WATTS	551	**423**	373	329
GTAMP	61	FENDER	**REVERB UNIT** BROWN TOLEX	1,068	**820**	725	639
GTAMP	62	FENDER	**REVERB UNIT** BROWN TOLEX	1,291	**991**	876	772
GTAMP	62	FENDER	**REVERB UNIT** WHITE TOLEX, MAROON GRILL	1,310	**1,006**	889	783
GTAMP	63	FENDER	**REVERB UNIT** WHITE TOLEX	976	**749**	662	584
GTAMP	63	FENDER	**REVERB UNIT** BLOND	1,252	**961**	849	749
GTAMP	63	FENDER	**REVERB UNIT** BROWN TOLEX	1,261	**968**	855	754
GTAMP	63	FENDER	**REVERB UNIT** WHITE TOLEX	1,310	**1,006**	889	783
GTAMP	64	FENDER	**REVERB UNIT**	976	**749**	662	584
GTAMP	64	FENDER	**REVERB UNIT** BLACK FACE	1,006	**773**	683	602
GTAMP	64	FENDER	**REVERB UNIT** BROWN TOLEX, TAN GRILL	1,067	**819**	724	638
GTAMP	65	FENDER	**REVERB UNIT** BLACK FACE, WHITE KNOBS	865	**664**	587	517
GTAMP	65	FENDER	**REVERB UNIT**	882	**677**	598	527
GTAMP	66	FENDER	**REVERB UNIT** BLACK FACE	838	**644**	569	501
GTAMP	70	FENDER	**REVERB UNIT**	657	**504**	446	393
GTAMP	72	FENDER	**REVERB UNIT**	582	**447**	395	348
GTAMP	75	FENDER	**REVERB UNIT** SILVER	565	**434**	383	338
GTAMP	71	FENDER	**SCORPIO** SOLID STATE, 2,x12", 56 WATTS	599	**460**	406	358
GTAMP	61	FENDER	**SHOWMAN** WHITE TOLEX, 12 AMP	1,697	**1,303**	1,152	1,015
GTAMP	61	FENDER	**SHOWMAN** BLOND, 15 AMP	2,126	**1,633**	1,443	1,272
GTAMP	62	FENDER	**SHOWMAN** BROWN, WHITE KNOBS/HEAD	1,775	**1,363**	1,204	1,061
GTAMP	64	FENDER	**SHOWMAN** BLOND, 15 AMP	1,718	**1,319**	1,165	1,027
GTAMP	65	FENDER	**SHOWMAN** BLACK FACE, TOP/BOTTOM, JBL	1,584	**1,216**	1,075	948
GTAMP	65	FENDER	**SHOWMAN** BLACK, HEAD ONLY, 15 AMP	3,057	**2,347**	2,074	1,829
GTAMP	66	FENDER	**SHOWMAN** BLACK FACE, HEAD AND CABINET	1,843	**1,415**	1,250	1,102
GTAMP	66	FENDER	**SHOWMAN** BLACK FACE, HEAD	2,027	**1,556**	1,375	1,212
GTAMP	68	FENDER	**SHOWMAN SINGLE** BOTTOM, JBL 15" CABINET	960	**737**	652	574
GTAMP	82	FENDER	**SUPER CHAMP** 2x10" SPEAKER	680	**522**	462	407
GTAMP	51	FENDER	**SUPER REVERB** TWEED	3,796	**2,915**	2,576	2,271
GTAMP	55	FENDER	**SUPER REVERB** TWEED	2,238	**1,719**	1,519	1,339
GTAMP	60	FENDER	**SUPER REVERB** BLACK TOLEX	1,476	**1,133**	1,001	883
GTAMP	60	FENDER	**SUPER REVERB** TWEED	2,974	**2,284**	2,018	1,779
GTAMP	62	FENDER	**SUPER REVERB** TOLEX, 2x10" M.L.D.	1,330	**1,021**	902	795
GTAMP	63	FENDER	**SUPER REVERB** BLACK FACE	1,723	**1,323**	1,169	1,031
GTAMP	64	FENDER	**SUPER REVERB** BLACK FACE, 24x25" SPEAKER	1,750	**1,344**	1,187	1,047
GTAMP	65	FENDER	**SUPER REVERB** BLACK FACE, 4x10" SPEAKERS	1,954	**1,500**	1,326	1,169
GTAMP	66	FENDER	**SUPER REVERB** 1-TONE NB, TV FRONT	2,059	**1,581**	1,397	1,232

TYPE	YR	MFG	PRICES--BASED ON 100% ORIGINAL MODEL	SELL EXC	SELL AVG	BUY EXC	BUY AVG
GTAMP	66	FENDER	**SUPER REVERB** BLACK FACE, 50 WATT TUBE COMBO, DUAL CHANNEL, TREMOLO, REVERB	2,208	**1,695**	1,498	1,321
GTAMP	67	FENDER	**SUPER REVERB** SILVER FACE	1,034	**794**	702	619
GTAMP	67	FENDER	**SUPER REVERB** BLACK FACE, VINYL COVER	1,785	**1,370**	1,211	1,067
GTAMP	69	FENDER	**SUPER REVERB** SILVER FACE, 4x10" SPEAKERS	1,030	**791**	699	616
GTAMP	70	FENDER	**SUPER REVERB** SILVER FACE	992	**761**	673	593
GTAMP	71	FENDER	**SUPER REVERB**	899	**690**	610	538
GTAMP	72	FENDER	**SUPER REVERB**	701	**538**	475	419
GTAMP	75	FENDER	**SUPER REVERB** SILVER FACE	726	**558**	493	434
GTAMP	76	FENDER	**SUPER REVERB** SILVER FACE	701	**538**	475	419
GTAMP	78	FENDER	**SUPER REVERB** SILVER FACE	726	**558**	493	434
GTAMP	79	FENDER	**SUPER REVERB** SILVER FACE	685	**526**	465	410
GTAMP	57	FENDER	**TREMOLUX** TWEED, 1x12"	2,008	**1,541**	1,362	1,201
GTAMP	58	FENDER	**TREMOLUX** TWEED	4,627	**3,553**	3,140	2,768
GTAMP	59	FENDER	**TREMOLUX** TWEED, 1x12"	2,082	**1,598**	1,412	1,245
GTAMP	60	FENDER	**TREMOLUX** TWEED	2,057	**1,579**	1,396	1,230
GTAMP	61	FENDER	**TREMOLUX** YELLOWED WHITE, PIGGY BACK, SINGLE 10" CABINET	1,794	**1,377**	1,217	1,073
GTAMP	62	FENDER	**TREMOLUX** BLOND, 1x10" CABINET	1,545	**1,186**	1,048	924
GTAMP	64	FENDER	**TREMOLUX** BLACK, HEAD ONLY	595	**457**	404	356
GTAMP	64	FENDER	**TREMOLUX** BLACK FACE, PIGGYBACK	847	**651**	575	507
GTAMP	65	FENDER	**TREMOLUX** BLACK, PIGGYBACK, 2x12"	1,571	**1,206**	1,066	940
GTAMP	66	FENDER	**TREMOLUX** HEAD	1,599	**1,228**	1,085	956
GTAMP	64	FENDER	**TUBE REVERB** WHITE TOLEX, CREAM GRILL	930	**714**	631	556
GTAMP	70	FENDER	**TUBE REVERB** BLACK	631	**485**	428	377
GTAMP	53	FENDER	**TWIN** TWEED	3,852	**2,958**	2,614	2,304
GTAMP	55	FENDER	**TWIN** TWEED, 1x12"	3,532	**2,712**	2,397	2,113
GTAMP	55	FENDER	**TWIN** TWEED, 100 WATT	11,429	**8,776**	7,755	6,837
GTAMP	57	FENDER	**TWIN** TWEED, 40 WATT, 2x12"	4,130	**3,171**	2,802	2,470
GTAMP	58	FENDER	**TWIN** TWEED, 100 WATT, 2x12"	10,750	**8,255**	7,295	6,431
GTAMP	59	FENDER	**TWIN** TWEED, 100 WATT	3,551	**2,727**	2,409	2,124
GTAMP	62	FENDER	**TWIN** WHITE TOLEX	4,389	**3,370**	2,978	2,625
GTAMP	63	FENDER	**TWIN** BLACK FACE, REVERB	1,254	**963**	851	750
GTAMP	63	FENDER	**TWIN** WHITE TOLEX	3,272	**2,512**	2,220	1,957
GTAMP	65	FENDER	**TWIN** BLACK FACE, 10" DEEP, REVERB	1,621	**1,245**	1,100	970
GTAMP	66	FENDER	**TWIN** BLACK FACE, 10" DEEP, REVERB	1,335	**1,025**	905	798
GTAMP	67	FENDER	**TWIN** REVERB	1,337	**1,026**	907	799
GTAMP	67	FENDER	**TWIN** BLACK FACE, REVERB	1,359	**1,044**	922	813
GTAMP	68	FENDER	**TWIN** SILVER, 9 3/4" DEEP, REVERB	796	**611**	540	476
GTAMP	69	FENDER	**TWIN** SILVER FACE, REVERB	791	**608**	537	473
GTAMP	69	FENDER	**TWIN** 85 RMS, 12" JENSENS, REVERB	1,029	**790**	698	615
GTAMP	70	FENDER	**TWIN** SILVER FACE, REVERB	773	**594**	525	462
GTAMP	70	FENDER	**TWIN** 100 RMS, REVERB	1,010	**775**	685	604
GTAMP	70	FENDER	**TWIN** REVERB	1,248	**958**	847	747
GTAMP	72	FENDER	**TWIN** SILVER FACE, REVERB, NON-MASTER VOLUME	449	**344**	304	268

TYPE	YR	MFG	PRICES--BASED ON 100% ORIGINAL MODEL	SELL EXC	SELL AVG	BUY EXC	BUY AVG
GTAMP	74	FENDER	**TWIN** SILVER FACE, REVERB	446	**343**	303	267
GTAMP	74	FENDER	**TWIN** CASTERS, MASTER VOLUME, REVERB	453	**348**	307	271
GTAMP	75	FENDER	**TWIN** MASTER VOLUME, REVERB	768	**589**	521	459
GTAMP	75	FENDER	**TWIN** CASTERS, REVERB	885	**680**	601	529
GTAMP	76	FENDER	**TWIN** REVERB	464	**356**	315	278
GTAMP	77	FENDER	**TWIN** REVERB	451	**346**	306	270
GTAMP	77	FENDER	**TWIN** SILVER FACE, SUPER REVERB	456	**350**	310	273
GTAMP	78	FENDER	**TWIN** REVERB	446	**343**	303	267
GTAMP	64	FENDER	**VIBRO CHAMP** BLACK FACE	700	**537**	475	418
GTAMP	65	FENDER	**VIBRO CHAMP** BLACK FACE	610	**468**	414	365
GTAMP	66	FENDER	**VIBRO CHAMP** BLACK FACE, SCRIPT NAME PLATE	579	**444**	392	346
GTAMP	67	FENDER	**VIBRO CHAMP** BLACK FACE, SCRIPT NAME PLATE	572	**439**	388	342
GTAMP	68	FENDER	**VIBRO CHAMP** SILVER FACE	566	**435**	384	339
GTAMP	70	FENDER	**VIBRO CHAMP** SILVER FACE	675	**518**	458	404
GTAMP	75	FENDER	**VIBRO CHAMP** SILVER FACE	520	**399**	353	311
GTAMP	78	FENDER	**VIBRO CHAMP** 8" SPEAKER	478	**367**	324	286
GTAMP	57	FENDER	**VIBROLUX** TWEED	1,688	**1,296**	1,146	1,010
GTAMP	58	FENDER	**VIBROLUX** TWEED, 1x10" SPEAKER	1,478	**1,135**	1,003	884
GTAMP	59	FENDER	**VIBROLUX** TWEED, 1x10" BLUE CAP SPEAKER	1,523	**1,169**	1,033	911
GTAMP	60	FENDER	**VIBROLUX** TWEED, 1x12" SPEAKER	1,484	**1,139**	1,007	887
GTAMP	61	FENDER	**VIBROLUX** BROWN, 12"	1,433	**1,100**	972	857
GTAMP	62	FENDER	**VIBROLUX** BROWN	1,540	**1,182**	1,045	921
GTAMP	63	FENDER	**VIBROLUX** BROWN	1,484	**1,139**	1,007	887
GTAMP	64	FENDER	**VIBROLUX** TWEED, 1x10" SPEAKER	1,349	**1,036**	915	807
GTAMP	64	FENDER	**VIBROLUX REVERB** BLACK FACE, 2x10"	1,928	**1,480**	1,308	1,153
GTAMP	65	FENDER	**VIBROLUX REVERB** BLACK FACE, 2x10"	1,864	**1,431**	1,265	1,115
GTAMP	66	FENDER	**VIBROLUX REVERB** BLACK FACE	1,860	**1,428**	1,262	1,112
GTAMP	67	FENDER	**VIBROLUX REVERB** BLACK FACE, 2x10"	1,852	**1,422**	1,257	1,108
GTAMP	69	FENDER	**VIBROLUX REVERB** SILVER FACE, 2x10"	838	**644**	569	501
GTAMP	70	FENDER	**VIBROLUX REVERB** 40 RMS	832	**638**	564	497
GTAMP	73	FENDER	**VIBROLUX REVERB**	735	**565**	499	440
GTAMP	75	FENDER	**VIBROLUX REVERB** SILVER FACE	827	**635**	561	495
GTAMP	78	FENDER	**VIBROLUX REVERB**	645	**495**	437	385
GTAMP	60	FENDER	**VIBROSONIC** BROWN TOLEX	1,580	**1,213**	1,072	945
GTAMP	62	FENDER	**VIBROSONIC** BROWN TOLEX	3,392	**2,604**	2,302	2,029
GTAMP	63	FENDER	**VIBROSONIC** M.L.D.	1,328	**1,019**	901	794
GTAMP	63	FENDER	**VIBROVERB** BROWN, 2x10"	3,942	**3,027**	2,675	2,358
GTAMP	64	FENDER	**VIBROVERB** BROWN or BLACK FACE	3,880	**2,979**	2,633	2,321
GTAMP	65	FENDER	**VIBROVERB** BLACK TOLEX	1,929	**1,481**	1,309	1,154
GUITAR (ACOUSTIC)	05	FENDER	**F-1040 CLASSICAL** SPRUCE TOP, MAHOGANY BACK/SIDES	118	**91**	80	71
GUIT	69	FENDER	**F-1050** SPRUCE TOP, MAHOGANY BACK/SIDES	114	**87**	77	68
GUITAR (ACOUSTIC)	64	FENDER	**CONCERT** ROSEWOOD, FLATTOP	777	**596**	527	464
GUITAR	65	FENDER	**CONCERT** MAHOGANY, FLATTOP	698	**528**	465	386

TYPE	YR	MFG	PRICES--BASED ON 100% ORIGINAL MODEL	SELL EXC	SELL AVG	BUY EXC	BUY AVG
GUITAR	68	FENDER	**CONCERT** ZEBRA BACK/SIDES, FLATTOP	636	**488**	431	380
GUITAR	69	FENDER	**CUSTOM** SUNBURST, SOLID BODY, SERIAL #232438-258071	1,354	**1,039**	918	810
GUITAR	79	FENDER	**DOVE** NATURAL	2,990	**2,296**	2,029	1,788
GUITAR	84	FENDER	**FLAME ULTRA** ALDER BODY, CARVED MAPLE TOP, INTERNAL TONE	1,041	**787**	694	575
GUITAR	62	FENDER	**KING** NATURAL, FLATTOP	824	**632**	559	493
GUITAR	63-65	FENDER	**KING** NATURAL, FLATTOP	762	**585**	517	456
GUITAR	64	FENDER	**KING** NATURAL, FLATTOP	750	**576**	509	448
GUITAR	66-68	FENDER	**KINGMAN** ANTIGUA, FLATTOP	816	**617**	544	451
GUITAR	66	FENDER	**KINGMAN** SUNBURST, FLATTOP	847	**651**	575	507
GUITAR	68	FENDER	**KINGMAN** NATURAL, FLATTOP	687	**528**	466	411
GUITAR	68	FENDER	**KINGMAN** ANTIGUA, FLATTOP	838	**644**	569	501
GUITAR	69-75	FENDER	**LTD** SUNBURST, CURLY MAPLE, GOLD HARDWARE	2,410	**1,850**	1,635	1,441
GUITAR	65-70	FENDER	**MALIBU** FLATTOP	579	**444**	392	346
GUITAR	66	FENDER	**MALIBU** FLATTOP	686	**527**	465	410
GUITAR	67	FENDER	**MALIBU** FLATTOP	685	**526**	465	410
GUITAR	68	FENDER	**MALIBU** FLATTOP	683	**524**	463	408
GUITAR	70	FENDER	**MALIBU**	670	**515**	455	401
GUITAR	65-68	FENDER	**NEWPORTER** SPRUCE TOP, MAHOG BACK/SIDES	313	**240**	212	187
GUITAR	67	FENDER	**NEWPORTER**	598	**459**	405	357
GUITAR	68-71	FENDER	**NEWPORTER** MAHOGANY, FLATTOP, SERIAL #232576	417	**320**	283	249
GUITAR	66	FENDER	**PALOMINO** NATURAL, FLATTOP	740	**568**	502	442
GUITAR	68	FENDER	**PALOMINO** NATURAL, FLATTOP	712	**546**	483	426
GUITAR	69	FENDER	**PALOMINO** NATURAL, FLATTOP	663	**509**	449	396
GUITAR	66	FENDER	**REDONDO** FLATTOP	686	**527**	465	410
GUITAR	66	FENDER	**SHENANDOAH** NATURAL, 12-STRING	743	**571**	504	444
GUITAR	68	FENDER	**SHENANDOAH** ANTIGUA, 12-STRING	640	**491**	434	383
GUITAR	68	FENDER	**SHENANDOAH** BLACK, 12-STRING	740	**568**	502	442
GUITAR	67	FENDER	**VILLAGER** 12-STRING, FLATTOP	704	**540**	478	421
GUITAR	68	FENDER	**VILLAGER** 12-STRING, FLATTOP	733	**563**	497	438
GUITAR	69	FENDER	**VILLAGER** 12-STRING, FLATTOP	734	**564**	498	439
GUITAR	71	FENDER	**VILLAGER** 12-STRING	598	**459**	405	357
GUITAR	66	FENDER	**WILDWOOD** SPRUCE TOP, DYED FIGURED BEECHWOOD BACK/SIDES	525	**403**	356	314
GUITAR	67	FENDER	**WILDWOOD** BLUE, FLATTOP	899	**690**	610	538
GUITAR	68	FENDER	**WILDWOOD** FLATTOP	870	**668**	590	520
GUITAR	67	FENDER	**WILDWOOD II**	1,361	**1,045**	924	814
GUITAR	68	FENDER	**WILDWOOD II** NATURAL TOP	856	**657**	581	512
GUITAR	67	FENDER	**WILDWOOD III** ROSEWOOD BACK/SIDES	1,199	**921**	813	717
GUITAR	68	FENDER	**WILDWOOD V** DREADNOUGHT, FLATTOP	1,070	**822**	726	640
GUITAR	67	FENDER	**WILDWOOD VI** GREEN, FLATTOP	1,201	**922**	815	718
GUITAR	68	FENDER	**WILDWOOD C II** HOLLOW BODY, THINLINE	770	**591**	522	460
GUITAR	68	FENDER	**WILDWOOD C XII** HOLLOW BODY, 12-STRING	764	**587**	519	457
MANDOLIN	56	FENDER	**ELECTRIC MANDOLIN** BLOND, TELECASTER, SERIAL #980-00985	2,184	**1,677**	1,482	1,306
MANDOL	57	FENDER	**ELECTRIC MANDOLIN** SUNBURST, 4-STRING, SERIAL #01308	1,862	**1,430**	1,263	1,114

TYPE	YR	MFG	PRICES--BASED ON 100% ORIGINAL MODEL	SELL EXC	SELL AVG	BUY EXC	BUY AVG
MANDOL	58	FENDER	**ELECTRIC MANDOLIN** SUNBURST 3-TONE, SERIAL #00541-00647	1,858	**1,426**	1,260	1,111
MANDOL	59	FENDER	**ELECTRIC MANDOLIN** SUNBURST 2-TONE, SERIAL #01253-027724	1,860	**1,428**	1,262	1,112
MANDOL	60	FENDER	**ELECTRIC MANDOLIN** SUNBURST. SERIAL #01407-03046	1,766	**1,356**	1,198	1,056
MANDOL	61	FENDER	**ELECTRIC MANDOLIN** SUNBURST 3-TONE	1,692	**1,299**	1,148	1,012
MANDOL	62	FENDER	**ELECTRIC MANDOLIN** SUNBURST	1,794	**1,377**	1,217	1,073
MANDOL	64	FENDER	**ELECTRIC MANDOLIN** SUNBURST, ROSEWOOD BOARD, SERIAL #01729-02027	1,659	**1,274**	1,126	992
MANDOL	69	FENDER	**ELECTRIC MANDOLIN** SUNBURST	1,290	**990**	875	771
MANDOL	74	FENDER	**ELECTRIC MANDOLIN** SUNBURST, ROSEWOOD BRIDGE	1,336	**1,025**	906	799
MANDOL	56	FENDER	**MANDOCASTER** BLOND, MAPLE NECK	3,589	**2,756**	2,435	2,147
MANDOL	59	FENDER	**MANDOCASTER** SUNBURST, ROSEWOOD FRETBOARD, SERIAL #01243	1,723	**1,323**	1,169	1,031
MANDOL	61	FENDER	**MANDOCASTER** SUNBURST, SLABOARD SPAGHETTI LOGO 9/10	3,110	**2,388**	2,110	1,860
MANDOL	62	FENDER	**MANDOCASTER** SUNBURST, 4-STRING, SERIAL #02217	1,485	**1,123**	990	821
MANDOL	63	FENDER	**MANDOCASTER** SUNBURST	2,750	**2,112**	1,866	1,645
MANDOL	66	FENDER	**MANDOCASTER** SUNBURST, SOLID BODY	1,256	**964**	852	751
MANDOL	57	FENDER	**MANDOLIN** BLOND, MAPLE NECK	3,019	**2,318**	2,048	1,806
STEEL GUITAR	58	FENDER	**400** FLAME MAPLE, 8-STRING, PEDAL STEEL	2,029	**1,558**	1,377	1,214
STGUIT	60	FENDER	**400** BROWN, 8-STRING, PEDAL STEEL	853	**655**	579	510
STGUIT	61	FENDER	**400** 8-STRING, PEDAL STEEL	725	**557**	492	434
STGUIT	62	FENDER	**400** BLACK, 8-STRING, PEDAL STEEL	723	**555**	490	432
STGUIT	65	FENDER	**400** SUNBURST, 8-STRING, PEDAL STEEL	638	**490**	433	381
STGUIT	64	FENDER	**800** SUNBURST, 10-STRING, PEDAL STEEL	648	**497**	440	387
STGUIT	60	FENDER	**1000** SUNBURST, (2)8-STRING, PEDAL STEEL	934	**717**	633	558
STGUIT	68	FENDER	**1000** SUNBURST, (2)8-STRING, PEDAL STEEL	800	**614**	543	479
STGUIT	65	FENDER	**2000** SUNBURST, (2)10-STRING NECKS	871	**669**	591	521
STGUIT	49	FENDER	**CHAMP LAP STEEL** YELLOW	833	**639**	565	498
STGUIT	50	FENDER	**CHAMP LAP STEEL** YELLOW PEARLOID	799	**614**	542	478
STGUIT	52	FENDER	**CHAMP LAP STEEL** YELLOW PEARLOID	751	**577**	509	449
STGUIT	54	FENDER	**CHAMP LAP STEEL** YELLOW PEARLOID	723	**555**	490	432
STGUIT	55	FENDER	**CHAMP LAP STEEL** DESERT FAWN	810	**622**	550	485
STGUIT	57	FENDER	**CHAMP LAP STEEL** BLOND	781	**600**	530	467
STGUIT	57	FENDER	**CHAMP LAP STEEL** DESERT FAWN	785	**602**	532	469
STGUIT	58	FENDER	**CHAMP LAP STEEL** DESERT FAWN	739	**567**	501	442
STGUIT	60	FENDER	**CHAMP LAP STEEL** DESERT FAWN	668	**513**	453	399
STGUIT	62	FENDER	**CHAMP LAP STEEL** DESERT FAWN	692	**531**	469	414
STGUIT	46	FENDER	**DELUXE** ELECTRIC STEEL	945	**725**	641	565
STGUIT	55	FENDER	**DELUXE** 8-STRING	724	**556**	491	433
STGUIT	68	FENDER	**DELUXE** 8-STRING	700	**537**	475	418
STGUIT	57	FENDER	**DELUXE 6** BLOND, ELECTRIC STEEL	668	**513**	453	399
STGUIT	65	FENDER	**DELUXE 6** ELECTRIC STEEL	703	**540**	477	420
STGUIT	52	FENDER	**DUAL 6 PROFESSIONAL** BLOND, (2)6-STRING NECKS	901	**692**	611	539
STGUIT	61	FENDER	**DUAL 6 PROFESSIONAL** DOUBLE NECK, TABLE STEEL	852	**654**	578	509
STGUIT	67	FENDER	**DUAL 6 PROFESSIONAL** DOUBLE NECK	706	**542**	479	422

TYPE	YR	MFG	PRICES--BASED ON 100% ORIGINAL MODEL	SELL EXC	SELL AVG	BUY EXC	BUY AVG
STGUIT	48	FENDER	DUAL 8 PROFESSIONAL WALNUT, (2)8-STRING	1,634	1,254	1,108	977
STGUIT	50	FENDER	DUAL 8 PROFESSIONAL BLOND, (2)8-STRING	1,001	768	679	598
STGUIT	50	FENDER	DUAL 8 PROFESSIONAL WALNUT, (2)8-STRING	1,003	770	680	600
STGUIT	52	FENDER	DUAL 8 PROFESSIONAL WALNUT, (2)8-STRING	929	713	630	556
STGUIT	54	FENDER	DUAL 8 PROFESSIONAL (2)8-STRING	1,023	786	694	612
STGUIT	58	FENDER	DUAL 8 PROFESSIONAL BLOND, (2)8-STRING	1,001	768	679	598
STGUIT	49	FENDER	LAP STEEL YELLOW PEARLOID, SN #5211	1,574	1,190	1,049	870
STGUIT	50	FENDER	LAP STEEL WHITE, SINGLE NECK	693	532	470	414
STGUIT	54	FENDER	LAP STEEL CREAM, 8-STRING, 3 LEGS	1,199	921	813	717
STGUIT	55	FENDER	LAP STEEL TAN, 6-STRING	693	532	470	414
STGUIT	47	FENDER	PRINCETON NATURAL, NON-PEDAL STEEL	674	517	457	403
STGUIT	48	FENDER	PRINCETON NATURAL, NON-PEDAL STEEL	673	516	456	402
STGUIT	55	FENDER	STRINGMASTER (2)8-STRING NECKS	1,051	807	713	629
STGUIT	56	FENDER	STRINGMASTER (3)8-STRING NECKS	1,979	1,519	1,342	1,183
STGUIT	57	FENDER	STRINGMASTER (4)8-STRING NECKS	1,281	983	869	766
STGUIT	58	FENDER	STRINGMASTER (2)8-STRING NECKS	1,266	972	859	757
STGUIT	59	FENDER	STRINGMASTER (3)8-STRING NECKS	1,330	1,021	902	795
STGUIT	60	FENDER	STRINGMASTER (2)8-STRING NECKS	1,001	768	679	598
STGUIT	61	FENDER	STRINGMASTER (3)8-STRING NECKS	941	723	639	563
STGUIT	65	FENDER	STRINGMASTER (2)8-STRING NECKS	940	722	638	562
STGUIT	68	FENDER	STRINGMASTER 4-NECK	922	708	626	552
STGUIT	71	FENDER	STRINGMASTER (2)8-STRING NECKS	977	750	663	584
STGUIT	76	FENDER	STRINGMASTER (3)8-STRING NECKS	973	747	660	582
STGUIT	80	FENDER	STRINGMASTER (3)8-STRING NECKS	717	551	487	429
STGUIT	56	FENDER	STUDIO DELUXE 3 LEGS	874	671	593	523
STGUIT	57	FENDER	STUDIO DELUXE 3 LEGS	891	684	604	533

FISHER

TYPE	YR	MFG	MODEL	SELL EXC	SELL AVG	BUY EXC	BUY AVG
PRE	73	FISHER	50C MONO TUBE	241	185	164	144
PRE	73-78	FISHER	50PR MONO TUBE	91	70	62	54
PRE	59-63	FISHER	400C TUBE STEREO	700	537	475	418
PRE	61	FISHER	400CX TUBE STEREO	668	513	453	399
PRE	63	FISHER	80C MONO TUBE	249	191	169	149
PWR	62-68	FISHER	20A MONO TUBE	266	204	180	159
PWR	62	FISHER	30A MONO TUBE	201	154	136	120
PWR	62	FISHER	50A TUBE	229	176	155	137
PWR	62-68	FISHER	55A MONO TUBE	545	418	370	326
PWR	55	FISHER	70-AZ TUBE	343	264	233	205
PWR	68-68	FISHER	80-AZ MONO TUBE	526	404	357	314
PWR	62	FISHER	90A MONO TUBE	179	137	121	107
PWR	62	FISHER	125A/AX MONO TUBE	416	319	282	249
PWR	62	FISHER	200 MONO TUBE	650	499	441	389
PWR	64-98	FISHER	KX-100 INTEGRATED 12 WATT	253	194	171	151

TYPE	YR	MFG	PRICES--BASED ON 100% ORIGINAL MODEL	SELL EXC	SELL AVG	BUY EXC	BUY AVG
PWR	60-61	FISHER	**SA-100** STEREO TUBE, 20 WATT	417	**320**	283	249
PWR	60-64	FISHER	**SA-300B** STEREO TUBE, 30 WATT	675	**518**	458	404
PWR	64-66	FISHER	**SA-300B** STEREO TUBE, 30 WATT	574	**441**	389	343
PWR	62	FISHER	**SA-1000** STEREO TUBE	633	**486**	430	379
PWR	62-68	FISHER	**SA-1000** STEREO TUBE, 65 WATT	1,029	**790**	698	615
PWR	61-62	FISHER	**X-100 INTEGRATED** STEREO TUBE, 15 WATT	281	**215**	190	168
TUNER	60	FISHER	**FM-50** TUBE	379	**291**	257	227
TUNER	62	FISHER	**FM-100** TUBE	346	**265**	234	207
TUNER	64	FISHER	**FM-100B** BLACK, TUBE	403	**309**	273	241
TUNER	64-66	FISHER	**FM-1000 CLASSIC** TUBE	971	**745**	658	580
TUNER	64	FISHER	**FMR-1** RACKMOUNT VERSION OF FM-1000 (TUBE)	1,350	**1,037**	916	808

FRAMUS (GERMANY)

TYPE	YR	MFG	MODEL	SELL EXC	SELL AVG	BUY EXC	BUY AVG
ELEC. GUITAR & BASS	74	FRAMUS	**36 COMBO BASS** LAMINATE	726	**558**	493	434
ELGUIT	74	FRAMUS	**APOLLO** TREMOLO, 2 PU's	225	**172**	152	134
ELGUIT	69	FRAMUS	**ATILLA ZOLLER** ARCHTOP	526	**404**	357	314
ELGUIT	62	FRAMUS	**BASS (WYMAN)**	313	**240**	212	187
ELGUIT	64	FRAMUS	**BASS IV**	579	**444**	392	346
ELGUIT	59	FRAMUS	**BILLY LORENTO**	918	**705**	623	549
ELGUIT	62	FRAMUS	**BILLY LORENTO**	635	**487**	430	379
ELGUIT	69	FRAMUS	**BILLY LORENTO**	657	**504**	446	393
ELGUIT	60	FRAMUS	**CARAVELLE**	545	**418**	370	326
ELGUIT	67	FRAMUS	**CARAVELLE** DOUBLE CUTAWAY, 2 PU's	604	**464**	410	361
ELGUIT	74	FRAMUS	**CARAVELLE** DOUBLE CUTAWAY, 2 PU's	459	**352**	311	274
ELGUIT	74	FRAMUS	**ELECTRONA** TREMOLO, ORGAN EFFECT SWITCH	542	**416**	367	324
ELGUIT	66	FRAMUS	**FRET JET** BLACK TO RED BURST, DOUBLE CUTAWAY	319	**245**	216	190
ELGUIT	74	FRAMUS	**GEORG HELLMER CARVED BASS**	1,551	**1,191**	1,052	927
ELGUIT	64	FRAMUS	**GOLDEN TELEVISION**	635	**487**	430	379
ELGUIT	74	FRAMUS	**GOLDEN TELEVISION** ORGAN EFFECT SWITCH	537	**412**	364	321
ELGUIT	74	FRAMUS	**J-144 SEMI ACOUSTIC BASS** 2 PU's	537	**412**	364	321
ELGUIT	74	FRAMUS	**JAN AKKERMAN** SINGLE CUTAWAY, 2 PU's	726	**558**	493	434
ELGUIT	75	FRAMUS	**JAN AKKERMAN**	645	**495**	437	385
ELGUIT	74	FRAMUS	**JOHANNES EBERLE CARVED BASS**	1,434	**1,101**	973	858
ELGUIT	74	FRAMUS	**JOSEF WILFER CARVED BASS**	3,006	**2,308**	2,039	1,798
ELGUIT	63	FRAMUS	**KING MODEL 5/98**	555	**426**	376	332
ELGUIT	64	FRAMUS	**MISSOURI** RED-BLACK SUNBURST, 2 PU's	551	**423**	373	329
ELGUIT	71	FRAMUS	**NASHVILLE**	553	**424**	375	330
ELGUIT	74	FRAMUS	**NEW SOUND** CUTAWAY, 2 or 3 PU's	346	**265**	234	207
ELGUIT	74	FRAMUS	**RHYTHM DELUXE BASS**	1,034	**794**	702	619
ELGUIT	60	FRAMUS	**SORELLA** RED SUNBURST	609	**467**	413	364
ELGUIT	64	FRAMUS	**SORELLA** BLACK TO RED BURST, ARCHTOP	400	**307**	272	239
ELGUIT	74	FRAMUS	**SORENTO** 12 STRING, 2 PU's	268	**206**	182	160
ELGUIT	66	FRAMUS	**SPORTSMAN**	226	**173**	153	135
ELGUIT	60	FRAMUS	**STAR BASS** SUNBURST, THIN BODY, 2 PU's	712	**546**	483	426
ELGUIT	65	FRAMUS	**STAR BASS** SUNBURST, THIN BODY, 2 PU's	473	**363**	321	283
ELGUIT	65	FRAMUS	**STRATO DELUXE** 12-STRING	604	**464**	410	361
ELGUIT	65	FRAMUS	**STRATO MELODIE** 9-STRING	670	**515**	455	401
ELGUIT	74	FRAMUS	**STRATO STAV BASS** 1 or 2 PU's	250	**192**	170	150
ELGUIT	74	FRAMUS	**STRATO SUPER** 2 PU's	178	**136**	120	106

TYPE	YR	MFG	PRICES--BASED ON 100% ORIGINAL MODEL	SELL EXC	SELL AVG	BUY EXC	BUY AVG
ELGUIT	74	FRAMUS	**TELEVISION** F HOLES, DBL CUTAWAY, 3 PU's	417	**320**	283	249
ELGUIT	74	FRAMUS	**WALTER LANGER CARVED BASS**	1,958	**1,504**	1,329	1,171
GUITAR (ACOUSTIC)	74	FRAMUS	**BLUE RIDGE DREADNOUGHT**	203	**156**	138	121
GUITAR	74	FRAMUS	**HOOTENANNY**	175	**135**	119	105
GUITAR	74	FRAMUS	**HUMMINGBIRD** 12-STRING	358	**275**	243	214
GUITAR	74	FRAMUS	**HUMMINGBIRD**	453	**348**	307	271
GUITAR	74	FRAMUS	**JUMBO**	402	**308**	272	240
GUITAR	75	FRAMUS	**SPORT 39"**	364	**279**	247	217
GUITAR	72	FRAMUS	**TEXAN** CHERRY SUNBURST, ENGRAVED PICKGUARD	712	**546**	483	426
GUITAR	75	FRAMUS	**TEXAN** FLAME CHERRY SUNBURST	592	**454**	402	354
MANDOLIN	74	FRAMUS	**GRACIELLA**	322	**247**	218	192
MANDOL	74	FRAMUS	**GRACIELLA** PICK UP	358	**275**	243	214
MANDOL	74	FRAMUS	**NEVADA** GUITAR SHAPED	358	**275**	243	214
UPRIG	46	FRAMUS	**UPRIGHT BASS** CARVED TOP	4,877	**3,745**	3,309	2,917

FUTTERMAN

TYPE	YR	MFG	MODEL	SELL EXC	SELL AVG	BUY EXC	BUY AVG
PWR	68-69	FUTT	**H-1** MONO, PAIR, 12 WATT	379	**291**	257	227
PWR	62-69	FUTT	**H-3** STEREO, 50 WATT	607	**466**	411	363
PWR	68-73	FUTT	**H-3** STEREO, 40 WATT	582	**447**	395	348
PWR	73-78	FUTT	**H-3A** STEREO, 60 WATT	601	**461**	408	359
PWR	78-82	FUTT	**H-3AA** DUAL MONO, 125 WATT, PAIR	794	**609**	538	475

G & L MUSIC SALES, INC

TYPE	YR	MFG	MODEL	SELL EXC	SELL AVG	BUY EXC	BUY AVG
EFFECTS	97	G&L	**ASAT CLASSIC** CUTAWAY, RSWD or MAPLE FNGRBRD, 2 G&L MAGNETIC FIELD PU's	947	**727**	642	566
EFFECTS	86	G&L	**BROADCASTER** EBONY, 2 SINGLE COIL PU, SIGNED BY LEO FENDER	1,744	**1,339**	1,184	1,043
EFFECTS	86	G&L	**BROADCASTER** MAPLE, 2 SINGLE COIL PU, SIGNED BY LEO FENDER	1,744	**1,339**	1,184	1,043
EFFECTS	84	G&L	**CAVALIER** EBONY NECK, NO VIBRATO, 2 HB	1,338	**1,027**	908	800
EFFECTS	84	G&L	**CAVALIER** EBONY NECK, VIBRATO, 2 HB	1,387	**1,065**	941	830
EFFECTS	84	G&L	**CAVALIER** MAPLE NECK, VIBRATO, 2 HB	1,393	**1,069**	945	833
EFFECTS	84	G&L	**CAVALIER** MAPLE NECK, NO VIBRATO, 2 HB	1,396	**1,072**	947	835
EFFECTS	88	G&L	**SC-3** MAPLE NECK, NO VIBRATO	853	**655**	579	510
EFFECTS	88	G&L	**SC-3** ROSEWOOD NECK, 3 SINGLE COIL PU, G & L VIBRATO	909	**698**	617	544
EFFECTS	84	G&L	**SKYHAWK** EBONY NECK, 3 SINGLE COIL PU	1,628	**1,250**	1,105	974
EFFECTS	84	G&L	**SKYHAWK** MAPLE or ROSEWOOD NEC, 3 SINGLE COIL PU, G & L VIBRATO	1,744	**1,339**	1,184	1,043
EFFECTS	85	G&L	**SKYHAWK** MAPLE or ROSEWOOD NECK, 3 SINGLE COIL PU, KAHLER TREMOLO	1,626	**1,248**	1,103	972
EFFECTS	88	G&L	**SKYHAWK** MAPLE or ROSEWOOD NECK, 3 SINGLE COIL PU, FENDER VIBRATO	1,628	**1,250**	1,105	974

GALLAGHER

TYPE	YR	MFG	MODEL	SELL EXC	SELL AVG	BUY EXC	BUY AVG
GUITAR (ACOUSTIC)	79	GALLAGHER	**71 SPECIAL** ROSEWOOD BACK/SIDES	1,792	**1,376**	1,216	1,072
GUITAR	65	GALLAGHER	**CUSTOM** MAHOGANY, 12-STRING, 12-FRET	1,531	**1,175**	1,038	915
GUITAR	81	GALLAGHER	**DOC WATSON** CUTAWAY	3,386	**2,600**	2,298	2,026
GUITAR	85	GALLAGHER	**DOC WATSON** CUTAWAY	1,921	**1,475**	1,304	1,149
GUITAR	67	GALLAGHER	**G-40** MAHOGANY BACK/SIDES, FLATTOP	1,206	**926**	818	721
GUITAR	80	GALLAGHER	**G-45** MAHOGANY	1,441	**1,106**	978	862
GUITAR	66	GALLAGHER	**G-50** MAHOGANY BACK/SIDES, DREADNOUGHT	1,461	**1,104**	974	807
GUITAR	67	GALLAGHER	**G-50** MAHOGANY, DREADNOUGHT	1,622	**1,246**	1,101	970
GUITAR	70	GALLAGHER	**G-50** MAHOGANY BACK/SIDES	1,301	**999**	883	778
GUITAR	66	GALLAGHER	**G-60**	1,008	**774**	684	603
GUITAR	68	GALLAGHER	**G-70** SUNBURST, DREADNOUGHT	1,688	**1,296**	1,146	1,010

TYPE	YR	MFG	PRICES--BASED ON 100% ORIGINAL MODEL	SELL EXC	SELL AVG	BUY EXC	BUY AVG
GUITAR	73	GALLAGHER	G-70	2,459	1,888	1,668	1,471
GUITAR	78	GALLAGHER	G-70 INDIAN ROSEWOOD	1,531	1,175	1,038	915
GUITAR	79	GALLAGHER	G-70 HERRINGBONE TRIM	1,747	1,341	1,185	1,045
GUITAR	70	GALLAGHER	G-70M FLATTOP	1,546	1,187	1,049	925
GUITAR	75	GALLAGHER	G-70M HERRINGBONE TRIM	1,656	1,271	1,124	990
GUITAR	73	GALLAGHER	G-71 SPECIAL INDIAN ROSEWOOD, HERRINGBONE	1,834	1,408	1,244	1,097
GUITAR	68	GALLAGHER	GC-65 ROSEWOOD BACK/SIDES, 12-FRET	2,345	1,800	1,591	1,402

GETZEN CO

TYPE	YR	MFG	MODEL	SELL EXC	SELL AVG	BUY EXC	BUY AVG
BANJO	60	GETZEN	SEVERENSEN 900 SEV Bb	805	618	546	481

GIBSON, SEE ALSO EPIPHONE, KALAMAZOO, RECORDING KING, RAMIRE

TYPE	YR	MFG	MODEL	SELL EXC	SELL AVG	BUY EXC	BUY AVG
BANJO	71	GIBSON	ALL AMERICAN	8,198	6,295	5,563	4,904
BANJO	72	GIBSON	ALL AMERICAN	8,309	6,380	5,638	4,970
BANJO	78	GIBSON	ALL AMERICAN	7,557	5,803	5,128	4,521
BANJO	24	GIBSON	BANJO-MANDOLIN TRAP DOOR, 8-STRING	1,252	961	849	749
BANJO	27	GIBSON	BELLA VOCE WHITE HOLLY, 5-STRING	11,586	8,896	7,862	6,931
BANJO	27	GIBSON	BELLA VOCE TENOR, ARCHTOP	11,883	9,124	8,063	7,108
BANJO	28	GIBSON	BELLA VOCE TENOR, WHITE HOLLY	13,138	10,088	8,915	7,859
BANJO	35	GIBSON	BU-2 BANJO-UKE LARGER HEAD	735	565	499	440
BANJO	32	GIBSON	BU-3 BANJO-UKE SUNBURST, 8" HEAD, MAPLE	972	746	659	581
BANJO	24	GIBSON	CB-4 CELLO-BANJO	2,309	1,773	1,567	1,381
BANJO	32	GIBSON	CUSTOM TENOR,12" HEAD, DBLECUT TB-4 STYLE PGHD,TBE&PLTE FLNGE	1,554	1,193	1,054	929
BANJO	38	GIBSON	ELECTRIC BANJO SUNBURST	4,794	3,681	3,253	2,868
BANJO	39	GIBSON	ETB ELECTRIC TENOR, INLAY LIKE TOP TENSION STYLE #7	5,323	4,087	3,612	3,184
BANJO	28	GIBSON	FLORENTINE TENOR	11,883	9,124	8,063	7,108
BANJO	30	GIBSON	FLORENTINE TENOR	12,162	9,338	8,252	7,275
BANJO	34	GIBSON	FLORENTINE RESONATOR	20,933	16,074	14,205	12,522
BANJO	72	GIBSON	FLORENTINE NATURAL MAPLE	9,791	7,518	6,643	5,857
BANJO	78	GIBSON	FLORENTINE	7,572	5,814	5,138	4,529
BANJO	28	GIBSON	FLORENTINE CUSTOM PLECTRUM, WHITE	13,040	10,012	8,848	7,800
BANJO	18	GIBSON	GB-1 GUITAR-BANJO OPEN BACK, 14" HEAD	971	745	658	580
BANJO	19	GIBSON	GB-1 GUITAR-BANJO	965	741	655	577
BANJO	20	GIBSON	GB-1 GUITAR-BANJO OPEN BACK, 14" HEAD, SERIAL #53800-62200	1,298	996	880	776
BANJO	27	GIBSON	GB-1 GUITAR-BANJO ROTOMATIC TUNERS	988	759	671	591
BANJO	32	GIBSON	GB-1 GUITAR-BANJO	972	746	659	581
BANJO	29	GIBSON	GB-3 GUITAR-BANJO MASTERTONE	2,427	1,863	1,646	1,451
BANJO	22	GIBSON	GB-4 GUITAR-BANJO SUNBURST	1,419	1,089	962	848
BANJO	25	GIBSON	GRANADA TENOR, 5-STRING, SERIAL #80300-82700	3,400	2,610	2,307	2,034
BANJO	26	GIBSON	GRANADA PLECTRUM, SERIAL #-85400	8,594	6,599	5,832	5,141
BANJO	28	GIBSON	GRANADA PLECTRUM, HEARTS & FLOWERS INLAY,NO-HOLE	8,594	6,599	5,832	5,141
BANJO	30	GIBSON	GRANADA TENOR, 2 PIECE FLANGE	8,594	6,599	5,832	5,141
BANJO	32	GIBSON	KEL KROYDEN TENOR, WALNUT, SERIAL #90400-90700	1,012	777	687	605
BANJO	34	GIBSON	KEL KROYDEN TENOR	1,331	1,022	903	796
BANJO	35	GIBSON	KEL KROYDEN TENOR, BLUE, SERIAL #92400-93500	1,005	772	682	601
BANJO	25	GIBSON	MASTERTONE TENOR, GRANADA, 18-FRET	3,457	2,654	2,346	2,068
BANJO	26	GIBSON	MASTERTONE TENOR	1,359	1,044	922	813
BANJO	28	GIBSON	MASTERTONE RESONATOR, 5-STRING, SERIAL #89800-90200	14,623	11,229	9,923	8,748

TYPE	YR	MFG	PRICES--BASED ON 100% ORIGINAL MODEL	SELL EXC	SELL AVG	BUY EXC	BUY AVG
BANJO	60	GIBSON	MASTERTONE FLATHEAD	1,300	998	882	777
BANJO	36	GIBSON	MB- 0 MANDOLIN-BANJO	786	603	533	470
BANJO	35	GIBSON	MB- 00 MANDOLIN-BANJO 1 PIECE FLANGE	870	668	590	520
BANJO	19	GIBSON	MB- 1 MANDOLIN-BANJO OPEN BACK	869	667	589	519
BANJO	20	GIBSON	MB- 1 MANDOLIN-BANJO	838	644	569	501
BANJO	22	GIBSON	MB- 1 MANDOLIN-BANJO TRAP DOOR RES	759	583	515	454
BANJO	28	GIBSON	MB- 1 MANDOLIN-BANJO SERIAL #85400-87300	756	580	513	452
BANJO	25	GIBSON	MB- 2 MANDOLIN-BANJO 10.5" HEAD	778	597	528	465
BANJO	24	GIBSON	MB- 3 MANDOLIN-BANJO SERIAL #74900-80300	869	667	589	519
BANJO	26	GIBSON	MB- 3 MANDOLIN-BANJO DIAMOND HOLE, SERIAL #82700-	870	668	590	520
BANJO	20	GIBSON	MB- 4 MANDOLIN-BANJO OPEN BACK	875	672	594	523
BANJO	21	GIBSON	MB- 4 MANDOLIN-BANJO TRAP DOOR RESONATOR	873	670	592	522
BANJO	24	GIBSON	MB- 4 MANDOLIN-BANJO	870	668	590	520
BANJO	24	GIBSON	MB-JR MANDOLIN-BANJO	764	587	519	457
BANJO	22	GIBSON	ORIOLE TENOR, OPEN BACK	972	746	659	581
BANJO	26	GIBSON	PB- 3 MASTERTONE PLECTRUM	2,037	1,564	1,382	1,218
BANJO	27	GIBSON	PB- 3 MASTERTONE PLECTRUM	1,557	1,177	1,038	860
BANJO	34	GIBSON	PB- 3 MASTERTONE FLATHEAD, 5-STRING	13,995	10,746	9,496	8,372
BANJO	31	GIBSON	PB- 6 FLATHEAD, RESONATOR	13,760	10,565	9,337	8,231
BANJO	37	GIBSON	PB- 7 FLATHEAD, ROSEWOOD BOARD, RESONATOR, WALNUT	1,229	944	834	735
BANJO	40	GIBSON	PB- 7 MASTERTONE	16,066	12,336	10,902	9,611
BANJO	66	GIBSON	PB-100 PLECTRUM	922	708	626	552
BANJO	67	GIBSON	PB-100 PLECTRUM, SUNBURST, RESONATOR	1,062	816	721	635
BANJO	69	GIBSON	PB-100 PLECTRUM	922	708	626	552
BANJO	72	GIBSON	PB-100 PLECTRUM	926	711	628	554
BANJO	62	GIBSON	PB-250 PLECTRUM	963	739	653	576
BANJO	65	GIBSON	PB-250 PLECTRUM	1,010	775	685	604
BANJO	66	GIBSON	PB-250 PLECTRUM	1,308	1,004	887	782
BANJO	67	GIBSON	PB-250 PLECTRUM	1,303	1,001	884	779
BANJO	66	GIBSON	PB-800 PLECTRUM. NATURAL	1,510	1,160	1,025	903
BANJO	24	GIBSON	PB-JUNIOR OPEN PACK	730	560	495	436
BANJO	29	GIBSON	PT-6 FLATHEAD, GOLD TRIM, HIGH PROFILE	17,476	13,419	11,859	10,454
BANJO	35	GIBSON	RB- 00 5-STRING	1,016	780	690	608
BANJO	34	GIBSON	RB- 1 5-STRING, FLATHEAD	4,126	3,168	2,799	2,468
BANJO	35	GIBSON	RB- 1 5-STRING, FLATHEAD	3,309	2,541	2,245	1,979
BANJO	25	GIBSON	RB- 3 5-STRING, RESONATOR	3,174	2,437	2,153	1,898
BANJO	27	GIBSON	RB- 3 5-STRING, RESONATOR	3,351	2,573	2,273	2,004
BANJO	28	GIBSON	RB- 3 5-STRING, RESONATOR	3,290	2,526	2,232	1,968
BANJO	29	GIBSON	RB- 3 5-STRING, RESONATOR	4,658	3,576	3,160	2,786
BANJO	31	GIBSON	RB- 3 5-STRING, RESONATOR	3,047	2,340	2,067	1,823
BANJO	32	GIBSON	RB- 4	6,025	4,626	4,088	3,604
BANJO	26	GIBSON	RB- 4 MASTERTONE 5-STRING	8,902	6,836	6,041	5,325
BANJO	26	GIBSON	RB- 4BB MASTERTONE 5-STRING, RESONATOR	10,271	7,887	6,969	6,144
BANJO	29	GIBSON	RB- 6 FLATHEAD	15,828	12,154	10,741	9,469
BANJO	32	GIBSON	RB- 6 MASTERTONE	18,167	13,950	12,327	10,868

TYPE	YR	MFG	PRICES--BASED ON 100% ORIGINAL MODEL	SELL EXC	SELL AVG	BUY EXC	BUY AVG
BANJO	35	GIBSON	RB- 75 5-STRING	7,766	5,963	5,269	4,645
BANJO	39	GIBSON	RB- 75 5-STRING, FLATHEAD, TONE RING	14,120	10,842	9,582	8,447
BANJO	61	GIBSON	RB-100 5-STRING	1,494	1,147	1,013	893
BANJO	62	GIBSON	RB-100 5-STRING	1,492	1,146	1,013	893
BANJO	64	GIBSON	RB-100 5-STRING	1,490	1,144	1,011	891
BANJO	67	GIBSON	RB-100 5-STRING	1,454	1,117	987	870
BANJO	70	GIBSON	RB-100 5-STRING	1,227	942	832	734
BANJO	73	GIBSON	RB-100 5-STRING	1,227	942	832	734
BANJO	50	GIBSON	RB-150 5-STRING	1,811	1,390	1,228	1,083
BANJO	64	GIBSON	RB-170 STANDARD LENGTH NECK, OPEN BACK	1,339	1,028	908	801
BANJO	67	GIBSON	RB-170 11" FIBERSKYN HEAD, DOT INLAY	1,299	997	881	777
BANJO	63	GIBSON	RB-175 LONG NECK	1,338	1,027	908	800
BANJO	64	GIBSON	RB-175 LONG NECK, OPEN BACK	1,303	1,001	884	779
BANJO	65	GIBSON	RB-175 LONG NECK, OPEN BACK	1,245	956	845	745
BANJO	66	GIBSON	RB-175 LONG NECK, OPEN BACK	1,220	937	828	730
BANJO	67	GIBSON	RB-175 LONG NECK, OPEN BACK	1,247	958	846	746
BANJO	65	GIBSON	RB-180 LONG NECK, OPEN BACK	1,421	1,091	964	850
BANJO	74	GIBSON	RB-200 CHERRY SUNBURST	2,322	1,783	1,576	1,389
BANJO	55	GIBSON	RB-250	2,316	1,778	1,571	1,385
BANJO	60	GIBSON	RB-250	2,035	1,562	1,380	1,217
BANJO	61	GIBSON	RB-250	1,795	1,378	1,218	1,074
BANJO	62	GIBSON	RB-250	1,872	1,437	1,270	1,120
BANJO	63	GIBSON	RB-250	1,872	1,437	1,270	1,120
BANJO	64	GIBSON	RB-250	1,849	1,419	1,254	1,106
BANJO	65	GIBSON	RB-250	1,869	1,435	1,268	1,118
BANJO	68	GIBSON	RB-250	1,644	1,262	1,115	983
BANJO	69	GIBSON	RB-250 5-STRING, RESONATOR	1,454	1,117	987	870
BANJO	70	GIBSON	RB-250	1,485	1,140	1,007	888
BANJO	71	GIBSON	RB-250	1,424	1,093	966	852
BANJO	72	GIBSON	RB-250	1,540	1,182	1,045	921
BANJO	74	GIBSON	RB-250	1,366	1,049	927	817
BANJO	75	GIBSON	RB-250	1,311	1,007	889	784
BANJO	75	GIBSON	RB-250	1,444	1,109	980	864
BANJO	77	GIBSON	RB-250	1,345	1,032	912	804
BANJO	78	GIBSON	RB-250	1,209	928	820	723
BANJO	79	GIBSON	RB-250	1,042	800	707	623
BANJO	80	GIBSON	RB-250	1,609	1,235	1,092	962
BANJO	62	GIBSON	RB-250 MASTERTONE	2,151	1,652	1,459	1,287
BANJO	65	GIBSON	RB-250 MASTERTONE	1,761	1,352	1,195	1,053
BANJO	76	GIBSON	RB-250 MASTERTONE	1,216	933	825	727
BANJO	70	GIBSON	RB-800 CHERRY SUNBURST	1,694	1,301	1,149	1,013
BANJO	72	GIBSON	RB-800 CHERRY SUNBURST	1,701	1,306	1,154	1,017
BANJO	77	GIBSON	RB-800 CHERRY SUNBURST	1,449	1,112	983	866
BANJO	72	GIBSON	RB-800 ARGENTINE GRAY SUNBURST	1,694	1,301	1,149	1,013
BANJO	75	GIBSON	RB-800 MASTERTONE CHERRY SUNBURST, GOLD HARDWARE	2,280	1,750	1,547	1,364
BANJO	72	GIBSON	RB-800 VICEROY SUNBURST	1,562	1,199	1,060	934
BANJO	24	GIBSON	RB-JUNIOR BLACK	958	736	650	573
BANJO	28	GIBSON	RECORDING KING TENOR	2,024	1,554	1,374	1,211
BANJO	30	GIBSON	STYLE 6 TENOR/PLECTRUM NECK	8,534	6,553	5,791	5,105
BANJO	24	GIBSON	TB- 0 TENOR	1,356	1,041	920	811
BANJO	40	GIBSON	TB- 00 TENOR, 1 PIECE FLANGE	1,301	999	883	778

TYPE	YR	MFG	PRICES--BASED ON 100% ORIGINAL MODEL	SELL EXC	SELL AVG	BUY EXC	BUY AVG
BANJO	18	GIBSON	TB- 1 TENOR, 5-STRING, HOLLOW RIM, SERIAL #39500-47900	4,141	3,180	2,810	2,477
BANJO	20	GIBSON	TB- 1 TENOR	1,361	1,045	924	814
BANJO	23	GIBSON	TB- 1 TENOR	1,356	1,041	920	811
BANJO	24	GIBSON	TB- 1 TENOR	1,359	1,044	922	813
BANJO	25	GIBSON	TB- 1 TENOR	1,356	1,041	920	811
BANJO	26	GIBSON	TB- 1 TENOR, DIAMOND HOLE FLANGE, SERIAL #82700-	1,896	1,455	1,286	1,134
BANJO	27	GIBSON	TB- 1 TENOR, DIAMOND HOLE FLANGE, SERIAL #-85400	1,895	1,455	1,285	1,133
BANJO	29	GIBSON	TB- 1 TENOR	1,359	1,044	922	813
BANJO	30	GIBSON	TB- 1 TENOR, 1 PIECE FLANGE	1,010	775	685	604
BANJO	30	GIBSON	TB- 1 TENOR, 1-PIECE FLANGE	1,027	788	696	614
BANJO	31	GIBSON	TB- 1 TENOR, HEXAGON HOLE FLANGE	1,896	1,455	1,286	1,134
BANJO	32	GIBSON	TB- 1 TENOR, 5-STRING, SERIAL #90400-90700	1,878	1,442	1,274	1,123
BANJO	38	GIBSON	TB- 1 TENOR	2,051	1,575	1,392	1,227
BANJO	30	GIBSON	TB- 1 REPLICA 5-STRING	1,615	1,240	1,095	966
BANJO	26	GIBSON	TB- 2 TENOR	1,396	1,072	947	835
BANJO	28	GIBSON	TB- 2 SERIAL #85400-87300	2,170	1,666	1,472	1,298
BANJO	30	GIBSON	TB- 2 CONVERSION 5-STRING, OPEN BACK	2,168	1,664	1,471	1,297
BANJO	29	GIBSON	TB- 2 TENOR	2,001	1,536	1,358	1,197
BANJO	23	GIBSON	TB- 3 TENOR, OPEN BACK	1,324	1,017	899	792
BANJO	24	GIBSON	TB- 3 TENOR, OPEN BACK, SERIAL #74900-80300	2,278	1,749	1,545	1,362
BANJO	25	GIBSON	TB- 3 TENOR, BALL BERING TONE RING	1,044	802	709	625
BANJO	25	GIBSON	TB- 3 TENOR, SERIAL #80300-82700	1,299	997	881	777
BANJO	26	GIBSON	TB- 3 5-STRING, SERIAL #82700-	1,758	1,350	1,193	1,051
BANJO	27	GIBSON	TB- 3 TENOR	3,308	2,540	2,245	1,979
BANJO	27	GIBSON	TB- 3 5-STRING CONVERSION, DUAL NECK	4,135	3,175	2,805	2,473
BANJO	28	GIBSON	TB- 3 5-STRING, SERIAL #85400-87300	2,340	1,797	1,588	1,400
BANJO	29	GIBSON	TB- 3 TENOR	2,047	1,572	1,389	1,224
BANJO	30	GIBSON	TB- 3 5-STRING, SERIAL #89800-90200	2,024	1,554	1,374	1,211
BANJO	25	GIBSON	TB- 3 MASTERTONE TENOR	3,170	2,434	2,151	1,896
BANJO	26	GIBSON	TB- 3 MASTERTONE TENOR	3,232	2,481	2,193	1,933
BANJO	27	GIBSON	TB- 3 MASTERTONE TENOR	3,020	2,319	2,049	1,806
BANJO	28	GIBSON	TB- 3 MASTERTONE TENOR, 2 PIECE FLANGE	2,988	2,294	2,027	1,787
BANJO	29	GIBSON	TB- 3 MASTERTONE TENOR	2,308	1,772	1,566	1,380
BANJO	30	GIBSON	TB- 3 MASTERTONE TENOR	1,802	1,383	1,222	1,078
BANJO	18	GIBSON	TB- 4 TENOR, SERIAL #39500-47900	1,624	1,247	1,102	971
BANJO	20	GIBSON	TB- 4 TENOR, 17-FRET, OPEN BACK	1,624	1,247	1,102	971
BANJO	22	GIBSON	TB- 4 TENOR	1,625	1,247	1,102	972
BANJO	23	GIBSON	TB- 4 TENOR	1,461	1,122	991	874
BANJO	24	GIBSON	TB- 4 TENOR, OPEN BACK	1,621	1,245	1,100	970
BANJO	25	GIBSON	TB- 4 TENOR, MAHOGANY NECK, RESONATOR	1,905	1,462	1,292	1,139
BANJO	26	GIBSON	TB- 4 TENOR, MAHOGANY NECK, RESONATOR, SERIAL #82700-	1,759	1,351	1,193	1,052
BANJO	29	GIBSON	TB- 4 TENOR, MAHOGANY, RESONATOR, SERIAL #87300-89800	2,139	1,642	1,451	1,279

TYPE	YR	MFG	PRICES--BASED ON 100% ORIGINAL MODEL	SELL EXC	SELL AVG	BUY EXC	BUY AVG
BANJO	32	GIBSON	TB- 4 TENOR	2,309	1,773	1,567	1,381
BANJO	32	GIBSON	TB- 4 TENOR, CURLY WALNUT NECK SERIAL #90400-90700	3,392	2,604	2,302	2,029
BANJO	32	GIBSON	TB- 4 WALNUT, FLYING EAGLE INLAY, 40-HOLE RAISED HEAD TONE RING	5,820	4,469	3,949	3,481
BANJO	24	GIBSON	TB- 4 JUNIOR TRAPDOOR TENOR	1,462	1,123	992	875
BANJO	25	GIBSON	TB- 4 MASTERTONE TENOR, SERIAL #80300-82700	2,038	1,565	1,383	1,219
BANJO	26	GIBSON	TB- 4 MASTERTONE TENOR	1,901	1,460	1,290	1,137
BANJO	24	GIBSON	TB- 4 TRAPDOOR TENOR, RESONATOR	1,621	1,245	1,100	970
BANJO	24	GIBSON	TB- 5 TENOR, SERIAL #74900-80300	3,594	2,759	2,438	2,150
BANJO	29	GIBSON	TB- 5 TENOR	4,794	3,681	3,253	2,868
BANJO	28	GIBSON	TB- 6 TENOR, SERIAL #85400-87300	10,273	7,888	6,971	6,145
BANJO	29	GIBSON	TB- 6 TENOR, SERIAL# 9226-34	8,215	6,308	5,574	4,914
BANJO	30	GIBSON	TB- 6 TENOR, 4 HOLE, RAISED HEAD, TONE RING	6,977	5,357	4,734	4,174
BANJO	31	GIBSON	TB- 6 TENOR	6,479	4,975	4,396	3,875
BANJO	35	GIBSON	TB- 11 5-STRING, SERIAL #92400-93500	3,300	2,534	2,239	1,974
BANJO	38	GIBSON	TB- 12 5-STRING, SERIAL #95400	11,186	8,589	7,590	6,691
BANJO	38	GIBSON	TB- 18 TENOR	30,572	23,475	20,745	18,288
BANJO	29	GIBSON	TB- 75 ARCHTOP	1,561	1,198	1,059	933
BANJO	50	GIBSON	TB-100 TENOR, SUNBURST, CURLY MAPLE	1,666	1,279	1,130	996
BANJO	62	GIBSON	TB-100 TENOR	984	755	668	588
BANJO	67	GIBSON	TB-100 TENOR	918	705	623	549
BANJO	68	GIBSON	TB-100 TENOR	842	646	571	503
BANJO	54	GIBSON	TB-250 MASTERTONE TENOR	1,506	1,156	1,022	901
BANJO	55	GIBSON	TB-250 MASTERTONE TENOR, SERIAL #A19000-A22000	1,494	1,147	1,013	893
BANJO	56	GIBSON	TB-250 MASTERTONE TENOR	1,572	1,207	1,067	940
BANJO	61	GIBSON	TB-250 MASTERTONE TENOR	1,230	945	835	736
BANJO	62	GIBSON	TB-250 MASTERTONE TENOR	1,256	964	852	751
BANJO	68	GIBSON	TB-250 MASTERTONE TENOR, SERIAL #959115	1,028	789	697	615
BANJO	69	GIBSON	TB-250 MASTERTONE TENOR, SERIAL #813724	1,018	781	690	609
BANJO	67	GIBSON	TB-500 MASTERTONE TENOR	1,568	1,204	1,064	938
BANJO	70	GIBSON	TB-800 TENOR, SUNBURST	1,534	1,178	1,041	917
BANJO	24	GIBSON	TB-JUNIOR TENOR, NATURAL, OPEN BACK	1,070	822	726	640
BANJO	30	GIBSON	TG- 1 TENOR, SUNBURST, SPRUCE TOP	1,324	1,017	899	792
BANJO	29	GIBSON	UB- 1 UKE-BANJO 8" HEAD	555	426	376	332
BANJO	30	GIBSON	UB- 1 UKE-BANJO FLAT RESONATOR, SERIAL #89800-90200	509	391	345	304
BANJO	28	GIBSON	UB- 2 UKE-BANJO 8" HEAD	567	436	385	339
BANJO	28	GIBSON	UB- 3 UKE-BANJO SUNBURST	1,016	780	690	608
BANJO	29	GIBSON	UB- 3 UKE-BANJO SUNBURST	1,012	777	687	605
ELEC. GUITAR & BASS	77	GIBSON	ARTISAN WALNUT	1,311	1,007	889	784
ELGUIT	81	GIBSON	B B KING CUSTOM	1,996	1,533	1,355	1,194
ELGUIT	85	GIBSON	B B KING CUSTOM	1,060	814	719	634
ELGUIT	85	GIBSON	B B KING STANDARD	1,335	1,025	905	798
ELGUIT	61	GIBSON	BARNEY KESSEL	5,913	4,540	4,012	3,537
ELGUIT	62	GIBSON	BARNEY KESSEL	3,032	2,328	2,058	1,814
ELGUIT	63	GIBSON	BARNEY KESSEL	3,160	2,426	2,144	1,890

TYPE	YR	MFG	PRICES--BASED ON 100% ORIGINAL MODEL	SELL EXC	SELL AVG	BUY EXC	BUY AVG
ELGUIT	64	GIBSON	**BARNEY KESSEL** NICKEL PARTS	3,763	**2,889**	2,553	2,251
ELGUIT	65	GIBSON	**BARNEY KESSEL**	2,197	**1,687**	1,491	1,314
ELGUIT	66	GIBSON	**BARNEY KESSEL** CHERRY SUNBURST	3,595	**2,760**	2,439	2,150
ELGUIT	67	GIBSON	**BARNEY KESSEL**	3,355	**2,576**	2,276	2,007
ELGUIT	68	GIBSON	**BARNEY KESSEL**	3,355	**2,576**	2,276	2,007
ELGUIT	69	GIBSON	**BARNEY KESSEL**	1,967	**1,511**	1,335	1,177
ELGUIT	61	GIBSON	**BARNEY KESSEL CUSTOM** SUNBURST	6,451	**4,953**	4,377	3,859
ELGUIT	66	GIBSON	**BARNEY KESSEL CUSTOM**	2,458	**1,887**	1,668	1,470
ELGUIT	66	GIBSON	**BARNEY KESSEL CUSTOM** SUNBURST, WHL MUSIC NOTE	3,763	**2,889**	2,553	2,251
ELGUIT	68	GIBSON	**BARNEY KESSEL CUSTOM** SUNBURST	2,345	**1,800**	1,591	1,402
ELGUIT	69	GIBSON	**BARNEY KESSEL CUSTOM** SUNBURST	3,320	**2,549**	2,253	1,986
ELGUIT	56	GIBSON	**BYRDLAND** NATURAL, P-90's, THINLINE ARCHTOP, SINGLE CUTAWAY	7,526	**5,779**	5,107	4,502
ELGUIT	56	GIBSON	**BYRDLAND** SUNBURST, P-90's, THINLINE ARCHTOP, SINGLE CUTAWAY	9,192	**7,058**	6,238	5,499
ELGUIT	57	GIBSON	**BYRDLAND** SUNBURST, P-90's, THINLINE ARCHTOP, SINGLE CUTAWAY	9,192	**7,058**	6,238	5,499
ELGUIT	57	GIBSON	**BYRDLAND** NATURAL, P-90's, THINLINE ARCHTOP, SINGLE CUTAWAY	11,886	**9,127**	8,065	7,110
ELGUIT	58	GIBSON	**BYRDLAND** SUNBURST, PAF's, THINLINE ARCHTOP, SINGLE CUTAWAY	9,438	**7,247**	6,404	5,646
ELGUIT	58	GIBSON	**BYRDLAND** NATURAL, PAF's, THINLINE ARCHTOP, SINGLE CUTAWAY	10,752	**8,256**	7,296	6,432
ELGUIT	59	GIBSON	**BYRDLAND** SUNBURST, PAF's, THINLINE ARCHTOP, SINGLE CUTAWAY	9,438	**7,247**	6,404	5,646
ELGUIT	59	GIBSON	**BYRDLAND** NATURAL, PAF's, THINLINE ARCHTOP, SINGLE CUTAWAY	10,752	**8,256**	7,296	6,432
ELGUIT	60	GIBSON	**BYRDLAND** NATURAL, PAF's, THINLINE ARCHTOP, SINGLE CUTAWAY	10,214	**7,843**	6,931	6,110
ELGUIT	60	GIBSON	**BYRDLAND** SUNBURST, PAF's, THINLINE ARCHTOP, SINGLE CUTAWAY	11,544	**8,864**	7,834	6,906
ELGUIT	61	GIBSON	**BYRDLAND** SUNBURST, PAF's, THINLINE ARCHTOP, SINGLE CUTAWAY	8,825	**6,776**	5,988	5,279
ELGUIT	61	GIBSON	**BYRDLAND** NATURAL, PAF's, THINLINE ARCHTOP, SINGLE CUTAWAY	9,676	**7,430**	6,566	5,788
ELGUIT	62	GIBSON	**BYRDLAND** SUNBURST, PAF's, THINLINE ARCHTOP, SINGLE CUTAWAY	8,825	**6,776**	5,988	5,279
ELGUIT	62	GIBSON	**BYRDLAND** NATURAL, PAF's, THINLINE ARCHTOP, SINGLE CUTAWAY	10,050	**7,717**	6,820	6,012
ELGUIT	63	GIBSON	**BYRDLAND** SUNBURST, PAF's, THINLINE ARCHTOP, SINGLE CUTAWAY	8,553	**6,567**	5,804	5,116
ELGUIT	63	GIBSON	**BYRDLAND** NATURAL, PAF's, THINLINE ARCHTOP, SINGLE CUTAWAY	9,139	**7,017**	6,201	5,467
ELGUIT	64	GIBSON	**BYRDLAND** SUNBURST, PAF's, THINLINE ARCHTOP, SINGLE CUTAWAY	8,550	**6,565**	5,801	5,114
ELGUIT	64	GIBSON	**BYRDLAND** NATURAL, PAF's, THINLINE ARCHTOP, SINGLE CUTAWAY	8,825	**6,776**	5,988	5,279
ELGUIT	65	GIBSON	**BYRDLAND** NATURAL, THINLINE ARCHTOP, SINGLE CUTAWAY	6,988	**5,366**	4,742	4,180
ELGUIT	65	GIBSON	**BYRDLAND** SUNBURST, THINLINE ARCHTOP, SINGLE CUTAWAY	7,776	**5,970**	5,276	4,651
ELGUIT	66	GIBSON	**BYRDLAND** SUNBURST, THINLINE ARCHTOP, SINGLE CUTAWAY	6,049	**4,644**	4,104	3,618
ELGUIT	66	GIBSON	**BYRDLAND** NATURAL, THINLINE ARCHTOP, SINGLE CUTAWAY	6,373	**4,894**	4,325	3,812
ELGUIT	67	GIBSON	**BYRDLAND** SUNBURST, THINLINE ARCHTOP, SINGLE CUTAWAY	5,718	**4,391**	3,880	3,421
ELGUIT	67	GIBSON	**BYRDLAND** NATURAL, THINLINE ARCHTOP, SINGLE CUTAWAY	6,666	**5,118**	4,523	3,987
ELGUIT	68	GIBSON	**BYRDLAND** SUNBURST, THINLINE ARCHTOP, SINGLE CUTAWAY	6,000	**4,607**	4,072	3,589
ELGUIT	68	GIBSON	**BYRDLAND** NATURAL, THINLINE ARCHTOP, SINGLE CUTAWAY	6,373	**4,894**	4,325	3,812
ELGUIT	69	GIBSON	**BYRDLAND** SUNBURST, THINLINE ARCHTOP, SINGLE CUTAWAY	5,147	**3,952**	3,492	3,079
ELGUIT	69	GIBSON	**BYRDLAND** NATURAL, THINLINE ARCHTOP, SINGLE CUTAWAY	6,373	**4,894**	4,325	3,812
ELGUIT	70	GIBSON	**BYRDLAND** VARIOUS COLORS, THINLINE ARCHTOP, SINGLE CUTAWAY	3,554	**2,729**	2,412	2,126
ELGUIT	70	GIBSON	**BYRDLAND** NATURAL, THINLINE ARCHTOP, SINGLE CUTAWAY	5,274	**4,049**	3,578	3,155
ELGUIT	71	GIBSON	**BYRDLAND** NATURAL, THINLINE ARCHTOP, SINGLE CUTAWAY	5,154	**3,957**	3,497	3,083
ELGUIT	72	GIBSON	**BYRDLAND** NATURAL, THINLINE ARCHTOP, SINGLE CUTAWAY	3,997	**3,069**	2,712	2,391
ELGUIT	72	GIBSON	**BYRDLAND** VARIOUS COLORS, THINLINE ARCHTOP, SINGLE CUTAWAY	4,363	**3,350**	2,960	2,610

TYPE	YR	MFG	PRICES--BASED ON 100% ORIGINAL MODEL	SELL EXC	SELL AVG	BUY EXC	BUY AVG
ELGUIT	73	GIBSON	**BYRDLAND** NATURAL, THINLINE ARCHTOP, SINGLE CUTAWAY	3,740	**2,872**	2,538	2,237
ELGUIT	74	GIBSON	**BYRDLAND** VARIOUS COLORS, THINLINE ARCHTOP, SINGLE CUTAWAY	3,676	**2,823**	2,495	2,199
ELGUIT	74	GIBSON	**BYRDLAND** NATURAL, THINLINE ARCHTOP, SINGLE CUTAWAY	4,307	**3,307**	2,922	2,576
ELGUIT	75	GIBSON	**BYRDLAND** NATURAL, THINLINE ARCHTOP, SINGLE CUTAWAY	4,908	**3,769**	3,331	2,936
ELGUIT	76	GIBSON	**BYRDLAND** NATURAL, THINLINE ARCHTOP, SINGLE CUTAWAY	3,676	**2,823**	2,495	2,199
ELGUIT	77	GIBSON	**BYRDLAND** NATURAL, THINLINE ARCHTOP, SINGLE CUTAWAY	4,300	**3,302**	2,918	2,572
ELGUIT	78	GIBSON	**BYRDLAND** NATURAL, THINLINE ARCHTOP, SINGLE CUTAWAY	3,554	**2,729**	2,412	2,126
ELGUIT	79	GIBSON	**BYRDLAND** NATURAL, THINLINE ARCHTOP, SINGLE CUTAWAY	3,615	**2,776**	2,453	2,162
ELGUIT	81	GIBSON	**BYRDLAND** VARIOUS COLORS, THINLINE ARCHTOP, SINGLE CUTAWAY	4,534	**3,482**	3,077	2,712
ELGUIT	59	GIBSON	**BYRDLAND CUSTOM** SUNBURST, 24 3/4", 2 PU's	10,752	**8,256**	7,296	6,432
ELGUIT	50	GIBSON	**CF-100 E** SUNBURST, FLATTOP, CUTAWAY, 1 PU	2,929	**2,249**	1,988	1,752
ELGUIT	51	GIBSON	**CF-100 E** SUNBURST, FLATTOP, CUTAWAY, 1 PU	2,158	**1,657**	1,464	1,291
ELGUIT	53	GIBSON	**CF-100 E** SUNBURST, FLATTOP, CUTAWAY, 1 PU, SERIAL #A13000-A16000	1,386	**1,064**	940	829
ELGUIT	54	GIBSON	**CF-100 E** SUNBURST, FLATTOP, CUTAWAY, 1 PU, SERIAL #A16000-A19000	1,385	**1,063**	940	828
ELGUIT	55	GIBSON	**CF-100 E** SUNBURST, FLATTOP, CUTAWAY, 1 PU	1,383	**1,062**	938	827
ELGUIT	56	GIBSON	**CF-100 E** SUNBURST, FLATTOP, CUTAWAY, 1 PU	1,380	**1,060**	937	826
ELGUIT	60	GIBSON	**CF-100 E** SUNBURST, FLATTOP, CUTAWAY, 1 PU	1,049	**805**	712	627
ELGUIT	34	GIBSON	**CHARLIE CHRISTIAN** SUNBURST	6,944	**5,332**	4,712	4,154
ELGUIT	82	GIBSON	**CHET ATKINS CE** NATURAL	1,211	**930**	822	724
ELGUIT	84	GIBSON	**CHET ATKINS CE** NATURAL	816	**626**	554	488
ELGUIT	84	GIBSON	**CHET ATKINS CE** WHITE	835	**641**	566	499
ELGUIT	85	GIBSON	**CHET ATKINS CEC** NATURAL	816	**626**	554	488
ELGUIT	87	GIBSON	**CHET ATKINS COUNTRY GENTLEMAN** WINE RED	2,016	**1,548**	1,368	1,206
ELGUIT	89	GIBSON	**CHET ATKINS SST-12** MAHOGANY/SPRUCE BODY, 12-STRING	1,680	**1,290**	1,140	1,005
ELGUIT	79	GIBSON	**CREST GOLD** BRAZILIAN RSWD BODY,DBL CUTAWAY,2 MINI HB,GOLD PLATED PARTS	3,993	**3,066**	2,710	2,389
ELGUIT	69	GIBSON	**CREST GOLD** BRAZILIAN RSWD BODY,DBL CUTAWAY,2 MINI HB,GOLD PLATED PARTS	2,996	**2,300**	2,033	1,792
ELGUIT	71	GIBSON	**CREST GOLD** BRAZILIAN RSWD BODY,DBL CUTAWAY,2 MINI HB,GOLD PLATED PARTS	2,996	**2,300**	2,033	1,792
ELGUIT	69	GIBSON	**CREST SILVER** BRAZILIAN ROSEWOOD, DBL CUTAWAY,SILVER PLATED PARTS	2,996	**2,300**	2,033	1,792
ELGUIT	70	GIBSON	**CREST SILVER** BRAZILIAN ROSEWOOD, DOUBLE CUTAWAY, SILVER PLATED PARTS	2,996	**2,300**	2,033	1,792
ELGUIT	71	GIBSON	**CREST SILVER** BRAZILIAN ROSEWOOD, DOUBLE CUTAWAY, SILVER PLATED PARTS	2,348	**1,803**	1,593	1,404
ELGUIT	72	GIBSON	**CREST SILVER** BRAZILIAN ROSEWOOD, DOUBLE CUTAWAY, SILVER PLATED PARTS	2,348	**1,803**	1,593	1,404
ELGUIT	59	GIBSON	**EB- 0 BASS** CHERRY, 1 HB, LES PAUL BODY	1,283	**985**	870	767
ELGUIT	60	GIBSON	**EB- 0 BASS** CHERRY, 1 HB, LES PAUL BODY	1,279	**982**	867	765
ELGUIT	61	GIBSON	**EB- 0 BASS** CHERRY, 1 HB, LES PAUL BODY	1,218	**935**	826	728
ELGUIT	62	GIBSON	**EB- 0 BASS** CHERRY, 1 HB, SINGLE BODY	563	**432**	382	337
ELGUIT	63	GIBSON	**EB- 0 BASS** CHERRY, 1 HB, SINGLE BODY	962	**738**	652	575
ELGUIT	64	GIBSON	**EB- 0 BASS** CHERRY, 1 HB, SINGLE BODY	957	**735**	649	572
ELGUIT	65	GIBSON	**EB- 0 BASS** CHERRY, 1 HB, SINGLE BODY	925	**710**	627	553
ELGUIT	65	GIBSON	**EB- 0 BASS** CARDINAL, 1 HB, SINGLE BODY	927	**712**	629	554
ELGUIT	66	GIBSON	**EB- 0 BASS** CHERRY, 1 HB, SINGLE BODY	963	**739**	653	576
ELGUIT	67	GIBSON	**EB- 0 BASS** CHERRY, 1 HB, SINGLE BODY	834	**640**	566	499
ELGUIT	68	GIBSON	**EB- 0 BASS** CHERRY, 1 HB, SINGLE BODY	695	**534**	471	416

TYPE	YR	MFG	PRICES--BASED ON 100% ORIGINAL MODEL	SELL EXC	SELL AVG	BUY EXC	BUY AVG
ELGUIT	69	GIBSON	**EB- 0 BASS** CHERRY, 1HB, SINGLE BODY	668	**513**	453	399
ELGUIT	69	GIBSON	**EB- 0 BASS** WALNUT, 1 HB, SINGLE BODY	668	**513**	453	399
ELGUIT	70	GIBSON	**EB- 0 BASS** CHERRY, 1 HB, SINGLE BODY	645	**495**	437	385
ELGUIT	70	GIBSON	**EB- 0 BASS** SPARKLING BURGUNDY. SINGLE BODY	645	**495**	437	385
ELGUIT	71	GIBSON	**EB- 0 BASS** WALNUT, 1 HB, SINGLE BODY	661	**508**	449	395
ELGUIT	72	GIBSON	**EB- 0 BASS** CHERRY, 1 HB, SINGLE BODY	669	**514**	454	400
ELGUIT	73	GIBSON	**EB- 0 BASS** CHERRY, 1HB, SINGLE BODY	663	**509**	449	396
ELGUIT	74	GIBSON	**EB- 0 BASS** CHERRY, 1 HB, SINGLE BODY	664	**509**	450	397
ELGUIT	63	GIBSON	**EB- 0F BASS**	1,013	**778**	687	606
ELGUIT	71	GIBSON	**EB- 0L BASS** CHERRY	657	**504**	446	393
ELGUIT	53	GIBSON	**EB- 1 BASS** NATURAL, 1 PU, VIOLIN SHAPE, SERIAL #A13000-A16000	3,472	**2,666**	2,356	2,077
ELGUIT	55	GIBSON	**EB- 1 BASS** VIOLIN SHAPE, SERIAL #A19000-A22000	1,779	**1,366**	1,207	1,064
ELGUIT	56	GIBSON	**EB- 1 BASS** BLACK, VIOLIN SHAPE, SERIAL #A22000-A24600	1,779	**1,366**	1,207	1,064
ELGUIT	57	GIBSON	**EB- 1 BASS** SOLID BODY	3,306	**2,538**	2,243	1,977
ELGUIT	58	GIBSON	**EB- 1 BASS** NATURAL, 1 PU, SOLID BODY	1,778	**1,365**	1,206	1,063
ELGUIT	69	GIBSON	**EB- 1 BASS** MOUNTAIN TONE, VIOLIN SHAPE	1,239	**952**	841	741
ELGUIT	70	GIBSON	**EB- 1 BASS** CONVENTIONAL TUNERS	963	**739**	653	576
ELGUIT	68	GIBSON	**EB- 2** SUNBURST	1,450	**1,113**	984	867
ELGUIT	58	GIBSON	**EB- 2 BASS** SUNBURST	2,117	**1,626**	1,437	1,266
ELGUIT	59	GIBSON	**EB- 2 BASS** NATURAL	1,958	**1,504**	1,329	1,171
ELGUIT	59	GIBSON	**EB- 2 BASS** SUNBURST	2,117	**1,626**	1,437	1,266
ELGUIT	60	GIBSON	**EB- 2 BASS** SUNBURST, SEMI-SOLID	1,304	**1,001**	885	780
ELGUIT	65	GIBSON	**EB- 2 BASS** SUNBURST, SEMI-SOLID	1,067	**819**	724	638
ELGUIT	65	GIBSON	**EB- 2 BASS** CHERRY	2,185	**1,677**	1,482	1,307
ELGUIT	66	GIBSON	**EB- 2 BASS** SUNBURST, HOLLOW BODY	955	**733**	648	571
ELGUIT	66	GIBSON	**EB- 2 BASS** TOBACCOBURST	1,041	**799**	706	623
ELGUIT	66	GIBSON	**EB- 2 BASS** CHERRY, 1 PU, RSWD FRTBRD, BARITONE SWITCH	1,386	**1,064**	940	829
ELGUIT	67	GIBSON	**EB- 2 BASS** SUNBURST, DOUBLE CUTAWAY	948	**728**	643	567
ELGUIT	67	GIBSON	**EB- 2 BASS** SPARKLING BURGUNDY	955	**733**	648	571
ELGUIT	67	GIBSON	**EB- 2 BASS** CHERRY	957	**735**	649	572
ELGUIT	67	GIBSON	**EB- 2 BASS** WALNUT	960	**737**	652	574
ELGUIT	68	GIBSON	**EB- 2 BASS** CHERRY	955	**733**	648	571
ELGUIT	68	GIBSON	**EB- 2 BASS** WALNUT	959	**737**	651	574
ELGUIT	69	GIBSON	**EB- 2 BASS** CHERRY	956	**734**	649	572
ELGUIT	70	GIBSON	**EB- 2 BASS** SUNBURST	954	**732**	647	570
ELGUIT	66	GIBSON	**EB- 2C BASS** CHERRY	1,252	**961**	849	749
ELGUIT	67	GIBSON	**EB- 2D BASS** SUNBURST	833	**639**	565	498
ELGUIT	67	GIBSON	**EB- 2D BASS** CHERRY, 2 PU's	1,324	**1,017**	899	792
ELGUIT	68	GIBSON	**EB- 2D BASS** SUNBURST, 2 PU's	1,033	**793**	701	618
ELGUIT	68	GIBSON	**EB- 2D BASS** WALNUT	1,311	**1,007**	889	784
ELGUIT	69	GIBSON	**EB- 2D BASS** WALNUT	1,069	**821**	725	639
ELGUIT	71	GIBSON	**EB- 2D BASS** WALNUT, 2 PU's	987	**758**	670	590

TYPE	YR	MFG	PRICES--BASED ON 100% ORIGINAL MODEL	SELL EXC	SELL AVG	BUY EXC	BUY AVG
ELGUIT	62	GIBSON	**EB- 3 BASS** CHERRY	1,995	**1,532**	1,354	1,193
ELGUIT	63	GIBSON	**EB- 3 BASS** CHERRY, SOLID PEGHEAD	1,324	**1,017**	899	792
ELGUIT	65	GIBSON	**EB- 3 BASS** SUNBURST, MUTE, 2 PU's	955	**733**	648	571
ELGUIT	65	GIBSON	**EB- 3 BASS** CHERRY, OWNED BY JEFFRY BEALS	1,271	**976**	862	760
ELGUIT	65	GIBSON	**EB- 3 BASS** CHERRY, SINGLE BODY	1,289	**989**	874	771
ELGUIT	67	GIBSON	**EB- 3 BASS** CHERRY	847	**651**	575	507
ELGUIT	68	GIBSON	**EB- 3 BASS** CHERRY	847	**651**	575	507
ELGUIT	69	GIBSON	**EB- 3 BASS** CHERRY	800	**614**	543	479
ELGUIT	70	GIBSON	**EB- 3 BASS** CHERRY	799	**614**	542	478
ELGUIT	71	GIBSON	**EB- 3 BASS** CHERRY	749	**575**	508	448
ELGUIT	71	GIBSON	**EB- 3 BASS** NATURAL/WALNUT FINISH,BLACK PICKGUARD,2 SINGLE COIL PU's	1,330	**1,021**	902	795
ELGUIT	72	GIBSON	**EB- 3 BASS** NATURAL MAHOGANY	776	**595**	526	464
ELGUIT	72	GIBSON	**EB- 3 BASS** WALNUT, SINGLE BODY, 2 PU's	835	**641**	566	499
ELGUIT	73	GIBSON	**EB- 3 BASS** WALNUT, SINGLE BODY	834	**640**	566	499
ELGUIT	73	GIBSON	**EB- 3 BASS** CHERRY, SOLID PEGHEAD	855	**657**	580	511
ELGUIT	74	GIBSON	**EB- 3 BASS** CHERRY STAIN, 2 PU's	742	**570**	503	444
ELGUIT	74	GIBSON	**EB- 3 BASS** WALNUT,BLACK PICKGUARD,RSWD FRTBRD, 2 HB, MED FRETS	1,218	**935**	826	728
ELGUIT	76	GIBSON	**EB- 3 BASS** WALNUT	803	**616**	544	480
ELGUIT	77	GIBSON	**EB- 3 BASS**	657	**504**	446	393
ELGUIT	70	GIBSON	**EB- 3L BASS** CHERRY	799	**614**	542	478
ELGUIT	71	GIBSON	**EB- 3L BASS** CHERRY	796	**611**	540	476
ELGUIT	71	GIBSON	**EB- 3L BASS** NATURAL	880	**675**	597	526
ELGUIT	73	GIBSON	**EB- 3L BASS** CHERRY	764	**587**	519	457
ELGUIT	72	GIBSON	**EB- 4L BASS** WALNUT	722	**554**	490	432
ELGUIT	60	GIBSON	**EB- 6 BASS** SUNBURST, SEMI-HOLLOW	3,204	**2,460**	2,174	1,916
ELGUIT	61	GIBSON	**EB- 6 BASS** SUNBURST	5,199	**3,992**	3,527	3,110
ELGUIT	63	GIBSON	**EB- 6 BASS** SINGLE BODY, 6-STRING	2,124	**1,631**	1,441	1,270
ELGUIT	65	GIBSON	**EB- 6 BASS** SINGLE BODY, 6-STRING	1,798	**1,381**	1,220	1,076
ELGUIT	62	GIBSON	**EBS-1250 DOUBLE BASS** DOUBLE CUTAWAY, SOLID BODY, DOUBLE NECK	8,457	**6,493**	5,738	5,059
ELGUIT	63	GIBSON	**EBS-1250 DOUBLE BASS** DOUBLE CUTAWAY, SOLID BODY, DOUBLE NECK	8,457	**6,493**	5,738	5,059
ELGUIT	64	GIBSON	**EBS-1250 DOUBLE BASS** DOUBLE CUTAWAY, SOLID BODY, DOUBLE NECK	8,457	**6,493**	5,738	5,059
ELGUIT	65	GIBSON	**EBS-1250 DOUBLE BASS** DBL CUTAWAY, SOLID BODY, DOUBLE NECK	6,006	**4,612**	4,075	3,593
ELGUIT	66	GIBSON	**EBS-1250 DOUBLE BASS** DBL CUTAWAY, SOLID BODY, DOUBLE NECK	6,006	**4,612**	4,075	3,593
ELGUIT	67	GIBSON	**EBS-1250 DOUBLE BASS** DBL CUTAWAY, SOLID BODY, DOUBLE NECK	5,392	**4,140**	3,659	3,226
ELGUIT	68	GIBSON	**EBS-1250 DOUBLE BASS** DBL CUTAWAY, SOLID BODY, DOUBLE NECK	5,392	**4,140**	3,659	3,226
ELGUIT	69	GIBSON	**EBS-1250 DOUBLE BASS** DBL CUTAWAY, SOLID BODY, DOUBLE NECK	5,392	**4,140**	3,659	3,226
ELGUIT	70	GIBSON	**EBS-1250 DOUBLE BASS** DBL CUTAWAY, SOLID BODY, DOUBLE NECK	4,167	**3,200**	2,827	2,493
ELGUIT	58	GIBSON	**EDS-1275 DOUBLE 12** SUNBURST, 6 & 12-STRING, DOUBLE CUTAWAY, DOUBLE NECK	15,014	**11,529**	10,188	8,982
ELGUIT	58	GIBSON	**EDS-1275 DOUBLE 12** BLACK or CHERRY, DBLE CUT DBL NECK, ONE 12, ONE 6 STRING	16,464	**12,642**	11,172	9,849
ELGUIT	59	GIBSON	**EDS-1275 DOUBLE 12** SUNBURST, 6 & 12-STRING, DOUBLE CUTAWAY, DOUBLE NECK	15,014	**11,529**	10,188	8,982
ELGUIT	59	GIBSON	**EDS-1275 DOUBLE 12** BLACK or CHERRY, DBLE CUT DBL NECK, ONE 12, ONE 6 STRING	17,517	**13,451**	11,887	10,479
ELGUIT	59	GIBSON	**EDS-1275 DOUBLE 12** WHITE, 6 & 12-STRING, DOUBLE CUTAWAY, DOUBLE NECK	19,208	**14,749**	13,034	11,490

TYPE	YR	MFG	PRICES--BASED ON 100% ORIGINAL MODEL	SELL EXC	SELL AVG	BUY EXC	BUY AVG
ELGUIT	60	GIBSON	**EDS-1275 DOUBLE 12** SUNBURST, 6 & 12-STRING, DOUBLE CUTAWAY, DOUBLE NECK	12,512	**9,607**	8,490	7,485
ELGUIT	60	GIBSON	**EDS-1275 DOUBLE 12** BLACK or CHERRY, DBLE CUT DBL NECK, ONE 12, ONE 6 STRING	16,266	**12,490**	11,038	9,731
ELGUIT	60	GIBSON	**EDS-1275 DOUBLE 12** WHITE, 6 & 12-STRING, DOUBLE CUTAWAY, DOUBLE NECK	17,517	**13,451**	11,887	10,479
ELGUIT	61	GIBSON	**EDS-1275 DOUBLE 12** SUNBURST, 6 & 12-STRING, DOUBLE CUTAWAY, DOUBLE NECK	12,512	**9,607**	8,490	7,485
ELGUIT	61	GIBSON	**EDS-1275 DOUBLE 12** BLACK or CHERRY, DBLE CUT DBL NECK, ONE 12, ONE 6 STRING	16,266	**12,490**	11,038	9,731
ELGUIT	61	GIBSON	**EDS-1275 DOUBLE 12** WHITE, 6 & 12-STRING, DOUBLE CUTAWAY, DOUBLE NECK	17,517	**13,451**	11,887	10,479
ELGUIT	62	GIBSON	**EDS-1275 DOUBLE 12** SUNBURST, 6 & 12-STRING, DOUBLE CUTAWAY, DOUBLE NECK	12,512	**9,607**	8,490	7,485
ELGUIT	62	GIBSON	**EDS-1275 DOUBLE 12** BLACK or CHERRY, DBLE CUT DBL NECK, ONE 12, ONE 6 STRING	16,266	**12,490**	11,038	9,731
ELGUIT	62	GIBSON	**EDS-1275 DOUBLE 12** WHITE, 6 & 12-STRING, DOUBLE CUTAWAY, DOUBLE NECK	17,517	**13,451**	11,887	10,479
ELGUIT	68	GIBSON	**EDS-1275 DOUBLE 12** BLACK or CHERRY, 6 & 12-STRING, DOUBLE CUTAWAY, DOUBLE NECK	6,128	**4,705**	4,158	3,666
ELGUIT	68	GIBSON	**EDS-1275 DOUBLE 12** WHITE, 6 & 12-STRING, DOUBLE CUTAWAY, DOUBLE NECK	7,231	**5,553**	4,907	4,326
ELGUIT	68	GIBSON	**EDS-1275 DOUBLE 12** JIMMY PAGE EXACT SPECS	8,457	**6,493**	5,738	5,059
ELGUIT	77	GIBSON	**EDS-1275 DOUBLE 12** SUNBURST, WHITE or WALNUT, 6 & 12-STRING, DBL CUT, DBL NECK	2,466	**1,893**	1,673	1,475
ELGUIT	78	GIBSON	**EDS-1275 DOUBLE 12** SUNBURST, WHITE or WALNUT, 6 & 12-STRING, DBL CUT, DBL NECK	2,466	**1,893**	1,673	1,475
ELGUIT	79	GIBSON	**EDS-1275 DOUBLE 12** SUNBURST, WHITE or WALNUT, 6 & 12 STRING, DDL CUT, DBL NECK	2,466	**1,893**	1,673	1,475
ELGUIT	80	GIBSON	**EDS-1275 DOUBLE 12** SUNBURST, WHITE or WALNUT, 6 & 12-STRING, DBL CUT DBL NECK	2,996	**2,300**	2,033	1,792
ELGUIT	81	GIBSON	**EDS-1275 DOUBLE 12** SUNBURST, WHITE or WALNUT, 6 & 12-STRING, DBL CUT, DBL NECK	2,231	**1,713**	1,513	1,334
ELGUIT	56	GIBSON	**ELECTRIC BASS** BROWN STAIN, BANJO TUNERS	2,381	**1,828**	1,615	1,424
ELGUIT	80	GIBSON	**ES ARTIST** SUNBURST, ACTIVE ELECTRONICS	1,005	**772**	682	601
ELGUIT	49	GIBSON	**ES- 5** SUNBURST, 3 PU's, SERIAL #A2800-A4400	6,084	**4,672**	4,129	3,640
ELGUIT	49	GIBSON	**ES- 5** NATURAL, 3 PU's, SERIAL #A2800-A4400	8,848	**6,794**	6,004	5,293
ELGUIT	50	GIBSON	**ES- 5** SUNBURST, 3 PU's, SERIAL #A4400-A6000	6,552	**5,031**	4,446	3,919
ELGUIT	51	GIBSON	**ES- 5** SUNBURST, 3 PU's, SERIAL #A6000-A9400	6,067	**4,658**	4,116	3,629
ELGUIT	51	GIBSON	**ES- 5** NATURAL, 3 PU's, SERIAL #A6000-A9400	7,508	**5,765**	5,095	4,491
ELGUIT	52	GIBSON	**ES- 5** SUNBURST, 3 PU's, SERIAL #A9400-A13000	6,868	**5,274**	4,661	4,109
ELGUIT	52	GIBSON	**ES- 5** NATURAL, 3 PU's, SERIAL #A9400-A13000	7,213	**5,539**	4,895	4,315
ELGUIT	53	GIBSON	**ES- 5** SUNBURST, 3 PU's, SERIAL #A13000-A16000	5,994	**4,602**	4,067	3,585
ELGUIT	53	GIBSON	**ES- 5** NATURAL, 3 PU's, SERIAL #A13000-A16000	7,340	**5,636**	4,981	4,391
ELGUIT	54	GIBSON	**ES- 5** SUNBURST, 3 PU's, SERIAL #A16000-A19000	5,909	**4,537**	4,009	3,534
ELGUIT	54	GIBSON	**ES- 5** NATURAL, 3 PU's, SERIAL #A16000-A19000	7,340	**5,636**	4,981	4,391
ELGUIT	55	GIBSON	**ES- 5 SWITCHMASTER** SUNBURST, 3 PU's, SERIAL #A19000-A22000	10,066	**7,729**	6,830	6,021
ELGUIT	56	GIBSON	**ES- 5 SWITCHMASTER** SUNBURST, 3 PU's, SERIAL #A22000-A24600	10,256	**7,875**	6,960	6,135
ELGUIT	57	GIBSON	**ES- 5 SWITCHMASTER** SUNBURST, 3 PU's, PAF	11,762	**9,031**	7,981	7,036
ELGUIT	57	GIBSON	**ES- 5 SWITCHMASTER** NATURAL 3 PU's, PAF	12,737	**9,780**	8,643	7,619
ELGUIT	58	GIBSON	**ES- 5 SWITCHMASTER** SUNBURST, 3 PU's, PAF	11,776	**9,042**	7,991	7,045
ELGUIT	59	GIBSON	**ES- 5 SWITCHMASTER** BLOND	9,836	**7,553**	6,675	5,884
ELGUIT	59	GIBSON	**ES- 5 SWITCHMASTER** NATURAL, 3 PU's, PAF	12,101	**9,292**	8,211	7,239
ELGUIT	59	GIBSON	**ES- 5 SWITCHMASTER** SUNBURST, 3 PU's, SERIAL #A28000/PAF	14,067	**10,801**	9,545	8,415
ELGUIT	60	GIBSON	**ES- 5 SWITCHMASTER** SUNBURST, PAF	11,404	**8,757**	7,739	6,822
ELGUIT	60	GIBSON	**ES- 5 SWITCHMASTER** NATURAL, 3 PU's, PAF	13,853	**10,637**	9,400	8,287
ELGUIT	60	GIBSON	**ES- 5 SWITCHMASTER** BLOND	17,137	**13,158**	11,628	10,251
ELGUIT	55	GIBSON	**ES- 5N** BLOND	10,416	**7,998**	7,068	6,231

TYPE	YR	MFG	PRICES--BASED ON 100% ORIGINAL MODEL	SELL EXC	SELL AVG	BUY EXC	BUY AVG
ELGUIT	57	GIBSON	**ES- 5N SWITCHMASTER** SUNBURST, 3 PAF's,	11,942	**9,170**	8,103	7,144
ELGUIT	57	GIBSON	**ES- 5N SWITCHMASTER** NATURAL, 3 PAF's, CURLY MAPLE	17,871	**13,723**	12,127	10,691
ELGUIT	38	GIBSON	**ES-100 ELECTRIC ACOUSTIC** SUNBURST, SERIAL #-96000	1,262	**969**	856	755
ELGUIT	39	GIBSON	**ES-100 ELECTRIC ACOUSTIC** SUNBURST, BAR PU	1,288	**989**	874	770
ELGUIT	41	GIBSON	**ES-100 ELECTRIC ACOUSTIC** SUNBURST, SERIAL #96000-96600	975	**749**	661	583
ELGUIT	61	GIBSON	**ES-120 T** SUNBURST, NON-CUTAWAY, THINLINE, 1 PU	645	**495**	437	385
ELGUIT	62	GIBSON	**ES-120 T** SUNBURST, NON-CUTAWAY, THINLINE, 1 PU	645	**495**	437	385
ELGUIT	63	GIBSON	**ES-120 T** SUNBURST, NON-CUTAWAY, THINLINE, 1 PU, SERIAL #118802	645	**495**	437	385
ELGUIT	64	GIBSON	**ES-120 T** SUNBURST, NON-CUTAWAY, THINLINE, 1 PU	618	**474**	419	369
ELGUIT	65	GIBSON	**ES-120 T** SUNBURST, NON-CUTAWAY, THINLINE, 1 PU	618	**474**	419	369
ELGUIT	66	GIBSON	**ES-120 T** SUNBURST, NON-CUTAWAY, THINLINE, 1 PU	591	**454**	401	353
ELGUIT	67	GIBSON	**ES-120 T** SUNBURST, NON-CUTAWAY, THINLINE 1 PU	591	**454**	401	353
ELGUIT	68	GIBSON	**ES-120 T** SUNBURST, NON-CUTAWAY, THINLINE 1 PU	591	**454**	401	353
ELGUIT	41	GIBSON	**ES-125** SUNBURST, NON-CUTAWAY, THICK, 1 PU	1,797	**1,380**	1,219	1,075
ELGUIT	47	GIBSON	**ES-125** MAHOGANY, NON-CUTAWAY, THICK, 1 PU	1,677	**1,288**	1,138	1,003
ELGUIT	47	GIBSON	**ES-125** SUNBURST, NON-CUTAWAY, THICK, 1 PU	1,677	**1,288**	1,138	1,003
ELGUIT	48	GIBSON	**ES-125** SUNBURST, NON-CUTAWAY, THICK, 1 PU	1,677	**1,288**	1,138	1,003
ELGUIT	49	GIBSON	**ES-125** MAHOGANY, NON-CUTAWAY, THICK, 1 PU	1,677	**1,288**	1,138	1,003
ELGUIT	49	GIBSON	**ES-125** SUNBURST, NON-CUTAWAY, THICK, 1 PU	1,677	**1,288**	1,138	1,003
ELGUIT	50	GIBSON	**ES-125** SUNBURST, NON-CUTAWAY, THICK, 1 PU	1,677	**1,288**	1,138	1,003
ELGUIT	51	GIBSON	**ES-125** SUNBURST, NON-CUTAWAY, THICK, 1 PU	1,677	**1,288**	1,138	1,003
ELGUIT	52	GIBSON	**ES-125** SUNBURST, NON-CUTAWAY, THICK, 1 PU	1,677	**1,288**	1,138	1,003
ELGUIT	53	GIBSON	**ES-125** SUNBURST, NON-CUTAWAY, THICK, 1 PU, SERIAL #A13000-A16000	1,677	**1,288**	1,138	1,003
ELGUIT	54	GIBSON	**ES-125** SUNBURST, NON-CUTAWAY, THICK, 1 PU, SERIAL #A16000-A19000	1,677	**1,288**	1,138	1,003
ELGUIT	55	GIBSON	**ES-125** SUNBURST, NON-CUTAWAY, THICK, 1 PU, SERIAL #A19000-A22000	1,677	**1,288**	1,138	1,003
ELGUIT	56	GIBSON	**ES-125** SUNBURST, NON-CUTAWAY, THICK, 1 PU	1,677	**1,288**	1,138	1,003
ELGUIT	57	GIBSON	**ES-125** SUNBURST, NON-CUTAWAY, THICK, 1 PU	1,677	**1,288**	1,138	1,003
ELGUIT	58	GIBSON	**ES-125** SUNBURST, NON-CUTAWAY, THICK, 1 PU, SERIAL #A26500-A28000	1,677	**1,288**	1,138	1,003
ELGUIT	59	GIBSON	**ES-125** SUNBURST, NON-CUTAWAY, THICK, 1 PU	1,677	**1,288**	1,138	1,003
ELGUIT	61	GIBSON	**ES-125** SUNBURST, NON-CUTAWAY, THICK, 1 PU	1,557	**1,196**	1,057	931
ELGUIT	62	GIBSON	**ES-125** SUNBURST, NON-CUTAWAY, THICK, 1 PU	1,557	**1,196**	1,057	931
ELGUIT	63	GIBSON	**ES-125** SUNUBRST, NON-CUTAWAY, THICK, 1 PU	1,557	**1,196**	1,057	931
ELGUIT	64	GIBSON	**ES-125** SUNBURST, NON-CUTAWAY, THICK, 1 PU	1,557	**1,196**	1,057	931
ELGUIT	65	GIBSON	**ES-125** SUNBURST, NON-CUTAWAY, THICK, 1 PU	1,557	**1,196**	1,057	931
ELGUIT	66	GIBSON	**ES-125** SUNBURST, NON-CUTAWAY, THICK, 1 PU	1,557	**1,196**	1,057	931
ELGUIT	67	GIBSON	**ES-125** SUNBURST, NON-CUTAWAY, THICK, 1 PU	1,557	**1,196**	1,057	931
ELGUIT	57	GIBSON	**ES-125 3/4** SUNBURST, NON-CUTAWAY, THIN, 13" WIDE	1,198	**920**	813	716
ELGUIT	59	GIBSON	**ES-125 3/4** SUNBURST, NON-CUTAWAY, THIN, 13" WIDE	1,198	**920**	813	716
ELGUIT	61	GIBSON	**ES-125 3/4** SUNBURST, NON-CUTAWAY, THIN, 13" WIDE	860	**660**	583	514
ELGUIT	64	GIBSON	**ES-125 3/4** SUNBURST, NON-CUTAWAY, THIN, 13" WIDE	860	**660**	583	514
ELGUIT	65	GIBSON	**ES-125 3/4** SUNBURST, NON-CUTAWAY, THIN, 13" WIDE	860	**660**	583	514
ELGUIT	67	GIBSON	**ES-125 3/4** SUNBURST, NON-CUTAWAY, THIN, 13" WIDE	806	**619**	547	482

2006 WINTER VINTAGE GUITARS & COLLECTIBLES BLUE BOOK

GIBSON

TYPE	YR	MFG	MODEL	SELL EXC	SELL AVG	BUY EXC	BUY AVG
ELGUIT	68	GIBSON	ES-125C SUNBURST, CUTAWAY, THICK 1 PU	1,071	**823**	727	641
ELGUIT	66	GIBSON	ES-125CD SUNBURST, THICK CUTAWAY, 2 PU's	1,591	**1,222**	1,079	952
ELGUIT	69	GIBSON	ES-125CD	1,253	**962**	850	749
ELGUIT	56	GIBSON	ES-125D SUNBURST, W/ ORIGINAL PU GUARD	2,010	**1,543**	1,364	1,202
ELGUIT	56	GIBSON	ES-125T SUNBURST, NON-CUTAWAY, THIN, 1 PU, SERIAL #A22000-A24600	1,438	**1,104**	975	860
ELGUIT	57	GIBSON	ES-125T SUNBURST, NON-CUTAWAY, THIN, 1 PU	1,438	**1,104**	975	860
ELGUIT	58	GIBSON	ES-125T SUNBURST, NON-CUTAWAY, THIN, 1 PU, SERIAL #A24600-A26500	1,438	**1,104**	975	860
ELGUIT	59	GIBSON	ES-125T SUNBURST, NON-CUTAWAY, THIN, 1 PU	1,438	**1,104**	975	860
ELGUIT	60	GIBSON	ES-125T SUNBURST, NON-CUTAWAY, THIN, 1 PU	1,318	**1,012**	894	788
ELGUIT	61	GIBSON	ES-125T SUNBURST, NON-CUTAWAY, THIN, 1 PU	1,318	**1,012**	894	788
ELGUIT	63	GIBSON	ES-125T SUNBURST, NON-CUTAWAY, THIN, 1 PU	1,318	**1,012**	894	788
ELGUIT	64	GIBSON	ES-125T SUNBURST, NON-CUTAWAY, THIN, 1 PU	1,318	**1,012**	894	788
ELGUIT	65	GIBSON	ES-125T SUNBURST, NON-CUTAWAY, THIN, 1 PU	764	**587**	519	457
ELGUIT	66	GIBSON	ES-125T SUNBURST, NON-CUTAWAY, THIN, 1 PU	756	**580**	513	452
ELGUIT	67	GIBSON	ES-125T SUNBURST, NON-CUTAWAY, THIN, 1 PU	745	**572**	506	446
ELGUIT	68	GIBSON	ES-125T SUNBURST, NON-CUTAWAY, THIN, 1 PU	1,198	**920**	813	716
ELGUIT	69	GIBSON	ES-125T SUNBURST, NON-CUTAWAY, THIN, 1 PU	725	**557**	492	434
ELGUIT	60	GIBSON	ES-125T 3/4	896	**688**	608	536
ELGUIT	61	GIBSON	ES-125T 3/4 SUNBURST, 1 P-90 PU	987	**758**	670	590
ELGUIT	60	GIBSON	ES-125TC SUNBURST, CUTAWAY, THIN, 1 PU	1,557	**1,196**	1,057	931
ELGUIT	61	GIBSON	ES-125TC CHERRY SUNBURST, CUTAWAY, THIN HOLLOW BODY, 1 P-90 PU	1,557	**1,196**	1,057	931
ELGUIT	62	GIBSON	ES-125TC SUNBURST, CUTAWAY, THIN, 1 PU	1,557	**1,196**	1,057	931
ELGUIT	63	GIBSON	ES-125TC CHERRY SUNBURST, CUTAWAY THIN BODY, 1 P-90 PU	1,226	**941**	832	733
ELGUIT	64	GIBSON	ES-125TC SUNBURST, CUTAWAY, THIN, 1 PU	1,498	**1,150**	1,016	896
ELGUIT	65	GIBSON	ES-125TC SUNBURST, CUTAWAY, THIN, 1 PU	1,498	**1,150**	1,016	896
ELGUIT	66	GIBSON	ES-125TC SUNBURST, CUTAWAY, THIN, 1 PU	1,438	**1,104**	975	860
ELGUIT	67	GIBSON	ES-125TC SUNBURST, CUTAWAY, THIN, 1 PU	1,438	**1,104**	975	860
ELGUIT	68	GIBSON	ES-125TC SUNBURST, CUTAWAY, THIN, 1 PU	1,438	**1,104**	975	860
ELGUIT	57	GIBSON	ES-125TD SUNBURST, NON-CUTAWAY, THIN, 2 PU's	975	**749**	661	583
ELGUIT	58	GIBSON	ES-125TD SUNBURST, NON-CUTAWAY, THIN, 2 PU's, SERIAL #A26500-A28000	1,008	**774**	684	603
ELGUIT	59	GIBSON	ES-125TD SUNBURST, NON-CUTAWAY, THIN, 2 PU's, SERIAL #A28000	992	**761**	673	593
ELGUIT	60	GIBSON	ES-125TD SUNBURST, NON-CUTAWAY, THIN, 2 PU's	969	**744**	658	580
ELGUIT	61	GIBSON	ES-125TD SUNBURST, NON-CUTAWAY, THIN, 2 PU's	909	**698**	617	544
ELGUIT	62	GIBSON	ES-125TD SUNBURST, NON-CUTAWAY, THIN, 2 PU's	1,226	**941**	832	733
ELGUIT	63	GIBSON	ES-125TD SUNBURST, NON-CUTAWAY, THIN, 2 PU's	990	**760**	671	592
ELGUIT	60	GIBSON	ES-125TDC	1,904	**1,462**	1,292	1,139
ELGUIT	61	GIBSON	ES-125TDC SUNBURST, CUTAWAY, THIN, 2 PU's	1,677	**1,288**	1,138	1,003
ELGUIT	62	GIBSON	ES-125TDC SUNBURST, CUTAWAY, THIN, 2 PU's	1,677	**1,288**	1,138	1,003
ELGUIT	63	GIBSON	ES-125TDC SUNBURST, CUTAWAY, THIN, 2 PU's	1,677	**1,288**	1,138	1,003
ELGUIT	65	GIBSON	ES-125TDC SUNBURST, CUTAWAY, THIN, 2 PU's	1,618	**1,242**	1,098	968
ELGUIT	67	GIBSON	ES-125TDC SUNBURST, CUTAWAY, THIN, 2 PU's	1,557	**1,196**	1,057	931
ELGUIT	69	GIBSON	ES-125TDC SUNBURST, CUTAWAY, THIN, 2 PU's	1,498	**1,150**	1,016	896
ELGUIT	70	GIBSON	ES-125TDC	1,568	**1,204**	1,064	938
ELGUIT	55	GIBSON	ES-130 SUNBURST, P-90 PU, INLAY, BOUND NECK	1,456	**1,118**	988	871

TYPE	YR	MFG	PRICES--BASED ON 100% ORIGINAL MODEL	SELL EXC	SELL AVG	BUY EXC	BUY AVG
ELGUIT	56	GIBSON	**ES-135**	881	**676**	598	527
ELGUIT	50	GIBSON	**ES-140 3/4** SUNBURST, SINGLE CUT, 1 PU	1,350	**1,037**	916	808
ELGUIT	51	GIBSON	**ES-140 3/4** SUNBURST, SINGLE CUT, 1 PU, SERIAL #A6000-A9400	1,382	**1,061**	937	826
ELGUIT	52	GIBSON	**ES-140 3/4** SUNBURST, SINGLE CUT, 1 PU. SERIAL #A9400-A13000	1,375	**1,056**	933	822
ELGUIT	53	GIBSON	**ES-140 3/4** SUNBURST, SINGLE CUT, 1 PU, SERIAL #A13000-A16000	1,453	**1,116**	986	869
ELGUIT	54	GIBSON	**ES-140 3/4** SUNBURST, SINGLE CUT, 1 PU, SERIAL #A16000-A19000	1,454	**1,117**	987	870
ELGUIT	55	GIBSON	**ES-140 3/4** SUNBURST, SINGLE, CUT, 1 PU, SERIAL #A19000-A22000	1,449	**1,112**	983	866
ELGUIT	56	GIBSON	**ES-140 3/4** SUNBURST, SINGLE, CUT, 1 PU, SERIAL #A22000-A24600	1,445	**1,110**	981	864
ELGUIT	57	GIBSON	**ES-140 3/4** SUNBURST, SINGLE CUTAWAY, THIN BODY, 1 PU	1,387	**1,065**	941	830
ELGUIT	57	GIBSON	**ES-140 3/4** NATURAL, SINGLE, CUT, 1 PU, SERIAL #A24600-A26500	1,725	**1,325**	1,171	1,032
ELGUIT	59	GIBSON	**ES-140 3/4T** SUNBURST, LEFT-HANDED	1,040	**798**	706	622
ELGUIT	59	GIBSON	**ES-140 3/4T** SUNBURST, SINGLE CUT, 1 PU, SERIAL #A28000	1,211	**930**	822	724
ELGUIT	60	GIBSON	**ES-140 3/4T** SUNBURST	1,013	**778**	687	606
ELGUIT	62	GIBSON	**ES-140 3/4T** SUNBURST, SINGLE CUT, 1 PU	1,038	**797**	704	621
ELGUIT	62	GIBSON	**ES-140 3/4T**	1,472	**1,130**	999	881
ELGUIT	63	GIBSON	**ES-140 3/4T** SUNBURST, SINGLE CUT	1,336	**1,025**	906	799
ELGUIT	65	GIBSON	**ES-140 3/4T** SUNBURST, SINGLE CUT, 1 PU	991	**761**	672	592
ELGUIT	66	GIBSON	**ES-140 3/4T** SUNBURST, SINGLE CUT, 1 PU	1,270	**975**	861	759
ELGUIT	68	GIBSON	**ES-140 3/4T** SUNBURST, 1 PU	1,265	**971**	858	757
ELGUIT	68	GIBSON	**ES-140 3/4T** SUNBURST, L5-STYLE	1,760	**1,351**	1,194	1,053
ELGUIT	61	GIBSON	**ES-140TC** TINY SUNBURST	1,065	**805**	710	588
ELGUIT	59	GIBSON	**ES-140TD** SUNBURST, 2 PU's	3,077	**2,363**	2,088	1,841
ELGUIT	35	GIBSON	**ES-150** SUNBURST, CHARLIE CHRISTIAN PU	5,615	**4,312**	3,810	3,359
ELGUIT	36	GIBSON	**ES-150** SUNBURST, CHARLIE CHRISTIAN PU	5,989	**4,599**	4,064	3,583
ELGUIT	37	GIBSON	**ES-150** CHARLIE CHRISTIAN PU	4,424	**3,397**	3,002	2,646
ELGUIT	38	GIBSON	**ES-150** SUNBURST, CHARLIE CHRISTIAN PU, SERIAL #95400	4,297	**3,299**	2,916	2,570
ELGUIT	39	GIBSON	**ES-150** SUNBURST, CHARLIE CHRISTIAN PU, SERIAL #-96000	3,311	**2,543**	2,247	1,981
ELGUIT	40	GIBSON	**ES-150** SUNBURST, CHARLIE CHRISTIAN PU, SERIAL #96000-96600	3,536	**2,715**	2,400	2,115
ELGUIT	46	GIBSON	**ES-150** SUNBURST, P-90 PU	3,454	**2,652**	2,343	2,066
ELGUIT	47	GIBSON	**ES-150** SUNBURST, P-90 PU, SERIAL #-A1400	3,188	**2,448**	2,163	1,907
ELGUIT	48	GIBSON	**ES-150** SUNBURST, P-90 PU, SERIAL #A1400-A2800	3,161	**2,427**	2,145	1,891
ELGUIT	49	GIBSON	**ES-150** SUNBURST, P-90 PU, SERIAL #A2800-A4400	3,297	**2,531**	2,237	1,972
ELGUIT	50	GIBSON	**ES-150** SUNBURST, P-90 PU, SERIAL #A4400-A6000	3,170	**2,434**	2,151	1,896
ELGUIT	51	GIBSON	**ES-150** SUNBURST, P-90 PU, SERIAL #A2800-A4400	3,153	**2,421**	2,140	1,886
ELGUIT	52	GIBSON	**ES-150** SUNBURST, P-90 PU	3,194	**2,452**	2,167	1,910
ELGUIT	53	GIBSON	**ES-150** SUNBURST, P-90 PU	2,276	**1,748**	1,545	1,362
ELGUIT	54	GIBSON	**ES-150** SUNBURST, P-90 PU, SERIAL #A16000-A19000	2,111	**1,621**	1,432	1,262
ELGUIT	69	GIBSON	**ES-150** WALNUT	1,574	**1,209**	1,068	942
ELGUIT	71	GIBSON	**ES-150** WALNUT	1,570	**1,205**	1,065	939
ELGUIT	70	GIBSON	**ES-150D** WALNUT	1,431	**1,099**	971	856
ELGUIT	52	GIBSON	**ES-150DC** SUNBURST, DOUBLE CUT, 1 PU	1,889	**1,450**	1,282	1,130
ELGUIT	69	GIBSON	**ES-150DC** WALNUT, DOUBLE CUT, 2 HB	1,484	**1,139**	1,007	887
ELGUIT	70	GIBSON	**ES-150DC** NATURAL, DOUBLE CUT, 2 HB	1,242	**953**	842	743

TYPE	YR	MFG	PRICES--BASED ON 100% ORIGINAL MODEL	SELL EXC	SELL AVG	BUY EXC	BUY AVG
ELGUIT	70	GIBSON	**ES-150DC** WALNUT, DOUBLE CUT, 2 HB	1,273	**977**	864	761
ELGUIT	70	GIBSON	**ES-150DC** CHERRY, DOUBLE CUT, 2 HB	1,448	**1,111**	982	866
ELGUIT	71	GIBSON	**ES-150DC** NATURAL, DOUBLE CUT, 2 HB	1,229	**944**	834	735
ELGUIT	71	GIBSON	**ES-150DC** WALNUT, DOUBLE CUT, 2 HB, SERIAL #727976	1,431	**1,099**	971	856
ELGUIT	72	GIBSON	**ES-150DC** WALNUT, DOUBLE CUT, 2 HB	1,052	**808**	714	629
ELGUIT	74	GIBSON	**ES-150DC** NATURAL, DOUBLE CUT, 2 HB	1,227	**942**	832	734
ELGUIT	70	GIBSON	**ES-150DW** WALNUT	1,264	**970**	858	756
ELGUIT	72	GIBSON	**ES-150DW** WALNUT	1,071	**823**	727	641
ELGUIT	40	GIBSON	**ES-150T** CHARLIE CHRISTIAN PU	3,343	**2,567**	2,268	1,999
ELGUIT	49	GIBSON	**ES-175** NATURAL, 1 PU, SERIAL #A4400-A6000	4,314	**3,312**	2,927	2,580
ELGUIT	49	GIBSON	**ES-175** SUNBURST, 1 PU, SERIAL #A2800-A4400	4,370	**3,355**	2,965	2,614
ELGUIT	50	GIBSON	**ES-175** SUNBURST, 1 PU, SERIAL #A4400-A6000	3,430	**2,634**	2,327	2,052
ELGUIT	50	GIBSON	**ES-175** NATURAL, 1 PU, SERIAL #A4400-A6000	4,122	**3,165**	2,797	2,466
ELGUIT	51	GIBSON	**ES-175** NATURAL, 1 PU	3,199	**2,457**	2,171	1,914
ELGUIT	51	GIBSON	**ES-175** SUNBURST, 1 PU, SERIAL #A6000-A9400	3,911	**3,003**	2,653	2,339
ELGUIT	52	GIBSON	**ES-175** NATURAL, 1 PU	2,436	**1,870**	1,653	1,457
ELGUIT	52	GIBSON	**ES-175** SUNBURST, 1 PU, SERIAL #A9400-A13000	3,326	**2,554**	2,257	1,989
ELGUIT	53	GIBSON	**ES-175** SUNBURST, 1 PU, SERIAL #A13000-A16000	3,071	**2,358**	2,083	1,837
ELGUIT	54	GIBSON	**ES-175** SUNBURST, 1 PU	3,233	**2,482**	2,194	1,934
ELGUIT	55	GIBSON	**ES-175** NATURAL, 1 PU	2,357	**1,810**	1,599	1,410
ELGUIT	55	GIBSON	**ES-175** SUNBURST, 1 PU	2,965	**2,277**	2,012	1,774
ELGUIT	55	GIBSON	**ES-175** SUNBURST, 2 P-90 PU's, BIGSBY, NON-FOLDING ARM	3,315	**2,545**	2,249	1,983
ELGUIT	56	GIBSON	**ES-175** SUNBURST, 1 PU	3,511	**2,696**	2,382	2,100
ELGUIT	57	GIBSON	**ES-175** NATURAL, 1 PU, SERIAL #A24600-A26500	2,437	**1,871**	1,653	1,457
ELGUIT	57	GIBSON	**ES-175** SUNBURST, 1 PU	3,898	**2,993**	2,645	2,332
ELGUIT	59	GIBSON	**ES-175** SUNBURST, 1 PU	2,404	**1,846**	1,631	1,438
ELGUIT	60	GIBSON	**ES-175** SUNBURST, 1 PU	2,347	**1,802**	1,592	1,404
ELGUIT	61	GIBSON	**ES-175** SUNBURST, 1 PU	3,513	**2,697**	2,384	2,101
ELGUIT	62	GIBSON	**ES-175** SUNBURST, 1 PU	1,796	**1,379**	1,219	1,074
ELGUIT	62	GIBSON	**ES-175** TOBACCO SUNBURST, 2 PU's, BRAZILIAN RSWD FNGRBRD, PEARL INLAY	4,448	**3,415**	3,018	2,661
ELGUIT	63	GIBSON	**ES-175** SUNBURST, 1 PU	1,864	**1,431**	1,265	1,115
ELGUIT	64	GIBSON	**ES-175** SUNBURST, 1 PU	1,776	**1,363**	1,205	1,062
ELGUIT	65	GIBSON	**ES-175** SUNBURST, 1 PU	1,723	**1,323**	1,169	1,031
ELGUIT	65	GIBSON	**ES-175** NATURAL, 1 PU	2,203	**1,691**	1,494	1,317
ELGUIT	66	GIBSON	**ES-175** SUNBURST, 1 PU	1,928	**1,480**	1,308	1,153
ELGUIT	67	GIBSON	**ES-175** SUNBURST, 1 PU	3,148	**2,417**	2,136	1,883
ELGUIT	68	GIBSON	**ES-175** NATURAL, 1 PU	2,115	**1,624**	1,435	1,265
ELGUIT	70	GIBSON	**ES-175** SUNBURST, 1 PU	1,620	**1,244**	1,099	969
ELGUIT	71	GIBSON	**ES-175** SUNBURST, 1 PU	1,989	**1,527**	1,349	1,189
ELGUIT	75	GIBSON	**ES-175** SUNBURST, 1 PU	1,496	**1,148**	1,015	895
ELGUIT	76	GIBSON	**ES-175** SUNBURST, 1 PU	1,340	**1,029**	909	801
ELGUIT	79	GIBSON	**ES-175** NICKEL HARDWARE	1,816	**1,394**	1,232	1,086

TYPE	YR	MFG	PRICES--BASED ON 100% ORIGINAL MODEL	SELL EXC	SELL AVG	BUY EXC	BUY AVG
ELGUIT	82	GIBSON	**ES-175** WHITE, 1 PU	1,219	**936**	827	729
ELGUIT	88	GIBSON	**ES-175** GOLD HARDWARE	1,657	**1,272**	1,124	991
ELGUIT	78	GIBSON	**ES-175CC** WALNUT, CHARLIE CHRISTIAN PU	2,105	**1,616**	1,428	1,259
ELGUIT	79	GIBSON	**ES-175CC** SUNBURST, CHARLIE CHRISTIAN PU	2,180	**1,674**	1,479	1,304
ELGUIT	79	GIBSON	**ES-175CC CUSTOM**	3,523	**2,705**	2,390	2,107
ELGUIT	52	GIBSON	**ES-175D** SUNBURST, 2 PU's	4,851	**3,725**	3,292	2,902
ELGUIT	53	GIBSON	**ES-175D** NATURAL, 2 PU's	4,838	**3,715**	3,283	2,894
ELGUIT	53	GIBSON	**ES-175D** SUNBURST, 2 PU's, LEFT-HANDED, SERIAL #A13000-A16000	5,473	**4,202**	3,714	3,274
ELGUIT	53	GIBSON	**ES-175D** SUNBURST, 2 PU's	5,719	**4,392**	3,881	3,421
ELGUIT	54	GIBSON	**ES-175D** NATURAL, 2 PU's, SERIAL #A16000-A19000	4,623	**3,550**	3,137	2,765
ELGUIT	55	GIBSON	**ES-175D** NATURAL, 2 PU's, SERIAL #A19000-A22000	4,623	**3,550**	3,137	2,765
ELGUIT	55	GIBSON	**ES-175D** SUNBURST, 2 PU's,	5,402	**4,148**	3,666	3,232
ELGUIT	56	GIBSON	**ES-175D** SUNBURST, 2 PU's, SERIAL #A22000-A24600	4,387	**3,368**	2,976	2,624
ELGUIT	56	GIBSON	**ES-175D** NATURAL, 2 PU's, SERIAL #A22000-A24600	4,623	**3,550**	3,137	2,765
ELGUIT	56	GIBSON	**ES-175D** CHERRY SUNBURST	5,936	**4,558**	4,028	3,551
ELGUIT	57	GIBSON	**ES-175D** SUNBURST, 2 PU's, LEFT-HANDED	5,053	**3,880**	3,429	3,023
ELGUIT	57	GIBSON	**ES-175D** SUNBURST, 2 PU's, SERIAL #A24600-A26500	5,137	**3,944**	3,486	3,073
ELGUIT	57	GIBSON	**ES-175D** NATURAL, 2 PU's, PAF'S, SERIAL #A24600-A26500	12,073	**9,270**	8,192	7,222
ELGUIT	58	GIBSON	**ES-175D** NATURAL, 2 PU's, SERIAL #A26500-A28000	12,073	**9,270**	8,192	7,222
ELGUIT	59	GIBSON	**ES-175D** SUNBURST, 2 PU's	4,984	**3,827**	3,382	2,981
ELGUIT	60	GIBSON	**ES-175D** SUNBURST, 2 PU's	5,176	**3,974**	3,512	3,096
ELGUIT	61	GIBSON	**ES-175D** SUNBURST, 2 PU's	5,453	**4,187**	3,700	3,262
ELGUIT	62	GIBSON	**ES-175D** SUNBURST	2,423	**1,861**	1,644	1,449
ELGUIT	62	GIBSON	**ES-175D** NATURAL, 2 PU's	4,300	**3,302**	2,918	2,572
ELGUIT	63	GIBSON	**ES-175D** SUNBURST, 2 PU's	3,287	**2,524**	2,230	1,966
ELGUIT	64	GIBSON	**ES-175D** SUNBURST, 2 PU's	3,701	**2,842**	2,511	2,214
ELGUIT	65	GIBSON	**ES-175D** SUNBURST, 2 PU's	3,430	**2,634**	2,327	2,052
ELGUIT	66	GIBSON	**ES-175D** SUNBURST, 2 PU's	3,032	**2,328**	2,058	1,814
ELGUIT	67	GIBSON	**ES-175D** SUNBURST, 2 PU's	3,081	**2,365**	2,090	1,843
ELGUIT	68	GIBSON	**ES-175D** SUNBURST, 2 PU's	2,879	**2,211**	1,953	1,722
ELGUIT	68	GIBSON	**ES-175D** NATURAL, 2 PU's	3,040	**2,334**	2,063	1,819
ELGUIT	69	GIBSON	**ES-175D** SUNBURST, 2 PU's	2,879	**2,211**	1,953	1,722
ELGUIT	70	GIBSON	**ES-175D** SUNBURST, 2 PU's	1,904	**1,462**	1,292	1,139
ELGUIT	70	GIBSON	**ES-175D** NATURAL, 2 PU's	3,595	**2,760**	2,439	2,150
ELGUIT	72	GIBSON	**ES-175D** SUNBURST, 2 PU's	1,442	**1,107**	978	862
ELGUIT	73	GIBSON	**ES-175D** SUNBURST, 2 PU's	1,440	**1,105**	977	861
ELGUIT	74	GIBSON	**ES-175D** SUNBURST, 2 PU's	1,435	**1,102**	974	858
ELGUIT	74	GIBSON	**ES-175D** NATURAL, 2 PU's	3,355	**2,576**	2,276	2,007
ELGUIT	75	GIBSON	**ES-175D** NATURAL, 2 PU's	3,296	**2,530**	2,236	1,971
ELGUIT	76	GIBSON	**ES-175D** SUNBURST, 2 PU's	1,340	**1,029**	909	801
ELGUIT	76	GIBSON	**ES-175D** NATURAL, 2 PU's	1,961	**1,505**	1,330	1,173
ELGUIT	77	GIBSON	**ES-175D** SUNBURST, 2 PU's	1,345	**1,032**	912	804

TYPE	YR	MFG	PRICES--BASED ON 100% ORIGINAL MODEL	SELL EXC	SELL AVG	BUY EXC	BUY AVG
ELGUIT	78	GIBSON	ES-175D SUNBURST, 2 PU's	1,340	**1,029**	909	801
ELGUIT	78	GIBSON	ES-175D NATURAL, 2 PU's	1,820	**1,397**	1,235	1,088
ELGUIT	78	GIBSON	ES-175D BLONDE	3,018	**2,317**	2,048	1,805
ELGUIT	79	GIBSON	ES-175D NATURAL, 2 PU's	1,319	**1,013**	895	789
ELGUIT	80	GIBSON	ES-175D SUNBURST, 2 PU's	1,494	**1,147**	1,013	893
ELGUIT	85	GIBSON	ES-175D BLOND	1,958	**1,504**	1,329	1,171
ELGUIT	86	GIBSON	ES-175D NATURAL	1,696	**1,302**	1,151	1,015
ELGUIT	54	GIBSON	ES-175DN BLOND, 2 PU's	4,360	**3,347**	2,958	2,608
ELGUIT	55	GIBSON	ES-175DN NATURAL, 2 PU's	4,475	**3,436**	3,036	2,677
ELGUIT	55	GIBSON	ES-175DN BLONDE	6,384	**4,902**	4,332	3,819
ELGUIT	57	GIBSON	ES-175DN PAF's	10,382	**7,972**	7,045	6,210
ELGUIT	59	GIBSON	ES-175DN BLOND, 2 PU's	3,582	**2,751**	2,431	2,143
ELGUIT	79	GIBSON	ES-175DN BLOND	2,900	**2,227**	1,968	1,735
ELGUIT	83	GIBSON	ES-175DN BLONDE, FLAME TOP	3,018	**2,317**	2,048	1,805
ELGUIT	63	GIBSON	ES-175DSPD WALNUT, 2 PU's	3,435	**2,637**	2,330	2,054
ELGUIT	77	GIBSON	ES-175T WINE RED, 2 PU's	1,372	**1,053**	931	820
ELGUIT	77	GIBSON	ES-175T NATURAL, 2 PU's	1,603	**1,231**	1,088	959
ELGUIT	78	GIBSON	ES-175T NATURAL, 2 PU's	1,280	**982**	868	765
ELGUIT	78	GIBSON	ES-175T WINE RED, 2 PU's	1,280	**982**	868	765
ELGUIT	78	GIBSON	ES-175T WINE RED	2,576	**1,978**	1,748	1,541
ELGUIT	79	GIBSON	ES-175T SUNBURST, 2 PU's	1,216	**933**	825	727
ELGUIT	79	GIBSON	ES-175T NATURAL, 2 PU's	1,265	**971**	858	757
ELGUIT	58	GIBSON	ES-225N BLOND	2,200	**1,689**	1,493	1,316
ELGUIT	55	GIBSON	ES-225T SUNBURST, 1 P-90 PU	1,490	**1,144**	1,011	891
ELGUIT	56	GIBSON	ES-225T SUNBURST	1,790	**1,375**	1,215	1,071
ELGUIT	57	GIBSON	ES-225T SUNBURST	1,768	**1,357**	1,200	1,057
ELGUIT	58	GIBSON	ES-225T SUNBURST	1,428	**1,096**	969	854
ELGUIT	58	GIBSON	ES-225T NATURAL	1,693	**1,300**	1,149	1,013
ELGUIT	59	GIBSON	ES-225T SUNBURST, SERIAL #S822314	1,232	**946**	836	737
ELGUIT	56	GIBSON	ES-225TD SUNBURST, 2 PU's, SERIAL #A22000-A24600	2,044	**1,569**	1,387	1,222
ELGUIT	56	GIBSON	ES-225TD NATURAL, 2 PU's, SERIAL #22000-A24600	2,363	**1,814**	1,603	1,413
ELGUIT	57	GIBSON	ES-225TD SUNBURST, 2 PU's, SERIAL #A24600-A26500	2,001	**1,536**	1,358	1,197
ELGUIT	57	GIBSON	ES-225TD NATURAL, 2 PU's, SERIAL #A24600-A26500	2,397	**1,841**	1,627	1,434
ELGUIT	58	GIBSON	ES-225TD SUNBURST, 2 PU's, SERIAL #A26500-A28000	2,001	**1,536**	1,358	1,197
ELGUIT	58	GIBSON	ES-225TD NATURAL, 2 PU's, SERIAL #A26500-A28000	2,375	**1,824**	1,611	1,421
ELGUIT	59	GIBSON	ES-225TD SUNBURST, 2 PU's, SERIAL #A28000	1,970	**1,512**	1,336	1,178
ELGUIT	59	GIBSON	ES-225TD NATURAL, 2 PU's	3,372	**2,589**	2,288	2,017
ELGUIT	62	GIBSON	ES-225TD SUNBURST, 2 PU's	1,563	**1,200**	1,060	935
ELGUIT	39	GIBSON	ES-250 SUNBURST	12,017	**9,227**	8,154	7,189
ELGUIT	40	GIBSON	ES-250 NATURAL, SERIAL #96000-96600	10,268	**7,884**	6,967	6,142
ELGUIT	80	GIBSON	ES-250T ANTIQUE SUNBURST	1,228	**943**	833	734
ELGUIT	55	GIBSON	ES-295 GOLD	6,086	**4,673**	4,129	3,640

TYPE	YR	MFG	PRICES--BASED ON 100% ORIGINAL MODEL	SELL EXC	SELL AVG	BUY EXC	BUY AVG
ELGUIT	56	GIBSON	**ES-295** GOLD, P-90 PU's	5,901	**4,531**	4,004	3,530
ELGUIT	58	GIBSON	**ES-295** HUMBUCKER PU's	10,164	**7,804**	6,897	6,080
ELGUIT	52	GIBSON	**ES-295TD** GOLD, SERIAL #A9400-A13000	5,873	**4,509**	3,985	3,513
ELGUIT	53	GIBSON	**ES-295TD** GOLD, SERIAL #A13000-A16000	5,760	**4,422**	3,908	3,445
ELGUIT	54	GIBSON	**ES-295TD** GOLD, SERIAL #A16000-A19000	5,755	**4,419**	3,905	3,443
ELGUIT	55	GIBSON	**ES-295TD** GOLD, SERIAL #A19000-A22000	6,000	**4,607**	4,072	3,589
ELGUIT	56	GIBSON	**ES-295TD** GOLD, SERIAL #A22000-A24600	5,998	**4,606**	4,070	3,588
ELGUIT	57	GIBSON	**ES-295TD** GOLD, SERIAL #A24600-A26500	5,989	**4,599**	4,064	3,583
ELGUIT	58	GIBSON	**ES-295TD** GOLD, PAF, SERIAL #A26500-A28000	8,005	**6,147**	5,432	4,789
ELGUIT	40	GIBSON	**ES-300** NATURAL, DIAGONAL PU, SERIAL #96000-96600	5,016	**3,851**	3,404	3,000
ELGUIT	41	GIBSON	**ES-300** NATURAL, DIAGONAL PU	3,447	**2,647**	2,339	2,062
ELGUIT	41	GIBSON	**ES-300** SUNBURST, DIAGONAL PU	3,531	**2,711**	2,396	2,112
ELGUIT	44	GIBSON	**ES-300** SUNBURST, P-90 PU	3,130	**2,403**	2,124	1,872
ELGUIT	45	GIBSON	**ES-300** SUNBURST, P-90 PU	3,105	**2,384**	2,107	1,857
ELGUIT	46	GIBSON	**ES-300** NATURAL, P-90 PU	2,154	**1,654**	1,462	1,289
ELGUIT	46	GIBSON	**ES-300** SUNBURST, P-90 PU, SERIAL #98600-99500	2,217	**1,702**	1,504	1,326
ELGUIT	47	GIBSON	**ES-300** NATURAL, P-90 PU	2,158	**1,657**	1,464	1,291
ELGUIT	47	GIBSON	**ES-300** SUNBURST, P-90 PU	2,162	**1,660**	1,467	1,293
ELGUIT	48	GIBSON	**ES-300** 1 P-90 PU	1,958	**1,504**	1,329	1,171
ELGUIT	49	GIBSON	**ES-300** 2 P-90 PU's	1,963	**1,507**	1,332	1,174
ELGUIT	50	GIBSON	**ES-300** SUNBURST, P-90 PU, SERIAL #A4400-A6000	2,296	**1,763**	1,558	1,373
ELGUIT	51	GIBSON	**ES-300** SUNBURST, P-90 PU, SERIAL #A9400-A13000	2,257	**1,733**	1,532	1,350
ELGUIT	52	GIBSON	**ES-300** SUNBURST, P-90 PU	2,236	**1,717**	1,517	1,337
ELGUIT	48	GIBSON	**ES-300N** BLOND	3,262	**2,505**	2,213	1,951
ELGUIT	71	GIBSON	**ES-320** CHERRY RED, MELODY MAKER STYLE PU's	910	**699**	617	544
ELGUIT	71	GIBSON	**ES-320TD** NATURAL, 2 MELODY MAKER PU's	815	**626**	553	487
ELGUIT	72	GIBSON	**ES-325TD** WALNUT, 1 F-HOLE, 2 MINI-HB	862	**662**	585	515
ELGUIT	72	GIBSON	**ES-325TD** CHERRY, 1 F-HOLE, 2 MINI-HB	881	**676**	598	527
ELGUIT	73	GIBSON	**ES-325TD** WALNUT, 1 F-HOLE, 2 MINI-HB	910	**699**	617	544
ELGUIT	76	GIBSON	**ES-325TD** CHERRY, 2 F-HOLE, 2 MINI-HB	803	**616**	544	480
ELGUIT	61	GIBSON	**ES-330** CHERRY, GOLD HARDWARE	5,936	**4,558**	4,028	3,551
ELGUIT	66	GIBSON	**ES-330** CHERRY RED	1,845	**1,417**	1,252	1,104
ELGUIT	67	GIBSON	**ES-330** CHERRY RED	1,967	**1,511**	1,335	1,177
ELGUIT	69	GIBSON	**ES-330** SUNBURST, ES-335 LENGTH NECK	1,970	**1,512**	1,336	1,178
ELGUIT	59	GIBSON	**ES-330D** SUNBURST	4,300	**3,302**	2,918	2,572
ELGUIT	60	GIBSON	**ES-330D** SUNBURST	4,300	**3,302**	2,918	2,572
ELGUIT	60	GIBSON	**ES-330D** CHERRY, DOT NECK	6,378	**4,897**	4,328	3,815
ELGUIT	61	GIBSON	**ES-330D** SUNBURST	4,085	**3,137**	2,772	2,444
ELGUIT	62	GIBSON	**ES-330D** SUNBURST, BLACK PU'S	3,018	**2,317**	2,048	1,805
ELGUIT	64	GIBSON	**ES-330D** SUNBURST, NICKLE HARDWARE	3,018	**2,317**	2,048	1,805
ELGUIT	64	GIBSON	**ES-330D** CHERRY, NICKLE HARDWARE	3,018	**2,317**	2,048	1,805
ELGUIT	66	GIBSON	**ES-330D** CHERRY	3,018	**2,317**	2,048	1,805

TYPE	YR	MFG	PRICES--BASED ON 100% ORIGINAL MODEL	SELL EXC	SELL AVG	BUY EXC	BUY AVG
ELGUIT	66	GIBSON	**ES-330D** SUNBURST	3,355	**2,576**	2,276	2,007
ELGUIT	68	GIBSON	**ES-330D** SUNBURST, LONG NECK	2,996	**2,300**	2,033	1,792
ELGUIT	59	GIBSON	**ES-330T** NATURAL	1,882	**1,445**	1,277	1,126
ELGUIT	59	GIBSON	**ES-330T** SUNBURST	2,112	**1,621**	1,433	1,263
ELGUIT	60	GIBSON	**ES-330T** SUNBURST	1,764	**1,354**	1,197	1,055
ELGUIT	60	GIBSON	**ES-330T** BLOND	4,300	**3,302**	2,918	2,572
ELGUIT	61	GIBSON	**ES-330T** SUNBURST	1,777	**1,364**	1,206	1,063
ELGUIT	61	GIBSON	**ES-330T** CHERRY	1,796	**1,379**	1,219	1,074
ELGUIT	62	GIBSON	**ES-330T** SUNBURST	1,380	**1,060**	937	826
ELGUIT	62	GIBSON	**ES-330T** NATURAL	1,524	**1,170**	1,034	911
ELGUIT	63	GIBSON	**ES-330T** SUNBURST	1,477	**1,134**	1,002	883
ELGUIT	66	GIBSON	**ES-330T** CHERRY, LONG NECK, HUMBUCKER	1,305	**1,002**	886	781
ELGUIT	60	GIBSON	**ES-330TD** CHERRY RED	4,300	**3,302**	2,918	2,572
ELGUIT	60	GIBSON	**ES-330TD** SUNBURST	4,300	**3,302**	2,918	2,572
ELGUIT	60	GIBSON	**ES-330TD** NATURAL	6,451	**4,953**	4,377	3,859
ELGUIT	61	GIBSON	**ES-330TD** CHERRY RED	4,300	**3,302**	2,918	2,572
ELGUIT	61	GIBSON	**ES-330TD** SUNBURST	4,300	**3,302**	2,918	2,572
ELGUIT	62	GIBSON	**ES-330TD** CHERRY RED	4,300	**3,302**	2,918	2,572
ELGUIT	62	GIBSON	**ES-330TD** SUNBURST	4,300	**3,302**	2,918	2,572
ELGUIT	63	GIBSON	**ES-330TD** CHERRY RED	4,300	**3,302**	2,918	2,572
ELGUIT	63	GIBSON	**ES-330TD** SUNBURST	4,300	**3,302**	2,918	2,572
ELGUIT	64	GIBSON	**ES-330TD** SUNBURST	3,595	**2,760**	2,439	2,150
ELGUIT	64	GIBSON	**ES-330TD** CHERRY RED	3,763	**2,889**	2,553	2,251
ELGUIT	65	GIBSON	**ES-330TD** SUNBURST	1,813	**1,392**	1,230	1,084
ELGUIT	65	GIBSON	**ES-330TD** CHERRY RED	3,355	**2,576**	2,276	2,007
ELGUIT	66	GIBSON	**ES-330TD** SUNBURST	1,373	**1,054**	931	821
ELGUIT	66	GIBSON	**ES-330TD** CHERRY RED	3,355	**2,576**	2,276	2,007
ELGUIT	66	GIBSON	**ES-330TD** SPARKLING BURGUNDY	4,300	**3,302**	2,918	2,572
ELGUIT	67	GIBSON	**ES-330TD** SUNBURST	1,911	**1,468**	1,297	1,143
ELGUIT	67	GIBSON	**ES-330TD** CHERRY RED	3,355	**2,576**	2,276	2,007
ELGUIT	67	GIBSON	**ES-330TD** SPARKLING BURGUNDY	4,085	**3,137**	2,772	2,444
ELGUIT	68	GIBSON	**ES-330TD** SUNBURST, NON-TREMOLO	1,350	**1,037**	916	808
ELGUIT	68	GIBSON	**ES-330TD** SUNBURST	1,422	**1,092**	965	850
ELGUIT	68	GIBSON	**ES-330TD** CHERRY RED, TRAPEZE TAIL, SERIAL #527101	3,115	**2,392**	2,114	1,863
ELGUIT	69	GIBSON	**ES-330TD** SUNBURST	1,277	**981**	867	764
ELGUIT	69	GIBSON	**ES-330TD** CHERRY RED	2,876	**2,208**	1,951	1,720
ELGUIT	70	GIBSON	**ES-330TD** WALNUT	1,015	**780**	689	607
ELGUIT	72	GIBSON	**ES-330TD** SUNBURST	985	**756**	668	589
ELGUIT	73	GIBSON	**ES-330TD** CHERRY RED	2,075	**1,593**	1,408	1,241
ELGUIT	67	GIBSON	**ES-330TDC**	1,421	**1,091**	964	850
ELGUIT	60	GIBSON	**ES-335** BLOND, DOT NECK, SLIM NECK	1,236	**949**	839	739
ELGUIT	61	GIBSON	**ES-335** SUNBURST, EXF, DOT INLAY, HB PU's	23,008	**17,666**	15,612	13,763

TYPE	YR	MFG	PRICES--BASED ON 100% ORIGINAL MODEL	SELL EXC	SELL AVG	BUY EXC	BUY AVG
ELGUIT	65	GIBSON	**ES-335** SUNBURST, 9/10	4,922	**3,779**	3,340	2,944
ELGUIT	67	GIBSON	**ES-335** BURGUNDY MIST	3,657	**2,808**	2,482	2,188
ELGUIT	67	GIBSON	**ES-335** CHERRY, 9/10	5,258	**4,037**	3,568	3,145
ELGUIT	68	GIBSON	**ES-335** NATURAL, 2-TONE BURGUNDY	1,276	**980**	866	763
ELGUIT	68	GIBSON	**ES-335** CHERRY	5,258	**4,037**	3,568	3,145
ELGUIT	69	GIBSON	**ES-335** SUNBURST	4,138	**3,177**	2,808	2,475
ELGUIT	71	GIBSON	**ES-335** CHERRY	3,466	**2,661**	2,352	2,073
ELGUIT	72	GIBSON	**ES-335** CHERRY	3,466	**2,661**	2,352	2,073
ELGUIT	74	GIBSON	**ES-335** WALNUT	1,535	**1,179**	1,041	918
ELGUIT	78	GIBSON	**ES-335** SUNBURST	3,018	**2,317**	2,048	1,805
ELGUIT	79	GIBSON	**ES-335** WINE RED	1,298	**996**	880	776
ELGUIT	81	GIBSON	**ES-335** BLOND, DOT NECK, BIG NECK	866	**665**	588	518
ELGUIT	81	GIBSON	**ES-335** BURGUNDY	3,018	**2,317**	2,048	1,805
ELGUIT	82	GIBSON	**ES-335** CHERRY, DOT	1,070	**822**	726	640
ELGUIT	82	GIBSON	**ES-335** BLOND, DOT NECK, BIG NECK	1,249	**959**	848	747
ELGUIT	86	GIBSON	**ES-335 CUSTOM** FAST PROFILE NECK	1,468	**1,127**	996	878
ELGUIT	78	GIBSON	**ES-335 DELUXE**	983	**755**	667	588
ELGUIT	83	GIBSON	**ES-335 DOT** NICKEL HARDWARE	2,021	**1,552**	1,371	1,209
ELGUIT	88	GIBSON	**ES-335 DOT** ALPINE, WHITE, GOLD HARDWARE	2,936	**2,254**	1,992	1,756
ELGUIT	79	GIBSON	**ES-335 PRO** ANTIQUE SUNBURST, 2 PU's	1,232	**946**	836	737
ELGUIT	81	GIBSON	**ES-335 PRO** CHERRY RED	1,237	**950**	839	740
ELGUIT	82	GIBSON	**ES-335 PRO** SUNBURST	1,060	**814**	719	634
ELGUIT	78	GIBSON	**ES-335 STANDARD**	805	**618**	546	481
ELGUIT	87	GIBSON	**ES-335 STUDIO** CHROME HARDWARE, GIG BAG	1,526	**1,172**	1,035	913
ELGUIT	87	GIBSON	**ES-335 STUDIO** KAHLER SUPERTUNE	1,526	**1,172**	1,035	913
ELGUIT	79	GIBSON	**ES-335 THING LINE PRO**	1,408	**1,081**	956	842
ELGUIT	65	GIBSON	**ES-335-12** SUNBURST, 12-STRING	1,603	**1,231**	1,088	959
ELGUIT	66	GIBSON	**ES-335-12** WINE, 12-STRING	1,589	**1,220**	1,078	950
ELGUIT	66	GIBSON	**ES-335-12** SUNBURST, 12-STRING	1,762	**1,353**	1,196	1,054
ELGUIT	67	GIBSON	**ES-335-12** CHERRY RED, 12-STRING	1,589	**1,220**	1,078	950
ELGUIT	67	GIBSON	**ES-335-12** SPARKLING BURGUNDY, 12-STRING	1,589	**1,220**	1,078	950
ELGUIT	67	GIBSON	**ES-335-12** SUNBURST, 12-STRING	1,620	**1,244**	1,099	969
ELGUIT	68	GIBSON	**ES-335-12** SPARKLING BURGUNDY, 12-STRING	1,589	**1,220**	1,078	950
ELGUIT	68	GIBSON	**ES-335-12** SUNBURST, 12-STRING	1,734	**1,332**	1,177	1,037
ELGUIT	69	GIBSON	**ES-335-12** CHERRY RED, 12-STRING	1,443	**1,108**	979	863
ELGUIT	58	GIBSON	**ES-335N** NATURAL, FIGURED BIGSBY	46,648	**35,819**	31,654	27,905
ELGUIT	59	GIBSON	**ES-335N** BLOND, NATURAL, STOP TAILPIECE	49,392	**37,926**	33,516	29,547
ELGUIT	60	GIBSON	**ES-335N** NATURAL	43,904	**33,712**	29,792	26,264
ELGUIT	80	GIBSON	**ES-335S CUSTOM**	1,364	**1,047**	925	816
ELGUIT	58	GIBSON	**ES-335TD** SUNBURST, DOT INLAY, LEFT-HANDED	16,596	**12,743**	11,261	9,928
ELGUIT	58	GIBSON	**ES-335TD** SUNBURST, DOT INLAY, SERIAL #A26500-A28000	18,139	**13,928**	12,308	10,851
ELGUIT	58	GIBSON	**ES-335TD** CHERRY RED	21,952	**16,856**	14,896	13,132
ELGUIT	58	GIBSON	**ES-335TD** NATURAL, DOT INLAY, SERIAL #A26500-A28000	42,300	**32,480**	28,703	25,304
ELGUIT	59	GIBSON	**ES-335TD** SUNBURST, DOT INLAY	17,372	**13,339**	11,788	10,392

TYPE	YR	MFG	PRICES--BASED ON 100% ORIGINAL MODEL	SELL EXC	SELL AVG	BUY EXC	BUY AVG
ELGUIT	59	GIBSON	ES-335TD CHERRY RED	21,952	16,856	14,896	13,132
ELGUIT	59	GIBSON	ES-335TD NATURAL, DOT INLAY	38,617	29,652	26,204	23,101
ELGUIT	60	GIBSON	ES-335TD SUNBURST, BIGSBY	14,692	11,281	9,969	8,789
ELGUIT	60	GIBSON	ES-335TD SUNBURST, DOT INLAY	14,836	11,392	10,067	8,875
ELGUIT	60	GIBSON	ES-335TD CHERRY RED	19,756	15,170	13,406	11,818
ELGUIT	60	GIBSON	ES-335TD NATURAL, DOT INLAY	32,244	24,759	21,880	19,289
ELGUIT	61	GIBSON	ES-335TD SUNBURST, DOT INLAY	13,403	10,291	9,094	8,017
ELGUIT	61	GIBSON	ES-335TD CHERRY RED, DOT INLAY	19,208	14,749	13,034	11,490
ELGUIT	62	GIBSON	ES-335TD SUNBURST, LEFT-HANDED	6,992	5,368	4,744	4,182
ELGUIT	62	GIBSON	ES-335TD SUNBURST, BLOCK INLAY	7,863	6,038	5,335	4,704
ELGUIT	62	GIBSON	ES-335TD CHERRY RED, BLOCK INLAY	10,376	7,967	7,041	6,207
ELGUIT	62	GIBSON	ES-335TD CHERRY RED, DOT INLAY	10,500	8,062	7,125	6,281
ELGUIT	62	GIBSON	ES-335TD SUNBURST	10,774	8,273	7,311	6,445
ELGUIT	62	GIBSON	ES-335TD SUNBURST, DOT INLAY	10,800	8,292	7,328	6,460
ELGUIT	63	GIBSON	ES-335TD CHERRY RED, BIGSBY VIB	5,372	4,125	3,645	3,213
ELGUIT	63	GIBSON	ES-335TD CHERRY RED	5,745	4,411	3,898	3,437
ELGUIT	63	GIBSON	ES-335TD SUNBURST	5,997	4,605	4,069	3,587
ELGUIT	64	GIBSON	ES-335TD SUNBURST	4,885	3,751	3,315	2,922
ELGUIT	64	GIBSON	ES-335TD CHERRY RED, NICKEL PARTS	8,601	6,604	5,836	5,145
ELGUIT	65	GIBSON	ES-335TD SUNBURST, TRAPEZE TAIL	2,418	1,856	1,640	1,446
ELGUIT	65	GIBSON	ES-335TD CHERRY RED, CHROME PARTS	4,085	3,137	2,772	2,444
ELGUIT	65	GIBSON	ES-335TD MAHOGANY, BIG NECK	5,174	3,973	3,511	3,095
ELGUIT	65	GIBSON	ES-335TD WHITE, GOLD-PLATED HARDWARE	6,799	5,221	4,613	4,067
ELGUIT	66	GIBSON	ES-335TD CHERRY RED	2,358	1,811	1,600	1,411
ELGUIT	66	GIBSON	ES-335TD SUNBURST	2,418	1,856	1,640	1,446
ELGUIT	66	GIBSON	ES-335TD CHERRY RED	3,060	2,350	2,077	1,831
ELGUIT	66	GIBSON	ES-335TD CHERRY RED, LEFT-HANDED	4,060	3,117	2,755	2,428
ELGUIT	66	GIBSON	ES-335TD SPARKLING BURGUNDY	6,042	4,639	4,100	3,614
ELGUIT	66	GIBSON	ES-335TD PELHAM BLUE	8,867	6,808	6,016	5,304
ELGUIT	67	GIBSON	ES-335TD SUNBURST	2,051	1,575	1,392	1,227
ELGUIT	67	GIBSON	ES-335TD CHERRY RED	2,304	1,769	1,564	1,378
ELGUIT	67	GIBSON	ES-335TD BLACK	3,763	2,889	2,553	2,251
ELGUIT	67	GIBSON	ES-335TD CHERRY RED, CHECKING, TRAPEZE	3,763	2,889	2,553	2,251
ELGUIT	67	GIBSON	ES-335TD SPARKLING BURGANDY	6,025	4,626	4,088	3,604
ELGUIT	68	GIBSON	ES-335TD WALNUT, BIGSBY VIBRATO	1,603	1,231	1,088	959
ELGUIT	68	GIBSON	ES-335TD SUNBURST	2,052	1,576	1,393	1,228
ELGUIT	68	GIBSON	ES-335TD CHERRY RED	2,288	1,756	1,552	1,368
ELGUIT	68	GIBSON	ES-335TD SPARKLING BURGUNDY	5,953	4,571	4,040	3,561
ELGUIT	69	GIBSON	ES-335TD WALNUT	1,622	1,246	1,101	970
ELGUIT	69	GIBSON	ES-335TD CHERRY RED, 3 PIECE NECK	2,059	1,581	1,397	1,232
ELGUIT	69	GIBSON	ES-335TD SUNBURST	2,225	1,708	1,510	1,331
ELGUIT	69	GIBSON	ES-335TD SPARKLING BURGUNDY	5,860	4,500	3,977	3,506

2006 WINTER VINTAGE GUITARS & COLLECTIBLES BLUE BOOK

GIBSON

TYPE	YR	MFG	PRICES--BASED ON 100% ORIGINAL MODEL	SELL EXC	SELL AVG	BUY EXC	BUY AVG
ELGUIT	70	GIBSON	ES-335TD WALNUT	1,389	1,067	943	831
ELGUIT	70	GIBSON	ES-335TD CHERRY RED, VALITE MADE WITH GUITAR AMP	1,674	1,285	1,136	1,001
ELGUIT	70	GIBSON	ES-335TD SUNBURST, LEFT-HANDED	1,992	1,529	1,352	1,191
ELGUIT	70	GIBSON	ES-335TD SUNBURST	2,275	1,747	1,544	1,361
ELGUIT	70	GIBSON	ES-335TD CHERRY RED	2,996	2,300	2,033	1,792
ELGUIT	71	GIBSON	ES-335TD WINE RED	1,431	1,099	971	856
ELGUIT	71	GIBSON	ES-335TD WALNUT	1,696	1,302	1,151	1,015
ELGUIT	71	GIBSON	ES-335TD CHERRY RED,MAHOGANY NECK,TRAPEZE TAILPIECE	2,876	2,208	1,951	1,720
ELGUIT	72	GIBSON	ES-335TD WALNUT	1,367	1,050	927	818
ELGUIT	72	GIBSON	ES-335TD WINE RED	1,389	1,067	943	831
ELGUIT	72	GIBSON	ES-335TD SUNBURST	1,797	1,380	1,219	1,075
ELGUIT	72	GIBSON	ES-335TD CHERRY RED	2,876	2,208	1,951	1,720
ELGUIT	72	GIBSON	ES-335TD SPARKLING BURGANDY	4,475	3,436	3,036	2,677
ELGUIT	73	GIBSON	ES-335TD WALNUT, SERIAL #055039	1,216	933	825	727
ELGUIT	73	GIBSON	ES-335TD CHERRY RED, SERIAL #055039	1,576	1,210	1,070	943
ELGUIT	74	GIBSON	ES-335TD WALNUT	1,336	1,025	906	799
ELGUIT	74	GIBSON	ES-335TD CHERRY RED	1,573	1,208	1,067	941
ELGUIT	75	GIBSON	ES-335TD WALNUT	984	755	668	588
ELGUIT	75	GIBSON	ES-335TD SUNBURST	1,394	1,070	946	834
ELGUIT	76	GIBSON	ES-335TD SUNBURST	1,028	789	697	615
ELGUIT	76	GIBSON	ES-335TD WALNUT	1,223	939	829	731
ELGUIT	76	GIBSON	ES-335TD WINE RED	1,242	953	842	743
ELGUIT	76	GIBSON	ES-335TD NATURAL	1,336	1,025	906	799
ELGUIT	77	GIBSON	ES-335TD WALNUT	1,067	819	724	638
ELGUIT	77	GIBSON	ES-335TD SUNBURST	1,346	1,033	913	805
ELGUIT	77	GIBSON	ES-335TD CHERRY RED	2,157	1,656	1,463	1,290
ELGUIT	78	GIBSON	ES-335TD WALNUT	990	760	671	592
ELGUIT	78	GIBSON	ES-335TD WINE RED	1,235	948	838	739
ELGUIT	78	GIBSON	ES-335TD SUNBURST	1,310	1,006	889	783
ELGUIT	79	GIBSON	ES-335TD WINE RED	1,206	926	818	721
ELGUIT	79	GIBSON	ES-335TD WALNUT	1,246	957	845	745
ELGUIT	79	GIBSON	ES-335TD SUNBURST	1,248	958	847	747
ELGUIT	79	GIBSON	ES-335TD CHERRY RED	1,320	1,013	896	789
ELGUIT	79	GIBSON	ES-335TD THIN LINE	1,408	1,081	956	842
ELGUIT	61	GIBSON	ES-335TDC CHERRY SUNBURST, 2 PAF's	10,324	7,806	6,883	5,707
ELGUIT	64	GIBSON	ES-335TDC CHERRY RED	8,148	6,256	5,529	4,874
ELGUIT	59	GIBSON	ES-335TDSV CHERRY RED, STEREO	7,869	6,042	5,339	4,707
ELGUIT	66	GIBSON	ES-335TDSV CHERRY RED, TREMOLO	3,035	2,330	2,059	1,815
ELGUIT	79	GIBSON	ES-335TDSV SUNBURST, STEREO	1,364	1,047	925	816
ELGUIT	79	GIBSON	ES-335TDSV THIN LINE	2,945	2,261	1,998	1,762
ELGUIT	69	GIBSON	ES-340TD NATURAL, 2 PU's	1,282	984	870	767
ELGUIT	69	GIBSON	ES-340TD WALNUT, 2 PU's	1,364	1,047	925	816
ELGUIT	70	GIBSON	ES-340TD NATURAL, 2 PU's	1,244	955	844	744

TYPE	YR	MFG	PRICES--BASED ON 100% ORIGINAL MODEL	SELL EXC	SELL AVG	BUY EXC	BUY AVG
ELGUIT	70	GIBSON	ES-340TD WALNUT	2,128	1,634	1,444	1,273
ELGUIT	72	GIBSON	ES-340TD NATURAL, 2 PU's	1,061	815	720	635
ELGUIT	61	GIBSON	ES-345 SUNBURST, LEFT-HANDED, PAF HB PU's.STEREO & VARITONE	12,796	9,825	8,683	7,654
ELGUIT	64	GIBSON	ES-345 SUNBURST, 9/10	6,378	4,897	4,328	3,815
ELGUIT	65	GIBSON	ES-345 SUNBURST	5,258	4,037	3,568	3,145
ELGUIT	68	GIBSON	ES-345 WALNUT FINISH, STEREO CORD	1,966	1,510	1,334	1,176
ELGUIT	70	GIBSON	ES-345 TRANS BURGUNDY	3,578	2,747	2,428	2,140
ELGUIT	72	GIBSON	ES-345 SUNBURST, 9/10	3,578	2,747	2,428	2,140
ELGUIT	79	GIBSON	ES-345 TRANS BURGUNDY	3,018	2,317	2,048	1,805
ELGUIT	81	GIBSON	ES-345 SUNBURST	3,018	2,317	2,048	1,805
ELGUIT	59	GIBSON	ES-345TD CHERRY, DOUBLE CUTAWAY, STEREO, 2 PU's	16,464	12,642	11,172	9,849
ELGUIT	59	GIBSON	ES-345TD SUNBURST, DOUBLE CUTAWAY, STEREO, 2 PU's	16,464	12,642	11,172	9,849
ELGUIT	59	GIBSON	ES-345TD NATURAL, DOUBLE CUTAWAY, STEREO, 2 PU's	19,756	15,170	13,406	11,818
ELGUIT	60	GIBSON	ES-345TD CHERRY, DOUBLE CUTAWAY, STEREO, 2 PU's	15,366	11,799	10,427	9,192
ELGUIT	60	GIBSON	ES-345TD SUNBURST, DOUBLE CUTAWAY, STEREO, 2 PU's	15,366	11,799	10,427	9,192
ELGUIT	61	GIBSON	ES-345TD CHERRY, DOUBLE CUTAWAY, STEREO, 2 PU's	14,817	11,377	10,054	8,864
ELGUIT	62	GIBSON	ES-345TD CHERRY, DOUBLE CUTAWAY, STEREO, 2 PU's	14,817	11,377	10,054	8,864
ELGUIT	62	GIBSON	ES-345TD CHERRY, DOUBLE CUATAWAY, STEREO, LEFT-HANDED, 2 PU's	14,817	11,377	10,054	8,864
ELGUIT	63	GIBSON	ES-345TD CHERRY, DOUBLE CUTAWAY, STEREO, 2 PU's	8,064	6,192	5,472	4,824
ELGUIT	63	GIBSON	ES-345TD SUNBURST, DOUBLE CUTAWAY, STEREO, 2 PU's	8,064	6,192	5,472	4,824
ELGUIT	64	GIBSON	ES-345TD CHERRY, DOUBLE CUTAWAY, STEREO, 2 PU's	8,064	6,192	5,472	4,824
ELGUIT	65	GIBSON	ES-345TD CHERRY, DOUBLE CUTAWAY, STEREO, 2 PU's	6,988	5,366	4,742	4,180
ELGUIT	66	GIBSON	ES-345TD SUNBURST, DOUBLE CUTAWAY, STEREO, 2 PU's	6,451	4,953	4,377	3,859
ELGUIT	66	GIBSON	ES-345TD CHERRY, DOUBLE CUTAWAY, STEREO, 2 PU's	6,720	5,160	4,560	4,020
ELGUIT	67	GIBSON	ES-345TD CHERRY, DOUBLE CUTAWAY, STEREO, 2 PU's	6,451	4,953	4,377	3,859
ELGUIT	68	GIBSON	ES-345TD WALNUT, DOUBLE CUTAWAY, STEREO, 2 PU's	3,595	2,760	2,439	2,150
ELGUIT	68	GIBSON	ES-345TD SUNBURST, DOUBLE CUTAWAY, STEREO, 2 PU's	5,913	4,540	4,012	3,537
ELGUIT	69	GIBSON	ES-345TD WALNUT, DOUBLE CUTAWAY, STEREO, 2 PU's	3,595	2,760	2,439	2,150
ELGUIT	69	GIBSON	ES-345TD SUNBURST, DOUBLE CUTAWAY, STEREO, 2 PU's	3,763	2,889	2,553	2,251
ELGUIT	70	GIBSON	ES-345TD SUNBURST, DOUBLE CUTAWAY, STEREO, 2 PU's	1,272	976	863	761
ELGUIT	70	GIBSON	ES-345TD WALNUT, DOUBLE CUTAWAY, STEREO, 2 PU's	1,460	1,121	991	873
ELGUIT	70	GIBSON	ES-345TD CHERRY, DOUBLE CUTAWAY, STEREO, 2 PU's	3,763	2,889	2,553	2,251
ELGUIT	71	GIBSON	ES-345TD WALNUT, DOUBLE CUTAWAY, STEREO, 2 PU's	1,443	1,108	979	863
ELGUIT	72	GIBSON	ES-345TD WALNUT, DOUBLE CUTAWAY, STEREO, 2 PU's	1,033	793	701	618
ELGUIT	73	GIBSON	ES-345TD WALNUT, DOUBLE CUTAWAY, STEREO, 2 PU's	1,373	1,054	931	821
ELGUIT	74	GIBSON	ES-345TD CHERRY, DOUBLE CUTAWAY, STEREO, 2 PU's	1,553	1,192	1,054	929
ELGUIT	77	GIBSON	ES-345TD WINE RED, DOUBLE CUTAWAY, 2 PU's	1,337	1,026	907	799
ELGUIT	78	GIBSON	ES-345TD WALNUT, DOUBLE CUTAWAY, STEREO, 2 PU's	1,248	958	847	747
ELGUIT	79	GIBSON	ES-345TD NATURAL, DOUBLE CUTAWAY, 2 PU's	1,270	975	861	759
ELGUIT	60	GIBSON	ES-345TDC CHERRY SUNBURST, BIGSBY	5,372	4,125	3,645	3,213
ELGUIT	68	GIBSON	ES-345TDC CHERRY, BIGSBY, VARITONE	1,431	1,099	971	856
ELGUIT	59	GIBSON	ES-345TDSV SUNBURST	7,404	5,685	5,024	4,429

TYPE	YR	MFG	PRICES--BASED ON 100% ORIGINAL MODEL	SELL EXC	SELL AVG	BUY EXC	BUY AVG
ELGUIT	67	GIBSON	**ES-345TDSV** CHERRY RED	2,054	**1,577**	1,393	1,228
ELGUIT	68	GIBSON	**ES-345TDSV** SUNBURST, SERIAL# 519851	1,611	**1,237**	1,093	964
ELGUIT	72	GIBSON	**ES-345TDSV** CHERRY RED	1,201	**922**	815	718
ELGUIT	78	GIBSON	**ES-345TDSV** WINE RED	996	**765**	676	596
ELGUIT	79	GIBSON	**ES-345TDSV** THIN LINE	2,994	**2,299**	2,032	1,791
ELGUIT	84	GIBSON	**ES-347** THIN LINE	1,060	**814**	719	634
ELGUIT	84	GIBSON	**ES-347 THIN LINE**	978	**751**	664	585
ELGUIT	78	GIBSON	**ES-347TD** NATURAL	2,696	**2,070**	1,830	1,613
ELGUIT	79	GIBSON	**ES-347TD** THIN LINE	1,544	**1,185**	1,048	923
ELGUIT	79	GIBSON	**ES-347TD** SUNBURST, DOUBLE CUTAWAY, TP-6, 2 PU's	2,396	**1,840**	1,626	1,433
ELGUIT	83	GIBSON	**ES-347TD**	1,996	**1,533**	1,355	1,194
ELGUIT	47	GIBSON	**ES-350** NATURAL, ROUNDED CUTAWAY, 1 PU	5,869	**4,507**	3,983	3,511
ELGUIT	47	GIBSON	**ES-350** SUNBURST, ROUNDED CUTAWAY, 1 PU	6,994	**5,370**	4,746	4,184
ELGUIT	48	GIBSON	**ES-350** SUNBURST, 1 P-90	5,574	**4,280**	3,782	3,334
ELGUIT	48	GIBSON	**ES-350** NATURAL, ROUNDED CUTAWAY, 1 PU	6,722	**5,161**	4,561	4,021
ELGUIT	48	GIBSON	**ES-350** SUNBURST, ROUNDED CUTAWAY, 2 PU's	6,724	**5,163**	4,563	4,022
ELGUIT	49	GIBSON	**ES-350** SUNBURST, ROUNDED CUTAWAY, 2 PU's	6,112	**4,693**	4,148	3,656
ELGUIT	49	GIBSON	**ES-350** NATURAL, 2 P-90's	6,361	**4,884**	4,316	3,805
ELGUIT	50	GIBSON	**ES-350** SUNBURST, ROUNDED CUTAWAY, 1 PU	5,768	**4,429**	3,914	3,450
ELGUIT	51	GIBSON	**ES-350** SUNBURST, ROUNDED CUTAWAY, 2 PU's	5,626	**4,320**	3,818	3,366
ELGUIT	52	GIBSON	**ES-350** SUNBURST, ROUNDED CUTAWAY, 2 PU's	5,746	**4,412**	3,899	3,437
ELGUIT	54	GIBSON	**ES-350** SUNBURST, ROUNDED CUTAWAY, 2 PU's	5,504	**4,226**	3,735	3,293
ELGUIT	56	GIBSON	**ES-350** BLOND, 2 P-90 PU's, SINGLE CUT, 1 OF 4 MADE	8,510	**6,535**	5,775	5,091
ELGUIT	57	GIBSON	**ES-350** SUNBURST	8,064	**6,192**	5,472	4,824
ELGUIT	56	GIBSON	**ES-350T** SUNBURST, ROUNDED CUTAWAY, 2 PU's, SERIAL #A22000-A24600	6,556	**5,034**	4,449	3,922
ELGUIT	56	GIBSON	**ES-350T** NATURAL, ROUNDED CUTAWAY, 2 PU's, SERIAL #A22000-A24600	7,869	**6,042**	5,339	4,707
ELGUIT	57	GIBSON	**ES-350T** SUNBURST, ROUNDED CUTAWAY, 2 PU's, PAF'S	8,064	**6,192**	5,472	4,824
ELGUIT	58	GIBSON	**ES-350T** SUNBURST, ROUNDED CUTAWAY, 2 PU's, PAF'S	8,064	**6,192**	5,472	4,824
ELGUIT	59	GIBSON	**ES-350T** BROWN, ROUNDED CUTAWAY, 2 PU's, STEREO VARITONE	8,064	**6,192**	5,472	4,824
ELGUIT	59	GIBSON	**ES-350T** SUNBURST, ROUNDED CUTAWAY, 2 PU's	8,064	**6,192**	5,472	4,824
ELGUIT	62	GIBSON	**ES-350T** SUNBURST, ROUNDED CUTAWAY, 2 PU's	6,267	**4,812**	4,252	3,749
ELGUIT	63	GIBSON	**ES-350T** NATURAL	6,267	**4,812**	4,252	3,749
ELGUIT	77	GIBSON	**ES-350T** NATURAL, ROUNDED CUTAWAY, 2 PU's	3,494	**2,683**	2,371	2,090
ELGUIT	77	GIBSON	**ES-350T** BLACK, ROUNDED CUTAWAY, 2 PU's	3,595	**2,760**	2,439	2,150
ELGUIT	77	GIBSON	**ES-350T** SUNBURST, ROUNDED CUTAWAY, 2 PU's	3,595	**2,760**	2,439	2,150
ELGUIT	78	GIBSON	**ES-350T** FIREBURST, ROUNDED CUTAWAY, 2 PU's	3,595	**2,760**	2,439	2,150
ELGUIT	78	GIBSON	**ES-350T** NATURAL	3,696	**2,838**	2,508	2,211
ELGUIT	58	GIBSON	**ES-350TD** SUNBURST, ROUNDED CUTAWAY, 2 PU's, SERIAL #A26500-A28000	5,872	**4,508**	3,984	3,512
ELGUIT	59	GIBSON	**ES-350TD** NATURAL, ROUNDED CUTAWAY, 2 PU's	5,831	**4,478**	3,957	3,488
ELGUIT	59	GIBSON	**ES-350TD** SUNBURST, ROUNDED CUTAWAY, 2 PU's	6,838	**5,251**	4,640	4,091
ELGUIT	60	GIBSON	**ES-350TD** SUNBURST, POINTED CUTAWAY, 2 PU's	5,600	**4,300**	3,800	3,350
ELGUIT	61	GIBSON	**ES-350TD** SUNBURST, POINTED CUTAWAY, 2 PU's	5,602	**4,301**	3,801	3,351
ELGUIT	62	GIBSON	**ES-350TD** NATURAL, POINTED CUTAWAY, 2 PU's	5,603	**4,302**	3,802	3,352

TYPE	YR	MFG	PRICES--BASED ON 100% ORIGINAL MODEL	SELL EXC	SELL AVG	BUY EXC	BUY AVG
ELGUIT	62	GIBSON	**ES-350TD** SUNBURST, POINTED CUTAWAY, 2 PU's	5,604	**4,303**	3,803	3,352
ELGUIT	58	GIBSON	**ES-355TD** CHERRY RED, MONO, BIGSBY	9,307	**7,146**	6,315	5,567
ELGUIT	59	GIBSON	**ES-355TD** CHERRY RED, BIGSBY, 2 PAF HB PU's, STEREO & VARITONE WIRING	9,836	**7,553**	6,675	5,884
ELGUIT	60	GIBSON	**ES-355TD** CHERRY RED, STEREO, 2 PU's	7,119	**5,467**	4,831	4,259
ELGUIT	61	GIBSON	**ES-355TD** CHERRY RED, MONO	1,688	**1,296**	1,146	1,010
ELGUIT	61	GIBSON	**ES-355TD** MONO, AMERICAN VINTAGE	7,809	**5,996**	5,299	4,671
ELGUIT	64	GIBSON	**ES-355TD** CHERRY RED, MONO	3,256	**2,500**	2,210	1,948
ELGUIT	64	GIBSON	**ES-355TD** CHERRY RED, MONO, BIGSBY	3,477	**2,670**	2,359	2,080
ELGUIT	66	GIBSON	**ES-355TD** CHERRY RED, MONO, BIGSBY	3,045	**2,338**	2,066	1,821
ELGUIT	67	GIBSON	**ES-355TD** CHERRY RED, MONO, VIBRATO	2,406	**1,848**	1,633	1,439
ELGUIT	67	GIBSON	**ES-355TD** SUNBURST, MONO	2,416	**1,855**	1,640	1,445
ELGUIT	69	GIBSON	**ES-355TD** WALNUT, MONO	1,359	**1,044**	922	813
ELGUIT	72	GIBSON	**ES-355TD** WALNUT, MONO	1,411	**1,083**	957	844
ELGUIT	74	GIBSON	**ES-355TD** BURGUNDY	1,481	**1,137**	1,005	886
ELGUIT	67	GIBSON	**ES-355TDC** BURGUNDY, MONO	2,416	**1,855**	1,640	1,445
ELGUIT	79	GIBSON	**ES-355TDS THIN LINE**	1,064	**817**	722	636
ELGUIT	59	GIBSON	**ES-355TDSV** FLAMED, STEREO, VARITONE, PAFS	7,017	**5,388**	4,762	4,198
ELGUIT	60	GIBSON	**ES-355TDSV** CHERRY RED, STEREO, BIGSBY	6,894	**5,294**	4,678	4,124
ELGUIT	61	GIBSON	**ES-355TDSV** CHERRY RED, STEREO, BIGSBY, PAF'S	5,424	**4,164**	3,680	3,244
ELGUIT	62	GIBSON	**ES-355TDSV** CHERRY RED, STEREO, BIGSBY	5,670	**4,354**	3,847	3,392
ELGUIT	63	GIBSON	**ES-355TDSV** CHERRY RED, STEREO, BIGSBY	4,883	**3,749**	3,313	2,921
ELGUIT	64	GIBSON	**ES-355TDSV** CHERRY RED, STEREO, VIBRATO	4,034	**3,097**	2,737	2,413
ELGUIT	65	GIBSON	**ES-355TDSV** RED, STEREO	3,289	**2,525**	2,232	1,967
ELGUIT	66	GIBSON	**ES-355TDSV** CHERRY RED, STEREO, VIBRATO	3,086	**2,370**	2,094	1,846
ELGUIT	67	GIBSON	**ES-355TDSV** CHERRY RED, STEREO, VIBRATO	2,933	**2,252**	1,990	1,754
ELGUIT	68	GIBSON	**ES-355TDSV** CHERRY RED, STEREO, VIBRATO	2,262	**1,737**	1,535	1,353
ELGUIT	69	GIBSON	**ES-355TDSV** CHERRY RED, STEREO, VIBRATO	2,076	**1,594**	1,409	1,242
ELGUIT	70	GIBSON	**ES-355TDSV** CHERRY RED, STEREO, BIGSBY	1,015	**780**	689	607
ELGUIT	71	GIBSON	**ES-355TDSV** CHERRY RED, STEREO	1,029	**790**	698	615
ELGUIT	71	GIBSON	**ES-355TDSV** WALNUT	2,066	**1,586**	1,402	1,236
ELGUIT	72	GIBSON	**ES-355TDSV** CHERRY RED, STEREO, BIGSBY	999	**767**	677	597
ELGUIT	72	GIBSON	**ES-355TDSV** WALNUT, STEREO, BIGSBY	1,318	**1,012**	894	788
ELGUIT	74	GIBSON	**ES-355TDSV** CHERRY RED, STEREO, BIGSBY	1,319	**1,013**	895	789
ELGUIT	74	GIBSON	**ES-355TDSV** WALNUT, STEREO, BIGSBY	1,883	**1,446**	1,278	1,126
ELGUIT	79	GIBSON	**ES-355TDSV** SUNBURST, STEREO, VIBRATO	1,039	**798**	705	621
ELGUIT	81	GIBSON	**ES-369** SUNBURST	1,365	**1,048**	926	816
ELGUIT	82	GIBSON	**ES-369** SUNBURST	1,624	**1,247**	1,102	971
ELGUIT	78	GIBSON	**ES-555TDSV** BURGUNDY, STEREO	1,808	**1,388**	1,227	1,082
ELGUIT	91	GIBSON	**ES-775 CLASSIC BEAUTY** EBONY, GOLD HARDWARE	2,936	**2,254**	1,992	1,756
ELGUIT	92	GIBSON	**ES-775 CLASSIC BEAUTY** VS/ANTIQUE NATURAL, GOLD HARDWARE	3,688	**2,831**	2,502	2,206
ELGUIT	79	GIBSON	**ES-ARTIST** BLACK, PEARL LOGO	1,980	**1,520**	1,343	1,184
ELGUIT	80	GIBSON	**ES-ARTIST** BLACK, PEARL LOGO	1,457	**1,118**	988	871

TYPE	YR	MFG	PRICES--BASED ON 100% ORIGINAL MODEL	SELL EXC	SELL AVG	BUY EXC	BUY AVG
ELGUIT	38	GIBSON	**EST-150** TENOR, 4-STRING	3,024	**2,322**	2,052	1,809
ELGUIT	40	GIBSON	**ETG-150** TENOR	1,541	**1,183**	1,045	921
ELGUIT	52	GIBSON	**ETG-150**	892	**685**	605	533
ELGUIT	55	GIBSON	**ETG-150** TENOR	1,053	**809**	715	630
ELGUIT	56	GIBSON	**ETG-150** TENOR	1,239	**952**	841	741
ELGUIT	57	GIBSON	**ETG-150** TENOR	1,038	**797**	704	621
ELGUIT	58	GIBSON	**ETG-150** TENOR	975	**749**	661	583
ELGUIT	62	GIBSON	**ETG-150**	812	**623**	551	485
ELGUIT	62	GIBSON	**ETG-150** TENOR	896	**688**	608	536
ELGUIT	66	GIBSON	**ETG-150** TENOR	827	**635**	561	495
ELGUIT	58	GIBSON	**EXPLORER** NATURAL, KORINA, SERIAL #A26500-A28000	145,465	**111,696**	98,708	87,019
ELGUIT	59	GIBSON	**EXPLORER** NATURAL, KORINA, SERIAL #A28000- (ONLY 3 SHIPPED IN 1959)	153,259	**117,681**	103,997	91,682
ELGUIT	63	GIBSON	**EXPLORER** NATURAL, KORINA	95,305	**73,180**	64,671	57,012
ELGUIT	76	GIBSON	**EXPLORER** WHITE, MAHOGANY	1,025	**787**	696	613
ELGUIT	76	GIBSON	**EXPLORER** BLACK, MAHOGANY	1,059	**813**	718	633
ELGUIT	76	GIBSON	**EXPLORER** NATURAL, MAHOGANY	1,244	**955**	844	744
ELGUIT	77	GIBSON	**EXPLORER** MAHOGANY	1,011	**776**	686	605
ELGUIT	78	GIBSON	**EXPLORER** MAHOGANY BODY	1,431	**1,099**	971	856
ELGUIT	79	GIBSON	**EXPLORER** WHITE, MAHOGANY	1,252	**961**	849	749
ELGUIT	79	GIBSON	**EXPLORER** NATURAL, MAHOGANY	1,290	**990**	875	771
ELGUIT	82	GIBSON	**EXPLORER** CURLY MAPLE TOP	985	**756**	668	589
ELGUIT	82	GIBSON	**EXPLORER** KORINA	2,301	**1,767**	1,561	1,376
ELGUIT	83	GIBSON	**EXPLORER** KORINA	2,988	**2,294**	2,027	1,787
ELGUIT	84	GIBSON	**EXPLORER** ALDER BODY	661	**508**	449	395
ELGUIT	89	GIBSON	**EXPLORER** CHERRY, 3 KNOB	840	**645**	570	502
ELGUIT	85	GIBSON	**EXPLORER BASS** WHITE	588	**451**	399	351
ELGUIT	81	GIBSON	**EXPLORER HERITAGE** WHITE	1,862	**1,430**	1,263	1,114
ELGUIT	81	GIBSON	**EXPLORER HERITAGE** MAHOGANY	1,909	**1,466**	1,295	1,142
ELGUIT	83	GIBSON	**EXPLORER HERITAGE** NATURAL	2,366	**1,817**	1,605	1,415
ELGUIT	83	GIBSON	**EXPLORER HERITAGE** WHITE	3,024	**2,322**	2,052	1,809
ELGUIT	81	GIBSON	**EXPLORER II** SUNBURST, EBONY BOARD	728	**559**	494	435
ELGUIT	84	GIBSON	**EXPLORER III**	870	**668**	590	520
ELGUIT	76	GIBSON	**FIREBIRD BICENTENNIAL 76** BLACK	2,396	**1,840**	1,626	1,433
ELGUIT	76	GIBSON	**FIREBIRD BICENTENNIAL 76** NATURAL, MAHOGANY	2,396	**1,840**	1,626	1,433
ELGUIT	76	GIBSON	**FIREBIRD BICENTENNIAL 76** SUNBURST	2,396	**1,840**	1,626	1,433
ELGUIT	76	GIBSON	**FIREBIRD BICENTENNIAL 76** NATURAL	2,396	**1,840**	1,626	1,433
ELGUIT	63	GIBSON	**FIREBIRD I** SUNBURST, REVERSE	5,376	**4,128**	3,648	3,216
ELGUIT	63	GIBSON	**FIREBIRD I** GOLD, REVERSE	5,600	**4,300**	3,800	3,350
ELGUIT	64	GIBSON	**FIREBIRD I** SUNBURST, REVERSE	4,838	**3,715**	3,283	2,894
ELGUIT	64	GIBSON	**FIREBIRD I** CARDINAL, REVERSE	5,913	**4,540**	4,012	3,537
ELGUIT	64	GIBSON	**FIREBIRD I** POLARIS WHITE, REVERSE	5,913	**4,540**	4,012	3,537
ELGUIT	65	GIBSON	**FIREBIRD I** CARDINAL, NON-REVERSE	2,458	**1,887**	1,668	1,470
ELGUIT	65	GIBSON	**FIREBIRD I** SUNBURST, REVERSE	4,232	**3,249**	2,872	2,531

TYPE	YR	MFG	PRICES--BASED ON 100% ORIGINAL MODEL	SELL EXC	SELL AVG	BUY EXC	BUY AVG
ELGUIT	65	GIBSON	FIREBIRD I GOLD, REVERSE	5,622	4,317	3,815	3,363
ELGUIT	66	GIBSON	FIREBIRD I SUNBURST, NON-REVERSE	1,370	1,052	930	820
ELGUIT	67	GIBSON	FIREBIRD I SUNBURST, NON-REVERSE	1,274	978	864	762
ELGUIT	67	GIBSON	FIREBIRD I POLARIS WHITE, NON-REVERSE	1,284	986	871	768
ELGUIT	68	GIBSON	FIREBIRD I CARDINAL, NON-REVERSE	1,244	955	844	744
ELGUIT	68	GIBSON	FIREBIRD I SUNBURST, NON-REVERSE	1,277	981	867	764
ELGUIT	63	GIBSON	FIREBIRD III CARDINAL RED	8,148	6,256	5,529	4,874
ELGUIT	63	GIBSON	FIREBIRD III GOLD, REVERSE	8,485	6,515	5,757	5,075
ELGUIT	63	GIBSON	FIREBIRD III SUNBURST, REVERSE	10,752	8,256	7,296	6,432
ELGUIT	63	GIBSON	FIREBIRD III FROST BLUE, REVERSE	13,171	10,113	8,937	7,879
ELGUIT	63	GIBSON	FIREBIRD III POLARIS WHITE, REVERSE	13,171	10,113	8,937	7,879
ELGUIT	64	GIBSON	FIREBIRD III POLARIS WHITE, BIG NECK	6,988	5,366	4,742	4,180
ELGUIT	64	GIBSON	FIREBIRD III METALLIC BRONZE, REVERSE	9,797	7,523	6,648	5,861
ELGUIT	64	GIBSON	FIREBIRD III SUNBURST, REVERSE	9,917	7,615	6,729	5,932
ELGUIT	64	GIBSON	FIREBIRD III CARDINAL, REVERSE	13,171	10,113	8,937	7,879
ELGUIT	65	GIBSON	FIREBIRD III SUNBURST, NON-REVERSE	1,386	1,064	940	829
ELGUIT	65	GIBSON	FIREBIRD III CARDINAL, REVERSE	5,628	4,321	3,819	3,366
ELGUIT	65	GIBSON	FIREBIRD III FROST BLUE, REVERSE	5,789	4,445	3,928	3,463
ELGUIT	65	GIBSON	FIREBIRD III SUNBURST, REVERSE	9,336	7,168	6,335	5,585
ELGUIT	66	GIBSON	FIREBIRD III SUNBURST, NON-REVERSE	2,415	1,855	1,639	1,445
ELGUIT	66	GIBSON	FIREBIRD III POLARIS WHITE, REVERSE	10,513	8,072	7,134	6,289
ELGUIT	67	GIBSON	FIREBIRD III SUNBURST, NON-REVERSE	2,191	1,683	1,487	1,311
ELGUIT	67	GIBSON	FIREBIRD III PELHAM BLUE, NON-REVERSE	3,856	2,960	2,616	2,306
ELGUIT	68	GIBSON	FIREBIRD III SUNBURST, NON-REVERSE	2,192	1,683	1,488	1,311
ELGUIT	69	GIBSON	FIREBIRD III CARDINAL, NON-REVERSE	2,190	1,682	1,486	1,310
ELGUIT	59	GIBSON	FIREBIRD V CARDINAL, REVERSE	7,751	5,952	5,259	4,637
ELGUIT	63	GIBSON	FIREBIRD V SUNBURST, REVERSE	7,526	5,779	5,107	4,502
ELGUIT	63	GIBSON	FIREBIRD V PELHAM BLUE, REVERSE	10,752	8,256	7,296	6,432
ELGUIT	64	GIBSON	FIREBIRD V CUSTOM ORANGE, REVERSE	8,162	6,267	5,538	4,882
ELGUIT	64	GIBSON	FIREBIRD V SUNBURST, REVERSE	8,220	6,312	5,578	4,917
ELGUIT	64	GIBSON	FIREBIRD V POLARIS WHITE, REVERSE	10,752	8,256	7,296	6,432
ELGUIT	64	GIBSON	FIREBIRD V FROST BLUE, REVERSE	13,171	10,113	8,937	7,879
ELGUIT	65	GIBSON	FIREBIRD V SUNBURST, NON-REVERSE	1,820	1,397	1,235	1,088
ELGUIT	65	GIBSON	FIREBIRD V KELLY GREEN, REVERSE	6,534	5,017	4,433	3,908
ELGUIT	65	GIBSON	FIREBIRD V CARDINAL RED, REVERSE	7,921	6,082	5,375	4,738
ELGUIT	66	GIBSON	FIREBIRD V SUNBURST, NON-REVERSE, 12-STRING	1,404	1,078	953	840
ELGUIT	67	GIBSON	FIREBIRD V SUNBURST, NON-REVERSE	2,190	1,682	1,486	1,310
ELGUIT	67	GIBSON	FIREBIRD V FROST BLUE, NON-REVERSE	2,195	1,685	1,489	1,313
ELGUIT	68	GIBSON	FIREBIRD V SUNBURST, NON-REVERSE	1,336	1,025	906	799
ELGUIT	71	GIBSON	FIREBIRD V MEDALLION SUNBURST, REVERSE	3,995	3,067	2,710	2,389
ELGUIT	72	GIBSON	FIREBIRD V MEDALLION SUNBURST, REVERSE	3,993	3,066	2,710	2,389
ELGUIT	73	GIBSON	FIREBIRD V MEDALLION LE REISSUE	2,177	1,671	1,477	1,302

TYPE	YR	MFG	PRICES--BASED ON 100% ORIGINAL MODEL	SELL EXC	SELL AVG	BUY EXC	BUY AVG
ELGUIT	63	GIBSON	FIREBIRD VII SUNBURST, REVERSE	10,752	8,256	7,296	6,432
ELGUIT	64	GIBSON	FIREBIRD VII SUNBURST, REVERSE	10,752	8,256	7,296	6,432
ELGUIT	64	GIBSON	FIREBIRD VII CARDINAL, REVERSE	13,720	10,535	9,310	8,207
ELGUIT	65	GIBSON	FIREBIRD VII SUNBURST, REVERSE	8,976	6,892	6,091	5,370
ELGUIT	68	GIBSON	FIREBIRD VII PELHAM BLUE, NON-REVERSE	4,949	3,800	3,358	2,960
ELGUIT	58	GIBSON	FLYING V NATURAL, KORINA, 2 PU's, SERIAL #A26500-A28000	126,054	96,792	85,537	75,407
ELGUIT	58	GIBSON	FLYING V KORINA "05"	129,814	99,679	88,088	77,657
ELGUIT	59	GIBSON	FLYING V NATURAL, KORINA, 2 PU's, SERIAL #A28000	125,106	96,063	84,893	74,840
ELGUIT	62	GIBSON	FLYING V NATURAL, KORINA, 2 PU's	42,959	32,987	29,151	25,699
ELGUIT	63	GIBSON	FLYING V NATURAL, KORINA, 2 PU's	40,316	30,957	27,357	24,117
ELGUIT	66	GIBSON	FLYING V SUNBURST, 2 PU's	6,092	4,678	4,134	3,644
ELGUIT	67	GIBSON	FLYING V TOBACCO SUNBURST, 2 PU's	4,308	3,308	2,923	2,577
ELGUIT	67	GIBSON	FLYING V CHERRY, 2 PU's	5,463	4,195	3,707	3,268
ELGUIT	71	GIBSON	FLYING V SUNBURST, MEDALLION, 2 PU's	1,356	1,041	920	811
ELGUIT	71	GIBSON	FLYING V CHERRY, MEDALLION, 2 PU's	3,610	2,772	2,450	2,160
ELGUIT	75	GIBSON	FLYING V BLACK, 2 PU's	770	591	522	460
ELGUIT	75	GIBSON	FLYING V NATURAL, MAHOGANY, 2 PU's	1,305	1,002	886	781
ELGUIT	76	GIBSON	FLYING V BLACK, 2 PU's	740	568	502	442
ELGUIT	76	GIBSON	FLYING V SUNBURST, 2 PU's	1,208	927	820	722
ELGUIT	76	GIBSON	FLYING V WHITE, 2 PU's	1,225	940	831	732
ELGUIT	76	GIBSON	FLYING V NATURAL, MAHOGANY, 2 PU's	1,295	995	879	775
ELGUIT	78	GIBSON	FLYING V	984	755	668	588
ELGUIT	79	GIBSON	FLYING V NATURAL, MAHOGANY, 2 PU's	1,237	950	839	740
ELGUIT	81	GIBSON	FLYING V SUNBURST, EBONY BOARD, 2 PU's	1,014	779	688	607
ELGUIT	82	GIBSON	FLYING V BLACK, KORINA BODY	1,591	1,222	1,079	952
ELGUIT	82	GIBSON	FLYING V MAHOGANY	2,016	1,548	1,368	1,206
ELGUIT	85	GIBSON	FLYING V ALDER BODY	687	528	466	411
ELGUIT	60	GIBSON	FLYING V 1957 PROTOTYPE	119,558	91,804	81,129	71,521
ELGUIT	83	GIBSON	FLYING V HERITAGE NATURAL	2,925	2,246	1,985	1,750
ELGUIT	79	GIBSON	FLYING V II NATURAL, V-SHAPED PU's	848	651	576	507
ELGUIT	81	GIBSON	FLYING V II V-SHAPED PU's	789	606	535	472
ELGUIT	88	GIBSON	FLYING V 90 DOUBLE	948	728	643	567
ELGUIT	82	GIBSON	FLYING V CMT SOLID BODY	1,001	768	679	598
ELGUIT	65	GIBSON	FOLK SINGER F-25 NATURAL, 12-FRET NECK	855	657	580	511
ELGUIT	67	GIBSON	FOLK SINGER FJ-N JUMBO	936	718	635	560
ELGUIT	72	GIBSON	G-3 BASS NATURAL	712	546	483	426
ELGUIT	74	GIBSON	G-3 BASS NATURAL	660	507	448	395
ELGUIT	76	GIBSON	G-3 BASS BLACK, SOLID MAPLE, 3 PU's	658	505	446	393
ELGUIT	78	GIBSON	G-3 BASS NATURAL, SOLID MAPLE, 3 PU's	658	505	446	393
ELGUIT	81	GIBSON	G-3 BASS NATURAL	611	469	414	365
ELGUIT	19	GIBSON	GB-1	1,449	1,112	983	866
ELGUIT	28	GIBSON	GB-1	1,341	1,030	910	802
ELGUIT	70	GIBSON	GOLD TOP LEFT-HANDED, 50"S P90'S	5,258	4,037	3,568	3,145
ELGUIT	74	GIBSON	GRABBER BASS NATURAL	668	513	453	399

TYPE	YR	MFG	PRICES--BASED ON 100% ORIGINAL MODEL	SELL EXC	SELL AVG	BUY EXC	BUY AVG
ELGUIT	75	GIBSON	**GRABBER BASS** SOLID MAPLE, 1 PU	810	**622**	550	485
ELGUIT	76	GIBSON	**GRABBER BASS** NATURAL	635	**487**	430	379
ELGUIT	77	GIBSON	**GRABBER BASS** SOLID MAPLE, 1 PU	730	**560**	495	436
ELGUIT	78	GIBSON	**GRABBER BASS** BURGUNDY, MAPLE NECK	666	**511**	452	398
ELGUIT	78	GIBSON	**GRABBER BASS** SOLID MAPLE, 1 PU	730	**560**	495	436
ELGUIT	79	GIBSON	**GRABBER BASS** BLACK, MAPLE	638	**490**	433	381
ELGUIT	79	GIBSON	**GRABBER BASS** SOLID MAPLE, 1 PU	695	**534**	471	416
ELGUIT	66	GIBSON	**GRANADA** SUNBURST	660	**507**	448	395
ELGUIT	77	GIBSON	**HOWARD ROBERTS ARTIST** SUNBURST	1,503	**1,154**	1,019	899
ELGUIT	78	GIBSON	**HOWARD ROBERTS ARTIST** SUNBURST	1,496	**1,148**	1,015	895
ELGUIT	78	GIBSON	**HOWARD ROBERTS ARTIST** CHERRY RED	1,498	**1,150**	1,016	896
ELGUIT	79	GIBSON	**HOWARD ROBERTS ARTIST** SUNBURST	1,426	**1,095**	968	853
ELGUIT	74	GIBSON	**HOWARD ROBERTS CUSTOM** WINE RED	1,494	**1,147**	1,013	893
ELGUIT	74	GIBSON	**HOWARD ROBERTS CUSTOM** CHERRY RED	1,496	**1,148**	1,015	895
ELGUIT	78	GIBSON	**HOWARD ROBERTS FUSION** SUNBURST	1,490	**1,144**	1,011	891
ELGUIT	81	GIBSON	**HOWARD ROBERTS FUSION** SUNBURST	1,389	**1,067**	943	831
ELGUIT	85	GIBSON	**INVADER**	579	**444**	392	346
ELGUIT	61	GIBSON	**JOHNNY SMITH** NATURAL, 1 PU	11,711	**8,993**	7,947	7,006
ELGUIT	61	GIBSON	**JOHNNY SMITH** TORTOISE SUNBURST, 1 PU	11,714	**8,994**	7,948	7,007
ELGUIT	62	GIBSON	**JOHNNY SMITH** SUNBURST, 1 PU	11,189	**8,592**	7,593	6,693
ELGUIT	63	GIBSON	**JOHNNY SMITH** SUNBURST, 1 PU	10,831	**8,317**	7,349	6,479
ELGUIT	64	GIBSON	**JOHNNY SMITH** SUNBURST, 1 PU	10,700	**8,216**	7,261	6,401
ELGUIT	65	GIBSON	**JOHNNY SMITH** SUNBURST, 1 PU	8,841	**6,788**	5,999	5,288
ELGUIT	66	GIBSON	**JOHNNY SMITH** SUNBURST, 2 PU's	6,459	**4,959**	4,382	3,863
ELGUIT	67	GIBSON	**JOHNNY SMITH** SUNBURST, 1 PU	8,868	**6,809**	6,017	5,305
ELGUIT	68	GIBSON	**JOHNNY SMITH** SUNBURST, 1 PU	7,890	**6,058**	5,354	4,720
ELGUIT	68	GIBSON	**JOHNNY SMITH** NATURAL, 1 PU	8,561	**6,573**	5,809	5,121
ELGUIT	69	GIBSON	**JOHNNY SMITH** SUNBURST, 1 PU	7,631	**5,860**	5,178	4,565
ELGUIT	69	GIBSON	**JOHNNY SMITH** NATURAL, 1 PU	7,862	**6,037**	5,335	4,703
ELGUIT	72	GIBSON	**JOHNNY SMITH** SUNBURST, 1 PU	6,804	**5,224**	4,617	4,070
ELGUIT	74	GIBSON	**JOHNNY SMITH** SUNBURST, 1 PU	7,397	**5,680**	5,019	4,425
ELGUIT	76	GIBSON	**JOHNNY SMITH** BLOND, 1 PU	5,664	**4,349**	3,844	3,388
ELGUIT	76	GIBSON	**JOHNNY SMITH** SUNBURST, 1 PU	6,129	**4,706**	4,159	3,666
ELGUIT	77	GIBSON	**JOHNNY SMITH** SUNBURST, 1 PU	5,191	**3,986**	3,522	3,105
ELGUIT	78	GIBSON	**JOHNNY SMITH** SUNBURST, 1 PU	5,682	**4,363**	3,856	3,399
ELGUIT	79	GIBSON	**JOHNNY SMITH** SUNBURST, 1 PU	5,839	**4,484**	3,962	3,493

TYPE	YR	MFG	PRICES--BASED ON 100% ORIGINAL MODEL	SELL EXC	SELL AVG	BUY EXC	BUY AVG
ELGUIT	81	GIBSON	**JOHNNY SMITH** FLAMED SUNBURST, 1 PU	6,064	**4,656**	4,115	3,628
ELGUIT	67	GIBSON	**JOHNNY SMITH D** SUNBURST, 2 PU's	8,022	**6,160**	5,443	4,799
ELGUIT	68	GIBSON	**JOHNNY SMITH D** SUNBURST, 2 PU's	8,836	**6,785**	5,996	5,286
ELGUIT	72	GIBSON	**JOHNNY SMITH D** SUNBURST, 2 PU's	6,805	**5,225**	4,617	4,070
ELGUIT	78	GIBSON	**JOHNNY SMITH D** NATURAL, 2 PU's	5,834	**4,479**	3,958	3,490
ELGUIT	78	GIBSON	**JOHNNY SMITH DOUBLE** CASE	4,742	**3,641**	3,217	2,836
ELGUIT	70	GIBSON	**JOHNNY SMITH H** SUNBURST, 1 PU	6,805	**5,225**	4,617	4,070
ELGUIT	78	GIBSON	**JOHNNY SMITH SINGLE** CASE	2,410	**1,850**	1,635	1,441
ELGUIT	78	GIBSON	**KALAMAZOO AWARD MODEL** NATURAL	7,311	**5,614**	4,961	4,373
ELGUIT	78	GIBSON	**L- 5 C**	3,523	**2,705**	2,390	2,107
ELGUIT	78	GIBSON	**L- 5 CES CUSTOM** CASE	4,742	**3,641**	3,217	2,836
ELGUIT	78	GIBSON	**L- 5 S CUSTOM**	2,936	**2,254**	1,992	1,756
ELGUIT	51	GIBSON	**L- 5CES** NATURAL	11,394	**8,749**	7,732	6,816
ELGUIT	51	GIBSON	**L- 5CES** SUNBURST, SERIAL #A6000-A9400	13,778	**10,579**	9,349	8,242
ELGUIT	53	GIBSON	**L- 5CES**	13,387	**10,279**	9,084	8,008
ELGUIT	55	GIBSON	**L- 5CES** SUNBURST, SERIAL #A19000-A22000	11,298	**8,675**	7,666	6,758
ELGUIT	56	GIBSON	**L- 5CES** NATURAL, P-90 PU	10,805	**8,297**	7,332	6,464
ELGUIT	57	GIBSON	**L- 5CES** SUNBURST	13,228	**10,157**	8,976	7,913
ELGUIT	60	GIBSON	**L- 5CES** SUNBURST, ROUNDED CUTAWAY	11,314	**8,687**	7,677	6,768
ELGUIT	61	GIBSON	**L- 5CES** NATURAL, PAF PU	13,190	**10,128**	8,950	7,890
ELGUIT	62	GIBSON	**L- 5CES** SUNBURST, FLORENTINE CUTAWAY, 2 PU's, INLAY	11,325	**8,696**	7,685	6,775
ELGUIT	63	GIBSON	**L- 5CES** SUNBURST	11,252	**8,640**	7,635	6,731
ELGUIT	64	GIBSON	**L- 5CES** SUNBURST, POINTED CUTAWAY	11,252	**8,640**	7,635	6,731
ELGUIT	65	GIBSON	**L- 5CES** NATURAL	8,158	**6,264**	5,535	4,880
ELGUIT	65	GIBSON	**L- 5CES** SUNBURST	8,486	**6,516**	5,758	5,076
ELGUIT	67	GIBSON	**L- 5CES** SUNBURST	8,131	**6,243**	5,517	4,864
ELGUIT	68	GIBSON	**L- 5CES** NATURAL	6,799	**5,221**	4,613	4,067
ELGUIT	68	GIBSON	**L- 5CES** SUNBURST, SHARP CUTAWAY	7,554	**5,800**	5,126	4,519
ELGUIT	69	GIBSON	**L- 5CES** NATURAL	6,797	**5,219**	4,612	4,066
ELGUIT	69	GIBSON	**L- 5CES** SUNBURST	7,427	**5,703**	5,040	4,443
ELGUIT	69	GIBSON	**L- 5CES** BLOND	9,798	**7,524**	6,649	5,861
ELGUIT	70	GIBSON	**L- 5CES** NATURAL	6,098	**4,682**	4,138	3,648
ELGUIT	70	GIBSON	**L- 5CES** SUNBURST	7,273	**5,584**	4,935	4,350
ELGUIT	71	GIBSON	**L- 5CES** NATURAL	5,615	**4,312**	3,810	3,359
ELGUIT	71	GIBSON	**L- 5CES** SUNBURST	6,993	**5,369**	4,745	4,183
ELGUIT	72	GIBSON	**L- 5CES** SUNBURST	6,344	**4,871**	4,305	3,795
ELGUIT	73	GIBSON	**L- 5CES** SUNBURST	6,388	**4,905**	4,335	3,821
ELGUIT	74	GIBSON	**L- 5CES** NATURAL	4,776	**3,667**	3,241	2,857
ELGUIT	75	GIBSON	**L- 5CES** SUNBURST	6,379	**4,898**	4,328	3,816
ELGUIT	76	GIBSON	**L- 5CES** SUNBURST, ARCHTOP	6,177	**4,743**	4,192	3,695
ELGUIT	77	GIBSON	**L- 5CES** NATURAL	4,776	**3,667**	3,241	2,857
ELGUIT	77	GIBSON	**L- 5CES** BURGUNDY	5,451	**4,185**	3,698	3,260
ELGUIT	77	GIBSON	**L- 5CES** SUNBURST	6,016	**4,619**	4,082	3,599

TYPE	YR	MFG	PRICES--BASED ON 100% ORIGINAL MODEL	SELL EXC	SELL AVG	BUY EXC	BUY AVG
ELGUIT	78	GIBSON	**L- 5CES** SUNBURST	5,992	**4,601**	4,066	3,584
ELGUIT	79	GIBSON	**L- 5CES** ANTIQUE SUNBURST	4,471	**3,433**	3,033	2,674
ELGUIT	69	GIBSON	**L- 5CESN** BLOND	8,407	**6,456**	5,705	5,029
ELGUIT	77	GIBSON	**L- 5CESN** ARCHTOP	6,323	**4,855**	4,290	3,782
ELGUIT	84	GIBSON	**L- 5CESN 50TH ANNIVERSARY** BLOND	5,900	**4,530**	4,003	3,529
ELGUIT	72	GIBSON	**L- 5S** CHERRY SUNBURST, CUTAWAY	3,842	**2,950**	2,607	2,298
ELGUIT	73	GIBSON	**L- 5S** CHERRY SUNBURST, CUTAWAY	2,061	**1,583**	1,399	1,233
ELGUIT	74	GIBSON	**L- 5S** CHERRY SUNBURST, CUTAWAY	2,065	**1,585**	1,401	1,235
ELGUIT	75	GIBSON	**L- 5S** CHERRY SUNBURST, CUTAWAY, HUMBUCKER	1,863	**1,431**	1,264	1,114
ELGUIT	76	GIBSON	**L- 5S** CHERRY SUNBURST, CUTAWAY	1,860	**1,428**	1,262	1,112
ELGUIT	76	GIBSON	**L- 5S** NATURAL	2,214	**1,700**	1,502	1,324
ELGUIT	76	GIBSON	**L- 5S** NATURAL, CUTAWAY	2,245	**1,724**	1,523	1,343
ELGUIT	77	GIBSON	**L- 5S** CHERRY SUNBURST, CUTAWAY	1,861	**1,429**	1,263	1,113
ELGUIT	77	GIBSON	**L- 5S** NATURAL, CUTAWAY	2,209	**1,696**	1,499	1,321
ELGUIT	78	GIBSON	**L- 5S** CHERRY SUNBURST, CUTAWAY	1,860	**1,428**	1,262	1,112
ELGUIT	78	GIBSON	**L- 5S** NATURAL, CUTAWAY	2,298	**1,764**	1,559	1,374
ELGUIT	79	GIBSON	**L- 5S** NATURAL, CUTAWAY	2,153	**1,653**	1,461	1,288
ELGUIT	70	GIBSON	**L- 6S** BLACK	660	**507**	448	395
ELGUIT	72	GIBSON	**L- 6S** NATURAL	652	**501**	443	390
ELGUIT	72	GIBSON	**L- 6S** BLACK	660	**507**	448	395
ELGUIT	73	GIBSON	**L- 6S** BLACK	593	**455**	402	355
ELGUIT	75	GIBSON	**L- 6S** NATURAL	612	**470**	415	366
ELGUIT	75	GIBSON	**L- 6S** BLACK	660	**507**	448	395
ELGUIT	75	GIBSON	**L- 6S**	673	**516**	456	402
ELGUIT	78	GIBSON	**L- 6S** NATURAL	645	**495**	437	385
ELGUIT	80	GIBSON	**L- 6S** SUNBURST	639	**491**	433	382
ELGUIT	75	GIBSON	**L- 6S CUSTOM** BLACK	673	**516**	456	402
ELGUIT	77	GIBSON	**L- 6S CUSTOM** NATURAL	658	**505**	446	393
ELGUIT	78	GIBSON	**L- 6S CUSTOM** SUNBURST	605	**465**	411	362
ELGUIT	78	GIBSON	**L- 6S CUSTOM** BLACK	661	**508**	449	395
ELGUIT	78	GIBSON	**L- 6S CUSTOM** NATURAL	742	**570**	503	444
ELGUIT	79	GIBSON	**L- 6S CUSTOM**	712	**546**	483	426
ELGUIT	74	GIBSON	**L- 6S DELUXE** NATURAL	664	**509**	450	397
ELGUIT	75	GIBSON	**L- 6S DELUXE** NATURAL	664	**509**	450	397
ELGUIT	76	GIBSON	**L- 6S DELUXE** BLACK	617	**473**	418	369
ELGUIT	80	GIBSON	**L- 6S DELUXE**	661	**508**	449	395
ELGUIT	36	GIBSON	**L-C/CENTURY**	3,614	**2,775**	2,452	2,162
ELGUIT	55	GIBSON	**LES PAUL** TV MAHOGANY, SINGLE CUTAWAY	4,904	**3,765**	3,328	2,933
ELGUIT	56	GIBSON	**LES PAUL** TV MAHOGANY, SINGLE CUTAWAY	4,932	**3,787**	3,347	2,950
ELGUIT	57	GIBSON	**LES PAUL** TV MAHOGANY, SINGLE CUTAWAY	5,174	**3,973**	3,511	3,095
ELGUIT	58	GIBSON	**LES PAUL** TV MAHOGANY, DOUBLE CUTAWAY	5,508	**4,229**	3,737	3,295
ELGUIT	59	GIBSON	**LES PAUL** TV MAHOGANY, DOUBLE CUTAWAY	5,626	**4,320**	3,818	3,366
ELGUIT	60	GIBSON	**LES PAUL** TV MAHOGANY, DOUBLE CUTAWAY	4,323	**3,319**	2,933	2,586
ELGUIT	77	GIBSON	**LES PAUL 25 50th ANNIVERSARY** SUNBURST	1,734	**1,332**	1,177	1,037

TYPE	YR	MFG	PRICES--BASED ON 100% ORIGINAL MODEL	SELL EXC	SELL AVG	BUY EXC	BUY AVG
ELGUIT	77	GIBSON	**LES PAUL 25 50th ANNIVERSARY** NATURAL	1,740	**1,336**	1,181	1,041
ELGUIT	78	GIBSON	**LES PAUL 25 50th ANNIVERSARY** WINE RED	1,391	**1,068**	943	832
ELGUIT	78	GIBSON	**LES PAUL 25 50th ANNIVERSARY** NATURAL	1,711	**1,314**	1,161	1,023
ELGUIT	78	GIBSON	**LES PAUL 25 50th ANNIVERSARY** TOBACCO SUNBURST	1,904	**1,462**	1,292	1,139
ELGUIT	78	GIBSON	**LES PAUL 25 50th ANNIVERSARY** CHERRY SUNBURST	1,917	**1,472**	1,301	1,147
ELGUIT	79	GIBSON	**LES PAUL 25 50th ANNIVERSARY** ANTIQUE	1,498	**1,150**	1,016	896
ELGUIT	79	GIBSON	**LES PAUL 25 50th ANNIVERSARY** SUNBURST	1,537	**1,180**	1,043	919
ELGUIT	79	GIBSON	**LES PAUL 25 50th ANNIVERSARY** NATURAL	1,750	**1,344**	1,187	1,047
ELGUIT	79	GIBSON	**LES PAUL 25 50th ANNIVERSARY** WINE RED	1,813	**1,392**	1,230	1,084
ELGUIT	82	GIBSON	**LES PAUL 30 ANNIVERSARY**	2,231	**1,713**	1,513	1,334
ELGUIT	76	GIBSON	**LES PAUL ARTISAN** WALNUT, 3 PU's	1,762	**1,353**	1,196	1,054
ELGUIT	77	GIBSON	**LES PAUL ARTISAN** WALNUT, 3 PU's, GOLD HARDWARE	1,440	**1,105**	977	861
ELGUIT	78	GIBSON	**LES PAUL ARTISAN** BLACK, 3 PU's	1,757	**1,349**	1,192	1,051
ELGUIT	78	GIBSON	**LES PAUL ARTISAN** WALNUT	1,813	**1,392**	1,230	1,084
ELGUIT	78	GIBSON	**LES PAUL ARTISAN** TOBACCO SUNBURST	1,904	**1,462**	1,292	1,139
ELGUIT	79	GIBSON	**LES PAUL ARTISAN** TOBACCO SUNBURST, 3 PU's	1,767	**1,357**	1,199	1,057
ELGUIT	79	GIBSON	**LES PAUL ARTISAN** BLACK, 3 PU's	1,776	**1,363**	1,205	1,062
ELGUIT	80	GIBSON	**LES PAUL ARTISAN** SUNBURST, 2 PU's	1,451	**1,114**	984	868
ELGUIT	80	GIBSON	**LES PAUL ARTISAN** BLACK	1,578	**1,211**	1,070	944
ELGUIT	81	GIBSON	**LES PAUL ARTISAN** TOBACCO SUNBURST	1,547	**1,188**	1,050	925
ELGUIT	78	GIBSON	**LES PAUL ARTIST**	1,761	**1,352**	1,195	1,053
ELGUIT	69	GIBSON	**LES PAUL BASS** NATURAL, TRIUMPH BASS	1,032	**792**	700	617
ELGUIT	70	GIBSON	**LES PAUL BASS** WALNUT, SOLID MAHOGANY	660	**507**	448	395
ELGUIT	72	GIBSON	**LES PAUL BASS** WALNUT	1,210	**929**	821	724
ELGUIT	73	GIBSON	**LES PAUL BASS** NATURAL, WALNUT	1,216	**933**	825	727
ELGUIT	54	GIBSON	**LES PAUL CUSTOM** EBONY, GOLD HARDWARE, 2 PU's	10,330	**7,932**	7,010	6,180
ELGUIT	55	GIBSON	**LES PAUL CUSTOM** EBONY, GOLD HARDWARE, 2 PU's	9,522	**7,311**	6,461	5,696
ELGUIT	55	GIBSON	**LES PAUL CUSTOM** BLACK	9,567	**7,346**	6,491	5,723
ELGUIT	55	GIBSON	**LES PAUL CUSTOM** EBONY, LEFT-HANDED	10,818	**8,306**	7,340	6,471
ELGUIT	56	GIBSON	**LES PAUL CUSTOM** EBONY, GOLD HARDWARE, 2 PU's	9,216	**7,076**	6,254	5,513
ELGUIT	56	GIBSON	**LES PAUL CUSTOM** BLACK, BIGSBY, 2 PU's	9,549	**7,332**	6,479	5,712
ELGUIT	56	GIBSON	**LES PAUL CUSTOM** NATURAL	13,121	**10,075**	8,904	7,849
ELGUIT	57	GIBSON	**LES PAUL CUSTOM** EBONY, GOLD HARDWARE, 2 PU's	9,181	**7,050**	6,230	5,492
ELGUIT	57	GIBSON	**LES PAUL CUSTOM** EBONY, GOLD HARDWARE, 3 PU's	13,351	**10,252**	9,059	7,987
ELGUIT	58	GIBSON	**LES PAUL CUSTOM** EBONY, GOLD HARDWARE, 3 PU's	13,048	**10,019**	8,854	7,805
ELGUIT	58	GIBSON	**LES PAUL CUSTOM** BLACK	13,112	**10,068**	8,898	7,844
ELGUIT	59	GIBSON	**LES PAUL CUSTOM** EBONY, GOLD HARDWARE, 3 PU's	13,351	**10,252**	9,059	7,987
ELGUIT	59	GIBSON	**LES PAUL CUSTOM** BLACK	13,700	**10,520**	9,297	8,196
ELGUIT	60	GIBSON	**LES PAUL CUSTOM** EBONY, GOLD HARDWARE, 3 PU's	12,690	**9,744**	8,611	7,591
ELGUIT	61	GIBSON	**LES PAUL CUSTOM** WHITE, 3 PU's, VIB, 3 PAF'S	6,086	**4,673**	4,129	3,640
ELGUIT	62	GIBSON	**LES PAUL CUSTOM** WHITE, 3 PU's, VIB	6,765	**5,195**	4,591	4,047
ELGUIT	68	GIBSON	**LES PAUL CUSTOM** BLACK, GOLD HARDWARE, 2 PU's	5,241	**4,024**	3,556	3,135
ELGUIT	69	GIBSON	**LES PAUL CUSTOM** BLACK, GOLD HARDWARE, 2 PU's, 3 PIECE NECK	3,638	**2,794**	2,469	2,176

TYPE	YR	MFG	PRICES--BASED ON 100% ORIGINAL MODEL	SELL EXC	SELL AVG	BUY EXC	BUY AVG
ELGUIT	70	GIBSON	**LES PAUL CUSTOM** BLACK, GOLD HARDWARE, 2 PU's, VALITE NECK MADE IN USA	1,750	**1,344**	1,187	1,047
ELGUIT	71	GIBSON	**LES PAUL CUSTOM** BLACK, GOLD HARDWARE, 2 PU's	1,805	**1,386**	1,225	1,080
ELGUIT	71	GIBSON	**LES PAUL CUSTOM** CHERRY SUNBURST, 2 PU's	1,907	**1,464**	1,294	1,141
ELGUIT	71	GIBSON	**LES PAUL CUSTOM** BLACK, LEFT-HANDED	2,334	**1,792**	1,583	1,396
ELGUIT	72	GIBSON	**LES PAUL CUSTOM** TOBACCO SUNBURST	1,576	**1,210**	1,070	943
ELGUIT	72	GIBSON	**LES PAUL CUSTOM** BLACK, GOLD HARDWARE, 2 PU's	1,597	**1,226**	1,083	955
ELGUIT	72	GIBSON	**LES PAUL CUSTOM** CHERRY SUNBURST, 2 PU's	2,172	**1,668**	1,474	1,299
ELGUIT	73	GIBSON	**LES PAUL CUSTOM** CHERRY SUNBURST	1,697	**1,303**	1,152	1,015
ELGUIT	73	GIBSON	**LES PAUL CUSTOM** BLACK, 2 PU's	1,769	**1,358**	1,200	1,058
ELGUIT	74	GIBSON	**LES PAUL CUSTOM** CHERRY SUNBURST, 2 PU's	1,322	**1,015**	897	791
ELGUIT	75	GIBSON	**LES PAUL CUSTOM** BLACK, GOLD HARDWARE, 2 PU's	1,307	**1,003**	886	781
ELGUIT	75	GIBSON	**LES PAUL CUSTOM** CHERRY SUNBURST, 2 PU's	1,322	**1,015**	897	791
ELGUIT	75	GIBSON	**LES PAUL CUSTOM** WINE RED	1,330	**1,021**	902	795
ELGUIT	75	GIBSON	**LES PAUL CUSTOM** WHITE, GOLD HARDWARE, 2 PU's	1,556	**1,195**	1,056	931
ELGUIT	75	GIBSON	**LES PAUL CUSTOM** SUNBURST	1,622	**1,246**	1,101	970
ELGUIT	76	GIBSON	**LES PAUL CUSTOM** NATURAL, 2 PU's	1,205	**925**	817	720
ELGUIT	76	GIBSON	**LES PAUL CUSTOM** WINE RED	1,299	**997**	881	777
ELGUIT	76	GIBSON	**LES PAUL CUSTOM** CHERRY SUNBURST, 2 PU's	1,312	**1,007**	890	785
ELGUIT	76	GIBSON	**LES PAUL CUSTOM** TOBACCO SUNBURST	1,316	**1,010**	893	787
ELGUIT	76	GIBSON	**LES PAUL CUSTOM** BLACK, GOLD HARDWARE, 2 PU's	1,322	**1,015**	897	791
ELGUIT	77	GIBSON	**LES PAUL CUSTOM** CHERRY SUNBURST, 2 PU's	1,274	**978**	864	762
ELGUIT	77	GIBSON	**LES PAUL CUSTOM** BLACK, GOLD HARDWARE, 2 PU's	1,322	**1,015**	897	791
ELGUIT	78	GIBSON	**LES PAUL CUSTOM** CHROME HARDWARE	1,028	**789**	697	615
ELGUIT	78	GIBSON	**LES PAUL CUSTOM** NATURAL, 2 PU's	1,068	**820**	725	639
ELGUIT	78	GIBSON	**LES PAUL CUSTOM** WINE RED, 2 PU's	1,300	**998**	882	777
ELGUIT	78	GIBSON	**LES PAUL CUSTOM** BLACK, GOLD HARDWARE, 2 PU's	1,301	**999**	883	778
ELGUIT	78	GIBSON	**LES PAUL CUSTOM** CHERRY SUNBURST, 2 PU's	1,305	**1,002**	886	781
ELGUIT	78	GIBSON	**LES PAUL CUSTOM** TOBACCO SUNBURST	1,305	**1,002**	886	781
ELGUIT	78	GIBSON	**LES PAUL CUSTOM** WHITE, GOLD HARDWARE, 2 PU's	1,501	**1,153**	1,019	898
ELGUIT	78	GIBSON	**LES PAUL CUSTOM** BLACK, LEFT-HANDED	1,535	**1,179**	1,041	918
ELGUIT	79	GIBSON	**LES PAUL CUSTOM** NATURAL, 2 PU's	1,025	**787**	696	613
ELGUIT	79	GIBSON	**LES PAUL CUSTOM** WINE RED	1,199	**921**	813	717
ELGUIT	79	GIBSON	**LES PAUL CUSTOM** CHERRY SUNBURST, 2 PU's	1,244	**955**	844	744
ELGUIT	79	GIBSON	**LES PAUL CUSTOM** CREAM, GOLD HARDWARE, 2 PU's	1,253	**962**	850	749
ELGUIT	79	GIBSON	**LES PAUL CUSTOM** BLACK, GOLD HARDWARE, 2 PU's	1,420	**1,090**	963	849
ELGUIT	79	GIBSON	**LES PAUL CUSTOM** SILVERBURST	1,475	**1,132**	1,000	882
ELGUIT	80	GIBSON	**LES PAUL CUSTOM** NATURAL, GOLD HARDWARE	1,027	**788**	696	614
ELGUIT	80	GIBSON	**LES PAUL CUSTOM** WINE RED	1,238	**951**	840	741
ELGUIT	80	GIBSON	**LES PAUL CUSTOM** WHITE, GOLD HARDWARE	1,242	**953**	842	743
ELGUIT	81	GIBSON	**LES PAUL CUSTOM** WINE RED	1,232	**946**	836	737
ELGUIT	81	GIBSON	**LES PAUL CUSTOM** BURGUNDY	1,235	**948**	838	739
ELGUIT	81	GIBSON	**LES PAUL CUSTOM** WINE RED, LEFT-HANDED	1,331	**1,022**	903	796

TYPE	YR	MFG	PRICES--BASED ON 100% ORIGINAL MODEL	SELL EXC	SELL AVG	BUY EXC	BUY AVG
ELGUIT	82	GIBSON	**LES PAUL CUSTOM** TOBACCO SUNBURST	1,003	**770**	680	600
ELGUIT	86	GIBSON	**LES PAUL CUSTOM** SUNBURST	1,472	**1,130**	999	881
ELGUIT	86	GIBSON	**LES PAUL CUSTOM** BLACK	1,495	**1,148**	1,014	894
ELGUIT	87	GIBSON	**LES PAUL CUSTOM** SUNBURST, GOLD SUPERTUNE, GOLD HARDWARE	2,701	**2,074**	1,833	1,616
ELGUIT	87	GIBSON	**LES PAUL CUSTOM** SUNBURST, GOLD HARDWARE	2,701	**2,074**	1,833	1,616
ELGUIT	72	GIBSON	**LES PAUL CUSTOM '54** 1954 REISSUE	2,214	**1,700**	1,502	1,324
ELGUIT	73	GIBSON	**LES PAUL CUSTOM '54** 1954 REISSUE	2,196	**1,686**	1,490	1,313
ELGUIT	74	GIBSON	**LES PAUL CUSTOM 20th ANNIVERSARY** WINE RED	1,615	**1,240**	1,095	966
ELGUIT	74	GIBSON	**LES PAUL CUSTOM 20th ANNIVERSARY** SUNBURST	1,914	**1,469**	1,298	1,145
ELGUIT	74	GIBSON	**LES PAUL CUSTOM 20th ANNIVERSARY** BLACK	2,167	**1,664**	1,470	1,296
ELGUIT	74	GIBSON	**LES PAUL CUSTOM 20th ANNIVERSARY** WHITE, RANDY RHONDEL STYLE	2,364	**1,815**	1,604	1,414
ELGUIT	68	GIBSON	**LES PAUL DELUXE** GOLD TOP	4,411	**3,387**	2,993	2,639
ELGUIT	69	GIBSON	**LES PAUL DELUXE** CHERRY SUNBURST	2,356	**1,809**	1,599	1,409
ELGUIT	69	GIBSON	**LES PAUL DELUXE** CHERRY SUNBURST, LEFT-HANDED	2,440	**1,873**	1,656	1,459
ELGUIT	69	GIBSON	**LES PAUL DELUXE** GOLD TOP	3,190	**2,450**	2,165	1,908
ELGUIT	70	GIBSON	**LES PAUL DELUXE** CHERRY SUNBURST	1,291	**991**	876	772
ELGUIT	70	GIBSON	**LES PAUL DELUXE** GOLD TOP	1,967	**1,511**	1,335	1,177
ELGUIT	70	GIBSON	**LES PAUL DELUXE** CHERRY SUNBURST, LEFT-HANDED	2,188	**1,680**	1,485	1,309
ELGUIT	71	GIBSON	**LES PAUL DELUXE** GOLD TOP	1,490	**1,144**	1,011	891
ELGUIT	71	GIBSON	**LES PAUL DELUXE** WINE RED	1,509	**1,159**	1,024	903
ELGUIT	71	GIBSON	**LES PAUL DELUXE** NATURAL, SERIAL # 678381	1,620	**1,244**	1,099	969
ELGUIT	71	GIBSON	**LES PAUL DELUXE** TOBACCO SUNBURST	1,886	**1,448**	1,279	1,128
ELGUIT	72	GIBSON	**LES PAUL DELUXE** GOLD TOP	1,405	**1,079**	953	840
ELGUIT	72	GIBSON	**LES PAUL DELUXE** CHERRY SUNBURST	1,433	**1,100**	972	857
ELGUIT	72	GIBSON	**LES PAUL DELUXE** SUNBURST	1,547	**1,188**	1,050	925
ELGUIT	72	GIBSON	**LES PAUL DELUXE** GOLD TOP, LEFT-HANDED	1,730	**1,328**	1,174	1,035
ELGUIT	73	GIBSON	**LES PAUL DELUXE** SUNBURST	1,356	**1,041**	920	811
ELGUIT	73	GIBSON	**LES PAUL DELUXE** NATURAL	1,562	**1,199**	1,060	934
ELGUIT	73	GIBSON	**LES PAUL DELUXE** GOLD TOP	1,682	**1,291**	1,141	1,006
ELGUIT	73	GIBSON	**LES PAUL DELUXE** CHERRY SUNBURST	2,027	**1,556**	1,375	1,212
ELGUIT	74	GIBSON	**LES PAUL DELUXE** GOLD TOP	1,781	**1,368**	1,209	1,065
ELGUIT	74	GIBSON	**LES PAUL DELUXE** CHERRY SUNBURST	1,841	**1,413**	1,249	1,101
ELGUIT	74	GIBSON	**LES PAUL DELUXE** RED SPARKLE	3,598	**2,763**	2,441	2,152
ELGUIT	74	GIBSON	**LES PAUL DELUXE** BLUE SPARKLE	4,159	**3,194**	2,822	2,488
ELGUIT	75	GIBSON	**LES PAUL DELUXE** WINE RED	1,212	**931**	823	725
ELGUIT	75	GIBSON	**LES PAUL DELUXE** GOLD TOP	1,505	**1,155**	1,021	900
ELGUIT	75	GIBSON	**LES PAUL DELUXE** NATURAL	1,573	**1,208**	1,067	941
ELGUIT	75	GIBSON	**LES PAUL DELUXE** BLUE SPARKLE	4,174	**3,205**	2,832	2,497
ELGUIT	76	GIBSON	**LES PAUL DELUXE** WINE RED	1,201	**922**	815	718
ELGUIT	76	GIBSON	**LES PAUL DELUXE** TOBACCO SUNBURST	1,206	**926**	818	721
ELGUIT	76	GIBSON	**LES PAUL DELUXE** BURGUNDY	1,300	**998**	882	777
ELGUIT	76	GIBSON	**LES PAUL DELUXE** SUNBURST	1,303	**1,001**	884	779

TYPE	YR	MFG	PRICES--BASED ON 100% ORIGINAL MODEL	SELL EXC	SELL AVG	BUY EXC	BUY AVG
ELGUIT	76	GIBSON	**LES PAUL DELUXE** NATURAL	1,368	**1,050**	928	818
ELGUIT	76	GIBSON	**LES PAUL DELUXE** GOLD TOP	1,408	**1,081**	956	842
ELGUIT	77	GIBSON	**LES PAUL DELUXE** WINE RED	981	**753**	665	586
ELGUIT	77	GIBSON	**LES PAUL DELUXE** BLACK	1,291	**991**	876	772
ELGUIT	77	GIBSON	**LES PAUL DELUXE** SUNBURST, 2 MINI PU's	1,336	**1,025**	906	799
ELGUIT	77	GIBSON	**LES PAUL DELUXE** NATURAL, BLOND	1,503	**1,154**	1,019	899
ELGUIT	78	GIBSON	**LES PAUL DELUXE** CHERRY SUNBURST	997	**766**	677	596
ELGUIT	78	GIBSON	**LES PAUL DELUXE** LEFT-HANDED	1,028	**789**	697	615
ELGUIT	78	GIBSON	**LES PAUL DELUXE** SUNBURST	1,291	**991**	876	772
ELGUIT	78	GIBSON	**LES PAUL DELUXE** WINE RED	1,295	**995**	879	775
ELGUIT	78	GIBSON	**LES PAUL DELUXE** GOLD TOP	1,713	**1,315**	1,162	1,025
ELGUIT	79	GIBSON	**LES PAUL DELUXE** BLACK, CREAM TRIM	1,056	**810**	716	631
ELGUIT	79	GIBSON	**LES PAUL DELUXE** SUNBURST	1,218	**935**	826	728
ELGUIT	79	GIBSON	**LES PAUL DELUXE** GOLD TOP	1,254	**963**	851	750
ELGUIT	79	GIBSON	**LES PAUL DELUXE** WINE RED	1,272	**976**	863	761
ELGUIT	80	GIBSON	**LES PAUL DELUXE** SUNBURST	963	**739**	653	576
ELGUIT	52	GIBSON	**LES PAUL GOLD TOP** TRAPEZE BRIDGE	13,171	**10,113**	8,937	7,879
ELGUIT	53	GIBSON	**LES PAUL GOLD TOP** TRAPEZE BRIDGE	13,171	**10,113**	8,937	7,879
ELGUIT	53	GIBSON	**LES PAUL GOLD TOP** STUD BRIDGE	27,440	**21,070**	18,620	16,415
ELGUIT	54	GIBSON	**LES PAUL GOLD TOP** STUD BRIDGE	27,440	**21,070**	18,620	16,415
ELGUIT	55	GIBSON	**LES PAUL GOLD TOP** STUD BRIDGE	30,184	**23,177**	20,482	18,056
ELGUIT	55	GIBSON	**LES PAUL GOLD TOP** TUNE-O-MATIC	43,904	**33,712**	29,792	26,264
ELGUIT	56	GIBSON	**LES PAUL GOLD TOP** TUNE-O-MATIC	43,904	**33,712**	29,792	26,264
ELGUIT	57	GIBSON	**LES PAUL GOLD TOP** 2 HB PU's	98,784	**75,852**	67,032	59,094
ELGUIT	58	GIBSON	**LES PAUL GOLD TOP** 2 HB PU's	98,784	**75,852**	67,032	59,094
ELGUIT	68	GIBSON	**LES PAUL GOLD TOP** 2 P-90's	8,601	**6,604**	5,836	5,145
ELGUIT	71	GIBSON	**LES PAUL GOLD TOP** CREAM	4,187	**3,215**	2,841	2,505
ELGUIT	82	GIBSON	**LES PAUL HERITAGE AWARD** CHERRY SUNBURST, GOLD HARDWARE	2,997	**2,301**	2,033	1,792
ELGUIT	81	GIBSON	**LES PAUL HERITAGE 80** BLACK	2,157	**1,656**	1,463	1,290
ELGUIT	81	GIBSON	**LES PAUL HERITAGE 80** CHERRY SUNBURST	3,309	**2,541**	2,245	1,979
ELGUIT	81	GIBSON	**LES PAUL HERITAGE 80 ELITE** SUNBURST	3,217	**2,470**	2,183	1,924
ELGUIT	82	GIBSON	**LES PAUL HERITAGE 80 ELITE**	2,107	**1,618**	1,430	1,260
ELGUIT	69	GIBSON	**LES PAUL JUMBO** CUTAWAY	1,290	**990**	875	771
ELGUIT	70	GIBSON	**LES PAUL JUMBO** CUTAWAY	1,505	**1,155**	1,021	900
ELGUIT	54	GIBSON	**LES PAUL JUNIOR** SUNBURST, SINGLE CUTAWAY	5,376	**4,128**	3,648	3,216
ELGUIT	55	GIBSON	**LES PAUL JUNIOR** SUNBURST, SINGLE CUTAWAY	4,838	**3,715**	3,283	2,894
ELGUIT	56	GIBSON	**LES PAUL JUNIOR** SUNBURST, SINGLE CUTAWAY	3,146	**2,415**	2,134	1,882
ELGUIT	57	GIBSON	**LES PAUL JUNIOR** CHERRY RED, SINGLE CUTAWAY	2,329	**1,788**	1,580	1,393
ELGUIT	57	GIBSON	**LES PAUL JUNIOR** SUNBURST, SINGLE CUTAWAY	3,150	**2,419**	2,137	1,884
ELGUIT	57	GIBSON	**LES PAUL JUNIOR** TV	6,022	**4,624**	4,086	3,602
ELGUIT	58	GIBSON	**LES PAUL JUNIOR** SUNBURST, SINGLE CUTAWAY	3,032	**2,328**	2,058	1,814
ELGUIT	58	GIBSON	**LES PAUL JUNIOR** CHERRY RED, DOUBLE CUTAWAY	4,300	**3,302**	2,918	2,572

TYPE	YR	MFG	PRICES--BASED ON 100% ORIGINAL MODEL	SELL EXC	SELL AVG	BUY EXC	BUY AVG
ELGUIT	59	GIBSON	**LES PAUL JUNIOR** SUNBURST, SINGLE CUTAWAY	2,318	**1,780**	1,573	1,386
ELGUIT	59	GIBSON	**LES PAUL JUNIOR** CHERRY RED, DOUBLE CUTAWAY	4,300	**3,302**	2,918	2,572
ELGUIT	59	GIBSON	**LES PAUL JUNIOR** TV MAHOGANY, DOUBLE CUTAWAY	5,491	**4,216**	3,726	3,285
ELGUIT	60	GIBSON	**LES PAUL JUNIOR** CHERRY RED, DOUBLE CUTAWAY	4,300	**3,302**	2,918	2,572
ELGUIT	60	GIBSON	**LES PAUL JUNIOR** TV YELLOW, SLIM NECK	5,847	**4,490**	3,967	3,498
ELGUIT	61	GIBSON	**LES PAUL JUNIOR** CHERRY RED, SINGLE CUTAWAY	1,495	**1,148**	1,014	894
ELGUIT	62	GIBSON	**LES PAUL JUNIOR** CHERRY, 1 BLACK P-90 PU, SG BODY STYLE	1,472	**1,130**	999	881
ELGUIT	86	GIBSON	**LES PAUL JUNIOR** DOUBLE CUTAWAY	712	**546**	483	426
ELGUIT	56	GIBSON	**LES PAUL JUNIOR 3/4** SUNBURST	1,842	**1,414**	1,250	1,102
ELGUIT	57	GIBSON	**LES PAUL JUNIOR 3/4** SUNBURST	2,315	**1,777**	1,570	1,384
ELGUIT	58	GIBSON	**LES PAUL JUNIOR 3/4** SUNBURST	1,852	**1,422**	1,257	1,108
ELGUIT	58	GIBSON	**LES PAUL JUNIOR 3/4** CHERRY RED	2,283	**1,753**	1,549	1,366
ELGUIT	59	GIBSON	**LES PAUL JUNIOR 3/4** CHERRY RED	1,828	**1,404**	1,241	1,094
ELGUIT	60	GIBSON	**LES PAUL JUNIOR 3/4** CHERRY RED	1,510	**1,160**	1,025	903
ELGUIT	61	GIBSON	**LES PAUL JUNIOR 3/4** CHERRY RED	1,324	**1,017**	899	792
ELGUIT	79	GIBSON	**LES PAUL KALAMAZOO** CHERRY SUNBURST	1,420	**1,090**	963	849
ELGUIT	79	GIBSON	**LES PAUL LIMITED EDITION #1** SS #73099116, FLAMED CARVED TOP, 2 GOLD GIBSON HB, FLAME MAPLE	14,871	**11,419**	10,091	8,896
ELGUIT	69	GIBSON	**LES PAUL PERSONAL** WALNUT	1,674	**1,285**	1,136	1,001
ELGUIT	69	GIBSON	**LES PAUL PROFESSIONAL** WALNUT	1,305	**1,002**	886	781
ELGUIT	69	GIBSON	**LES PAUL PROFESSIONAL**	1,341	**1,030**	910	802
ELGUIT	69	GIBSON	**LES PAUL PROFESSIONAL** TERRY KATH STYLE	1,361	**1,045**	924	814
ELGUIT	70	GIBSON	**LES PAUL PROFESSIONAL**	1,028	**789**	697	615
ELGUIT	71	GIBSON	**LES PAUL PROFESSIONAL** WALNUT	1,298	**996**	880	776
ELGUIT	77	GIBSON	**LES PAUL PROFESSIONAL DELUXE** SUNBURST	1,341	**1,030**	910	802
ELGUIT	77	GIBSON	**LES PAUL PROFESSIONAL DELUXE** BLACK	1,449	**1,112**	983	866
ELGUIT	78	GIBSON	**LES PAUL PROFESSIONAL DELUXE**	1,008	**774**	684	603
ELGUIT	82	GIBSON	**LES PAUL PROFESSIONAL DELUXE**	1,305	**1,002**	886	781
ELGUIT	70	GIBSON	**LES PAUL RECORDING** WALNUT	1,301	**999**	883	778
ELGUIT	71	GIBSON	**LES PAUL RECORDING** WALNUT	1,282	**984**	870	767
ELGUIT	72	GIBSON	**LES PAUL RECORDING** WALNUT	1,265	**971**	858	757
ELGUIT	72	GIBSON	**LES PAUL RECORDING** MAHOGANY	1,323	**1,016**	898	791
ELGUIT	73	GIBSON	**LES PAUL RECORDING**	990	**760**	671	592
ELGUIT	73	GIBSON	**LES PAUL RECORDING** WALNUT	1,265	**971**	858	757
ELGUIT	74	GIBSON	**LES PAUL RECORDING** WALNUT	1,265	**971**	858	757
ELGUIT	75	GIBSON	**LES PAUL RECORDING** WHITE	1,011	**776**	686	605
ELGUIT	75	GIBSON	**LES PAUL RECORDING** WALNUT	1,265	**971**	858	757
ELGUIT	76	GIBSON	**LES PAUL RECORDING** WHITE	1,050	**806**	712	628
ELGUIT	76	GIBSON	**LES PAUL RECORDING** WALNUT	1,277	**981**	867	764
ELGUIT	78	GIBSON	**LES PAUL RECORDING** WHITE	1,041	**799**	706	623
ELGUIT	78	GIBSON	**LES PAUL RECORDING** SUNBURST	1,051	**807**	713	629
ELGUIT	78	GIBSON	**LES PAUL RECORDING** WALNUT	1,204	**924**	817	720
ELGUIT	61	GIBSON	**LES PAUL SG** TV YELLOW, SINGLE CUTAWAY	6,093	**4,679**	4,135	3,645
ELGUIT	62	GIBSON	**LES PAUL SG** CHERRY RED, TREMOLO	3,872	**2,973**	2,628	2,316
ELGUIT	62	GIBSON	**LES PAUL SG** BROWN	4,068	**3,124**	2,761	2,434

TYPE	YR	MFG	PRICES--BASED ON 100% ORIGINAL MODEL	SELL EXC	SELL AVG	BUY EXC	BUY AVG
ELGUIT	62	GIBSON	**LES PAUL SG** RED, VIBROLA	4,447	**3,415**	3,017	2,660
ELGUIT	63	GIBSON	**LES PAUL SG CUSTOM** WHITE	4,812	**3,695**	3,265	2,878
ELGUIT	63	GIBSON	**LES PAUL SG CUSTOM** BLACK, 2 PAG's	5,783	**4,441**	3,924	3,459
ELGUIT	61	GIBSON	**LES PAUL SG SPECIAL** CHERRY RED, 2 PU's	3,104	**2,383**	2,106	1,857
ELGUIT	60	GIBSON	**LES PAUL SG STANDARD** CHERRY RED	16,464	**12,642**	11,172	9,849
ELGUIT	61	GIBSON	**LES PAUL SG STANDARD** CHERRY RED	16,464	**12,642**	11,172	9,849
ELGUIT	62	GIBSON	**LES PAUL SG STANDARD** CHERRY RED, EBONY BLACK	5,660	**4,346**	3,841	3,386
ELGUIT	62	GIBSON	**LES PAUL SG STANDARD** CHERRY RED	16,464	**12,642**	11,172	9,849
ELGUIT	63	GIBSON	**LES PAUL SG STANDARD** CHERRY RED	10,752	**8,256**	7,296	6,432
ELGUIT	73	GIBSON	**LES PAUL SIGNATURE** GOLD TOP	2,121	**1,628**	1,439	1,268
ELGUIT	74	GIBSON	**LES PAUL SIGNATURE** GOLD TOP, SIGNED BY LES PAUL	3,018	**2,317**	2,048	1,805
ELGUIT	77	GIBSON	**LES PAUL SIGNATURE** GOLD	1,384	**1,062**	939	828
ELGUIT	71	GIBSON	**LES PAUL SIGNATURE GOLD TOP**	2,421	**1,859**	1,643	1,448
ELGUIT	72	GIBSON	**LES PAUL SIGNATURE GOLD TOP**	2,261	**1,736**	1,534	1,352
ELGUIT	74	GIBSON	**LES PAUL SIGNATURE GOLD TOP** LOW IMP PICKUPS	1,768	**1,357**	1,200	1,057
ELGUIT	74	GIBSON	**LES PAUL SIGNATURE GOLD TOP BASS**	1,700	**1,305**	1,153	1,017
ELGUIT	55	GIBSON	**LES PAUL SPECIAL** TV MAHOGANY, SINGLE CUTAWAY	7,526	**5,779**	5,107	4,502
ELGUIT	56	GIBSON	**LES PAUL SPECIAL** NATURAL	7,526	**5,779**	5,107	4,502
ELGUIT	56	GIBSON	**LES PAUL SPECIAL** TV MAHOGANY, SINGLE CUTAWAY	7,526	**5,779**	5,107	4,502
ELGUIT	56	GIBSON	**LES PAUL SPECIAL** TV YELLOW	8,618	**6,617**	5,848	5,155
ELGUIT	57	GIBSON	**LES PAUL SPECIAL** TV MAHOGANY, SINGLE CUTAWAY	7,526	**5,779**	5,107	4,502
ELGUIT	57	GIBSON	**LES PAUL SPECIAL** TV YELLOW, SINGLE CUTAWAY	7,526	**5,779**	5,107	4,502
ELGUIT	58	GIBSON	**LES PAUL SPECIAL** TV MAHOGANY, SINGLE CUTAWAY	7,526	**5,779**	5,107	4,502
ELGUIT	59	GIBSON	**LES PAUL SPECIAL** CHERRY RED, DOUBLE CUTAWAY	4,838	**3,715**	3,283	2,894
ELGUIT	60	GIBSON	**LES PAUL SPECIAL** CHERRY RED, DOUBLE CUTAWAY	4,838	**3,715**	3,283	2,894
ELGUIT	60	GIBSON	**LES PAUL SPECIAL** TV MAHOGANY, DOUBLE CUTAWAY	4,838	**3,715**	3,283	2,894
ELGUIT	60	GIBSON	**LES PAUL SPECIAL** TV YELLOW, DOUBLE CUT	9,738	**7,477**	6,608	5,825
ELGUIT	61	GIBSON	**LES PAUL SPECIAL** CHERRY SUNBURST, DOUBLE CUTAWAY	4,838	**3,715**	3,283	2,894
ELGUIT	76	GIBSON	**LES PAUL SPECIAL** DOUBLE CUTAWAY	882	**677**	598	527
ELGUIT	78	GIBSON	**LES PAUL SPECIAL** TOBACCO SUNBURST, DOUBLE CUTAWAY	864	**663**	586	517
ELGUIT	79	GIBSON	**LES PAUL SPECIAL** SUNBURST, DOUBLE CUTAWAY	855	**657**	580	511
ELGUIT	59	GIBSON	**LES PAUL SPECIAL 3/4** CHERRY RED	2,998	**2,302**	2,034	1,793
ELGUIT	60	GIBSON	**LES PAUL SPECIAL 3/4** CHERRY RED	1,332	**1,023**	904	797
ELGUIT	58	GIBSON	**LES PAUL STANDARD** FLAME SUNBURST	109,760	**84,280**	74,480	65,660
ELGUIT	59	GIBSON	**LES PAUL STANDARD** SUNBURST, NO FLAME	51,235	**39,341**	34,766	30,649
ELGUIT	59	GIBSON	**LES PAUL STANDARD** CHERRY SUNBURST, PAF/TUNE-O-MATIC BRIDGE/2 PU/JUMBO FRETS	109,760	**84,280**	74,480	65,660
ELGUIT	59	GIBSON	**LES PAUL STANDARD** CURLY MAPLE	131,712	**101,136**	89,376	78,792
ELGUIT	59	GIBSON	**LES PAUL STANDARD** FLAME SUNBURST, LEFT-HANDED, ONLY 3 MADE	131,712	**101,136**	89,376	78,792
ELGUIT	59	GIBSON	**LES PAUL STANDARD** FLAME SUNBURST, HIGH FLAME	137,200	**105,350**	93,100	82,075
ELGUIT	60	GIBSON	**LES PAUL STANDARD** CHERRY, LEFT-HANDED	77,563	**59,557**	52,632	46,399
ELGUIT	60	GIBSON	**LES PAUL STANDARD** CHERRY SUNBURST, NO FLAME/THIN NECK	109,760	**84,280**	74,480	65,660
ELGUIT	60	GIBSON	**LES PAUL STANDARD** FLAME SUNBURST	131,712	**101,136**	89,376	78,792
ELGUIT	61	GIBSON	**LES PAUL STANDARD** CHERRY SUNBURST, SG STYLE	16,464	**12,642**	11,172	9,849

TYPE	YR	MFG	PRICES--BASED ON 100% ORIGINAL MODEL	SELL EXC	SELL AVG	BUY EXC	BUY AVG
ELGUIT	70	GIBSON	**LES PAUL STANDARD**	2,262	**1,737**	1,535	1,353
ELGUIT	72	GIBSON	**LES PAUL STANDARD** TOBACCO SUNBURST	2,115	**1,624**	1,435	1,265
ELGUIT	73	GIBSON	**LES PAUL STANDARD** TOBACCO SUNBURST	2,017	**1,548**	1,368	1,206
ELGUIT	74	GIBSON	**LES PAUL STANDARD** TOBACCO SUNBURST	1,869	**1,435**	1,268	1,118
ELGUIT	75	GIBSON	**LES PAUL STANDARD** NATURAL	1,049	**805**	712	627
ELGUIT	75	GIBSON	**LES PAUL STANDARD** TOBACCO SUNBURST	1,336	**1,025**	906	799
ELGUIT	75	GIBSON	**LES PAUL STANDARD** BLACK	1,481	**1,137**	1,005	886
ELGUIT	76	GIBSON	**LES PAUL STANDARD** NATURAL	984	**755**	668	588
ELGUIT	76	GIBSON	**LES PAUL STANDARD** CHERRY SUNBURST	1,018	**781**	690	609
ELGUIT	76	GIBSON	**LES PAUL STANDARD** WINE RED	1,028	**789**	697	615
ELGUIT	76	GIBSON	**LES PAUL STANDARD** TOBACCO SUNBURST	1,289	**989**	874	771
ELGUIT	77	GIBSON	**LES PAUL STANDARD** NATURAL	971	**745**	658	580
ELGUIT	77	GIBSON	**LES PAUL STANDARD** WINE RED	996	**765**	676	596
ELGUIT	78	GIBSON	**LES PAUL STANDARD** BLACK	975	**749**	661	583
ELGUIT	78	GIBSON	**LES PAUL STANDARD** CHERRY SUNBURST	982	**754**	666	587
ELGUIT	78	GIBSON	**LES PAUL STANDARD** BURGUNDY	996	**765**	676	596
ELGUIT	78	GIBSON	**LES PAUL STANDARD** NATURAL	1,229	**944**	834	735
ELGUIT	78	GIBSON	**LES PAUL STANDARD** TOBACCO SUNBURST	1,233	**946**	836	737
ELGUIT	78	GIBSON	**LES PAUL STANDARD** WINE RED	1,389	**1,067**	943	831
ELGUIT	79	GIBSON	**LES PAUL STANDARD** CHERRY SUNBURST	1,319	**1,013**	895	789
ELGUIT	79	GIBSON	**LES PAUL STANDARD** TOBACCO SUNBURST	1,319	**1,013**	895	789
ELGUIT	81	GIBSON	**LES PAUL STANDARD** WINE RED	1,263	**970**	857	755
ELGUIT	81	GIBSON	**LES PAUL STANDARD** TOBACOC SUNBURST	1,271	**976**	862	760
ELGUIT	83	GIBSON	**LES PAUL STANDARD** BLACK	992	**761**	673	593
ELGUIT	83	GIBSON	**LES PAUL STANDARD** CHERRY SUNBURST	1,225	**940**	831	732
ELGUIT	71	GIBSON	**LES PAUL STANDARD '54 REISSUE**	2,194	**1,684**	1,488	1,312
ELGUIT	71	GIBSON	**LES PAUL STANDARD '58 REISSUE**	1,967	**1,511**	1,335	1,177
ELGUIT	72	GIBSON	**LES PAUL STANDARD '58 REISSUE**	2,164	**1,662**	1,469	1,295
ELGUIT	58	GIBSON	**LES PAUL STANDARD GOLD TOP** PAF's	39,952	**30,677**	27,110	23,900
ELGUIT	68	GIBSON	**LES PAUL STANDARD GOLD TOP**	5,276	**4,051**	3,580	3,156
ELGUIT	69	GIBSON	**LES PAUL STANDARD GOLD TOP**	3,269	**2,510**	2,218	1,955
ELGUIT	71	GIBSON	**LES PAUL STANDARD GOLD TOP**	1,704	**1,308**	1,156	1,019
ELGUIT	87	GIBSON	**LES PAUL STUDIO LITE**	841	**645**	570	503
ELGUIT	75	GIBSON	**LES PAUL TRIUMPH BASS** BROWN	827	**635**	561	495
ELGUIT	55	GIBSON	**LES PAUL TV**	4,169	**3,201**	2,829	2,494
ELGUIT	56	GIBSON	**LES PAUL TV**	6,228	**4,782**	4,226	3,725
ELGUIT	81	GIBSON	**LES PAUL XR-1**	572	**439**	388	342
ELGUIT	82	GIBSON	**LES PAUL XR-2**	555	**426**	376	332
ELGUIT	76	GIBSON	**MARAUDER FINGERBOARD** ROSEWOOD	563	**432**	382	337
ELGUIT	78	GIBSON	**MARAUDER FINGERBOARD** MAPLE	608	**466**	412	363
ELGUIT	79	GIBSON	**MARAUDER FINGERBOARD** MAPLE	604	**464**	410	361
ELGUIT	59	GIBSON	**MELODY MAKER** SUNBURST, SINGLE CUTAWAY	978	**751**	664	585
ELGUIT	60	GIBSON	**MELODY MAKER** SUNBURST, SINGLE CUTAWAY, 1 PU	908	**697**	616	543
ELGUIT	61	GIBSON	**MELODY MAKER** SUNBURST, SINGLE CUTAWAY	842	**646**	571	503
ELGUIT	62	GIBSON	**MELODY MAKER** SUNBURST, DOUBLE CUTAWAY, 1 PU	864	**663**	586	517
ELGUIT	63	GIBSON	**MELODY MAKER** SUNBURST, DOUBLE CUTAWAY, 1 PU	850	**652**	576	508
ELGUIT	64	GIBSON	**MELODY MAKER** SUNBURST, 1 PU	864	**663**	586	517

TYPE	YR	MFG	PRICES--BASED ON 100% ORIGINAL MODEL	SELL EXC	SELL AVG	BUY EXC	BUY AVG
ELGUIT	64	GIBSON	MELODY MAKER CHERRY RED, 1 PU	1,226	**941**	832	733
ELGUIT	65	GIBSON	MELODY MAKER SUNBURST, 1 PU	841	**645**	570	503
ELGUIT	65	GIBSON	MELODY MAKER CHERRY RED, 1 PU	963	**739**	653	576
ELGUIT	65	GIBSON	MELODY MAKER CHERRY RED, DOUBLE CUTAWAY	963	**739**	653	576
ELGUIT	65	GIBSON	MELODY MAKER CARDINAL RED, 1 PU	1,198	**920**	813	716
ELGUIT	65	GIBSON	MELODY MAKER PELHAM BLUE, 12-STRNG	1,438	**1,104**	975	860
ELGUIT	66	GIBSON	MELODY MAKER OPAQUE RED, 1 PU, DOUBLE CUTAWAY	617	**473**	418	369
ELGUIT	66	GIBSON	MELODY MAKER PELHAM BLUE, 2 PU's	855	**657**	580	511
ELGUIT	67	GIBSON	MELODY MAKER CARDINAL RED, 1 PU	967	**743**	656	578
ELGUIT	67	GIBSON	MELODY MAKER PELHAM BLUE, 1 PU	1,211	**930**	822	724
ELGUIT	67	GIBSON	MELODY MAKER PELHAM BLUE, 12-STRING	1,438	**1,104**	975	860
ELGUIT	68	GIBSON	MELODY MAKER CARDINAL RED, 1 PU	655	**503**	444	391
ELGUIT	68	GIBSON	MELODY MAKER WALNUT	841	**645**	570	503
ELGUIT	68	GIBSON	MELODY MAKER PELHAM BLUE, 1 PU	1,009	**774**	684	603
ELGUIT	68	GIBSON	MELODY MAKER PELHAM BLUE, 12-STRING	1,438	**1,104**	975	860
ELGUIT	68	GIBSON	MELODY MAKER BURGUNDY, 12-STRING	1,438	**1,104**	975	860
ELGUIT	70	GIBSON	MELODY MAKER WALNUT, 2 PU's	794	**609**	538	475
ELGUIT	59	GIBSON	MELODY MAKER 3/4 SUNBURST	860	**660**	583	514
ELGUIT	60	GIBSON	MELODY MAKER 3/4 SINGLE CUTAWAY	635	**487**	430	379
ELGUIT	60	GIBSON	MELODY MAKER 3/4 SUNBURST	860	**660**	583	514
ELGUIT	62	GIBSON	MELODY MAKER 3/4 DOUBLE CUTAWAY	617	**473**	418	369
ELGUIT	62	GIBSON	MELODY MAKER 3/4 SUNBURST	752	**577**	510	450
ELGUIT	63	GIBSON	MELODY MAKER 3/4 SUNBURST	752	**577**	510	450
ELGUIT	64	GIBSON	MELODY MAKER 3/4 SUNBURST	698	**536**	474	418
ELGUIT	65	GIBSON	MELODY MAKER 3/4 SUNBURST	698	**536**	474	418
ELGUIT	68	GIBSON	MELODY MAKER 3/4 PELHAM BLUE	806	**619**	547	482
ELGUIT	60	GIBSON	MELODY MAKER D SUNBURST, SINGLE CUTAWAY	967	**743**	656	578
ELGUIT	61	GIBSON	MELODY MAKER D SUNBURST, SINGLE CUTAWAY, 2 PU's	1,198	**920**	813	716
ELGUIT	62	GIBSON	MELODY MAKER D SUNBURST, DOUBLE CUTAWAY	588	**451**	399	351
ELGUIT	64	GIBSON	MELODY MAKER D SUNBURST, 2 PU's	850	**652**	576	508
ELGUIT	65	GIBSON	MELODY MAKER D CHERRY RED, 2 PU's	860	**660**	583	514
ELGUIT	65	GIBSON	MELODY MAKER D PELHAM BLUE, 2 PU's	860	**660**	583	514
ELGUIT	65	GIBSON	MELODY MAKER D RED, 2 PU's	860	**660**	583	514
ELGUIT	67	GIBSON	MELODY MAKER D PELHAM BLUE, 2 PU's	806	**619**	547	482
ELGUIT	67	GIBSON	MELODY MAKER D RED, 2 PU's	806	**619**	547	482
ELGUIT	68	GIBSON	MELODY MAKER D BURGUNDY, 2 PU's	670	**515**	455	401
ELGUIT	70	GIBSON	MELODY MAKER D WALNUT	658	**505**	446	393
ELGUIT	76	GIBSON	MELODY MAKER D CHERRY RED, 2 PU's	661	**508**	449	395
ELGUIT	77	GIBSON	MELODY MAKER DOUBLE REISSUE	645	**495**	437	385
ELGUIT	66	GIBSON	MELODY MAKER III SPARKLING BURGUNDY, 3 PU's	1,438	**1,104**	975	860
ELGUIT	68	GIBSON	MELODY MAKER III PELHAM BLUE, 3 PU's	1,438	**1,104**	975	860
ELGUIT	68	GIBSON	MELODY MAKER III SPARKLING BURGUNDY, 3 PU'S	1,438	**1,104**	975	860

Copyright 2006 - Orion Research Corp., Scottsdale, AZ (480) 951-1114
FAX (480) 951-1117 - e-mail: sales@orionbluebook.com

TYPE	YR	MFG	PRICES--BASED ON 100% ORIGINAL MODEL	SELL EXC	SELL AVG	BUY EXC	BUY AVG
ELGUIT	69	GIBSON	**MELODY MAKER III** PELHAM BLUE	779	**598**	528	466
ELGUIT	82	GIBSON	**MODERNE** BLACK, KORINA	2,263	**1,711**	1,508	1,251
ELGUIT	82	GIBSON	**MODERNE** NATURAL, KORINA	3,016	**2,315**	2,046	1,804
ELGUIT	83	GIBSON	**MODERNE** WHITE, KORINA	1,569	**1,204**	1,064	938
ELGUIT	83	GIBSON	**MODERNE** NATURAL, KORINA	2,243	**1,722**	1,522	1,342
ELGUIT	82	GIBSON	**MODERNE HERITAGE** BLACK, KORINA WOOD	2,157	**1,656**	1,463	1,290
ELGUIT	83	GIBSON	**MODERNE HERITAGE** BLACK	1,753	**1,346**	1,190	1,049
ELGUIT	83	GIBSON	**MODERNE HERITAGE** WHITE	2,996	**2,300**	2,033	1,792
ELGUIT	83	GIBSON	**MODERNE HERITAGE** NATURAL, KORINA WOOD	3,355	**2,576**	2,276	2,007
ELGUIT	87	GIBSON	**Q-80 BASS**	577	**443**	392	345
ELGUIT	77	GIBSON	**RD ARTIST** NATURAL	677	**520**	459	405
ELGUIT	78	GIBSON	**RD ARTIST** NATURAL	580	**445**	393	347
ELGUIT	78	GIBSON	**RD ARTIST** SUNBURST	607	**466**	411	363
ELGUIT	79	GIBSON	**RD ARTIST** SUNBURST	598	**459**	405	357
ELGUIT	77	GIBSON	**RD ARTIST BASS** SUNBURST	762	**585**	517	456
ELGUIT	77	GIBSON	**RD ARTIST BASS** NATURAL	871	**669**	591	521
ELGUIT	78	GIBSON	**RD ARTIST BASS** SUNBURST	673	**516**	456	402
ELGUIT	78	GIBSON	**RD ARTIST BASS** BLACK	764	**587**	519	457
ELGUIT	79	GIBSON	**RD ARTIST BASS** SUNBURST	723	**555**	490	432
ELGUIT	81	GIBSON	**RD ARTIST BASS** FIREBURST	728	**559**	494	435
ELGUIT	78	GIBSON	**RD CUSTOM**	722	**554**	490	432
ELGUIT	78	GIBSON	**RD CUSTOM** NATURAL	725	**557**	492	434
ELGUIT	78	GIBSON	**RD STANDARD** BLACK	711	**546**	482	425
ELGUIT	78	GIBSON	**RD STANDARD** BROWN SUNBURST	749	**575**	508	448
ELGUIT	78	GIBSON	**RD STANDARD** WALNUT	762	**585**	517	456
ELGUIT	79	GIBSON	**RD STANDARD BASS** NATURAL	715	**549**	485	428
ELGUIT	73	GIBSON	**RIPPER BASS** NATURAL	758	**582**	514	453
ELGUIT	74	GIBSON	**RIPPER BASS** NATURAL	590	**453**	400	353
ELGUIT	75	GIBSON	**RIPPER BASS** NATURAL	647	**497**	439	387
ELGUIT	75	GIBSON	**RIPPER BASS** BLACK, FRETLESS	668	**513**	453	399
ELGUIT	76	GIBSON	**RIPPER BASS** SUNBURST, EBONY FINGERBOARD	596	**458**	405	357
ELGUIT	76	GIBSON	**RIPPER BASS** BLACK	757	**581**	513	452
ELGUIT	78	GIBSON	**RIPPER BASS** NATURAL	596	**458**	405	357
ELGUIT	78	GIBSON	**RIPPER BASS** BLACK	623	**479**	423	373
ELGUIT	79	GIBSON	**RIPPER BASS** NATURAL	567	**436**	385	339
ELGUIT	79	GIBSON	**RIPPER BASS** SUNBURST	571	**438**	387	341
ELGUIT	81	GIBSON	**RIPPER BASS** NATURAL	570	**437**	386	341
ELGUIT	53	GIBSON	**ROYALTONE**	563	**432**	382	337
ELGUIT	76	GIBSON	**S-1** NATURAL, 3 PU's	613	**471**	416	367
ELGUIT	77	GIBSON	**S-1** SUNBURST, 3 PU's	617	**473**	418	369
ELGUIT	78	GIBSON	**S-1** BLACK, 3 PU's	620	**476**	421	371
ELGUIT	40	GIBSON	**SB-350 BASS** WALNUT, SG BODY SHAPE	704	**540**	478	421
ELGUIT	72	GIBSON	**SB-450 BASS** CHERRY RED, SG BODY SHAPE	652	**501**	443	390

TYPE	YR	MFG	PRICES--BASED ON 100% ORIGINAL MODEL	SELL EXC	SELL AVG	BUY EXC	BUY AVG
ELGUIT	59	GIBSON	**SG** TV, DOUBLE CUT	4,343	**3,335**	2,947	2,598
ELGUIT	60	GIBSON	**SG** TV YELLOW, DOUBLE CUTAWAY	5,913	**4,540**	4,012	3,537
ELGUIT	61	GIBSON	**SG** TV MAHOGANY, 1 PU	1,323	**1,016**	898	791
ELGUIT	62	GIBSON	**SG** TV WHITE, 1 PU	1,298	**996**	880	776
ELGUIT	63	GIBSON	**SG** TV WHITE, 1 PU	1,298	**996**	880	776
ELGUIT	72	GIBSON	**SG** WINE RED, BIGSBY	1,302	**1,000**	883	779
ELGUIT	74	GIBSON	**SG** WALNUT, 3 PU's	1,261	**968**	855	754
ELGUIT	87	GIBSON	**SG '62 REISSUE**	1,018	**781**	690	609
ELGUIT	89	GIBSON	**SG 90** DOUBLE	641	**492**	435	383
ELGUIT	73	GIBSON	**SG 100** WALNUT	668	**513**	453	399
ELGUIT	79	GIBSON	**SG 100** WALNUT	635	**487**	430	379
ELGUIT	70	GIBSON	**SG 200** WALNUT	658	**505**	446	393
ELGUIT	71	GIBSON	**SG 250** CHERRY RED	612	**470**	415	366
ELGUIT	61	GIBSON	**SG CUSTOM** WHITE	8,601	**6,604**	5,836	5,145
ELGUIT	62	GIBSON	**SG CUSTOM** WHITE	3,763	**2,889**	2,553	2,251
ELGUIT	63	GIBSON	**SG CUSTOM** WHITE	3,763	**2,889**	2,553	2,251
ELGUIT	64	GIBSON	**SG CUSTOM** WHITE	3,763	**2,889**	2,553	2,251
ELGUIT	65	GIBSON	**SG CUSTOM** WHITE, GOLD HARDWARE	3,310	**2,542**	2,246	1,980
ELGUIT	66	GIBSON	**SG CUSTOM** WHITE	3,655	**2,807**	2,480	2,186
ELGUIT	67	GIBSON	**SG CUSTOM** WHITE	3,595	**2,760**	2,439	2,150
ELGUIT	68	GIBSON	**SG CUSTOM** WALNUT	2,396	**1,840**	1,626	1,433
ELGUIT	68	GIBSON	**SG CUSTOM** WHITE	3,595	**2,760**	2,439	2,150
ELGUIT	68	GIBSON	**SG CUSTOM** WHITE, GOLD HARDWARE, 3 PU'S	8,618	**6,617**	5,848	5,155
ELGUIT	69	GIBSON	**SG CUSTOM** WALNUT	2,396	**1,840**	1,626	1,433
ELGUIT	70	GIBSON	**SG CUSTOM** WHITE	3,235	**2,484**	2,195	1,935
ELGUIT	71	GIBSON	**SG CUSTOM** WHITE	3,115	**2,392**	2,114	1,863
ELGUIT	72	GIBSON	**SG CUSTOM** WALNUT	2,157	**1,656**	1,463	1,290
ELGUIT	72	GIBSON	**SG CUSTOM** METALLIC GREEN	2,396	**1,840**	1,626	1,433
ELGUIT	73	GIBSON	**SG CUSTOM** WALNUT, 3 PU's, TREMOLO	2,396	**1,840**	1,626	1,433
ELGUIT	74	GIBSON	**SG CUSTOM** WALNUT	2,157	**1,656**	1,463	1,290
ELGUIT	75	GIBSON	**SG CUSTOM** WALNUT	2,157	**1,656**	1,463	1,290
ELGUIT	76	GIBSON	**SG CUSTOM** WALNUT	2,157	**1,656**	1,463	1,290
ELGUIT	76	GIBSON	**SG CUSTOM** WHITE	2,996	**2,300**	2,033	1,792
ELGUIT	77	GIBSON	**SG CUSTOM** CHERRY RED	2,157	**1,656**	1,463	1,290
ELGUIT	78	GIBSON	**SG CUSTOM** WALNUT	2,037	**1,564**	1,382	1,218
ELGUIT	78	GIBSON	**SG CUSTOM** CHERRY RED	2,157	**1,656**	1,463	1,290
ELGUIT	71	GIBSON	**SG DELUXE** CHERRY RED	980	**752**	665	586
ELGUIT	71	GIBSON	**SG DELUXE** WALNUT	1,014	**779**	688	607
ELGUIT	72	GIBSON	**SG DELUXE**	695	**534**	471	416
ELGUIT	87	GIBSON	**SG ELITE** GOLD HARDWARE	1,761	**1,352**	1,195	1,053
ELGUIT	87	GIBSON	**SG ELITE** GOLD HARDWARE, SUPERTUNE	1,761	**1,352**	1,195	1,053
ELGUIT	78	GIBSON	**SG EXCLUSIVE** BLACK, CREAM PARTS	992	**761**	673	593
ELGUIT	73	GIBSON	**SG I** CHERRY RED	882	**677**	598	527

TYPE	YR	MFG	PRICES--BASED ON 100% ORIGINAL MODEL	SELL EXC	SELL AVG	BUY EXC	BUY AVG
ELGUIT	75	GIBSON	SG I	540	415	367	323
ELGUIT	72	GIBSON	SG II WALNUT	673	516	456	402
ELGUIT	73	GIBSON	SG II WALNUT	804	617	545	481
ELGUIT	74	GIBSON	SG II CHERRY, 2 MINI HB PU's, SOLID BODY	674	517	457	403
ELGUIT	61	GIBSON	SG JUNIOR CHERRY RED	1,797	1,380	1,219	1,075
ELGUIT	61	GIBSON	SG JUNIOR TV	5,376	4,128	3,648	3,216
ELGUIT	62	GIBSON	SG JUNIOR CHERRY RED	1,797	1,380	1,219	1,075
ELGUIT	62	GIBSON	SG JUNIOR WHITE, 1 PU	2,876	2,208	1,951	1,720
ELGUIT	63	GIBSON	SG JUNIOR CHERRY RED	1,797	1,380	1,219	1,075
ELGUIT	64	GIBSON	SG JUNIOR CHERRY RED	1,677	1,288	1,138	1,003
ELGUIT	64	GIBSON	SG JUNIOR WHITE	2,396	1,840	1,626	1,433
ELGUIT	65	GIBSON	SG JUNIOR CHERRY RED	1,677	1,288	1,138	1,003
ELGUIT	65	GIBSON	SG JUNIOR WHITE	2,396	1,840	1,626	1,433
ELGUIT	66	GIBSON	SG JUNIOR CHERRY RED	1,557	1,196	1,057	931
ELGUIT	66	GIBSON	SG JUNIOR PELHAM BLUE	2,396	1,840	1,626	1,433
ELGUIT	67	GIBSON	SG JUNIOR CHERRY RED	1,557	1,196	1,057	931
ELGUIT	68	GIBSON	SG JUNIOR CHERRY RED, LARGE GUARD, MAESTRO VIBROLA	1,557	1,196	1,057	931
ELGUIT	69	GIBSON	SG JUNIOR CHERRY RED	1,498	1,150	1,016	896
ELGUIT	71	GIBSON	SG JUNIOR WALNUT	698	536	474	418
ELGUIT	71	GIBSON	SG PRO WALNUT	864	663	586	517
ELGUIT	72	GIBSON	SG PRO WALNUT, SERIAL #685131	862	662	585	515
ELGUIT	73	GIBSON	SG PRO	695	534	471	416
ELGUIT	74	GIBSON	SG PRO WALNUT	748	574	507	447
ELGUIT	60	GIBSON	SG SPECIAL CHERRY RED	2,636	2,024	1,789	1,577
ELGUIT	61	GIBSON	SG SPECIAL CHERRY RED	2,396	1,840	1,626	1,433
ELGUIT	62	GIBSON	SG SPECIAL CHERRY RED	2,396	1,840	1,626	1,433
ELGUIT	62	GIBSON	SG SPECIAL WHITE	2,996	2,300	2,033	1,792
ELGUIT	63	GIBSON	SG SPECIAL CHERRY RED	2,396	1,840	1,626	1,433
ELGUIT	63	GIBSON	SG SPECIAL WHITE	2,996	2,300	2,033	1,792
ELGUIT	64	GIBSON	SG SPECIAL CHERRY RED	2,396	1,840	1,626	1,433
ELGUIT	64	GIBSON	SG SPECIAL WHITE	2,996	2,300	2,033	1,792
ELGUIT	64	GIBSON	SG SPECIAL LIMED MAHOGANY	4,300	3,302	2,918	2,572
ELGUIT	65	GIBSON	SG SPECIAL CHERRY RED, CHROME HARDWARE	2,396	1,840	1,626	1,433
ELGUIT	65	GIBSON	SG SPECIAL WHITE	2,996	2,300	2,033	1,792
ELGUIT	65	GIBSON	SG SPECIAL LIMED MAHOGANY	4,300	3,302	2,918	2,572
ELGUIT	66	GIBSON	SG SPECIAL CHERRY RED	2,396	1,840	1,626	1,433
ELGUIT	66	GIBSON	SG SPECIAL WHITE	2,876	2,208	1,951	1,720
ELGUIT	67	GIBSON	SG SPECIAL CHERRY RED	2,037	1,564	1,382	1,218
ELGUIT	67	GIBSON	SG SPECIAL WHITE	2,636	2,024	1,789	1,577
ELGUIT	68	GIBSON	SG SPECIAL WINE RED	1,039	798	705	621
ELGUIT	68	GIBSON	SG SPECIAL CHERRY RED	2,037	1,564	1,382	1,218
ELGUIT	69	GIBSON	SG SPECIAL WALNUT	1,312	1,007	890	785
ELGUIT	69	GIBSON	SG SPECIAL CHERRY RED	1,797	1,380	1,219	1,075

TYPE	YR	MFG	PRICES--BASED ON 100% ORIGINAL MODEL	SELL EXC	SELL AVG	BUY EXC	BUY AVG
ELGUIT	70	GIBSON	**SG SPECIAL** WALNUT	1,006	**773**	683	602
ELGUIT	70	GIBSON	**SG SPECIAL** CHERRY RED	1,438	**1,104**	975	860
ELGUIT	71	GIBSON	**SG SPECIAL** WALNUT	984	**755**	668	588
ELGUIT	72	GIBSON	**SG SPECIAL** CHERRY RED	922	**708**	626	552
ELGUIT	72	GIBSON	**SG SPECIAL** WALNUT	969	**744**	658	580
ELGUIT	73	GIBSON	**SG SPECIAL** WALNUT	803	**616**	544	480
ELGUIT	76	GIBSON	**SG SPECIAL** CHERRY RED	776	**595**	526	464
ELGUIT	63	GIBSON	**SG STANDARD** CHERRY RED	5,320	**4,085**	3,610	3,182
ELGUIT	64	GIBSON	**SG STANDARD** CHERRY RED	5,320	**4,085**	3,610	3,182
ELGUIT	65	GIBSON	**SG STANDARD** CHERRY RED	5,320	**4,085**	3,610	3,182
ELGUIT	66	GIBSON	**SG STANDARD** CHERRY RED	4,085	**3,137**	2,772	2,444
ELGUIT	67	GIBSON	**SG STANDARD** CHERRY RED	3,870	**2,972**	2,626	2,315
ELGUIT	68	GIBSON	**SG STANDARD** CHERRY RED	3,763	**2,889**	2,553	2,251
ELGUIT	69	GIBSON	**SG STANDARD** WALNUT, LEFT-HANDED	1,467	**1,126**	995	877
ELGUIT	69	GIBSON	**SG STANDARD** CHERRY RED	2,178	**1,672**	1,478	1,303
ELGUIT	70	GIBSON	**SG STANDARD** SUNBURST	987	**758**	670	590
ELGUIT	70	GIBSON	**SG STANDARD** CHERRY RED	1,340	**1,029**	909	801
ELGUIT	70	GIBSON	**SG STANDARD** WALNUT	1,373	**1,054**	931	821
ELGUIT	71	GIBSON	**SG STANDARD** CHERRY RED, LEFT-HANDED	969	**744**	658	580
ELGUIT	71	GIBSON	**SG STANDARD** SUNBURST	1,008	**774**	684	603
ELGUIT	71	GIBSON	**SG STANDARD** WALNUT	1,032	**792**	700	617
ELGUIT	71	GIBSON	**SG STANDARD**	1,282	**984**	870	767
ELGUIT	71	GIBSON	**SG STANDARD** CHERRY RED	1,310	**1,006**	889	783
ELGUIT	72	GIBSON	**SG STANDARD** WALNUT	1,216	**933**	825	727
ELGUIT	72	GIBSON	**SG STANDARD** NATURAL	1,562	**1,199**	1,060	934
ELGUIT	72	GIBSON	**SG STANDARD** CHERRY RED	2,636	**2,024**	1,789	1,577
ELGUIT	73	GIBSON	**SG STANDARD** WHITE	910	**699**	617	544
ELGUIT	73	GIBSON	**SG STANDARD** NATURAL	1,005	**772**	682	601
ELGUIT	73	GIBSON	**SG STANDARD** CHERRY RED	2,636	**2,024**	1,789	1,577
ELGUIT	74	GIBSON	**SG STANDARD** WALNUT, PRO-INSTALLED KAHLER, BIG FRETS	907	**696**	615	542
ELGUIT	74	GIBSON	**SG STANDARD** CHERRY RED	2,636	**2,024**	1,789	1,577
ELGUIT	75	GIBSON	**SG STANDARD** MAHOGANY BODY/NECK, 2# PAH HB's	962	**738**	652	575
ELGUIT	76	GIBSON	**SG STANDARD** WHITE	909	**698**	617	544
ELGUIT	77	GIBSON	**SG STANDARD** SUNBURST, LEFT-HANDED	1,028	**789**	697	615
ELGUIT	78	GIBSON	**SG STANDARD** WALNUT	588	**451**	399	351
ELGUIT	78	GIBSON	**SG STANDARD** NATURAL	825	**633**	560	493
ELGUIT	78	GIBSON	**SG STANDARD** BLACK	1,201	**922**	815	718
ELGUIT	78	GIBSON	**SG STANDARD** CHERRY RED	2,157	**1,656**	1,463	1,290
ELGUIT	79	GIBSON	**SG STANDARD** WALNUT	689	**529**	468	412
ELGUIT	79	GIBSON	**SG STANDARD** CHERRY RED	2,037	**1,564**	1,382	1,218
ELGUIT	80	GIBSON	**SG STANDARD** WALNUT	795	**610**	539	475
ELGUIT	81	GIBSON	**SG STANDARD**	678	**521**	460	406
ELGUIT	82	GIBSON	**SG STANDARD** SOLID BODY, LEFT-HANDED	1,198	**920**	813	716

TYPE	YR	MFG	PRICES--BASED ON 100% ORIGINAL MODEL	SELL EXC	SELL AVG	BUY EXC	BUY AVG
ELGUIT	81	GIBSON	**SONEX-180 CUSTOM**	546	**419**	370	326
ELGUIT	81	GIBSON	**SONEX-180 DELUXE**	500	**384**	339	299
ELGUIT	82	GIBSON	**SONEX-180 DELUXE** CANDY APPLE RED	644	**494**	437	385
ELGUIT	82	GIBSON	**SONEX-180 DELUXE** LEFT-HANDED	685	**526**	465	410
ELGUIT	83	GIBSON	**SONEX-180 DELUXE**	473	**363**	321	283
ELGUIT	83	GIBSON	**SONEX-180 STANDARD**	582	**447**	395	348
ELGUIT	83	GIBSON	**SPIRT i** SINGLE PU, SOLID BODY	579	**444**	392	346
ELGUIT	39	GIBSON	**SUPER 100 JUMBO** MOUSTACHE BRIDGE, STAIRSTEP PEGHEAD	19,573	**15,029**	13,281	11,708
ELGUIT	51	GIBSON	**SUPER 400 CES** SUNBURST, ROUNDED CUTAWAY	15,288	**11,739**	10,374	9,145
ELGUIT	52	GIBSON	**SUPER 400 CES** NATURAL, ROUNDED CUTAWAY, SERIAL #A9400-A13000	13,720	**10,535**	9,310	8,207
ELGUIT	53	GIBSON	**SUPER 400 CES** NATURAL, ROUNDED CUTAWAY, SERIAL #A13000-A16000	13,720	**10,535**	9,310	8,207
ELGUIT	53	GIBSON	**SUPER 400 CES** SUNBURST, ROUNDED CUTAWAY, SERIAL #A13000-A16000	16,472	**12,648**	11,178	9,854
ELGUIT	54	GIBSON	**SUPER 400 CES** SUNBURST, ROUNDED CUATWAY, ALNICO V PU's	16,066	**12,336**	10,902	9,611
ELGUIT	55	GIBSON	**SUPER 400 CES** SUNBURST, ROUNDED CUTAWAY, SERIAL #A19000-A22000	16,484	**12,657**	11,185	9,861
ELGUIT	56	GIBSON	**SUPER 400 CES** SUNBURST, ROUNDED CUTAWAY, SERIAL #A22000-A24600	16,470	**12,647**	11,176	9,853
ELGUIT	57	GIBSON	**SUPER 400 CES** HUMBUCKERS	20,081	**15,419**	13,626	12,013
ELGUIT	58	GIBSON	**SUPER 400 CES** NATURAL, ROUNDED CUTAWAY	15,366	**11,799**	10,427	9,192
ELGUIT	58	GIBSON	**SUPER 400 CES** SUNBURST, HB	17,842	**13,700**	12,107	10,673
ELGUIT	60	GIBSON	**SUPER 400 CES** SUNBURST, VENETIAN CUTAWAY	14,483	**11,121**	9,828	8,664
ELGUIT	60	GIBSON	**SUPER 400 CES** NATURAL, ROUNDED CUTAWAY	15,366	**11,799**	10,427	9,192
ELGUIT	61	GIBSON	**SUPER 400 CES** SUNBURST, POINTED CUTAWAY	14,384	**11,044**	9,760	8,604
ELGUIT	62	GIBSON	**SUPER 400 CES** SUNBURST, POINTED CUTAWAY	14,579	**11,194**	9,892	8,721
ELGUIT	63	GIBSON	**SUPER 400 CES** NATURAL, POINTED CUTAWAY	12,896	**9,902**	8,751	7,715
ELGUIT	63	GIBSON	**SUPER 400 CES** SUNBURST	15,865	**12,182**	10,766	9,491
ELGUIT	64	GIBSON	**SUPER 400 CES** NATURAL, POINTED CUTAWAY	12,894	**9,901**	8,749	7,713
ELGUIT	64	GIBSON	**SUPER 400 CES** SUNBURST, POINTED CUTAWAY	14,151	**10,866**	9,602	8,465
ELGUIT	65	GIBSON	**SUPER 400 CES** NATURAL, POINTED CUTAWAY	12,457	**9,565**	8,453	7,452
ELGUIT	66	GIBSON	**SUPER 400 CES**	11,196	**8,597**	7,597	6,697
ELGUIT	68	GIBSON	**SUPER 400 CES** SUNBURST, LEFT-HANDED	9,479	**7,279**	6,432	5,670
ELGUIT	68	GIBSON	**SUPER 400 CES** SUNBURST, POINTED CUTAWAY	11,189	**8,592**	7,593	6,693
ELGUIT	68	GIBSON	**SUPER 400 CES** NATURAL, POINTED CUTAWAY, SERIAL #523714	11,537	**8,858**	7,828	6,901
ELGUIT	69	GIBSON	**SUPER 400 CES** SUNBURST, POINTED CUTAWAY	11,252	**8,640**	7,635	6,731
ELGUIT	70	GIBSON	**SUPER 400 CES** NATURAL, ROUNDED CUTAWAY	7,953	**6,106**	5,396	4,757
ELGUIT	71	GIBSON	**SUPER 400 CES** SUNBURST, ROUNDED CUTAWAY	8,370	**6,427**	5,680	5,007
ELGUIT	72	GIBSON	**SUPER 400 CES** SUNBURST, ROUNDED CUTAWAY	8,265	**6,346**	5,608	4,944
ELGUIT	73	GIBSON	**SUPER 400 CES** SUNBURST, ROUNDED CUTAWAY	8,219	**6,311**	5,577	4,917
ELGUIT	74	GIBSON	**SUPER 400 CES** NATURAL, ROUNDED CUTAWAY	6,662	**5,116**	4,521	3,985
ELGUIT	76	GIBSON	**SUPER 400 CES** SUNBURST, ROUNDED CUTAWAY	7,921	**6,082**	5,375	4,738
ELGUIT	77	GIBSON	**SUPER 400 CES** SUNBURST, ROUNDED CUTAWAY	8,211	**6,305**	5,572	4,912
ELGUIT	79	GIBSON	**SUPER 400 CES** SUNBURST, ROUNDED CUTAWAY	6,902	**5,300**	4,683	4,129
ELGUIT	80	GIBSON	**SUPER 400 CES** SUNBURST	6,984	**5,362**	4,739	4,178
ELGUIT	87	GIBSON	**SUPER 400 CES**	5,803	**4,456**	3,938	3,471
ELGUIT	61	GIBSON	**SUPER 400 CES SPECIAL** SUNBURST, PAF's	13,171	**10,113**	8,937	7,879
ELGUIT	52	GIBSON	**SUPER 400 CESN** NATURAL, P-90's	18,743	**14,392**	12,718	11,212

TYPE	YR	MFG	PRICES--BASED ON 100% ORIGINAL MODEL	SELL EXC	SELL AVG	BUY EXC	BUY AVG
ELGUIT	54	GIBSON	**SUPER 400 CESN** ALNICO V PU's	18,074	**13,878**	12,264	10,812
ELGUIT	62	GIBSON	**SUPER 400 CESN** NATURAL, ROUNDED CUTAWAY	17,715	**13,602**	12,020	10,597
ELGUIT	63	GIBSON	**SUPER 400 CESN** NATURAL, POINTED CUTAWAY	17,052	**13,093**	11,571	10,200
ELGUIT	66	GIBSON	**SUPER 400 CESN**	12,752	**9,791**	8,653	7,628
ELGUIT	69	GIBSON	**SUPER 400 CESN** NATURAL, 2 HB's	15,425	**11,844**	10,467	9,227
ELGUIT	70	GIBSON	**SUPER 400 CESN** NATURAL	8,249	**6,334**	5,598	4,935
ELGUIT	74	GIBSON	**SUPER 400 CESN** NATURAL	8,238	**6,326**	5,590	4,928
ELGUIT	80	GIBSON	**SUPER 400 CESN**	8,124	**6,238**	5,513	4,860
ELGUIT	48	GIBSON	**SUPER 400 N**	12,048	**9,251**	8,176	7,207
ELGUIT	83	GIBSON	**SUPER V** NATURAL	8,161	**6,266**	5,538	4,882
ELGUIT	78	GIBSON	**SUPER V CES** ANTIQUE SUNBURST	6,162	**4,731**	4,181	3,686
ELGUIT	79	GIBSON	**SUPER V CES** ANTIQUE SUNBURST, HOLLOW BODY	5,480	**4,207**	3,718	3,278
ELGUIT	80	GIBSON	**SUPER V CES** SUNBURST	5,803	**4,456**	3,938	3,471
ELGUIT	62	GIBSON	**TAL FARLOW** HOLLOW BODY	9,938	**7,631**	6,744	5,945
ELGUIT	64	GIBSON	**TAL FARLOW** HOLLOW BODY	8,638	**6,633**	5,861	5,167
ELGUIT	65	GIBSON	**TAL FARLOW** HOLLOW BODY	8,452	**6,490**	5,735	5,056
ELGUIT	66	GIBSON	**TAL FARLOW** HOLLOW BODY	8,263	**6,345**	5,607	4,943
ELGUIT	63	GIBSON	**TAL FARROW** FLAMEY	12,953	**9,946**	8,790	7,749
ELGUIT	76	GIBSON	**THUNDERBIRD '76 BASS** SUNBURST	984	**755**	668	588
ELGUIT	76	GIBSON	**THUNDERBIRD '76 BASS** BLACK, 2 PU's	1,202	**923**	816	719
ELGUIT	76	GIBSON	**THUNDERBIRD '76 BASS** NATURAL, MAHOGANY, 2 PU's	1,216	**933**	825	727
ELGUIT	76	GIBSON	**THUNDERBIRD '76 BASS** WHITE, 2 PU's	1,233	**946**	836	737
ELGUIT	79	GIBSON	**THUNDERBIRD '79 BASS** SUNBURST	1,261	**968**	855	754
ELGUIT	63	GIBSON	**THUNDERBIRD II BASS** SUNBURST, 1 PU	3,195	**2,453**	2,168	1,911
ELGUIT	64	GIBSON	**THUNDERBIRD II BASS** SUNBURST, 1 PU	2,418	**1,856**	1,640	1,446
ELGUIT	65	GIBSON	**THUNDERBIRD II BASS** SUNBURST, 1 PU	3,296	**2,530**	2,236	1,971
ELGUIT	66	GIBSON	**THUNDERBIRD II BASS** SUNBURST, 1 PU	1,220	**937**	828	730
ELGUIT	67	GIBSON	**THUNDERBIRD II BASS** SUNBURST, 1 PU	1,277	**981**	867	764
ELGUIT	68	GIBSON	**THUNDERBIRD II BASS** CARDINAL RED, 1 PU	1,279	**982**	867	765
ELGUIT	63	GIBSON	**THUNDERBIRD IV BASS** SUNBURST, 2 PU's	4,145	**3,182**	2,812	2,479
ELGUIT	64	GIBSON	**THUNDERBIRD IV BASS** SUNBURST, 2 PU's	4,104	**3,151**	2,785	2,455
ELGUIT	64	GIBSON	**THUNDERBIRD IV BASS** PELHAM BLUE METALLIC, REVERSE BODY	5,201	**3,993**	3,529	3,111
ELGUIT	65	GIBSON	**THUNDERBIRD IV BASS** INVERNESS GREEN, NON-REVERSE BODY	3,148	**2,417**	2,136	1,883
ELGUIT	67	GIBSON	**THUNDERBIRD IV BASS** SUNBURST, 2 PU's	1,281	**983**	869	766
ELGUIT	68	GIBSON	**THUNDERBIRD IV BASS** SUNBURST, 2 PU's	1,274	**978**	864	762
ELGUIT	68	GIBSON	**THUNDERBIRD IV BASS** CUSTOM BLUE, 2 PU's	1,286	**988**	873	769
ELGUIT	89	GIBSON	**THUNDERBIRD IV BASS REISSUE** SUNBURST	941	**723**	639	563
ELGUIT	65	GIBSON	**TRINI LOPEZ CUSTOM** CHERRY RED	4,113	**3,158**	2,791	2,460
ELGUIT	66	GIBSON	**TRINI LOPEZ CUSTOM** SUNBURST	5,376	**4,128**	3,648	3,216
ELGUIT	68	GIBSON	**TRINI LOPEZ CUSTOM** SUNBURST	3,199	**2,457**	2,171	1,914
ELGUIT	66	GIBSON	**TRINI LOPEZ DELUXE** CHERRY SUNBURST	3,589	**2,756**	2,435	2,147
ELGUIT	67	GIBSON	**TRINI LOPEZ DELUXE** CHERRY SUNBURST	2,433	**1,868**	1,651	1,455
ELGUIT	68	GIBSON	**TRINI LOPEZ DELUXE** CHERRY SUNBURST	2,362	**1,813**	1,602	1,413

TYPE	YR	MFG	PRICES--BASED ON 100% ORIGINAL MODEL	SELL EXC	SELL AVG	BUY EXC	BUY AVG
ELGUIT	69	GIBSON	TRINI LOPEZ DELUXE	2,124	**1,631**	1,441	1,270
ELGUIT	65	GIBSON	TRINI LOPEZ STANDARD CHERRY RED	1,761	**1,352**	1,195	1,053
ELGUIT	66	GIBSON	TRINI LOPEZ STANDARD CHERRY RED	1,967	**1,511**	1,335	1,177
ELGUIT	67	GIBSON	TRINI LOPEZ STANDARD PELHAM BLUE	2,022	**1,553**	1,372	1,210
ELGUIT	67	GIBSON	TRINI LOPEZ STANDARD CHERRY RED	2,031	**1,560**	1,378	1,215
ELGUIT	68	GIBSON	TRINI LOPEZ STANDARD CHERRY RED	1,846	**1,418**	1,253	1,104
ELGUIT	69	GIBSON	TRINI LOPEZ STANDARD CHERRY RED	1,779	**1,366**	1,207	1,064
ELGUIT	83	GIBSON	V CURLY MAPLE TOP	1,761	**1,352**	1,195	1,053
ELGUIT	81	GIBSON	VICTORY SILVER	612	**470**	415	366
ELGUIT	81	GIBSON	VICTORY SUNBURST	722	**554**	490	432
ELGUIT	82	GIBSON	VICTORY PELHAM BLUE	547	**420**	371	327
ELGUIT	82	GIBSON	VICTORY BASS RED FINISH, BLACK PICKGUARD,RSWD FRTBRD,1 ACTIVE PU	570	**437**	386	341
ELGUIT	81	GIBSON	VICTORY ARTIST BASS FIREBURST	588	**451**	399	351
ELGUIT	82	GIBSON	VICTORY CUSTOM BASS	645	**495**	437	385
ELGUIT	81	GIBSON	VICTORY MV X 3 PU's	661	**508**	449	395
ELGUIT	85	GIBSON	XPL CUSTOM	712	**546**	483	426
GUITAR AMP	45	GIBSON	BR- 1 BROWN TOLEX, 10" SPEAKER	588	**451**	399	351
GTAMP	47	GIBSON	BR- 6 BROWN, WHITE GRILL, 10" SPEAKER	589	**452**	399	352
GTAMP	49	GIBSON	BR- 6 10" SPEAKER	605	**465**	411	362
GTAMP	52	GIBSON	BR- 6 10" SPEAKER	582	**447**	395	348
GTAMP	48	GIBSON	BR- 9 BROWN	739	**567**	501	442
GTAMP	50	GIBSON	BR- 9	605	**465**	411	362
GTAMP	52	GIBSON	BR- 9 BROWN	517	**397**	351	309
GTAMP	53	GIBSON	BR- 9	501	**385**	340	300
GTAMP	54	GIBSON	BR- 9 TAN	593	**455**	402	355
GTAMP	55	GIBSON	BR- 9 1x8" JENSEN, TV FRONT	753	**578**	511	450
GTAMP	40	GIBSON	EH-125	539	**414**	366	322
GTAMP	41	GIBSON	EH-125	605	**465**	411	362
GTAMP	38	GIBSON	EH-150 TWEED, 12" SPEAKER	778	**597**	528	465
GTAMP	54	GIBSON	EXPLORER TWEED, 1x10" SPEAKERS	750	**576**	509	448
GTAMP	60	GIBSON	FALCON BROWN TOLEX, 1x12" SPEAKER	805	**618**	546	481
GTAMP	63	GIBSON	FALCON BROWN TOLEX, 12" JENSEN, REVERB	804	**617**	545	481
GTAMP	64	GIBSON	FALCON BLACK TOLEX, 12" REV, TREMOLO	801	**615**	544	479
GTAMP	62	GIBSON	FALCON GA- 19RVT TWEED	801	**615**	544	479
GTAMP	64	GIBSON	FALCON GA- 19RVT BROWN	799	**614**	542	478
GTAMP	65	GIBSON	FALCON GA- 19RVT 12" SPEAKER	779	**598**	528	466
GTAMP	66	GIBSON	G-100 100 WATTS, 2 SPEAKER BOTTOMS,2x10" SPEAKERS IN EACH BOTTOM	650	**499**	441	389
GTAMP	62	GIBSON	GA- 3RV TUBE REVERB	554	**425**	376	331
GTAMP	72	GIBSON	GA- 3RV TUBE REVERB II, SOLID STATE	470	**361**	319	281
GTAMP	55	GIBSON	GA- 5 LES PAUL JR.	739	**567**	501	442
GTAMP	56	GIBSON	GA- 5 LES PAUL JR.	700	**537**	475	418
GTAMP	57	GIBSON	GA- 5 LES PAUL JR.	750	**576**	509	448
GTAMP	58	GIBSON	GA- 5 SKYLARK	745	**572**	506	446
GTAMP	60	GIBSON	GA- 5 SKYLARK 10" SPEAKER	246	**189**	167	147
GTAMP	62	GIBSON	GA- 5 SKYLARK	243	**186**	164	145
GTAMP	63	GIBSON	GA- 5 SKYLARK 1x10" SPEAKER	241	**185**	164	144
GTAMP	65	GIBSON	GA- 5 SKYLARK	230	**177**	156	138

TYPE	YR	MFG	PRICES--BASED ON 100% ORIGINAL MODEL	SELL EXC	SELL AVG	BUY EXC	BUY AVG
GTAMP	66	GIBSON	**GA- 5 SKYLARK** BLACK	319	**245**	216	190
GTAMP	64	GIBSON	**GA- 5T SKYLARK** BLOND	387	**297**	262	231
GTAMP	65	GIBSON	**GA- 5T SKYLARK** 10" JENSEN SPEAKER	281	**215**	190	168
GTAMP	66	GIBSON	**GA- 5T SKYLARK**	266	**204**	180	159
GTAMP	75	GIBSON	**GA- 5T SKYLARK** 10" SPEAKER	238	**183**	161	142
GTAMP	58	GIBSON	**GA- 6** 12" SPEAKER	731	**561**	496	437
GTAMP	60	GIBSON	**GA- 8 DISCOVERER**	383	**294**	259	229
GTAMP	64	GIBSON	**GA- 8 DISCOVERER** TREMOLO	256	**196**	174	153
GTAMP	52	GIBSON	**GA- 8 GIBSONETTE** 1x10" SPEAKER	508	**390**	345	304
GTAMP	55	GIBSON	**GA- 9**	517	**397**	351	309
GTAMP	67	GIBSON	**GA- 15RT** BLACK TOLEX, 10" SPEAKER	239	**184**	162	143
GTAMP	64	GIBSON	**GA- 15RVT**	408	**313**	277	244
GTAMP	66	GIBSON	**GA- 15RVT EXPLORER**	321	**246**	218	192
GTAMP	59	GIBSON	**GA- 18** 1x10" SPEAKER, 14 WATTS	639	**491**	433	382
GTAMP	62	GIBSON	**GA- 18T EXPLORER**	567	**436**	385	339
GTAMP	50	GIBSON	**GA- 20** TWEED, RANGER, 1x12" SPEAKER	760	**583**	516	454
GTAMP	52	GIBSON	**GA- 20** BROWN, P12-R JENSEN	751	**577**	509	449
GTAMP	55	GIBSON	**GA- 20** BROWN, P12-R JENSEN	692	**531**	469	414
GTAMP	57	GIBSON	**GA- 20**	274	**210**	186	164
GTAMP	60	GIBSON	**GA- 20** WHITE, CABINET ONLY	132	**101**	89	79
GTAMP	60	GIBSON	**GA- 20** TWEED	602	**462**	408	360
GTAMP	66	GIBSON	**GA- 20** RANTER, TREMOLO	554	**425**	376	331
GTAMP	70	GIBSON	**GA- 20** BLACK, REVERB, SOLID STATE	231	**178**	157	138
GTAMP	65	GIBSON	**GA- 20RVT MINUTEMAN** REVERB	512	**393**	348	306
GTAMP	67	GIBSON	**GA- 20RVT MINUTEMAN** 1x12" SPEAKER	601	**461**	408	359
GTAMP	55	GIBSON	**GA- 20T** 12" SPEAKER	733	**563**	497	438
GTAMP	59	GIBSON	**GA- 20T** TWEED, RANGER, 12" SPEAKER	740	**568**	502	442
GTAMP	60	GIBSON	**GA- 20T** TWEED, RANTER, 12" SPEAKER	672	**516**	456	402
GTAMP	61	GIBSON	**GA- 20T** TWEED	629	**483**	427	376
GTAMP	64	GIBSON	**GA- 20TVT MINUTEMAN** BLACK, REVERB, TREMOLO	328	**251**	222	196
GTAMP	50	GIBSON	**GA- 25 HAWK** 1x12", 1x8" JENSEN	476	**365**	323	284
GTAMP	49	GIBSON	**GA- 30** JENSEN SPEAKERS	724	**556**	491	433
GTAMP	51	GIBSON	**GA- 30** BROWN COVERED CAB, 8", 12" JENSEN SPEAKERS	686	**527**	465	410
GTAMP	52	GIBSON	**GA- 30**	724	**556**	491	433
GTAMP	54	GIBSON	**GA- 30** TWEED, 12" JENSEN SPEAKERS	712	**546**	483	426
GTAMP	59	GIBSON	**GA- 30**	645	**495**	437	385
GTAMP	63	GIBSON	**GA- 30** 10" AND 12" SPEAKERS	731	**561**	496	437
GTAMP	61	GIBSON	**GA- 30RV INVADER** 1x12" JENSEN SPEAKERS	329	**252**	223	196
GTAMP	65	GIBSON	**GA- 35 LANCER** 2x12" SPEAKERS, REVERB, TREMOLO	319	**245**	216	190
GTAMP	65	GIBSON	**GA- 35RVT** GREY	319	**245**	216	190
GTAMP	53	GIBSON	**GA- 40 LES PAUL**	735	**565**	499	440
GTAMP	54	GIBSON	**GA- 40 LES PAUL**	1,046	**803**	709	625
GTAMP	55	GIBSON	**GA- 40 LES PAUL** TWEED, 2 CHANNEL, 20 WATTS	962	**738**	652	575
GTAMP	60	GIBSON	**GA- 40 LES PAUL**	1,233	**946**	836	737
GTAMP	50	GIBSON	**GA- 50** 8" AND 12" SPEAKERS, 25 WATTS	724	**556**	491	433
GTAMP	63	GIBSON	**GA- 50T** 8" AND 12" BLUE JENSENS	815	**626**	553	487
GTAMP	65	GIBSON	**GA- 55RVT RANGER** 4x10" COMBO	702	**539**	476	420

TYPE	YR	MFG	PRICES--BASED ON 100% ORIGINAL MODEL	SELL EXC	SELL AVG	BUY EXC	BUY AVG
GTAMP	66	GIBSON	**GA- 55RVT RANGER**	658	**505**	446	393
GTAMP	52	GIBSON	**GA- 75** 15" JENSEN	1,225	**940**	831	732
GTAMP	61	GIBSON	**GA- 77 VANGUARD**	1,228	**943**	833	734
GTAMP	61	GIBSON	**GA- 79RV** TREMOLO	1,283	**985**	870	767
GTAMP	61	GIBSON	**GA- 79RVT** TWEED, STEREO	975	**749**	661	583
GTAMP	64	GIBSON	**GA- 79RVT** STEREO	2,030	**1,559**	1,377	1,214
GTAMP	56	GIBSON	**GA- 90** BURGUNDY, 6x6" SPEAKERS	663	**509**	449	396
GTAMP	61	GIBSON	**GA-100 BASS** TWEED	701	**538**	475	419
GTAMP	66	GIBSON	**GSS-100** GREY, 2x12" SPEAKERS	663	**509**	449	396
GTAMP	60	GIBSON	**GT- 8T DISCOVERER** 1x12" SPEAKER	582	**447**	395	348
GTAMP	62	GIBSON	**GT- 8T DISCOVERER** TREMOLO 1x12", 15 WATTS	624	**479**	424	373
GTAMP	62	GIBSON	**HAWK** 15" SPEAKER, REVERB	426	**327**	289	255
GTAMP	60	GIBSON	**MINUTEMAN** BLACK, REVERB	328	**251**	222	196
GTAMP	66	GIBSON	**REVERB III** SOLID STATE	399	**307**	271	239
GTAMP	64	GIBSON	**VANGUARD** 1x15" SPEAKER, 2 CHANNEL	415	**319**	281	248
GUITAR (ACOUSTIC)	36	GIBSON	**ADVANCED JUMBO DREADNOUGHT** SUNBURST, BRAZILIAN ROSEWOOD B/.S, 16" WIDE	43,563	**33,450**	29,560	26,060
GUITAR	37	GIBSON	**ADVANCED JUMBO DREADNOUGHT** SUNBURST, BRAZILIAN ROSEWOOD B/.S, 16" WIDE	43,563	**33,450**	29,560	26,060
GUITAR	38	GIBSON	**ADVANCED JUMBO DREADNOUGHT** BRAZILIAN RSWD B/S, SUNBURST, 16" WIDE, ROUND SHOULDERS	39,790	**30,553**	27,000	23,803
GUITAR	39	GIBSON	**ADVANCED JUMBO DREADNOUGHT** BRAZILIAN RSWD B/S, SUNBURST, ROUND SHOULDERS, 16" WIDE	39,664	**30,456**	26,915	23,728
GUITAR	40	GIBSON	**ADVANCED JUMBO DREADNOUGHT** BRAZILIAN RSWD B/S, SUNBURST, ROUND SHOULDERS, 16" WIDE	39,664	**30,456**	26,915	23,728
GUITAR	68	GIBSON	**B- 15** NATURAL, FLATTOP	743	**571**	504	444
GUITAR	69	GIBSON	**B- 15 STUDENT MODEL**	712	**546**	483	426
GUITAR	62	GIBSON	**B- 25** CHERRY SUNBURST, FLATTOP	987	**758**	670	590
GUITAR	63	GIBSON	**B- 25** CHERRY SUNBURST, FLATTOP	981	**753**	665	586
GUITAR	64	GIBSON	**B- 25** CHERRY SUNBURST, FLATTOP	971	**745**	658	580
GUITAR	65	GIBSON	**B- 25** CHERRY SUNBURST, FLATTOP	920	**706**	624	550
GUITAR	66	GIBSON	**B- 25** CHERRY SUNBURST, FLATTOP	910	**699**	617	544
GUITAR	66	GIBSON	**B- 25** CHERRY BACK/SIDES, BLOND TOP, FLATTOP	975	**749**	661	583
GUITAR	67	GIBSON	**B- 25** CHERRY SUNBURST, FLATTOP	685	**526**	465	410
GUITAR	68	GIBSON	**B- 25** CHERRY SUNBURST, FLATTOP	876	**673**	595	524
GUITAR	69	GIBSON	**B- 25** CHERRY SUNBURST, FLATTOP	869	**667**	589	519
GUITAR	70	GIBSON	**B- 25** CHERRY SUNBURST, FLATTOP	863	**663**	585	516
GUITAR	61	GIBSON	**B- 25 3/4** SUNBURST, FLATTOP	949	**729**	644	568
GUITAR	63	GIBSON	**B- 25 3/4** SUNBURST, FLATTOP	917	**704**	622	548
GUITAR	64	GIBSON	**B- 25 3/4** SUNBURST, FLATTOP	862	**662**	585	515
GUITAR	68	GIBSON	**B- 25 3/4** NATURAL, FLATTOP	736	**565**	500	440
GUITAR	63	GIBSON	**B- 25-12** SUNBURST, 12-STRING	766	**588**	519	458
GUITAR	65	GIBSON	**B- 25-12** SUNBURST, 12-STRING	706	**542**	479	422
GUITAR	67	GIBSON	**B- 25-12** SUNBURST, 12-STRING	683	**524**	463	408
GUITAR	68	GIBSON	**B- 25-12** SUNBURST, 12-STRING	668	**513**	453	399
GUITAR	69	GIBSON	**B- 25-12** SUNBURST, 12-STRING	658	**505**	446	393
GUITAR	62	GIBSON	**B- 25-12N**	1,232	**946**	836	737
GUITAR	63	GIBSON	**B- 25-12N** NATURAL, 12-STRING	754	**579**	512	451
GUITAR	65	GIBSON	**B- 25-12N** NATURAL, 12-STRING	655	**503**	444	391

TYPE	YR	MFG	PRICES--BASED ON 100% ORIGINAL MODEL	SELL EXC	SELL AVG	BUY EXC	BUY AVG
GUITAR	66	GIBSON	**B- 25-12N** NATURAL, 12-STRING	658	**505**	446	393
GUITAR	67	GIBSON	**B- 25-12N** NATURAL, 12-STRING	652	**501**	443	390
GUITAR	68	GIBSON	**B- 25-12N** NATURAL, 12-STRING	640	**491**	434	383
GUITAR	69	GIBSON	**B- 25-12N** NATURAL, 12-STRING	642	**493**	436	384
GUITAR	72	GIBSON	**B- 25-12N** NATURAL, 12-STRING	686	**527**	465	410
GUITAR	75	GIBSON	**B- 25-12N** NATURAL, 12-STRING	658	**505**	446	393
GUITAR	63	GIBSON	**B- 25N** NATURAL, FLATTOP	1,310	**1,006**	889	783
GUITAR	64	GIBSON	**B- 25N** NATURAL, FLATTOP	1,280	**982**	868	765
GUITAR	65	GIBSON	**B- 25N** NATURAL, FLATTOP	1,262	**969**	856	755
GUITAR	67	GIBSON	**B- 25N** NATURAL, FLATTOP	808	**620**	548	483
GUITAR	68	GIBSON	**B- 25N** NATURAL, FLATTOP	1,242	**953**	842	743
GUITAR	69	GIBSON	**B- 25N** NATURAL, FLATTOP	1,000	**767**	678	598
GUITAR	71	GIBSON	**B- 25N** NATURAL, FLATTOP	956	**734**	649	572
GUITAR	74	GIBSON	**B- 25N**	749	**575**	508	448
GUITAR	66	GIBSON	**B- 25N 3/4**	683	**524**	463	408
GUITAR	61	GIBSON	**B- 45-12** CHERRY SUNBURST, FLATTOP, 12-STRING	1,288	**989**	874	770
GUITAR	63	GIBSON	**B- 45-12** SQUARE SHOULDERS	1,034	**794**	702	619
GUITAR	64	GIBSON	**B- 45-12** CHERRY SUNBURST, FLATTOP, 12-STRING	1,295	**995**	879	775
GUITAR	66	GIBSON	**B- 45-12** SUNBURST, 12-STRING	1,401	**1,075**	950	838
GUITAR	67	GIBSON	**B- 45-12** CHERRY SUNBURST, FLATTOP, 12-STRING	999	**767**	677	597
GUITAR	68	GIBSON	**B- 45-12** CHERRY SUNBURST, FLATTOP, 12-STRING	992	**761**	673	593
GUITAR	69	GIBSON	**B- 45-12** CHERRY SUNBURST, FLATTOP, 12-STRING	940	**722**	638	562
GUITAR	73	GIBSON	**B- 45-12** CHERRY SUNBURST, FLATTOP, 12-STRING	947	**727**	642	566
GUITAR	75	GIBSON	**B- 45-12**	769	**590**	522	460
GUITAR	63	GIBSON	**B- 45-12N** NATURAL, FLATTOP, 12-STRING	1,219	**936**	827	729
GUITAR	67	GIBSON	**B- 45-12N** NATURAL, FLATTOP, 12-STRING	999	**767**	677	597
GUITAR	68	GIBSON	**B- 45-12N** NATURAL, FLATTOP, 12-STRING	992	**761**	673	593
GUITAR	69	GIBSON	**B- 45-12N** NATURAL, FLATTOP, 12-STRING	940	**722**	638	562
GUITAR	70	GIBSON	**B- 45-12N** NATURAL, FLATTOP, 12-STRING	843	**647**	572	504
GUITAR	73	GIBSON	**B- 45-12N** NATURAL, FLATTOP, 12-STRING	817	**627**	554	489
GUITAR	74	GIBSON	**B- 45-12N**	1,344	**1,032**	912	804
GUITAR	76	GIBSON	**B- 45-12N** NATURAL, FLATTOP, 12-STRING	827	**635**	561	495
GUITAR	68	GIBSON	**BLUE RIDGE** ROSEWOOD BACK/SIDES, FLATTOP	1,008	**774**	684	603
GUITAR	69	GIBSON	**BLUE RIDGE** ROSEWOOD BACK/SIDES, FLATTOP	977	**750**	663	584
GUITAR	70	GIBSON	**BLUE RIDGE** ROSEWOOD BACK/SIDES, FLATTOP	1,068	**820**	725	639
GUITAR	72	GIBSON	**BLUE RIDGE** ROSEWOOD BACK/SIDES, FLATTOP	1,235	**948**	838	739
GUITAR	73	GIBSON	**BLUE RIDGE** ROSEWOOD BACK/SIDES, FLATTOP	1,319	**1,013**	895	789
GUITAR	74	GIBSON	**BLUE RIDGE** ROSEWOOD BACK/SIDES, FLATTOP	1,021	**784**	693	611
GUITAR	75	GIBSON	**BLUE RIDGE** ROSEWOOD BACK/SIDES, FLATTOP	1,000	**767**	678	598
GUITAR	73	GIBSON	**BLUE RIDGE CUSTOM** INDIAN ROSEWOOD	1,324	**1,017**	899	792
GUITAR	52	GIBSON	**BURL IVES 6004** NATURAL, FLATTOP	992	**761**	673	593
GUITAR	62	GIBSON	**C-0 CLASSICAL** MAHOGANY BACK/SIDES	735	**565**	499	440
GUITAR	64	GIBSON	**C-0 CLASSICAL** MAHOGANY BACK/SIDES	766	**588**	519	458
GUITAR	65	GIBSON	**C-0 CLASSICAL** MAHOGANY BACK/SIDES	712	**546**	483	426

TYPE	YR	MFG	PRICES--BASED ON 100% ORIGINAL MODEL	SELL EXC	SELL AVG	BUY EXC	BUY AVG
GUITAR	66	GIBSON	**C-0 CLASSICAL** MAHOGANY BACK/SIDES	680	**522**	462	407
GUITAR	59	GIBSON	**C-1 CLASSICAL** MAHOGANY BACK/SIDES	863	**663**	585	516
GUITAR	60	GIBSON	**C-1 CLASSICAL** MAHOGANY BACK/SIDES	761	**584**	516	455
GUITAR	64	GIBSON	**C-1 CLASSICAL** MAHOGANY BACK/SIDES. 3/4 SIZE	613	**471**	416	367
GUITAR	66	GIBSON	**C-1 CLASSICAL** MAHOGANY BACK/SIDES	739	**567**	501	442
GUITAR	69	GIBSON	**C-1 CLASSICAL** MAHOGANY BACK/SIDES	732	**562**	497	438
GUITAR	67	GIBSON	**C-2 CLASSICAL**	712	**546**	483	426
GUITAR	63	GIBSON	**C-4 CLASSICAL** MAPLE BACK/SIDES	792	**608**	538	474
GUITAR	65	GIBSON	**C-6 CLASSICAL** BRAZILIAN ROSEWOOD	1,212	**931**	823	725
GUITAR	58	GIBSON	**C-6 CLASSICAL CUSTOM** BRAZILIAN ROSEWOOD BACK/SIDES	1,247	**958**	846	746
GUITAR	60	GIBSON	**C-6 CLASSICAL CUSTOM** BRAZILIAN ROSEWOOD BACK/SIDES	1,067	**819**	724	638
GUITAR	64	GIBSON	**C-6 CLASSICAL CUSTOM** BRAZILIAN ROSEWOOD BACK/SIDES	1,049	**805**	712	627
GUITAR	62	GIBSON	**C-8 CLASSICAL** NATURAL, ROSEWOOD BACK/SIDES	948	**728**	643	567
GUITAR	63	GIBSON	**C-8 CLASSICAL** NATURAL, ROSEWOOD BACK/SIDES	948	**728**	643	567
GUITAR	64	GIBSON	**C-8 CLASSICAL** NATURAL, ROSEWOOD BACK/SIDES	948	**728**	643	567
GUITAR	65	GIBSON	**C-8 CLASSICAL** NATURAL, ROSEWOOD BACK/SIDES	948	**728**	643	567
GUITAR	66	GIBSON	**C-8 CLASSICAL** NATURAL, ROSEWOOD BACK/SIDES	948	**728**	643	567
GUITAR	67	GIBSON	**C-8 CLASSICAL** NATURAL, ROSEWOOD BACK/SIDES	948	**728**	643	567
GUITAR	68	GIBSON	**C-8 CLASSICAL** NATURAL, ROSEWOOD BACK/SIDES	1,036	**795**	703	619
GUITAR	69	GIBSON	**C-8 CLASSICAL** NATURAL, ROSEWOOD BACK/SIDES	948	**728**	643	567
GUITAR	33	GIBSON	**CENTURY OF PROGRESS**	1,688	**1,296**	1,146	1,010
GUITAR	50	GIBSON	**CF-100** SUNBURST, POINTED CUTAWAY, FLATTOP, MAHOG BACK/SIDES	3,006	**2,308**	2,039	1,798
GUITAR	51	GIBSON	**CF-100** SUNBURST, POINTED CUTAWAY, FLATTOP, MAHOG BACK/SIDES	3,006	**2,308**	2,039	1,798
GUITAR	52	GIBSON	**CF-100** SUNBURST, POINTED CUTAWAY, MAHOG BACK/SIDES, FLATTOP	2,922	**2,243**	1,982	1,748
GUITAR	53	GIBSON	**CF-100** SUNBURST, POINTED CUTAWAY, MAHOG BACK/SIDES, FLATTOP	3,006	**2,308**	2,039	1,798
GUITAR	54	GIBSON	**CF-100** SUNBURST, POINTED CUTAWAY, MAHOG BACK/SIDES, FLATTOP	3,006	**2,308**	2,039	1,798
GUITAR	55	GIBSON	**CF-100** SUNBURST, POINTED CUTAWAY, MAHOG BACK/SIDES, FLATTOP	3,006	**2,308**	2,039	1,798
GUITAR	56	GIBSON	**CF-100** SUNBURST, POINTED CUTAWAY, MAHOG BACK/SIDES, FLATTOP	3,006	**2,308**	2,039	1,798
GUITAR	57	GIBSON	**CF-100** SUNBURST, POINTED CUTAWAY, MAHOG BACK/SIDES, FLATTOP	3,006	**2,308**	2,039	1,798
GUITAR	58	GIBSON	**CF-100** SUNBURST, POINTED CUTAWAY, MAHOG BACK/SIDES, FLATTOP	3,006	**2,308**	2,039	1,798
GUITAR	53	GIBSON	**CF-100E**	2,083	**1,599**	1,413	1,246
GUITAR	58	GIBSON	**CF-100E** CUTAWAY, GOLD KNOBS	3,435	**2,637**	2,330	2,054
GUITAR	67	GIBSON	**CHALLENGER I**	598	**459**	405	357
GUITAR	83	GIBSON	**CHALLENGER II**	564	**433**	383	337
GUITAR	69	GIBSON	**CITATION** BLOND	19,008	**14,595**	12,898	11,371
GUITAR	69	GIBSON	**CITATION** SUNBURST	19,009	**14,596**	12,899	11,371
GUITAR	55	GIBSON	**COUNTRY WESTERN** NATURAL	2,312	**1,775**	1,569	1,383
GUITAR	56	GIBSON	**COUNTRY WESTERN** NATURAL	2,335	**1,793**	1,584	1,396
GUITAR	57	GIBSON	**COUNTRY WESTERN** NATURAL, SERIAL #A24600-A26500	2,347	**1,802**	1,592	1,404
GUITAR	59	GIBSON	**COUNTRY WESTERN** NATURAL, SERIAL #A28000-	2,362	**1,813**	1,602	1,413
GUITAR	62	GIBSON	**COUNTRY WESTERN** NATURAL	2,055	**1,578**	1,394	1,229
GUITAR	63	GIBSON	**COUNTRY WESTERN** NATURAL	1,989	**1,527**	1,349	1,189
GUITAR	64	GIBSON	**COUNTRY WESTERN** NATURAL	1,638	**1,258**	1,111	980
GUITAR	65	GIBSON	**COUNTRY WESTERN** NATURAL	2,210	**1,697**	1,500	1,322

TYPE	YR	MFG	PRICES--BASED ON 100% ORIGINAL MODEL	SELL EXC	SELL AVG	BUY EXC	BUY AVG
GUITAR	66	GIBSON	**COUNTRY WESTERN** NATURAL, SERIAL #403787	1,774	**1,362**	1,203	1,061
GUITAR	67	GIBSON	**COUNTRY WESTERN** NATURAL	1,324	**1,017**	899	792
GUITAR	68	GIBSON	**COUNTRY WESTERN** NATURAL	2,011	**1,544**	1,364	1,203
GUITAR	69	GIBSON	**COUNTRY WESTERN** NATURAL	1,283	**985**	870	767
GUITAR	70	GIBSON	**D-12-20** LEFT-HANDED, 12-STRING	1,458	**1,119**	989	872
GUITAR	62	GIBSON	**DOVE** SUNBURST, FLATTOP, MAPLE B/S, SQUARE SHOULDERS	4,289	**3,293**	2,910	2,566
GUITAR	63	GIBSON	**DOVE** SUNBURST, FLATTOP, MAPLE B/S, SQUARE SHOULDERS	4,289	**3,293**	2,910	2,566
GUITAR	63	GIBSON	**DOVE** NATURAL, FLATTOP, MAPLE B/S, SQUARE SHOULDERS	4,780	**3,670**	3,243	2,859
GUITAR	64	GIBSON	**DOVE** SUNBURST, FLATTOP, MAPLE B/S, SQUARE SHOULDERS	4,289	**3,293**	2,910	2,566
GUITAR	64	GIBSON	**DOVE** NATURAL, FLATTOP, MAPLE B/S, SQUARE SHOULDERS	4,780	**3,670**	3,243	2,859
GUITAR	65	GIBSON	**DOVE** SUNBURST, FLATTOP, MAPLE BACK/SIDES, SQUARE SHOULDERS	4,217	**3,238**	2,862	2,523
GUITAR	65	GIBSON	**DOVE** NATURAL, FLATTOP, MAPLE BACK/SIDES, SQUARE SHOULDERS	4,289	**3,293**	2,910	2,566
GUITAR	66	GIBSON	**DOVE** SUNBURST, FLATTOP, MAPLE BACIK/SIDES, SQUARE SHOULDERS	3,431	**2,635**	2,328	2,052
GUITAR	66	GIBSON	**DOVE** NATURAL, FLATTOP, MAPLE BACK/SIDES, SQUARE SHOULDERS	3,800	**2,917**	2,578	2,273
GUITAR	67	GIBSON	**DOVE** SUNBURST, FLATTOP, MAPLE BACK/SIDES, SQUARE SHOULDERS	3,142	**2,413**	2,132	1,880
GUITAR	67	GIBSON	**DOVE** NATURAL, FLATTOP, MAPLE BACK/SIDES, SQUARE SHOULDERS	3,279	**2,518**	2,225	1,961
GUITAR	68	GIBSON	**DOVE** SUNBURST, FLATTOP, MAPLE BACK/SIDES, SQUARE SHOULDERS	2,466	**1,893**	1,673	1,475
GUITAR	68	GIBSON	**DOVE** NATURAL, FLATTOP, MAPLE BACK/SIDES, SQUARE SHOULDERS	3,142	**2,413**	2,132	1,880
GUITAR	69	GIBSON	**DOVE** SUNBURST, FLATTOP, MAPLE BACK/SIDES, SQUARE SHOULDERS	2,192	**1,683**	1,488	1,311
GUITAR	69	GIBSON	**DOVE** NATURAL, FLATTOP, MAPLE BACK/SIDES, SQUARE SHOULDERS	2,215	**1,701**	1,503	1,325
GUITAR	70	GIBSON	**DOVE** SUNBURST, FLATTOP, MAPLE BACK/SIDES, SQUARE SHOULDERS	2,113	**1,622**	1,434	1,264
GUITAR	70	GIBSON	**DOVE** NATURAL, FLATTOP, MAPLE BACK/SIDES, SQUARE SHOULDERS	2,231	**1,713**	1,513	1,334
GUITAR	72	GIBSON	**DOVE** SUNBURST, FLATTOP, MAPLE BACK/SIDES, SQUARE SHOULDERS	2,141	**1,644**	1,453	1,281
GUITAR	73	GIBSON	**DOVE** SUNBURST, FLATTOP, MAPLE BACK SIDES, SQUARE SHOULDERS	2,141	**1,644**	1,453	1,281
GUITAR	74	GIBSON	**DOVE** NATURAL, FLATTOP, MAPLE BACK/SIDES, SQUARE SHOULDERS	1,850	**1,420**	1,255	1,106
GUITAR	76	GIBSON	**DOVE** SUNBURST, FLATTOP, MAPLE BACK/SIDES, SQUARE SHOULDERS	1,644	**1,262**	1,115	983
GUITAR	76	GIBSON	**DOVE** NATURAL, FLATTOP, MAPLE BACK/SIDES, SQUARE SHOULDERS	1,802	**1,383**	1,222	1,078
GUITAR	77	GIBSON	**DOVE** NATURAL, FLATTOP, MAPLE BACK SIDES, SQUARE SHOULDERS	1,761	**1,352**	1,195	1,053
GUITAR	62	GIBSON	**EVERLY BROTHERS** BLACK, FLATTOP	11,549	**8,868**	7,837	6,909
GUITAR	63	GIBSON	**EVERLY BROTHERS** BLACK, FLATTOP	9,962	**7,649**	6,760	5,959
GUITAR	63	GIBSON	**EVERLY BROTHERS** NATURAL, FLATTOP, CHERRY RED BACK/SIDES	14,963	**11,489**	10,153	8,951
GUITAR	64	GIBSON	**EVERLY BROTHERS** BLACK, FLATTOP	11,621	**8,923**	7,885	6,951
GUITAR	65	GIBSON	**EVERLY BROTHERS** BLACK, FLATTOP	10,698	**8,214**	7,259	6,399
GUITAR	66	GIBSON	**EVERLY BROTHERS** BLACK, FLATTOP	10,594	**8,134**	7,188	6,337
GUITAR	68	GIBSON	**EVERLY BROTHERS** NATURAL, FLATTOP	9,953	**7,642**	6,754	5,954
GUITAR	68	GIBSON	**EVERLY BROTHERS** BLACK, FLATTOP	10,202	**7,833**	6,922	6,103
GUITAR	69	GIBSON	**EVERLY BROTHERS** NATURAL, FLATTOP	9,779	**7,509**	6,636	5,850
GUITAR	70	GIBSON	**EVERLY BROTHERS** BLACK, FLATTOP	9,737	**7,476**	6,607	5,824
GUITAR	71	GIBSON	**EVERLY BROTHERS** NATURAL, FLATTOP	9,648	**7,408**	6,547	5,772
GUITAR	41	GIBSON	**EXPERIMENTAL MODEL** 17" WIDE	3,270	**2,511**	2,219	1,956
GUITAR	63	GIBSON	**F-25 FOLKSINGER**	1,227	**942**	832	734
GUITAR	64	GIBSON	**F-25 FOLKSINGER**	1,201	**922**	815	718
GUITAR	65	GIBSON	**F-25 FOLKSINGER**	1,244	**955**	844	744

TYPE	YR	MFG	PRICES--BASED ON 100% ORIGINAL MODEL	SELL EXC	SELL AVG	BUY EXC	BUY AVG
GUITAR	68	GIBSON	**F-25 FOLKSINGER**	1,208	**927**	820	722
GUITAR	55	GIBSON	**GF-100E** SUNBURST, 1 PU	2,418	**1,856**	1,640	1,446
GUITAR	73	GIBSON	**GOSPEL** NATURAL	964	**740**	654	576
GUITAR	74	GIBSON	**GOSPEL** NATURAL	1,226	**941**	832	733
GUITAR	76	GIBSON	**GOSPEL** NATURAL	1,347	**1,034**	914	806
GUITAR	73	GIBSON	**GOSPEL DREADNOUGHT** BLOND, MAPLE BACK/SIDES, SPRUCE TOP	1,462	**1,123**	992	875
GUITAR	55	GIBSON	**GS- 1 CLASSICAL** MAHOGANY BACK/SIDES	544	**417**	369	325
GUITAR	39	GIBSON	**GS-35 CLASSICAL** SPRUCE TOP, MAHOGANY BACK/SIDES	1,042	**800**	707	623
GUITAR	18	GIBSON	**GY ARMY-NAVY** FLAT TOP	1,644	**1,262**	1,115	983
GUITAR	18	GIBSON	**GY ARMY-NAVY SPECIAL** MAHOGANY	1,816	**1,394**	1,232	1,086
GUITAR	66	GIBSON	**HERITAGE** ROSEWOOD BACK/SIDES, FLATTOP	1,899	**1,458**	1,288	1,136
GUITAR	68	GIBSON	**HERITAGE** ROSEWOOD BACK/SIDES, FLATTOP	1,932	**1,483**	1,311	1,155
GUITAR	68	GIBSON	**HERITAGE** NATURAL, FLATTOP	1,934	**1,485**	1,312	1,157
GUITAR	69	GIBSON	**HERITAGE** ROSEWOOD BACK/SIDES, FLATTOP	1,919	**1,474**	1,302	1,148
GUITAR	70	GIBSON	**HERITAGE** NATURAL, FLATTOP	1,986	**1,525**	1,348	1,188
GUITAR	73	GIBSON	**HERITAGE** ROSEWOOD BACK/SIDES, FLATTOP	1,420	**1,090**	963	849
GUITAR	74	GIBSON	**HERITAGE** ROSEWOOD BACK/SIDES, FLATTOP	1,425	**1,094**	967	852
GUITAR	75	GIBSON	**HERITAGE** ROSEWOOD BACK/SIDES, FLATTOP	1,364	**1,047**	925	816
GUITAR	76	GIBSON	**HERITAGE** NATURAL, FLATTOP	1,312	**1,007**	890	785
GUITAR	76	GIBSON	**HERITAGE**	1,673	**1,284**	1,135	1,000
GUITAR	80	GIBSON	**HERITAGE** NATURAL, FLATTOP	1,031	**792**	699	617
GUITAR	69	GIBSON	**HERITAGE-12** NATURAL, 12-STRING	1,064	**817**	722	636
GUITAR	37	GIBSON	**HG-00**	1,615	**1,240**	1,095	966
GUITAR	39	GIBSON	**HG-00** SUNBURST, SERIAL #-96000	1,316	**1,010**	893	787
GUITAR	32	GIBSON	**HG-20 HAWAIIAN** BLACK	1,762	**1,353**	1,196	1,054
GUITAR	37	GIBSON	**HG-CENTURY** ROSEWOOD AND PEARL INLAYS	3,250	**2,495**	2,205	1,944
GUITAR	39	GIBSON	**HG-CENTURY** ROSEWOOD AND PEARL INLAYS	3,417	**2,623**	2,318	2,044
GUITAR	78	GIBSON	**HOWARD ROBERTS ARTIST** 1 PU	1,673	**1,284**	1,135	1,000
GUITAR	74	GIBSON	**HOWARD ROBERTS CUSTOM** SUNBURST	1,766	**1,356**	1,198	1,056
GUITAR	76	GIBSON	**HOWARD ROBERTS CUSTOM**	1,568	**1,204**	1,064	938
GUITAR	60	GIBSON	**HUMMINGBIRD** CHERRY SUNBURST	3,480	**2,672**	2,362	2,082
GUITAR	61	GIBSON	**HUMMINGBIRD** CHERRY SUNBURST	3,300	**2,534**	2,239	1,974
GUITAR	62	GIBSON	**HUMMINGBIRD** CHERRY SUNBURST	3,300	**2,534**	2,239	1,974
GUITAR	63	GIBSON	**HUMMINGBIRD** CHERRY SUNBURST	3,239	**2,487**	2,197	1,937
GUITAR	64	GIBSON	**HUMMINGBIRD** NATURAL	3,202	**2,458**	2,172	1,915
GUITAR	64	GIBSON	**HUMMINGBIRD** CHERRY SUNBURST	3,270	**2,511**	2,219	1,956
GUITAR	65	GIBSON	**HUMMINGBIRD** CHERRY SUNBURST	3,778	**2,901**	2,564	2,260
GUITAR	66	GIBSON	**HUMMINGBIRD** CHERRY SUNBURST	2,348	**1,803**	1,593	1,404
GUITAR	67	GIBSON	**HUMMINGBIRD** CHERRY SUNBURST	1,858	**1,426**	1,260	1,111
GUITAR	67	GIBSON	**HUMMINGBIRD** NATURAL	2,946	**2,262**	1,999	1,762
GUITAR	68	GIBSON	**HUMMINGBIRD** CHERRY SUNBURST	1,858	**1,426**	1,260	1,111
GUITAR	68	GIBSON	**HUMMINGBIRD** NATURAL BLOND	2,890	**2,219**	1,961	1,729
GUITAR	69	GIBSON	**HUMMINGBIRD** CHERRY SUNBURST	1,667	**1,280**	1,131	997
GUITAR	70	GIBSON	**HUMMINGBIRD** CHERRY SUNBURST	3,239	**2,487**	2,197	1,937

TYPE	YR	MFG	PRICES--BASED ON 100% ORIGINAL MODEL	SELL EXC	SELL AVG	BUY EXC	BUY AVG
GUITAR	72	GIBSON	**HUMMINGBIRD** CHERRY SUNBURST	3,085	**2,369**	2,093	1,845
GUITAR	73	GIBSON	**HUMMINGBIRD** CHERRY SUNBURST	2,993	**2,298**	2,031	1,790
GUITAR	74	GIBSON	**HUMMINGBIRD** CHERRY SUNBURST	2,459	**1,888**	1,668	1,471
GUITAR	75	GIBSON	**HUMMINGBIRD** NATURAL	1,971	**1,513**	1,337	1,179
GUITAR	75	GIBSON	**HUMMINGBIRD** CHERRY SUNBURST	2,430	**1,866**	1,649	1,453
GUITAR	76	GIBSON	**HUMMINGBIRD** CHERRY SUNBURST	2,352	**1,806**	1,596	1,407
GUITAR	76	GIBSON	**HUMMINGBIRD** BURGUNDY	2,458	**1,887**	1,668	1,470
GUITAR	76	GIBSON	**HUMMINGBIRD** NATURAL	2,458	**1,887**	1,668	1,470
GUITAR	77	GIBSON	**HUMMINGBIRD** WINE RED	2,064	**1,584**	1,400	1,234
GUITAR	79	GIBSON	**HUMMINGBIRD** BURGUNDY	1,780	**1,367**	1,208	1,065
GUITAR	83	GIBSON	**J- 25** NATURAL	720	**552**	488	430
GUITAR	87	GIBSON	**J- 25**	677	**520**	459	405
GUITAR	84	GIBSON	**J- 30**	901	**692**	611	539
GUITAR	37	GIBSON	**J- 35** SUNBURST, SERIAL #-95400	5,483	**4,210**	3,720	3,280
GUITAR	38	GIBSON	**J- 35** NATURAL, SERIAL #95400-	10,251	**7,871**	6,956	6,132
GUITAR	39	GIBSON	**J- 35** SUNBURST, SERIAL #-96000	5,264	**4,042**	3,572	3,149
GUITAR	39	GIBSON	**J- 35** NATURAL	10,237	**7,861**	6,947	6,124
GUITAR	40	GIBSON	**J- 35** NATURAL, SERIAL #96000-96600	4,266	**3,275**	2,894	2,552
GUITAR	40	GIBSON	**J- 35** SUNBURST	5,298	**4,068**	3,595	3,169
GUITAR	41	GIBSON	**J- 35** NATURAL, SERIAL #96600-97400	6,674	**5,124**	4,528	3,992
GUITAR	71	GIBSON	**J- 40** NATURAL	1,013	**778**	687	606
GUITAR	72	GIBSON	**J- 40** NATURAL	863	**663**	585	516
GUITAR	74	GIBSON	**J- 40** NATURAL	1,294	**994**	878	774
GUITAR	75	GIBSON	**J- 40** NATURAL	1,293	**993**	877	773
GUITAR	78	GIBSON	**J- 40** NATURAL	947	**727**	642	566
GUITAR	42	GIBSON	**J- 45** SUNBURST, BANNER PEGHEAD LOGO	4,081	**3,133**	2,769	2,441
GUITAR	43	GIBSON	**J- 45** SUNBURST	4,463	**3,427**	3,028	2,669
GUITAR	43	GIBSON	**J- 45** MAHOGANY	9,716	**7,460**	6,593	5,812
GUITAR	44	GIBSON	**J- 45** SUNBURST	4,297	**3,299**	2,916	2,570
GUITAR	45	GIBSON	**J- 45** SUNBURST	4,379	**3,362**	2,971	2,619
GUITAR	45	GIBSON	**J- 45** MAPLE	9,990	**7,671**	6,779	5,976
GUITAR	46	GIBSON	**J- 45** SUNBURST, BANNER LOGO	4,193	**3,219**	2,845	2,508
GUITAR	47	GIBSON	**J- 45** STANDARD LOGO	3,532	**2,712**	2,397	2,113
GUITAR	47	GIBSON	**J- 45** SUNBURST	4,441	**3,410**	3,014	2,657
GUITAR	47	GIBSON	**J- 45** MAPLE	9,402	**7,219**	6,380	5,624
GUITAR	48	GIBSON	**J- 45** SUNBURST	4,047	**3,108**	2,746	2,421
GUITAR	49	GIBSON	**J- 45** SUNBURST	3,354	**2,575**	2,276	2,006
GUITAR	50	GIBSON	**J- 45** SUNBURST	3,595	**2,760**	2,439	2,150
GUITAR	51	GIBSON	**J- 45** SUNBURST	3,595	**2,760**	2,439	2,150
GUITAR	52	GIBSON	**J- 45** SUNBURST	3,595	**2,760**	2,439	2,150
GUITAR	53	GIBSON	**J- 45** SUNBURST	3,595	**2,760**	2,439	2,150
GUITAR	55	GIBSON	**J- 45** SUNBURST	3,595	**2,760**	2,439	2,150
GUITAR	57	GIBSON	**J- 45** SUNBURST	3,355	**2,576**	2,276	2,007

TYPE	YR	MFG	PRICES--BASED ON 100% ORIGINAL MODEL	SELL EXC	SELL AVG	BUY EXC	BUY AVG
GUITAR	58	GIBSON	J- 45 SUNBURST	3,355	2,576	2,276	2,007
GUITAR	59	GIBSON	J- 45 NATURAL	1,408	1,081	956	842
GUITAR	59	GIBSON	J- 45 SUNBURST	3,355	2,576	2,276	2,007
GUITAR	60	GIBSON	J- 45 SUNBURST	3,296	2,530	2,236	1,971
GUITAR	61	GIBSON	J- 45 SUNBURST	3,296	2,530	2,236	1,971
GUITAR	62	GIBSON	J- 45 SUNBURST	3,296	2,530	2,236	1,971
GUITAR	63	GIBSON	J- 45 SUNBURST	3,296	2,530	2,236	1,971
GUITAR	64	GIBSON	J- 45 SUNBURST	3,296	2,530	2,236	1,971
GUITAR	65	GIBSON	J- 45 SUNBURST	2,996	2,300	2,033	1,792
GUITAR	66	GIBSON	J- 45 SUNBURST	2,876	2,208	1,951	1,720
GUITAR	67	GIBSON	J- 45 SUNBURST	2,636	2,024	1,789	1,577
GUITAR	68	GIBSON	J- 45 SUNBURST	2,636	2,024	1,789	1,577
GUITAR	69	GIBSON	J- 45 SUNBURST	2,636	2,024	1,789	1,577
GUITAR	70	GIBSON	J- 45 SUNBURST	1,319	1,013	895	789
GUITAR	71	GIBSON	J- 45 SUNBURST	1,336	1,025	906	799
GUITAR	72	GIBSON	J- 45 SUNBURST	1,319	1,013	895	789
GUITAR	73	GIBSON	J- 45 SUNBURST	1,317	1,011	893	787
GUITAR	74	GIBSON	J- 45 SUNBURST	1,321	1,014	896	790
GUITAR	75	GIBSON	J- 45 SUNBURST	1,326	1,018	899	793
GUITAR	76	GIBSON	J- 45 SUNBURST	1,276	980	866	763
GUITAR	77	GIBSON	J- 45 SUNBURST	1,256	964	852	751
GUITAR	78	GIBSON	J- 45 SUNBURST	1,242	953	842	743
GUITAR	79	GIBSON	J- 45 SUNBURST	1,023	786	694	612
GUITAR	85	GIBSON	J- 45 CELEBRITY	1,692	1,299	1,148	1,012
GUITAR	49	GIBSON	J- 50 NATURAL	3,133	2,406	2,126	1,874
GUITAR	50	GIBSON	J- 50 NATURAL	2,915	2,238	1,978	1,744
GUITAR	51	GIBSON	J- 50 NATURAL	3,037	2,332	2,061	1,817
GUITAR	52	GIBSON	J- 50 NATURAL	3,133	2,406	2,126	1,874
GUITAR	53	GIBSON	J- 50 NATURAL	2,922	2,243	1,982	1,748
GUITAR	54	GIBSON	J- 50 NATURAL	2,920	2,242	1,982	1,747
GUITAR	56	GIBSON	J- 50 NATURAL	3,076	2,362	2,087	1,840
GUITAR	57	GIBSON	J- 50 NATURAL	2,363	1,814	1,603	1,413
GUITAR	58	GIBSON	J- 50 NATURAL	2,465	1,892	1,672	1,474
GUITAR	59	GIBSON	J- 50 NATURAL	2,362	1,813	1,602	1,413
GUITAR	60	GIBSON	J- 50 NATURAL	2,107	1,618	1,430	1,260
GUITAR	61	GIBSON	J- 50 NATURAL	2,041	1,567	1,385	1,221
GUITAR	62	GIBSON	J- 50 NATURAL	1,989	1,527	1,349	1,189
GUITAR	63	GIBSON	J- 50 NATURAL	1,893	1,454	1,285	1,132
GUITAR	63	GIBSON	J- 50 SUNBURST	1,944	1,492	1,319	1,163
GUITAR	64	GIBSON	J- 50 NATURAL	1,747	1,341	1,185	1,045
GUITAR	65	GIBSON	J- 50 NATURAL	1,664	1,277	1,129	995
GUITAR	66	GIBSON	J- 50 NATURAL	1,589	1,220	1,078	950

TYPE	YR	MFG	PRICES--BASED ON 100% ORIGINAL MODEL	SELL EXC	SELL AVG	BUY EXC	BUY AVG
GUITAR	67	GIBSON	J- 50 NATURAL	1,504	**1,154**	1,020	899
GUITAR	68	GIBSON	J- 50 NATURAL	1,442	**1,107**	978	862
GUITAR	68	GIBSON	J- 50 NATURAL, LEFT-HANDED	1,444	**1,109**	980	864
GUITAR	69	GIBSON	J- 50 NATURAL	1,337	**1,026**	907	799
GUITAR	70	GIBSON	J- 50 NATURAL	685	**526**	465	410
GUITAR	71	GIBSON	J- 50 NATURAL	1,204	**924**	817	720
GUITAR	72	GIBSON	J- 50 NATURAL	1,062	**816**	721	635
GUITAR	73	GIBSON	J- 50 NATURAL	1,000	**767**	678	598
GUITAR	74	GIBSON	J- 50 NATURAL	963	**739**	653	576
GUITAR	74	GIBSON	J- 50 NATURAL, LEFT-HANDED	971	**745**	658	580
GUITAR	76	GIBSON	J- 50 NATURAL	1,208	**927**	820	722
GUITAR	39	GIBSON	J- 55 SUNBURST	9,758	**7,493**	6,621	5,837
GUITAR	40	GIBSON	J- 55 SUNBURST	4,141	**3,180**	2,810	2,477
GUITAR	41	GIBSON	J- 55 SUNBURST	4,141	**3,180**	2,810	2,477
GUITAR	66	GIBSON	J- 55 BLOND	1,394	**1,070**	946	834
GUITAR	70	GIBSON	J- 55 NATURAL	1,587	**1,218**	1,076	949
GUITAR	74	GIBSON	J- 55 SUNBURST	1,354	**1,039**	918	810
GUITAR	74	GIBSON	J- 55 NATURAL	1,475	**1,132**	1,000	882
GUITAR	76	GIBSON	J- 55 NATURAL	1,475	**1,132**	1,000	882
GUITAR	79	GIBSON	J- 55	1,256	**964**	852	751
GUITAR	40	GIBSON	J- 55R SITKA SPRUCE, INDIAN ROSEWOOD	10,752	**8,256**	7,296	6,432
GUITAR	40	GIBSON	J-100 NATURAL	11,577	**8,889**	7,856	6,925
GUITAR	72	GIBSON	J-100 SUNBURST	1,606	**1,233**	1,089	960
GUITAR	74	GIBSON	J-100 NATURAL	1,308	**1,004**	887	782
GUITAR	89	GIBSON	J-100 MAPLE BACK/SIDES	1,071	**823**	727	641
GUITAR	54	GIBSON	J-160E SUNBURST, ADJUSTABLE BRIDGE, SERIAL #A16000-A19000	4,015	**3,083**	2,724	2,401
GUITAR	55	GIBSON	J-160E SUNBURST, SERIAL #A19000-A22000	3,460	**2,657**	2,348	2,070
GUITAR	56	GIBSON	J-160E SUNBURST	3,423	**2,629**	2,323	2,048
GUITAR	57	GIBSON	J-160E SUNBURST	3,421	**2,627**	2,321	2,046
GUITAR	58	GIBSON	J-160E SUNBURST	3,419	**2,625**	2,320	2,045
GUITAR	59	GIBSON	J-160E SUNBURST	4,020	**3,087**	2,728	2,405
GUITAR	60	GIBSON	J-160E SUNBURST	2,946	**2,262**	1,999	1,762
GUITAR	62	GIBSON	J-160E SUNBURST	2,428	**1,864**	1,647	1,452
GUITAR	62	GIBSON	J-160E NATURAL	4,586	**3,521**	3,112	2,743
GUITAR	63	GIBSON	J-160E SUNBURST	3,503	**2,690**	2,377	2,095
GUITAR	64	GIBSON	J-160E SUNBURST	2,936	**2,254**	1,992	1,756
GUITAR	65	GIBSON	J-160E SUNBURST	2,278	**1,749**	1,545	1,362
GUITAR	66	GIBSON	J-160E SUNBURST	2,340	**1,797**	1,588	1,400
GUITAR	67	GIBSON	J-160E SUNBURST	1,790	**1,375**	1,215	1,071
GUITAR	68	GIBSON	J-160E SUNBURST	2,141	**1,644**	1,453	1,281
GUITAR	69	GIBSON	J-160E SUNBURST	1,967	**1,511**	1,335	1,177
GUITAR	70	GIBSON	J-160E SUNBURST	1,775	**1,363**	1,204	1,061

TYPE	YR	MFG	PRICES--BASED ON 100% ORIGINAL MODEL	SELL EXC	SELL AVG	BUY EXC	BUY AVG
GUITAR	72	GIBSON	J-160E SUNBURST	1,712	**1,314**	1,162	1,024
GUITAR	73	GIBSON	J-160E SUNBURST	1,712	**1,314**	1,162	1,024
GUITAR	75	GIBSON	J-160E SUNBURST	1,475	**1,132**	1,000	882
GUITAR	51	GIBSON	J-185 SUNBURST, FLATTOP	12,764	**9,801**	8,661	7,635
GUITAR	52	GIBSON	J-185 SUNBURST, FLATTOP	11,439	**8,784**	7,762	6,843
GUITAR	53	GIBSON	J-185 SUNBURST, FLATTOP, SERIAL #A13000-A16000	9,222	**7,081**	6,257	5,516
GUITAR	55	GIBSON	J-185 NATURAL, FLATTOP	12,057	**9,258**	8,182	7,213
GUITAR	58	GIBSON	J-185 SUNBURST, FLATTOP	10,419	**8,000**	7,070	6,233
GUITAR	58	GIBSON	J-185 NATURAL, FLATTOP	12,056	**9,257**	8,181	7,212
GUITAR	40	GIBSON	J-200 SUNBURST	15,401	**11,825**	10,450	9,213
GUITAR	50	GIBSON	J-200 SUNBURST, SERIAL #A4400-A6000	13,623	**10,461**	9,244	8,149
GUITAR	50	GIBSON	J-200 NATURAL	15,149	**11,632**	10,279	9,062
GUITAR	51	GIBSON	J-200 SUNBURST, SERIAL #A28000-	12,159	**9,337**	8,251	7,274
GUITAR	51	GIBSON	J-200 NATURAL	15,150	**11,633**	10,280	9,063
GUITAR	52	GIBSON	J-200 SUNBURST	12,159	**9,337**	8,251	7,274
GUITAR	53	GIBSON	J-200 SUNBURST	10,591	**8,133**	7,187	6,336
GUITAR	53	GIBSON	J-200 NATURAL	14,332	**11,005**	9,725	8,573
GUITAR	54	GIBSON	J-200 NATURAL	10,207	**7,838**	6,926	6,106
GUITAR	55	GIBSON	J-200 SUNBURST, SERIAL #A19000-A22000	11,401	**8,754**	7,736	6,820
GUITAR	55	GIBSON	J-200 NATURAL	13,345	**10,247**	9,056	7,983
GUITAR	56	GIBSON	J-200 SUNBURST	11,689	**8,975**	7,932	6,992
GUITAR	56	GIBSON	J-200 NATURAL	12,962	**9,953**	8,796	7,754
GUITAR	57	GIBSON	J-200 SUNBURST	10,265	**7,882**	6,966	6,141
GUITAR	57	GIBSON	J-200 NATURAL, SERIAL #A24600-A26500	11,439	**8,784**	7,762	6,843
GUITAR	58	GIBSON	J-200 SUNBURST, SERIAL #A26500-A28000	10,015	**7,690**	6,795	5,991
GUITAR	58	GIBSON	J-200 BROWN SUNBURST	12,962	**9,953**	8,796	7,754
GUITAR	59	GIBSON	J-200 SUNBURST	9,067	**6,962**	6,152	5,424
GUITAR	59	GIBSON	J-200 NATURAL	11,296	**8,673**	7,665	6,757
GUITAR	60	GIBSON	J-200 SUNBURST	8,541	**6,558**	5,795	5,109
GUITAR	61	GIBSON	J-200 SUNBURST	5,706	**4,381**	3,872	3,413
GUITAR	61	GIBSON	J-200 NATURAL	8,568	**6,579**	5,814	5,125
GUITAR	62	GIBSON	J-200 SUNBURST	6,146	**4,719**	4,170	3,676
GUITAR	63	GIBSON	J-200 SUNBURST	5,789	**4,445**	3,928	3,463
GUITAR	63	GIBSON	J-200 NATURAL	7,142	**5,484**	4,846	4,272
GUITAR	64	GIBSON	J-200 SUNBURST	4,431	**3,403**	3,007	2,651
GUITAR	64	GIBSON	J-200 NATURAL	4,960	**3,808**	3,366	2,967
GUITAR	65	GIBSON	J-200 SUNBURST	4,859	**3,731**	3,297	2,907
GUITAR	65	GIBSON	J-200 NATURAL	5,085	**3,905**	3,451	3,042
GUITAR	66	GIBSON	J-200 SUNBURST	3,572	**2,743**	2,424	2,137
GUITAR	66	GIBSON	J-200 NATURAL	4,006	**3,076**	2,718	2,396
GUITAR	67	GIBSON	J-200 NATURAL	3,390	**2,603**	2,300	2,028
GUITAR	67	GIBSON	J-200 SUNBURST	4,315	**3,313**	2,928	2,581

TYPE	YR	MFG	PRICES--BASED ON 100% ORIGINAL MODEL	SELL EXC	SELL AVG	BUY EXC	BUY AVG
GUITAR	68	GIBSON	J-200 NATURAL	3,390	2,603	2,300	2,028
GUITAR	68	GIBSON	J-200 SUNBURST	4,001	3,072	2,715	2,393
GUITAR	69	GIBSON	J-200 NATURAL	3,388	2,601	2,299	2,026
GUITAR	69	GIBSON	J-200 SUNBURST	3,589	2,756	2,435	2,147
GUITAR	70	GIBSON	J-200 NATURAL	1,870	1,436	1,269	1,118
GUITAR	72	GIBSON	J-200 NATURAL	1,807	1,388	1,226	1,081
GUITAR	73	GIBSON	J-200 NATURAL	1,751	1,345	1,188	1,047
GUITAR	74	GIBSON	J-200 SUNBURST	2,467	1,894	1,674	1,476
GUITAR	70	GIBSON	J-200 ARTIST CHERRY SUNBURST	1,725	1,325	1,171	1,032
GUITAR	85	GIBSON	J-200 CELEBRITY	3,231	2,481	2,192	1,932
GUITAR	54	GIBSON	J-200N	5,740	4,407	3,895	3,433
GUITAR	84	GIBSON	J-25 CASE	843	647	572	504
GUITAR	72	GIBSON	J-250R	2,091	1,605	1,418	1,250
GUITAR	77	GIBSON	J-250R	2,253	1,730	1,529	1,348
GUITAR	62	GIBSON	JOHNNY SMITH NATURAL	8,814	6,768	5,981	5,272
GUITAR	62	GIBSON	JOHNNY SMITH SUNBURST ICE TEA	8,817	6,770	5,983	5,274
GUITAR	63	GIBSON	JOHNNY SMITH NATURAL	8,310	6,381	5,639	4,971
GUITAR	63	GIBSON	JOHNNY SMITH SUNBURST	9,294	7,137	6,307	5,560
GUITAR	67	GIBSON	JOHNNY SMITH NATURAL	7,442	5,714	5,050	4,452
GUITAR	67	GIBSON	JOHNNY SMITH SUNBURST	8,391	6,443	5,693	5,019
GUITAR	75	GIBSON	JOHNNY SMITH NATURAL	6,512	5,000	4,419	3,896
GUITAR	77	GIBSON	JOHNNY SMITH WINE RED	6,224	4,779	4,224	3,723
GUITAR	81	GIBSON	JOHNNY SMITH SUNBURST	5,315	4,081	3,606	3,179
GUITAR	88	GIBSON	JOHNNY SMITH SUNBURST, DOUBLE PU	5,663	4,349	3,843	3,388
GUITAR	69	GIBSON	JUBILEE NATURAL	1,029	790	698	615
GUITAR	69	GIBSON	JUBILEE MAHOGANY BACK/SIDES	1,038	797	704	621
GUITAR	71	GIBSON	JUBILEE NATURAL, 12-STRING	919	706	623	550
GUITAR	70	GIBSON	JUBILEE DELUXE ROSEWOOD BACK/SIDES	925	710	627	553
GUITAR	34	GIBSON	JUMBO SUNBURST, MAHOGANY BACK/SIDES, SERIAL #91500-92400	14,230	10,927	9,656	8,513
GUITAR	35	GIBSON	JUMBO SUNBURST	16,564	12,719	11,240	9,909
GUITAR	36	GIBSON	JUMBO SUNBURST	11,841	9,092	8,035	7,083
GUITAR	37	GIBSON	JUMBO SUNBURST	14,665	11,260	9,951	8,772
GUITAR	36	GIBSON	JUMBO 35 SUNBURST	10,594	8,134	7,188	6,337
GUITAR	38	GIBSON	JUMBO 35 SUNBURST	10,876	8,351	7,380	6,506
GUITAR	40	GIBSON	JUMBO 35 NATURAL	6,006	4,612	4,075	3,593
GUITAR	39	GIBSON	JUMBO 55 SUNBURST	12,808	9,834	8,691	7,662
GUITAR	78	GIBSON	KALAMAZOO AWARD MODEL NATURAL	13,295	10,209	9,021	7,953
GUITAR	80	GIBSON	KALAMAZOO AWARD MODEL SUNBURST	15,223	11,689	10,329	9,106
GUITAR	81	GIBSON	KALAMAZOO AWARD MODEL NATURAL	16,280	12,500	11,047	9,739
GUITAR	85	GIBSON	KENNY BURRELL PROTYPE DARK BLUE, WOODEN PICKGUARD, 17 7/8" BODY	46,150	35,437	31,316	27,608
GUITAR	26	GIBSON	L- 0 AMBER, FLATTOP, EBONY FRETBOARD & BRIDGE/DIAGONAL LOGO	1,018	781	690	609
GUITAR	27	GIBSON	L- 0 AMBER, FLATTOP	1,308	1,004	887	782
GUITAR	28	GIBSON	L- 0 AMBER, FLATTOP	1,265	971	858	757
GUITAR	29	GIBSON	L- 0 AMBER, FLATTOP, SERIAL #87300-89800	1,253	962	850	749

TYPE	YR	MFG	PRICES--BASED ON 100% ORIGINAL MODEL	SELL EXC	SELL AVG	BUY EXC	BUY AVG
GUITAR	30	GIBSON	L- 0 AMBER, FLATTOP, SERIAL #89800-90200	1,072	823	728	641
GUITAR	31	GIBSON	L- 0 AMBER, FLATTOP	1,276	980	866	763
GUITAR	35	GIBSON	L- 0 SUNBURST, FLATTOP	1,266	972	859	757
GUITAR	36	GIBSON	L- 0 SUNBURST, FLATTOP, SERIAL #93500	1,265	971	858	757
GUITAR	37	GIBSON	L- 0 BLACK, FLATTOP	1,244	955	844	744
GUITAR	37	GIBSON	L- 0 SUNBURST, FLATTOP, SERIAL #-95400	1,246	957	845	745
GUITAR	38	GIBSON	L- 0 BLACK, FLATTOP, SERIAL #95400	1,033	793	701	618
GUITAR	41	GIBSON	L- 0 BLACK, FLATTOP, SERIAL #96600-97400	1,198	920	813	716
GUITAR	42	GIBSON	L- 0 BLACK, FLATTOP	977	750	663	584
GUITAR	30	GIBSON	L- 00 BLACK, FLATTOP, SERIAL #89800-90200	1,366	1,049	927	817
GUITAR	31	GIBSON	L- 00 BLACK, FLATTOP	1,316	1,010	893	787
GUITAR	32	GIBSON	L- 00 BLACK, FLATTOP	1,366	1,049	927	817
GUITAR	33	GIBSON	L- 00 BLACK, FLATTOP	1,366	1,049	927	817
GUITAR	34	GIBSON	L- 00 SUNBURST, FLATTOP	2,036	1,563	1,381	1,218
GUITAR	34	GIBSON	L- 00 MAPLE, FLATTOP	3,417	2,623	2,318	2,044
GUITAR	35	GIBSON	L- 00 BLACK, FLATTOP, SERIAL #92400-93500	1,611	1,237	1,093	964
GUITAR	35	GIBSON	L- 00 SUNBURST, FLATTOP, SERIAL #92400-93500	1,889	1,450	1,282	1,130
GUITAR	36	GIBSON	L- 00 SUNBURST, FLATTOP	1,778	1,365	1,206	1,063
GUITAR	37	GIBSON	L- 00 SUNBURST, FLATTOP, SERIAL #-95400	2,416	1,855	1,640	1,445
GUITAR	38	GIBSON	L- 00 SUNBURST, FLATTOP, SERIAL #95400-	1,715	1,317	1,164	1,026
GUITAR	39	GIBSON	L- 00 SUNBURST, FLATTOP	1,646	1,264	1,117	984
GUITAR	41	GIBSON	L- 00 BLACK, FLATTOPSERIAL #96600-97400	1,288	989	874	770
GUITAR	05	GIBSON	L- 1 1905, BLACK, ARCHTOP, SERIAL #1850-2550	1,434	1,101	973	858
GUITAR	07	GIBSON	L- 1 1907, BLACK, ARCHTOP	1,436	1,103	975	859
GUITAR	14	GIBSON	L- 1 ORANGE, ARCHTOP, SERIAL #16100-20150	1,434	1,101	973	858
GUITAR	15	GIBSON	L- 1 NATURAL, ARCHTOP, SERIAL #20150-25150	1,321	1,014	896	790
GUITAR	15	GIBSON	L- 1 BLACK, ARCHTOP	1,408	1,081	956	842
GUITAR	16	GIBSON	L- 1 NATURAL, ARCHTOP	1,282	984	870	767
GUITAR	16	GIBSON	L- 1 ORANGE, ARCHTOP	1,764	1,354	1,197	1,055
GUITAR	17	GIBSON	L- 1 NATURAL, ARCHTOP	1,481	1,137	1,005	886
GUITAR	17	GIBSON	L- 1 NATURAL, CARVED TOP	1,963	1,507	1,332	1,174
GUITAR	18	GIBSON	L- 1 NATURAL, ARCHTOP, SERIAL #32000-39500	1,436	1,103	975	859
GUITAR	19	GIBSON	L- 1 BROWN, ARCHTOP, SERIAL #47900-53800	1,454	1,117	987	870
GUITAR	20	GIBSON	L- 1 BROWN, ARCHTOP, SERIAL #53800-62200	1,434	1,101	973	858
GUITAR	21	GIBSON	L- 1 BROWN, ARCHTOP, SERIAL #62200-69300	2,263	1,738	1,535	1,354
GUITAR	21	GIBSON	L- 1 NATURAL TOP	2,415	1,855	1,639	1,445
GUITAR	26	GIBSON	L- 1 FLATTOP	1,967	1,511	1,335	1,177
GUITAR	27	GIBSON	L- 1 AMBER, FLATTOP	1,966	1,510	1,334	1,176
GUITAR	29	GIBSON	L- 1 FLATTOP, CONCERT SIZE, SERIAL #87300-89800	1,697	1,303	1,152	1,015
GUITAR	29	GIBSON	L- 1 SUNBURST, FLATTOP	2,108	1,619	1,431	1,261
GUITAR	29	GIBSON	L- 1 SUNBURST, 12-FRET	3,382	2,597	2,295	2,023
GUITAR	30	GIBSON	L- 1 SUNBURST, 12-FRET	3,400	2,610	2,307	2,034

TYPE	YR	MFG	PRICES--BASED ON 100% ORIGINAL MODEL	SELL EXC	SELL AVG	BUY EXC	BUY AVG
GUITAR	31	GIBSON	L- 1 SUNBURST, 12-FRET	3,217	2,470	2,183	1,924
GUITAR	35	GIBSON	L- 1 SUNBURST, FLATTOP, SERIAL #9240-93500	1,697	1,303	1,152	1,015
GUITAR	37	GIBSON	L- 1	1,880	1,443	1,276	1,124
GUITAR	42	GIBSON	L- 1 NATURAL, FLATTOP	1,881	1,444	1,276	1,125
GUITAR	62	GIBSON	L- 1 NATURAL, WALNUT STAINED BACK	1,798	1,381	1,220	1,076
GUITAR	05	GIBSON	L- 2 1905, ORANGE, ARCHTOP, SERIAL #1850-2550	1,044	802	709	625
GUITAR	24	GIBSON	L- 2 AMBER, ARCHTOP	1,053	809	715	630
GUITAR	25	GIBSON	L- 2 SNAKEHEAD BROWN, ARCHTOP	3,519	2,702	2,387	2,105
GUITAR	30	GIBSON	L- 2 NATURAL, FLATTOP, SERIAL #89800-90200	2,915	2,238	1,978	1,744
GUITAR	31	GIBSON	L- 2 SUNBURST, FLATTOP, SERIAL #90200-90400	2,394	1,838	1,624	1,432
GUITAR	32	GIBSON	L- 2 SUNBURST, FLATTOP	2,394	1,838	1,624	1,432
GUITAR	15	GIBSON	L- 3 ARCHTOP, SERIAL #20150-25150	2,173	1,669	1,475	1,300
GUITAR	16	GIBSON	L- 3 RED MAHOGANY, ARCHTOP, SERIAL #25150-32000	1,889	1,450	1,282	1,130
GUITAR	17	GIBSON	L- 3 RED SUNBURST, ARCHTOP, SERIAL #32000-39500	1,848	1,419	1,254	1,105
GUITAR	18	GIBSON	L- 3 RED SUNBURST, ARCHTOP	1,850	1,420	1,255	1,106
GUITAR	19	GIBSON	L- 3 RED SUNBURST, ARCHTOP, SERIAL #47900-53800	1,848	1,419	1,254	1,105
GUITAR	20	GIBSON	L- 3 RED SUNBURST, ARCHTOP, SERIAL #53800-62200	1,848	1,419	1,254	1,105
GUITAR	21	GIBSON	L- 3 RED SUNBURST, ARCHTOP	1,944	1,492	1,319	1,163
GUITAR	24	GIBSON	L- 3 RED SUNBURST, ARCHTOP	1,738	1,334	1,179	1,039
GUITAR	25	GIBSON	L- 3 RED SUNBURST, SNAKE HEAD	1,917	1,472	1,301	1,147
GUITAR	26	GIBSON	L- 3 RED SUNBURST, ARCHTOP, SERIAL #82700	1,738	1,334	1,179	1,039
GUITAR	27	GIBSON	L- 3 RED SUNBURST, ARCHTOP, SERIAL #85400	1,740	1,336	1,181	1,041
GUITAR	28	GIBSON	L- 3 IVORY, ARCHTOP, SERIAL #85400-87300	1,965	1,509	1,333	1,175
GUITAR	29	GIBSON	L- 3 RED SUNBURST, ARCHTOP, SERIAL #87300-89800	1,630	1,252	1,106	975
GUITAR	29	GIBSON	L- 3 IVORY, ARCHTOP	1,963	1,507	1,332	1,174
GUITAR	12	GIBSON	L- 4 BLACK, ARCHTOP	6,050	4,645	4,105	3,619
GUITAR	13	GIBSON	L- 4 BLACK	2,056	1,578	1,395	1,230
GUITAR	14	GIBSON	L- 4 SUNBURST, ARCHTOP, SERIAL #16100-20150	2,133	1,638	1,447	1,276
GUITAR	15	GIBSON	L- 4 SUNBURST, ARCHTOP, SERIAL #20150-25150	2,134	1,639	1,448	1,277
GUITAR	17	GIBSON	L- 4 SUNBURST, ARCHTOP	2,907	2,232	1,972	1,739
GUITAR	18	GIBSON	L- 4 SUNBURST, ARCHTOP	1,572	1,207	1,067	940
GUITAR	19	GIBSON	L- 4 SUNBURST, ARCHTOP	1,585	1,217	1,076	948
GUITAR	20	GIBSON	L- 4 SUNBURST, ARCHTOP	1,573	1,208	1,067	941
GUITAR	24	GIBSON	L- 4 SUNBURST, ARCHTOP	1,966	1,510	1,334	1,176
GUITAR	24	GIBSON	L- 4 RED SUNBURST	2,232	1,713	1,514	1,335
GUITAR	25	GIBSON	L- 4 SUNBURST, ARCHTOP	1,575	1,210	1,069	942
GUITAR	27	GIBSON	L- 4 SUNBURST, ARCHTOP	1,568	1,204	1,064	938
GUITAR	28	GIBSON	L- 4 SUNBURST, ARCHTOP, SERIAL #85400-87300	1,571	1,206	1,066	940
GUITAR	29	GIBSON	L- 4 SUNBURST, ARCHTOP, SERIAL #87300-89800	1,572	1,207	1,067	940
GUITAR	31	GIBSON	L- 4 SUNBURST, ARCHTOP	1,568	1,204	1,064	938
GUITAR	32	GIBSON	L- 4 SUNBURST, ARCHTOP	1,573	1,208	1,067	941
GUITAR	33	GIBSON	L- 4 SUNBURST, ARCHTOP	1,572	1,207	1,067	940

TYPE	YR	MFG	PRICES--BASED ON 100% ORIGINAL MODEL	SELL EXC	SELL AVG	BUY EXC	BUY AVG
GUITAR	34	GIBSON	L- 4 SUNBURST, ARCHTOP, SERIAL #91500-92400	1,573	1,208	1,067	941
GUITAR	35	GIBSON	L- 4 SUNBURST, F-HOLES	2,143	1,646	1,454	1,282
GUITAR	36	GIBSON	L- 4 SUNBURST, ARCHTOP, SERIAL #93500	1,572	1,207	1,067	940
GUITAR	37	GIBSON	L- 4 SUNBURST, ARCHTOP, SERIAL #93500-95400	1,644	1,262	1,115	983
GUITAR	38	GIBSON	L- 4 SUNBURST, ARCHTOP	1,573	1,208	1,067	941
GUITAR	39	GIBSON	L- 4 SUNBURST, ARCHTOP	2,008	1,541	1,362	1,201
GUITAR	40	GIBSON	L- 4 BLOND, ARCHTOP, NON-CUTAWAY	1,732	1,330	1,175	1,036
GUITAR	46	GIBSON	L- 4 SUNBURST, SUNBURST	1,505	1,155	1,021	900
GUITAR	47	GIBSON	L- 4 NATURAL, ARCHTOP, TRIPLE BOUND	2,945	2,261	1,998	1,762
GUITAR	48	GIBSON	L- 4 SUNBURST, ARCHTOP, SERIAL #A1400-A2800	1,467	1,126	995	877
GUITAR	48	GIBSON	L- 4 BLOND, SOLID CARVED TOP, NON-CUTAWAY, ARCHTOP	2,962	2,274	2,010	1,772
GUITAR	49	GIBSON	L- 4 SUNBURST, ARCHTOP	1,349	1,036	915	807
GUITAR	49	GIBSON	L- 4 NATURAL, ARCHTOP, SERIAL #A2801-A4400	2,121	1,628	1,439	1,268
GUITAR	51	GIBSON	L- 4 SUNBURST, ARCHTOP, SERIAL #A6000-A9400	1,417	1,088	962	848
GUITAR	54	GIBSON	L- 4 SUNBURST, ARCHTOP	1,239	952	841	741
GUITAR	49	GIBSON	L- 4C SUNBURST, CUTAWAY	4,463	3,427	3,028	2,669
GUITAR	50	GIBSON	L- 4C SUNBURST, CUTAWAY, SERIAL #A4400-A6000	2,929	2,249	1,988	1,752
GUITAR	51	GIBSON	L- 4C SUNBURST, CUTAWAY, SERIAL #A6000-A9400	2,937	2,255	1,993	1,757
GUITAR	51	GIBSON	L- 4C NATURAL, CUTAWAY	3,301	2,535	2,240	1,975
GUITAR	52	GIBSON	L- 4C SUNBURST, CUTAWAY, SERIAL #A9400-A13000	2,920	2,242	1,982	1,747
GUITAR	53	GIBSON	L- 4C SUNBURST, CUTAWAY, SERIAL #A13000-A16000	2,048	1,572	1,390	1,225
GUITAR	53	GIBSON	L- 4C NATURAL, CUTAWAY, SERIAL #A13000-A16000	3,279	2,518	2,225	1,961
GUITAR	54	GIBSON	L- 4C SUNBURST, CUTAWAY	2,920	2,242	1,982	1,747
GUITAR	55	GIBSON	L- 4C NATURAL, CUTAWAY	3,076	2,362	2,087	1,840
GUITAR	55	GIBSON	L- 4C SUNBURST, CUTAWAY	3,161	2,427	2,145	1,891
GUITAR	56	GIBSON	L- 4C SUNBURST	2,945	2,261	1,998	1,762
GUITAR	56	GIBSON	L- 4C NATURAL, CUTAWAY, SERIAL #A22000-A24600	3,011	2,312	2,043	1,801
GUITAR	58	GIBSON	L- 4C SUNBURST, CUTAWAY, SERIAL #A26500-A28000	2,929	2,249	1,988	1,752
GUITAR	60	GIBSON	L- 4C SUNBURST, CUTAWAY	2,345	1,800	1,591	1,402
GUITAR	63	GIBSON	L- 4C NATURAL, CUTAWAY	3,002	2,305	2,037	1,796
GUITAR	65	GIBSON	L- 4C SUNBURST, CUTAWAY	2,288	1,756	1,552	1,368
GUITAR	66	GIBSON	L- 4C SUNBURST, CUTAWAY	2,300	1,766	1,561	1,376
GUITAR	68	GIBSON	L- 4C SUNBURST, CUTAWAY	1,807	1,388	1,226	1,081
GUITAR	69	GIBSON	L- 4CES SPRUCE, ROSEWOOD, ARCHTOP	5,181	3,978	3,515	3,099
GUITAR	87	GIBSON	L- 4CES NATURAL	3,011	2,312	2,043	1,801
GUITAR	22	GIBSON	L- 5 SUNBURST, LLOYD LOAR	48,233	37,036	32,730	28,854
GUITAR	23	GIBSON	L- 5 SUNBURST, NON-CUTAWAY, SERIAL #53800-62200	12,744	9,785	8,648	7,623
GUITAR	24	GIBSON	L- 5 SUNBURST, NON-CUTAWAY, SERIAL #74900-80300	12,744	9,785	8,648	7,623
GUITAR	24	GIBSON	L- 5 SUNBURST, SIGNED BY LLOYD LOAR	68,177	52,350	46,263	40,784
GUITAR	25	GIBSON	L- 5 SUNBURST, NON-CUTAWAY, SERIAL #80300-82700	17,360	13,330	11,780	10,385
GUITAR	27	GIBSON	L- 5 SUNBURST	9,758	7,493	6,621	5,837
GUITAR	27	GIBSON	L- 5 SUNBURST, NON-CUTAWAY	17,360	13,330	11,780	10,385

TYPE	YR	MFG	PRICES--BASED ON 100% ORIGINAL MODEL	SELL EXC	SELL AVG	BUY EXC	BUY AVG
GUITAR	28	GIBSON	L- 5 SUNBURST, NON-CUTAWAY, SERIAL #85400-87300	10,455	**8,028**	7,094	6,254
GUITAR	29	GIBSON	L- 5 DOT INLAY	11,740	**9,015**	7,967	7,023
GUITAR	29	GIBSON	L- 5 SUNBURST, NON-CUTAWAY	12,094	**9,287**	8,207	7,235
GUITAR	30	GIBSON	L- 5 SUNBURST, NON-CUTAWAY	9,061	**6,958**	6,149	5,420
GUITAR	31	GIBSON	L- 5 BLOCK INLAY, GOLD HARDWARE	8,457	**6,493**	5,738	5,059
GUITAR	33	GIBSON	L- 5 SUNBURST, NON-CUTAWAY	9,061	**6,958**	6,149	5,420
GUITAR	34	GIBSON	L- 5 BLOCK INLAY, NON-CUTAWAY	6,222	**4,778**	4,222	3,722
GUITAR	34	GIBSON	L- 5 SUNBURST, NON-CUTAWAY, SERIAL #91500-92400	10,427	**8,006**	7,075	6,237
GUITAR	35	GIBSON	L- 5 SUNBURST, NON-CUTAWAYSERIAL #92400-93500	9,645	**7,406**	6,545	5,770
GUITAR	36	GIBSON	L- 5 SUNBURST, NON-CUTAWAY, SERIAL #93500	9,042	**6,943**	6,136	5,409
GUITAR	37	GIBSON	L- 5 SUNBURST, NON-CUTAWAY	7,318	**5,619**	4,965	4,377
GUITAR	38	GIBSON	L- 5 SUNBURST, NON-CUTAWAY	8,363	**6,421**	5,674	5,002
GUITAR	38	GIBSON	L- 5 NATURAL, NON-CUTAWAY, SERIAL #95400	9,834	**7,551**	6,673	5,883
GUITAR	39	GIBSON	L- 5 SUNBURST, NON-CUTAWAY	7,680	**5,897**	5,212	4,594
GUITAR	39	GIBSON	L- 5 NATURAL, NON-CUTAWAY	9,825	**7,544**	6,667	5,877
GUITAR	40	GIBSON	L- 5 SUNBURST, NON-CUTAWAY, SERIAL #96000	6,948	**5,335**	4,715	4,156
GUITAR	40	GIBSON	L- 5 NATURAL, NON-CUTAWAY	8,676	**6,662**	5,887	5,190
GUITAR	41	GIBSON	L- 5 SUNBURST, NON-CUTAWAY	7,112	**5,461**	4,826	4,254
GUITAR	43	GIBSON	L- 5 SUNBURST, NON-CUTAWAY	6,703	**5,147**	4,548	4,009
GUITAR	45	GIBSON	L- 5 SUNBURST, NON-CUTAWAY	6,606	**5,073**	4,483	3,952
GUITAR	46	GIBSON	L- 5 SUNBURST, NON-CUTAWAY	6,550	**5,030**	4,445	3,918
GUITAR	46	GIBSON	L- 5 NATURAL, NON-CUTAWAY, SERIAL #95400	8,108	**6,226**	5,502	4,850
GUITAR	47	GIBSON	L- 5 SUNBURST, NON-CUTAWAY, SERIAL #99500-A1400	6,303	**4,840**	4,277	3,770
GUITAR	47	GIBSON	L- 5 NATURAL, NON-CUTAWAY	7,676	**5,894**	5,209	4,592
GUITAR	48	GIBSON	L- 5 SUNBURST, NON-CUTAWAY, SERIAL #A1400-A2800	6,179	**4,744**	4,192	3,696
GUITAR	49	GIBSON	L- 5 SUNBURST, NON-CUTAWAY	6,180	**4,745**	4,193	3,697
GUITAR	49	GIBSON	L- 5 NATURAL, NON-CUTAWAY, SERIAL #A2800-A4400	6,706	**5,149**	4,550	4,011
GUITAR	51	GIBSON	L- 5 NATURAL, NON-CUTAWAY, SERIAL #A6000-A9400	7,676	**5,894**	5,209	4,592
GUITAR	52	GIBSON	L- 5 SUNBURST, NON-CUTAWAY	8,009	**6,149**	5,434	4,791
GUITAR	53	GIBSON	L- 5 SUNBURST, NON-CUTAWAY, SERIAL #A13000-A16000	5,799	**4,453**	3,935	3,469
GUITAR	55	GIBSON	L- 5 NATURAL, NON-CUTAWAY	6,700	**5,145**	4,547	4,008
GUITAR	56	GIBSON	L- 5 SUNBURST	8,476	**6,508**	5,751	5,070
GUITAR	71	GIBSON	L- 5 SUNBURST, NON-CUTAWAY	5,036	**3,867**	3,417	3,012
GUITAR	77	GIBSON	L- 5 SUNBURST, NON-CUTAWAY	4,418	**3,392**	2,998	2,643
GUITAR	78	GIBSON	L- 5 SUNBURST, NON-CUTAWAY	4,351	**3,341**	2,952	2,602
GUITAR	34	GIBSON	L- 5 CUSTOM MAHOGANY	7,128	**5,473**	4,837	4,264
GUITAR	28	GIBSON	L- 5 SPECIAL 16" SNAKE HEAD	9,061	**6,958**	6,149	5,420
GUITAR	28	GIBSON	L- 5C CURLY MAPLE FIGURED, CUTAWAY	21,343	**16,389**	14,483	12,768
GUITAR	39	GIBSON	L- 5C NATURAL, CUTAWAY, PREMIER	17,987	**13,811**	12,205	10,760
GUITAR	40	GIBSON	L- 5C BLOND, CUTAWAY	15,835	**12,159**	10,745	9,473
GUITAR	48	GIBSON	L- 5C SUNBURST	15,669	**12,032**	10,633	9,373
GUITAR	49	GIBSON	L- 5C NATURAL, CUTAWAY, SERIAL #A2800-A4400	16,502	**12,671**	11,197	9,871

TYPE	YR	MFG	PRICES--BASED ON 100% ORIGINAL MODEL	SELL EXC	SELL AVG	BUY EXC	BUY AVG
GUITAR	50	GIBSON	L- 5C SUNBURST, CUTAWAY, SERIAL #A4400-A6000	12,203	9,370	8,280	7,300
GUITAR	51	GIBSON	L- 5C SUNBURST, CUTAWAY	11,581	8,893	7,859	6,928
GUITAR	54	GIBSON	L- 5C SUNBURST, CUTAWAY	12,701	9,753	8,619	7,598
GUITAR	55	GIBSON	L- 5C NATURAL, CUTAWAY, SERIAL #A19000-A22000	16,499	12,669	11,196	9,870
GUITAR	57	GIBSON	L- 5C NATURAL, CUTAWAY, PAF's	13,037	10,011	8,847	7,799
GUITAR	58	GIBSON	L- 5C SUNBURST, CUTAWAY	12,083	9,278	8,199	7,228
GUITAR	58	GIBSON	L- 5C SUNBURST	13,694	10,515	9,292	8,192
GUITAR	58	GIBSON	L- 5C NATURAL, CUTAWAY, SERIAL #A26500-A28000	19,033	14,614	12,915	11,385
GUITAR	59	GIBSON	L- 5C SUNBURST, CUTAWAY	9,308	7,147	6,316	5,568
GUITAR	60	GIBSON	L- 5C NATURAL, CUTAWAY	12,144	9,324	8,240	7,264
GUITAR	62	GIBSON	L- 5C SUNBURST, CUTAWAY	8,581	6,589	5,823	5,133
GUITAR	64	GIBSON	L- 5C FLAMEY SUNBURST, 1 PU	7,654	5,877	5,193	4,578
GUITAR	64	GIBSON	L- 5C SUNBURST, CUTAWAY	8,551	6,566	5,802	5,115
GUITAR	67	GIBSON	L- 5C SUNBURST, CUTAWAY	8,312	6,382	5,640	4,972
GUITAR	68	GIBSON	L- 5C NATURAL, CUTAWAY	8,683	6,667	5,892	5,194
GUITAR	68	GIBSON	L- 5C SUNBURST, CUTAWAY	9,429	7,240	6,398	5,640
GUITAR	69	GIBSON	L- 5C SUNBURST, CUTAWAY	9,158	7,032	6,214	5,478
GUITAR	70	GIBSON	L- 5C SUNBURST, CUTAWAY	8,895	6,830	6,035	5,321
GUITAR	72	GIBSON	L- 5C SUNBURST, CUTAWAY	8,664	6,652	5,879	5,183
GUITAR	74	GIBSON	L- 5C SUNBURST, CUTAWAY	7,814	6,000	5,302	4,674
GUITAR	75	GIBSON	L- 5C SUNBURST, CUTAWAY	7,343	5,639	4,983	4,393
GUITAR	76	GIBSON	L- 5C SUNBURST, CUTAWAY	6,882	5,284	4,670	4,117
GUITAR	77	GIBSON	L- 5C SUNBURST, CUTAWAY	6,825	5,240	4,631	4,082
GUITAR	78	GIBSON	L- 5C SUNBURST, CUTAWAY	6,787	5,211	4,605	4,060
GUITAR	54	GIBSON	L- 5CN ARCHTOP	13,612	10,452	9,237	8,143
GUITAR	76	GIBSON	L- 5CN SUNBURST, TUNE-O-MATIC	4,270	3,279	2,897	2,554
GUITAR	59	GIBSON	L- 5CT GEORGE GOBEL CHERRY RED	29,798	22,881	20,220	17,826
GUITAR	60	GIBSON	L- 5CT GEORGE GOBEL CHERRY RED	20,315	15,599	13,785	12,153
GUITAR	61	GIBSON	L- 5CT GEORGE GOBEL CHERRY RED	28,481	21,869	19,326	17,038
GUITAR	38	GIBSON	L- 5P PREMIER BLOND	22,005	16,897	14,932	13,164
GUITAR	39	GIBSON	L- 5P PREMIER NATURAL BLOND, SERIAL #-96000	24,436	18,763	16,581	14,618
GUITAR	40	GIBSON	L- 5P PREMIER SUNBURST, SERIAL #96000-96600	16,461	12,640	11,170	9,847
GUITAR	40	GIBSON	L- 5P PREMIER NATURAL BLOND, SERIAL #96000-96600	19,278	14,803	13,081	11,532
GUITAR	41	GIBSON	L- 5P PREMIER NATURAL BLOND, SERIAL #96600-97400	13,259	10,181	8,997	7,932
GUITAR	47	GIBSON	L- 5P PREMIER SUNBURST	8,632	6,628	5,858	5,164
GUITAR	33	GIBSON	L- 7 SUNBURST, NON-CUTAWAY, SERIAL #90700-91500	3,310	2,542	2,246	1,980
GUITAR	34	GIBSON	L- 7 SUNBURST, NON-CUTAWAY, SERIAL #91500-92400	2,442	1,875	1,657	1,461
GUITAR	35	GIBSON	L- 7 SUNBURST, NON-CUTAWAY, SERIAL #92400-93500	3,060	2,350	2,077	1,831
GUITAR	36	GIBSON	L- 7 SUNBURST, NON-CUTAWAY, SERIAL #93500	2,436	1,870	1,653	1,457
GUITAR	37	GIBSON	L- 7 NATURAL, NON-GUITAWAY, SERIAL #-95400	2,194	1,684	1,488	1,312
GUITAR	37	GIBSON	L- 7 SUNBURST, NON-CUTAWAY, SERIAL #-95400	2,976	2,285	2,020	1,780
GUITAR	38	GIBSON	L- 7 SUNBURST, NON-CUTAWAY, SERIAL #95400	2,914	2,237	1,977	1,743

TYPE	YR	MFG	MODEL	SELL EXC	SELL AVG	BUY EXC	BUY AVG
GUITAR	39	GIBSON	L- 7 NATURAL, NON-CUTAWAY	3,063	2,352	2,078	1,832
GUITAR	39	GIBSON	L- 7 SUNBURST, NON-CUTAWAY, SERIAL #-96000	3,204	2,460	2,174	1,916
GUITAR	40	GIBSON	L- 7 NATURAL, NON-CUTAWAY	2,922	2,243	1,982	1,748
GUITAR	42	GIBSON	L- 7 SUNBURST, NON-CUTAWAY, SERIAL #97400-97600	3,013	2,314	2,045	1,802
GUITAR	43	GIBSON	L- 7 SUNBURST, NON-CUTAWAY	3,065	2,353	2,080	1,833
GUITAR	44	GIBSON	L- 7 SUNBURST, NON-CUTAWAY, SERIAL #97800-98300	2,928	2,248	1,987	1,752
GUITAR	45	GIBSON	L- 7 NATURAL, NON-CUTAWAY, SERIAL #98300-98600	2,924	2,245	1,984	1,749
GUITAR	46	GIBSON	L- 7 SUNBURST, NON-CUTAWAY	2,418	1,856	1,640	1,446
GUITAR	46	GIBSON	L- 7 NATURAL, NON-CUTAWAY, SERIAL #98600-99500	2,924	2,245	1,984	1,749
GUITAR	47	GIBSON	L- 7 SUNBURST, NON-CUTAWAY, SERIAL #99500-A1400	2,437	1,871	1,653	1,457
GUITAR	48	GIBSON	L- 7 SUNBURST, NON-CUTAWAY, SERIAL #A1400-A2800	1,584	1,216	1,075	948
GUITAR	48	GIBSON	L- 7 NATURAL, NON-CUTAWAY, SERIAL #A1400-A2800	2,922	2,243	1,982	1,748
GUITAR	49	GIBSON	L- 7 BLACK, NON-CUTAWAY, SERIAL #A2800-A4400	1,584	1,216	1,075	948
GUITAR	49	GIBSON	L- 7 SUNBURST, NON-CUTAWAY, SERIAL #A2800-A4400	1,587	1,218	1,076	949
GUITAR	50	GIBSON	L- 7 SUNBURST, NON-CUTAWAY, SERIAL #A4400-A6000	1,560	1,197	1,058	933
GUITAR	50	GIBSON	L- 7 NATURAL, NON-CUTAWAY, SERIAL #A4400-A6000	3,386	2,600	2,298	2,026
GUITAR	51	GIBSON	L- 7 SUNBURST, NON-CUTAWAY, SERIAL #A6000-A9400	1,547	1,188	1,050	925
GUITAR	52	GIBSON	L- 7 SUNBURST, NON-CUTAWAY, SERIAL #A9400-A13000	1,544	1,185	1,048	923
GUITAR	54	GIBSON	L- 7 SUNBURST, NON-CUTAWAY	2,879	2,211	1,953	1,722
GUITAR	55	GIBSON	L- 7 SUNBURST, NON-CUTAWAY	2,055	1,578	1,394	1,229
GUITAR	48	GIBSON	L- 7C SUNBURST	4,244	3,259	2,880	2,539
GUITAR	48	GIBSON	L- 7C NATURAL, CUTAWAY	5,673	4,356	3,850	3,394
GUITAR	50	GIBSON	L- 7C SUNBURST, CUTAWAY	7,440	5,712	5,048	4,450
GUITAR	51	GIBSON	L- 7C SUNBURST, CUTAWAY, SERIAL #A6000-A9400	5,964	4,579	4,047	3,567
GUITAR	52	GIBSON	L- 7C NATURAL, CUTAWAY, SERIAL #A9400-A13000	3,289	2,525	2,232	1,967
GUITAR	52	GIBSON	L- 7C SUNBURST, CUTAWAY, SERIAL #A9400-A13000	5,505	4,227	3,736	3,293
GUITAR	53	GIBSON	L- 7C SUNBURST, CUTAWAY	6,276	4,819	4,259	3,754
GUITAR	54	GIBSON	L- 7C NATURAL, CUTAWAY, SERIAL #16000-A19000	5,206	3,998	3,533	3,114
GUITAR	56	GIBSON	L- 7C NATURAL, CUTAWAY, SERIAL #A22000-A24600	5,200	3,992	3,528	3,110
GUITAR	58	GIBSON	L- 7C SUNBURST, CUTAWAY	4,421	3,395	3,000	2,645
GUITAR	60	GIBSON	L- 7C SUNBURST	3,440	2,641	2,334	2,058
GUITAR	60	GIBSON	L- 7C SUNBURST, CUTAWAY	4,972	3,818	3,374	2,974
GUITAR	61	GIBSON	L- 7C SUNBURST, CUTAWAY	4,972	3,818	3,374	2,974
GUITAR	63	GIBSON	L- 7C VINTAGE SUNBURST, DeARMOND	4,183	3,212	2,838	2,502
GUITAR	67	GIBSON	L- 7C NATURAL, CUTAWAY	2,064	1,584	1,400	1,234
GUITAR	67	GIBSON	L- 7C SUNBURST, CUTAWAY	3,762	2,888	2,552	2,250
GUITAR	69	GIBSON	L- 7C SUNBURST, CUTAWAY	4,006	3,076	2,718	2,396
GUITAR	49	GIBSON	L- 7CE NATURAL, CUTAWAY, SERIAL #A2800-A4400	5,959	4,576	4,043	3,565
GUITAR	51	GIBSON	L- 7CED SUNBURST, CUTAWAY, SERIAL #A6000-A9400	5,799	4,453	3,935	3,469
GUITAR	50	GIBSON	L- 7CN BROWN, 1 PU	5,873	4,509	3,985	3,513
GUITAR	51	GIBSON	L- 7CN CARMEL, 2 PU's	5,006	3,844	3,397	2,994
GUITAR	56	GIBSON	L- 7CN BLONDE	6,125	4,703	4,156	3,664

TYPE	YR	MFG	PRICES--BASED ON 100% ORIGINAL MODEL	SELL EXC	SELL AVG	BUY EXC	BUY AVG
GUITAR	52	GIBSON	L- 7CT TENOR, SUNBURST, CUTAWAY	4,295	**3,298**	2,914	2,569
GUITAR	52	GIBSON	L- 7E SUNBURST, NO-CUTAWAY	2,926	**2,247**	1,985	1,750
GUITAR	49	GIBSON	L- 7ED SUNBURST, NON-CUTAWAY, SERIAL #A2800-A4400	4,299	**3,301**	2,917	2,572
GUITAR	50	GIBSON	L- 7ED SUNBURST, CUTAWAY, SERIAL #A4400-A6000	3,263	**2,506**	2,214	1,952
GUITAR	41	GIBSON	L- 7N NATURAL	3,142	**2,413**	2,132	1,880
GUITAR	30	GIBSON	L- 10 SUNBURST, DOT INLAY, MAPLE BACK/SIDES	2,520	**1,935**	1,710	1,507
GUITAR	31	GIBSON	L- 10	1,762	**1,353**	1,196	1,054
GUITAR	31	GIBSON	L- 10 BLACK, ARCHTOP, SERIAL #90200-90400	2,167	**1,664**	1,470	1,296
GUITAR	32	GIBSON	L- 10 BLACK, ARCHTOP	3,542	**2,720**	2,403	2,119
GUITAR	33	GIBSON	L- 10 BLACK, ARCHTOP	3,678	**2,824**	2,495	2,200
GUITAR	34	GIBSON	L- 10 BLACK, ARCHTOP	2,464	**1,892**	1,672	1,474
GUITAR	34	GIBSON	L- 10 SUNBURST, ARCHTOP	3,114	**2,391**	2,113	1,863
GUITAR	35	GIBSON	L- 10 BLACK, ARCHTOP, SERIAL #92400-93500	2,408	**1,849**	1,634	1,440
GUITAR	35	GIBSON	L- 10 SUNBURST, ARCHTOP	2,957	**2,271**	2,007	1,769
GUITAR	36	GIBSON	L- 10 SUNBURST, ARCHTOP, SERIAL #93500	2,298	**1,764**	1,559	1,374
GUITAR	37	GIBSON	L- 10 ARCHTOP, CHECKER BINDING	2,102	**1,614**	1,426	1,257
GUITAR	39	GIBSON	L- 10 SUNBURST, ARCHTOP, SERIAL #96000	2,189	**1,681**	1,485	1,309
GUITAR	32	GIBSON	L- 12 SUNBURST, ARCHTOP, SERIAL #90400-90700	3,599	**2,764**	2,442	2,153
GUITAR	33	GIBSON	L- 12 SUNBURST, ARCHTOP	3,678	**2,824**	2,495	2,200
GUITAR	34	GIBSON	L- 12 SUNBURST, ARCHTOP, SERIAL #91500-92400	3,599	**2,764**	2,442	2,153
GUITAR	35	GIBSON	L- 12 SUNBURST, ARCHTOP	3,500	**2,687**	2,375	2,093
GUITAR	36	GIBSON	L- 12 SUNBURST, ARCHTOP	3,613	**2,774**	2,451	2,161
GUITAR	37	GIBSON	L- 12 SUNBURST, ARCHTOP, NON-CUTAWAY	3,409	**2,617**	2,313	2,039
GUITAR	37	GIBSON	L- 12 SUNBURST, ARCHTOP, SERIAL #95400	3,601	**2,765**	2,444	2,154
GUITAR	39	GIBSON	L- 12 SUNBURST, ARCHTOP	2,430	**1,866**	1,649	1,453
GUITAR	40	GIBSON	L- 12 SUNBURST, ARCHTOP, SERIAL #96000	3,449	**2,648**	2,340	2,063
GUITAR	41	GIBSON	L- 12 SUNBURST, ARCHTOP, SERIAL #97400	3,449	**2,648**	2,340	2,063
GUITAR	46	GIBSON	L- 12	4,179	**3,209**	2,836	2,500
GUITAR	47	GIBSON	L- 12 SUNBURST, CUTAWAY, SERIAL #99500-A1400	3,080	**2,365**	2,090	1,842
GUITAR	48	GIBSON	L- 12 SUNBURST, ARCHTOP, SERIAL #A1400-A2800	3,455	**2,653**	2,344	2,066
GUITAR	52	GIBSON	L- 12 SUNBURST, ARCHTOP	3,080	**2,365**	2,090	1,842
GUITAR	49	GIBSON	L- 12C SUNBURST	7,342	**5,638**	4,982	4,392
GUITAR	48	GIBSON	L- 12P PREMIER SUNBURST, ARCHTOP, SERIAL #A1400-A2800	3,082	**2,366**	2,091	1,843
GUITAR	48	GIBSON	L- 12P PREMIER BROWN	3,290	**2,526**	2,232	1,968
GUITAR	49	GIBSON	L- 12P PREMIER SUNBURST, ARCHTOP, SERIAL #A2800-A4400	3,467	**2,662**	2,352	2,074
GUITAR	35	GIBSON	L- 30 BLACK, ARCHTOP, SERIAL #92400-93500	1,643	**1,261**	1,114	982
GUITAR	37	GIBSON	L- 30 BLACK, ARCHTOP	1,369	**1,051**	929	819
GUITAR	37	GIBSON	L- 30 SUNBURST, ARCHTOP, SERIAL #95400	1,372	**1,053**	931	820
GUITAR	38	GIBSON	L- 30 BLACK, ARCHTOP, SERIAL #95400	1,365	**1,048**	926	816
GUITAR	38	GIBSON	L- 30 SUNBURST, ARCHTOP	1,378	**1,058**	935	824
GUITAR	39	GIBSON	L- 30 SUNBURST, ARCHTOP	1,351	**1,038**	917	808
GUITAR	40	GIBSON	L- 30 SUNBURST, ARCHTOP, SERIAL #96000-96600	987	**758**	670	590
GUITAR	41	GIBSON	L- 30 SUNBURST, ARCHTOP	987	**758**	670	590

TYPE	YR	MFG	PRICES--BASED ON 100% ORIGINAL MODEL	SELL EXC	SELL AVG	BUY EXC	BUY AVG
GUITAR	42	GIBSON	L-30 SUNBURST, ARCHTOP	1,337	1,026	907	799
GUITAR	37	GIBSON	L-37 BROWN SUNBURST, SERIAL #95400	1,660	1,275	1,127	993
GUITAR	39	GIBSON	L-37 BROWN SUNBURST	1,656	1,271	1,124	990
GUITAR	41	GIBSON	L-47 NATURAL BLOND, SERIAL #97400	1,326	1,018	899	793
GUITAR	46	GIBSON	L-48	1,049	805	712	627
GUITAR	47	GIBSON	L-48 SUNBURST	1,022	785	693	611
GUITAR	48	GIBSON	L-48 SUNBURST	955	733	648	571
GUITAR	49	GIBSON	L-48 SUNBURST	990	760	671	592
GUITAR	50	GIBSON	L-48 SUNBURST	976	749	662	584
GUITAR	51	GIBSON	L-48 SUNBURST	948	728	643	567
GUITAR	52	GIBSON	L-48 SUNBURST	957	735	649	572
GUITAR	53	GIBSON	L-48 SUNBURST	947	727	642	566
GUITAR	54	GIBSON	L-48 SUNBURST	929	713	630	556
GUITAR	55	GIBSON	L-48 SUNBURST	916	703	621	548
GUITAR	56	GIBSON	L-48 SUNBURST	899	690	610	538
GUITAR	57	GIBSON	L-48 SUNBURST	880	675	597	526
GUITAR	58	GIBSON	L-48 SUNBURST	870	668	590	520
GUITAR	59	GIBSON	L-48 SUNBURST	955	733	648	571
GUITAR	61	GIBSON	L-48 SUNBURST	818	628	555	489
GUITAR	62	GIBSON	L-48 SUNBURST	826	634	560	494
GUITAR	63	GIBSON	L-48 SUNBURST	791	608	537	473
GUITAR	65	GIBSON	L-48 SUNBURST	968	743	657	579
GUITAR	67	GIBSON	L-48 SUNBURST	739	567	501	442
GUITAR	70	GIBSON	L-48	769	590	522	460
GUITAR	32	GIBSON	L-50 SUNBURST, ARCHTOP	1,028	789	697	615
GUITAR	33	GIBSON	L-50 SUNBURST, ARCHTOP	1,329	1,020	902	795
GUITAR	34	GIBSON	L-50 SUNBURST, ARCHTOP	1,321	1,014	896	790
GUITAR	35	GIBSON	L-50 SUNBURST, ARCHTOP	972	746	659	581
GUITAR	36	GIBSON	L-50 SUNBURST, ARCHTOP	1,310	1,006	889	783
GUITAR	37	GIBSON	L-50 SUNBURST, ARCHTOP	1,303	1,001	884	779
GUITAR	39	GIBSON	L-50 SUNBURST, ARCHTOP	1,296	995	880	775
GUITAR	40	GIBSON	L-50 SUNBURST, ARCHTOP	1,235	948	838	739
GUITAR	41	GIBSON	L-50 SUNBURST, ARCHTOP	1,228	943	833	734
GUITAR	42	GIBSON	L-50 SUNBURST, ARCHTOP	1,219	936	827	729
GUITAR	43	GIBSON	L-50 SUNBURST, ARCHTOP	1,215	933	824	726
GUITAR	46	GIBSON	L-50 SUNBURST, ARCHTOP	973	747	660	582
GUITAR	47	GIBSON	L-50 SUNBURST, ARCHTOP	1,028	789	697	615
GUITAR	48	GIBSON	L-50 SUNBURST, ARCHTOP	1,072	823	728	641
GUITAR	49	GIBSON	L-50 SUNBURST, ARCHTOP	1,064	817	722	636
GUITAR	50	GIBSON	L-50 SUNBURST, ARCHTOP	1,060	814	719	634
GUITAR	51	GIBSON	L-50 SUNBURST, ARCHTOP	1,057	811	717	632
GUITAR	52	GIBSON	L-50 SUNBURST, ARCHTOP	1,052	808	714	629
GUITAR	54	GIBSON	L-50 SUNBURST, ARCHTOP	1,047	804	710	626

TYPE	YR	MFG	PRICES--BASED ON 100% ORIGINAL MODEL	SELL EXC	SELL AVG	BUY EXC	BUY AVG
GUITAR	55	GIBSON	L-50 SUNBURST, ARCHTOP	1,038	**797**	704	621
GUITAR	56	GIBSON	L-50 SUNBURST, ARCHTOP	1,029	**790**	698	615
GUITAR	57	GIBSON	L-50 SUNBURST, ARCHTOP	1,060	**814**	719	634
GUITAR	58	GIBSON	L-50 SUNBURST, ARCHTOP	1,016	**780**	690	608
GUITAR	59	GIBSON	L-50 SUNBURST, ARCHTOP	1,011	**776**	686	605
GUITAR	60	GIBSON	L-50 SUNBURST, DeARMOND FLOATING PU	1,200	**921**	814	718
GUITAR	62	GIBSON	L-50 SUNBURST, ARCHTOP	1,323	**1,016**	898	791
GUITAR	66	GIBSON	L-50 SUNBURST, ARCHTOP	922	**708**	626	552
GUITAR	34	GIBSON	L-75 SUNBURST, SERIAL #91500-92400	3,129	**2,402**	2,123	1,871
GUITAR	35	GIBSON	L-75 SUNBURST	2,188	**1,680**	1,485	1,309
GUITAR	35	GIBSON	L-75 SUNBURST, SERIAL #144A-10	2,203	**1,691**	1,494	1,317
GUITAR	36	GIBSON	L-75 SUNBURST, SERIAL #93500	2,039	**1,566**	1,383	1,220
GUITAR	30	GIBSON	**L-C CENTURY** MAPLE BACK/SIDES, SERIAL #89800-90200	5,436	**4,174**	3,689	3,252
GUITAR	33	GIBSON	**L-C CENTURY** SUNBURST	3,426	**2,630**	2,324	2,049
GUITAR	34	GIBSON	**L-C CENTURY** SUNBURST, SERIAL #91500-92400	3,414	**2,622**	2,317	2,042
GUITAR	36	GIBSON	**L-C CENTURY** SUNBURST	4,249	**3,262**	2,883	2,541
GUITAR	37	GIBSON	**L-C CENTURY** SUNBURST, SERIAL #95400	3,446	**2,646**	2,338	2,061
GUITAR	38	GIBSON	**L-C CENTURY** CURLY MAPLE	5,252	**4,033**	3,564	3,142
GUITAR	22	GIBSON	**L-JR** BROWN, ARCHTOP, ROUND HOLE, SERIAL #69300-71400	1,563	**1,200**	1,060	935
GUITAR	23	GIBSON	**L-JR** BLOND, ARCHTOP	981	**753**	665	586
GUITAR	24	GIBSON	**L-JR** BROWN, ARCHTOP, ROUND HOLE	981	**753**	665	586
GUITAR	58	GIBSON	LG-0 SERIAL #A26500-A28000	588	**451**	399	351
GUITAR	59	GIBSON	LG-0 SERIAL #A28000	776	**595**	526	464
GUITAR	60	GIBSON	LG-0	728	**559**	494	435
GUITAR	61	GIBSON	LG-0	686	**527**	465	410
GUITAR	62	GIBSON	LG-0	607	**466**	411	363
GUITAR	63	GIBSON	LG-0	657	**504**	446	393
GUITAR	64	GIBSON	LG-0 NATURAL, FLAT TOP	972	**746**	659	581
GUITAR	65	GIBSON	LG-0	527	**405**	357	315
GUITAR	66	GIBSON	LG-0	610	**468**	414	365
GUITAR	67	GIBSON	LG-0	582	**447**	395	348
GUITAR	68	GIBSON	LG-0	588	**451**	399	351
GUITAR	69	GIBSON	LG-0	499	**383**	338	298
GUITAR	70	GIBSON	LG-0	556	**427**	377	332
GUITAR	47	GIBSON	LG-1 SUNBURST	1,051	**807**	713	629
GUITAR	48	GIBSON	LG-1	955	**733**	648	571
GUITAR	49	GIBSON	LG-1 SUNBURST	1,037	**796**	703	620
GUITAR	50	GIBSON	LG-1 SUNBURST	1,037	**796**	703	620
GUITAR	51	GIBSON	LG-1 SUNBURST	1,033	**793**	701	618
GUITAR	52	GIBSON	LG-1 SUNBURST, SERIAL #A9400-A13000	994	**763**	674	594
GUITAR	53	GIBSON	LG-1 SUNBURST	1,049	**805**	712	627
GUITAR	54	GIBSON	LG-1 SUNBURST, SERIAL #A16000-A19000	992	**761**	673	593
GUITAR	55	GIBSON	LG-1 SUNBURST	987	**758**	670	590
GUITAR	56	GIBSON	LG-1 SUNBURST, SERIAL #A22000-A24600	981	**753**	665	586
GUITAR	57	GIBSON	LG-1 SUNBURST, SERIAL #A24600-A26500	711	**546**	482	425
GUITAR	58	GIBSON	LG-1 SUNBURST	968	**743**	657	579
GUITAR	59	GIBSON	LG-1 SUNBURST	967	**743**	656	578

TYPE	YR	MFG	PRICES--BASED ON 100% ORIGINAL MODEL	SELL EXC	SELL AVG	BUY EXC	BUY AVG
GUITAR	60	GIBSON	LG- 1 SUNBURST	885	680	601	529
GUITAR	62	GIBSON	LG- 1 SUNBURST	882	677	598	527
GUITAR	63	GIBSON	LG- 1 SUNBURST	855	657	580	511
GUITAR	64	GIBSON	LG- 1 SUNBURST	855	657	580	511
GUITAR	65	GIBSON	LG- 1 SUNBURST	827	635	561	495
GUITAR	66	GIBSON	LG- 1 SUNBURST	801	615	544	479
GUITAR	67	GIBSON	LG- 1 SUNBURST	797	612	541	477
GUITAR	68	GIBSON	LG- 1	712	546	483	426
GUITAR	42	GIBSON	LG- 2 FIRESTRIPE GUARD	1,852	1,422	1,257	1,108
GUITAR	43	GIBSON	LG- 2 SUNBURST	2,204	1,692	1,495	1,318
GUITAR	43	GIBSON	LG- 2 MAHOGANY	2,345	1,800	1,591	1,402
GUITAR	44	GIBSON	LG- 2 SUNBURST	2,204	1,692	1,495	1,318
GUITAR	45	GIBSON	LG- 2 SUNBURST	2,198	1,688	1,491	1,315
GUITAR	46	GIBSON	LG- 2 SUNBURST	2,197	1,687	1,491	1,314
GUITAR	49	GIBSON	LG- 2 SUNBURST	2,358	1,811	1,600	1,411
GUITAR	50	GIBSON	LG- 2 SUNBURST	2,097	1,610	1,423	1,254
GUITAR	52	GIBSON	LG- 2 SUNBURST	1,993	1,530	1,352	1,192
GUITAR	53	GIBSON	LG- 2 SUNBURST	1,889	1,450	1,282	1,130
GUITAR	54	GIBSON	LG- 2 SUNBURST	2,014	1,547	1,367	1,205
GUITAR	56	GIBSON	LG- 2 SUNBURST	1,673	1,284	1,135	1,000
GUITAR	57	GIBSON	LG- 2 SUNBURST	1,571	1,206	1,066	940
GUITAR	59	GIBSON	LG- 2 SUNBURST	1,508	1,158	1,023	902
GUITAR	66	GIBSON	LG- 2 SUNBURST	1,341	1,030	910	802
GUITAR	50	GIBSON	LG- 2 3/4 SUNBURST	1,467	1,126	995	877
GUITAR	52	GIBSON	LG- 2 3/4	1,019	782	691	609
GUITAR	58	GIBSON	LG- 2 3/4 SUNBURST	1,279	982	867	765
GUITAR	60	GIBSON	LG- 2 3/4 SUNBURST	1,208	927	820	722
GUITAR	61	GIBSON	LG- 2 3/4 SUNBURST	1,040	798	706	622
GUITAR	62	GIBSON	LG- 2 3/4 CHERRY SUNBURST	977	750	663	584
GUITAR	49	GIBSON	LG- 3 NATURAL	1,557	1,196	1,057	931
GUITAR	50	GIBSON	LG- 3 NATURAL	1,499	1,151	1,017	897
GUITAR	51	GIBSON	LG- 3 NATURAL	1,276	980	866	763
GUITAR	53	GIBSON	LG- 3 NATURAL	1,266	972	859	757
GUITAR	54	GIBSON	LG- 3 NATURAL	1,265	971	858	757
GUITAR	55	GIBSON	LG- 3	1,348	1,035	915	806
GUITAR	58	GIBSON	LG- 3 NATURAL	1,268	974	861	759
GUITAR	68	GIBSON	LG- 12 NATURAL, 12-STRING	1,055	810	715	631
GUITAR	61	GIBSON	LG-2 CHERRY SUNBURST	1,435	1,102	974	858
GUITAR	36	GIBSON	LOAR ARCHTOP	2,798	2,115	1,865	1,547
GUITAR	75	GIBSON	MARK 35 MAHOGANY BACK/SIDES	759	583	515	454
GUITAR	76	GIBSON	MARK 35	590	453	400	353
GUITAR	77	GIBSON	MARK 35 NATURAL	582	447	395	348
GUITAR	77	GIBSON	MARK 35 SUNBURST	747	573	506	446
GUITAR	75	GIBSON	MARK 53	797	612	541	477

TYPE	YR	MFG	PRICES--BASED ON 100% ORIGINAL MODEL	SELL EXC	SELL AVG	BUY EXC	BUY AVG
GUITAR	77	GIBSON	**MARK 53** NATURAL, MAPLE BACK/SIDES	827	**635**	561	495
GUITAR	75	GIBSON	**MARK 72**	1,008	**774**	684	603
GUITAR	76	GIBSON	**MARK 72** ROSEWOOD BACK/SIDES	1,056	**810**	716	631
GUITAR	77	GIBSON	**MARK 72** ROSEWOOD BACK/SIDES	1,047	**804**	710	626
GUITAR	75	GIBSON	**MARK 81**	1,228	**943**	833	734
GUITAR	76	GIBSON	**MARK 81**	1,205	**925**	817	720
GUITAR	77	GIBSON	**MARK 81** ROSEWOOD BACK/SIDES	984	**755**	668	588
GUITAR	78	GIBSON	**MARK 81**	1,018	**781**	690	609
GUITAR	26	GIBSON	**NICK LUCAS** SUNBURST, FLATTOP	5,305	**4,073**	3,600	3,173
GUITAR	27	GIBSON	**NICK LUCAS** SUNBURST, FLATTOP, SERIAL #-85400	5,299	**4,069**	3,596	3,170
GUITAR	28	GIBSON	**NICK LUCAS** SUNBURST, FLATTOP	5,157	**3,960**	3,499	3,085
GUITAR	29	GIBSON	**NICK LUCAS** SUNBURST, FLATTOP, SERIAL #87300-89800	5,304	**4,072**	3,599	3,173
GUITAR	30	GIBSON	**NICK LUCAS** SUNBURST, FLATTOP, SERIAL #89800-90200	5,043	**3,872**	3,422	3,017
GUITAR	32	GIBSON	**NICK LUCAS** SUNBURST, BRAZILIAN ROSEWOOD BACK/SIDES	5,784	**4,441**	3,925	3,460
GUITAR	33	GIBSON	**NICK LUCAS** SUNBURST, FLATTOP, SERIAL #90700-91500	5,043	**3,872**	3,422	3,017
GUITAR	34	GIBSON	**NICK LUCAS** SUNBURST, FLATTOP, SERIAL #91500-92400	5,040	**3,870**	3,420	3,015
GUITAR	35	GIBSON	**NICK LUCAS** SUNBURST, FLATTOP, SERIAL #92400-93500	5,036	**3,867**	3,417	3,012
GUITAR	36	GIBSON	**NICK LUCAS** SUNBURST, FLATTOP	5,032	**3,863**	3,414	3,010
GUITAR	28	GIBSON	**PG-1** PLECTRUM, SUNBURST, FLATTOP, SERIAL #85400-87300	1,217	**934**	826	728
GUITAR	34	GIBSON	**ROY SMECK RADIO GRANDE** NATURAL	5,035	**3,866**	3,416	3,012
GUITAR	35	GIBSON	**ROY SMECK RADIO GRANDE** NATURAL	4,421	**3,395**	3,000	2,645
GUITAR	34	GIBSON	**ROY SMECK STAGE DELUXE**	3,212	**2,466**	2,179	1,921
GUITAR	34	GIBSON	**ROY SMECK STAGE DELUXE** SUNBURST	5,709	**4,384**	3,874	3,415
GUITAR	35	GIBSON	**ROY SMECK STAGE DELUXE** SERIAL #92400-93500	5,619	**4,314**	3,812	3,361
GUITAR	37	GIBSON	**ROY SMECK STAGE DELUXE** SERIAL #95400	6,829	**5,244**	4,634	4,085
GUITAR	42	GIBSON	**SJ** SUNBURST	7,064	**5,424**	4,794	4,226
GUITAR	43	GIBSON	**SJ** SUNBURST, SERIAL #97600-97800	5,942	**4,563**	4,032	3,555
GUITAR	44	GIBSON	**SJ** SUNBURST, SERIAL #97800-98300	5,948	**4,567**	4,036	3,558
GUITAR	45	GIBSON	**SJ** SUNBURST, SERIAL #98300-98600	5,932	**4,555**	4,025	3,548
GUITAR	46	GIBSON	**SJ** SUNBURST, SERIAL #98600-99500	5,932	**4,555**	4,025	3,548
GUITAR	47	GIBSON	**SJ** SUNBURST	4,421	**3,395**	3,000	2,645
GUITAR	48	GIBSON	**SJ** SUNBURST	4,856	**3,671**	3,237	2,684
GUITAR	49	GIBSON	**SJ** SUNBURST	6,082	**4,670**	4,127	3,638
GUITAR	50	GIBSON	**SJ** SUNBURST	3,298	**2,532**	2,238	1,973
GUITAR	51	GIBSON	**SJ** SUNBURST	3,292	**2,528**	2,234	1,969
GUITAR	52	GIBSON	**SJ** SUNBURST	3,286	**2,523**	2,229	1,965
GUITAR	53	GIBSON	**SJ** SUNBURST, SERIAL #A13000-A16000	3,276	**2,515**	2,223	1,959
GUITAR	54	GIBSON	**SJ** SUNBURST	3,287	**2,524**	2,230	1,966
GUITAR	55	GIBSON	**SJ** SUNBURST, SERIAL #A19000-A22000	3,267	**2,508**	2,216	1,954
GUITAR	56	GIBSON	**SJ** SUNBURST	3,265	**2,507**	2,216	1,953
GUITAR	58	GIBSON	**SJ** SUNBURST, SERIAL #A26500-A28000	3,265	**2,507**	2,216	1,953
GUITAR	59	GIBSON	**SJ** SUNBURST	3,315	**2,545**	2,249	1,983
GUITAR	61	GIBSON	**SJ** SUNBURST	1,439	**1,105**	976	860
GUITAR	62	GIBSON	**SJ** SUNBURST	1,436	**1,103**	975	859

TYPE	YR	MFG	PRICES--BASED ON 100% ORIGINAL MODEL	SELL EXC	SELL AVG	BUY EXC	BUY AVG
GUITAR	63	GIBSON	SJ SUNBURST	1,442	1,107	978	862
GUITAR	65	GIBSON	SJ SUNBURST	1,411	1,083	957	844
GUITAR	66	GIBSON	SJ SUNBURST	1,406	1,080	954	841
GUITAR	67	GIBSON	SJ SUNBURST	1,398	1,074	949	836
GUITAR	67	GIBSON	SJ SUNBURST, FLATTOP	1,848	1,419	1,254	1,105
GUITAR	68	GIBSON	SJ SUNBURST	1,396	1,072	947	835
GUITAR	68	GIBSON	SJ SUNBURST, FLATTOP	1,848	1,419	1,254	1,105
GUITAR	70	GIBSON	SJ SUNBURST	1,356	1,041	920	811
GUITAR	72	GIBSON	SJ SUNBURST	1,355	1,040	919	810
GUITAR	73	GIBSON	SJ SUNBURST	1,352	1,038	918	809
GUITAR	74	GIBSON	SJ SUNBURST	1,352	1,038	918	809
GUITAR	72	GIBSON	SJ DELUXE	1,008	774	684	603
GUITAR	73	GIBSON	SJ DELUXE NATURAL	887	681	601	530
GUITAR	73	GIBSON	SJ DELUXE FLATTOP	1,319	1,013	895	789
GUITAR	50	GIBSON	SJ NATURAL	5,072	3,894	3,442	3,034
GUITAR	60	GIBSON	SJ SOUTHERN JUMBO SUNBURST	2,072	1,591	1,406	1,239
GUITAR	68	GIBSON	SJ SOUTHERN JUMBO DELUXE SUNBURST	1,588	1,219	1,077	950
GUITAR	34	GIBSON	SJ- 40 SERIAL #94400-94957	9,061	6,958	6,149	5,420
GUITAR	39	GIBSON	SJ- 44	2,467	1,894	1,674	1,476
GUITAR	41	GIBSON	SJ- 45 SERIAL #96600-97400	4,865	3,735	3,301	2,910
GUITAR	46	GIBSON	SJ- 45 BANNER MAHOGANY BACK/SIDES	5,605	4,304	3,803	3,353
GUITAR	40	GIBSON	SJ-100 MAHOGANY BACK/SIDES, FLATTOP, SERIAL #96000	12,755	9,794	8,655	7,630
GUITAR	41	GIBSON	SJ-100 SUNBURST	8,808	6,763	5,977	5,269
GUITAR	39	GIBSON	SJ-100 CENTENNIAL ONLY 100 MADE/STAIRSTEP HEAD STACK/MOUSTACHE BRIDGE	18,231	13,999	12,371	10,906
GUITAR	38	GIBSON	SJ-200 SUNBURST, ROSEWOOD BACK/SIDES	51,264	39,363	34,786	30,667
GUITAR	38	GIBSON	SJ-200 ROSEWOOD, FLATTOP	54,456	41,814	36,952	32,576
GUITAR	39	GIBSON	SJ-200 SUNBURST, ROSEWOOD BACK/SIDES	48,233	37,036	32,730	28,854
GUITAR	40	GIBSON	SJ-200 SUNBURST	48,811	37,480	33,122	29,199
GUITAR	41	GIBSON	SJ-200 SUNBURST	48,680	37,379	33,033	29,121
GUITAR	48	GIBSON	SJ-200 SUNBURST, SERIAL #A1400-A2800	12,071	9,269	8,191	7,221
GUITAR	49	GIBSON	SJ-200 SUNBURST, SERIAL #A2800-A4400	9,815	7,537	6,660	5,871
GUITAR	49	GIBSON	SJ-200 BLOND, SERIAL #A2800-A4400	19,710	15,135	13,375	11,791
GUITAR	50	GIBSON	SJ-200 SUNBURST	10,550	8,101	7,159	6,311
GUITAR	51	GIBSON	SJ-200 SUNBURST, SERIAL #A6000-A9400	9,278	7,124	6,295	5,550
GUITAR	51	GIBSON	SJ-200 NATURAL, SERIAL #A9400-A13000	10,513	8,072	7,134	6,289
GUITAR	52	GIBSON	SJ-200 SUNBURST	10,384	7,973	7,046	6,212
GUITAR	53	GIBSON	SJ-200 NATURAL	7,286	5,595	4,944	4,359
GUITAR	53	GIBSON	SJ-200 SUNBURST	11,308	8,683	7,673	6,764
GUITAR	54	GIBSON	SJ-200 SUNBURST	9,875	7,582	6,700	5,907
GUITAR	41	GIBSON	SP-TG4 CUSTOM TENOR, NATURAL, 6-STRING	1,631	1,253	1,107	976
GUITAR	83	GIBSON	SPIRIT I CHERRY, ROUND BODY	570	437	386	341
GUITAR	08	GIBSON	STYLE O ARTIST 1908, BLACK, OVAL HOLE	5,364	4,119	3,640	3,209
GUITAR	12	GIBSON	STYLE O ARTIST BLACK, OVAL HOLE, SERIAL #10850-13350	4,850	3,724	3,291	2,901

TYPE	YR	MFG	PRICES--BASED ON 100% ORIGINAL MODEL	SELL EXC	SELL AVG	BUY EXC	BUY AVG
GUITAR	13	GIBSON	**STYLE O ARTIST** BLACK, OVAL HOLE	5,768	**4,429**	3,914	3,450
GUITAR	14	GIBSON	**STYLE O ARTIST** BLACK, OVAL HOLE	5,764	**4,426**	3,911	3,448
GUITAR	15	GIBSON	**STYLE O ARTIST** BLACK, OVAL HOLE	5,629	**4,322**	3,819	3,367
GUITAR	16	GIBSON	**STYLE O ARTIST** BLACK, OVAL HOLE	5,517	**4,236**	3,743	3,300
GUITAR	18	GIBSON	**STYLE O ARTIST** BLACK, OVAL HOLE, SERIAL #39500-47900	6,759	**5,190**	4,586	4,043
GUITAR	19	GIBSON	**STYLE O ARTIST**	2,095	**1,609**	1,421	1,253
GUITAR	20	GIBSON	**STYLE O ARTIST** SUNBURST, OVAL HOLE, RED MAHOGANY, SERIAL #53800-62200	5,465	**4,196**	3,708	3,269
GUITAR	21	GIBSON	**STYLE O ARTIST** SUNBURST, OVAL HOLE, RED MAHOGANY	5,463	**4,195**	3,707	3,268
GUITAR	22	GIBSON	**STYLE O ARTIST** SUNBURST, OVAL HOLE, RED MAHOGANY, SERIAL #69300-71400	5,461	**4,193**	3,705	3,266
GUITAR	23	GIBSON	**STYLE O ARTIST** SUNBURST, OVAL HOLE, RED MAHOGANY	6,377	**4,896**	4,327	3,814
GUITAR	07	GIBSON	**STYLE O-1** 1907, BLACK TOP, SERIAL #3350-4250	5,414	**4,157**	3,673	3,238
GUITAR	04	GIBSON	**STYLE O-2** 1904, BLACK TOP, SERIAL #1150-1850	5,417	**4,159**	3,676	3,240
GUITAR	06	GIBSON	**STYLE O-2** 1906, BLACK TOP, SERIAL #2550-3350	5,417	**4,159**	3,676	3,240
GUITAR	05	GIBSON	**STYLE O-3** 1905, BLACK TOP, SERIAL #1850-2550	5,434	**4,172**	3,687	3,250
GUITAR	02	GIBSON	**STYLE R HARP GUITAR** 1902, ORANGE, SERIAL #1850-2550	5,037	**3,868**	3,418	3,013
GUITAR	02	GIBSON	**STYLE R-1 HARP GUITAR** 1902, BLACK, SERIAL #2550-3350	5,035	**3,866**	3,416	3,012
GUITAR	09	GIBSON	**STYLE U HARP GUITAR** 1909, BLACK TOP, SERIAL #5450-6950	5,041	**3,870**	3,420	3,015
GUITAR	10	GIBSON	**STYLE U HARP GUITAR** BLACK TOP, SERIAL #6950-8750	4,440	**3,409**	3,013	2,656
GUITAR	12	GIBSON	**STYLE U HARP GUITAR** BLACK TOP, SERIAL #10850-13350	4,439	**3,409**	3,012	2,655
GUITAR	13	GIBSON	**STYLE U HARP GUITAR** BLACK TOP, SERIAL #13350-16100	5,507	**4,228**	3,736	3,294
GUITAR	15	GIBSON	**STYLE U HARP GUITAR** ORANGE	4,219	**3,239**	2,862	2,523
GUITAR	15	GIBSON	**STYLE U HARP GUITAR** BLACK TOP	4,437	**3,407**	3,011	2,654
GUITAR	15	GIBSON	**STYLE U HARP GUITAR** SUNBURST, RED MAHOGANY, SERIAL #20150-25150	5,463	**4,195**	3,707	3,268
GUITAR	16	GIBSON	**STYLE U HARP GUITAR** BLACK TOP	4,431	**3,403**	3,007	2,651
GUITAR	16	GIBSON	**STYLE U HARP GUITAR** SUNBURST, RED MAHOGANY	4,444	**3,412**	3,015	2,658
GUITAR	17	GIBSON	**STYLE U HARP GUITAR** SUNBURST, RED MAHOGANY, SERIAL #32000-39500	8,579	**6,587**	5,821	5,132
GUITAR	18	GIBSON	**STYLE U HARP GUITAR** SUNBURST, RED MAHOGANY	8,578	**6,586**	5,820	5,131
GUITAR	19	GIBSON	**STYLE U HARP GUITAR** SUNBURST, RED MAHOGANY	8,581	**6,589**	5,823	5,133
GUITAR	20	GIBSON	**STYLE U HARP GUITAR** SUNBURST, RED MAHOGANY	8,580	**6,588**	5,822	5,132
GUITAR	06	GIBSON	**STYLE U-1 HARP GUITAR** 1906, BLACK TOP, SERIAL #2550-3350	5,037	**3,868**	3,418	3,013
GUITAR	50	GIBSON	**SUPER 300** SUNBURST, ARCHTOP, SERIAL #A4400-A6000	5,210	**4,000**	3,535	3,116
GUITAR	51	GIBSON	**SUPER 300** SUNBURST, ARCHTOP	5,143	**3,949**	3,489	3,076
GUITAR	52	GIBSON	**SUPER 300** SUNBURST, ARCHTOP, SERIAL #A9400-A13000	5,089	**3,907**	3,453	3,044
GUITAR	54	GIBSON	**SUPER 300** SUNBURST, ARCHTOP, SERIAL #A16000-A19000	5,089	**3,907**	3,453	3,044
GUITAR	57	GIBSON	**SUPER 300** SUNBURST, CUTAWAY	8,676	**6,662**	5,887	5,190
GUITAR	58	GIBSON	**SUPER 300C** SUNBURST	7,342	**5,638**	4,982	4,392
GUITAR	34	GIBSON	**SUPER 400** SUNBURST, NON-CUTAWAY	13,363	**10,261**	9,068	7,994
GUITAR	35	GIBSON	**SUPER 400** SUNBURST, NON-CUTAWAY, SERIAL #92400-93500	13,200	**10,135**	8,957	7,896
GUITAR	36	GIBSON	**SUPER 400** SUNBURST, NON-CUTAWAY, SERIAL #95400	13,940	**10,704**	9,459	8,339
GUITAR	37	GIBSON	**SUPER 400** SUNBURST, NON-CUTAWAY, SERIAL #95400	13,787	**10,586**	9,355	8,247
GUITAR	38	GIBSON	**SUPER 400** SUNBURST, NON-CUTAWAY, SERIAL #96000	17,076	**13,112**	11,587	10,215
GUITAR	40	GIBSON	**SUPER 400** SUNBURST, NON-CUTAWAY	10,548	**8,099**	7,157	6,310

TYPE	YR	MFG	PRICES--BASED ON 100% ORIGINAL MODEL	SELL EXC	SELL AVG	BUY EXC	BUY AVG
GUITAR	41	GIBSON	**SUPER 400** NATURAL, NON-CUTAWAY	12,295	**9,441**	8,343	7,355
GUITAR	46	GIBSON	**SUPER 400** SUNBURST, NON-CUTAWAY	11,443	**8,786**	7,764	6,845
GUITAR	47	GIBSON	**SUPER 400** SUNBURST, NON-CUTAWAY	11,521	**8,846**	7,818	6,892
GUITAR	48	GIBSON	**SUPER 400** SUNBURST, NON-CUTAWAY	11,278	**8,660**	7,653	6,746
GUITAR	48	GIBSON	**SUPER 400** NATURAL, NON-CUTAWAY	11,415	**8,765**	7,745	6,828
GUITAR	49	GIBSON	**SUPER 400** SUNBURST, NON-CUTAWAY, SERIAL #A2800-A4400	11,277	**8,659**	7,652	6,746
GUITAR	50	GIBSON	**SUPER 400** NATURAL, NON-CUTAWAY	12,819	**9,843**	8,698	7,668
GUITAR	51	GIBSON	**SUPER 400** SUNBURST, NON-CUTAWAY	10,886	**8,359**	7,387	6,512
GUITAR	51	GIBSON	**SUPER 400** NATURAL, NON-CUTAWAY	10,889	**8,361**	7,389	6,514
GUITAR	77	GIBSON	**SUPER 400** BLOND	7,032	**5,399**	4,772	4,206
GUITAR	39	GIBSON	**SUPER 400C** NATURAL, CUTAWAY	20,680	**15,879**	14,033	12,371
GUITAR	41	GIBSON	**SUPER 400C** PREMIER	21,120	**16,217**	14,332	12,634
GUITAR	46	GIBSON	**SUPER 400C** SUNBURST, CUTAWAY	14,508	**11,140**	9,845	8,679
GUITAR	49	GIBSON	**SUPER 400C** NATURAL, CUTAWAY	13,955	**10,715**	9,469	8,348
GUITAR	50	GIBSON	**SUPER 400C** SUNBURST, CUTAWAY	14,059	**10,795**	9,540	8,410
GUITAR	52	GIBSON	**SUPER 400C** SUNBURST, CUTAWAY	14,988	**11,509**	10,171	8,966
GUITAR	54	GIBSON	**SUPER 400C** SUNBURST, CUTAWAY	12,941	**9,937**	8,781	7,741
GUITAR	56	GIBSON	**SUPER 400C** SUNBURST, CUTAWAY	12,924	**9,924**	8,770	7,731
GUITAR	58	GIBSON	**SUPER 400C** SUNBURST, CUTAWAY	12,924	**9,924**	8,770	7,731
GUITAR	59	GIBSON	**SUPER 400C** SUNBURST, CUTAWAY	13,451	**10,328**	9,127	8,046
GUITAR	60	GIBSON	**SUPER 400C** SUNBURST	13,776	**10,578**	9,348	8,241
GUITAR	61	GIBSON	**SUPER 400C** NATURAL, CUTAWAY	12,137	**9,319**	8,236	7,260
GUITAR	62	GIBSON	**SUPER 400C** SUNBURST, CUTAWAY	12,373	**9,501**	8,396	7,402
GUITAR	63	GIBSON	**SUPER 400C** NATURAL, CUTAWAY	12,128	**9,312**	8,230	7,255
GUITAR	64	GIBSON	**SUPER 400C** CHARLIE CHRISTIAN PU	9,429	**7,240**	6,398	5,640
GUITAR	64	GIBSON	**SUPER 400C** SUNBURST, CUTAWAY, FLOATING PU	12,162	**9,338**	8,252	7,275
GUITAR	66	GIBSON	**SUPER 400C** SUNBURST, CUTAWAY	9,001	**6,911**	6,108	5,384
GUITAR	67	GIBSON	**SUPER 400C** SUNBURST	9,972	**7,657**	6,767	5,965
GUITAR	68	GIBSON	**SUPER 400C** NATURAL, CUTAWAY	9,535	**7,322**	6,470	5,704
GUITAR	69	GIBSON	**SUPER 400C** SUNBURST, CUTAWAY	8,900	**6,834**	6,039	5,324
GUITAR	70	GIBSON	**SUPER 400C** SUNBURST, CUTAWAY	7,598	**5,834**	5,155	4,545
GUITAR	72	GIBSON	**SUPER 400C** SUNBURST, CUTAWAY	7,399	**5,682**	5,021	4,426
GUITAR	73	GIBSON	**SUPER 400C** SUNBURST, CUTAWAY	9,303	**7,144**	6,313	5,565
GUITAR	74	GIBSON	**SUPER 400C** SUNBURST, CUTAWAY	8,683	**6,667**	5,892	5,194
GUITAR	76	GIBSON	**SUPER 400C** NATURAL, CUTAWAY	4,472	**3,433**	3,034	2,675
GUITAR	77	GIBSON	**SUPER 400C** SUNBURST, CUTAWAY	5,834	**4,479**	3,958	3,490
GUITAR	41	GIBSON	**SUPER 400CN**	21,050	**16,163**	14,284	12,592
GUITAR	50	GIBSON	**SUPER 400CN** BLOND	18,366	**14,103**	12,463	10,987
GUITAR	57	GIBSON	**SUPER 400CN** BLOND	15,536	**11,929**	10,542	9,294
GUITAR	59	GIBSON	**SUPER 400CN** BLOND	15,736	**12,083**	10,678	9,413
GUITAR	61	GIBSON	**SUPER 400CN** FLAMEY BACK/SIDES	49,843	**38,272**	33,822	29,817
GUITAR	69	GIBSON	**SUPER 400CN** NATURAL, CUTAWAY	11,245	**8,635**	7,631	6,727

TYPE	YR	MFG	PRICES--BASED ON 100% ORIGINAL MODEL	SELL EXC	SELL AVG	BUY EXC	BUY AVG
GUITAR	49	GIBSON	**SUPER 400N** QUILTED MAPLE BACK, NON-CUTAWAY	12,853	**9,869**	8,721	7,688
GUITAR	36	GIBSON	**SUPER 400P PREMIER** SUNBURST, CUTAWAY, SERIAL #93500	22,159	**17,015**	15,036	13,255
GUITAR	39	GIBSON	**SUPER 400P PREMIER** SUNBURST, CUTAWAY, SERIAL #96000	18,180	**13,960**	12,337	10,876
GUITAR	41	GIBSON	**SUPER 400P PREMIER** SUNBURST, CUTAWAYSERIAL #96600-97400	18,536	**14,233**	12,578	11,088
GUITAR	75	GIBSON	**SUPER V CES** SUNBURST	10,543	**8,096**	7,154	6,307
GUITAR	27	GIBSON	**TG- 0** TENOR, MAHOGANY, FLATTOP	557	**428**	378	333
GUITAR	28	GIBSON	**TG- 0** TENOR, MAHOGANY, FLATTOP, SERIAL #85400-87300	1,234	**947**	837	738
GUITAR	30	GIBSON	**TG- 0** TENOR, MAHOGANY, FLATTOP, SERIAL #89800-90200	1,228	**943**	833	734
GUITAR	60	GIBSON	**TG- 0** TENOR, MAHOGANY, FLATTOP	995	**764**	675	595
GUITAR	61	GIBSON	**TG- 0** TENOR, MAHOGANY, FLATTOP	999	**767**	677	597
GUITAR	63	GIBSON	**TG- 0** TENOR, MAHOGANY, FLATTOP	994	**763**	674	594
GUITAR	64	GIBSON	**TG- 0** TENOR, MAHOGANY, FLATTOP	995	**764**	675	595
GUITAR	65	GIBSON	**TG- 0** TENOR, MAHOGANY, FLATTOP	969	**744**	658	580
GUITAR	70	GIBSON	**TG- 0** TENOR	712	**546**	483	426
GUITAR	30	GIBSON	**TG- 00** TENOR, BLACK, FLATTOLP, SERIAL #89800-90200	715	**549**	485	428
GUITAR	30	GIBSON	**TG- 00** TENOR, SUNBURST, FLATTOP, SERIAL #89800-90200	831	**638**	563	497
GUITAR	32	GIBSON	**TG- 00** TENOR, BLACK, FLATTOP, SERIAL #90400-90700	670	**515**	455	401
GUITAR	34	GIBSON	**TG- 00** TENOR, SUNBURST, FLATTOP, SERIAL #91500-92400	792	**608**	538	474
GUITAR	35	GIBSON	**TG- 00** TENOR, SUNBURST, FLATTOP	797	**612**	541	477
GUITAR	37	GIBSON	**TG- 00** TENOR, SUNBURST, FLATTOP, SERIAL #95400	712	**546**	483	426
GUITAR	40	GIBSON	**TG- 00** TENOR, SUNBURST, FLATTOP, SERIAL #96000-96600	647	**497**	439	387
GUITAR	27	GIBSON	**TG- 1** TENOR, SUNBURST, FLATTOP, SERIAL #85400	822	**631**	557	491
GUITAR	28	GIBSON	**TG- 1** TENOR, SUNBURST, FLATTOP, SERIAL #85400-87300	803	**616**	544	480
GUITAR	30	GIBSON	**TG- 1** TENOR, SUNBURST, FLATTOP	801	**615**	544	479
GUITAR	31	GIBSON	**TG- 1** TENOR, SUNBURST, FLATTOP	831	**638**	563	497
GUITAR	36	GIBSON	**TG- 1** TENOR	865	**664**	587	517
GUITAR	33	GIBSON	**TG- 7** TENOR, SUNBURST, FLATTOP	2,022	**1,553**	1,372	1,210
GUITAR	35	GIBSON	**TG- 7** TENOR, SUNBURST, FLATTOP, SERIAL #92400-93500	2,070	**1,590**	1,405	1,238
GUITAR	38	GIBSON	**TG- 7** TENOR, SUNBURST, FLATTOP	1,938	**1,488**	1,315	1,159
GUITAR	39	GIBSON	**TG- 7** TENOR	1,762	**1,353**	1,196	1,054
GUITAR	65	GIBSON	**TG- 25** TENOR, SUNBURST, FLATTOP	652	**501**	443	390
GUITAR	66	GIBSON	**TG- 25** TENOR, SUNBURST, FLATTOP	712	**546**	483	426
GUITAR	64	GIBSON	**TG- 25N** TENOR, NATURAL, FLATTOP	717	**542**	478	396
GUITAR	65	GIBSON	**TG- 25N** TENOR, NATURAL, FLATTOP	683	**524**	463	408
GUITAR	36	GIBSON	**TG- 50** TENOR, SUNBURST, ARCHTOP, SERIAL #93500	1,042	**800**	707	623
GUITAR	40	GIBSON	**TG- 50** TENOR, SUNBURST, ARCHTOP, SERIAL #96000	1,002	**769**	680	599
GUITAR	46	GIBSON	**TG- 50** TENOR, SUNBURST, ARCHTOP, SERIAL #98600-99500	948	**728**	643	567
GUITAR	47	GIBSON	**TG- 50** TENOR, SUNBURST, ARCHTOP, SERIAL #A1400	932	**716**	633	558
GUITAR	48	GIBSON	**TG- 50** TENOR, SUNBURST, ARCHTOP	919	**706**	623	550
GUITAR	50	GIBSON	**TG- 50** TENOR, SUNBURST, ARCHTOP	827	**635**	561	495
GUITAR	52	GIBSON	**TG- 50** TENOR, SUNBURST, ARCHTOP	846	**650**	574	506
GUITAR	54	GIBSON	**TG- 50** TENOR--SUNBURST, ARCHTOP, SERIAL #A16000-A19000	820	**630**	557	491

TYPE	YR	MFG	PRICES--BASED ON 100% ORIGINAL MODEL	SELL EXC	SELL AVG	BUY EXC	BUY AVG
GUITAR	57	GIBSON	**TG- 50** TENOR, SUNBURST, ARCHTOP	1,206	**926**	818	721
GUITAR	64	GIBSON	**TG- 50** TENOR, SUNBURST	1,066	**818**	723	637
MANDOLA	36	GIBSON	**H-0** SUNBURST, F-HOLES, FLAT BACK	997	**766**	677	596
MANDLA	06	GIBSON	**H-1** 1906, NATURAL	1,713	**1,315**	1,162	1,025
MANDLA	07	GIBSON	**H-1** 1907, BLOND TOP, INLAID PICKGUARD	1,584	**1,216**	1,075	948
MANDLA	09	GIBSON	**H-1** 1909, BLACK TOP, SERIAL #5450-6950	1,647	**1,265**	1,117	985
MANDLA	12	GIBSON	**H-1** BLOND TOP	1,478	**1,135**	1,003	884
MANDLA	14	GIBSON	**H-1** SHERIDAN BROWN, SERIAL #16100-20150	1,413	**1,085**	959	845
MANDLA	14	GIBSON	**H-1** BLOND TOP	1,524	**1,170**	1,034	911
MANDLA	16	GIBSON	**H-1** NATURAL	1,715	**1,317**	1,164	1,026
MANDLA	16	GIBSON	**H-1** PUMPKIN, SERIAL #25485	2,105	**1,592**	1,403	1,164
MANDLA	18	GIBSON	**H-1** NATURAL	2,107	**1,618**	1,430	1,260
MANDLA	20	GIBSON	**H-1** BROWN	19,180	**14,727**	13,015	11,473
MANDLA	22	GIBSON	**H-1** BROWN, SERIAL #69300-71400	13,718	**10,534**	9,309	8,206
MANDLA	26	GIBSON	**H-1** BLACK TOP	2,312	**1,775**	1,569	1,383
MANDLA	29	GIBSON	**H-1** BLACK TOP, SERIAL #87300-89800	1,596	**1,225**	1,083	954
MANDLA	13	GIBSON	**H-2** BLACK TOP, SERIAL #13350-16100	1,709	**1,312**	1,159	1,022
MANDLA	15	GIBSON	**H-2** RED SUNBURST	1,580	**1,213**	1,072	945
MANDLA	17	GIBSON	**H-2** BLACK TOP	1,641	**1,260**	1,114	982
MANDLA	18	GIBSON	**H-2** RED SUNBURST	1,669	**1,282**	1,133	998
MANDLA	20	GIBSON	**H-2** RED SUNBURST	1,715	**1,317**	1,164	1,026
MANDLA	21	GIBSON	**H-2** RED SUNBURST	1,560	**1,197**	1,058	933
MANDLA	14	GIBSON	**H-4** RED SUNBURST	6,838	**5,251**	4,640	4,091
MANDLA	15	GIBSON	**H-4** RED SUNBURST	7,434	**5,708**	5,044	4,447
MANDLA	18	GIBSON	**H-4** RED MAHOGANY	5,210	**4,000**	3,535	3,116
MANDLA	19	GIBSON	**H-4** RED SUNBURST	6,512	**5,000**	4,419	3,896
MANDLA	20	GIBSON	**H-4** RED SUNBURST	6,512	**5,000**	4,419	3,896
MANDLA	21	GIBSON	**H-4** RED SUNBURST	8,591	**6,597**	5,829	5,139
MANDLA	23	GIBSON	**H-4** RED SUNBURST	8,728	**6,701**	5,922	5,221
MANDLA	24	GIBSON	**H-4** RED SUNBURST	7,488	**5,749**	5,081	4,479
MANDLA	24	GIBSON	**H-4** NATURAL, VIRZI TONE	7,808	**5,995**	5,298	4,671
MANDLA	25	GIBSON	**H-4** RED SUNBURST	7,427	**5,703**	5,040	4,443
MANDLA	27	GIBSON	**H-4** RED SUNBURST	6,942	**5,331**	4,711	4,153
MANDOLIN	n/a	GIBSON	**A** 1899, BLACK, HANDMADE BY ORVILLE GIBSON, PRE GIBSON COMPANY	37,477	**28,777**	25,431	22,419
MANDOL	06	GIBSON	**A** 1906, GOLDEN ORANGE	1,932	**1,483**	1,311	1,155
MANDOL	11	GIBSON	**A** NATURAL TOP	1,466	**1,125**	994	877
MANDOL	12	GIBSON	**A** NATURAL TOP	1,289	**989**	874	771
MANDOL	13	GIBSON	**A** NATURAL TOP	1,011	**776**	686	605
MANDOL	13	GIBSON	**A** BLACK TOP	1,286	**988**	873	769
MANDOL	13	GIBSON	**A** PUMPKIN TOP, SERIAL #14841	1,286	**988**	873	769
MANDOL	13	GIBSON	**A** BLOND TOP, SERIAL #13350-16100	1,546	**1,187**	1,049	925
MANDOL	14	GIBSON	**A** NATURAL TOP, SERIAL #16100-20150	1,289	**989**	874	771

TYPE	YR	MFG	PRICES--BASED ON 100% ORIGINAL MODEL	SELL EXC	SELL AVG	BUY EXC	BUY AVG
MANDOL	14	GIBSON	A PUMPKIN TOP	1,291	991	876	772
MANDOL	14	GIBSON	A BROWN	1,294	994	878	774
MANDOL	15	GIBSON	A NATURAL TOP, SERIAL #20150-25150	1,285	987	872	769
MANDOL	15	GIBSON	A BLOND TOP, SERIAL #20150-25150	1,289	989	874	771
MANDOL	15	GIBSON	A AMBER TOP	1,484	1,139	1,007	887
MANDOL	16	GIBSON	A PUMPKIN TOP	993	762	674	594
MANDOL	16	GIBSON	A AMBER TOP	1,293	993	877	773
MANDOL	16	GIBSON	A BLOND TOP	1,296	995	880	775
MANDOL	16	GIBSON	A BLACK TOP	1,391	1,068	943	832
MANDOL	17	GIBSON	A PUMPKIN TOP, SERIAL #32000-39500	993	762	674	594
MANDOL	17	GIBSON	A BROWN	1,293	993	877	773
MANDOL	17	GIBSON	A NATURAL TOP, SERIAL #32000-39500	1,293	993	877	773
MANDOL	18	GIBSON	A BROWN, SERIAL #39500-47900	1,289	989	874	771
MANDOL	18	GIBSON	A NATURAL TOP, SERIAL #39500-47900	1,352	1,038	918	809
MANDOL	19	GIBSON	A BLOND TOP	1,286	988	873	769
MANDOL	20	GIBSON	A BLACK TOP	1,011	776	686	605
MANDOL	20	GIBSON	A PUMPKIN	1,260	967	855	753
MANDOL	20	GIBSON	A WALNUT	1,263	970	857	755
MANDOL	20	GIBSON	A BROWN	1,286	988	873	769
MANDOL	21	GIBSON	A BROWN	1,296	995	880	775
MANDOL	21	GIBSON	A WALNUT	1,373	1,054	931	821
MANDOL	22	GIBSON	A BROWN, SERIAL #69300-71400	1,336	1,025	906	799
MANDOL	22	GIBSON	A BROWN, SNAKEHEAD	1,683	1,292	1,142	1,007
MANDOL	23	GIBSON	A GOLDEN ORANGE	1,205	925	817	720
MANDOL	23	GIBSON	A BROWN, SNAKEHEAD	1,748	1,342	1,186	1,045
MANDOL	23	GIBSON	A BROWN, LEFT-HANDED, SERIAL #71400-74900	2,143	1,646	1,454	1,282
MANDOL	24	GIBSON	A BROWN, SNAKEHEAD	1,742	1,338	1,182	1,042
MANDOL	24	GIBSON	A BLACK TOP, SNAKEHEAD PEGHEAD	1,757	1,349	1,192	1,051
MANDOL	26	GIBSON	A BLACK TOP, SNAKEHEAD PEGHEAD, SERIAL #82700	1,834	1,408	1,244	1,097
MANDOL	27	GIBSON	A BLACK TOP	1,205	925	817	720
MANDOL	28	GIBSON	A BLACK TOP	1,296	995	880	775
MANDOL	20	GIBSON	A JUNIOR BROWN	1,426	1,095	968	853
MANDOL	21	GIBSON	A JUNIOR BROWN	1,011	776	686	605
MANDOL	22	GIBSON	A JUNIOR BROWN	1,426	1,095	968	853
MANDOL	24	GIBSON	A JUNIOR BROWN	993	762	674	594
MANDOL	25	GIBSON	A JUNIOR BROWN	1,256	964	852	751
MANDOL	26	GIBSON	A JUNIOR BROWN	1,021	784	693	611
MANDOL	26	GIBSON	A JUNIOR BROWN, SNAKEHEAD	1,021	784	693	611
MANDOL	32	GIBSON	A JUNIOR BROWN	1,330	1,021	902	795
MANDOL	29	GIBSON	A-0 BROWN	1,260	967	855	753
MANDOL	35	GIBSON	A-00 SUNBURST	878	674	595	525
MANDOL	36	GIBSON	A-00 SUNBURST, FLAT BACK, SERIAL #93500	1,286	988	873	769

TYPE	YR	MFG	PRICES--BASED ON 100% ORIGINAL MODEL	SELL EXC	SELL AVG	BUY EXC	BUY AVG
MANDOL	41	GIBSON	A-00 SUNBURST	1,036	**795**	703	619
MANDOL	05	GIBSON	A-1 1905, BLOND	3,192	**2,451**	2,166	1,909
MANDOL	07	GIBSON	A-1 1907, BLOND	2,270	**1,743**	1,540	1,358
MANDOL	08	GIBSON	A-1 1908, SERIAL #4250-5450	1,974	**1,516**	1,339	1,181
MANDOL	10	GIBSON	A-1	980	**752**	665	586
MANDOL	13	GIBSON	A-1 BLOND	1,392	**1,068**	944	832
MANDOL	13	GIBSON	A-1 NATURAL	1,547	**1,188**	1,050	925
MANDOL	14	GIBSON	A-1 BLOND	1,294	**994**	878	774
MANDOL	14	GIBSON	A-1 NATURAL	1,547	**1,188**	1,050	925
MANDOL	15	GIBSON	A-1 PUMPKIN TOP	1,067	**819**	724	638
MANDOL	15	GIBSON	A-1 BLOND	1,272	**976**	863	761
MANDOL	15	GIBSON	A-1 NATURAL, SERIAL #20150-25150	1,551	**1,191**	1,052	927
MANDOL	16	GIBSON	A-1 BLOND	1,299	**997**	881	777
MANDOL	17	GIBSON	A-1 NATURAL, SERIAL #32000-39500	1,551	**1,191**	1,052	927
MANDOL	18	GIBSON	A-1 NATURAL, SERIAL #39500-47900	984	**755**	668	588
MANDOL	23	GIBSON	A-1 BLACK, SNAKEHEAD, SERIAL #71400-74900	1,932	**1,483**	1,311	1,155
MANDOL	24	GIBSON	A-1 BLACK, SNAKEHEAD, SERIAL #74900-80300	1,881	**1,444**	1,276	1,125
MANDOL	25	GIBSON	A-1 BLACK, SNAKEHEAD	1,917	**1,472**	1,301	1,147
MANDOL	35	GIBSON	A-1 SUNBURST, F-HOLES, SERIAL #93500	1,550	**1,190**	1,051	927
MANDOL	37	GIBSON	A-1 SUNBURST, F-HOLES, CURLY MAPLE	1,321	**1,014**	896	790
MANDOL	38	GIBSON	A-1 SUNBURST, F-HOLES	1,312	**1,007**	890	785
MANDOL	39	GIBSON	A-1	1,300	**998**	882	777
MANDOL	40	GIBSON	A-1 SUNBURST	1,232	**946**	836	737
MANDOL	41	GIBSON	A-1 SUNBURST	1,221	**938**	829	730
MANDOL	42	GIBSON	A-1 SUNBURST	1,210	**929**	821	724
MANDOL	51	GIBSON	A-1 PUMPKIN	1,211	**930**	822	724
MANDOL	18	GIBSON	A-2 BROWN, SERIAL #39500-47900	1,550	**1,190**	1,051	927
MANDOL	19	GIBSON	A-2 BROWN, SERIAL #47900-53800	1,553	**1,192**	1,054	929
MANDOL	20	GIBSON	A-2 BROWN, SERIAL #53800-62200	1,444	**1,109**	980	864
MANDOL	21	GIBSON	A-2 BROWN	1,341	**1,030**	910	802
MANDOL	22	GIBSON	A-2 BROWN	2,030	**1,559**	1,377	1,214
MANDOL	23	GIBSON	A-2Z BROWN	1,554	**1,193**	1,054	929
MANDOL	24	GIBSON	A-2Z BLOND, SNAKEHEAD	4,819	**3,700**	3,270	2,883
MANDOL	05	GIBSON	A-3 1905, BLACK, FANCY INLAY	3,280	**2,518**	2,226	1,962
MANDOL	07	GIBSON	A-3 1907, NATURAL	1,844	**1,416**	1,251	1,103
MANDOL	07	GIBSON	A-3 1907, BLOND	2,115	**1,624**	1,435	1,265
MANDOL	14	GIBSON	A-3 NATURAL, SERIAL #16100-20150	1,934	**1,485**	1,312	1,157
MANDOL	15	GIBSON	A-3 BLOND	1,939	**1,489**	1,316	1,160
MANDOL	16	GIBSON	A-3 BLOND	1,940	**1,490**	1,317	1,161
MANDOL	16	GIBSON	A-3 GOLDEN ORANGE	2,057	**1,579**	1,396	1,230
MANDOL	17	GIBSON	A-3 NATURAL, SERIAL #32000-39500	1,932	**1,483**	1,311	1,155
MANDOL	18	GIBSON	A-3 WHITE FACE	1,939	**1,489**	1,316	1,160
MANDOL	19	GIBSON	A-3 WHITE FACE, SERIAL #47900-53800	1,939	**1,489**	1,316	1,160

TYPE	YR	MFG	PRICES--BASED ON 100% ORIGINAL MODEL	SELL EXC	SELL AVG	BUY EXC	BUY AVG
MANDOL	20	GIBSON	A- 3 WHITE FACE, SERIAL #53800-62200	1,811	1,390	1,228	1,083
MANDOL	21	GIBSON	A- 3 WHITE FACE	1,939	1,489	1,316	1,160
MANDOL	22	GIBSON	A- 3 WHITE FACE, IVORY PICKGUARD	1,938	1,488	1,315	1,159
MANDOL	22	GIBSON	A- 3 IVORY, WHITE IVORY PICKGUARD	2,113	1,622	1,434	1,264
MANDOL	06	GIBSON	A- 4 1906, BLACK TOP	2,195	1,685	1,489	1,313
MANDOL	07	GIBSON	A- 4 1907, BLACK TOP	2,274	1,746	1,543	1,360
MANDOL	08	GIBSON	A- 4 1908, BLACK TOP	2,936	2,254	1,992	1,756
MANDOL	09	GIBSON	A- 4 1909, BLACK TOP, INLAID TUNERS, SERIAL #5450-6950	3,002	2,305	2,037	1,796
MANDOL	12	GIBSON	A- 4 BLACK TOP, INLAID TUNERS, MAROON BACK/SIDES	2,896	2,223	1,965	1,732
MANDOL	13	GIBSON	A- 4 BLACK TOP	2,291	1,759	1,554	1,370
MANDOL	13	GIBSON	A- 4 BLACK TOP	2,320	1,781	1,574	1,388
MANDOL	14	GIBSON	A- 4 BLACK TOP, INLAID TUNERS	2,433	1,868	1,651	1,455
MANDOL	15	GIBSON	A- 4 BLACK TOP, INLAID TUNERS, SERIAL #20150-25150	2,346	1,801	1,592	1,403
MANDOL	16	GIBSON	A- 4 BLACK TOP, SERIAL #25308	2,191	1,683	1,487	1,311
MANDOL	16	GIBSON	A- 4 RED SUNBURST	2,356	1,809	1,599	1,409
MANDOL	17	GIBSON	A- 4 RED SUNBURST, INLAID TUNER BUTTONS, SERIAL #32000-39500	2,013	1,546	1,366	1,204
MANDOL	18	GIBSON	A- 4 RED MAHOGANY	2,142	1,645	1,453	1,281
MANDOL	19	GIBSON	A- 4 RED SUNBURST, SERIAL #47900-53800	2,284	1,754	1,550	1,366
MANDOL	20	GIBSON	A- 4 RED MAHOGANY	2,013	1,546	1,366	1,204
MANDOL	20	GIBSON	A- 4 RED SUNBURST	2,074	1,592	1,407	1,240
MANDOL	20	GIBSON	A- 4 RED SUNBURST	2,101	1,613	1,425	1,256
MANDOL	20	GIBSON	A- 4 MAROON SUNBURST	3,151	2,420	2,138	1,885
MANDOL	21	GIBSON	A- 4 RED SUNBURST, SERIAL #62200-69300	1,752	1,345	1,189	1,048
MANDOL	21	GIBSON	A- 4 MAROON SUNBURST, SERIAL #62200-69300	2,164	1,662	1,469	1,295
MANDOL	22	GIBSON	A- 4 BLACK TOP	1,858	1,426	1,260	1,111
MANDOL	22	GIBSON	A- 4 RED SUNBURST	1,888	1,449	1,281	1,129
MANDOL	23	GIBSON	A- 4 RED SUNBURST, SERIAL #71400-74900	1,811	1,390	1,228	1,083
MANDOL	23	GIBSON	A- 4 RED MAHOGANY, SNAKEHEAD	3,923	3,012	2,662	2,347
MANDOL	24	GIBSON	A- 4 RED MAHOGANY, SNAKEHEAD, SERIAL #74900-80300	3,319	2,549	2,252	1,985
MANDOL	27	GIBSON	A- 4 RED MAHOGANY	2,195	1,685	1,489	1,313
MANDOL	28	GIBSON	A- 4 RED SUNBURST, SERIAL #85400-87300	1,501	1,153	1,019	898
MANDOL	34	GIBSON	A- 5 SUNBURST, SERIAL #91500-92400	2,993	2,298	2,031	1,790
MANDOL	51	GIBSON	A- 5 SUNBURST	2,115	1,624	1,435	1,265
MANDOL	60	GIBSON	A- 5 CHERRY SUNBURST	1,570	1,205	1,065	939
MANDOL	63	GIBSON	A- 5 CHERRY SUNBURST	2,027	1,556	1,375	1,212
MANDOL	64	GIBSON	A- 5 CHERRY SUNBURST	1,776	1,363	1,205	1,062
MANDOL	71	GIBSON	A- 5 CHERRY SUNBURST	1,466	1,125	994	877
MANDOL	72	GIBSON	A- 5 SUNBURST, LUMP SCROLL	1,724	1,324	1,170	1,031
MANDOL	73	GIBSON	A- 5 SUNBURST, LUMP SCROLL	1,723	1,323	1,169	1,031
MANDOL	74	GIBSON	A- 5 SUNBURST	984	755	668	588
MANDOL	79	GIBSON	A- 5 GOLDEN SUNBURST, LUMP SCROLL	1,644	1,262	1,115	983
MANDOL	52	GIBSON	A- 5L A STYLE, LEFT HANDED	2,231	1,713	1,513	1,334

TYPE	YR	MFG	PRICES--BASED ON 100% ORIGINAL MODEL	SELL EXC	SELL AVG	BUY EXC	BUY AVG
MANDOL	71	GIBSON	A-12 LUMP SCROLL	1,221	**938**	829	730
MANDOL	72	GIBSON	A-12 LUMP SCROLL	1,380	**1,060**	937	826
MANDOL	73	GIBSON	A-12 SUNBURST, SOLID SCROLLS	1,268	**974**	861	759
MANDOL	74	GIBSON	A-12 LUMP SCROLL	1,525	**1,171**	1,035	912
MANDOL	75	GIBSON	A-12 LUMP SCROLL	1,154	**873**	769	638
MANDOL	78	GIBSON	A-12 LUMP SCROLL	1,383	**1,062**	938	827
MANDOL	35	GIBSON	A-40 NATURAL	1,294	**994**	878	774
MANDOL	48	GIBSON	A-40 SUNBURST	967	**743**	656	578
MANDOL	49	GIBSON	A-40 NATURAL, SERIAL #A2800-A4400	1,312	**1,007**	890	785
MANDOL	50	GIBSON	A-40 NATURAL, SERIAL #A4400-A6000	1,338	**1,027**	908	800
MANDOL	52	GIBSON	A-40 NATURAL	1,324	**1,017**	899	792
MANDOL	54	GIBSON	A-40 NATURAL	1,290	**990**	875	771
MANDOL	59	GIBSON	A-40 NATURAL	1,228	**943**	833	734
MANDOL	60	GIBSON	A-40 NATURAL	1,053	**809**	715	630
MANDOL	63	GIBSON	A-40 SUNBURST	1,001	**768**	679	598
MANDOL	64	GIBSON	A-40 SUNBURST	1,001	**768**	679	598
MANDOL	65	GIBSON	A-40 SUNBURST	964	**740**	654	576
MANDOL	66	GIBSON	A-40 SUNBURST	972	**746**	659	581
MANDOL	68	GIBSON	A-40 SUNBURST	645	**495**	437	385
MANDOL	68	GIBSON	A-40 NATURAL	838	**644**	569	501
MANDOL	69	GIBSON	A-40 SUNBURST	865	**664**	587	517
MANDOL	32	GIBSON	A-50 SUNBURST	1,934	**1,485**	1,312	1,157
MANDOL	33	GIBSON	A-50 SUNBURST	1,936	**1,486**	1,314	1,158
MANDOL	34	GIBSON	A-50 SUNBURST, SERIAL #91500-92400	1,929	**1,481**	1,309	1,154
MANDOL	35	GIBSON	A-50 SUNBURST	1,929	**1,481**	1,309	1,154
MANDOL	38	GIBSON	A-50 SUNBURST, SERIAL #95400	2,997	**2,301**	2,033	1,792
MANDOL	39	GIBSON	A-50 SUNBURST, SERIAL #96000	2,972	**2,282**	2,017	1,778
MANDOL	40	GIBSON	A-50 SUNBURST, WIDE BODY	1,525	**1,171**	1,035	912
MANDOL	41	GIBSON	A-50 SUNBURST	1,561	**1,198**	1,059	933
MANDOL	43	GIBSON	A-50 SUNBURST	1,402	**1,076**	951	838
MANDOL	45	GIBSON	A-50 SUNBURST	1,485	**1,140**	1,007	888
MANDOL	47	GIBSON	A-50 SUNBURST	1,481	**1,137**	1,005	886
MANDOL	48	GIBSON	A-50 SUNBURST	1,305	**1,002**	886	781
MANDOL	49	GIBSON	A-50 SUNBURST	1,305	**1,002**	886	781
MANDOL	50	GIBSON	A-50 SUNBURST	1,232	**946**	836	737
MANDOL	51	GIBSON	A-50 SUNBURST	967	**743**	656	578
MANDOL	53	GIBSON	A-50 SUNBURST	1,014	**779**	688	607
MANDOL	60	GIBSON	A-50 SUNBURST	1,238	**951**	840	741
MANDOL	61	GIBSON	A-50 SUNBURST	1,238	**951**	840	741
MANDOL	63	GIBSON	A-50 SUNBURST	1,218	**935**	826	728
MANDOL	64	GIBSON	A-50 SUNBURST	1,217	**934**	826	728
MANDOL	66	GIBSON	A-50 SUNBURST	1,286	**988**	873	769

TYPE	YR	MFG	PRICES--BASED ON 100% ORIGINAL MODEL	SELL EXC	SELL AVG	BUY EXC	BUY AVG
MANDOL	67	GIBSON	**A-50** SUNBURST	893	**686**	606	534
MANDOL	68	GIBSON	**A-50** SUNBURST	1,285	**987**	872	769
MANDOL	35	GIBSON	**A-C CENTURY** SUNBURST, PEARLOID INLAY	3,321	**2,550**	2,254	1,987
MANDOL	36	GIBSON	**A-C CENTURY** SUNBURST, PEARLOID	2,415	**1,855**	1,639	1,445
MANDOL	17	GIBSON	**ALRITE STYLE D** ORANGE, FLATTOP	1,319	**1,013**	895	789
MANDOL	18	GIBSON	**ALRITE STYLE D** ORANGE, FLATTOP AND BACK	1,318	**1,012**	894	788
MANDOL	12	GIBSON	**ARMY-NAVY MODEL** DARK BROWN, SERIAL #10850-13350	1,313	**1,008**	891	785
MANDOL	30	GIBSON	**ARMY-NAVY MODEL** BROWN	1,318	**1,012**	894	788
MANDOL	07	GIBSON	**ARTIST MODEL** 1907, 3-POINT BODY, SERIAL #3350-4250	6,546	**5,026**	4,442	3,916
MANDOL	32	GIBSON	**C-1** FLATTOP	984	**755**	668	588
MANDOL	58	GIBSON	**DOUBLE MANDOLIN** SUNBURST, 2-NECK	1,630	**1,252**	1,106	975
MANDOL	62	GIBSON	**DOUBLE MANDOLIN** SUNBURST, 2-NECK	6,646	**5,103**	4,509	3,975
MANDOL	65	GIBSON	**ELECTRIC FLORETINE**	1,973	**1,515**	1,339	1,180
MANDOL	39	GIBSON	**EM-150 ELECTRIC**	1,761	**1,352**	1,195	1,053
MANDOL	52	GIBSON	**EM-150 ELECTRIC**	1,347	**1,034**	914	806
MANDOL	54	GIBSON	**EM-150 ELECTRIC**	1,209	**928**	820	723
MANDOL	55	GIBSON	**EM-150 ELECTRIC**	1,341	**1,030**	910	802
MANDOL	56	GIBSON	**EM-150 ELECTRIC**	1,027	**788**	696	614
MANDOL	57	GIBSON	**EM-150 ELECTRIC**	1,024	**786**	695	613
MANDOL	63	GIBSON	**EM-150 ELECTRIC**	977	**750**	663	584
MANDOL	66	GIBSON	**EM-150 ELECTRIC**	1,233	**946**	836	737
MANDOL	68	GIBSON	**EM-150 ELECTRIC**	1,235	**948**	838	739
MANDOL	69	GIBSON	**EM-150 ELECTRIC**	1,221	**938**	829	730
MANDOL	50	GIBSON	**EM-250 ELECTRIC** SERIAL #A4400-A6000	1,756	**1,348**	1,191	1,050
MANDOL	58	GIBSON	**EMS-1235 DOUBLE** WHITE	1,404	**1,078**	953	840
MANDOL	66	GIBSON	**EMS-1235 DOUBLE**	3,744	**2,874**	2,540	2,239
MANDOL	05	GIBSON	**F-2** 1905, BLACK TOP	3,652	**2,804**	2,478	2,184
MANDOL	06	GIBSON	**F-2** 1906, BLACK TOP	3,646	**2,800**	2,474	2,181
MANDOL	08	GIBSON	**F-2** 1908, BLACK TOP, SERIAL #4250-5450	3,648	**2,801**	2,476	2,182
MANDOL	09	GIBSON	**F-2** 1909, BLACK TOP	3,643	**2,797**	2,472	2,179
MANDOL	11	GIBSON	**F-2** BLACK TOP, TORTOISE PICKGUARD, SERIAL #10762	3,641	**2,795**	2,470	2,178
MANDOL	12	GIBSON	**F-2** BLACK TOP, SERIAL #10850-13350	3,636	**2,792**	2,467	2,175
MANDOL	13	GIBSON	**F-2** RED SUNBURST, SERIAL #53800-62200	3,633	**2,789**	2,465	2,173
MANDOL	13	GIBSON	**F-2** BLACK TOP, SERIAL #13350-16100	3,634	**2,790**	2,466	2,174
MANDOL	14	GIBSON	**F-2** BLACK TOP, INLAID TUNERS	3,629	**2,787**	2,463	2,171
MANDOL	15	GIBSON	**F-2** BLACK TOP, INLAID TUNERS, SERIAL #20150-25150	3,633	**2,789**	2,465	2,173
MANDOL	16	GIBSON	**F-2** BLACK TOP	3,623	**2,782**	2,458	2,167
MANDOL	17	GIBSON	**F-2** BLACK TOP	3,618	**2,778**	2,455	2,164
MANDOL	18	GIBSON	**F-2** RED SUNBURST	4,352	**3,341**	2,953	2,603
MANDOL	19	GIBSON	**F-2** RED SUNBURST	3,168	**2,432**	2,150	1,895
MANDOL	20	GIBSON	**F-2** SUNBURST	2,101	**1,613**	1,425	1,256
MANDOL	21	GIBSON	**F-2** RED SUNBURST	3,162	**2,428**	2,146	1,892
MANDOL	23	GIBSON	**F-2** RED SUNBURST	2,944	**2,260**	1,998	1,761
MANDOL	24	GIBSON	**F-2** RED SUNBURST	2,427	**1,863**	1,646	1,451
MANDOL	26	GIBSON	**F-2** RED SUNBURST, SERIAL #82700	2,348	**1,803**	1,593	1,404
MANDOL	07	GIBSON	**F-4** 1907, BLACK TOP, ORNATE INLAY	4,884	**3,750**	3,314	2,921
MANDOL	10	GIBSON	**F-4** BLACK TOP, SERIAL #6950-8750	3,225	**2,476**	2,188	1,929

TYPE	YR	MFG	PRICES--BASED ON 100% ORIGINAL MODEL	SELL EXC	SELL AVG	BUY EXC	BUY AVG
MANDOL	10	GIBSON	F- 4 ORANGE, 3-POINT SHALLOW BODY, ELABORATE PEGHEAD INLAY	4,459	3,424	3,026	2,667
MANDOL	12	GIBSON	F- 4 ORANGE, FLOWERPOT INLAY	5,315	4,081	3,606	3,179
MANDOL	14	GIBSON	F- 4 BLACK TOP	3,960	3,040	2,687	2,369
MANDOL	14	GIBSON	F- 4 ORANGE, 1-PIECE HIGHLY FIGURED MAPLE BACK	4,263	3,274	2,893	2,550
MANDOL	14	GIBSON	F- 4 RED MAHOGANY, SERIAL #16100-20150	4,341	3,333	2,945	2,596
MANDOL	15	GIBSON	F- 4 RED MAHOGANY SUNBURST, SERIAL #20150-25150	3,363	2,582	2,282	2,012
MANDOL	16	GIBSON	F- 4 BLACK TOP	3,192	2,451	2,166	1,909
MANDOL	16	GIBSON	F- 4 RED MAHOGANY SUNBURST, INLAID TUNERS	3,351	2,573	2,273	2,004
MANDOL	17	GIBSON	F- 4 RED SUNBURST, FLOWER INLAY, SERIAL #35590	4,438	3,408	3,011	2,655
MANDOL	17	GIBSON	F- 4 RED MAHOGANY	5,085	3,905	3,451	3,042
MANDOL	18	GIBSON	F- 4 RED SUNBURST	4,608	3,538	3,127	2,757
MANDOL	19	GIBSON	F- 4 RED SUNBURST	4,264	3,274	2,894	2,551
MANDOL	20	GIBSON	F- 4 RED SUNBURST, CURLY MAPLE	2,592	1,960	1,728	1,433
MANDOL	20	GIBSON	F- 4 RED MAHOGANY	3,438	2,640	2,333	2,056
MANDOL	20	GIBSON	F- 4 RED SUNBURST, FLAMEY, FLORAL, SERIAL #53800-62200	5,183	3,980	3,517	3,100
MANDOL	21	GIBSON	F- 4 RED SUNBURST, DOUBLE FLOWER-POT PEGHEAD INLAY	3,256	2,500	2,210	1,948
MANDOL	22	GIBSON	F- 4 RED SUNBURST, 2-PC CURLY MAPLE, SERIAL #69300-71400	4,490	3,447	3,046	2,686
MANDOL	23	GIBSON	F- 4 RED SUNBURST, SERIAL #71400-74900	3,858	2,962	2,618	2,308
MANDOL	24	GIBSON	F- 4 RED SUNBURST	4,261	3,272	2,891	2,549
MANDOL	26	GIBSON	F- 4 RED SUNBURST	5,707	4,382	3,872	3,414
MANDOL	28	GIBSON	F- 4 RED SUNBURST	3,385	2,599	2,297	2,025
MANDOL	29	GIBSON	F- 4 RED SUNBURST	3,594	2,759	2,438	2,150
MANDOL	37	GIBSON	F- 4 RED SUNBURST	3,139	2,410	2,130	1,878
MANDOL	42	GIBSON	F- 4 RED SUNBURST	2,975	2,285	2,019	1,780
MANDOL	23	GIBSON	F- 5 FLAMED MAPLE, FLOWERPOT INLAY	61,990	47,600	42,065	37,083
MANDOL	24	GIBSON	F- 5 FLOWERPOT INLAY	62,492	47,985	42,405	37,383
MANDOL	26	GIBSON	F- 5 FERN PEGHEAD INLAY	39,985	30,702	27,132	23,919
MANDOL	27	GIBSON	F- 5 SUNBURST, SERIAL #85400	18,618	14,296	12,634	11,138
MANDOL	29	GIBSON	F- 5 FERN PEGHEAD INLAY, SERIAL #87300-89800	35,538	27,288	24,115	21,259
MANDOL	34	GIBSON	F- 5 FERN SUNBURST	38,791	29,786	26,322	23,205
MANDOL	41	GIBSON	F- 5 SUNBURST	18,428	14,150	12,505	11,024
MANDOL	41	GIBSON	F- 5 SUNBURST, FLOWERPOT INLAY	19,887	15,271	13,495	11,897
MANDOL	42	GIBSON	F- 5 FLEUR-DE-LIS PEGHEAD INLAY	15,918	12,223	10,801	9,522
MANDOL	42	GIBSON	F- 5 SUNBURST, SERIAL #97418	20,280	15,572	13,762	12,132
MANDOL	65	GIBSON	F- 5 3-PC MAPLE NECK	4,212	3,234	2,858	2,519
MANDOL	67	GIBSON	F- 5 SUNBURST	4,083	3,135	2,770	2,442
MANDOL	71	GIBSON	F- 5 2-PC CURLY MAPLE BACK	1,822	1,399	1,236	1,090
MANDOL	71	GIBSON	F- 5 TOBACCO SUNBURST, FLAMED BACK/NECK	3,972	3,050	2,695	2,376
MANDOL	74	GIBSON	F- 5 CURLY MAPLE	3,348	2,571	2,272	2,003
MANDOL	75	GIBSON	F- 5 SUNBURST	2,920	2,242	1,982	1,747
MANDOL	76	GIBSON	F- 5 2-PC QUILTED MAPLE BACK	2,038	1,565	1,383	1,219
MANDOL	77	GIBSON	F- 5 2-PC FLAMED MAPLE BACK	1,808	1,388	1,227	1,082

TYPE	YR	MFG	PRICES--BASED ON 100% ORIGINAL MODEL	SELL EXC	SELL AVG	BUY EXC	BUY AVG
MANDOL	77	GIBSON	F- 5 CURLY MAPLE	1,821	1,398	1,235	1,089
MANDOL	64	GIBSON	F- 5 CUSTOM FIGURED MAPLE BACK/SIDES	4,910	3,770	3,331	2,937
MANDOL	67	GIBSON	F- 5 CUSTOM	3,430	2,634	2,327	2,052
MANDOL	79	GIBSON	F- 5 L MAPLE SUNBURST	3,255	2,500	2,209	1,947
MANDOL	22	GIBSON	F- 5 LLOYD LOAR	67,780	52,045	45,993	40,547
MANDOL	23	GIBSON	F- 5 LLOYD LOAR	67,207	51,606	45,605	40,204
MANDOL	24	GIBSON	F- 5 LLOYD LOAR	58,158	44,657	39,464	34,791
MANDOL	25	GIBSON	F- 5 LLOYD LOAR	36,615	28,115	24,845	21,903
MANDOL	35	GIBSON	F- 7 FLEUR-DE-LIS PEGHEAD INLAY, "F" HOLES (RARE)	6,101	4,685	4,140	3,650
MANDOL	37	GIBSON	F- 7 SERIAL #95400	6,779	5,205	4,600	4,055
MANDOL	89	GIBSON	F- 7 SUNBURST	5,579	4,284	3,786	3,337
MANDOL	36	GIBSON	F-10 BLACK, SERIAL #93500	5,227	4,013	3,546	3,126
MANDOL	35	GIBSON	F-12 SUNBURST, SERIAL #92400-93500	5,875	4,511	3,986	3,514
MANDOL	49	GIBSON	F-12 SERIAL #A2800-A4400	4,038	3,101	2,740	2,416
MANDOL	50	GIBSON	F-12 SUNBURST	3,259	2,502	2,211	1,949
MANDOL	52	GIBSON	F-12 SUNBURST	4,307	3,307	2,922	2,576
MANDOL	54	GIBSON	F-12 SUNBURST	3,240	2,487	2,198	1,938
MANDOL	65	GIBSON	F-12 SUNBURST	2,440	1,873	1,656	1,459
MANDOL	67	GIBSON	F-12 SUNBURST	2,150	1,651	1,459	1,286
MANDOL	71	GIBSON	F-12 SUNBURST	2,187	1,679	1,484	1,308
MANDOL	00	GIBSON	F-MODEL ORVILLE 1900, OVAL SOUNDHOLE	19,629	15,072	13,319	11,742
MANDOL	03	GIBSON	F-MODEL ORVILLE 1903, OVAL SOUNDHOLE, SERIAL #1150	16,237	12,468	11,018	9,713
MANDOL	59	GIBSON	FLORENTINE ELECTRIC 8 STRINGS, TOBACCO SUNBURST,DOUBLE CUTAWAY,MAHOG BODY	1,812	1,391	1,229	1,084
MANDOL	62	GIBSON	FLORENTINE ELECTRIC	1,824	1,400	1,238	1,091
MANDOL	63	GIBSON	FLORENTINE ELECTRIC	1,861	1,429	1,263	1,113
MANDOL	64	GIBSON	FLORENTINE ELECTRIC	2,331	1,790	1,582	1,394
MANDOL	65	GIBSON	FLORENTINE ELECTRIC	1,934	1,485	1,312	1,157
MANDOL	66	GIBSON	FLORENTINE ELECTRIC	1,839	1,412	1,247	1,100
MANDOL	68	GIBSON	FLORENTINE ELECTRIC	1,792	1,376	1,216	1,072
MANDOL	69	GIBSON	FLORENTINE ELECTRIC	1,509	1,159	1,024	903
MANDOL	16	GIBSON	H-1 PUMPKIN TOP	1,882	1,445	1,277	1,126
MANDOL	18	GIBSON	J MANDO-BASS RED SUNBURST, SERIAL #39500-47900	2,001	1,536	1,358	1,197
MANDOL	20	GIBSON	J MANDO-BASS	3,192	2,451	2,166	1,909
MANDOL	27	GIBSON	J MANDO-BASS BLACK TOP, SERIAL #85400	1,369	1,051	929	819
MANDOL	14	GIBSON	K- 1 MANDOCELLO ORANGE TOP	3,372	2,589	2,288	2,017
MANDOL	15	GIBSON	K- 1 MANDOCELLO	3,364	2,583	2,283	2,012
MANDOL	16	GIBSON	K- 1 MANDOCELLO PUMPKIN	2,143	1,646	1,454	1,282
MANDOL	17	GIBSON	K- 1 MANDOCELLO PUMPKIN	2,195	1,685	1,489	1,313
MANDOL	17	GIBSON	K- 1 MANDOCELLO ORANGE TOP	3,897	2,992	2,644	2,331
MANDOL	18	GIBSON	K- 1 MANDOCELLO BROWN, SERIAL #39500-47900	3,991	3,065	2,708	2,387
MANDOL	27	GIBSON	K- 1 MANDOCELLO BLACK TOP	3,375	2,592	2,290	2,019
MANDOL	14	GIBSON	K- 2 MANDOCELLO BLACK, SERIAL #19359	3,386	2,600	2,298	2,026
MANDOL	16	GIBSON	K- 2 MANDOCELLO RED SUNBURST	2,448	1,879	1,661	1,464
MANDOL	18	GIBSON	K- 2 MANDOCELLO RED SUNBURST, SERIAL #39500-47900	2,231	1,713	1,513	1,334
MANDOL	19	GIBSON	K- 2 MANDOCELLO RED SUNBURST, SERIAL #47900-53800	3,377	2,593	2,292	2,020
MANDOL	15	GIBSON	K- 4 MANDOCELLO BLACK, SERIAL #20150-25150	7,260	5,575	4,927	4,343
MANDOL	16	GIBSON	K- 4 MANDOCELLO SUNBURST, FLAME MAPLE BACK/SIDES	8,453	6,491	5,736	5,057
MANDOL	17	GIBSON	K- 4 MANDOCELLO RED SUNBURST	7,815	6,001	5,303	4,675

TYPE	YR	MFG	PRICES--BASED ON 100% ORIGINAL MODEL	SELL EXC	SELL AVG	BUY EXC	BUY AVG
MANDOL	20	GIBSON	**K- 4 MANDOCELLO** RED SUNBURST, SERIAL #53800-62200	6,826	**5,241**	4,632	4,083
MANDOL	21	GIBSON	**K- 4 MANDOCELLO** RED SUNBURST	3,869	**2,971**	2,625	2,314
MANDOL	24	GIBSON	**K- 4 MANDOCELLO** RED SUNBURST, SERIAL #74900-80300	3,519	**2,702**	2,387	2,105
MANDOL	37	GIBSON	**KALAMAZOO** SUNBURST, SERIAL #95400	1,031	**792**	699	617
MANDOL	38	GIBSON	**KALAMAZOO** SUNBURST, F-HOLES, SERIAL #95400	1,031	**792**	699	617
MANDOL	39	GIBSON	**KALAMAZOO C** SUNBURST	1,032	**792**	700	617
MANDOL	10	GIBSON	**MANDO BASS**	3,513	**2,697**	2,384	2,101
MANDOL	24	GIBSON	**MB-JUNIOR** BLACK	747	**573**	506	446
MANDOL	38	GIBSON	**RECORDING KING** SUNBURST, SERIAL #95400	1,313	**1,008**	891	785
MANDOL	24	GIBSON	**TL-1 TENOR LUTE-MANDOLIN** 4-STRING	1,757	**1,349**	1,192	1,051
STEEL GUITAR	46	GIBSON	**BR-4 LAP STEEL** SUNBURST, MAHOGANY	665	**510**	451	397
STGUIT	46	GIBSON	**BR-6 LAP STEEL** BLACK	805	**618**	546	481
STGUIT	47	GIBSON	**BR-6 LAP STEEL** BLACK	805	**618**	546	481
STGUIT	48	GIBSON	**BR-6 LAP STEEL** BLACK	747	**573**	506	446
STGUIT	49	GIBSON	**BR-6 LAP STEEL**	682	**523**	462	408
STGUIT	50	GIBSON	**BR-6 LAP STEEL** SUNBURST	603	**463**	409	361
STGUIT	52	GIBSON	**BR-6 LAP STEEL** SUNBURST, SERIAL #A9400-A13000	633	**486**	430	379
STGUIT	55	GIBSON	**BR-6 LAP STEEL** MAHOGANY	560	**430**	380	335
STGUIT	58	GIBSON	**BR-6 LAP STEEL** SUNBURST	570	**437**	386	341
STGUIT	50	GIBSON	**BR-9 LAP STEEL** BEIGE, SERIAL #A4400-A6000	642	**493**	436	384
STGUIT	51	GIBSON	**BR-9 LAP STEEL** SUNBURST	620	**476**	421	371
STGUIT	52	GIBSON	**BR-9 LAP STEEL** BEIGE	666	**511**	452	398
STGUIT	53	GIBSON	**BR-9 LAP STEEL** SUNBURST	745	**572**	506	446
STGUIT	54	GIBSON	**BR-9 LAP STEEL** SUNBURST	757	**581**	513	452
STGUIT	56	GIBSON	**BR-9 LAP STEEL** BEIGE	724	**556**	491	433
STGUIT	57	GIBSON	**BR-9 LAP STEEL** BEIGE	724	**556**	491	433
STGUIT	58	GIBSON	**BR-9 LAP STEEL**	570	**437**	386	341
STGUIT	54	GIBSON	**CENTURY** SALMON	724	**556**	491	433
STGUIT	56	GIBSON	**CENTURY 6 LAP STEEL** 6-STRING	781	**600**	530	467
STGUIT	57	GIBSON	**CENTURY 6 LAP STEEL** 6-STRING, SERIAL #A24600-A26500	745	**572**	506	446
STGUIT	61	GIBSON	**CENTURY 6 LAP STEEL** 6-STRING	716	**550**	486	428
STGUIT	48	GIBSON	**CENTURY 10 LAP STEEL** BLACK, 10-STRING, 1 PU	724	**556**	491	433
STGUIT	55	GIBSON	**CENTURY 10 LAP STEEL** 10-STRING	693	**532**	470	414
STGUIT	56	GIBSON	**CENTURY 10 LAP STEEL** 10-STRING, SERIAL #A22000-A24600	848	**651**	576	507
STGUIT	56	GIBSON	**CG 520 DOUBLE NECK STEEL** NATURAL, 8-STRING	1,263	**970**	857	755
STGUIT	64	GIBSON	**CG 520 DOUBLE NECK STEEL** NATURAL, 8-STRING	1,579	**1,212**	1,071	944
STGUIT	59	GIBSON	**CG 523 STEEL** NATURAL, 8-STRING, TRIPLE NECK	1,239	**952**	841	741
STGUIT	35	GIBSON	**CONSOLE GRANDE** SUNBURST, 2 PU, (1)7-STRING, (1)8-STRING	1,239	**952**	841	741
STGUIT	39	GIBSON	**CONSOLE GRANDE 2** NATURAL, 8-STRING, SERIAL #95400-96000	948	**728**	643	567
STGUIT	46	GIBSON	**CONSOLE GRANDE 2** SUNBURST, 8-STRING	852	**654**	578	509
STGUIT	49	GIBSON	**CONSOLE GRANDE 2** SUNBURST, 8-STRING, SERIAL #A2800-A4400	753	**578**	511	450
STGUIT	50	GIBSON	**CONSOLE GRANDE 2** MAPLE, 8-STRING	757	**581**	513	452
STGUIT	51	GIBSON	**CONSOLE GRANDE 2** SUNBURST, 8-STRING	753	**578**	511	450

TYPE	YR	MFG	PRICES--BASED ON 100% ORIGINAL MODEL	SELL EXC	SELL AVG	BUY EXC	BUY AVG
STGUIT	52	GIBSON	**CONSOLE GRANDE 2** SUNBURST, 8-STRING, SERIAL #A9400-A13000	723	**555**	490	432
STGUIT	53	GIBSON	**CONSOLE GRANDE 2** SUNBURST, 8-STRING	717	**551**	487	429
STGUIT	52	GIBSON	**CONSOLETTE 2** KORINA WOOD, 8-STRING, SERIAL #A9400-13000	1,067	**819**	724	638
STGUIT	53	GIBSON	**CONSOLETTE 2** KORINA WOOD, 8-STRING	1,009	**774**	684	603
STGUIT	54	GIBSON	**CONSOLETTE 2** KORINA WOOD, 8-STRING	1,001	**768**	679	598
STGUIT	55	GIBSON	**CONSOLETTE 2** KORINA WOOD, 8-STRING	883	**678**	599	528
STGUIT	36	GIBSON	**EH-100 LAP STEEL** BLACK	884	**679**	600	529
STGUIT	36	GIBSON	**EH-100 LAP STEEL** SUNBURST	975	**749**	661	583
STGUIT	38	GIBSON	**EH-100 LAP STEEL** BLACK, BAR PU	817	**627**	554	489
STGUIT	39	GIBSON	**EH-100 LAP STEEL** SUNBURST	700	**537**	475	418
STGUIT	40	GIBSON	**EH-100 LAP STEEL** SUNBURST	724	**556**	491	433
STGUIT	38	GIBSON	**EH-125 LAP STEEL** BLACK	842	**646**	571	503
STGUIT	39	GIBSON	**EH-125 LAP STEEL** SUNBURST	789	**606**	535	472
STGUIT	40	GIBSON	**EH-125 LAP STEEL** SUNBURST	665	**510**	451	397
STGUIT	35	GIBSON	**EH-150 CHARLIE** SUNBURST, CHRISTIAN PU	973	**747**	660	582
STGUIT	36	GIBSON	**EH-150 CHARLIE** SUNBURST, CHRISTIAN PU	1,006	**773**	683	602
STGUIT	37	GIBSON	**EH-150 CHARLIE** SUNBURST, CHRISTIAN PU, SERIAL #95400	991	**761**	672	592
STGUIT	38	GIBSON	**EH-150 CHARLIE** SUNBURST, CHRISTIAN PU	817	**627**	554	489
STGUIT	39	GIBSON	**EH-150 CHARLIE** SUNBURST, CHRISTIAN PU	801	**615**	544	479
STGUIT	40	GIBSON	**EH-150 CHARLIE** ORANGE, CHRISTIAN PU	781	**600**	530	467
STGUIT	40	GIBSON	**EH-150 CHARLIE** SUNBURST, CHRISTIAN PU	792	**608**	538	474
STGUIT	39	GIBSON	**EH-185 LAP STEEL** SUNBURST	1,070	**822**	726	640
STGUIT	40	GIBSON	**EH-185 LAP STEEL** SUNBURST	955	**733**	648	571
STGUIT	40	GIBSON	**EH-185 LAP STEEL** SUNBURST	1,046	**803**	709	625
STGUIT	41	GIBSON	**EH-185 LAP STEEL** SUNBURST	990	**760**	671	592
STGUIT	42	GIBSON	**EH-185 LAP STEEL** SUNBURST	978	**751**	664	585
STGUIT	60	GIBSON	**EH-820 LAP STEEL**	833	**639**	565	498
STGUIT	39	GIBSON	**ELECTRAHARP** 8-STRING	1,350	**1,037**	916	808
STGUIT	41	GIBSON	**ELECTRAHARP** 8-STRING	1,263	**970**	857	755
STGUIT	49	GIBSON	**ELECTRAHARP** MAPLE, 8-STRING	984	**755**	668	588
STGUIT	53	GIBSON	**ELECTRAHARP** 8-STRING	901	**692**	611	539
STGUIT	60	GIBSON	**ELECTRAHARP** SUNBURST, 8-STRING	771	**592**	523	461
STGUIT	63	GIBSON	**ELECTRAHARP** 8-STRING	768	**589**	521	459
STGUIT	37	GIBSON	**HG-CENTURY HAWAIIAN** SUNBURST	2,195	**1,685**	1,489	1,313
STGUIT	39	GIBSON	**KALAMAZOO** BAR PU	554	**425**	376	331
STGUIT	68	GIBSON	**MODEL 400 PEDAL STEEL** SUNBURST	1,317	**1,011**	893	787
STGUIT	49	GIBSON	**PEDAL HARP** MAPLE, 8-STRING, 4-PEDAL	1,366	**1,049**	927	817
STGUIT	56	GIBSON	**SKYHAWK LAP STEEL** NATURAL, KORINA	773	**594**	525	462
STGUIT	56	GIBSON	**SKYHAWK LAP STEEL** NATURAL, KORINA	792	**608**	538	474
STGUIT	56	GIBSON	**SKYLARK LAP STEEL** NATURAL, KORINA	751	**577**	509	449
STGUIT	57	GIBSON	**SKYLARK LAP STEEL** NATURAL, KORINA	754	**579**	512	451
STGUIT	58	GIBSON	**SKYLARK LAP STEEL** NATURAL, KORINA	692	**531**	469	414

TYPE	YR	MFG	PRICES--BASED ON 100% ORIGINAL MODEL	SELL EXC	SELL AVG	BUY EXC	BUY AVG
STGUIT	59	GIBSON	**SKYLARK LAP STEEL** NATURAL, KORINA	670	**515**	455	401
STGUIT	60	GIBSON	**SKYLARK LAP STEEL** NATURAL, KORINA	706	**542**	479	422
STGUIT	61	GIBSON	**SKYLARK LAP STEEL** NATURAL, KORINA	666	**511**	452	398
STGUIT	62	GIBSON	**SKYLARK LAP STEEL** NATURAL, KORINA	617	**473**	418	369
STGUIT	64	GIBSON	**SKYLARK LAP STEEL** NATURAL, KORINA	565	**434**	383	338
STGUIT	66	GIBSON	**SKYLARK LAP STEEL** NATURAL, KORINA	502	**386**	341	300
STGUIT	48	GIBSON	**ULTRATONE 6 LAP STEEL** WHITE, 6-STRING	754	**579**	512	451
STGUIT	50	GIBSON	**ULTRATONE 6 LAP STEEL** BLACK, 6-STRING	693	**532**	470	414
STGUIT	53	GIBSON	**ULTRATONE 6 LAP STEEL** BLUE GREEN, 6-STRING	731	**561**	496	437
UKULELE	29	GIBSON	**TU** TENOR	1,260	**967**	855	753
UKE	30	GIBSON	**TU** TENOR	889	**682**	603	531
UKE	39	GIBSON	**TU** TENOR	756	**580**	513	452
UKE	50	GIBSON	**TU-1** TENOR	734	**564**	498	439
UKE	53	GIBSON	**TU-1** TENOR	734	**564**	498	439
UKE	55	GIBSON	**TU-1** TENOR	632	**485**	429	378
UKE	56	GIBSON	**TU-1** TENOR	632	**485**	429	378
UKE	58	GIBSON	**TU-1** TENOR	669	**514**	454	400
UKE	25	GIBSON	**UKE-1** PLAIN, NO BINDING	712	**546**	483	426
UKE	30	GIBSON	**UKE-1** MAHOGANY	745	**572**	506	446
UKE	34	GIBSON	**UKE-1** SUNBURST	710	**545**	481	424
UKE	27	GIBSON	**UKE-2** MAHOGANY	697	**535**	473	417
UKE	30	GIBSON	**UKE-2** TRIPLE BOUND	554	**425**	376	331
UKE	28	GIBSON	**UKE-3** MAHOGANY	700	**537**	475	418

GLAESEL, DIST by CONN-SELMER INC

TYPE	YR	MFG	MODEL	SELL EXC	SELL AVG	BUY EXC	BUY AVG
CELLO	78	GLAESEL	**DB-70 DOUBLE BASS** 3/4, INSTRUMENT ONLY, HANDCRAFTED, SPRUCE TOP MAPLE B/S	7,889	**6,057**	5,353	4,719

GLEEMAN

TYPE	YR	MFG	MODEL	SELL EXC	SELL AVG	BUY EXC	BUY AVG
SYNTHESIZER	82	GLEE	**PENTAPHONIC** BLACK, CLEAR	1,961	**1,505**	1,330	1,173

GOWER

TYPE	YR	MFG	MODEL	SELL EXC	SELL AVG	BUY EXC	BUY AVG
GUITAR (ACOUSTIC)	65	GOWER	**DREADNOUGHT** NATURAL	465	**357**	316	278
GUITAR	60	GOWER	**G-55-2** 3-PIECE MAHOGANY BACK	613	**471**	416	367
GUITAR	65	GOWER	**G-55-2** SUNBURST, BRAZILIAN ROSEWOOD BACK/SIDES	551	**423**	373	329
GUITAR	60	GOWER	**G-65** NATURAL, MAHOGANY BACK/SIDES	608	**466**	412	363

GOYA by MARTIN GUITAR CO

TYPE	YR	MFG	MODEL	SELL EXC	SELL AVG	BUY EXC	BUY AVG
ELEC. GUITAR & BASS	69	GOYA	**JAGUAR** 2 PU's, CHERRY SUNBURST	235	**180**	159	140
ELGUIT	69	GOYA	**JAGUAR BASS** 2 PU's, RED TO BLACK SUNBURST	227	**174**	154	136
ELGUIT	65	GOYA	**P-26** 4-PRESETS, 2 PU's	343	**264**	233	205
ELGUIT	62	GOYA	**P-46** 6-PRESETS, 4 PU's	472	**362**	320	282
ELGUIT	60	GOYA	**PANTHER** WHITE, VIBRATO, 3 PU's	160	**122**	108	95
ELGUIT	68	GOYA	**PANTHER** 2 PU's	183	**141**	124	109
ELGUIT	68	GOYA	**PANTHER BASS**	155	**119**	105	93
ELGUIT	60	GOYA	**RANGEMASTER** LIME GREEN	160	**122**	108	95
ELGUIT	64	GOYA	**RANGEMASTER** SUNBURST	162	**124**	110	97
ELGUIT	65	GOYA	**RANGEMASTER**	229	**176**	155	137

TYPE	YR	MFG	PRICES--BASED ON 100% ORIGINAL MODEL	SELL EXC	SELL AVG	BUY EXC	BUY AVG
ELGUIT	67	GOYA	RANGEMASTER RED TO BLACK SUNBURST, 2 PU's	155	119	105	93
ELGUIT	67	GOYA	RANGEMASTER RED TO BLACK SUNBURST	163	125	110	97
ELGUIT	67	GOYA	RANGEMASTER 2 PU's, SEMI-HOLLOW, CUTAWAY	180	138	122	107
ELGUIT	68	GOYA	RANGEMASTER CHERRY SUNBURST	155	119	105	93
ELGUIT	69	GOYA	RANGEMASTER 2 PU's	155	119	105	93
ELGUIT	60	GOYA	RANGEMASTER 12-STRING SUNBURST	670	515	455	401
ELGUIT	62	GOYA	SPARKLE SOLID BODY, INLAY, 2 PU's	842	646	571	503
GUITAR (ACOUSTIC)	60	GOYA	F-11 WHITE, DOUBLE PICKGUARD	608	466	412	363
GUITAR	65	GOYA	GG-10 CLASSICAL	191	147	129	114
GUITAR	72	GOYA	N-26 SUNBURST, DREADNOUGHT	598	459	405	357

GRAMMER

TYPE	YR	MFG	MODEL	SELL EXC	SELL AVG	BUY EXC	BUY AVG
GUITAR (ACOUSTIC)	67	GRAMMER	DREADNOUGHT BRAZILIAN ROSEWOOD BACK/SIDES	1,834	1,408	1,244	1,097
GUITAR	67	GRAMMER	G-10 NATURAL	922	708	626	552
GUITAR	68	GRAMMER	G-10 SUNBURST, BRAZILIAN ROSEWOOD BACK/SIDES	712	546	483	426
GUITAR	68	GRAMMER	G-10 ROSEWOOD BODY, FLATTOP	1,319	1,013	895	789
GUITAR	69	GRAMMER	G-10 SUNBURST, FLATTOP	672	508	448	371
GUITAR	69	GRAMMER	G-10 NATURAL	857	658	582	513
GUITAR	70	GRAMMER	G-10 NATURAL, ROSEWOOD BACK/SIDES	739	567	501	442
GUITAR	66	GRAMMER	G-20 MAPLE BODY, FLATTOP	652	501	443	390
GUITAR	67	GRAMMER	G-20 NATURAL, FLATTOP	703	540	477	420
GUITAR	68	GRAMMER	G-20 NATURAL, FLATTOP	558	429	379	334
GUITAR	66	GRAMMER	G-30 MAHOGANY, FLATTOP	601	461	408	359
GUITAR	67	GRAMMER	G-30 MAHOGANY, FLATTOP	715	549	485	428
GUITAR	68	GRAMMER	G-58 FLATTOP	740	568	502	442
GUITAR	70	GRAMMER	G-S	3,304	2,537	2,242	1,976
GUITAR	68	GRAMMER	H-10 MERLE HAGGARD MODEL FLATTOP	880	665	587	486
GUITAR	70	GRAMMER	PROTOTYPE BRAZILIAN ROSEWOOD, FLATTOP	1,448	1,095	965	801
GUITAR	68	GRAMMER	S-20 NATURAL, MAPLE BACK/SIDES	650	491	433	359
GUITAR	65	GRAMMER	S-30 MAHOGANY BACK/SIDES, FLATTOP	616	473	418	368
GUITAR	67	GRAMMER	S-40 NATURAL, AFRICAN WALNUT BACK/SIDES, FLATTOP	670	515	455	401

GRETSCH

TYPE	YR	MFG	MODEL	SELL EXC	SELL AVG	BUY EXC	BUY AVG
BANJO	61	GRETSCH	APPALACHIA MOUNTAIN BOWL 5-STRING TENOR, RESONATOR, WALNUT NECK	997	766	677	596
BANJO	52	GRETSCH	B&D SENORITA PEARLOID PEGHEAD VENEER, FINGERBOARD, RIM, RESONATOR	1,061	815	720	635
BANJO	66	GRETSCH	BACON LONG NECK, OPEN BACK	1,221	938	829	730
BANJO	55	GRETSCH	BACON BELMONT ORIGINAL 5-STRING	1,268	974	861	759
BANJO	60	GRETSCH	BACON FOLK MODEL 5-STRING, OPEN BACK	1,290	990	875	771
BANJO	61	GRETSCH	KENTUCKY MOUNTAIN BOWL 5-STRING, RESONATOR, WALNUT NECK	937	719	636	560
BANJO	50	GRETSCH	NEW YORKER TENOR	842	646	571	503
BANJO	51	GRETSCH	NEW YORKER	505	387	342	302
BANJO	79	GRETSCH	ODE STYLE D	735	565	499	440
BANJO	25	GRETSCH	ORCHESTRELLA TENOR, PEGHEAD INLAY	911	700	618	545
BANJO	29	GRETSCH	PRESIDENT TENOR,WALNUT NECK,ORNAMENTAL ENGRVNG,PEARLOID PEGHEAD	1,002	769	680	599
BANJO	56	GRETSCH	TENNESSEE MOUNTAIN BOWL 5-STRING, RESONATOR	930	714	631	556
BANJO	69	GRETSCH	TENOR 5-STRING	665	510	451	397

TYPE	YR	MFG	MODEL	SELL EXC	SELL AVG	BUY EXC	BUY AVG
ELEC. GUITAR & BASS	60	GRETSCH	12-STRING SUNBURST	822	631	557	491
ELGUIT	36	GRETSCH	65 AMBER	810	622	550	485
ELGUIT	69	GRETSCH	6009 JUMBO SUNBURST	672	516	456	402
ELGUIT	67	GRETSCH	6071 BASS MAHOGANY, HOLLOW, SINGLE CUTAWAY 1 PU	1,069	821	725	639
ELGUIT	68	GRETSCH	6071 BASS MAHOGANY, HOLLOW, SINGLE CUTAWAY, 1 PU	636	488	431	380
ELGUIT	68	GRETSCH	6072 BASS SUNBURST, HOLLOW, DOUBLE CUTAWAY, 2 PU's	1,251	960	848	748
ELGUIT	69	GRETSCH	6072 BASS SUNBURST, HOLLOW, DOUBLE CUTAWAY, 2 PU's	668	513	453	399
ELGUIT	69	GRETSCH	6072 BASS SUNBURST, LONG SCALE, 34" LENGTH, 17" WIDE BODY	950	730	645	568
ELGUIT	68	GRETSCH	6073 BASS MAHOGANY, HOLLOW, SINGLE CUTAWAY, 2 PU's	647	497	439	387
ELGUIT	66	GRETSCH	6075 SUNBURST, 12-STRING	650	499	441	389
ELGUIT	67	GRETSCH	6075 SUNBURST, 12-STRING	647	497	439	387
ELGUIT	68	GRETSCH	6075 SUNBURST, 12-STRING	812	623	551	485
ELGUIT	69	GRETSCH	6076 NATURAL, 12-STRING	611	469	414	365
ELGUIT	55	GRETSCH	6120	3,875	2,975	2,629	2,318
ELGUIT	63	GRETSCH	6162	389	299	264	233
ELGUIT	57	GRETSCH	6187 METALLIC GREY BACK/SIDES, CUTAWAY	932	716	633	558
ELGUIT	81	GRETSCH	7010 FENDER STYLE 1 PU	103	79	69	61
ELGUIT	81	GRETSCH	7012 S.G. STYLE 1 PU	103	79	69	61
ELGUIT	58	GRETSCH	ANNIVERSARY 6124 SUNBURST	745	572	506	446
ELGUIT	59	GRETSCH	ANNIVERSARY 6124 SUNBURST	708	544	481	424
ELGUIT	60	GRETSCH	ANNIVERSARY 6124 SUNBURST	628	482	426	375
ELGUIT	61	GRETSCH	ANNIVERSARY 6124 SUNBURST	619	475	420	370
ELGUIT	62	GRETSCH	ANNIVERSARY 6124 SUNBURST	672	516	456	402
ELGUIT	64	GRETSCH	ANNIVERSARY 6124 SUNBURST	655	503	444	391
ELGUIT	65	GRETSCH	ANNIVERSARY 6124 SUNBURST	604	464	410	361
ELGUIT	67	GRETSCH	ANNIVERSARY 6124 SUNBURST	596	458	405	357
ELGUIT	67	GRETSCH	ANNIVERSARY 6124 SUNBURST, LEFT-HANDED	621	477	421	371
ELGUIT	71	GRETSCH	ANNIVERSARY 6124 SUNBURST	647	497	439	387
ELGUIT	58	GRETSCH	ANNIVERSARY 6125 SMOKE GREEN 2-TONE	1,336	1,025	906	799
ELGUIT	59	GRETSCH	ANNIVERSARY 6125 SMOKE GREEN 2-TONE	739	567	501	442
ELGUIT	62	GRETSCH	ANNIVERSARY 6125 SMOKE GREEN 2-TONE	720	552	488	430
ELGUIT	63	GRETSCH	ANNIVERSARY 6125 SMOKE GREEN 2-TONE	679	522	461	406
ELGUIT	64	GRETSCH	ANNIVERSARY 6125 SMOKE GREEN 2-TONE	740	568	502	442
ELGUIT	67	GRETSCH	ANNIVERSARY 6125 SMOKE GREEN 2-TONE	657	504	446	393
ELGUIT	68	GRETSCH	ANNIVERSARY 6125 SMOKE GREEN 2-TONE	618	474	419	369
ELGUIT	70	GRETSCH	ANNIVERSARY 6125 SMOKE GREEN 2-TONE	611	469	414	365
ELGUIT	65	GRETSCH	ASTRO JET 6126 RED, BLACK BACK/SIDES	585	449	397	350
ELGUIT	66	GRETSCH	ASTRO JET 6126 RED, BLACK BACK/SIDES	579	444	392	346
ELGUIT	67	GRETSCH	ASTRO JET 6126 RED, BLACK BACK/SIDES	611	469	414	365
ELGUIT	61	GRETSCH	BIKINI 6023 BLACK	397	305	269	237
ELGUIT	62	GRETSCH	BIKINI 6023 BLACK	327	251	221	195
ELGUIT	62	GRETSCH	BIKINI 6024 BASS BLACK	437	336	297	261
ELGUIT	61	GRETSCH	BIKINI 6025 BLACK, DOUBLE NECK	975	749	661	583

TYPE	YR	MFG	PRICES--BASED ON 100% ORIGINAL MODEL	SELL EXC	SELL AVG	BUY EXC	BUY AVG
ELGUIT	68	GRETSCH	**BLACK HAWK** BLACK	3,589	**2,756**	2,435	2,147
ELGUIT	69	GRETSCH	**BLACKHAWK 6101** BLACK, FLOATING BRIDGE	574	**441**	389	343
ELGUIT	69	GRETSCH	**BOSSA NOVA CLASSICAL ELECTRIC**	639	**491**	433	382
ELGUIT	75	GRETSCH	**BROADKASTER** SOLID BODY	729	**559**	494	436
ELGUIT	75	GRETSCH	**BROADKASTER** HOLLOW BODY	800	**614**	543	479
ELGUIT	78	GRETSCH	**BROADKASTER** SOLID BODY	789	**606**	535	472
ELGUIT	79	GRETSCH	**BROADKASTER** HOLLOWBODY	710	**545**	481	424
ELGUIT	79	GRETSCH	**BST-1000**	430	**330**	291	257
ELGUIT	80	GRETSCH	**BST-1000**	415	**319**	281	248
ELGUIT	79	GRETSCH	**BST-2000**	389	**299**	264	233
ELGUIT	80	GRETSCH	**BST-2000** WALNUT BROWN	396	**304**	269	237
ELGUIT	78	GRETSCH	**BST-5000** NATURAL	400	**307**	272	239
ELGUIT	79	GRETSCH	**BST-5000** NATURAL	368	**282**	250	220
ELGUIT	80	GRETSCH	**BST-5000** NATURAL	338	**259**	229	202
ELGUIT	76	GRETSCH	**CHET ATKINS AXE** ROSEWOOD	875	**672**	594	523
ELGUIT	79	GRETSCH	**CHET ATKINS AXE**	955	**733**	648	571
ELGUIT	70	GRETSCH	**CHET ATKINS JUNIOR** ORANGE	764	**587**	519	457
ELGUIT	77	GRETSCH	**CHET ATKINS SUPER AXE** BLACK	701	**538**	475	419
ELGUIT	80	GRETSCH	**CHET ATKINS SUPER AXE**	820	**679**	585	484
ELGUIT	58	GRETSCH	**CHET ATKINS 6119 TENNESSEAN**	1,634	**1,254**	1,108	977
ELGUIT	59	GRETSCH	**CHET ATKINS 6119 TENNESSEAN**	1,621	**1,245**	1,100	970
ELGUIT	60	GRETSCH	**CHET ATKINS 6119 TENNESSEAN**	1,545	**1,186**	1,048	924
ELGUIT	61	GRETSCH	**CHET ATKINS 6119 TENNESSEAN**	1,711	**1,314**	1,161	1,023
ELGUIT	62	GRETSCH	**CHET ATKINS 6119 TENNESSEAN**	1,688	**1,296**	1,146	1,010
ELGUIT	63	GRETSCH	**CHET ATKINS 6119 TENNESSEAN**	1,682	**1,291**	1,141	1,006
ELGUIT	64	GRETSCH	**CHET ATKINS 6119 TENNESSEAN**	1,643	**1,261**	1,114	982
ELGUIT	65	GRETSCH	**CHET ATKINS 6119 TENNESSEAN**	1,561	**1,198**	1,059	933
ELGUIT	66	GRETSCH	**CHET ATKINS 6119 TENNESSEAN**	1,373	**1,054**	931	821
ELGUIT	67	GRETSCH	**CHET ATKINS 6119 TENNESSEAN**	1,357	**1,042**	921	812
ELGUIT	68	GRETSCH	**CHET ATKINS 6119 TENNESSEAN**	1,339	**1,028**	908	801
ELGUIT	69	GRETSCH	**CHET ATKINS 6119 TENNESSEAN**	1,321	**1,014**	896	790
ELGUIT	71	GRETSCH	**CHET ATKINS 6119 TENNESSEAN**	1,303	**1,001**	884	779
ELGUIT	72	GRETSCH	**CHET ATKINS 6119 TENNESSEAN**	1,293	**993**	877	773
ELGUIT	75	GRETSCH	**CHET ATKINS 6119 TENNESSEAN**	1,288	**989**	874	770
ELGUIT	54	GRETSCH	**CHET ATKINS 6120 NASHVILLE**	6,213	**4,771**	4,216	3,717
ELGUIT	55	GRETSCH	**CHET ATKINS 6120 NASHVILLE** WHITE CASS COWBOY STRAP, COW & CACTUS INLAYS	6,391	**4,908**	4,337	3,823
ELGUIT	56	GRETSCH	**CHET ATKINS 6120 NASHVILLE** HOLLOW BODY	5,976	**4,588**	4,055	3,575
ELGUIT	57	GRETSCH	**CHET ATKINS 6120 NASHVILLE**	5,630	**4,323**	3,820	3,368
ELGUIT	58	GRETSCH	**CHET ATKINS 6120 NASHVILLE** HOLLOW BODY	5,280	**4,054**	3,583	3,159
ELGUIT	59	GRETSCH	**CHET ATKINS 6120 NASHVILLE** HOLLOW BODY	5,268	**4,045**	3,575	3,151
ELGUIT	60	GRETSCH	**CHET ATKINS 6120 NASHVILLE** ORANGE, HOLLOW BODY	4,167	**3,200**	2,827	2,493
ELGUIT	61	GRETSCH	**CHET ATKINS 6120 NASHVILLE** THINBODY	1,518	**1,166**	1,030	908
ELGUIT	62	GRETSCH	**CHET ATKINS 6120 NASHVILLE**	1,516	**1,164**	1,029	907
ELGUIT	63	GRETSCH	**CHET ATKINS 6120 NASHVILLE**	1,500	**1,152**	1,018	897
ELGUIT	64	GRETSCH	**CHET ATKINS 6120 NASHVILLE**	1,495	**1,148**	1,014	894
ELGUIT	65	GRETSCH	**CHET ATKINS 6120 NASHVILLE**	1,435	**1,102**	974	858
ELGUIT	66	GRETSCH	**CHET ATKINS 6120 NASHVILLE**	1,420	**1,090**	963	849
ELGUIT	67	GRETSCH	**CHET ATKINS 6120 NASHVILLE**	1,382	**1,061**	937	826
ELGUIT	68	GRETSCH	**CHET ATKINS 6120 NASHVILLE**	1,374	**1,055**	932	822
ELGUIT	69	GRETSCH	**CHET ATKINS 6120 NASHVILLE**	1,350	**1,037**	916	808
ELGUIT	72	GRETSCH	**CHET ATKINS 6120 NASHVILLE**	754	**579**	512	451
ELGUIT	73	GRETSCH	**CHET ATKINS 6120 NASHVILLE**	739	**567**	501	442
ELGUIT	79	GRETSCH	**CHET ATKINS 6120 NASHVILLE**	701	**538**	475	419
ELGUIT	55	GRETSCH	**CHET ATKINS 6121** SOLID BODY	5,047	**3,876**	3,425	3,019
ELGUIT	56	GRETSCH	**CHET ATKINS 6121** SOLID BODY	4,762	**3,656**	3,231	2,848
ELGUIT	57	GRETSCH	**CHET ATKINS 6121** SOLID BODY	4,346	**3,337**	2,949	2,600
ELGUIT	58	GRETSCH	**CHET ATKINS 6121** SOLID BODY	4,598	**3,531**	3,120	2,751

TYPE	YR	MFG	PRICES--BASED ON 100% ORIGINAL MODEL	SELL EXC	SELL AVG	BUY EXC	BUY AVG
ELGUIT	58	GRETSCH	CHET ATKINS 6121 SOLID BODY, LEFT-HANDED	4,716	3,621	3,200	2,821
ELGUIT	59	GRETSCH	CHET ATKINS 6121 SOLID BODY	4,683	3,596	3,178	2,801
ELGUIT	60	GRETSCH	CHET ATKINS 6121 SOLID BODY	4,431	3,403	3,007	2,651
ELGUIT	62	GRETSCH	CHET ATKINS 6121 SOLID BOLDY	4,378	3,361	2,970	2,619
ELGUIT	57	GRETSCH	CHET ATKINS 6122 COUNTRY GENT	4,242	3,257	2,878	2,537
ELGUIT	58	GRETSCH	CHET ATKINS 6122 COUNTRY GENT	4,137	3,176	2,807	2,474
ELGUIT	59	GRETSCH	CHET ATKINS 6122 COUNTRY GENT	3,239	2,487	2,197	1,937
ELGUIT	60	GRETSCH	CHET ATKINS 6122 COUNTRY GENT LEFT-HANDED	3,505	2,691	2,378	2,097
ELGUIT	61	GRETSCH	CHET ATKINS 6122 COUNTRY GENT	2,380	1,827	1,615	1,423
ELGUIT	62	GRETSCH	CHET ATKINS 6122 COUNTRY GENT	2,878	2,210	1,953	1,721
ELGUIT	63	GRETSCH	CHET ATKINS 6122 COUNTRY GENT	2,457	1,886	1,667	1,469
ELGUIT	64	GRETSCH	CHET ATKINS 6122 COUNTRY GENT	2,427	1,863	1,646	1,451
ELGUIT	65	GRETSCH	CHET ATKINS 6122 COUNTRY GENT	2,325	1,785	1,577	1,390
ELGUIT	66	GRETSCH	CHET ATKINS 6122 COUNTRY GENT	2,300	1,766	1,561	1,376
ELGUIT	67	GRETSCH	CHET ATKINS 6122 COUNTRY GENT WALNUT	2,276	1,748	1,545	1,362
ELGUIT	69	GRETSCH	CHET ATKINS 6122 COUNTRY GENT	2,250	1,727	1,526	1,346
ELGUIT	70	GRETSCH	CHET ATKINS 6122 COUNTRY GENT	1,900	1,459	1,289	1,136
ELGUIT	71	GRETSCH	CHET ATKINS 6122 COUNTRY GENT	1,886	1,448	1,279	1,128
ELGUIT	72	GRETSCH	CHET ATKINS 6122 COUNTRY GENT	1,861	1,429	1,263	1,113
ELGUIT	73	GRETSCH	CHET ATKINS 6122 COUNTRY GENT	1,828	1,404	1,241	1,094
ELGUIT	74	GRETSCH	CHET ATKINS 6122 COUNTRY GENT	1,674	1,285	1,136	1,001
ELGUIT	75	GRETSCH	CHET ATKINS 6122 COUNTRY GENT	1,653	1,269	1,121	988
ELGUIT	76	GRETSCH	CHET ATKINS 6122 COUNTRY GENT	1,626	1,248	1,103	972
ELGUIT	79	GRETSCH	CHET ATKINS 6122 COUNTRY GENT	638	490	433	381
ELGUIT	71	GRETSCH	CLIPPER 1 PU	542	416	367	324
ELGUIT	56	GRETSCH	CLIPPER 6186 SUNBURST	575	442	390	344
ELGUIT	57	GRETSCH	CLIPPER 6186 SUNBURST	580	445	393	347
ELGUIT	58	GRETSCH	CLIPPER 6186 SUNBURST	712	546	483	426
ELGUIT	59	GRETSCH	CLIPPER 6186 SUNBURST	673	516	456	402
ELGUIT	60	GRETSCH	CLIPPER 6186 SUNBURST	611	469	414	365
ELGUIT	61	GRETSCH	CLIPPER 6186 SUNBURST	603	463	409	361
ELGUIT	62	GRETSCH	CLIPPER 6186 SUNBURST	570	437	386	341
ELGUIT	63	GRETSCH	CLIPPER 6186 SUNBURST	600	460	407	359
ELGUIT	64	GRETSCH	CLIPPER 6186 SUNBURST	603	463	409	361
ELGUIT	67	GRETSCH	CLIPPER 6186 SUNBURST	491	377	333	294
ELGUIT	69	GRETSCH	CLIPPER 6186 SUNBURST	523	401	354	312
ELGUIT	59	GRETSCH	CLIPPER 6187 NATURAL	712	546	483	426
ELGUIT	72	GRETSCH	CLIPPER 6187 NATURAL	579	444	392	346
ELGUIT	77	GRETSCH	COMMITTEE 7628 NATURAL	460	353	312	275
ELGUIT	77	GRETSCH	COMMITTEE 7628 ROSEWOOD, DOUBLE HB	497	381	337	297
ELGUIT	78	GRETSCH	COMMITTEE 7628 NATURAL	458	351	310	274
ELGUIT	79	GRETSCH	COMMITTEE 7628 NATURAL	412	316	279	246
ELGUIT	55	GRETSCH	CONVERTIBLE 6199 LOTUS IVORY TOP	1,389	1,067	943	831
ELGUIT	56	GRETSCH	CONVERTIBLE 6199 IVORY FINISH TOP,COPPER MIST FINISH B/S/NECK,DBL BOUND	3,818	2,931	2,590	2,284
ELGUIT	57	GRETSCH	CONVERTIBLE 6199 LOTUS IVORY TOP	1,365	1,048	926	816
ELGUIT	56	GRETSCH	CORSAIR NATURAL	712	546	483	426
ELGUIT	60	GRETSCH	CORSAIR	720	552	488	430
ELGUIT	57	GRETSCH	CORVETTE HOLLOWBODY, ELECTROMATIC	741	569	503	443
ELGUIT	76	GRETSCH	CORVETTE SOLID BODY	555	426	376	332
ELGUIT	61	GRETSCH	CORVETTE 6132 MAHOGANY, SOLID BODY, 1 PU	677	520	459	405

TYPE	YR	MFG	PRICES--BASED ON 100% ORIGINAL MODEL	SELL EXC	SELL AVG	BUY EXC	BUY AVG
ELGUIT	62	GRETSCH	**CORVETTE 6132** CHERRY RED, 1 PU	715	**549**	485	428
ELGUIT	63	GRETSCH	**CORVETTE 6132** CHERRY RED, 1 PU	580	**445**	393	347
ELGUIT	64	GRETSCH	**CORVETTE 6132** CHERRY RED, 1 PU	595	**457**	404	356
ELGUIT	65	GRETSCH	**CORVETTE 6132** CHERRY RED, 1 PU	556	**427**	377	332
ELGUIT	66	GRETSCH	**CORVETTE 6132** CHERRY RED, 1 PU	574	**441**	389	343
ELGUIT	62	GRETSCH	**CORVETTE 6134** CHERRY RED, VIBRATO, 1 PU	577	**443**	392	345
ELGUIT	66	GRETSCH	**CORVETTE 6134** CHERRY RED, VIBRATO, 1 PU	604	**464**	410	361
ELGUIT	62	GRETSCH	**CORVETTE 6135** CHERRY RED, 2 PU's	664	**509**	450	397
ELGUIT	64	GRETSCH	**CORVETTE 6135** CHERRY RED, 2 PU's	510	**392**	346	305
ELGUIT	65	GRETSCH	**CORVETTE 6135** CHERRY RED, 2 PU's	549	**422**	373	328
ELGUIT	66	GRETSCH	**CORVETTE 6135** CHERRY RED, 2 PU's	605	**465**	411	362
ELGUIT	68	GRETSCH	**CORVETTE 6135** CHERRY RED, 2 PU's	549	**422**	373	328
ELGUIT	55	GRETSCH	**CORVETTE 6182** SUNBURST, HOLLOW BODY	764	**587**	519	457
ELGUIT	55	GRETSCH	**CORVETTE 6183** NATURAL, HOLLOW BODY	785	**602**	532	469
ELGUIT	56	GRETSCH	**CORVETTE 6183** NATURAL, HOLLOW BODY	769	**590**	522	460
ELGUIT	57	GRETSCH	**CORVETTE 6183** NATURAL, HOLLOW BODY	789	**606**	535	472
ELGUIT	71	GRETSCH	**CORVETTE 6183** SOLID BODY, BIGSBY	642	**493**	436	384
ELGUIT	53	GRETSCH	**COUNTRY CLUB** NATURAL	3,326	**2,554**	2,257	1,989
ELGUIT	53	GRETSCH	**COUNTRY CLUB** CADILLAC GREEN	4,407	**3,384**	2,990	2,636
ELGUIT	54	GRETSCH	**COUNTRY CLUB** NATURAL	3,305	**2,537**	2,242	1,977
ELGUIT	54	GRETSCH	**COUNTRY CLUB** CADILLAC GREEN	3,339	**2,564**	2,266	1,997
ELGUIT	55	GRETSCH	**COUNTRY CLUB** SUNBURST	2,383	**1,830**	1,617	1,425
ELGUIT	55	GRETSCH	**COUNTRY CLUB** NATURAL	2,938	**2,256**	1,994	1,758
ELGUIT	55	GRETSCH	**COUNTRY CLUB** CADILLAC GREEN	4,064	**3,120**	2,758	2,431
ELGUIT	56	GRETSCH	**COUNTRY CLUB** NATURAL	2,153	**1,628**	1,435	1,190
ELGUIT	56	GRETSCH	**COUNTRY CLUB** SUNBURST	2,115	**1,624**	1,435	1,265
ELGUIT	56	GRETSCH	**COUNTRY CLUB** CADILLAC GREEN	3,370	**2,587**	2,286	2,016
ELGUIT	57	GRETSCH	**COUNTRY CLUB** SUNBURST	1,884	**1,447**	1,279	1,127
ELGUIT	57	GRETSCH	**COUNTRY CLUB** NATURAL	2,260	**1,735**	1,533	1,352
ELGUIT	57	GRETSCH	**COUNTRY CLUB** CADILLAC GREEN	3,964	**3,044**	2,690	2,371
ELGUIT	58	GRETSCH	**COUNTRY CLUB** SUNBURST, PROJECT-O-SONIC	3,057	**2,347**	2,074	1,829
ELGUIT	58	GRETSCH	**COUNTRY CLUB** NATURAL	3,318	**2,548**	2,251	1,985
ELGUIT	58	GRETSCH	**COUNTRY CLUB** CADILLAC GREEN	3,654	**2,806**	2,479	2,186
ELGUIT	59	GRETSCH	**COUNTRY CLUB** SUNBURST	1,865	**1,432**	1,266	1,116
ELGUIT	59	GRETSCH	**COUNTRY CLUB** NATURAL	2,192	**1,683**	1,488	1,311
ELGUIT	59	GRETSCH	**COUNTRY CLUB** CADILLAC GREEN	3,423	**2,629**	2,323	2,048
ELGUIT	60	GRETSCH	**COUNTRY CLUB** SUNBURST	1,792	**1,376**	1,216	1,072
ELGUIT	61	GRETSCH	**COUNTRY CLUB** BLOND	1,985	**1,524**	1,347	1,187
ELGUIT	61	GRETSCH	**COUNTRY CLUB** SUNBURST	2,128	**1,634**	1,444	1,273
ELGUIT	61	GRETSCH	**COUNTRY CLUB** CADILLAC GREEN	3,123	**2,398**	2,119	1,868
ELGUIT	62	GRETSCH	**COUNTRY CLUB** SUNBURST	1,682	**1,291**	1,141	1,006
ELGUIT	62	GRETSCH	**COUNTRY CLUB** CADILLAC GREEN	1,870	**1,436**	1,269	1,118

TYPE	YR	MFG	PRICES--BASED ON 100% ORIGINAL MODEL	SELL EXC	SELL AVG	BUY EXC	BUY AVG
ELGUIT	62	GRETSCH	**COUNTRY CLUB** BLOND	2,026	**1,555**	1,374	1,212
ELGUIT	64	GRETSCH	**COUNTRY CLUB** SUNBURST	1,565	**1,202**	1,062	936
ELGUIT	64	GRETSCH	**COUNTRY CLUB** CADILLAC GREEN	1,870	**1,436**	1,269	1,118
ELGUIT	65	GRETSCH	**COUNTRY CLUB** SUNBURST, TRON PU	1,403	**1,077**	952	839
ELGUIT	66	GRETSCH	**COUNTRY CLUB** SUNBURST	1,403	**1,077**	952	839
ELGUIT	67	GRETSCH	**COUNTRY CLUB** NATURAL	1,081	**817**	720	597
ELGUIT	67	GRETSCH	**COUNTRY CLUB** SUNBURST	1,402	**1,076**	951	838
ELGUIT	71	GRETSCH	**COUNTRY CLUB** SUNBURST	922	**708**	626	552
ELGUIT	72	GRETSCH	**COUNTRY CLUB** NATURAL	1,342	**1,031**	911	803
ELGUIT	74	GRETSCH	**COUNTRY CLUB** NATURAL	1,340	**1,029**	909	801
ELGUIT	75	GRETSCH	**COUNTRY CLUB** NATURAL	1,039	**798**	705	621
ELGUIT	76	GRETSCH	**COUNTRY CLUB** SUNBURST	1,421	**1,091**	964	850
ELGUIT	77	GRETSCH	**COUNTRY CLUB** NATURAL	1,311	**1,007**	889	784
ELGUIT	78	GRETSCH	**COUNTRY CLUB** NATURAL	1,296	**995**	880	775
ELGUIT	79	GRETSCH	**COUNTRY CLUB** NATURAL	1,218	**935**	826	728
ELGUIT	79	GRETSCH	**COUNTRY CLUB** BLOND, GOLD HARDWARE	1,268	**974**	861	759
ELGUIT	80	GRETSCH	**COUNTRY CLUB** NATURAL	1,200	**921**	814	718
ELGUIT	57	GRETSCH	**COUNTRY CLUB 6193** NATURAL,CUTAWAY,EBONY FRTBRD,GORVER TUNERS,GOLD HDWR	3,833	**2,943**	2,601	2,293
ELGUIT	64	GRETSCH	**COUNTRY GENTLEMAN BASS 6070** SUNBURST, HOLLOW, DOUBLE CUTAWAY, 1 U	634	**479**	423	350
ELGUIT	64	GRETSCH	**COUNTRY GENTLEMAN BASS 6070** 1 PU	991	**761**	672	592
ELGUIT	68	GRETSCH	**COUNTRY GENTLEMAN BASS 6070** 1 PU	803	**616**	544	480
ELGUIT	72	GRETSCH	**COUNTRY GENTLEMAN BASS 6070** 1 PU	572	**439**	388	342
ELGUIT	74	GRETSCH	**COUNTRY ROC**	1,363	**1,046**	924	815
ELGUIT	78	GRETSCH	**COUNTRY ROC G-BRAND**	1,242	**953**	842	743
ELGUIT	71	GRETSCH	**DOUBLE ANNIVERSARY**	2,016	**1,548**	1,368	1,206
ELGUIT	58	GRETSCH	**DOUBLE ANNIVERSARY 6117** SUNBURST	937	**719**	636	560
ELGUIT	59	GRETSCH	**DOUBLE ANNIVERSARY 6117** SUNBURST	1,526	**1,172**	1,035	913
ELGUIT	60	GRETSCH	**DOUBLE ANNIVERSARY 6117** SUNBURST	807	**620**	547	483
ELGUIT	61	GRETSCH	**DOUBLE ANNIVERSARY 6117** SUNBURST	817	**627**	554	489
ELGUIT	62	GRETSCH	**DOUBLE ANNIVERSARY 6117** SUNBURST	812	**623**	551	485
ELGUIT	64	GRETSCH	**DOUBLE ANNIVERSARY 6117** SUNBURST	754	**579**	512	451
ELGUIT	65	GRETSCH	**DOUBLE ANNIVERSARY 6117** SUNBURST	944	**724**	640	564
ELGUIT	66	GRETSCH	**DOUBLE ANNIVERSARY 6117** SUNBURST	940	**722**	638	562
ELGUIT	67	GRETSCH	**DOUBLE ANNIVERSARY 6117** SUNBURST	940	**722**	638	562
ELGUIT	68	GRETSCH	**DOUBLE ANNIVERSARY 6117** SUNBURST	939	**721**	637	562
ELGUIT	73	GRETSCH	**DOUBLE ANNIVERSARY 6117** SUNBURST	977	**750**	663	584
ELGUIT	58	GRETSCH	**DOUBLE ANNIVERSARY 6118** SMOKE GREEN 2-TONE	1,323	**1,016**	898	791
ELGUIT	59	GRETSCH	**DOUBLE ANNIVERSARY 6118** SMOKE GREEN 2-TONE	992	**761**	673	593
ELGUIT	61	GRETSCH	**DOUBLE ANNIVERSARY 6118** SMOKE GREEN 2-TONE	736	**565**	500	440
ELGUIT	62	GRETSCH	**DOUBLE ANNIVERSARY 6118** SMOKE GREEN 2-TONE	850	**652**	576	508
ELGUIT	63	GRETSCH	**DOUBLE ANNIVERSARY 6118** SMOKE GREEN 2-TONE	864	**663**	586	517
ELGUIT	64	GRETSCH	**DOUBLE ANNIVERSARY 6118** SMOKE GREEN 2-TONE	863	**663**	585	516
ELGUIT	67	GRETSCH	**DOUBLE ANNIVERSARY 6118** SMOKE GREEN 2-TONE	725	**557**	492	434

TYPE	YR	MFG	PRICES--BASED ON 100% ORIGINAL MODEL	SELL EXC	SELL AVG	BUY EXC	BUY AVG
ELGUIT	69	GRETSCH	**DOUBLE ANNIVERSARY 6118** SMOKE GREEN 2-TONE	770	**591**	522	460
ELGUIT	58	GRETSCH	**DOUBLE ANNIVERSARY 7560** SUNBURST	1,378	**1,058**	935	824
ELGUIT	73	GRETSCH	**DOUBLE ANNIVERSARY 7560** SUNBURST	668	**513**	453	399
ELGUIT	59	GRETSCH	**DUO JET 6127** TENOR, 4-STRING	1,608	**1,234**	1,091	962
ELGUIT	54	GRETSCH	**DUO JET 6128** BLACK, 2 PU's	2,332	**1,791**	1,583	1,395
ELGUIT	55	GRETSCH	**DUO JET 6128** BLACK, 2 PU's	1,526	**1,172**	1,035	913
ELGUIT	56	GRETSCH	**DUO JET 6128** BLACK, 2 PU's, BLACK INLAY	3,132	**2,405**	2,125	1,873
ELGUIT	56	GRETSCH	**DUO JET 6128** CADILLAC GREEN, 2 PU's	5,737	**4,405**	3,893	3,432
ELGUIT	57	GRETSCH	**DUO JET 6128** BLACK, 2 PU's	3,316	**2,546**	2,250	1,983
ELGUIT	57	GRETSCH	**DUO JET 6128** CADILLAC GREEN, 2 PU's	4,874	**3,742**	3,307	2,915
ELGUIT	58	GRETSCH	**DUO JET 6128** BLACK, 2 PU's	2,905	**2,230**	1,971	1,737
ELGUIT	59	GRETSCH	**DUO JET 6128** BLACK, 2 PU's	1,526	**1,172**	1,035	913
ELGUIT	60	GRETSCH	**DUO JET 6128** BLACK, 2 PU's	1,676	**1,287**	1,137	1,002
ELGUIT	61	GRETSCH	**DUO JET 6128** BLACK, DOUBLE CUTAWAY	1,338	**1,027**	908	800
ELGUIT	62	GRETSCH	**DUO JET 6128** BLACK, DOUBLE CUTAWAY, 2 PU's	1,305	**1,002**	886	781
ELGUIT	63	GRETSCH	**DUO JET 6128** BLACK, DOUBLE CUTAWAY, 2 PU's	1,450	**1,113**	984	867
ELGUIT	65	GRETSCH	**DUO JET 6128** BLACK, DOUBLE CUTAWAY, 2 PU's	1,059	**813**	718	633
ELGUIT	69	GRETSCH	**DUO JET 6128** BLACK, DOUBLE CUTAWAY, 2 PU's	1,484	**1,139**	1,007	887
ELGUIT	53	GRETSCH	**DUO-JET 6128** BLACK, 2 PU's	3,878	**2,978**	2,631	2,320
ELGUIT	52	GRETSCH	**ELECTRO II 6193** SUNBURST, CUTAWAY	2,919	**2,242**	1,981	1,746
ELGUIT	53	GRETSCH	**ELECTRO II 6193** SUNBURST, CUTAWAY	1,634	**1,254**	1,108	977
ELGUIT	56	GRETSCH	**ELECTROMATIC** SUNBURST	1,283	**985**	870	767
ELGUIT	48	GRETSCH	**ELECTROMATIC 6185** SUNBURST, NON-CUTAWAY	922	**708**	626	552
ELGUIT	51	GRETSCH	**ELECTROMATIC 6185** SUNBURST, CUTAWAY	720	**552**	488	430
ELGUIT	51	GRETSCH	**ELECTROMATIC 6185** NATURAL, NON-CUTAWAY	922	**708**	626	552
ELGUIT	51	GRETSCH	**ELECTROMATIC 6185** CUTAWAY, 2 PU's	1,010	**775**	685	604
ELGUIT	52	GRETSCH	**ELECTROMATIC 6185** SUNBURST, NON-CUTAWAY	922	**708**	626	552
ELGUIT	52	GRETSCH	**ELECTROMATIC 6185** NATURAL, CUTAWAY	1,034	**794**	702	619
ELGUIT	53	GRETSCH	**ELECTROMATIC 6185** NATURAL, CUTAWAY	1,019	**782**	691	609
ELGUIT	54	GRETSCH	**ELECTROMATIC 6185** TENOR, SUNBURST	807	**620**	547	483
ELGUIT	54	GRETSCH	**ELECTROMATIC 6185** PLECTRUM, BLOND	1,295	**995**	879	775
ELGUIT	56	GRETSCH	**ELECTROMATIC 6185** TENOR, NATURAL	1,276	**980**	866	763
ELGUIT	54	GRETSCH	**ELECTROMATIC 6190-1** SUNBURST	1,803	**1,384**	1,223	1,078
ELGUIT	66	GRETSCH	**GOLD DUKE** GOLD SPARKLE	3,604	**2,767**	2,445	2,156
ELGUIT	56	GRETSCH	**JET FIREBIRD 6131** RED	4,407	**3,384**	2,990	2,636
ELGUIT	57	GRETSCH	**JET FIREBIRD 6131** RED	5,666	**4,350**	3,844	3,389
ELGUIT	58	GRETSCH	**JET FIREBIRD 6131** RED	3,809	**2,924**	2,584	2,278
ELGUIT	60	GRETSCH	**JET FIREBIRD 6131** RED	3,588	**2,755**	2,435	2,146
ELGUIT	61	GRETSCH	**JET FIREBIRD 6131** SINGLE CUTAWAY	3,101	**2,381**	2,104	1,855
ELGUIT	62	GRETSCH	**JET FIREBIRD 6131** RED	2,412	**1,852**	1,637	1,443
ELGUIT	63	GRETSCH	**JET FIREBIRD 6131** RED	3,571	**2,742**	2,423	2,136
ELGUIT	64	GRETSCH	**JET FIREBIRD 6131** RED	3,506	**2,692**	2,379	2,097

TYPE	YR	MFG	MODEL	SELL EXC	SELL AVG	BUY EXC	BUY AVG
ELGUIT	65	GRETSCH	JET FIREBIRD 6131 RED	3,151	2,420	2,138	1,885
ELGUIT	68	GRETSCH	JET FIREBIRD 6131 RED	3,150	2,419	2,137	1,884
ELGUIT	69	GRETSCH	JET FIREBIRD 6131 RED	3,149	2,418	2,137	1,884
ELGUIT	66	GRETSCH	MONKEES RED	1,744	1,339	1,184	1,043
ELGUIT	67	GRETSCH	MONKEES RED	2,303	1,769	1,563	1,378
ELGUIT	68	GRETSCH	MONKEES RED	1,601	1,229	1,086	958
ELGUIT	63	GRETSCH	NASHVILLE ORANGE	3,542	2,720	2,403	2,119
ELGUIT	60	GRETSCH	NIGHTHAWK BLACK	2,309	1,773	1,567	1,381
ELGUIT	63	GRETSCH	PRINCESS 6106 PINK	2,086	1,602	1,415	1,248
ELGUIT	63	GRETSCH	PRINCESS 6106 WHITE	2,107	1,618	1,430	1,260
ELGUIT	69	GRETSCH	RALLY 6104 CADILLAC GREEN	1,574	1,209	1,068	942
ELGUIT	67	GRETSCH	RALLY 6105 BAMBOO YELLOW	1,584	1,216	1,075	948
ELGUIT	68	GRETSCH	RALLY 6105 BAMBOO YELLOW	1,308	1,004	887	782
ELGUIT	57	GRETSCH	RAMBLER 6115 IVORY TOP	1,385	1,063	940	828
ELGUIT	58	GRETSCH	RAMBLER 6115 IVORY TOP	1,321	1,014	896	790
ELGUIT	59	GRETSCH	RAMBLER 6115 IVORY TOP	1,330	1,021	902	795
ELGUIT	76	GRETSCH	ROC I	917	704	622	548
ELGUIT	77	GRETSCH	ROC II MAHOGANY	918	705	623	549
ELGUIT	73	GRETSCH	ROC JET	909	698	617	544
ELGUIT	70	GRETSCH	ROC JET 6127 PUMPKIN	1,018	781	690	609
ELGUIT	70	GRETSCH	ROC JET 6130 BLACK	1,021	784	693	611
ELGUIT	71	GRETSCH	ROC JET 7610 BLACK	1,339	1,028	908	801
ELGUIT	72	GRETSCH	ROC JET 7610 BLACK	1,215	933	824	726
ELGUIT	71	GRETSCH	ROC JET 7611 PUMPKIN	1,223	939	829	731
ELGUIT	54	GRETSCH	ROUND UP 6130 ORANGE, WESTERN INLAY G BRAND	8,786	6,746	5,962	5,256
ELGUIT	55	GRETSCH	ROUND UP 6130 ORANGE, WESTERN INLAY G BRAND	8,052	6,183	5,464	4,817
ELGUIT	57	GRETSCH	ROUND UP 6130 ORANGE	8,207	6,302	5,569	4,909
ELGUIT	59	GRETSCH	ROUND UP 6130 ORANGE	4,376	3,360	2,970	2,618
ELGUIT	58	GRETSCH	SAL SALVADOR 6199 SUNBURST	3,027	2,324	2,054	1,811
ELGUIT	60	GRETSCH	SAL SALVADOR 6199 SUNBURST	2,880	2,211	1,954	1,723
ELGUIT	61	GRETSCH	SAL SALVADOR 6199 SUNBURST	2,224	1,707	1,509	1,330
ELGUIT	62	GRETSCH	SAL SALVADOR 6199 SUNBURST	1,804	1,385	1,224	1,079
ELGUIT	65	GRETSCH	SAL SALVADOR 6199 SUNBURST, ARCHTOP	1,637	1,257	1,111	979
ELGUIT	78	GRETSCH	SHO-BUD III	855	657	580	511
ELGUIT	70	GRETSCH	SHO-BUD PRO II	969	744	658	580
ELGUIT	66	GRETSCH	SILVER DUKE SILVER SPARKLE	3,306	2,538	2,243	1,977
ELGUIT	54	GRETSCH	SILVER JET 6129 SILVER SPARKLE	6,704	5,147	4,549	4,010
ELGUIT	55	GRETSCH	SILVER JET 6129 SILVER SPARKLE	6,560	5,037	4,452	3,924
ELGUIT	56	GRETSCH	SILVER JET 6129 SILVER SPARKLE	6,426	4,934	4,360	3,844
ELGUIT	57	GRETSCH	SILVER JET 6129 SILVER SPARKLE	7,286	5,595	4,944	4,359
ELGUIT	58	GRETSCH	SILVER JET 6129 SILVER SPARKLE	6,384	4,902	4,332	3,819
ELGUIT	60	GRETSCH	SILVER JET 6129 SILVER SPARKLE, SINGLE CUTAWAY	4,763	3,657	3,232	2,849
ELGUIT	61	GRETSCH	SILVER JET 6129 SILVER SPARKLE, DOUBLE CUTAWAY	4,373	3,358	2,967	2,616
ELGUIT	62	GRETSCH	SILVER JET 6129 SILVER SPARKLE	4,238	3,254	2,875	2,535

TYPE	YR	MFG	PRICES--BASED ON 100% ORIGINAL MODEL	SELL EXC	SELL AVG	BUY EXC	BUY AVG
ELGUIT	63	GRETSCH	**SILVER JET 6129** SILVER SPARKLE	4,118	**3,162**	2,794	2,463
ELGUIT	64	GRETSCH	**SILVER JET 6129** SILVER SPARKLE	5,009	**3,846**	3,399	2,996
ELGUIT	83	GRETSCH	**SOUTHERN BELL 7177** WALNUT	1,249	**959**	848	747
ELGUIT	69	GRETSCH	**STREAMLINER 6102** SUNBURST, DOUBLE CUTAWAY	894	**687**	607	535
ELGUIT	70	GRETSCH	**STREAMLINER 6102** SUNBURST, DOUBLE CUTAWAY	894	**687**	607	535
ELGUIT	71	GRETSCH	**STREAMLINER 6102** SUNBURST, DOUBLE CUTAWAY	897	**688**	608	536
ELGUIT	72	GRETSCH	**STREAMLINER 6102** SUNBURST, DOUBLE CUTAWAY	841	**645**	570	503
ELGUIT	66	GRETSCH	**STREAMLINER 6103** SUNBURST, DOUBLE CUTAWAY	953	**731**	646	570
ELGUIT	68	GRETSCH	**STREAMLINER 6103** CHERRY, DOUBLE CUTAWAY	950	**730**	645	568
ELGUIT	69	GRETSCH	**STREAMLINER 6103** CHERRY, DOUBLE CUTAWAY	950	**730**	645	568
ELGUIT	71	GRETSCH	**STREAMLINER 6103** CHERRY, DOUBLE CUTAWAY	841	**645**	570	503
ELGUIT	55	GRETSCH	**STREAMLINER 6189** BAMBOO YELLOW	1,498	**1,150**	1,016	896
ELGUIT	55	GRETSCH	**STREAMLINER 6189** JAGUAR TAN	1,634	**1,254**	1,108	977
ELGUIT	56	GRETSCH	**STREAMLINER 6189** BAMBOO YELLOW	1,631	**1,253**	1,107	976
ELGUIT	57	GRETSCH	**STREAMLINER 6189** BAMBOO YELLOW	1,629	**1,251**	1,105	974
ELGUIT	58	GRETSCH	**STREAMLINER 6189** BAMBOO YELLOW, DOUBLE CUTAWAY	1,893	**1,454**	1,285	1,132
ELGUIT	56	GRETSCH	**STREAMLINER 6190** SUNBURST	1,631	**1,253**	1,107	976
ELGUIT	57	GRETSCH	**STREAMLINER 6190** SUNBURST	1,725	**1,325**	1,171	1,032
ELGUIT	58	GRETSCH	**STREAMLINER 6190** SUNBURST	1,602	**1,230**	1,087	958
ELGUIT	71	GRETSCH	**STREAMLINER 6190** SUNBURST	950	**730**	645	568
ELGUIT	56	GRETSCH	**STREAMLINER 6191** NATURAL	1,659	**1,274**	1,126	992
ELGUIT	57	GRETSCH	**STREAMLINER 6191** NATURAL	1,615	**1,240**	1,095	966
ELGUIT	77	GRETSCH	**SUPER AXE 7680** RED	1,313	**1,008**	891	785
ELGUIT	79	GRETSCH	**SUPER AXE 7680** RED	1,025	**787**	696	613
ELGUIT	76	GRETSCH	**SUPER AXE 7681** EBONY	1,069	**821**	725	639
ELGUIT	78	GRETSCH	**SUPER AXE 7681** EBONY	1,029	**790**	698	615
ELGUIT	79	GRETSCH	**SUPER AXE 7681** EBONY	1,070	**822**	726	640
ELGUIT	72	GRETSCH	**SUPER CHET 7690** CHERRY RED	2,130	**1,635**	1,445	1,274
ELGUIT	72	GRETSCH	**SUPER CHET 7690** AUTUMN RED, LEFT-HANDED	3,347	**2,570**	2,271	2,002
ELGUIT	73	GRETSCH	**SUPER CHET 7690** CHERRY RED	2,170	**1,666**	1,472	1,298
ELGUIT	74	GRETSCH	**SUPER CHET 7690** CHERRY RED	2,130	**1,635**	1,445	1,274
ELGUIT	75	GRETSCH	**SUPER CHET 7690** CHERRY RED	2,098	**1,611**	1,424	1,255
ELGUIT	76	GRETSCH	**SUPER CHET 7690** CHERRY RED	2,101	**1,613**	1,425	1,256
ELGUIT	77	GRETSCH	**SUPER CHET 7690** CHERRY RED	1,779	**1,366**	1,207	1,064
ELGUIT	79	GRETSCH	**SUPER CHET 7690** CHERRY RED	2,054	**1,577**	1,393	1,228
ELGUIT	73	GRETSCH	**SUPER CHET 7691** WALNUT	2,040	**1,566**	1,384	1,220
ELGUIT	76	GRETSCH	**SUPER CHET 7691** WALNUT	2,016	**1,548**	1,368	1,206
ELGUIT	77	GRETSCH	**SUPER CHET 7691** WALNUT	2,007	**1,541**	1,361	1,200
ELGUIT	49	GRETSCH	**SYNCHROMATIC ARCHTOP** SUNBURST	2,100	**1,612**	1,425	1,256
ELGUIT	67	GRETSCH	**TENNESSEAN** CHERRY	3,589	**2,756**	2,435	2,147
ELGUIT	76	GRETSCH	**TK 300 7625** NATURAL	668	**513**	453	399
ELGUIT	80	GRETSCH	**TK 300 7625** NATURAL	546	**419**	370	326

TYPE	YR	MFG	PRICES--BASED ON 100% ORIGINAL MODEL	SELL EXC	SELL AVG	BUY EXC	BUY AVG
ELGUIT	68	GRETSCH	**VAN EPPS 6079** SUNBURST, 7-STRING	3,440	**2,641**	2,334	2,058
ELGUIT	69	GRETSCH	**VAN EPPS 6079** SUNBURST, 7-STRING	3,022	**2,321**	2,051	1,808
ELGUIT	70	GRETSCH	**VAN EPPS 6080** WALNUT, 7-STRING	1,649	**1,266**	1,119	986
ELGUIT	70	GRETSCH	**VAN EPPS 6081** SUNBURST, 6-STRING	938	**720**	636	561
ELGUIT	69	GRETSCH	**VAN EPPS 6082** WALNUT, 6-STRING	1,088	**823**	725	601
ELGUIT	75	GRETSCH	**VAN EPPS 7580** SUNBURST, 7-STRING	3,562	**2,735**	2,417	2,131
ELGUIT	79	GRETSCH	**VAN EPPS 7580** SUNBURST, 7-STRING	2,084	**1,600**	1,414	1,246
ELGUIT	67	GRETSCH	**VIKING 6187** SUNBURST	1,899	**1,458**	1,288	1,136
ELGUIT	68	GRETSCH	**VIKING 6187** SUNBURST	1,487	**1,142**	1,009	889
ELGUIT	69	GRETSCH	**VIKING 6187** SUNBURST	1,451	**1,114**	984	868
ELGUIT	65	GRETSCH	**VIKING 6188** NATURAL BLOND	1,592	**1,222**	1,080	952
ELGUIT	66	GRETSCH	**VIKING 6189** CADILLAC GREEN	3,384	**2,598**	2,296	2,024
ELGUIT	54	GRETSCH	**WHITE FALCON** SINGLE CUTAWAY	3,159	**2,426**	2,143	1,890
ELGUIT	55	GRETSCH	**WHITE FALCON** SINGLE CUTAWAY	26,253	**20,159**	17,815	15,705
ELGUIT	56	GRETSCH	**WHITE FALCON** SINGLE CUTAWAY	23,430	**17,991**	15,899	14,016
ELGUIT	57	GRETSCH	**WHITE FALCON** SINGLE CUTAWAY	24,858	**19,087**	16,868	14,870
ELGUIT	58	GRETSCH	**WHITE FALCON** SINGLE CUTAWAY	23,461	**18,015**	15,920	14,035
ELGUIT	59	GRETSCH	**WHITE FALCON** SINGLE CUTAWAY	24,767	**19,018**	16,806	14,816
ELGUIT	60	GRETSCH	**WHITE FALCON** SINGLE CUTAWAY	21,091	**16,195**	14,312	12,617
ELGUIT	61	GRETSCH	**WHITE FALCON** SINGLE CUTAWAY	14,437	**11,086**	9,797	8,636
ELGUIT	62	GRETSCH	**WHITE FALCON** DOUBLE CUTAWAY	6,371	**4,892**	4,323	3,811
ELGUIT	63	GRETSCH	**WHITE FALCON** DOUBLE CUTAWAY, STEREO	3,446	**2,646**	2,338	2,061
ELGUIT	63	GRETSCH	**WHITE FALCON** DOUBLE CUTAWAY, MONO WIRING	3,591	**2,758**	2,437	2,148
ELGUIT	64	GRETSCH	**WHITE FALCON** DOUBLE CUTAWAY	2,468	**1,895**	1,675	1,476
ELGUIT	65	GRETSCH	**WHITE FALCON** DOUBLE CUTAWAY, STEREO	2,401	**1,843**	1,629	1,436
ELGUIT	66	GRETSCH	**WHITE FALCON** DOUBLE CUTAWAY	2,275	**1,747**	1,544	1,361
ELGUIT	67	GRETSCH	**WHITE FALCON** DOUBLE CUTAWAY, STEREO	1,699	**1,304**	1,152	1,016
ELGUIT	67	GRETSCH	**WHITE FALCON** DOUBLE CUTAWAY	2,160	**1,658**	1,466	1,292
ELGUIT	68	GRETSCH	**WHITE FALCON** DOUBLE CUTAWAY	2,160	**1,658**	1,466	1,292
ELGUIT	69	GRETSCH	**WHITE FALCON** DOUBLE CUTAWAY, STEREO	2,158	**1,657**	1,464	1,291
ELGUIT	70	GRETSCH	**WHITE FALCON** DOUBLE CUTAWAY	1,789	**1,374**	1,214	1,070
ELGUIT	71	GRETSCH	**WHITE FALCON** DOUBLE CUTAWAY	1,764	**1,354**	1,197	1,055
ELGUIT	72	GRETSCH	**WHITE FALCON** DOUBLE CUTAWAY	1,734	**1,332**	1,177	1,037
ELGUIT	74	GRETSCH	**WHITE FALCON** DOUBLE CUTAWAY, STEREO	1,694	**1,301**	1,149	1,013
ELGUIT	75	GRETSCH	**WHITE FALCON** SINGLE CUTAWAY	1,639	**1,259**	1,112	980
ELGUIT	75	GRETSCH	**WHITE FALCON** DOUBLE CUTAWAY, STEREO	1,674	**1,285**	1,136	1,001
ELGUIT	75	GRETSCH	**WHITE FALCON** DOUBLE CUTAWAY	1,677	**1,288**	1,138	1,003
ELGUIT	76	GRETSCH	**WHITE FALCON** DOUBLE CUTAWAY, STEREO	1,626	**1,248**	1,103	972
ELGUIT	77	GRETSCH	**WHITE FALCON** SINGLE CUTAWAY	1,587	**1,218**	1,076	949
ELGUIT	77	GRETSCH	**WHITE FALCON** DOUBLE CUTAWAY, STEREO	1,603	**1,231**	1,088	959
ELGUIT	79	GRETSCH	**WHITE FALCON** DOUBLE CUTAWAY	1,459	**1,120**	990	873
ELGUIT	79	GRETSCH	**WHITE FALCON** DOUBLE CUTAWAY, STEREO	1,495	**1,148**	1,014	894

TYPE	YR	MFG	PRICES--BASED ON 100% ORIGINAL MODEL	SELL EXC	SELL AVG	BUY EXC	BUY AVG
ELGUIT	80	GRETSCH	**WHITE FALCON** DOUBLE CUTAWAY	1,439	**1,105**	976	860
ELGUIT	55	GRETSCH	**WHITE PENGUIN 6134**	112,810	**86,622**	76,550	67,485
ELGUIT	56	GRETSCH	**WHITE PENGUIN 6134**	94,736	**72,743**	64,285	56,672
ELGUIT	57	GRETSCH	**WHITE PENGUIN 6134**	137,024	**105,214**	92,980	81,969
ELGUIT	58	GRETSCH	**WHITE PENGUIN 6134**	124,262	**95,416**	84,321	74,335
ELGUIT	59	GRETSCH	**WHITE PENGUIN 6134**	123,969	**95,190**	84,122	74,160
ELGUIT	60	GRETSCH	**WHITE PENGUIN 6134**	80,706	**61,970**	54,764	48,279
GUITAR AMP	68	GRETSCH	**6144** REVERB UNIT	198	**152**	134	118
GTAMP	63	GRETSCH	**6149** POWER REVERB UNIT	351	**270**	238	210
GTAMP	59	GRETSCH	**6150** 1x8" ROLA SPEAKER	448	**344**	304	268
GTAMP	60	GRETSCH	**6150** 1x9" JENSEN SPEAKER	412	**316**	279	246
GTAMP	60	GRETSCH	**6156** 1x10" JENSEN SPEAKER	329	**252**	223	196
GTAMP	65	GRETSCH	**6159** GREY, 2x12" JENSENS	538	**413**	365	322
GTAMP	62	GRETSCH	**6159 DUAL BASS** GREY, TOLEX, 2x12" SPEAKERS	574	**441**	389	343
GTAMP	63	GRETSCH	**6159 DUAL BASS**	542	**416**	367	324
GTAMP	56	GRETSCH	**6161** 3 SPEAKERS, TUBE, TREMOLO	585	**449**	397	350
GTAMP	59	GRETSCH	**6161 DUAL TWIN** 2 OVAL, 1 ROUND SPEAKER	605	**465**	411	362
GTAMP	57	GRETSCH	**6161 ELECTROMATIC** TWIN AMP, WRAP AROUND GRILL	509	**391**	345	304
GTAMP	58	GRETSCH	**6169 FURY MODEL** PIGGYBACK, 2x12" SPEAKERS	590	**453**	400	353
GTAMP	67	GRETSCH	**6169 FURY MODEL** PIGGYBACK, 2x12" SPEAKERS	547	**420**	371	327
GTAMP	60	GRETSCH	**CAROSEL** 10" SPEAKER, TWEETER	332	**255**	225	198
GTAMP	65	GRETSCH	**COMPACT** 8" SPEAKER	250	**192**	170	150
GTAMP	50	GRETSCH	**ELECTROMAT** WESTERN FINISH	626	**480**	424	374
GTAMP	54	GRETSCH	**ELECTROMAT** (2)6x9" AND 1x5" SPEAKERS	571	**438**	387	341
GTAMP	55	GRETSCH	**ELECTROMAT** 10" SPEAKER	552	**423**	374	330
GTAMP	68	GRETSCH	**TWIN REVERB** GREY, 2 CHANNEL, 2x10" SPEAKERS	502	**386**	341	300
GUITAR (ACOUSTIC)	40	GRETSCH	**20** SPRUCE TOP, FLATTOP	786	**603**	533	470
GUITAR	30	GRETSCH	**30** SUNBURST, ARCHTOP	938	**720**	636	561
GUITAR	38	GRETSCH	**35** SUNBURST, ARCHTOP	825	**633**	560	493
GUITAR	40	GRETSCH	**35** SUNBURST, ARCHTOP	794	**609**	538	475
GUITAR	41	GRETSCH	**35** SUNBURST, ARCHTOP	901	**692**	611	539
GUITAR	39	GRETSCH	**40** HAWAIIAN, FLATTOP	579	**438**	386	320
GUITAR	40	GRETSCH	**40** HAWAIIAN, FLATTOP	581	**446**	394	347
GUITAR	40	GRETSCH	**50** SUNBURST, ARCHTOP	605	**457**	403	334
GUITAR	53	GRETSCH	**50** SUNBURST, ARCHTOP, NON-CUTAWAY	884	**679**	600	529
GUITAR	36	GRETSCH	**65** PEARL DOTS, ARCHTOP	1,768	**1,357**	1,200	1,057
GUITAR	38	GRETSCH	**75F** SUNBURST, FLATTOP	715	**549**	485	428
GUITAR	41	GRETSCH	**80S** FLATTOP	992	**761**	673	593
GUITAR	69	GRETSCH	**6020** FLATTOP, 12-STRING	658	**505**	446	393
GUITAR	49	GRETSCH	**BURL IVES 6004** NATURAL, FLATTOP	3,063	**2,352**	2,078	1,832
GUITAR	52	GRETSCH	**BURL IVES 6004**	3,028	**2,325**	2,055	1,811
GUITAR	53	GRETSCH	**BURL IVES 6004** NATURAL, FLATTOP	2,369	**1,819**	1,608	1,417
GUITAR	54	GRETSCH	**BURL IVES 6004** NATURAL, FLATTOP	2,352	**1,806**	1,596	1,407
GUITAR	55	GRETSCH	**BURL IVES 6004** NATURAL, FLATTOP	2,238	**1,719**	1,519	1,339
GUITAR	64	GRETSCH	**CLIPPER 6186** SUNBURST	687	**528**	466	411
GUITAR	59	GRETSCH	**CONSTELLATION**	3,063	**2,352**	2,078	1,832

TYPE	YR	MFG	PRICES--BASED ON 100% ORIGINAL MODEL	SELL EXC	SELL AVG	BUY EXC	BUY AVG
GUITAR	56	GRETSCH	**CONSTELLATION 603** NATURAL, ARCHTOP	3,886	**2,984**	2,637	2,324
GUITAR	55	GRETSCH	**CORSAIR 6014** SUNBURST, ARCHTOP	1,546	**1,187**	1,049	925
GUITAR	56	GRETSCH	**CORSAIR 6014** SUNBURST, ARCHTOP	1,552	**1,191**	1,053	928
GUITAR	62	GRETSCH	**CORSAIR 6014** SUNBURST, ARCHTOP, CUTAWAY	1,356	**1,041**	920	811
GUITAR	56	GRETSCH	**CORSAIR 6015** NATURAL, ARCHTOP	1,540	**1,182**	1,045	921
GUITAR	55	GRETSCH	**CORSAIR 6016** BURGUNDY, ARCHTOP	1,552	**1,191**	1,053	928
GUITAR	55	GRETSCH	**ELDORADO 6040** SUNBURST, NON-CUTAWAY	2,369	**1,819**	1,608	1,417
GUITAR	57	GRETSCH	**ELDORADO 6040** SUNBURST, ARCHTOP	3,103	**2,383**	2,105	1,856
GUITAR	58	GRETSCH	**ELDORADO 6040** SUNBURST	5,339	**4,099**	3,622	3,193
GUITAR	59	GRETSCH	**ELDORADO 6040** SUNBURST, ARCHTOP	4,046	**3,107**	2,745	2,420
GUITAR	66	GRETSCH	**ELDORADO 6040** SUNBURST	2,201	**1,690**	1,494	1,317
GUITAR	68	GRETSCH	**ELDORADO 6040** SUNBURST, ARCHTOP	2,358	**1,811**	1,600	1,411
GUITAR	69	GRETSCH	**ELDORADO 6040** SUNBURST	2,447	**1,879**	1,660	1,463
GUITAR	55	GRETSCH	**ELDORADO 6041** NATURAL, ARCHTOP	3,510	**2,695**	2,381	2,099
GUITAR	60	GRETSCH	**ELDORADO 6041** NATURAL, ARCHTOP	3,477	**2,670**	2,359	2,080
GUITAR	51	GRETSCH	**ELECTRO II SYNCHROMATIC 6192** SUNBURST, CUTAWAY	1,730	**1,328**	1,174	1,035
GUITAR	52	GRETSCH	**ELECTRO II SYNCHROMATIC 6193** NATURAL, CUTAWAY	1,878	**1,442**	1,274	1,123
GUITAR	56	GRETSCH	**FLEETWOOD 6038** SUNBURST, ARCHTOP	1,338	**1,027**	908	800
GUITAR	54	GRETSCH	**FLEETWOOD 6039** NATURAL, ARCHTOP	1,466	**1,125**	994	877
GUITAR	69	GRETSCH	**FOLK 6002** SUNBURST, FLATTOP	731	**561**	496	437
GUITAR	60	GRETSCH	**FOLK 6003** NATURAL, FLATTOP	884	**679**	600	529
GUITAR	67	GRETSCH	**FOLK 6003** NATURAL, FLATTOP	861	**661**	584	515
GUITAR	69	GRETSCH	**FOLK 6004** MAHOGANY, FLATTOP	739	**567**	501	442
GUITAR	58	GRETSCH	**J-200** NATURAL	899	**690**	610	538
GUITAR	47	GRETSCH	**JUMBO SYNCHROMATIC 6021-125F** NATURAL SUNBURST	3,063	**2,352**	2,078	1,832
GUITAR	48	GRETSCH	**JUMBO SYNCHROMATIC 6021-125F** NATURAL SUNBURST	3,027	**2,324**	2,054	1,811
GUITAR	49	GRETSCH	**JUMBO SYNCHROMATIC 6021-125F** NATURAL SUNBURST	2,972	**2,282**	2,017	1,778
GUITAR	51	GRETSCH	**JUMBO SYNCHROMATIC 6021-125F** NATURAL SUNBURST	2,905	**2,230**	1,971	1,737
GUITAR	49	GRETSCH	**NEW YORKER 6050** SUNBURST, ARCHTOP	1,235	**948**	838	739
GUITAR	50	GRETSCH	**NEW YORKER 6050** SUNBURST, ARCHTOP	1,225	**940**	831	732
GUITAR	51	GRETSCH	**NEW YORKER 6050** SUNBURST, ARCHTOP	1,219	**936**	827	729
GUITAR	54	GRETSCH	**NEW YORKER 6050** SUNBURST, ARCHTOP	1,208	**927**	820	722
GUITAR	55	GRETSCH	**NEW YORKER 6050** SUNBURST, ARCHTOP	1,204	**924**	817	720
GUITAR	56	GRETSCH	**NEW YORKER 6050** SUNBURST, ARCHTOP	1,072	**823**	728	641
GUITAR	62	GRETSCH	**NEW YORKER 6050** SUNBURST, ARCHTOP	1,021	**784**	693	611
GUITAR	63	GRETSCH	**NEW YORKER 6050** SUNBURST, ARCHTOP	1,013	**778**	687	606
GUITAR	69	GRETSCH	**NEW YORKER 6050** SUNBURST, ARCHTOP	982	**754**	666	587
GUITAR	55	GRETSCH	**RANCHER 6022** ORANGE, HUMP TOP 17" JUMBO	3,920	**3,010**	2,660	2,345
GUITAR	56	GRETSCH	**RANCHER 6022** ORANGE	3,528	**2,709**	2,394	2,110
GUITAR	57	GRETSCH	**RANCHER 6022** ORANGE, 'G' BRAND	3,431	**2,635**	2,328	2,052
GUITAR	61	GRETSCH	**RANCHER 6022** ORANGE	3,545	**2,722**	2,406	2,121
GUITAR	62	GRETSCH	**RANCHER 6022** ORANGE	2,999	**2,303**	2,035	1,794

TYPE	YR	MFG	PRICES--BASED ON 100% ORIGINAL MODEL	SELL EXC	SELL AVG	BUY EXC	BUY AVG
GUITAR	63	GRETSCH	RANCHER 6022 ORANGE	3,114	2,391	2,113	1,863
GUITAR	67	GRETSCH	RANCHER 6022 ORANGE	2,243	1,722	1,522	1,342
GUITAR	68	GRETSCH	RANCHER 6022 ORANGE	2,909	2,234	1,974	1,740
GUITAR	69	GRETSCH	RANCHER 6022 ORANGE	2,418	1,828	1,612	1,336
GUITAR	75	GRETSCH	RANCHER 6022 ORANGE	2,391	1,836	1,622	1,430
GUITAR	67	GRETSCH	SAM GOODY GREEN SUNBURST, "G" F-HOLES	3,072	2,358	2,084	1,837
GUITAR	67	GRETSCH	SHO BRO 6030 SPANISH, FLATTOP	1,038	797	704	621
GUITAR	69	GRETSCH	SHO BRO 6030 SPANISH, FLATTOP	1,064	817	722	636
GUITAR	69	GRETSCH	SHO BRO 6031 HAWAIIAN, FLATTOP	813	614	542	449
GUITAR	70	GRETSCH	SHO BRO 6031 HAWAIIAN, FLATTOP	917	704	622	548
GUITAR	71	GRETSCH	SHO BRO 7715 NATURAL TOP, 6-STRING	1,324	1,017	899	792
GUITAR	75	GRETSCH	SHO BRO 7715 NATURAL TOP, 6-STRING	977	750	663	584
GUITAR	78	GRETSCH	SHO BRO DIAMOND ROSEWOOD	743	571	504	444
GUITAR	78	GRETSCH	SHO BRO GRAND SLAM MAHOGANY	712	546	483	426
GUITAR	72	GRETSCH	SHO BRO HAWAIIAN	1,319	1,013	895	789
GUITAR	78	GRETSCH	SHO BRO SPADE ROSEWOOD	743	571	504	444
GUITAR	75	GRETSCH	SHO BRO SPANISH NATURAL, RESONATOR, ROUND NECK	947	727	642	566
GUITAR	78	GRETSCH	SHO BUD PRO 1	797	612	541	477
GUITAR	78	GRETSCH	SHO BUD SUPER PRO DOUBLE NECK, 10-STRING	1,453	1,116	986	869
GUITAR	47	GRETSCH	SIERRA 6007 SUNBURST, FLATTOP	2,273	1,745	1,542	1,360
GUITAR	58	GRETSCH	STREAMLINER 1689 CREAM & COPPER	2,164	1,662	1,469	1,295
GUITAR	59	GRETSCH	SUN VALLEY NATURAL	805	618	546	481
GUITAR	65	GRETSCH	SUN VALLEY	701	538	475	419
GUITAR	75	GRETSCH	SUN VALLEY	670	515	455	401
GUITAR	61	GRETSCH	SUN VALLEY 6010 NATURAL, FLATTOP	1,554	1,193	1,054	929
GUITAR	67	GRETSCH	SUN VALLEY 6010 NATURAL, FLATTOP	1,319	1,013	895	789
GUITAR	68	GRETSCH	SUN VALLEY 6010 NATURAL, FLATTOP	1,245	956	845	745
GUITAR	70	GRETSCH	SUN VALLEY 6010 NATURAL, FLATTOP	1,242	953	842	743
GUITAR	39	GRETSCH	SYNCHROMATIC 75 CAT'S EYE SUNBURST	1,537	1,180	1,043	919
GUITAR	40	GRETSCH	SYNCHROMATIC 75 CAT'S EYE SUNBURST	2,320	1,781	1,574	1,388
GUITAR	47	GRETSCH	SYNCHROMATIC 75 CAT'S EYE SUNBURST	1,304	1,001	885	780
GUITAR	48	GRETSCH	SYNCHROMATIC 75 CAT'S EYE SUNBURST	1,708	1,311	1,159	1,021
GUITAR	49	GRETSCH	SYNCHROMATIC 75XF BLACK	1,472	1,130	999	881
GUITAR	46	GRETSCH	SYNCHROMATIC 100	1,276	980	866	763
GUITAR	39	GRETSCH	SYNCHROMATIC 100 6014 SUNBURST, ARCHTOP	1,543	1,185	1,047	923
GUITAR	47	GRETSCH	SYNCHROMATIC 100 6014 SUNBURST, ARCHTOP	1,554	1,193	1,054	929
GUITAR	51	GRETSCH	SYNCHROMATIC 100 6014 SUNBURST, ARCHTOP	1,458	1,119	989	872
GUITAR	52	GRETSCH	SYNCHROMATIC 100 6014 SUNBURST, ARCHTOP	1,553	1,192	1,054	929
GUITAR	53	GRETSCH	SYNCHROMATIC 100 6014 SUNBURST, ARCHTOP	1,445	1,110	981	864
GUITAR	54	GRETSCH	SYNCHROMATIC 100 6014 SUNBURST, ARCHTOP	1,552	1,191	1,053	928
GUITAR	51	GRETSCH	SYNCHROMATIC 100 6015 NATURAL, ARCHTOP	1,560	1,197	1,058	933
GUITAR	53	GRETSCH	SYNCHROMATIC 100 6015 NATURAL, ARCHTOP	1,554	1,193	1,054	929
GUITAR	54	GRETSCH	SYNCHROMATIC 100 6015 NATURAL, ARCHTOP	1,540	1,182	1,045	921
GUITAR	46	GRETSCH	SYNCHROMATIC 115 TRANSPARENT BLOND, ARCHTOP	1,867	1,433	1,266	1,116

TYPE	YR	MFG	PRICES--BASED ON 100% ORIGINAL MODEL	SELL EXC	SELL AVG	BUY EXC	BUY AVG
GUITAR	51	GRETSCH	SYNCHROMATIC 125F SUNBURST	2,306	1,770	1,564	1,379
GUITAR	39	GRETSCH	SYNCHROMATIC 160 CAT'S EYE SUNBURST	1,649	1,266	1,119	986
GUITAR	48	GRETSCH	SYNCHROMATIC 160 CAT'S EYE SUNBURST	1,681	1,290	1,140	1,005
GUITAR	49	GRETSCH	SYNCHROMATIC 160 CAT'S EYE SUNBURST	3,239	2,487	2,197	1,937
GUITAR	51	GRETSCH	SYNCHROMATIC 160	3,433	2,636	2,330	2,054
GUITAR	55	GRETSCH	SYNCHROMATIC 160 SUNBURST, NON-CUTAWAY	4,396	3,375	2,983	2,629
GUITAR	55	GRETSCH	SYNCHROMATIC 160 CAT'S EYE SUNBURST	4,421	3,395	3,000	2,645
GUITAR	39	GRETSCH	SYNCHROMATIC 200 CAT'S EYE SUNBURST	2,406	1,848	1,633	1,439
GUITAR	41	GRETSCH	SYNCHROMATIC 200 CAT'S EYE NATURAL	3,372	2,589	2,288	2,017
GUITAR	47	GRETSCH	SYNCHROMATIC 200 CAT'S EYE SUNBURST	3,344	2,567	2,269	2,000
GUITAR	48	GRETSCH	SYNCHROMATIC 200 CAT'S EYE NATURAL	3,063	2,352	2,078	1,832
GUITAR	46	GRETSCH	SYNCHROMATIC 250 ARCHTOP	2,222	1,706	1,507	1,329
GUITAR	39	GRETSCH	SYNCHROMATIC 300 CAT'S EYE SUNBURST	3,342	2,566	2,267	1,999
GUITAR	40	GRETSCH	SYNCHROMATIC 300 CAT'S EYE SUNBURST	4,221	3,241	2,864	2,525
GUITAR	40	GRETSCH	SYNCHROMATIC 400 CAT'S EYE SUNBURST	8,363	6,421	5,674	5,002
GUITAR	50	GRETSCH	SYNCHROMATIC 400 CAT'S EYE NATURAL	9,046	6,946	6,138	5,411
GUITAR	51	GRETSCH	SYNCHROMATIC 6029-160 CAT'S EYE NATURAL	3,231	2,481	2,192	1,932
GUITAR	53	GRETSCH	SYNCHROMATIC 6030 CONSTELLATION SUNBURST	3,228	2,479	2,191	1,931
GUITAR	55	GRETSCH	SYNCHROMATIC 6031 SUNBURST, CUTAWAY	3,060	2,350	2,077	1,831
GUITAR	49	GRETSCH	SYNCHROMATIC 6036-300 CAT'S EYE SUNBURST	3,923	3,012	2,662	2,347
GUITAR	52	GRETSCH	SYNCHROMATIC 6036-300 CAT'S EYE SUNBURST	3,920	3,010	2,660	2,345
GUITAR	54	GRETSCH	SYNCHROMATIC 6036-300 CAT'S EYE SUNBURST	3,384	2,598	2,296	2,024
GUITAR	47	GRETSCH	SYNCHROMATIC 6037-300 CAT'S EYE NATURAL	4,189	3,217	2,843	2,506
GUITAR	51	GRETSCH	SYNCHROMATIC 6037-300 CAT'S EYE NATURAL	3,510	2,695	2,381	2,099
GUITAR	53	GRETSCH	SYNCHROMATIC 6038 SUNBURST, CUTAWAY	3,571	2,742	2,423	2,136
GUITAR	48	GRETSCH	SYNCHROMATIC 6040-400 CAT'S EYE SUNBURST	6,891	5,291	4,676	4,122
GUITAR	52	GRETSCH	SYNCHROMATIC 6040-400 CAT'S EYE SUNBURST	6,648	5,104	4,511	3,977
GUITAR	53	GRETSCH	SYNCHROMATIC 6040-400 CAT'S EYE SUNBURST	6,497	4,988	4,408	3,886
GUITAR	49	GRETSCH	SYNCHROMATIC 6041-400 CAT'S EYE NATURAL	8,088	6,210	5,488	4,838
GUITAR	51	GRETSCH	SYNCHROMATIC 6041-400 CAT'S EYE NATURAL	8,049	6,180	5,462	4,815
GUITAR	50	GRETSCH	SYNCHROMATIC 6042-400F NATURAL, FLATTOP	1,314	1,009	892	786
GUITAR	54	GRETSCH	SYNCHROMATIC FLEETWOOD SUNBURST, CUTAWAY	5,139	3,946	3,487	3,074
GUITAR	48	GRETSCH	SYNCHROMATIC X75F	1,019	782	691	609
GUITAR	53	GRETSCH	TOWN & COUNTRY 6021 SUNBURST	3,232	2,481	2,193	1,933
GUITAR	53	GRETSCH	TOWN & COUNTRY 6021 NATURAL	3,233	2,482	2,194	1,934
GUITAR	54	GRETSCH	TOWN & COUNTRY 6021 NATURAL	3,236	2,485	2,196	1,936
GUITAR	56	GRETSCH	TOWN & COUNTRY 6021 NATURAL	3,589	2,756	2,435	2,147
GUITAR	57	GRETSCH	TOWN & COUNTRY 6021 NATURAL	3,232	2,481	2,193	1,933
GUITAR	69	GRETSCH	WAYFARER 6008 NATURAL, CHERRY BACK/SIDES, FLATTOP	879	675	596	525
GUITAR	70	GRETSCH	WAYFARER 6008 NATURAL, CHERRY BACK/SIDES, FLATTOP	807	620	547	483
STEEL GUITAR	49	GRETSCH	ELECTROMATIC CONSOLE 6158 DOUBLE 6	1,023	786	694	612
UKULELE	55	GRETSCH	MAHOGANY NO BINDING	605	465	411	362

TYPE	YR	MFG	PRICES--BASED ON 100% ORIGINAL MODEL	SELL EXC	SELL AVG	BUY EXC	BUY AVG

GRYPHON

TYPE	YR	MFG	MODEL	SELL EXC	SELL AVG	BUY EXC	BUY AVG
PWR	98	GRYPHON	TABU 2-CHANNEL	5,772	**4,432**	3,917	3,453

GUILD MUSIC CORP.

TYPE	YR	MFG	MODEL	SELL EXC	SELL AVG	BUY EXC	BUY AVG
EFFECTS	69	GUILD	FOXEY LADY FUZZ 2 KNOBS	453	**348**	307	271
EFFECTS	77	GUILD	FOXEY LADY FUZZ 3 KNOBS IN ROW	294	**226**	199	176
EFFECTS	76	GUILD	HH ECHO UNIT	421	**323**	285	251
ELEC. GUITAR & BASS	79	GUILD	B-300 BLACK, LEFT-HANDED, 1 PU	908	**697**	616	543
ELGUIT	78	GUILD	B-301 BLACK	535	**411**	363	320
ELGUIT	77	GUILD	B-301 BASS WALNUT	561	**430**	380	335
ELGUIT	79	GUILD	B-301 BASS BLACK	507	**389**	344	303
ELGUIT	61	GUILD	BLACKFIRE BLACK-GREEN TRANSPARENT, SERIAL #14713-18419	878	**674**	595	525
ELGUIT	94	GUILD	BRIAN MAY STANDARD STOP TAILPIECE, 3 SINGLE COIL PU's or 2 HB's	976	**749**	662	584
ELGUIT	94	GUILD	BRIAN MAY STANDARD SOLID MAHOG, NO VIBRATO SYSTEM, BLACK/WHITE/GREEN	1,332	**1,023**	904	797
ELGUIT	61	GUILD	CE-100 SUNBURST, BIGBSY VIBRATO, SERIAL #14714-18419	980	**752**	665	586
ELGUIT	65	GUILD	CE-100 SUNBURST, SINGLE CUTAWAY, SERIAL #EF101-211	487	**374**	330	291
ELGUIT	67	GUILD	CE-100 SUNBURST, CUTAWAY, SERIAL #EF397-549	478	**367**	324	286
ELGUIT	68	GUILD	CE-100 SUNBURST	677	**520**	459	405
ELGUIT	79	GUILD	CE-100 SUNBURST	567	**436**	385	339
ELGUIT	79	GUILD	CE-100 SUNBURST, 2 PU's, LEFT-HANDED	797	**612**	541	477
ELGUIT	57	GUILD	CE-100 CAPRI HOLLOW BODY, SERIAL #12035	1,410	**1,082**	956	843
ELGUIT	58	GUILD	CE-100 CAPRI BLOND, HOLLOW BODY, SERIAL #12035	1,024	**786**	695	613
ELGUIT	58	GUILD	CE-100D	716	**550**	486	428
ELGUIT	66	GUILD	CE-100D SUNBURST	664	**509**	450	397
ELGUIT	73	GUILD	CE-100D SUNBURST	560	**430**	380	335
ELGUIT	68	GUILD	CE-100D CAPRI SUNBURST, HOLLOW BODY, SERIAL #EF650-719	441	**338**	299	263
ELGUIT	65	GUILD	DE-400 DUANE EDDY SUNBURST, SERIAL #EH101-126	2,132	**1,637**	1,447	1,275
ELGUIT	66	GUILD	DE-400 DUANE EDDY SERIAL #EH127-233	2,128	**1,634**	1,444	1,273
ELGUIT	64	GUILD	DE-500 DUANE EDDY	660	**507**	448	395
ELGUIT	66	GUILD	DE-500 DUANE EDDY SERIAL #EI108-116	2,974	**2,284**	2,018	1,779
ELGUIT	78	GUILD	DE-500 DUANE EDDY SERIAL #169867-195067	1,326	**1,018**	899	793
ELGUIT	63	GUILD	DE-500 DUANE EDDY DELUXE	3,571	**2,742**	2,423	2,136
ELGUIT	64	GUILD	DE-500 DUANE EDDY SPECIAL BLACK	3,060	**2,350**	2,077	1,831
ELGUIT	67	GUILD	GEORGE BARNES HOLLOW BODY, SERIAL #46609-46637	3,214	**2,468**	2,181	1,922
ELGUIT	64	GUILD	GEORGE BARNES H HOLLOW BODY, SERIAL #28944-38636	3,458	**2,655**	2,346	2,068
ELGUIT	77	GUILD	HOWARD ROBERTS CHERRY SUNBURST	1,316	**1,010**	893	787
ELGUIT	70	GUILD	J.S. BASS II NATURAL, MAHOGANY, 2 PU's	588	**451**	399	351
ELGUIT	77	GUILD	JOHNNY SMITH BLOND	2,303	**1,769**	1,563	1,378
ELGUIT	78	GUILD	JOHNNY SMITH SUNBURST	2,297	**1,763**	1,558	1,374
ELGUIT	57	GUILD	M- 65 SUNBURST, 1 PU, SERIAL #-12035	1,454	**1,117**	987	870
ELGUIT	58	GUILD	M- 65 NATURAL, 1 PU	1,504	**1,154**	1,020	899
ELGUIT	72	GUILD	M- 65 SUNBURST, THINLINE, SINGLE CUTAWAY, HARP STYLE TAILPIECE	716	**550**	486	428
ELGUIT	73	GUILD	M- 65 BLUESBIRD NATURAL, SOLID MAHOGANY	731	**561**	496	437
ELGUIT	60	GUILD	M- 65 FRESHMAN HOLLOW BODY, F-HOLE, SERIAL #12036-14713	859	**659**	582	513

TYPE	YR	MFG	PRICES--BASED ON 100% ORIGINAL MODEL	SELL EXC	SELL AVG	BUY EXC	BUY AVG
ELGUIT	60	GUILD	**M- 65 3/4** SUNBURST	846	**650**	574	506
ELGUIT	64	GUILD	**M- 65 3/4** CHERRY RED, SINGLE CUTAWAY, SERIAL #28944-38636	969	**744**	658	580
ELGUIT	65	GUILD	**M- 65 3/4** WINE RED, SINGLE CUTAWAY	660	**507**	448	395
ELGUIT	59	GUILD	**M- 65 3/4 FRESHMAN**	864	**663**	586	517
ELGUIT	73	GUILD	**M- 65 3/4 FRESHMAN** ARCHTOP, SERIAL #75603-95496	816	**626**	554	488
ELGUIT	70	GUILD	**M- 70** HOLLOW BODY, 2 HB's	1,008	**774**	684	603
ELGUIT	56	GUILD	**M- 75 ARISTOCRAT** SUNBURST, SERIAL #12035	613	**471**	416	367
ELGUIT	57	GUILD	**M- 75 ARISTOCRAT** SUNBURST, SERIAL #12035	611	**469**	414	365
ELGUIT	58	GUILD	**M- 75 ARISTOCRAT** SUNBURST, SERIAL #12035	610	**468**	414	365
ELGUIT	59	GUILD	**M- 75 ARISTOCRAT** SUNBURST	609	**467**	413	364
ELGUIT	60	GUILD	**M- 75 ARISTOCRAT** BLOND, SERIAL#12325	579	**444**	392	346
ELGUIT	60	GUILD	**M- 75 ARISTOCRAT** SUNBURST	579	**444**	392	346
ELGUIT	71	GUILD	**M- 75 BLUESBIRD**	3,495	**2,684**	2,371	2,091
ELGUIT	75	GUILD	**M- 80 CS** DOUBLE CUTAWAY, SERIAL #112804-130304	668	**513**	453	399
ELGUIT	54	GUILD	**M- 85 BLUESBIRD**	720	**552**	488	430
ELGUIT	66	GUILD	**M- 85 BLUESBIRD** BLACK, SERIAL #46607-46608	441	**338**	299	263
ELGUIT	68	GUILD	**M- 85 BLUESBIRD** SERIAL #DD139-237	478	**367**	324	286
ELGUIT	68	GUILD	**M- 85 BLUESBIRD** CHERRY RED	596	**458**	405	357
ELGUIT	69	GUILD	**M- 85 BLUESBIRD** SUNBURST	441	**338**	299	263
ELGUIT	71	GUILD	**M- 85 BLUESBIRD** 2 HUMBUCKER PU's, SERIAL #50978-61463	398	**306**	270	238
ELGUIT	71	GUILD	**M- 85 BLUESBIRD** SUNBURST, SERIAL #50979-61463	472	**362**	320	282
ELGUIT	75	GUILD	**M- 85 BLUESBIRD** BLACK, GOLD HARDWARE	414	**318**	281	247
ELGUIT	73	GUILD	**M- 85 BLUESBIRD II BASS** WALNUT, SERIAL #75603-95496	631	**485**	428	377
ELGUIT	79	GUILD	**MUSICIAN BASS** NATURAL	720	**552**	488	430
ELGUIT	79	GUILD	**MUSICIAN MC-500** NATURAL	722	**554**	490	432
ELGUIT	64	GUILD	**S- 50 JET STAR BASS**	781	**600**	530	467
ELGUIT	65	GUILD	**S- 50 JET STAR BASS** SERIAL #38637-46606	761	**584**	516	455
ELGUIT	66	GUILD	**S- 50 JET STAR BASS**	757	**581**	513	452
ELGUIT	67	GUILD	**S- 50 JET STAR BASS** SERIAL #46609-46637	754	**579**	512	451
ELGUIT	68	GUILD	**S- 50 JET STAR BASS**	750	**576**	509	448
ELGUIT	78	GUILD	**S- 60**	540	**415**	367	323
ELGUIT	79	GUILD	**S- 60** NATURAL, MAHOGANY, 1 PU	510	**392**	346	305
ELGUIT	75	GUILD	**S- 60D** WALNUT	658	**505**	446	393
ELGUIT	78	GUILD	**S- 60D** MAHOGANY	660	**507**	448	395
ELGUIT	76	GUILD	**S- 60DD** WALNUT, 2 PU's	607	**466**	411	363
ELGUIT	80	GUILD	**S- 65D** SOLID BODY	473	**363**	321	283
ELGUIT	78	GUILD	**S- 70** SERIAL #169868-195067	635	**487**	430	379
ELGUIT	65	GUILD	**S-100 POLARA** LEFT-HANDED	319	**245**	216	190
ELGUIT	65	GUILD	**S-100 POLARA** SERIAL #SB101-169	817	**627**	554	489
ELGUIT	66	GUILD	**S-100 POLARA** SUNBURST	720	**552**	488	430
ELGUIT	67	GUILD	**S-100 POLARA** VIBRATO	723	**555**	490	432
ELGUIT	68	GUILD	**S-100 POLARA**	650	**499**	441	389
ELGUIT	69	GUILD	**S-100 POLARA** SERIAL #46657-46695	598	**459**	405	357
ELGUIT	70	GUILD	**S-100 POLARA**	695	**534**	471	416
ELGUIT	72	GUILD	**S-100 POLARA**	655	**503**	444	391
ELGUIT	64	GUILD	**S-200 THUNDERBIRD** SERIAL #28944-38636	412	**316**	279	246

TYPE	YR	MFG	PRICES--BASED ON 100% ORIGINAL MODEL	SELL EXC	SELL AVG	BUY EXC	BUY AVG
ELGUIT	77	GUILD	**S-300** SUNBURST, 2 HB's	573	**440**	389	343
ELGUIT	77	GUILD	**S-300D** NATURAL	607	**466**	411	363
ELGUIT	65	GUILD	**STARFIRE** SERIAL #38637-46606	647	**497**	439	387
ELGUIT	62	GUILD	**STARFIRE II**	770	**591**	522	460
ELGUIT	63	GUILD	**STARFIRE II**	825	**633**	560	493
ELGUIT	65	GUILD	**STARFIRE II** HOLLOW BODY, SERIAL #EK101-387	736	**565**	500	440
ELGUIT	66	GUILD	**STARFIRE II** CHERRY RED, SERIAL #EK388-2098	796	**611**	540	476
ELGUIT	61	GUILD	**STARFIRE III** SINGLE CUT	582	**447**	395	348
ELGUIT	62	GUILD	**STARFIRE III** CHERRY RED	881	**676**	598	527
ELGUIT	66	GUILD	**STARFIRE III** SERIAL #EK388-2098	589	**452**	399	352
ELGUIT	67	GUILD	**STARFIRE III**	749	**575**	508	448
ELGUIT	72	GUILD	**STARFIRE III** RED, MAHOGANY, SINGLE CUT, 2 PU's	598	**459**	405	357
ELGUIT	70	GUILD	**STARFIRE III SPECIAL** CHERRY RED, CUTAWAY	595	**457**	404	356
ELGUIT	62	GUILD	**STARFIRE IV** SERIAL #18419-22722	682	**523**	462	408
ELGUIT	67	GUILD	**STARFIRE IV** SUNBURST, LEFT-HANDED	658	**505**	446	393
ELGUIT	67	GUILD	**STARFIRE IV** SERIAL #EL1168-1840	1,420	**1,090**	963	849
ELGUIT	69	GUILD	**STARFIRE IV** SUNBURST, SERIAL #EL2224-2272	657	**504**	446	393
ELGUIT	70	GUILD	**STARFIRE IV** SUNBURST	645	**495**	437	385
ELGUIT	74	GUILD	**STARFIRE IV** SUNBURST	651	**500**	442	389
ELGUIT	76	GUILD	**STARFIRE IV** SUNBURST	673	**516**	456	402
ELGUIT	79	GUILD	**STARFIRE IV** SUNBURST, SERIAL #195067	638	**490**	433	381
ELGUIT	64	GUILD	**STARFIRE V** CHERRY RED, SERIAL #28944-38636	723	**555**	490	432
ELGUIT	65	GUILD	**STARFIRE V** SERIAL #EN101-194	705	**541**	478	422
ELGUIT	66	GUILD	**STARFIRE V** LEFT-HANDED, SERIAL #EN195-927	649	**498**	440	388
ELGUIT	66	GUILD	**STARFIRE V** SERIAL #EN195-927	697	**535**	473	417
ELGUIT	68	GUILD	**STARFIRE V** CHERRY RED	665	**510**	451	397
ELGUIT	70	GUILD	**STARFIRE V**	1,253	**962**	850	749
ELGUIT	68	GUILD	**STARFIRE VI** SERIAL #DB 275-329	724	**556**	491	433
ELGUIT	75	GUILD	**STARFIRE VI** CHERRY RED, SERIAL #112803-130304	701	**538**	475	419
ELGUIT	66	GUILD	**STARFIRE XII** CHERRY RED, 12-STRING, SERIAL #DC101-586	925	**710**	627	553
ELGUIT	67	GUILD	**STARFIRE XII** CHERRY RED, 12-STRING, SERIAL #DC587-896	808	**620**	548	483
ELGUIT	68	GUILD	**STARFIRE XII** 12-STRING, SERIAL #DC897	789	**606**	535	472
ELGUIT	70	GUILD	**STARFIRE XII**	855	**657**	580	511
ELGUIT	65	GUILD	**STARFIRE BASS** WINE RED, SEMI-HOLLOW	661	**508**	449	395
ELGUIT	66	GUILD	**STARFIRE BASS** CHERRY RED	560	**430**	380	335
ELGUIT	67	GUILD	**STARFIRE BASS** CHERRY RED, 2 PU's, SERIAL #BA655-1696	556	**427**	377	332
ELGUIT	67	GUILD	**STARFIRE BASS** SUNBURST, 1 PU, SERIAL #BA655-1696	661	**508**	449	395
ELGUIT	73	GUILD	**STARFIRE BASS** CHERRY RED, 1 PU	452	**347**	307	270
ELGUIT	67	GUILD	**STARFIRE BASS II** SUNBURST	663	**509**	449	396
ELGUIT	69	GUILD	**STARFIRE BASS II** SERIAL #BA1947-2043	689	**529**	468	412
ELGUIT	71	GUILD	**STARFIRE BASS II** CHERRY RED, 2 PU's, SERIAL #50978-61463	551	**423**	373	329
ELGUIT	75	GUILD	**STARFIRE BASS II** SUNBURST, SERIAL #112804-130304	687	**528**	466	411
ELGUIT	61	GUILD	**STARSONG**	1,320	**1,013**	896	789
ELGUIT	65	GUILD	**T- 50 CORDOBA SLIM** SERIAL #EB101-196	751	**577**	509	449

TYPE	YR	MFG	PRICES--BASED ON 100% ORIGINAL MODEL	SELL EXC	SELL AVG	BUY EXC	BUY AVG
ELGUIT	67	GUILD	T- 50 CORDOBA SLIM SUNBURST, SERIAL #EB392-558	636	488	431	380
ELGUIT	74	GUILD	T- 50 CORDOBA SLIM CHERRY RED	635	487	430	379
ELGUIT	58	GUILD	T-100 SLIM JIM SUNBURST, SINGLE CUTAWAY	1,219	936	827	729
ELGUIT	59	GUILD	T-100 SLIM JIM SUNBURST, 1 PU	1,008	774	684	603
ELGUIT	61	GUILD	T-100 SLIM JIM	715	549	485	428
ELGUIT	64	GUILD	T-100 SLIM JIM SUNBURST, CUTAWAY	692	531	469	414
ELGUIT	69	GUILD	T-100 SLIM JIM SUNBURST, ARCHTOP, SERIAL #EE3004-3109	754	579	512	451
ELGUIT	70	GUILD	T-100 SLIM JIM CHERRY RED, 2 PU's, SINGLE CUTAWAY	736	557	491	407
ELGUIT	60	GUILD	T-100D SLIM JIM SUNBURST	984	755	668	588
ELGUIT	61	GUILD	T-100D SLIM JIM SUNBURST	715	549	485	428
ELGUIT	61	GUILD	T-100D SLIM JIM SUNBURST, SERIAL #14713-18419	826	634	560	494
ELGUIT	66	GUILD	T-100D SLIM JIM HOLLOW BODY, SERIAL #EE602-1939	626	480	424	374
ELGUIT	69	GUILD	T-100D SLIM JIM SINGLE CUT, SERIAL #95496-112803	648	497	440	387
ELGUIT	68	GUILD	THUNDERBIRD BASS BUILT-IN STAND	1,053	809	715	630
ELGUIT	55	GUILD	X- 50 SUNBURST, ARCHTOP	554	425	376	331
ELGUIT	57	GUILD	X- 50 SUNBURST, 1 PU, THICK BODY	1,205	925	817	720
ELGUIT	62	GUILD	X- 50 SUNBURST, 1 PU, NON-CUTAWAY, SERIAL #18420-22722	673	516	456	402
ELGUIT	65	GUILD	X- 50 SUNBURST, 1 PU	663	509	449	396
ELGUIT	67	GUILD	X- 50 HOLLOW BODY	742	570	503	444
ELGUIT	64	GUILD	X- 50 CORDOBA	990	760	671	592
ELGUIT	67	GUILD	X- 50 CORDOBA HOLLOW BODY, SERIAL #EA327-491	756	580	513	452
ELGUIT	58	GUILD	X- 50 GRANADA HOLLOW BODY, SERIAL #12035	1,205	925	817	720
ELGUIT	53	GUILD	X-150 JAZZ SUNBURST, ARCHTOP, SERIAL #12035	1,276	980	866	763
ELGUIT	57	GUILD	X-150 SAVOY HOLLOW BODY, SERIAL #12035	1,208	927	820	722
ELGUIT	61	GUILD	X-150 SAVOY	1,724	1,324	1,170	1,031
ELGUIT	57	GUILD	X-150B NATURAL, SINGLE CUTAWAY, 17" WIDE	1,208	927	820	722
ELGUIT	59	GUILD	X-150LH SUNBURST, SINGLE CUTAWAY, LEFT-HANDED	1,413	1,085	959	845
ELGUIT	54	GUILD	X-175 SUNBURST	1,781	1,368	1,209	1,065
ELGUIT	55	GUILD	X-175 SUNBURST, SERIAL #12035	1,769	1,358	1,200	1,058
ELGUIT	59	GUILD	X-175 SUNBURST	2,204	1,692	1,495	1,318
ELGUIT	62	GUILD	X-175 BLOND, SINGLE CUTAWAY, 2 PU's, SERIAL #18419-22722	1,682	1,291	1,141	1,006
ELGUIT	63	GUILD	X-175 SUNBURST	1,789	1,374	1,214	1,070
ELGUIT	67	GUILD	X-175 NATURAL	1,728	1,326	1,172	1,033
ELGUIT	75	GUILD	X-175 NATURAL, SERIAL #112803-130304	792	608	538	474
ELGUIT	77	GUILD	X-175 NATURAL	791	608	537	473
ELGUIT	79	GUILD	X-175 SUNBURST, 2 PU's, CUTAWAY	632	485	429	378
ELGUIT	55	GUILD	X-175 MANHATTAN HOLLOW BODY, SERIAL #12035	702	539	476	420
ELGUIT	58	GUILD	X-175 MANHATTAN	2,292	1,760	1,555	1,371
ELGUIT	69	GUILD	X-175 MANHATTAN HOLLOW BODY, SERIAL #EG323-346	677	520	459	405
ELGUIT	78	GUILD	X-175 MANHATTAN	1,398	1,074	949	836
ELGUIT	54	GUILD	X-350 STRATFORD SUNBURST, 3 BLACK PU's	3,394	2,606	2,303	2,030
ELGUIT	55	GUILD	X-350 STRATFORD SUNBURST, WHITE, 3 SINGLE COIL PU's	3,396	2,608	2,305	2,032
ELGUIT	56	GUILD	X-350 STRATFORD HOLLOW BODY, SERIAL #12035	3,217	2,470	2,183	1,924
ELGUIT	57	GUILD	X-350 STRATFORD BLOND, ARCHTOP, SERIAL #12035	3,384	2,598	2,296	2,024

TYPE	YR	MFG	PRICES--BASED ON 100% ORIGINAL MODEL	SELL EXC	SELL AVG	BUY EXC	BUY AVG
ELGUIT	58	GUILD	**X-350 STRATFORD** SUNBURST, 3 WHITE PU's	3,394	**2,606**	2,303	2,030
ELGUIT	61	GUILD	**X-350 STRATFORD** SUNBURST	2,014	**1,547**	1,367	1,205
ELGUIT	62	GUILD	**X-350B** BLOND, PUSH BUTTONS	3,661	**2,811**	2,484	2,190
ELGUIT	55	GUILD	**X-375** SUNBURST, 3 PU's	2,353	**1,806**	1,596	1,407
ELGUIT	58	GUILD	**X-375** NATURL, 3 PU's	1,980	**1,497**	1,320	1,094
ELGUIT	60	GUILD	**X-375 STRATFORD**	2,368	**1,818**	1,607	1,417
ELGUIT	55	GUILD	**X-440** HOLLOW BODY, SERIAL #12035	2,181	**1,675**	1,480	1,305
ELGUIT	57	GUILD	**X-500 STUART** NATURAL, SERIAL #12035	3,533	**2,713**	2,397	2,113
ELGUIT	61	GUILD	**X-500 STUART**	2,250	**1,727**	1,526	1,346
ELGUIT	62	GUILD	**X-500 STUART** SUNBURST, WHITE DEARMOND	1,226	**941**	832	733
ELGUIT	65	GUILD	**X-500 STUART** NATURAL	1,311	**1,007**	889	784
ELGUIT	68	GUILD	**X-500 STUART** NATURAL, CURLY MAPLE BACK/SIDE, SERIAL #DA231	1,298	**996**	880	776
ELGUIT	70	GUILD	**X-500 STUART**	1,043	**801**	708	624
ELGUIT	73	GUILD	**X-500 STUART** NATURAL	991	**761**	672	592
ELGUIT	74	GUILD	**X-500 STUART** NATURAL, SERIAL #95496-112803	963	**739**	653	576
ELGUIT	75	GUILD	**X-500 STUART** SUNBURST	910	**699**	617	544
ELGUIT	77	GUILD	**X-500 STUART** NATURAL, CURLY MAPLE	909	**698**	617	544
ELGUIT	79	GUILD	**X-500 STUART** NATURAL, SERIAL #195067-	812	**623**	551	485
ELGUIT	79	GUILD	**X-500 STUART** SUNBURST	812	**623**	551	485
ELGUIT	79	GUILD	**X-500 STUART** NATURAL, GOLD TAILPIECE	871	**669**	591	521
ELGUIT	55	GUILD	**X-550 STUART** NATURAL	3,840	**2,948**	2,606	2,297
GUITAR AMP	69	GUILD	**FOXY LADY** 2 KNOBS	399	**307**	271	239
GTAMP	58	GUILD	**MASTER AMP** 12" SPEAKER	600	**460**	407	359
GTAMP	71	GUILD	**STARFIRE V** WALNUT, MAHOGANY	1,006	**773**	683	602
GTAMP	76	GUILD	**STARFIRE VI** NATURAL, MAHOGANY	1,245	**956**	845	745
GTAMP	64	GUILD	**THUNDER 1-12** 12" SPEAKER	305	**234**	207	182
GTAMP	67	GUILD	**THUNDER 1-12** 12" SPEAKER	318	**244**	215	190
GUITAR (ACOUSTIC)	55	GUILD	**A- 50 GRANADA**	827	**635**	561	495
GUITAR	57	GUILD	**A- 50 GRANADA** SUNBURST	1,380	**1,060**	937	826
GUITAR	59	GUILD	**A- 50 GRANADA** SUNBURST	1,457	**1,118**	988	871
GUITAR	62	GUILD	**A- 50 GRANADA** BLOND	1,003	**770**	680	600
GUITAR	65	GUILD	**A- 50 GRANADA** SUNBURST, SERIAL #AB101-136	1,281	**983**	869	766
GUITAR	51	GUILD	**A- 50 STUART** SUNBURST	1,552	**1,191**	1,053	928
GUITAR	60	GUILD	**A-150 SAVOY** SUNBURST	2,282	**1,752**	1,548	1,365
GUITAR	62	GUILD	**A-150 SAVOY** SUNBURST, SERIAL #18420-22722	1,936	**1,486**	1,314	1,158
GUITAR	55	GUILD	**A-350 STRATFORD** ARCHTOP, SERIAL #12035	1,348	**1,035**	915	806
GUITAR	61	GUILD	**A-350 STRATFORD** NATURAL	1,826	**1,402**	1,239	1,092
GUITAR	60	GUILD	**A-500 STUART** SUNBURST, ARCHTOP, SERIAL #12035	1,047	**792**	698	579
GUITAR	61	GUILD	**A-500 STUART** SUNBURST, ARCHTOP	2,390	**1,835**	1,621	1,429
GUITAR	62	GUILD	**A-500 STUART** BLOND, ARCHTOP, SERIAL #18420-22722	1,279	**982**	867	765
GUITAR	63	GUILD	**A-500 STUART** SUNBURST, ARCHTOP, SERIAL #22723-28943	1,802	**1,383**	1,222	1,078
GUITAR	63	GUILD	**ARTIST AWARD** SUNBURST, ARCHTOP	5,565	**4,273**	3,776	3,329
GUITAR	65	GUILD	**ARTIST AWARD** BLOND, ARCHTOP, SERIAL #AA101	5,560	**4,269**	3,773	3,326
GUITAR	69	GUILD	**ARTIST AWARD** SUNBURST, ARCHTOP	4,941	**3,794**	3,353	2,956

TYPE	YR	MFG	PRICES--BASED ON 100% ORIGINAL MODEL	SELL EXC	SELL AVG	BUY EXC	BUY AVG
GUITAR	69	GUILD	**ARTIST AWARD** NATURAL, ARCHTOP	5,252	**4,033**	3,564	3,142
GUITAR	70	GUILD	**ARTIST AWARD** BLOND, ARCHTOP, SERIAL #46695-50978	3,177	**2,439**	2,156	1,900
GUITAR	70	GUILD	**ARTIST AWARD** SUNBURST, ARCHTOP, SERIAL #46696-50978	3,521	**2,703**	2,389	2,106
GUITAR	72	GUILD	**ARTIST AWARD** ARCHTOP, SERIAL #61464-75602	2,915	**2,238**	1,978	1,744
GUITAR	76	GUILD	**ARTIST AWARD** SUNBURST, ARCHTOP	3,894	**2,990**	2,642	2,329
GUITAR	77	GUILD	**ARTIST AWARD** NATURAL, ARCHTOP, SERIAL #149626-169867	3,505	**2,691**	2,378	2,097
GUITAR	77	GUILD	**ARTIST AWARD** SUNBURST, ARCHTOP, MAPLE, ORIGINAL DeARMOND FLOATING PICKUP	3,892	**2,988**	2,641	2,328
GUITAR	80	GUILD	**ARTIST AWARD** NATURAL, ARCHTOP	3,501	**2,688**	2,375	2,094
GUITAR	76	GUILD	**B-50 BASS** MAHOGANY	1,317	**1,011**	893	787
GUITAR	60	GUILD	**CA-100 CAPRI**	1,339	**1,028**	908	801
GUITAR	64	GUILD	**CA-100 CAPRI** SUNBURST, CUTAWAY	1,256	**964**	852	751
GUITAR	66	GUILD	**CA-100 CAPRI** ARCHTOP, SERIAL #46607-46608	1,029	**790**	698	615
GUITAR	61	GUILD	**CE-100 CAPRI**	1,219	**936**	827	729
GUITAR	77	GUILD	**CLASSICAL MK2**	725	**557**	492	434
GUITAR	70	GUILD	**D-25** MAHOGANY	665	**510**	451	397
GUITAR	70	GUILD	**D-25** CHERRY RED	668	**513**	453	399
GUITAR	71	GUILD	**D-25** MAHOGANY	657	**504**	446	393
GUITAR	71	GUILD	**D-25** CHERRY RED, SERIAL #50979-61463	658	**505**	446	393
GUITAR	72	GUILD	**D-25** CHERRY RED	784	**602**	532	469
GUITAR	72	GUILD	**D-25** NATURAL	787	**604**	534	471
GUITAR	73	GUILD	**D-25** CHERRY RED, SERIAL #75603-95496	786	**603**	533	470
GUITAR	74	GUILD	**D-25** SUNBURST	784	**602**	532	469
GUITAR	75	GUILD	**D-25** NATURAL	781	**600**	530	467
GUITAR	75	GUILD	**D-25** MAHOGANY	784	**602**	532	469
GUITAR	75	GUILD	**D-25** SUNBURST	864	**653**	576	478
GUITAR	76	GUILD	**D-25** MAHOGANY	779	**598**	528	466
GUITAR	77	GUILD	**D-25** BROWN	778	**597**	528	465
GUITAR	78	GUILD	**D-25** CHERRY RED, SERIAL #169867-195067	554	**425**	376	331
GUITAR	78	GUILD	**D-25** BLACK	777	**596**	527	464
GUITAR	78	GUILD	**D-25** MAHOGANY	787	**604**	534	471
GUITAR	79	GUILD	**D-25** MAHOGANY, SERIAL #195068	786	**603**	533	470
GUITAR	72	GUILD	**D-25 BLUEGRASS**	720	**552**	488	430
GUITAR	78	GUILD	**D-25-12**	787	**604**	534	471
GUITAR	76	GUILD	**D-25M**	657	**504**	446	393
GUITAR	73	GUILD	**D-30** MAHOGANY	827	**635**	561	495
GUITAR	70	GUILD	**D-35** NATURAL, SERIAL #46696-50978	1,061	**815**	720	635
GUITAR	74	GUILD	**D-35** NATURAL	1,056	**810**	716	631
GUITAR	76	GUILD	**D-35** NATURAL	1,061	**815**	720	635
GUITAR	76	GUILD	**D-35** NATURAL LEFT-HANDED	1,064	**817**	722	636
GUITAR	77	GUILD	**D-35** NATURAL	1,061	**815**	720	635
GUITAR	78	GUILD	**D-35** NATURAL, SERIAL #169867-195067	1,059	**813**	718	633
GUITAR	78	GUILD	**D-35** NATURAL, LEFT-HANDED	1,062	**816**	721	635
GUITAR	79	GUILD	**D-35** NATURAL	1,057	**811**	717	632
GUITAR	67	GUILD	**D-35 BLUEGRASS** SERIAL #46609-46637	1,048	**804**	711	627

TYPE	YR	MFG	MODEL	SELL EXC	SELL AVG	BUY EXC	BUY AVG
GUITAR	68	GUILD	**D- 35 BLUEGRASS** SERIAL #OJ101-1003	1,046	**803**	709	625
GUITAR	71	GUILD	**D- 35 BLUEGRASS** SERIAL #50979-61463	1,041	**799**	706	623
GUITAR	72	GUILD	**D- 35 BLUEGRASS** SERIAL #61463-75602	1,040	**798**	706	622
GUITAR	73	GUILD	**D- 35 BLUEGRASS**	1,037	**796**	703	620
GUITAR	72	GUILD	**D- 35NT**	1,048	**804**	711	627
GUITAR	66	GUILD	**D- 40** SERIAL #AJ334-1136	1,426	**1,095**	968	853
GUITAR	71	GUILD	**D- 40**	1,249	**959**	848	747
GUITAR	72	GUILD	**D- 40**	1,249	**959**	848	747
GUITAR	75	GUILD	**D- 40**	1,246	**957**	845	745
GUITAR	78	GUILD	**D- 40**	1,244	**955**	844	744
GUITAR	79	GUILD	**D- 40**	1,243	**954**	843	743
GUITAR	79	GUILD	**D- 40** LEFT-HANDED	1,258	**966**	854	753
GUITAR	80	GUILD	**D- 40** NATURAL FINISH, MEDIUM FRETS, ROSEWOOD FRETBOARD, CASE	1,345	**1,032**	912	804
GUITAR	79	GUILD	**D- 40CNT**	1,243	**954**	843	743
GUITAR	70	GUILD	**D- 40NT** SERIAL #46696-50978	1,254	**963**	851	750
GUITAR	75	GUILD	**D- 40NT**	1,253	**962**	850	749
GUITAR	78	GUILD	**D- 40NT** SERIAL #169868-195067	1,246	**957**	845	745
GUITAR	79	GUILD	**D- 40NT**	1,243	**954**	843	743
GUITAR	68	GUILD	**D- 44**	1,575	**1,210**	1,069	942
GUITAR	76	GUILD	**D- 44 BLUEGRASS JUBILEE**	1,008	**774**	684	603
GUITAR	74	GUILD	**D- 44M**	936	**718**	635	560
GUITAR	76	GUILD	**D- 44M**	1,064	**817**	722	636
GUITAR	73	GUILD	**D- 44NT**	917	**704**	622	548
GUITAR	84	GUILD	**D- 46**	901	**692**	611	539
GUITAR	70	GUILD	**D- 50** NATURAL, SERIAL #46696-50978	1,341	**1,030**	910	802
GUITAR	72	GUILD	**D- 50** NATURAL	1,337	**1,026**	907	799
GUITAR	73	GUILD	**D- 50** NATURAL	1,329	**1,020**	902	795
GUITAR	74	GUILD	**D- 50** NATURAL	1,324	**1,017**	899	792
GUITAR	75	GUILD	**D- 50** NATURAL	1,321	**1,014**	896	790
GUITAR	76	GUILD	**D- 50** NATURAL, SERIAL #130304-149625	1,320	**1,013**	896	789
GUITAR	78	GUILD	**D- 50** NATURAL	1,317	**1,011**	893	787
GUITAR	78	GUILD	**D- 50** NATURAL, LEFT-HANDED, SERIAL #181399	1,345	**1,032**	912	804
GUITAR	79	GUILD	**D- 50** SUNBURST	1,319	**1,013**	895	789
GUITAR	79	GUILD	**D- 50** NATURAL, LEFT-HANDED	1,342	**1,031**	911	803
GUITAR	68	GUILD	**D- 55**	1,640	**1,259**	1,113	981
GUITAR	73	GUILD	**D- 55** ROSEWOOD, SERIAL #75603-95496	1,627	**1,249**	1,104	973
GUITAR	78	GUILD	**D- 55**	1,622	**1,246**	1,101	970
GUITAR	66	GUILD	**DE-500 DUANE EDDY DELUXE**	2,263	**1,738**	1,535	1,354
GUITAR	75	GUILD	**F- 4-12 JUMBO** MAHOGANY BACK/SIDES, 12-STRING, SERIAL #112803-130304	975	**749**	661	583
GUITAR	55	GUILD	**F- 20 TROUBADOR** SUNBURST, SERIAL #12035	947	**727**	642	566
GUITAR	56	GUILD	**F- 20 TROUBADOR** MAPLE	1,006	**773**	683	602
GUITAR	58	GUILD	**F- 20 TROUBADOR** NATURAL, SERIAL #12035	1,005	**772**	682	601
GUITAR	58	GUILD	**F- 20 TROUBADOR** SUNBURST, SERIAL #12035	1,015	**780**	689	607
GUITAR	59	GUILD	**F- 20 TROUBADOR** MAPLE	1,001	**768**	679	598
GUITAR	62	GUILD	**F- 20 TROUBADOR** NATURAL	932	**716**	633	558
GUITAR	67	GUILD	**F- 20 TROUBADOR** NATURAL, SERIAL #AG1535-2499	588	**451**	399	351
GUITAR	68	GUILD	**F- 20 TROUBADOR** SUNBURST, SERIAL #AG2500-2793	761	**584**	516	455
GUITAR	73	GUILD	**F- 20 TROUBADOR**	797	**612**	541	477
GUITAR	75	GUILD	**F- 20 TROUBADOR** SUNBURST, LEFT-HANDED, SERIAL #112804-130304	663	**509**	449	396
GUITAR	75	GUILD	**F- 20 TROUBADOR** SUNBURST	683	**524**	463	408
GUITAR	78	GUILD	**F- 20 TROUBADOR** NATURAL	712	**546**	483	426

TYPE	YR	MFG	PRICES--BASED ON 100% ORIGINAL MODEL	SELL EXC	SELL AVG	BUY EXC	BUY AVG
GUITAR	79	GUILD	F- 20 TROUBADOR SUNBURST	621	477	421	371
GUITAR	79	GUILD	F- 20 TROUBADOR NATURAL	685	526	465	410
GUITAR	80	GUILD	F- 20 TROUBADOR NATURAL	679	522	461	406
GUITAR	82	GUILD	F- 20 TROUBADOR	733	563	497	438
GUITAR	65	GUILD	F- 30 ARAGON SUNBURST, SERIAL #AI101-351	1,008	774	684	603
GUITAR	67	GUILD	F- 30 ARAGON NATURAL, SERIAL #AI1143-1855	975	749	661	583
GUITAR	68	GUILD	F- 30 ARAGON MAHOGANY, SERIAL #AI1856-2270	887	681	601	530
GUITAR	78	GUILD	F- 30 ARAGON SUNBURST	739	567	501	442
GUITAR	79	GUILD	F- 30 ARAGON	710	545	481	424
GUITAR	74	GUILD	F- 30R ARAGON SERIAL #95497-112803	822	631	557	491
GUITAR	54	GUILD	F- 40 VALENCIA MAPLE BACK/SIDES	1,579	1,212	1,071	944
GUITAR	57	GUILD	F- 40 VALENCIA MAPLE BACK/SIDES, SERIAL #12035	1,046	803	709	625
GUITAR	59	GUILD	F- 40 VALENCIA MAPLE BACK/SIDES, SERIAL #12035	893	686	606	534
GUITAR	65	GUILD	F- 47 BLUEGRASS NATURAL, SERIAL #AK101-128	1,551	1,191	1,052	927
GUITAR	72	GUILD	F- 47 BLUEGRASS NATURAL	1,254	963	851	750
GUITAR	57	GUILD	F- 50 NAVARRE NATURAL, SERIAL #12035	1,535	1,179	1,041	918
GUITAR	58	GUILD	F- 50 NAVARRE SUNBURST, SERIAL #12035	1,734	1,311	1,156	958
GUITAR	65	GUILD	F- 50 NAVARRE SUNBURST	1,330	1,021	902	795
GUITAR	67	GUILD	F- 50 NAVARRE	1,834	1,408	1,244	1,097
GUITAR	71	GUILD	F- 50 NAVARRE NATURAL, SERIAL #50979-61463	1,319	1,013	895	789
GUITAR	72	GUILD	F- 50 NAVARRE SUNBURST	1,313	1,008	891	785
GUITAR	74	GUILD	F- 50 NAVARRE NATURAL	1,007	761	671	556
GUITAR	75	GUILD	F- 50 NAVARRE NATURAL	1,254	963	851	750
GUITAR	77	GUILD	F- 50 NAVARRE	1,453	1,116	986	869
GUITAR	67	GUILD	F- 50R NAVARRE ROSEWOOD, SERIAL #AD191-291	1,288	989	874	770
GUITAR	70	GUILD	F- 50R NAVARRE ROSEWOOD	1,453	1,116	986	869
GUITAR	73	GUILD	F- 50R NAVARRE ROSEWOOD	1,456	1,118	988	871
GUITAR	74	GUILD	F- 50R NAVARRE ROSEWOOD	1,392	1,068	944	832
GUITAR	75	GUILD	F- 50R NAVARRE ROSEWOOD	1,288	989	874	770
GUITAR	77	GUILD	F- 50R NAVARRE ROSEWOOD, SERIAL #149625-169867	1,285	987	872	769
GUITAR	79	GUILD	F- 50R NAVARRE ROSEWOOD, SERIAL #195067	1,071	823	727	641
GUITAR	78	GUILD	F- 50RNT NATURAL, FLATTOP	1,245	956	845	745
GUITAR	68	GUILD	F-112 NATURAL, 12-STRING	1,219	936	827	729
GUITAR	71	GUILD	F-112 NATURAL, 12-STRING	975	749	661	583
GUITAR	73	GUILD	F-112 NATURAL, 12-STRING	950	730	645	568
GUITAR	76	GUILD	F-112 NATURAL, 12-STRING	443	340	300	265
GUITAR	69	GUILD	F-212 12-STRING, SERIAL #AN2010-2271	919	706	623	550
GUITAR	75	GUILD	F-212 12-STRING	1,358	1,043	921	812
GUITAR	77	GUILD	F-212 12-STRING	901	692	611	539
GUITAR	78	GUILD	F-212 12-STRING	899	690	610	538
GUITAR	77	GUILD	F-212C NATURAL, CUTAWAY, 12-STRING, SERIAL #149625-169867	1,285	987	872	769
GUITAR	65	GUILD	F-212XL 12-STRING, SERIAL #AN101-228	972	746	659	581
GUITAR	67	GUILD	F-212XL 12-STRING	975	749	661	583
GUITAR	75	GUILD	F-212XL 12-STRING	808	620	548	483

TYPE	YR	MFG	PRICES--BASED ON 100% ORIGINAL MODEL	SELL EXC	SELL AVG	BUY EXC	BUY AVG
GUITAR	79	GUILD	F-212XL 12-STRING	789	606	535	472
GUITAR	82	GUILD	F-212XL 12-STRING	1,419	1,089	962	848
GUITAR	65	GUILD	F-312 12-STRING, SERIAL #AS101-141	1,428	1,096	969	854
GUITAR	67	GUILD	F-312 12-STRING	1,254	963	851	750
GUITAR	73	GUILD	F-412 NATURAL, 12-STRING	1,415	1,087	960	846
GUITAR	75	GUILD	F-412 NATURAL, 12-STRING	1,321	1,014	896	790
GUITAR	76	GUILD	F-412 NATURAL, 12-STRING	1,254	963	851	750
GUITAR	76	GUILD	F-412 CUSTOM 12-STRING	1,653	1,269	1,121	988
GUITAR	72	GUILD	F-512 ROSEWOOD BACK/SIDES, 12-STRING, SERIAL #61463-75602	1,467	1,126	995	877
GUITAR	73	GUILD	F-512 ROSEWOOD BACK/SIDES, 12-STRING	1,477	1,134	1,002	883
GUITAR	74	GUILD	F-512 ROSEWOOD BACK/SIDES, 12-STRING	1,392	1,068	944	832
GUITAR	77	GUILD	F-512 ROSEWOOD BACK/SIDES, 12-STRING	1,384	1,062	939	828
GUITAR	79	GUILD	F-512 ROSEWOOD BACK/SIDES, 12-STRING	1,256	964	852	751
GUITAR	70	GUILD	F-512 CUSTOM 12-STRING	1,453	1,116	986	869
GUITAR	74	GUILD	G-37 NATURAL	677	520	459	405
GUITAR	76	GUILD	G-37 NATURAL	743	571	504	444
GUITAR	79	GUILD	G-37	789	606	535	472
GUITAR	75	GUILD	G-41	874	671	593	523
GUITAR	74	GUILD	G-75 NATURAL	1,251	960	848	748
GUITAR	77	GUILD	G-75 NATURAL	1,008	774	684	603
GUITAR	80	GUILD	G-75 NATURAL	903	694	613	540
GUITAR	75	GUILD	G-212 12-STRING, SERIAL #112803-130304	563	432	382	337
GUITAR	78	GUILD	G-212 12-STRING	887	681	601	530
GUITAR	80	GUILD	G-212 12-STRING	1,339	1,028	908	801
GUITAR	76	GUILD	G-312NT ROSEWOOD, 12-STRING	1,242	953	842	743
GUITAR	77	GUILD	G-312NT ROSEWOOD, 12-STRING	1,330	1,021	902	795
GUITAR	76	GUILD	GT-312 NATURAL	841	645	570	503
GUITAR	63	GUILD	JF-65-12 JUMBO NATURAL	1,507	1,157	1,022	901
GUITAR	87	GUILD	JF-65R	1,514	1,162	1,027	905
GUITAR	59	GUILD	JOHNNY SMITH ARTIST ARCHTOP, SERIAL #12035	2,991	2,297	2,029	1,789
GUITAR	62	GUILD	M-20 ECONOMY	766	588	519	458
GUITAR	66	GUILD	M-20 ECONOMY MAHOGANY, SERIAL #46607-46608	837	643	568	501
GUITAR	67	GUILD	M-20 ECONOMY MAHOGANY	887	681	601	530
GUITAR	77	GUILD	M-20 ECONOMY MAHOGANY	733	563	497	438
GUITAR	66	GUILD	MARK I	712	546	483	426
GUITAR	65	GUILD	MARK I CLASSICAL MAHOGANY	739	567	501	442
GUITAR	65	GUILD	MARK III CLASSICAL MAHOGANY	731	561	496	437
GUITAR	69	GUILD	MARK III CLASSICAL MAHOGANY, SERIAL #46657-46695	704	540	478	421
GUITAR	72	GUILD	MARK III CLASSICAL MAHOGANY	664	509	450	397
GUITAR	74	GUILD	MARK III CLASSICAL MAHOGANY, SERIAL #111926	613	464	409	339
GUITAR	78	GUILD	MARK IV	683	524	463	408
GUITAR	60	GUILD	S-200 THUNDERBIRD SERIAL #12036-14713	1,609	1,235	1,092	962
GUITAR	67	GUILD	S-200 THUNDERBIRD SERIAL #46609-46637	883	678	599	528
GUITAR	68	GUILD	S-200 THUNDERBIRD SERIAL #46638-46656	801	615	544	479

TYPE	YR	MFG	PRICES--BASED ON 100% ORIGINAL MODEL	SELL EXC	SELL AVG	BUY EXC	BUY AVG
GUITAR	24	GUILD	**STUDIO 24** DOUBLE CUTAWAY, FLATTOP	2,329	**1,788**	1,580	1,393
UKULELE	60	GUILD	**B-11 BARITONE**	412	**316**	279	246
UKE	65	GUILD	**BARITONE**	568	**436**	386	340

DAWSON HADLEY

TYPE	YR	MFG	MODEL	SELL EXC	SELL AVG	BUY EXC	BUY AVG
PWR	70	HADLEY	**H-601**	950	**730**	645	568

HAGSTROM

TYPE	YR	MFG	MODEL	SELL EXC	SELL AVG	BUY EXC	BUY AVG
ELEC. GUITAR & BASS	65	HAGSTROM	**135** HOLLOW BODY, 2 PU's	535	**411**	363	320
ELGUIT	66	HAGSTROM	**BASS** SUNBURST, 8-STRING	621	**477**	421	371
ELGUIT	67	HAGSTROM	**BASS** RED, 8-STRING	730	**560**	495	436
ELGUIT	68	HAGSTROM	**BASS** SUNBURST, 8-STRING	613	**471**	416	367
ELGUIT	72	HAGSTROM	**BASS** SUNBURST, 8-STRING	668	**513**	453	399
ELGUIT	73	HAGSTROM	**BASS** SUNBURST,BLACK PICKGUARD,MAPLE NECK,RSWD FNGRBRD,2 PU	405	**311**	275	242
ELGUIT	62	HAGSTROM	**BASS I** RED, PLASTIC TOP, RAISED LABEL	584	**448**	396	349
ELGUIT	65	HAGSTROM	**BASS I** BLACK	469	**360**	318	280
ELGUIT	66	HAGSTROM	**BASS I** RED, 2 PU's	464	**356**	315	278
ELGUIT	71	HAGSTROM	**BASS I** SUNBURST	564	**433**	383	337
ELGUIT	61	HAGSTROM	**BASS II** RED, SOLID BODY, 2 PU's	551	**423**	373	329
ELGUIT	67	HAGSTROM	**BASS II** HOLLOW BODY, 2 PU's	530	**407**	360	317
ELGUIT	62	HAGSTROM	**H- 22** SINGLE CUTAWAY, THINLINE, 1 PU	346	**265**	234	207
ELGUIT	60	HAGSTROM	**HAGSTROM II** RED	333	**256**	226	199
ELGUIT	70	HAGSTROM	**HAGSTROM II** SUNBURST	333	**256**	226	199
ELGUIT	66	HAGSTROM	**KING BASS** 2 PU's	381	**293**	259	228
ELGUIT	66	HAGSTROM	**MODEL I**	453	**348**	307	271
ELGUIT	71	HAGSTROM	**MODEL I**	499	**383**	338	298
ELGUIT	75	HAGSTROM	**MODEL II**	523	**401**	354	312
ELGUIT	65	HAGSTROM	**MODEL III**	389	**299**	264	233
ELGUIT	76	HAGSTROM	**NORWAY** NATURAL, CHERRY	596	**458**	405	357
ELGUIT	71	HAGSTROM	**NORWAY BASS**	571	**438**	387	341
ELGUIT	65	HAGSTROM	**SUPER III** WOOD BACK, PLASTIC TOP	530	**407**	360	317
ELGUIT	78	HAGSTROM	**SUPER SWEDE**	660	**507**	448	395
ELGUIT	76	HAGSTROM	**SWEDE** NATURAL	588	**451**	399	351
ELGUIT	71	HAGSTROM	**SWEDE BASS**	588	**451**	399	351
ELGUIT	67	HAGSTROM	**V-I** SUNBURST	607	**466**	411	363
ELGUIT	74	HAGSTROM	**VIKING**	588	**451**	399	351

HALES

TYPE	YR	MFG	MODEL	SELL EXC	SELL AVG	BUY EXC	BUY AVG
SPKR	97	HALES	**REVELATION** (2)6.5" WOOD	922	**708**	626	552

HAMMOND SUZUKI USA, INC.

TYPE	YR	MFG	MODEL	SELL EXC	SELL AVG	BUY EXC	BUY AVG
ORGAN	35	HAMMOND	**A** (2)61-KEY MANUALS, 25-PEDS, 18-PRESET KEYS, 4-SETS DRAWBARS	527	**405**	357	315
ORGAN	59- 65	HAMMOND	**A- 100** (2)61-KEY MANUALS, 25-PEDS, SPLIT/CHORUS VIB, STEREO REVERB	1,432	**1,099**	972	856
ORGAN	61	HAMMOND	**A- 105 LOCKING TOP** (2)61-KEY MANUALS, 25-PEDS, SPLIT VIB, VIB/STEREO CHORUS	1,032	**792**	700	617
ORGAN	38	HAMMOND	**AB** (2)61-KEY MANUALS, 25-PEDS, 18-PRESET KEYS, 4-SETS DRAWBARS	501	**385**	340	300
ORGAN	49- 54	HAMMOND	**B- 2 CHORUS, 2-TONE GENERATORS** (2)61-KEY MANUALS, 25-PEDS, MANUAL SPLIT VIB, STEREO REVERB	1,244	**955**	844	744
ORGAN	55	HAMMOND	**B- 3** (2)61-KEY MANUALS, 25-PEDS, SPLIT/CHORUS VIB, TOUCH PERC.	3,736	**2,868**	2,535	2,235
ORGAN	36- 42	HAMMOND	**BC CHORUS, 2-TONE GENERATORS** (2)61-KEY MANUALS, 25-PEDS, SPLIT VIB, VIB/STEREO CHORUS	930	**714**	631	556
ORGAN	46- 49	HAMMOND	**BV CHORUS, 2-TONE GENERATORS** (2)61-KEY MANUALS, 25-PEDS, VARIABLE/CHORUS VIB, STEREO REV	1,732	**1,330**	1,175	1,036
ORGAN	39- 42	HAMMOND	**C LOWER CABINET ENCLOSED** (2)61-KEY MANUALS, 25-PEDS, 18-PRESET KEYS, 4-SETS DRAWBARS	1,809	**1,389**	1,228	1,082
ORGAN	49- 54	HAMMOND	**C- 2 LOWER CABINET ENCLOSED** (2)61-KEY MANUALS, 25-PEDS, MAN. SPLIT VIBRATO, STEREO REV.	897	**688**	608	536

TYPE	YR	MFG	PRICES--BASED ON 100% ORIGINAL MODEL	SELL EXC	SELL AVG	BUY EXC	BUY AVG
ORGAN	55	HAMMOND	**C- 3 LOWER CABINET ENCLOSED** (2)61-KEY MANUALS, 25-PEDS, SPLIT/CHORUS VIB, TOUCH PERC.	1,352	**1,038**	918	809
ORGAN	45- 49	HAMMOND	**CV LOWER CABINET ENCLOSED** (2)61-KEY MANUALS, 25-PEDS, VARIABLE/CHORUS VIB, STEREO REV	413	**317**	280	247

HARMAN/KARDON

TYPE	YR	MFG	MODEL	SELL EXC	SELL AVG	BUY EXC	BUY AVG
PRE	60- 63	HARM	**CITATION 1 KIT** STEREO TUBE	588	**451**	399	351
PRE	60	HARM	**CITATION 2** STEREO TUBE	660	**507**	448	395
PRE	60- 63	HARM	**CITATION 4 KIT** STEREO TUBE	392	**301**	266	234
PRE	60	HARM	**CITATION 5 KIT** STEREO TUBE	573	**440**	389	343
PWR	60- 64	HARM	**CITATION 2** STEREO TUBE, 60 WATT	829	**637**	563	496
PWR	60- 64	HARM	**CITATION 5 KIT** STEREO TUBE	723	**555**	490	432
PWR	60	HARM	**HK- 20** MONO TUBE	120	**92**	82	72
PWR	73	HARM	**HK-250**	201	**154**	136	120
TUNER	59	HARM	**T-220** TUBE	219	**168**	148	131
TUNER	59	HARM	**T-230** TUBE	219	**168**	148	131

HARMONY, SEE ALSO STELLA

TYPE	YR	MFG	MODEL	SELL EXC	SELL AVG	BUY EXC	BUY AVG
ELEC. GUITAR & BASS	56	HARMONY	**AIRLINE** BLACK w/WHITE, SEMI-HOLLOW	314	**241**	213	188
ELGUIT	65	HARMONY	**H- 14**	381	**293**	259	228
ELGUIT	66	HARMONY	**H- 27** TOBACCO SUNBURST	273	**209**	185	163
ELGUIT	60	HARMONY	**H- 61** SUNBURST	260	**200**	177	156
ELGUIT	57	HARMONY	**H- 62** BLOND	517	**397**	351	309
ELGUIT	58	HARMONY	**H- 62** BLOND	264	**202**	179	158
ELGUIT	58	HARMONY	**H- 62** SUNBURST	316	**243**	215	189
ELGUIT	60	HARMONY	**H- 62** BLOND, SINGLE CUTAWAY, ROSEWOOD	421	**323**	285	251
ELGUIT	63	HARMONY	**H- 62** BLOND, CUTAWAY, ARCHTOP, INLAID BOARD	388	**298**	263	232
ELGUIT	67	HARMONY	**H- 71**	236	**181**	160	141
ELGUIT	60	HARMONY	**H- 72** RED	329	**252**	223	196
ELGUIT	69	HARMONY	**H- 72** RED	309	**237**	209	184
ELGUIT	70	HARMONY	**H- 72** RED, DOUBLE CUTAWAY, SEMI-HOLLOW, 2 PU's	302	**232**	205	180
ELGUIT	63	HARMONY	**H- 73** SUNBURST, SINGLE CUTAWAY, 2 PU's	492	**378**	334	294
ELGUIT	66	HARMONY	**H- 73** SUNBURST, DOUBLE CUTAWAY, 2 PU's	478	**367**	324	286
ELGUIT	58	HARMONY	**H- 75** RED, SINGLE CUTAWAY, SEMI-HOLLOW, 3 PU's	605	**465**	411	362
ELGUIT	67	HARMONY	**H- 75** SUNBURST, 3 PU's	498	**382**	338	298
ELGUIT	60	HARMONY	**H- 77** SUNBURST	624	**479**	424	373
ELGUIT	65	HARMONY	**H- 77** SUNBURST, DOUBLE CUTAWAY, THIN	563	**432**	382	337
ELGUIT	64	HARMONY	**H-116**	641	**492**	435	383
ELGUIT	60	HARMONY	**HOLIDAY** SUNBURST, 1 PU	392	**301**	266	234
ELGUIT	60	HARMONY	**HOLLYWOOD** SUNBURST, NON-CUT, 1 PU	312	**239**	212	186
ELGUIT	58	HARMONY	**METEOR** SUNBURST, SINGLE CUTAWAY, SEMI-HOLLOW	327	**251**	221	195
ELGUIT	65	HARMONY	**METEOR** SUNBURST, 2 PU's	381	**293**	259	228
ELGUIT	63	HARMONY	**METEOR S-60**	383	**294**	259	229
ELGUIT	63	HARMONY	**MONTEREY**	404	**310**	274	241
ELGUIT	65	HARMONY	**R-70** CHERRY RED, 12-STRING	451	**346**	306	270
ELGUIT	65	HARMONY	**R-79** CHERRY RED, 12-STRING	500	**384**	339	299
ELGUIT	60	HARMONY	**ROCKET** RED SUNBURST	418	**321**	284	250
ELGUIT	62	HARMONY	**ROCKET** RED SUNBURST	416	**319**	282	249
ELGUIT	63	HARMONY	**ROCKET** RED SUNBURST	417	**320**	283	249

TYPE	YR	MFG	PRICES--BASED ON 100% ORIGINAL MODEL	SELL EXC	SELL AVG	BUY EXC	BUY AVG
ELGUIT	64	HARMONY	**ROCKET** RED SUNBURST	415	**319**	281	248
ELGUIT	65	HARMONY	**ROCKET** RED SUNBURST	423	**325**	287	253
ELGUIT	66	HARMONY	**ROCKET** RED SUNBURST	423	**325**	287	253
ELGUIT	68	HARMONY	**ROCKET** RED SUNBURST	417	**320**	283	249
ELGUIT	62	HARMONY	**ROCKET F-65**	278	**214**	189	166
ELGUIT	62	HARMONY	**ROCKET F-70**	277	**213**	188	166
ELGUIT	60	HARMONY	**ROCKET III**	361	**277**	245	216
ELGUIT	50	HARMONY	**ROY SMECK** MIDNIGHT BLUE	642	**493**	436	384
ELGUIT	71	HARMONY	**ROY SMECK** BLACK & WHITE	604	**464**	410	361
ELGUIT	60	HARMONY	**SILVERTONE** BLACK, SEMI-HOLLOW	243	**186**	164	145
ELGUIT	62	HARMONY	**SILVERTONE** BLACK, SEMI-HOLLOW	236	**181**	160	141
ELGUIT	64	HARMONY	**SILVERTONE** BLACK, SEMI-HOLLOW	228	**175**	155	136
ELGUIT	53	HARMONY	**STRAT-O-TONE**	426	**327**	289	255
ELGUIT	55	HARMONY	**STRAT-O-TONE** COPPER MIST	412	**316**	279	246
ELGUIT	56	HARMONY	**STRAT-O-TONE**	600	**460**	407	359
ELGUIT	59	HARMONY	**STRAT-O-TONE**	407	**313**	276	243
ELGUIT	60	HARMONY	**STRAT-O-TONE** MARS SUNBURST	423	**325**	287	253
ELGUIT	60	HARMONY	**STRAT-O-TONE** JUPITER BLACK	481	**369**	326	288
ELGUIT	61	HARMONY	**STRAT-O-TONE** JUPITER SPRUCE	435	**334**	295	260
ELGUIT	62	HARMONY	**STRAT-O-TONE** MERCURY BLOND	432	**331**	293	258
ELGUIT	63	HARMONY	**STRAT-O-TONE**	369	**283**	250	221
GUITAR AMP	67	HARMONY	**H-420** 115" SPEAKER, 20 WATTS, TUBE, COMBO	399	**307**	271	239
GUITAR (ACOUSTIC)	54	HARMONY	**BRILLIANT**	505	**387**	342	302
GUITAR	57	HARMONY	**BRILLIANT** SERIAL #631	628	**482**	426	375
GUITAR	69	HARMONY	**BUCK OWENS** RED, WHITE & BLUE	495	**380**	335	296
GUITAR	44	HARMONY	**CREMONA** ARCHTOP	488	**374**	331	292
GUITAR	50	HARMONY	**CREMONA VI** SUNBURST, MAPLE BACK/SIDES, PEARL INLAY	680	**522**	462	407
GUITAR	60	HARMONY	**ESPANADA**	441	**338**	299	263
GUITAR	59	HARMONY	**F-66GM** SPRUCE TOP	362	**278**	246	217
GUITAR	20	HARMONY	**FLATTOP** PEARL ROSETTE	586	**450**	398	351
GUITAR	62	HARMONY	**FLATTOP** NATURAL	286	**216**	191	158
GUITAR	58	HARMONY	**JAMBOREE**	361	**277**	245	216
GUITAR	50	HARMONY	**K-11** SUNBURST, CUTAWAY, ARCHTOP, 17", SOLID SPRUCE TOP	803	**616**	544	480
GUITAR	60	HARMONY	**MONTCLAIR** BLACK, ARCHTOP	434	**333**	294	259
GUITAR	30	HARMONY	**PATRICIAN** ARCHTOP	665	**510**	451	397
GUITAR	38	HARMONY	**PATRICIAN** NATURAL, MAHOGANY, ARCHTOP	758	**582**	514	453
GUITAR	40	HARMONY	**PATRICIAN**	778	**597**	528	465
GUITAR	50	HARMONY	**PATRICIAN** NATURAL, MAHOGANY, ARCHTOP	827	**635**	561	495
GUITAR	54	HARMONY	**PATRICIAN** ARCHTOP, F-HOLES	679	**522**	461	406
GUITAR	55	HARMONY	**PATRICIAN** NATURAL, SPRUCE, ARCHTOP	739	**567**	501	442
GUITAR	63	HARMONY	**PATRICIAN** NATURAL, MAHOGANY, ARCHTOP	670	**515**	455	401
GUITAR	50	HARMONY	**REGAL** SUNBURST, ARCHTOP	460	**353**	312	275
GUITAR	60	HARMONY	**SILVERTONE** NATURAL, ARCHTOP	344	**264**	234	206
GUITAR	60	HARMONY	**SILVERTONE** SUNBURST, FLATTOP	348	**267**	236	208
GUITAR	57	HARMONY	**SINGING COWBOY**	319	**245**	216	190
GUITAR	59	HARMONY	**SOVEREIGN** FLATTOP	333	**256**	226	199
GUITAR	60	HARMONY	**SOVEREIGN** FLATTOP	712	**546**	483	426

	TYPE	YR	MFG	PRICES--BASED ON 100% ORIGINAL MODEL	SELL EXC	SELL AVG	BUY EXC	BUY AVG
	GUITAR	62	HARMONY	**SOVEREIGN** FLATTOP	708	**544**	481	424
	GUITAR	63	HARMONY	**SOVEREIGN** FLATTOP	706	**542**	479	422
	GUITAR	65	HARMONY	**SOVEREIGN** FLATTOP	687	**528**	466	411
	GUITAR	68	HARMONY	**SOVEREIGN** FLATTOP	278	**214**	189	166
	GUITAR	70	HARMONY	**SOVEREIGN**	380	**292**	258	227
MANDOLIN		50	HARMONY	**410**	388	**298**	263	232
	MANDOL	40	HARMONY	**F-47** SUNBURST, A STYLE F-HOLES	430	**330**	291	257
	MANDOL	76	HARMONY	**MODEL A** F-HOLES	319	**245**	216	190
	MANDOL	30	HARMONY	**MONTEREY** SUNBURST, TEARDROP SHAPE	380	**292**	258	227
	MANDOL	60	HARMONY	**MONTEREY** SUNBURST, A STYLE F-HOLES	351	**270**	238	210
STEEL GUITAR		53	HARMONY	**LAP STEEL** GREY PEARLOID	361	**277**	245	216
UKULELE		54	HARMONY	**BARITONE**	227	**174**	154	136
	UKE	55	HARMONY	**BARITONE**	309	**237**	209	184
	UKE	25	HARMONY	**JOHNNY MARVIN** TENOR	441	**338**	299	263
	UKE	35	HARMONY	**ROY SMECK CONCERT**	278	**214**	189	166
	UKE	25	HARMONY	**ROY SMECK VITA-UKE** TEARDROP SHAPE	605	**465**	411	362
	UKE	26	HARMONY	**ROY SMECK VITA-UKE** PEAR SHAPED, SEAL SHAPED F-HOLES	364	**279**	247	217
	UKE	33	HARMONY	**ROY SMECK VITA-UKE** TEARDROP SHAPE	472	**357**	314	261

HAYNES OF BOSTON

	TYPE	YR	MFG	MODEL	SELL EXC	SELL AVG	BUY EXC	BUY AVG
GUITAR (ACOUSTIC)		10	HAYNES	**BAY STATE** BRAZILIAN ROSEWOOD BACK/SIDES	632	**485**	429	378
	GUITAR	01	HAYNES	**STYLE 6** 1901, BRAZILIAN ROSEWOOD BACK/SIDES	670	**515**	455	401
	GUITAR	01	HAYNES	**WURLITZER** 1901, SPRUCE TOP, OAK BACK/SIDES	380	**292**	258	227

HEATHKIT

	TYPE	YR	MFG	MODEL	SELL EXC	SELL AVG	BUY EXC	BUY AVG
PRE		72	HEATH	**WAP-2** MONO TUBE	132	**101**	89	79
PWR		51	HEATH	**W-1** MONO TUBE	142	**109**	96	85
	PWR	54	HEATH	**W-2** MONO TUBE	154	**118**	104	92
	PWR	54	HEATH	**W-3** MONO TUBE	1,234	**947**	837	738
	PWR	72	HEATH	**W-4AM** MONO TUBE	318	**244**	215	190
	PWR	58-62	HEATH	**W-4M** MONO TUBE, 20 WATT	390	**300**	265	233
	PWR	58	HEATH	**W-5 KIT** MONO TUBE	694	**533**	471	415
	PWR	72	HEATH	**W-5AM** TUBE	318	**244**	215	190
	PWR	58-62	HEATH	**W-5M** MONO TUBE, 25 WATT	170	**130**	115	101
	PWR	72	HEATH	**W-5M** MONO TUBE, 25 WATTS	319	**245**	216	190
	PWR	58-62	HEATH	**W-6 KIT** MONO TUBE, 70 WATT	443	**340**	300	265
	PWR	73	HEATH	**W-6M** MONO 70, PAIR	893	**686**	606	534
	PWR	58-62	HEATH	**W-7 KIT** MONO TUBE, 55 WATT	333	**256**	226	199

HIEL

	TYPE	YR	MFG	MODEL	SELL EXC	SELL AVG	BUY EXC	BUY AVG
EFFECTS		74	HIEL	**SQUAWKBOX "ORANGE"**	726	**558**	493	434
	EFFECTS	74	HIEL	**TALKBOX "PURPLE"**	742	**570**	503	444

HIWATT AMPLIFICATION

	TYPE	YR	MFG	MODEL	SELL EXC	SELL AVG	BUY EXC	BUY AVG
GUITAR AMP		71	HIWATT	**4x12" CAB FANE SPEAKERS**	838	**644**	569	501
	GTAMP	72	HIWATT	**50 WATT HEAD**	780	**599**	529	466
	GTAMP	72	HIWATT	**100 WATT HEAD**	960	**737**	652	574
	GTAMP	70	HIWATT	**100 WATT PA HEAD**	797	**612**	541	477
	GTAMP	75	HIWATT	**DR-504** AMP HEAD	645	**495**	437	385

HOFNER

	TYPE	YR	MFG	MODEL	SELL EXC	SELL AVG	BUY EXC	BUY AVG
BANJO		75	HOFNER	**STRAD ARTIST MODEL** 2 PC BACK/SHADED RED VARNISH, MATCHING EBONY FITTINGS	1,244	**955**	844	744

TYPE	YR	MFG	PRICES--BASED ON 100% ORIGINAL MODEL	SELL EXC	SELL AVG	BUY EXC	BUY AVG
ELEC. GUITAR & BASS	58	HOFNER	125 HOLLOW BODY, SINGLE CUTAWAY, 1 PU	903	694	613	540
ELGUIT	60	HOFNER	126 HOLLOW BODY, SINGLE CUTAWAY, 2 PU's	889	682	603	531
ELGUIT	56	HOFNER	160 NATURAL, SOLID BODY, 1 PU	692	531	469	414
ELGUIT	57	HOFNER	162 BLACK, SOLID BODY, 2 PU's	714	548	484	427
ELGUIT	65	HOFNER	164 DOUBLE CUTAWAY, 2 PU's	635	487	430	379
ELGUIT	60	HOFNER	175 VINYL COVER	651	500	442	389
ELGUIT	67	HOFNER	176 RED, SOLID BODY	565	434	383	338
ELGUIT	65	HOFNER	**185 BASS**	724	556	491	433
ELGUIT	64	HOFNER	335 SUNBURST	688	528	467	412
ELGUIT	67	HOFNER	427 SUNBURST, DOUBLE NECK 4/6	2,303	1,769	1,563	1,378
ELGUIT	74	HOFNER	**448 ELECTRIC UPRIGHT** NATURAL, SPRUCE	834	640	566	499
ELGUIT	65	HOFNER	**470 SE2** NATURAL, CUTAWAY, 2 PU's	540	415	367	323
ELGUIT	62	HOFNER	**500 1** CLOSE DIAMOND PU, SERIAL #317-349	9,421	7,234	6,393	5,636
ELGUIT	57	HOFNER	**500 1 BASS** PRE-BEATLE SPRUCE	5,901	4,531	4,004	3,530
ELGUIT	58	HOFNER	**500 1 BEATLE BASS** SUNBURST, 2 BLACK PU'S	6,378	4,897	4,328	3,815
ELGUIT	62	HOFNER	**500 1 BEATLE BASS** LEFT-HANDED, SERIAL #191-292	7,473	5,738	5,071	4,470
ELGUIT	63	HOFNER	**500 1 BEATLE BASS**	4,151	3,188	2,817	2,483
ELGUIT	64	HOFNER	**500 1 BEATLE BASS** SUNBURST	4,597	3,530	3,119	2,750
ELGUIT	64	HOFNER	**500 1 BEATLE BASS** LEFT-HANDED	5,382	4,133	3,652	3,220
ELGUIT	65	HOFNER	**500 1 BEATLE BASS** SERIAL #402-500	2,320	1,781	1,574	1,388
ELGUIT	65	HOFNER	**500 1 BEATLE BASS** LEFT-HANDED	5,220	4,008	3,542	3,122
ELGUIT	66	HOFNER	**500 1 BEATLE BASS**	2,226	1,709	1,510	1,331
ELGUIT	67	HOFNER	**500 1 BEATLE BASS**	2,170	1,666	1,472	1,298
ELGUIT	68	HOFNER	**500 1 BEATLE BASS**	2,349	1,804	1,594	1,405
ELGUIT	69	HOFNER	**500 1 BEATLE BASS**	1,774	1,362	1,203	1,061
ELGUIT	70	HOFNER	**500 1 BEATLE BASS** ICED TEA SUNBURST	1,784	1,369	1,210	1,067
ELGUIT	71	HOFNER	**500 1 BEATLE BASS** LEFT-HANDED	1,526	1,172	1,035	913
ELGUIT	71	HOFNER	**500 1 BEATLE BASS**	1,592	1,222	1,080	952
ELGUIT	73	HOFNER	**500 1 BEATLE BASS**	1,545	1,186	1,048	924
ELGUIT	74	HOFNER	**500 1 BEATLE BASS**	1,543	1,185	1,047	923
ELGUIT	75	HOFNER	**500 1 BEATLE BASS**	1,544	1,185	1,048	923
ELGUIT	78	HOFNER	**500 1 BEATLE BASS**	1,385	1,063	940	828
ELGUIT	79	HOFNER	**500 1 BEATLE BASS**	1,313	1,008	891	785
ELGUIT	56	HOFNER	**500 1 VIOLIN BASS**	10,492	8,056	7,119	6,276
ELGUIT	59	HOFNER	**500 1 VIOLIN BASS** SERIAL #107-191	6,942	5,331	4,711	4,153
ELGUIT	60	HOFNER	**500 1 VIOLIN BASS**	6,650	5,106	4,512	3,978
ELGUIT	61	HOFNER	**500 1 VIOLIN BASS**	6,634	5,094	4,502	3,969
ELGUIT	62	HOFNER	**500 1 VIOLIN BASS**	6,267	4,812	4,252	3,749
ELGUIT	63	HOFNER	**500 1 VIOLIN BASS** SERIAL #293-401	7,520	5,774	5,103	4,499
ELGUIT	57	HOFNER	**500 2 CLUB BASS** SUNBURST, SINGLE CUT, 2 PU's, STARTING SERIAL #29900	3,316	2,546	2,250	1,983
ELGUIT	58	HOFNER	**500 2 CLUB BASS** SUNBURST, SINGLE CUT, 2 PU's	3,808	2,924	2,584	2,278
ELGUIT	60	HOFNER	**500 2 CLUB BASS** SUNBURST, SINGLE CUT, 2 PU's, STARTING SERIAL #30290	3,239	2,487	2,197	1,937
ELGUIT	60	HOFNER	**500 3 BEATLE BASS** SUNBURST, SEMI-HOLLOW BODY, 2 PU's	2,113	1,622	1,434	1,264
ELGUIT	62	HOFNER	**500 3 BEATLE BASS** SEMI-HOLLOW BODY	1,611	1,237	1,093	964
ELGUIT	62	HOFNER	**500 6 BEATLE BASS** SUNBURST, DOUBLE CUTAWAY, 2 PU's	2,036	1,563	1,381	1,218
ELGUIT	67	HOFNER	**500 6 BEATLE BASS** SUNBURST, DOUBLE CUTAWAY	1,370	1,052	930	820
ELGUIT	67	HOFNER	527 6/4 DOUBLE NECK, SOLID BODY	1,697	1,303	1,152	1,015
ELGUIT	69	HOFNER	**BEATLE BASS**	1,784	1,369	1,210	1,067
ELGUIT	58	HOFNER	**CLUB 40** ONE PU	1,681	1,290	1,140	1,005

TYPE	YR	MFG	PRICES--BASED ON 100% ORIGINAL MODEL	SELL EXC	SELL AVG	BUY EXC	BUY AVG
ELGUIT	59	HOFNER	**CLUB 50** BLOND	1,312	**1,007**	890	785
ELGUIT	61	HOFNER	**CLUB 50** SUNBURST	1,215	**933**	824	726
ELGUIT	58-62	HOFNER	**CLUB 60** FLAME MAPLE BACK	2,881	**2,212**	1,955	1,723
ELGUIT	58	HOFNER	**CLUB 60 BASS** BLACK or NATURAL, 2 PU's, SERIAL #101-147	6,183	**4,748**	4,195	3,699
ELGUIT	59	HOFNER	**CLUB 60 BASS** NATURAL, 2 PU's	3,878	**2,978**	2,631	2,320
ELGUIT	59	HOFNER	**CLUB 60 BASS** BLACK, VERTICAL LOGO, 2 PU's, SERIAL #147-165	5,246	**4,028**	3,559	3,138
ELGUIT	60	HOFNER	**CLUB 60 BASS** VERTICAL LOGO, 2 PU's	4,151	**3,188**	2,817	2,483
ELGUIT	59	HOFNER	**COMMITTEE** F-HOLE, 2 PU's	1,444	**1,109**	980	864
ELGUIT	63	HOFNER	**COMMITTEE BASS** NATURAL	2,250	**1,727**	1,526	1,346
ELGUIT	61	HOFNER	**GOLDEN HOFNER**	1,206	**926**	818	721
ELGUIT	59	HOFNER	**PRESIDENT** F-HOLES, 2 PU's	3,480	**2,672**	2,362	2,082
ELGUIT	60	HOFNER	**PRESIDENT** NATURAL	2,899	**2,226**	1,967	1,734
ELGUIT	66	HOFNER	**PRESIDENT**	1,069	**821**	725	639
ELGUIT	63	HOFNER	**PRESIDENT BASS** NATURAL	1,441	**1,106**	978	862
ELGUIT	65	HOFNER	**PRESIDENT BASS** SUNBURST	1,069	**821**	725	639
ELGUIT	68	HOFNER	**PRESIDENT BASS** SUNBURST, SINGLE CUTAWAY	1,743	**1,339**	1,183	1,043
ELGUIT	65	HOFNER	**RANGER** RAISED LOGO, SINGLE CUTAWAY, TINA WEYMOUTH TALKING HEADS	1,256	**964**	852	751
ELGUIT	67	HOFNER	**VERI-THIN** RUST	650	**499**	441	389
ELGUIT	67	HOFNER	**VIOLIN GUITAR** FUZZ TONE	645	**495**	437	385
GUITAR AMP	70	HOFNER	**KV-40**	334	**257**	227	200
GUITAR (ACOUSTIC)	51	HOFNER	**463-S** SPRUCE, ARCHTOP, CUTAWAY	3,778	**2,901**	2,564	2,260
GUITAR	72	HOFNER	**974** SPRUCE TOP, MAHOGANY BACK/SIDES	1,545	**1,186**	1,048	924
GUITAR	70	HOFNER	**SLAP-BASS STANDARD**	592	**454**	402	354
UPRIG	71	HOFNER	**UPRIGHT BASS** SPRUCE TOP, MAPLE BACK/SIDES	4,387	**3,368**	2,976	2,624

HOHNER

TYPE	YR	MFG	MODEL	SELL EXC	SELL AVG	BUY EXC	BUY AVG
EFFECTS	78	HOHNER	**DIRTY WAH WAH'ER**	163	**125**	110	97
GUITAR AMP	65	HOHNER	**6149 DELUXE REVERB UNIT**	399	**307**	271	239
SYNTHESIZER	72	HOHNER	**C-86 63 KEY**	295	**227**	200	176
SYNTH	70	HOHNER	**C-88 63 KEY**	303	**233**	205	181

TOM HOLMES

TYPE	YR	MFG	MODEL	SELL EXC	SELL AVG	BUY EXC	BUY AVG
ELEC. GUITAR & BASS	72	HOLMES	**THC** BLACK	343	**264**	233	205

HOYER

TYPE	YR	MFG	MODEL	SELL EXC	SELL AVG	BUY EXC	BUY AVG
ELEC. GUITAR & BASS	67	HOYER	**150** SUNBURST, SEMI-HOLLOW BODY, 2 PU's	459	**352**	311	274
ELGUIT	62	HOYER	**SOLOIST** BLOND, CUTAWAY	906	**685**	604	501
ELGUIT	65	HOYER	**VIOLIN BASS** 1 PU	661	**508**	449	395
ELGUIT	66	HOYER	**VIOLIN BASS** 2 PU's	743	**571**	504	444
GUITAR AMP	64	HOYER	**J-45**	495	**380**	335	296

IBANEZ

TYPE	YR	MFG	MODEL	SELL EXC	SELL AVG	BUY EXC	BUY AVG
EFFECTS	80	IBANEZ	**AD-80** MAGENTA, ANALOG DELAY	280	**215**	190	167
EFFECTS	79	IBANEZ	**MUSICIAN EQUALIZER BASS**	672	**516**	456	402
EFFECTS	79	IBANEZ	**PT-909**	196	**150**	133	117
EFFECTS	80	IBANEZ	**PT-909** PHASE TONE	258	**198**	175	154
EFFECTS	75	IBANEZ	**PT-999** PHASE TONE, SLANT TOP	252	**193**	171	150
EFFECTS	79	IBANEZ	**TS- 9**	221	**170**	150	132
EFFECTS	78	IBANEZ	**TS-808** TUBE SCREAMER	678	**521**	460	406
EFFECTS	78	IBANEZ	**UE-300** MULTI-EFFECTS	421	**323**	285	251
ELEC. GUITAR & BASS	74	IBANEZ	**175 COPY** SUNBURST or BLOND	588	**451**	399	351
ELGUIT	73	IBANEZ	**2355**	773	**594**	525	462

TYPE	YR	MFG	PRICES--BASED ON 100% ORIGINAL MODEL	SELL EXC	SELL AVG	BUY EXC	BUY AVG
ELGUIT	74	IBANEZ	**2402**	855	**657**	580	511
ELGUIT	75	IBANEZ	**2404**	749	**575**	508	448
ELGUIT	76	IBANEZ	**2460**	1,340	**1,029**	909	801
ELGUIT	78	IBANEZ	**2680 BOB WEIR STANDARD** CARVED SOLID ASH BODY,6-STRING,MAPLE NECK,EBONY FRTBRD	573	**440**	389	343
ELGUIT	79	IBANEZ	**2681 BOB WEIR** CARVED SOLID ASH BODY,6-STRING,MAPLE NECK,EBONY FRTBRD	1,251	**960**	848	748
ELGUIT	80	IBANEZ	**AM-205**	804	**617**	545	481
ELGUIT	78	IBANEZ	**AR- 50 ARTIST** MAHOG BODY,CARVED MAPLE TOP,BIRCH NECK,CHROME HDWR	652	**501**	443	390
ELGUIT	78	IBANEZ	**AR-100 ARTIST**	631	**485**	428	377
ELGUIT	79	IBANEZ	**AR-200 ARTIST**	995	**764**	675	595
ELGUIT	76	IBANEZ	**ARTIST** SCROLL VINE INLAYS	803	**616**	544	480
ELGUIT	79	IBANEZ	**ARTIST** SEMI HOLLOWBODY	712	**546**	483	426
ELGUIT	80	IBANEZ	**AS- 50 ARTIST SEMI-ACOUSTIC**	639	**491**	433	382
ELGUIT	80	IBANEZ	**AS- 80**	640	**491**	434	383
ELGUIT	78	IBANEZ	**CN-250 CONCERT** VINE INLAY ON BOARD	673	**516**	456	402
ELGUIT	80	IBANEZ	**CUSTOM AGENT LES PAUL STYLE**	741	**569**	503	443
ELGUIT	76	IBANEZ	**DESTROYER** KORINA	1,025	**787**	696	613
ELGUIT	77	IBANEZ	**DESTROYER** KORINA, NATURAL, MADE IN JAPAN	927	**712**	629	554
ELGUIT	82	IBANEZ	**DESTROYER II**	629	**483**	427	376
ELGUIT	69	IBANEZ	**DOUBLE NECK** SG STYLE, 6+4-STRING	608	**460**	405	336
ELGUIT	78	IBANEZ	**FA-100 JAZZ MODEL** 2 PU's	852	**654**	578	509
ELGUIT	78	IBANEZ	**FA-300 JAZZ MODEL** 2 PU's	976	**749**	662	584
ELGUIT	78	IBANEZ	**FA-500 JAZZ MODEL** 2 FLOATING PU's	1,308	**1,004**	887	782
ELGUIT	78	IBANEZ	**FA-510 JAZZ MODEL** FLOATING PU's	1,307	**1,003**	886	781
ELGUIT	78	IBANEZ	**FA-700 JAZZ MODEL** CARVED TOP, 2 PU's	1,851	**1,421**	1,256	1,107
ELGUIT	76	IBANEZ	**FIREBIRD COPY** NON-REVERSE	545	**418**	370	326
ELGUIT	77	IBANEZ	**GB-10 GEORGE BENSON**	1,201	**922**	815	718
ELGUIT	78	IBANEZ	**GB-10 GEORGE BENSON** SUNBURST	1,201	**922**	815	718
ELGUIT	79	IBANEZ	**GB-10 GEORGE BENSON** NATURAL	1,256	**964**	852	751
ELGUIT	80	IBANEZ	**GB-10 GEORGE BENSON** SUNBURST	1,201	**922**	815	718
ELGUIT	76	IBANEZ	**ICEMAN** RICK NELSON, KORINA	1,672	**1,283**	1,134	1,000
ELGUIT	77	IBANEZ	**ICEMAN** PAUL STANLEY	1,339	**1,028**	908	801
ELGUIT	78	IBANEZ	**ICEMAN** BOLT-ON NECK	540	**415**	367	323
ELGUIT	77	IBANEZ	**JAZZ BASS SILVER SERIES** BROWN	645	**495**	437	385
ELGUIT	92	IBANEZ	**JOE SATRINI SIGNATURE JS** ONLY 12 MADE,BASSWD BODY,MAPLE NECK,INLAY,2 DIMARZIO HB's	2,936	**2,254**	1,992	1,756
ELGUIT	76	IBANEZ	**JOHNNY SMITH** BLOND	1,792	**1,376**	1,216	1,072
ELGUIT	82	IBANEZ	**JP-20 JOE PASS**	1,518	**1,166**	1,030	908
ELGUIT	76	IBANEZ	**KORINA V**	1,031	**792**	699	617
ELGUIT	79	IBANEZ	**KORINA V**	973	**747**	660	582
ELGUIT	80	IBANEZ	**LES PAUL DELUXE** 2 PU's	312	**239**	212	186
ELGUIT	78	IBANEZ	**LES PAUL PERFORMER COPY** 3 PU's	353	**271**	240	211
ELGUIT	79	IBANEZ	**LES PAUL TV JUNIOR COPY** GLUED-IN	360	**276**	244	215
ELGUIT	80	IBANEZ	**LES PAUL TV SPECIAL COPY** GLUED-IN	405	**311**	275	242
ELGUIT	76	IBANEZ	**MODERNERE** NATURAL, MADE IN JAPAN	1,293	**993**	877	773
ELGUIT	80	IBANEZ	**MODERNERE** MAHOGANY	956	**734**	649	572
ELGUIT	78	IBANEZ	**PF-100** WALNUT	443	**340**	300	265
ELGUIT	70	IBANEZ	**PF-200** SUNBURST	465	**357**	316	278
ELGUIT	78	IBANEZ	**PF-200** BOLT-ON	459	**352**	311	274
ELGUIT	78	IBANEZ	**PF-300** SET NECK	749	**575**	508	448

TYPE	YR	MFG	MODEL	SELL EXC	SELL AVG	BUY EXC	BUY AVG
ELGUIT	78	IBANEZ	PROFESSIONAL BOB WEIR	1,404	1,078	953	840
ELGUIT	78	IBANEZ	PS-10 PAUL STANLEY SIGNATURE	894	687	607	535
ELGUIT	76	IBANEZ	SCRUGGS NATURAL	1,428	1,096	969	854
ELGUIT	78	IBANEZ	ST-300NT STUDIO NATURAL	612	470	415	366
ELGUIT	62	IBANEZ	TULIO RED	741	569	503	443
SIGNAL PROCESSOR	82	IBANEZ	SD-9 SONIC DISTORTION	84	64	57	50
SGNPRO	82	IBANEZ	TS- 9 TUBE SCREAMER	176	135	120	105
SGNPRO	80	IBANEZ	TS-808 TUBE SCREAMER	245	188	166	146
UPRIG	76	IBANEZ	CONCORD NATURAL, CURLY MAPLE, MADE IN JAPAN, COPY OF GUILD F-50	621	477	421	371

JBL LOUDSPEAKERS

TYPE	YR	MFG	MODEL	SELL EXC	SELL AVG	BUY EXC	BUY AVG
RAW	76	JBL	002 SYSTEM NO CABINET	365	280	247	218
RAW	64	JBL	075 HORN TWEETER RING RADIATOR	296	227	201	177
RAW	71	JBL	077 TWEETER SLOT HORN	302	232	205	180
RAW	64	JBL	130A 15"	458	351	310	274
RAW	64-72	JBL	130B	435	334	295	260
RAW	60-72	JBL	150-4C 15" WOOFER	516	396	350	308
RAW	75	JBL	2202 12" WOOFER	262	201	177	156
RAW	70	JBL	D-110 10" LEAD GUITAR	148	114	101	89
RAW	62	JBL	D-123 12"	200	153	136	119
RAW	68-82	JBL	D-130 15"	328	251	222	196
RAW	60	JBL	D-216 8" PAIR	268	206	182	160
RAW	60	JBL	LE- 8 8" PAIR	274	210	186	164
RAW	68	JBL	LE-15A 15" WOOFER	356	273	241	213
SPKR	73	JBL	375 2" HORN DRIVER	806	619	547	482
SPKR	85	JBL	2204H,J CONE TRANSDUCER 12"	412	316	279	246
SPKR	80	JBL	2215 CONDE TRANSDUCER 15"	323	248	219	193
SPKR	75	JBL	2220 15" WOOFER	148	114	101	89
SPKR	83	JBL	2385A HORN	826	634	560	494
SPKR	82	JBL	2404H BI-RADIAL TWEETER	418	321	284	250
SPKR	75	JBL	2405 TWEETER HORN	201	154	136	120
SPKR	80	JBL	4311 (PAIR) 3-QWAY, 12" WOOFER	480	368	326	287
SPKR	80	JBL	4343 (PAIR) 4-WAY, 15" WOOFER	2,824	2,168	1,916	1,689
SPKR	64	JBL	C-34 SPEAKER ENCLOSURE	184	141	125	110
SPKR	64	JBL	C-35 SPEAKER ENCLOSURE	280	215	190	167
SPKR	64-68	JBL	D-30085 HARTSFIELD (PAIR)	6,174	4,741	4,189	3,693
XOVER	77	JBL	N-1200 FREQUENCY NETWORK	138	106	94	83

JENSEN

TYPE	YR	MFG	MODEL	SELL EXC	SELL AVG	BUY EXC	BUY AVG
RAW	60	JENSEN	C-12NF 12" PAIR	198	152	134	118
RAW	60	JENSEN	DX-120 12" PAIR	196	150	133	117
RAW	73	JENSEN	G-610B	594	456	403	355
RAW	60	JENSEN	K-210 12" PAIR	193	148	131	115
RAW	60	JENSEN	RP-302A TWEETER PAIR	192	147	130	115

JUZEK

TYPE	YR	MFG	MODEL	SELL EXC	SELL AVG	BUY EXC	BUY AVG
UPRIG	47	JUZEK	UPRIGHT STRING BASS FULLY CARVE, SPRUCE TOP, FLAMED MAPLE BACK/SIDES	5,953	4,571	4,040	3,561
UPRIGHT	50	JUZEK	UPRIGHT STRING BASS FULLY CARVED, VIOLIN CORNERS	7,940	6,097	5,388	4,750

KALAMAZOO

TYPE	YR	MFG	MODEL	SELL EXC	SELL AVG	BUY EXC	BUY AVG
BANJO	37	KALAMAZOO	KALAMAZOO 5-STRING	1,756	1,348	1,191	1,050
ELEC. GUITAR & BASS	67	KALAMAZOO	KB BASS RED, 1 PU	610	468	414	365
ELGUIT	68	KALAMAZOO	KB BASS RED, 1 PU	564	433	383	337
ELGUIT	66	KALAMAZOO	KG-1A BLUE, 1 PU	599	460	406	358
ELGUIT	68	KALAMAZOO	SG SOLID BODY RED, 1 PU, ROSEWOOD FRETBOARD	458	351	310	274
GUITAR AMP	67	KALAMAZOO	REVERB 12	319	245	216	190
GUITAR (ACOUSTIC)	40	KALAMAZOO	HG-00 SUNBURST	623	479	423	373

TYPE	YR	MFG	PRICES--BASED ON 100% ORIGINAL MODEL	SELL EXC	SELL AVG	BUY EXC	BUY AVG
GUITAR	38	KALAMAZOO	**K-14** SUNBURST	817	**627**	554	489
GUITAR	36	KALAMAZOO	**KG- 3/4** SUNBURST, FLATTOP	603	**463**	409	361
GUITAR	35	KALAMAZOO	**KG- 1**	788	**605**	535	471
GUITAR	39	KALAMAZOO	**KG-10** SUNBURST, ARCHTOP	837	**643**	568	501
GUITAR	37	KALAMAZOO	**KG-11** SUNBURST, FLATTOP	741	**569**	503	443
GUITAR	37	KALAMAZOO	**KG-14** SUNBURST, FLATTOP	741	**569**	503	443
GUITAR	39	KALAMAZOO	**KG-16** SUNBURST, ARCHTOP	728	**559**	494	435
GUITAR	36	KALAMAZOO	**KG-21** SUNBURST FINISH, BLACK PICKGUARD,RSWD FRTBRD,MED FRETS,CASE	1,313	**1,008**	891	785
GUITAR	37	KALAMAZOO	**KG-31** SUNBURST, ARCHTOP	826	**634**	560	494
GUITAR	41	KALAMAZOO	**KGN-12** NATURAL, FLATTOP	618	**474**	419	369
GUITAR	40	KALAMAZOO	**KGN-32** BLOND, ORIOLE ARCHTOP	768	**589**	521	459
GUITAR	41	KALAMAZOO	**KGN-32** NATURAL	530	**407**	360	317
GUITAR	36	KALAMAZOO	**KHG-11** SUNBURST, HAWAIIAN	610	**468**	414	365
GUITAR	38	KALAMAZOO	**KTG-14 SENIOR L-0 SIZE TENOR** SUNBURST	670	**515**	455	401
GUITAR	35	KALAMAZOO	**ORIOLE ARCHTOP**	610	**468**	414	365
GUITAR	37	KALAMAZOO	**SPORT MODEL**	663	**509**	449	396
GUITAR	30	KALAMAZOO	**TENOR** SUNBURST, FLATTOP, MAHOGANY BACK/SIDES	540	**415**	367	323
GUITAR	31	KALAMAZOO	**TENOR** SUNBURST, FLATTOP	549	**422**	373	328
MANDOLIN	37	KALAMAZOO	**KM- 2** SUNBURST, A STYLE F-HOLES, MAPLE BACK/SIDES	644	**494**	437	385
MANDOL	36	KALAMAZOO	**KM-21** SUNBURST, F-HOLES	770	**591**	522	460
STEEL GUITAR	39	KALAMAZOO	**KEH LAP STEEL** BROWN	488	**374**	331	292
STGUIT	40	KALAMAZOO	**KEH LAP STEEL** WALNUT, SERIAL #FKE731	599	**460**	406	358

KAMAKA

UKULELE	70	KAMAKA	**PINEAPPLE**	564	**433**	383	337
UKE	30	KAMAKA	**PLAIN KOA**	573	**440**	389	343
UKE	65	KAMAKA	**PLAIN STANDARD SHAPE**	415	**319**	281	248
UKE	50	KAMAKA	**PLAIN TENOR**	560	**430**	380	335

KAY GUITAR COMPANY

BANJO	30	KAY	**KRAFT** KEY-CHORD	779	**598**	528	466
BANJO	35	KAY	**KRAFT** SUNBURST, WOOD BODY, RESONATOR	770	**591**	522	460
BANJO	36	KAY	**KRAFT TENOR**	347	**266**	235	207
BANJO	15	KAY	**ORPHEUM #1 TENOR** OPEN BACK	605	**465**	411	362
BANJO	60	KAY	**SILVERTONE** 5-STRING	332	**255**	225	198
BANJO	50	KAY	**SILVERTONE TENOR**	181	**139**	123	108
BANJO	40	KAY	**TENOR** MAHOGANY NECK	277	**213**	188	166
BANJO	50	KAY	**TENOR** DEEP RESONATOR	227	**174**	154	136
BANJO	60	KAY	**TENOR** 19-FRET, RESONATOR, SERIAL #2847-28	172	**132**	117	103
ELEC. GUITAR & BASS	58	KAY	**BARNEY KESSEL STYLE** MAPLE, ARCHTOP	467	**358**	316	279
ELGUIT	58	KAY	**BARNEY KESSEL STYLE** BLACK	524	**402**	355	313
ELGUIT	61	KAY	**CATALINA** SUNBURST	499	**383**	338	298
ELGUIT	60	KAY	**JAZZ SPECIAL**	510	**392**	346	305
ELGUIT	58	KAY	**JUMBO** SUNBURST, CUTAWAY, ARCHTOP, 2 PU's	446	**343**	303	267
ELGUIT	54	KAY	**K- 21S SPEED DEMON** SOLID BODY	628	**482**	426	375
ELGUIT	52	KAY	**K- 161 THIN TWIN**	316	**243**	215	189
ELGUIT	53	KAY	**K- 161 THIN TWIN** LES PAUL SHAPE, 2 PU's	278	**214**	189	166
ELGUIT	58	KAY	**K- 161 THIN TWIN** LES PAUL SHAPE	254	**195**	172	152
ELGUIT	58	KAY	**K- 161 THIN TWIN** JIMMY REED, NATURAL	264	**202**	179	158

TYPE	YR	MFG	PRICES--BASED ON 100% ORIGINAL MODEL	SELL EXC	SELL AVG	BUY EXC	BUY AVG
ELGUIT	58	KAY	**K- 161 THIN TWIN** BLOND, CURLY MAPLE	268	**206**	182	160
ELGUIT	59	KAY	**K- 161 THIN TWIN** SEMI-ACOUSTIC	271	**208**	183	162
ELGUIT	67	KAY	**K- 405** WHITE, BIGSBY VIBRATO	235	**180**	159	140
ELGUIT	60	KAY	**K- 535** DOUBLE CUTAWAY, VIBRATO, 2 PU's	362	**278**	246	217
ELGUIT	62	KAY	**K- 671 OLD KRAFTSMAN** FLAME MAPLE	283	**217**	192	169
ELGUIT	63	KAY	**K- 671 OLD KRAFTSMAN** SUNBURST	250	**192**	170	150
ELGUIT	66	KAY	**K-5935** BROWN SUNBURST, STRAT, 1 PU	198	**152**	134	118
ELGUIT	64	KAY	**K-5953 BASS** SOLIDBODY	357	**274**	242	213
ELGUIT	59	KAY	**K-6000**	319	**245**	216	190
ELGUIT	60	KAY	**K-8900 JAZZ SPECIAL**	431	**331**	292	257
ELGUIT	52	KAY	**K-8901** SUNBURST, CUTAWAY, ARCHTOP	464	**356**	315	278
ELGUIT	62	KAY	**KAY** RED, SEMI-HOLLOW, CUTAWAY, 2 PU's	278	**214**	189	166
ELGUIT	55	KAY	**KAY SB** SEMI-SOLLOW, CUTAWAY, 3 PU's	452	**342**	301	250
ELGUIT	30	KAY	**KRAFT RECORDING KING**	547	**420**	371	327
ELGUIT	40	KAY	**O-100 SWING BASS**	997	**766**	677	596
ELGUIT	62	KAY	**SEMI HOLLOW** TRANSPARENT RED, CUTAWAY, 2 PU's	394	**302**	267	235
ELGUIT	58	KAY	**SEMI-HOLLOW** SUNBURST, CUTAWAY, NP F-HOLES	486	**373**	329	290
ELGUIT	62	KAY	**SEMI-HOLLOW** WALNUT, BIGSBY, MAPLE NECK, 3 PU's	459	**352**	311	274
ELGUIT	52	KAY	**SHERWOOD DELUXE** SUNBURST, 16", SINGLE PU	492	**378**	334	294
ELGUIT	55	KAY	**SILVERTONE** SUNBURST, JIMMY REED MODEL	572	**439**	388	342
ELGUIT	60	KAY	**SILVERTONE** NATURAL	313	**240**	212	187
ELGUIT	62	KAY	**SILVERTONE** NATURAL, ARCHED TOP/BACK	235	**180**	159	140
ELGUIT	62	KAY	**SILVERTONE** NATURAL, HOLLOW, CUTAWAY	235	**180**	159	140
ELGUIT	50	KAY	**SOLID BODY** BOLT-ON NECK, 2 MIRROW PU's	288	**221**	196	172
ELGUIT	62	KAY	**SWINGMASTER**	511	**393**	347	306
ELGUIT	50	KAY	**THIN** HOLLOW BODY, ELEC, F-HOLE, 1 PU	369	**283**	250	221
ELGUIT	62	KAY	**THIN** BROWN SUNBURST, HOLLOW BODY, SINGLE CUTAWAY	309	**237**	209	184
ELGUIT	65	KAY	**THIN** HOLLOW BODY, DOUBLE CUTAWAY	389	**299**	264	233
ELGUIT	52	KAY	**TRUETONE** SUNBURST	327	**251**	221	195
ELGUIT	55	KAY	**UPBEAT** SUNBURST, 2 PU's	527	**405**	357	315
GUITAR AMP	60	KAY	**K-503A** BLACK-WHITE, 1x8" SPEAKER	221	**170**	150	132
GTAMP	60	KAY	**K-507** TWIN 10" SPEAKERS, "REFRIGERATOR HANDLE MODEL"	1,201	**922**	815	718
GTAMP	60	KAY	**MODEL 703** 1x8" SPEAKER, 6 WATTS	178	**136**	120	106
GUITAR (ACOUSTIC)	60	KAY	**CLASSICAL STRING BASS**	1,219	**936**	827	729
GUITAR	30	KAY	**DELUXE** SUNBURST, ROUND SOUND HOLE	801	**615**	544	479
GUITAR	29	KAY	**GABRIEL** FLATTOP	705	**541**	478	422
GUITAR	62	KAY	**JAZZ II**	424	**325**	288	253
GUITAR	55	KAY	**JUMBO** SPRUCE, ARCHTOP, NON-CUTAWAY, 1 PU	362	**278**	246	217
GUITAR	56	KAY	**JUMBO** SPRUCE TOP, MAHOGANY, FLATTOP	472	**362**	320	282
GUITAR	57	KAY	**K- 18**	453	**348**	307	271
GUITAR	48	KAY	**K- 21** SILVERTONE BLOND, SPRUCE TOP	635	**487**	430	379
GUITAR	50	KAY	**K- 21** BLOND	605	**465**	411	362
GUITAR	52	KAY	**K- 21** CHERRY SUNBURST	599	**460**	406	358
GUITAR	53	KAY	**K- 21** BLOND	601	**461**	408	359
GUITAR	60	KAY	**K- 21S SPEED DEMON**	441	**338**	299	263
GUITAR	50	KAY	**K- 24**	453	**348**	307	271

TYPE	YR	MFG	PRICES--BASED ON 100% ORIGINAL MODEL	SELL EXC	SELL AVG	BUY EXC	BUY AVG
GUITAR	53	KAY	K- 27	460	353	312	275
GUITAR	38	KAY	K- 40 SUNBURST, ARCHTOP	759	583	515	454
GUITAR	25	KAY	KAYKRAFT SUNBURST, FLATTOP	527	405	357	315
GUITAR	32	KAY	KAYKRAFT ARCHTOP	364	279	247	217
GUITAR	36	KAY	KAYKRAFT "A"	527	405	357	315
GUITAR	38	KAY	KAYKRAFT "B"	551	423	373	329
GUITAR	38	KAY	KAYKRAFT "C"	649	491	432	359
GUITAR	59	KAY	KESSEL ARTIST	571	438	387	341
GUITAR	57	KAY	KESSEL JAZZ SP	499	383	338	298
GUITAR	58	KAY	KESSEL JAZZ SP	543	417	368	324
GUITAR	59	KAY	KESSEL JAZZ SP	511	393	347	306
GUITAR	58	KAY	KESSEL PRO	189	143	126	104
GUITAR	42	KAY	LOUISE MASSEY FLATTOP	683	524	463	408
GUITAR	70	KAY	M-1 MAESTRO STRING BASS	1,319	1,013	895	789
GUITAR	70	KAY	M-5 STRING BASS	2,201	1,690	1,494	1,317
GUITAR	30	KAY	MODEL A	672	516	456	402
GUITAR	58	KAY	N-1 CUT FLATTOP JUMBO	546	419	370	326
GUITAR	60	KAY	N-1 CUT FLATTOP JUMBO SOLID SPRUCE	555	426	376	332
GUITAR	36	KAY	O SUNBURST	379	291	257	227
GUITAR	40	KAY	ORPHEUM SUNBURST, ARCHTOP	426	327	289	255
GUITAR	62	KAY	P-3 JUMBO ORANGE	568	436	386	340
GUITAR	50	KAY	PLECTRUM 1 PU	301	231	204	180
GUITAR	30	KAY	RECORDING KING FLATTOP, ASYMMETRICAL	635	487	430	379
GUITAR	34	KAY	RECORDING KING 2 POINT ARCHTOP	627	481	425	375
GUITAR	55	KAY	RESONATOR MAHOGANY BODY, 14-FRET	596	458	405	357
GUITAR	55	KAY	SIERRA SUNBURST, SOLID SPRUCE, CUTAWAY, FLAME MAPLE BACK/SIDES	545	418	370	326
GUITAR	50	KAY	SILVERTONE SUNBURST, ARCHTOP	404	310	274	241
GUITAR	55	KAY	SILVERTONE SUNBURST, FLATTOP	435	334	295	260
GUITAR	60	KAY	SILVERTONE SUNBURST, SINGLE CUTAWAY	685	526	465	410
GUITAR	49	KAY	SPECIAL 40	595	457	404	356
MANDOLIN	30	KAY	KRAFT SUNBURST	529	406	359	316
STEEL GUITAR	58	KAY	K- 24	448	344	304	268
STGUIT	61	KAY	K- 24	412	316	279	246
UPRIG	60	KAY	BASS FIDDLE ROSEWOOD FINGERBOARD	1,312	1,007	890	785
UPRIGHT	45	KAY	MODEL C-1	1,336	1,025	906	799
UPRIGHT	45	KAY	UPRIGHT BASS SN-10711	1,634	1,254	1,108	977
UPRIGHT	55	KAY	UPRIGHT BASS	1,242	953	842	743

KENTUCKY

MANDOLIN	93	KENTUCKY	KM-60 STANDARD FLAT	266	204	180	159
MANDOL	88	KENTUCKY	KM-JR A-MODEL CARVED, TOP-MATCHED SOLID SPRUCE, SOLID MAPLE BACK/SIDES	273	209	185	163

KOLSTEIN

STEEL GUITAR	79	KOLSTEIN	PANORMO STRING BASS COPY HARD MAPLE	26,920	20,670	18,267	16,104
UPRIG	80	KOLSTEIN	MAGANTAL 5-STRING	35,117	26,965	23,829	21,007

KORG USA

SYNTHESIZER	81	KORG	MS-50 PATCHABLE EXPANDER MODULE	870	668	590	520

KRAMER

ELEC. GUITAR & BASS	77	KRAMER	250-B SPECIAL BASS	617	473	418	369
ELGUIT	77	KRAMER	ARTIST 650-G ALUMINUM NECK, DOUBLE CUTAWAY	607	466	411	363
ELGUIT	78	KRAMER	DMZ 1000	612	470	415	366
ELGUIT	78	KRAMER	DMZ 3000 ALUMINUM NECK, SOLID BODY	666	511	452	398
ELGUIT	78	KRAMER	DMZ 4000 BASS	612	470	415	366
ELGUIT	80	KRAMER	XL-8 BASS 8-STRING, SOLID BODY, 2 PU's	937	719	636	560

TYPE	YR	MFG	PRICES--BASED ON 100% ORIGINAL MODEL	SELL EXC	SELL AVG	BUY EXC	BUY AVG

KRK

| TUNER | 78 | KRK | ES-335 CUSTOM | 1,053 | 809 | 715 | 630 |

KUSTOM

GUITAR AMP	68	KUSTOM	100 COMBO BLUE SPARKLE, 50 WATTS	333	256	226	199
GTAMP	70	KUSTOM	200 AMP 2x15" or 3x12" CABINET	443	340	300	265
GTAMP	73	KUSTOM	220 AMP 3x12"	389	299	264	233
GTAMP	67	KUSTOM	CHALLENGER BLUE, SINGLE 12" COMBO	221	170	150	132
GTAMP	68	KUSTOM	ENDEAVOR GREEN, SINGLE 12" COMBO	221	170	150	132
GTAMP	68	KUSTOM	ENDEAVOR GOLD GOLD, 2X12" COMBO	333	256	226	199

LAB SERIES AMPLIFIERS

GUITAR AMP	77	LAB	L-3 60 WATT COMBO	333	256	226	199
GTAMP	77	LAB	L-5	389	299	264	233
GTAMP	77	LAB	L-7 100 WATT, 20" SPEAKERS	416	319	282	249

LAFAYETTE

| PWR | 69 | LAF | KT-550 KIT | 399 | 307 | 271 | 239 |
| PWR | 73 | LAF | KT-600A KIT | 129 | 99 | 88 | 77 |

LARSON BROTHERS

GUITAR (ACOUSTIC)	10	LARSON	DYER	2,098	1,611	1,424	1,255
GUITAR	17	LARSON	DYER	2,442	1,875	1,657	1,461
GUITAR	34	LARSON	EUPHONON MAHOGANY BODY, 14"	694	525	463	384
GUITAR	37	LARSON	EUPHONON ROSEWOOD BACK/SIDES, 18"	23,478	18,028	15,931	14,045
GUITAR	38	LARSON	EUPHONON DREADNOUGHT, MOP NECK	12,398	9,520	8,413	7,416
GUITAR	38	LARSON	EUPHONON ROSEWOOD, DREADNOUGHT	13,519	10,381	9,173	8,087
GUITAR	39	LARSON	EUPHONON ROSEWOOD BODY, 16" JUMBO	1,669	1,262	1,112	922
GUITAR	40	LARSON	EUPHONON TONE BAR	8,009	6,149	5,434	4,791
GUITAR	41	LARSON	EUPHONON	3,470	2,665	2,355	2,076
GUITAR	42	LARSON	EUPHONON CARL FISHER LABEL	4,042	3,103	2,742	2,418
GUITAR	44	LARSON	EUPHONON KIMBALL HALL LABEL	4,042	3,103	2,742	2,418
GUITAR	10	LARSON	HARP GUITAR KNUTSON STYLE CONSTRUCTION, 7 SUB-BASS STRINGS	8,144	6,253	5,526	4,872
GUITAR	22	LARSON	J.F. STETSON ROSEWOOD	5,576	4,281	3,784	3,335
GUITAR	14	LARSON	MAURER FLATTOP	1,333	1,024	905	797
GUITAR	15	LARSON	MAURER	5,542	4,256	3,761	3,315
GUITAR	16	LARSON	MAURER	3,454	2,652	2,343	2,066
GUITAR	19	LARSON	MAURER	5,544	4,257	3,762	3,316
GUITAR	20	LARSON	MAURER BRAZILIAN ROSEWOOD BACK/SIDES	4,878	3,746	3,310	2,918
GUITAR	32	LARSON	MAURER ROSEWOOD	4,220	3,240	2,863	2,524
GUITAR	33	LARSON	MAURER	3,339	2,524	2,226	1,846
GUITAR	30	LARSON	MAURER 000 ROSEWOOD, ABALONE TRIM	1,512	1,161	1,026	904
GUITAR	10	LARSON	MAURER 531 SPRUCE TOP, ROSEWOOD BACK/SIDES	2,200	1,689	1,493	1,316
GUITAR	20	LARSON	PRAIRIE STATE ROSEWOOD BACK/SIDES	6,969	5,351	4,729	4,169
GUITAR	32	LARSON	PRAIRIE STATE	6,549	5,029	4,444	3,918
GUITAR	33	LARSON	PRAIRIE STATE	6,555	5,033	4,448	3,921
GUITAR	35	LARSON	PRAIRIE STATE	5,357	4,051	3,571	2,962
GUITAR	38	LARSON	PRAIRIE STATE	4,878	3,746	3,310	2,918
GUITAR	40	LARSON	PRAIRIE STATE MAPLE BACK/SIDES, F-HOLE, 17"	17,590	13,507	11,936	10,523
GUITAR	20	LARSON	STAHL BRAZILIAN ROSEWOOD BACK/SIDES, FLATTOP	1,641	1,260	1,114	982
GUITAR	22	LARSON	STAHL ROSEWOOD	2,416	1,827	1,611	1,336
GUITAR	32	LARSON	STAHL ROSEWOOD	6,272	4,816	4,256	3,752
GUITAR	30	LARSON	STAHL 0 SIZE ROSEWOOD, PEARL TRIM	1,757	1,349	1,192	1,051

TYPE	YR	MFG	PRICES--BASED ON 100% ORIGINAL MODEL	SELL EXC	SELL AVG	BUY EXC	BUY AVG
MANDOLIN	38	LARSON	**EUPHONON** ROSEWOOD	4,950	**3,801**	3,359	2,961
MANDOL	15	LARSON	**MAURER BOWL-BACK** ROSEWOOD RIBS	745	**572**	506	446
MANDOL	10	LARSON	**STAHL BOWL-BACK**	1,542	**1,184**	1,046	922
MANDOL	15	LARSON	**STAHL BOWL-BACK**	1,671	**1,283**	1,133	999
MANDOL	20	LARSON	**STAHL BOWL-BACK** ROSEWOOD	1,613	**1,239**	1,095	965
MANDOL	25	LARSON	**STAHL BOWL-BACK** ROSEWOOD	1,330	**1,021**	902	795
MANDOL	30	LARSON	**STAHL MANDO-CELLO** MAPLE	6,251	**4,800**	4,242	3,739

LEAK by ERCONA CORPORATION

TYPE	YR	MFG	MODEL	SELL EXC	SELL AVG	BUY EXC	BUY AVG
PRE	58	LEAK	**POINT 1** STEREO TUBE	375	**288**	254	224
PWR	59	LEAK	**STEREO 20** TUBE, 25 WATT	581	**446**	394	347
PWR	59	LEAK	**STEREO 50** 25 WATTS	571	**438**	387	341
PWR	64	LEAK	**STEREO 60** TUBE, 30 WATT	547	**420**	371	327
PWR	55	LEAK	**TL-50 MONO** TUBE, 45 WATT	327	**251**	221	195
TUNER	56	LEAK	**TROUGH LINE**	134	**103**	91	80
TUNER	58	LEAK	**TROUGH LINE 2**	137	**105**	93	82
TUNER	60	LEAK	**TROUGH LINE 3**	142	**109**	96	85

LEVIN (MADE IN SWEDEN)

TYPE	YR	MFG	MODEL	SELL EXC	SELL AVG	BUY EXC	BUY AVG
GUITAR (ACOUSTIC)	49	LEVIN	**DELUXE** NATURAL, CUTAWAY, 18 1/4" WIDE	6,414	**4,849**	4,276	3,546
GUITAR	52	LEVIN	**SOLOIST** NATURAL, CUTAWAY, 17 1/8" WIDE	3,771	**2,851**	2,514	2,084
TUNER	72	LEVIN	**JC-1 CARTRIDGE**	271	**208**	183	162

LEXICON

TYPE	YR	MFG	MODEL	SELL EXC	SELL AVG	BUY EXC	BUY AVG
SIGNAL PROCESSOR	83	LEXICON	**PCM-42**	1,266	**972**	859	757
SGNPRO	04	LEXICON	**PCM-42MEO**	1,634	**1,254**	1,108	977

LINN ELECTRONICS

TYPE	YR	MFG	MODEL	SELL EXC	SELL AVG	BUY EXC	BUY AVG
PRE	64	LINN	**NAJIK LINE ONLY**	3,642	**2,796**	2,471	2,178

LUXMAN

TYPE	YR	MFG	MODEL	SELL EXC	SELL AVG	BUY EXC	BUY AVG
PWR	76	LUX	**MB-3045 TUBE MONO** 50 WATT	698	**536**	474	418
XOVER	73	LUX	**A-2003** 3-WAY ACTIVE, STEREO, TUBE	704	**540**	478	421

LYON & HEALY

TYPE	YR	MFG	MODEL	SELL EXC	SELL AVG	BUY EXC	BUY AVG
BANJO	00	LYON	**L&H STAR** 1900	789	**606**	535	472
BANJO	15	LYON	**STYLE A** 5-STRING	972	**746**	659	581
BANJO	10	LYON	**TENOR** OPEN BACK	665	**503**	443	367
BANJO	20	LYON	**TENOR LUTE** MAHOGANY BACK/SIDES, PEAR SHAPED BODY, ATTRACTIVE INLAY	539	**414**	366	322
BANJO	20	LYON	**VAN EPS RECORDING** 5-STRING	1,037	**796**	703	620
BANJO	20	LYON	**VAN EPS RECORDING PLECTRUM**	1,011	**776**	686	605
BANJO	22	LYON	**VAN EPS RECORDING PLECTRUM**	1,014	**779**	688	607
GUITAR (ACOUSTIC)	10	LYON	**AMERICAN CONSERVATORY** BRAZILIAN ROSEWD BACK/SIDES,12" WIDE,12-FRET SLOT HEAD NECK	1,064	**817**	722	636
GUITAR	20	LYON	**AMERICAN CONSERVATORY TENOR**	474	**364**	322	284
GUITAR	05	LYON	**PARLOR GUITAR** 1905, SPRUCE TOP, OAK BACK/SIDES	819	**629**	556	490
MANDOLIN	20	LYON	**2-POINT BODY** OVAL SOUND HOLE	817	**627**	554	489
MANDOL	01	LYON	**AMERICAN CONSERVATORY BOWL-BACK** 1901	682	**523**	462	408
MANDOL	20	LYON	**DITSON STYLE A**	3,030	**2,327**	2,056	1,813
MANDOL	20	LYON	**DITSON STYLE B** SYMMETRICAL 2-POINT BODY SHAPE, OVAL SOUND HOLE	1,068	**820**	725	639
MANDOL	01	LYON	**HOMER WARREN BOWL-BACK** 1901, ROSEWOOD RIBS	1,313	**1,008**	891	785
MANDOL	12	LYON	**STYLE A MANDOCELLO**	7,163	**5,500**	4,860	4,285
MANDOL	20	LYON	**STYLE A MANDOCELLO** SCROLL PEGHEAD	9,744	**7,482**	6,612	5,829
MANDOL	18	LYON	**STYLE A PROFESSIONAL** SCROLL PEGHEAD	4,314	**3,312**	2,927	2,580
MANDOL	12	LYON	**STYLE B** SERIAL #39	3,393	**2,605**	2,302	2,030
MANDOL	20	LYON	**STYLE B** MAPLE BACK/SIDES	1,927	**1,480**	1,307	1,153

TYPE	YR	MFG	MODEL	SELL EXC	SELL AVG	BUY EXC	BUY AVG
MANDOL	20	LYON	STYLE C — A BODY STYLE	1,508	1,158	1,023	902
MANDOL	20	LYON	STYLE C — OVAL SOUND HOLE	1,601	1,229	1,086	958
UKULELE	25	LYON	CAMP — SMALL BODY	358	275	243	214
UKE	30	LYON	TENOR — BOUND TOP	225	172	152	134
UKE	30	LYON	TENOR	343	264	233	205

MacCAFERRI/SELMER

TYPE	YR	MFG	MODEL	SELL EXC	SELL AVG	BUY EXC	BUY AVG
ELEC. GUITAR & BASS	52	MAC/SEL	MAESTRO — PLASTIC, ROUND SOUND HOLE, 1 PU	288	221	196	172
GUITAR (ACOUSTIC)	53	MAC/SEL	G-40 — ARCHTOP	315	242	214	188
GUITAR	56	MAC/SEL	ISLANDER — PLASTIC BODY	273	209	185	163
GUITAR	54	MAC/SEL	MACCAFERRI — PLASTIC BODY	269	207	183	161
GUITAR	56	MAC/SEL	MACCAFERRI — PLASTIC BODY, ARCHTOP	292	224	198	174
GUITAR	31	MAC/SEL	MODELE CONCERT — D SHAPED SOUND HOLE	56,679	43,522	38,461	33,906
GUITAR	32	MAC/SEL	MODELE CONCERT — D SHAPED SOUND HOLE	54,386	41,760	36,904	32,534
GUITAR	53	MAC/SEL	PLASTIC — FLATTOP	179	137	121	107
GUITAR	35	MAC/SEL	SELMER	12,808	9,834	8,691	7,662
GUITAR	38	MAC/SEL	SELMER	14,066	10,635	9,377	7,776
GUITAR	40	MAC/SEL	SELMER — MADE IN FRANCE, ROSEWOOD B/S, 12-FRET, CUTWY, ROUND SOUND HOLE	37,250	28,602	25,276	22,283
GUITAR	47	MAC/SEL	SELMER — MADE IN FRANCE, CUTAWAY, SMALL OVAL SOUND HOLE	29,798	22,881	20,220	17,826
GUITAR	59	MAC/SEL	SHOWTIME CLASSICAL	409	314	278	245
UKULELE	50	MAC/SEL	ISLANDER — PLASTIC	137	105	93	82
UKE	55	MAC/SEL	PLAYTUNE SENIOR — WHITE STYRENE	257	197	174	154

MAESTRO

TYPE	YR	MFG	MODEL	SELL EXC	SELL AVG	BUY EXC	BUY AVG
EFFECTS	72	MAESTRO	BG-2 BOOMER 2 WAH	274	210	186	164
EFFECTS	70	MAESTRO	BOOMERANG WAH	264	202	179	158
EFFECTS	73	MAESTRO	ECHOPLEX EP-3 SOLID STATE	741	569	503	443
EFFECTS	62	MAESTRO	ECHOPLEX TUBE	1,243	954	843	743
EFFECTS	67	MAESTRO	FG-1A FUZZ TONE	337	258	228	201
EFFECTS	76	MAESTRO	FP-1 FUZZ PHASER	316	243	215	189
EFFECTS	70	MAESTRO	FZ-1B FUZZ TONE	221	170	150	132
EFFECTS	70	MAESTRO	G-2 RHYTHM AND SOUND	378	290	256	226
EFFECTS	71	MAESTRO	G-2 RHYTHM AND SOUND	421	323	285	251
EFFECTS	72	MAESTRO	ME-1 ENVELOPE MODIFIER	252	193	171	150
EFFECTS	75	MAESTRO	MINI PHASE	193	148	131	115
EFFECTS	78	MAESTRO	MPP-1 STAGE PHASER	176	135	120	105
GUITAR AMP	65	MAESTRO	FZ-1A	399	307	271	239
GTAMP	66	MAESTRO	FZ-1A	399	307	271	239
GTAMP	68	MAESTRO	FZ-1A	460	353	312	275
GTAMP	69	MAESTRO	FZ-1A	460	353	312	275

MANLEY

TYPE	YR	MFG	MODEL	SELL EXC	SELL AVG	BUY EXC	BUY AVG
SIGNAL PROCESSOR	94	MANLEY	STEREO TUBE DIRECT INTERFACE W/EQ	1,011	776	686	605

MARANTZ AMERICA, INC

TYPE	YR	MFG	MODEL	SELL EXC	SELL AVG	BUY EXC	BUY AVG
PRE	54	MARANTZ	1-C	1,263	970	857	755
PRE	53-59	MARANTZ	1-C CONSOLE — MONO TUBE, #4 POWER SUPPLY	2,294	1,762	1,557	1,372
PRE	78	MARANTZ	3650	1,223	939	829	731
PRE	59-66	MARANTZ	7-C — STEREO TUBE	3,783	2,905	2,567	2,263
PRE	60	MARANTZ	7-C — TUBE	2,468	1,895	1,675	1,476
PRE	67	MARANTZ	7-T CLASSIC U.S. VERSION	977	750	663	584
PWR	56-62	MARANTZ	2 — MONO TUBE, 40 WATT	2,327	1,787	1,579	1,392
PWR	55-62	MARANTZ	5 — MONO TUBE, 30 WATT	2,029	1,558	1,377	1,214
PWR	59	MARANTZ	5 — MONO, 30 WATTS	1,273	977	864	761
PWR	60-62	MARANTZ	8 — STEREO TUBE, 30 WATT	2,147	1,648	1,456	1,284
PWR	61	MARANTZ	8 — 30 WATTS	1,422	1,092	965	850
PWR	61-67	MARANTZ	9 — MONO TUBE, PAIR, 70 WATT, RACK MOUNT PANEL OPTIONAL	9,179	7,048	6,228	5,491

TYPE	YR	MFG	PRICES--BASED ON 100% ORIGINAL MODEL	SELL EXC	SELL AVG	BUY EXC	BUY AVG
PWR	68	MARANTZ	**15** DUAL MONO, 60 WATT	462	**355**	313	276
PWR	73	MARANTZ	**32 VARIABLE OVERLAP DRIVE**	584	**448**	396	349
PWR	60-67	MARANTZ	**8B** STEREO TUBE, 35 WATT	1,925	**1,478**	1,306	1,151
PWR	64	MARANTZ	**8B** 35 WATTS	2,352	**1,806**	1,596	1,407
PWR	64	MARANTZ	**9A** MONO	8,189	**6,288**	5,557	4,899
PWR	92	MARANTZ	**MA-500BL MONO/THX CERTIFIED**	554	**425**	376	331
PWR	79	MARANTZ	**SM-7 ESOTEC**	1,339	**1,028**	908	801
RCV	68	MARANTZ	**18 CLASSIC U.S. VERSION**	564	**433**	383	337
RCV	73	MARANTZ	**19**	673	**516**	456	402
RCV	77	MARANTZ	**2500**	1,989	**1,527**	1,349	1,189
RCV	78	MARANTZ	**2600** SCOPE,TOROIDAL DUAL PWR SUPPLY,DOLBY CAPABLE,QTZ LOCK FM	2,177	**1,671**	1,477	1,302
SIGNAL PROCESSOR	76	MARANTZ	**SQA-2B DECODER**	171	**131**	116	102
SPKR	77	MARANTZ	**HD-440**	201	**154**	136	120
SPKR	73	MARANTZ	**IMPERIAL 4G**	204	**157**	139	122
SPKR	77	MARANTZ	**MODEL 4 MKII**	200	**153**	136	119
SPKR	77	MARANTZ	**MODEL 6 MKII**	266	**204**	180	159
TUNER	62-63	MARANTZ	**10** STEREO TUBE, SCOPE	3,353	**2,574**	2,275	2,005
TUNER	64	MARANTZ	**10** SCOPE	2,120	**1,627**	1,438	1,268
TUNER	63-67	MARANTZ	**10B** STEREO TUBE, SCOPE	3,528	**2,709**	2,394	2,110
TUNER	64	MARANTZ	**10B** SCOPE	2,352	**1,806**	1,596	1,407
TUNER	73	MARANTZ	**112**	266	**204**	180	159
TUNER	76	MARANTZ	**150** SCOPE	946	**726**	642	566
TUNER	78-80	MARANTZ	**2130 QUARTZ LOCK** SCOPE, MULTIPLEX DEMODULATOR	842	**646**	571	503
TUNER	79	MARANTZ	**ST-7 ESOTEC** SCOPE	1,488	**1,142**	1,010	890
TUNER	79	MARANTZ	**ST-8 ESOTEC** SCOPE	1,601	**1,229**	1,086	958
XOVER	55	MARANTZ	**3 MONO TUBE**	2,515	**1,931**	1,706	1,504

MARSHALL AMPS

TYPE	YR	MFG	MODEL	SELL EXC	SELL AVG	BUY EXC	BUY AVG
GUITAR AMP	68	MARSHALL	**JMP- 50 WATT** RED, SMALL BOX, PLEXI 4x12" CABINET	1,650	**1,267**	1,120	987
GTAMP	72	MARSHALL	**JMP- 50 WATT**	816	**626**	554	488
GTAMP	74	MARSHALL	**JMP- 50 WATT** MK II LEAD HEAD	694	**533**	471	415
GTAMP	74	MARSHALL	**JMP- 50 WATT**	706	**542**	479	422
GTAMP	75	MARSHALL	**JMP- 50 WATT**	650	**499**	441	389
GTAMP	77	MARSHALL	**JMP- 50 WATT**	682	**523**	462	408
GTAMP	78	MARSHALL	**JMP- 50 WATT**	668	**513**	453	399
GTAMP	79	MARSHALL	**JMP- 50 WATT**	612	**470**	415	366
GTAMP	79	MARSHALL	**JMP- 50 WATT** BEIGE, COMBO	649	**498**	440	388
GTAMP	59	MARSHALL	**JMP-100 WATT**	751	**577**	509	449
GTAMP	75	MARSHALL	**JMP-100 WATT** BLACK	656	**503**	445	392
GTAMP	79	MARSHALL	**JMP-100 WATT**	658	**505**	446	393
GTAMP	80	MARSHALL	**JMP-100 WATT** MK II LEAD	641	**492**	435	383
GTAMP	81	MARSHALL	**JMP-100 WATT**	648	**497**	440	387
GTAMP	63	MARSHALL	**JTM- 45** WHITE PANEL/BACK	1,912	**1,468**	1,298	1,144
GTAMP	63	MARSHALL	**JTM- 45** BLACK AND WHITE FACE, HEAD	2,134	**1,639**	1,448	1,277
GTAMP	64	MARSHALL	**JTM- 45** GOLD PLEXIGLASS, LARGE LETTERS, NAME PLATE	1,738	**1,334**	1,179	1,039
GTAMP	64	MARSHALL	**JTM- 45** HALF STACK, G12-15's	2,928	**2,248**	1,987	1,752
GTAMP	65	MARSHALL	**JTM- 45** WHITE BACK, PLEXI, 4x12" CABINET	1,419	**1,089**	962	848
GTAMP	66	MARSHALL	**JTM- 45** WHITE BACK, PLEXI	1,826	**1,402**	1,239	1,092
GTAMP	66	MARSHALL	**JTM- 45** HALF STACK, STRIPE FRONT	3,899	**2,994**	2,646	2,332
GTAMP	62	MARSHALL	**JTM- 45 HEAD** 45 WATT	8,376	**6,431**	5,684	5,010
GTAMP	63	MARSHALL	**JTM- 45 HEAD** 45 WATT	8,373	**6,429**	5,681	5,008
GTAMP	64	MARSHALL	**JTM- 45 HEAD** 45 WATT	8,359	**6,419**	5,672	5,000
GTAMP	73	MARSHALL	**JTM- 45 HEAD**	1,245	**956**	845	745

TYPE	YR	MFG	PRICES--BASED ON 100% ORIGINAL MODEL	SELL EXC	SELL AVG	BUY EXC	BUY AVG
GTAMP	65	MARSHALL	**JTM- 45 HEAD MODEL 1987** 45 WATT	8,335	**6,400**	5,655	4,986
GTAMP	66	MARSHALL	**JTM- 45 HEAD MODEL 1987** 45 WATT	8,335	**6,400**	5,655	4,986
GTAMP	66	MARSHALL	**JTM-100**	847	**651**	575	507
GTAMP	77	MARSHALL	**MASTER MARK II** 50 WATT COMBO	786	**603**	533	470
GTAMP	69	MARSHALL	**MODEL 1930** 10 WATT, 2x10", COMBO	910	**699**	617	544
GTAMP	66	MARSHALL	**MODEL 1959 SUPER LEAD MATCHING SET** 100 WATT, HALF STACK, BLACK, PLEXI, WEAVE	7,109	**5,459**	4,824	4,253
GTAMP	67	MARSHALL	**MODEL 1959 SUPER LEAD MATCHING SET** 100 WATT, HALF STACK, BLACK, PLEXI, WEAVE	7,098	**5,450**	4,816	4,246
GTAMP	68	MARSHALL	**MODEL 1959 SUPER LEAD MATCHING SET** 100 WATT, HALF STACK, BLACK, PLEXI, WEAVE	7,080	**5,436**	4,804	4,235
GTAMP	69	MARSHALL	**MODEL 1959 SUPER LEAD MATCHING SET** 100 WATT, HALF STACK, BLACK, PLEXI, WEAVE	7,048	**5,411**	4,782	4,216
GTAMP	72	MARSHALL	**MODEL 1960** BLACK, 4x12" SLANT SPEAKER	682	**523**	462	408
GTAMP	68	MARSHALL	**MODEL 1967** MAJOR AMP HEAD	1,223	**939**	829	731
GTAMP	67	MARSHALL	**MODEL 1987** 50 WATT, HEAD, PLEXI	1,678	**1,289**	1,139	1,004
GTAMP	77	MARSHALL	**MODEL 1987** 50 WATT, HEAD	663	**509**	449	396
GTAMP	67	MARSHALL	**MODEL 1992** SUPER BASS HEAD, PLEXI	1,473	**1,131**	1,000	881
GTAMP	72	MARSHALL	**MODEL 1992** 100 WATT, SUPER BASS HEAD	972	**746**	659	581
GTAMP	73	MARSHALL	**MODEL 1992** 100 WATT, SUPER BASS HEAD	907	**696**	615	542
GTAMP	75	MARSHALL	**MODEL 1992** BLACK, SUPER BASS HEAD	629	**483**	427	376
GTAMP	75	MARSHALL	**MODEL 1992** 100 WATT, SUPER BASS HEAD	702	**539**	476	420
GTAMP	80	MARSHALL	**MODEL 2203** LEAD HEAD	632	**485**	429	378
GTAMP	72	MARSHALL	**SLANT "PURPLE TOLEX"** 100 WATT SPEAKERS	929	**713**	630	556
GTAMP	72	MARSHALL	**SPECIALIST 2046** 15" SPEAKER	574	**441**	389	343
GTAMP	72	MARSHALL	**STRAIGHT & SLANT** 4x12" 25 WATT GREEN CELESTIONS	666	**511**	452	398
GTAMP	68	MARSHALL	**SUPER BASS 100 WATT** PLEXI, LAY DOWN TRANSFORMER	1,342	**1,031**	911	803
GTAMP	70	MARSHALL	**SUPER BASS 100 WATT** PLEXI, LAY DOWN TRANSFORMER	937	**719**	636	560
GTAMP	73	MARSHALL	**SUPER BASS 100 WATT**	609	**467**	413	364
GTAMP	75	MARSHALL	**SUPER BASS 100 WATT**	694	**533**	471	415
GTAMP	69	MARSHALL	**SUPER LEAD 100 WATT** HEAD, PLEXI, LAY DOWN TRANSFORMER	1,775	**1,363**	1,204	1,061
GTAMP	70	MARSHALL	**SUPER LEAD 100 WATT** HEAD, LAY DOWN TRANSFORMER	1,229	**944**	834	735
GTAMP	71	MARSHALL	**SUPER LEAD 100 WATT** HEAD, LAY DOWN TRANSFORMER	1,227	**942**	832	734
GTAMP	72	MARSHALL	**SUPER LEAD 100 WATT**	924	**709**	627	552
GTAMP	73	MARSHALL	**SUPER LEAD 100 WATT**	797	**612**	541	477
GTAMP	75	MARSHALL	**SUPER LEAD 100 WATT**	648	**497**	440	387
GTAMP	79	MARSHALL	**SUPER LEAD 100 WATT**	641	**492**	435	383
GTAMP	79	MARSHALL	**SUPER LEAD 100 WATT CUSTOM** WHITE	658	**505**	446	393
SIGNAL PROCESSOR	87	MARSHALL	**AR-300 TAPE ELIMINATOR**	1,860	**1,428**	1,262	1,112

MARTIN GUITAR COMPANY

TYPE	YR	MFG	MODEL	SELL EXC	SELL AVG	BUY EXC	BUY AVG
BANJO	70	MARTIN	**VEGA** LONG NECK, 5-STRING, SERIAL #256003-271633	1,018	**781**	690	609
BANJO	70	MARTIN	**VEGA VIP** SERIAL #256004-271633	864	**663**	586	517
BANJO	72	MARTIN	**VEGA VIP** SERIAL #294271-313302	835	**641**	566	499
ELEC. GUITAR & BASS	73	MARTIN	**D- 12-18**	1,363	**1,046**	924	815
ELGUIT	59	MARTIN	**D- 18E** FLATTOP, 2 PU's, SERIAL #165577-171047	1,892	**1,453**	1,284	1,132
ELGUIT	59	MARTIN	**D- 28E** FLATTOP, 2 PU's, SERIAL #165577-171047	4,166	**3,199**	2,827	2,492
ELGUIT	69	MARTIN	**D- 41** INDIAN ROSEWOOD	3,604	**2,767**	2,445	2,156
ELGUIT	69	MARTIN	**D- 41** BRAZILIAN ROSEWOOD	12,439	**9,552**	8,441	7,441
ELGUIT	68	MARTIN	**D-1235** BRAZILIAN ROSEWOOD	3,477	**2,670**	2,359	2,080
ELGUIT	64	MARTIN	**D-28E** ROSEWOOD, GOLD-PLATED,	3,808	**2,924**	2,584	2,278

TYPE	YR	MFG	PRICES--BASED ON 100% ORIGINAL MODEL	SELL EXC	SELL AVG	BUY EXC	BUY AVG
ELGUIT	79	MARTIN	**E-18** NATURAL,MAPLE/ROSEWOOD BODY,2 DIMARZIO PU's	784	**602**	532	469
ELGUIT	61	MARTIN	**F-50** SUNBURST, ARCHTOP, CUTAWAY, 1 PU, SERIAL #175690-181297	794	**609**	538	475
ELGUIT	64	MARTIN	**F-50** SUNBURST, ARCHTOP, CUTAWAY, 1 PU, SERIAL #193328-199626	795	**610**	539	475
ELGUIT	62	MARTIN	**F-55** SUNBURST, ARCHTOP, CUTAWAY, 1 PU, SERIAL #181298-187384	607	**466**	411	363
ELGUIT	62	MARTIN	**F-65**	852	**654**	578	509
ELGUIT	64	MARTIN	**F-65** SUNBURST,ARCHTOP, 2 PU's,DBL CUTAWAY,SERIAL #193328-199626	934	**717**	633	558
ELGUIT	65	MARTIN	**GT-70** BURGUNDY, ARCHTOP, 2 PU's, CUTAWAY, SERIAL #199627-207030	928	**712**	630	555
ELGUIT	66	MARTIN	**GT-70** BURGUNDY, ARCHTOP, 2 PU's, CUTAWAY, SERIAL #207031-217215	931	**715**	632	557
ELGUIT	66	MARTIN	**GT-70** BLACK, ARCHTOP, 2 PU's, CUTAWAY, SERIAL #207031-217215	936	**718**	635	560
ELGUIT	67	MARTIN	**GT-70** BURGUNDY, ARCHTOP, 2 PU's, CUTAWAY, SERIAL #217216-230095	665	**510**	451	397
ELGUIT	65	MARTIN	**GT-75** BURGUNDY, ARCHTOP, 2 PU's,DBL CUTAWAY,SERIAL #199627-207030	663	**509**	449	396
ELGUIT	66	MARTIN	**GT-75** BURGUNDY,ARCHTOP, 2 PU's,DBL CUTAWAY,SERIAL #207031-217215	664	**509**	450	397
ELGUIT	67	MARTIN	**GT-75** BURGUNDY, ARCHTOP, 2 PU's,DBL CUTAWAY,SERIAL #217216-230095	661	**508**	449	395
GUITAR (ACOUSTIC)	11	MARTIN	**1-17** SERIAL #11204-11413	1,622	**1,246**	1,101	970
GUITAR	31	MARTIN	**1-17**	1,792	**1,376**	1,216	1,072
GUITAR	32	MARTIN	**1-17** SERIAL #49590-52590	1,792	**1,376**	1,216	1,072
GUITAR	29	MARTIN	**1-17P** PLECTRUM, SERIAL #37569-40843	1,302	**1,000**	883	779
GUITAR	30	MARTIN	**1-17P** PLECTRUM, SERIAL #40844-45317	1,317	**1,011**	893	787
GUITAR	31	MARTIN	**1-17P** PLECTRUM, SERIAL #45318-49589	1,267	**973**	860	758
GUITAR	18	MARTIN	**1-18** SERIAL #12989-13450	2,576	**1,978**	1,748	1,541
GUITAR	20	MARTIN	**1-18**	3,287	**2,524**	2,230	1,966
GUITAR	26	MARTIN	**1-18** SERIAL #24117-28689	2,576	**1,978**	1,748	1,541
GUITAR	19	MARTIN	**1-18K HAWAIIAN** KOA WOOD, SERIAL #13451-14512	1,276	**980**	866	763
GUITAR	20	MARTIN	**1-21** SERIAL #14513-15848	3,136	**2,408**	2,128	1,876
GUITAR	25	MARTIN	**1-21** SERIAL #22009-24116	3,136	**2,408**	2,128	1,876
GUITAR	34	MARTIN	**1-21** SERIAL #55085-58679	3,381	**2,596**	2,294	2,022
GUITAR	15	MARTIN	**1-28** SERIAL #12048-12209	5,264	**4,042**	3,572	3,149
GUITAR	19	MARTIN	**1-28** SERIAL #13451-14512	5,264	**4,042**	3,572	3,149
GUITAR	29	MARTIN	**1-28P** PLECTRUM, SERIAL #37569-40843	2,207	**1,695**	1,497	1,320
GUITAR	02	MARTIN	**1-42** 1902, SERIAL #9311-9528	4,868	**3,738**	3,303	2,912
GUITAR	70	MARTIN	**2 1/2-17** 1870	4,878	**3,746**	3,310	2,918
GUITAR	17	MARTIN	**2 1/2-17** SERIAL #12391-12988	1,329	**1,020**	902	795
GUITAR	41	MARTIN	**2 1/2-17** SERIAL #76735-80013	1,282	**984**	870	767
GUITAR	42	MARTIN	**2 1/2-18** SERIAL #80014-83107	1,611	**1,218**	1,074	890
GUITAR	09	MARTIN	**2 1/2-26** 1909, HARDSHELL CASE, SERIAL #11002	5,024	**3,857**	3,409	3,005
GUITAR	09	MARTIN	**2 1/2-28** 1909, SERIAL #11002	5,018	**3,853**	3,405	3,002
GUITAR	22	MARTIN	**2-17** SERIAL #16759-17839	1,537	**1,180**	1,043	919
GUITAR	23	MARTIN	**2-17** SERIAL #17840-19891	1,426	**1,095**	968	853
GUITAR	25	MARTIN	**2-17** SERIAL #22009-24116	1,364	**1,047**	925	816
GUITAR	26	MARTIN	**2-17** SERIAL #24117-28689	1,392	**1,068**	944	832
GUITAR	27	MARTIN	**2-17** SERIAL #28690-34435	1,388	**1,066**	942	830
GUITAR	28	MARTIN	**2-17** SERIAL #34436-37568	1,345	**1,032**	912	804
GUITAR	29	MARTIN	**2-17** SERIAL #37569-40843	1,312	**1,007**	890	785

TYPE	YR	MFG	PRICES--BASED ON 100% ORIGINAL MODEL	SELL EXC	SELL AVG	BUY EXC	BUY AVG
GUITAR	30	MARTIN	2-17 SERIAL #40844-45317	1,286	988	873	769
GUITAR	31	MARTIN	2-17 SERIAL #45318-49589	1,347	1,034	914	806
GUITAR	29	MARTIN	2-17K HAWAIIAN KOA WOOD, SERIAL #37569-40843	1,200	921	814	718
GUITAR	41	MARTIN	2-18 SERIAL #76735-80013	1,258	966	854	753
GUITAR	28	MARTIN	2-18T TENOR, SERIAL #34436-37568	1,410	1,082	956	843
GUITAR	29	MARTIN	2-18T TENOR, SERIAL #37569-40843	1,525	1,171	1,035	912
GUITAR	30	MARTIN	2-18T TENOR, SERIAL #40844-45317	1,525	1,171	1,035	912
GUITAR	50	MARTIN	2-20 1850's	3,198	2,456	2,170	1,913
GUITAR	36	MARTIN	2-20	3,580	2,749	2,429	2,141
GUITAR	91	MARTIN	2-21 1891	4,353	3,342	2,954	2,604
GUITAR	03	MARTIN	2-27 1903	3,920	3,010	2,660	2,345
GUITAR	29	MARTIN	2-28T TENOR, SERIAL #37569-40843	2,464	1,892	1,672	1,474
GUITAR	30	MARTIN	2-44 OLCOTT BIKFORD MODEL SERIAL #40844-45317	5,321	4,085	3,610	3,183
GUITAR	60	MARTIN	3-17 1860's, CUSTOM WOOD AND METAL CASE	3,660	2,810	2,483	2,189
GUITAR	90	MARTIN	3-17 1890's, BRAZILIAN ROSEWOOD	1,680	1,290	1,140	1,005
GUITAR	96	MARTIN	3-17 1896	1,680	1,290	1,140	1,005
GUITAR	27	MARTIN	5-15T TENOR, SERIAL #28690-34435	1,244	955	844	744
GUITAR	50	MARTIN	5-15T TENOR, SERIAL #112962-117961	1,456	1,118	988	871
GUITAR	52	MARTIN	5-15T TENOR, SERIAL #122800-128436	1,456	1,118	988	871
GUITAR	55	MARTIN	5-15T TENOR, SERIAL #141346-147328	1,456	1,118	988	871
GUITAR	58	MARTIN	5-15T TENOR	1,456	1,118	988	871
GUITAR	62	MARTIN	5-16 SPRUCE TOP, SERIAL #181298-187384	1,216	933	825	727
GUITAR	27	MARTIN	5-17T TENOR, SERIAL #28690-34435	1,456	1,118	988	871
GUITAR	28	MARTIN	5-17T TENOR	1,456	1,118	988	871
GUITAR	29	MARTIN	5-17T TENOR	1,456	1,118	988	871
GUITAR	30	MARTIN	5-17T TENOR, SERIAL #40844-45317	1,456	1,118	988	871
GUITAR	37	MARTIN	5-17T TENOR, SERIAL #65177-68865	1,456	1,118	988	871
GUITAR	22	MARTIN	5-18 SMALL BODY	1,996	1,533	1,355	1,194
GUITAR	37	MARTIN	5-18	2,061	1,583	1,399	1,233
GUITAR	45	MARTIN	5-18 SERIAL #90150-93623	2,352	1,806	1,596	1,407
GUITAR	46	MARTIN	5-18 SERIAL #93624-98158	2,352	1,806	1,596	1,407
GUITAR	48	MARTIN	5-18 SERIAL #103469-108269	2,352	1,806	1,596	1,407
GUITAR	50	MARTIN	5-18 SERIAL #112962-117961	2,128	1,634	1,444	1,273
GUITAR	56	MARTIN	5-18 SERIAL #147329-152775	2,128	1,634	1,444	1,273
GUITAR	57	MARTIN	5-18	1,579	1,212	1,071	944
GUITAR	58	MARTIN	5-18 SERIAL #159062-165576	2,128	1,634	1,444	1,273
GUITAR	60	MARTIN	5-18	1,792	1,376	1,216	1,072
GUITAR	68	MARTIN	5-18 SERIAL #230096-241925	1,792	1,376	1,216	1,072
GUITAR	72	MARTIN	5-18 SERIAL #294271-313302	1,344	1,032	912	804
GUITAR	73	MARTIN	5-18 SERIAL #313303-333873	1,344	1,032	912	804
GUITAR	75	MARTIN	5-18 SERIAL #353388-371828	1,344	1,032	912	804
GUITAR	77	MARTIN	5-18 SERIAL #389235	1,344	1,032	912	804
GUITAR	70	MARTIN	5-18S SERIAL #256004-271633	1,061	815	720	635
GUITAR	55	MARTIN	5-18T TENOR, SERIAL #141346-147328	1,266	972	859	757

TYPE	YR	MFG	PRICES--BASED ON 100% ORIGINAL MODEL	SELL EXC	SELL AVG	BUY EXC	BUY AVG
GUITAR	27	MARTIN	5-21 SERIAL #28690-34435	1,329	1,020	902	795
GUITAR	27	MARTIN	5-21T TENOR, SERIAL #28690-34435	2,352	1,806	1,596	1,407
GUITAR	39	MARTIN	5-28T TENOR, SERIAL #71867-74061	1,265	971	858	757
GUITAR	21	MARTIN	5-45 PEARL INLAY, SERIAL #15849-16758	14,013	10,760	9,509	8,383
GUITAR	32	MARTIN	C-1 ARCHTOP, SERIAL #49590-52590	2,240	1,720	1,520	1,340
GUITAR	34	MARTIN	C-1 ARCHTOP, F-HOLES, SERIAL #55085-58679	2,240	1,720	1,520	1,340
GUITAR	35	MARTIN	C-1 ARCHTOP, F-HOLES, SERIAL #58680-61947	2,240	1,720	1,520	1,340
GUITAR	36	MARTIN	C-1 ARCHTOP, SERIAL #61948-65176	2,240	1,720	1,520	1,340
GUITAR	42	MARTIN	C-1 ARCHTOP, F-HOLES, SERIAL #80014-83107	2,240	1,720	1,520	1,340
GUITAR	32	MARTIN	C-1P PLECTRUM, SERIAL #49590-52590	2,308	1,772	1,566	1,380
GUITAR	33	MARTIN	C-1P PLECTRUM, SERIAL #52591-55084	2,301	1,767	1,561	1,376
GUITAR	33	MARTIN	C-1T TENOR, SERIAL #52591-55084	2,298	1,764	1,559	1,374
GUITAR	34	MARTIN	C-1T TENOR, SERIAL #55085-58679	2,292	1,760	1,555	1,371
GUITAR	31	MARTIN	C-2 ARCHTOP, ROUND HOLE, SERIAL #45318-49589	3,212	2,466	2,179	1,921
GUITAR	32	MARTIN	C-2 ARCHTOP, ROUND HOLE, SERIAL #49590-52590	3,202	2,458	2,172	1,915
GUITAR	34	MARTIN	C-2 ARCHTOP, F-HOLES, SERIAL #55085-58679	3,195	2,453	2,168	1,911
GUITAR	35	MARTIN	C-2 ARCHTOP	3,131	2,404	2,124	1,873
GUITAR	36	MARTIN	C-2 SUNBURST, ARCHTOP, F-HOLES, SERIAL #61948-65176	3,472	2,666	2,356	2,077
GUITAR	37	MARTIN	C-2 ARCHTOP, F-HOLES, SERIAL #65177-68865	3,200	2,457	2,172	1,914
GUITAR	39	MARTIN	C-2 ARCHTOP, F-HOLES, SERIAL #71867-74061	3,059	2,349	2,076	1,830
GUITAR	32	MARTIN	C-2T TENOR, SERIAL #49590-52590	2,960	2,272	2,008	1,770
GUITAR	32	MARTIN	C-3 ARCHTOP, ROUND HOLE, SERIAL #49590-52590	5,488	4,214	3,724	3,283
GUITAR	33	MARTIN	C-3 ARCHTOP, SERIAL #52591-55084	5,488	4,214	3,724	3,283
GUITAR	34	MARTIN	C-3 ARCHTOP, SERIAL #55085-58679 F-HOLES	5,488	4,214	3,724	3,283
GUITAR	72	MARTIN	D-12-18 12-STRING	1,361	1,045	924	814
GUITAR	75	MARTIN	D-12-18 12-STRING	1,512	1,161	1,026	904
GUITAR	64	MARTIN	D-12-20 12-STRING	1,904	1,462	1,292	1,139
GUITAR	65	MARTIN	D-12-20	1,380	1,060	937	826
GUITAR	66	MARTIN	D-12-20 12-STRING, SERIAL #207031-217215	1,904	1,462	1,292	1,139
GUITAR	67	MARTIN	D-12-20 12-STRING, SERIAL #217216-230095	1,904	1,462	1,292	1,139
GUITAR	68	MARTIN	D-12-20 12-STRING, SERIAL #230096-241925	1,904	1,462	1,292	1,139
GUITAR	69	MARTIN	D-12-20 12-STRING, SERIAL #241926-256003	1,904	1,462	1,292	1,139
GUITAR	70	MARTIN	D-12-20 12-STRING, SERIAL #256004-271633	1,624	1,247	1,102	971
GUITAR	70	MARTIN	D-12-20 12-STRING, LEFT-HANDED	1,624	1,247	1,102	971
GUITAR	71	MARTIN	D-12-20 12-STRING, SERIAL #271634-294270	1,624	1,247	1,102	971
GUITAR	72	MARTIN	D-12-20 12-STRING, SERIAL #294271-313302	1,624	1,247	1,102	971
GUITAR	75	MARTIN	D-12-20	1,319	1,013	895	789
GUITAR	68	MARTIN	D-12-28 INDIAN ROSEWOOD, 12-STRING	1,680	1,290	1,140	1,005
GUITAR	73	MARTIN	D-12-28 NATURAL TOP, 12-STRING	1,792	1,376	1,216	1,072
GUITAR	75	MARTIN	D-12-28 12-STRING, SERIAL #353388-371828	1,792	1,376	1,216	1,072
GUITAR	66	MARTIN	D-12-35 12-STRING, SERIAL #207031-217215	3,472	2,666	2,356	2,077
GUITAR	67	MARTIN	D-12-35 12-STRING, SERIAL #217216-230095	3,472	2,666	2,356	2,077
GUITAR	68	MARTIN	D-12-35 12-STRING, SERIAL #230096-241925	3,472	2,666	2,356	2,077

TYPE	YR	MFG	PRICES--BASED ON 100% ORIGINAL MODEL	SELL EXC	SELL AVG	BUY EXC	BUY AVG
GUITAR	69	MARTIN	D-12-35 12-STRING, SERIAL #241926-256003	3,472	2,666	2,356	2,077
GUITAR	70	MARTIN	D-12-35 12-STRING, SERIAL #256004-271633	1,792	1,376	1,216	1,072
GUITAR	71	MARTIN	D-12-35 12-STRING, SERIAL #271634-294270	1,792	1,376	1,216	1,072
GUITAR	72	MARTIN	D-12-35 12-STRING, SERIAL #294271-313302	1,792	1,376	1,216	1,072
GUITAR	73	MARTIN	D-12-35 12-STRING, SERIAL #313303-333873	1,792	1,376	1,216	1,072
GUITAR	74	MARTIN	D-12-35 12-STRING, SERIAL #333874-353387	1,792	1,376	1,216	1,072
GUITAR	75	MARTIN	D-12-35 12-STRING, SERIAL #353388-371828	1,792	1,376	1,216	1,072
GUITAR	70	MARTIN	D-12-41 12-STRING, SERIAL #256004-271633	3,057	2,347	2,074	1,829
GUITAR	70	MARTIN	D-12-45 12-STRING, SERIAL #256004-271633	5,600	4,300	3,800	3,350
GUITAR	32	MARTIN	D-18 12-FRET NECK	25,760	19,780	17,480	15,410
GUITAR	33	MARTIN	D-18 SERIAL #52591-55084	25,760	19,780	17,480	15,410
GUITAR	34	MARTIN	D-18 SERIAL #55085-58679	22,161	17,016	15,038	13,257
GUITAR	35	MARTIN	D-18 SERIAL #58680-61947	22,161	17,016	15,038	13,257
GUITAR	36	MARTIN	D-18 SERIAL #61948-65176	21,280	16,340	14,440	12,730
GUITAR	37	MARTIN	D-18 SERIAL #65177-68865	21,280	16,340	14,440	12,730
GUITAR	38	MARTIN	D-18 SERIAL #68866-71866	21,280	16,340	14,440	12,730
GUITAR	39	MARTIN	D-18 SERIAL #71867-74061	21,280	16,340	14,440	12,730
GUITAR	40	MARTIN	D-18 SERIAL #74062-76734	15,680	12,040	10,640	9,380
GUITAR	41	MARTIN	D-18 SERIAL #76735-80013	16,800	12,900	11,400	10,050
GUITAR	42	MARTIN	D-18 SERIAL #80014-83107, SCALLOPED BRACES	11,200	8,600	7,600	6,700
GUITAR	43	MARTIN	D-18 SERIAL #83108-86724, SCALLOPED BRACES	11,200	8,600	7,600	6,700
GUITAR	44	MARTIN	D-18 SERIAL #86725-90149	7,840	6,020	5,320	4,690
GUITAR	45	MARTIN	D-18 SERIAL #90150-93623	7,840	6,020	5,320	4,690
GUITAR	46	MARTIN	D-18 SERIAL #93624-98158	7,840	6,020	5,320	4,690
GUITAR	47	MARTIN	D-18 SERIAL #98159-103468	6,496	4,988	4,408	3,886
GUITAR	48	MARTIN	D-18 SERIAL #103469-108269	6,482	4,977	4,398	3,877
GUITAR	49	MARTIN	D-18 SERIAL #108270-112961	6,459	4,959	4,382	3,863
GUITAR	51	MARTIN	D-18 SERIAL #117962-122799	4,766	3,660	3,234	2,851
GUITAR	52	MARTIN	D-18 SERIAL #122800-128436	4,704	3,612	3,192	2,814
GUITAR	53	MARTIN	D-18 SERIAL #128437-134501	4,480	3,440	3,040	2,680
GUITAR	54	MARTIN	D-18 SERIAL #134502-141345	4,480	3,440	3,040	2,680
GUITAR	55	MARTIN	D-18 SERIAL #141346-147328	4,480	3,440	3,040	2,680
GUITAR	56	MARTIN	D-18 SERIAL #147329-152775	4,480	3,440	3,040	2,680
GUITAR	57	MARTIN	D-18 SERIAL #152776-159061	4,480	3,440	3,040	2,680
GUITAR	58	MARTIN	D-18 SERIAL #159062-165576	4,480	3,440	3,040	2,680
GUITAR	59	MARTIN	D-18 SERIAL #165577-171047	4,480	3,440	3,040	2,680
GUITAR	60	MARTIN	D-18 SERIAL #171048-175689	4,032	3,096	2,736	2,412
GUITAR	61	MARTIN	D-18 SERIAL #175690-181297	4,032	3,096	2,736	2,412
GUITAR	62	MARTIN	D-18 SERIAL #181298-187384	4,032	3,096	2,736	2,412
GUITAR	63	MARTIN	D-18	3,511	2,696	2,382	2,100
GUITAR	64	MARTIN	D-18 SERIAL #193328-199626	3,248	2,494	2,204	1,943
GUITAR	65	MARTIN	D-18 TORTOISE PICKGUARD	3,248	2,494	2,204	1,943

TYPE	YR	MFG	PRICES--BASED ON 100% ORIGINAL MODEL	SELL EXC	SELL AVG	BUY EXC	BUY AVG
GUITAR	66	MARTIN	D-18 BLACK GUARD	2,688	**2,064**	1,824	1,608
GUITAR	67	MARTIN	D-18 SERIAL #217216-230095	2,464	**1,892**	1,672	1,474
GUITAR	68	MARTIN	D-18 SERIAL #230096-241925	2,352	**1,806**	1,596	1,407
GUITAR	69	MARTIN	D-18 SERIAL #241926-256003	1,919	**1,474**	1,302	1,148
GUITAR	70	MARTIN	D-18 SERIAL #256004-271633	1,680	**1,290**	1,140	1,005
GUITAR	71	MARTIN	D-18 SERIAL #271634-294270	1,716	**1,318**	1,165	1,027
GUITAR	72	MARTIN	D-18 SERIAL #294271-313302	1,580	**1,213**	1,072	945
GUITAR	73	MARTIN	D-18 SERIAL #313303-333873	1,551	**1,191**	1,052	927
GUITAR	74	MARTIN	D-18 SERIAL #333874-353387	1,456	**1,118**	988	871
GUITAR	75	MARTIN	D-18 SERIAL #353388-371828	1,587	**1,218**	1,076	949
GUITAR	67	MARTIN	D-18S SERIAL #217216-230095	2,128	**1,634**	1,444	1,273
GUITAR	69	MARTIN	D-18S SERIAL #241926-256003	2,128	**1,634**	1,444	1,273
GUITAR	70	MARTIN	D-18S SERIAL #256004-271633	1,596	**1,225**	1,083	954
GUITAR	71	MARTIN	D-18S	1,593	**1,223**	1,081	953
GUITAR	73	MARTIN	D-18S	1,589	**1,220**	1,078	950
GUITAR	56	MARTIN	D-21 SERIAL #147329-152775	6,384	**4,902**	4,332	3,819
GUITAR	58	MARTIN	D-21	6,384	**4,902**	4,332	3,819
GUITAR	60	MARTIN	D-21 SERIAL #171048-175689	5,376	**4,128**	3,648	3,216
GUITAR	61	MARTIN	D-21 SERIAL #175690-181297	5,376	**4,128**	3,648	3,216
GUITAR	63	MARTIN	D-21 SERIAL# 187385-193327	5,040	**3,870**	3,420	3,015
GUITAR	64	MARTIN	D-21 SERIAL #193328-199626	5,040	**3,870**	3,420	3,015
GUITAR	65	MARTIN	D-21 SERIAL #199627-207030	5,040	**3,870**	3,420	3,015
GUITAR	66	MARTIN	D-21 SERIAL #207031-217215	4,480	**3,440**	3,040	2,680
GUITAR	67	MARTIN	D-21 SERIAL #217216-230095	4,480	**3,440**	3,040	2,680
GUITAR	68	MARTIN	D-21 SERIAL #230096-241925	3,934	**3,021**	2,669	2,353
GUITAR	69	MARTIN	D-21 SERIAL #241926-256003	3,920	**3,010**	2,660	2,345
GUITAR	31	MARTIN	D-28	70,016	**53,762**	47,511	41,885
GUITAR	32	MARTIN	D-28 SERIAL #49590-52590	67,200	**51,600**	45,600	40,200
GUITAR	33	MARTIN	D-28 SERIAL #52591-55084	61,600	**47,300**	41,800	36,850
GUITAR	34	MARTIN	D-28 SERIAL #55085-58679	47,040	**36,120**	31,920	28,140
GUITAR	35	MARTIN	D-28 SERIAL #58680-61947	46,120	**35,413**	31,296	27,589
GUITAR	36	MARTIN	D-28 SERIAL #61948-65176	47,040	**36,120**	31,920	28,140
GUITAR	37	MARTIN	D-28 SERIAL #65177-68865	39,200	**30,100**	26,600	23,450
GUITAR	38	MARTIN	D-28 HERRINGBONE	16,578	**12,729**	11,249	9,917
GUITAR	38	MARTIN	D-28 SERIAL #68866-71866	39,200	**30,100**	26,600	23,450
GUITAR	39	MARTIN	D-28 SERIAL #71867-74061	42,804	**32,867**	29,045	25,606
GUITAR	40	MARTIN	D-28 SERIAL #74062-76734	34,720	**26,660**	23,560	20,770
GUITAR	41	MARTIN	D-28 SERIAL #76735-80013	34,720	**26,660**	23,560	20,770
GUITAR	42	MARTIN	D-28 SERIAL #80014-83107	30,240	**23,220**	20,520	18,090
GUITAR	43	MARTIN	D-28 SERIAL #83108-86724, SCALLOPED BRACES	30,598	**23,495**	20,763	18,304
GUITAR	44	MARTIN	D-28 SERIAL #86725-90149, NON-SCALLOPED	20,160	**15,480**	13,680	12,060
GUITAR	45	MARTIN	D-28 SERIAL #90150-93623, NON-SCALLOPED	19,040	**14,620**	12,920	11,390
GUITAR	46	MARTIN	D-28 SERIAL #93624-98158, NON-SCALLOPED	19,040	**14,620**	12,920	11,390
GUITAR	47	MARTIN	D-28 SERIAL #98159-103468	11,200	**8,600**	7,600	6,700

TYPE	YR	MFG	PRICES--BASED ON 100% ORIGINAL MODEL	SELL EXC	SELL AVG	BUY EXC	BUY AVG
GUITAR	48	MARTIN	**D-28** SERIAL #103469-108269	11,200	**8,600**	7,600	6,700
GUITAR	49	MARTIN	**D-28** SERIAL #108270-112961	11,200	**8,600**	7,600	6,700
GUITAR	50	MARTIN	**D-28** SERIAL #112962-117961	8,970	**6,887**	6,086	5,366
GUITAR	51	MARTIN	**D-28** SERIAL #117962-122799	8,588	**6,594**	5,827	5,137
GUITAR	52	MARTIN	**D-28** SERIAL #122800-128436	8,960	**6,880**	6,080	5,360
GUITAR	53	MARTIN	**D-28** SERIAL #128437-134501	8,176	**6,278**	5,548	4,891
GUITAR	54	MARTIN	**D-28** SERIAL #134502-141345	8,176	**6,278**	5,548	4,891
GUITAR	55	MARTIN	**D-28** SERIAL #141346-147328	8,176	**6,278**	5,548	4,891
GUITAR	56	MARTIN	**D-28** SERIAL #147329-152775	8,176	**6,278**	5,548	4,891
GUITAR	57	MARTIN	**D-28** SERIAL #152776-159061	8,176	**6,278**	5,548	4,891
GUITAR	58	MARTIN	**D-28** SERIAL #159062-165576	7,504	**5,762**	5,092	4,489
GUITAR	59	MARTIN	**D-28** SERIAL #165577-171047	7,504	**5,762**	5,092	4,489
GUITAR	60	MARTIN	**D-28** SERIAL #171048-175689	7,141	**5,483**	4,845	4,271
GUITAR	61	MARTIN	**D-28** SERIAL #175690-181297	7,133	**5,477**	4,840	4,267
GUITAR	62	MARTIN	**D-28** SERIAL #181298-187384	7,120	**5,467**	4,832	4,259
GUITAR	63	MARTIN	**D-28** SERIAL #187385-193327	6,384	**4,902**	4,332	3,819
GUITAR	64	MARTIN	**D-28** SERIAL #193328-199626	6,384	**4,902**	4,332	3,819
GUITAR	65	MARTIN	**D-28** SERIAL #199627-207030	6,384	**4,902**	4,332	3,819
GUITAR	66	MARTIN	**D-28** SERIAL #207031-217215	5,712	**4,386**	3,876	3,417
GUITAR	67	MARTIN	**D-28** SERIAL #217216-230095	5,600	**4,300**	3,800	3,350
GUITAR	68	MARTIN	**D-28** SERIAL #230096-241925	5,152	**3,956**	3,496	3,082
GUITAR	69	MARTIN	**D-28** SERIAL #241926-256003	4,704	**3,612**	3,192	2,814
GUITAR	69	MARTIN	**D-28** LEFT-HANDED, SERIAL #241926-256003	4,816	**3,698**	3,268	2,881
GUITAR	70	MARTIN	**D-28** SERIAL #256004-271633	2,016	**1,548**	1,368	1,206
GUITAR	71	MARTIN	**D-28** SERIAL #271634-294270	2,016	**1,548**	1,368	1,206
GUITAR	72	MARTIN	**D-28** SERIAL #294271-313302	2,016	**1,548**	1,368	1,206
GUITAR	73	MARTIN	**D-28** SERIAL #313303-333873	2,016	**1,548**	1,368	1,206
GUITAR	74	MARTIN	**D-28** SERIAL #333874-353387	2,016	**1,548**	1,368	1,206
GUITAR	75	MARTIN	**D-28** SERIAL #353388-371828	2,016	**1,548**	1,368	1,206
GUITAR	75	MARTIN	**D-28** LEFT-HANDED	2,016	**1,548**	1,368	1,206
GUITAR	76	MARTIN	**D-28**	2,016	**1,548**	1,368	1,206
GUITAR	78	MARTIN	**D-28**	2,016	**1,548**	1,368	1,206
GUITAR	79	MARTIN	**D-28**	2,016	**1,548**	1,368	1,206
GUITAR	34	MARTIN	**D-28H** SERIAL #56435	24,545	**18,847**	16,656	14,683
GUITAR	65	MARTIN	**D-28S** SERIAL #199627-207030	5,936	**4,558**	4,028	3,551
GUITAR	66	MARTIN	**D-28S** SERIAL #207031-217215	5,812	**4,463**	3,944	3,477
GUITAR	67	MARTIN	**D-28S** LEFT-HANDED	5,221	**4,009**	3,543	3,123
GUITAR	67	MARTIN	**D-28S** SERIAL #217216-230095	5,804	**4,457**	3,939	3,472
GUITAR	68	MARTIN	**D-28S** SERIAL #230096-241925	5,792	**4,447**	3,930	3,465
GUITAR	70	MARTIN	**D-28S** SERIAL#263662	2,107	**1,618**	1,430	1,260
GUITAR	71	MARTIN	**D-28S** SERIAL #271634-294270	2,016	**1,548**	1,368	1,206
GUITAR	72	MARTIN	**D-28S** SERIAL #294271-313302	2,103	**1,615**	1,427	1,258
GUITAR	74	MARTIN	**D-28S** SERIAL #333874-353387	2,093	**1,607**	1,420	1,252

TYPE	YR	MFG	PRICES--BASED ON 100% ORIGINAL MODEL	SELL EXC	SELL AVG	BUY EXC	BUY AVG
GUITAR	75	MARTIN	**D-28S** SERIAL #353388-371828	2,080	**1,597**	1,412	1,244
GUITAR	65	MARTIN	**D-35** SERIAL #199627-207030	5,040	**3,870**	3,420	3,015
GUITAR	66	MARTIN	**D-35** SERIAL #210490	4,144	**3,182**	2,812	2,479
GUITAR	67	MARTIN	**D-35** SERIAL #217216-230095	4,011	**3,080**	2,722	2,399
GUITAR	68	MARTIN	**D-35** SERIAL #230096-241925	3,716	**2,853**	2,521	2,223
GUITAR	69	MARTIN	**D-35** SITKA TOP, BRAZILIAN SIDES/CENTER OF BACK	3,472	**2,666**	2,356	2,077
GUITAR	70	MARTIN	**D-35** SERIAL #256004-271633	2,128	**1,634**	1,444	1,273
GUITAR	71	MARTIN	**D-35** SERIAL #271634-294270	2,058	**1,580**	1,396	1,231
GUITAR	72	MARTIN	**D-35** SERIAL #294271-313302	2,287	**1,756**	1,551	1,368
GUITAR	73	MARTIN	**D-35** SERIAL #313303-333873	2,115	**1,624**	1,435	1,265
GUITAR	74	MARTIN	**D-35** SERIAL #333874-353387	2,016	**1,548**	1,368	1,206
GUITAR	75	MARTIN	**D-35** SERIAL #353388-371828	2,016	**1,548**	1,368	1,206
GUITAR	67	MARTIN	**D-35-12** 12-STRING	3,336	**2,561**	2,264	1,995
GUITAR	70	MARTIN	**D-35-12** NATURAL, 12-STRING	1,604	**1,232**	1,089	960
GUITAR	67	MARTIN	**D-35S** SERIAL #217216-230095	4,207	**3,231**	2,855	2,517
GUITAR	69	MARTIN	**D-35S** SERIAL #2431100	4,256	**3,268**	2,888	2,546
GUITAR	70	MARTIN	**D-35S** SERIAL #256004-271633	2,016	**1,548**	1,368	1,206
GUITAR	72	MARTIN	**D-35S**	1,988	**1,526**	1,349	1,189
GUITAR	73	MARTIN	**D-35S** SERIAL #313303-333873	1,939	**1,489**	1,316	1,160
GUITAR	74	MARTIN	**D-35S** SERIAL #333874-353387	1,960	**1,505**	1,330	1,172
GUITAR	75	MARTIN	**D-35S** SERIAL #353388-371828	2,016	**1,548**	1,368	1,206
GUITAR	69	MARTIN	**D-41** BRAZILIAN ROSEWOOD, SERIAL #241926-256003	12,320	**9,460**	8,360	7,370
GUITAR	70	MARTIN	**D-41** SERIAL #256004-271633	3,696	**2,838**	2,508	2,211
GUITAR	72	MARTIN	**D-41** SERIAL #294271-313302	3,696	**2,838**	2,508	2,211
GUITAR	73	MARTIN	**D-41** SERIAL #313303-333873	3,696	**2,838**	2,508	2,211
GUITAR	74	MARTIN	**D-41** SERIAL #333874-353387	3,696	**2,838**	2,508	2,211
GUITAR	36	MARTIN	**D-45** SNOWFLAKE, SERIAL #61948-65176	259,062	**198,923**	175,792	154,975
GUITAR	38	MARTIN	**D-45** BRAZILIAN ROSEWOOD, SNOWFLAKE	223,554	**171,657**	151,697	133,733
GUITAR	39	MARTIN	**D-45** SERIAL #71867-74061	188,160	**144,480**	127,680	112,560
GUITAR	40	MARTIN	**D-45** SERIAL #74062-76734	179,200	**137,600**	121,600	107,200
GUITAR	41	MARTIN	**D-45** SERIAL #76735-80013	168,000	**129,000**	114,000	100,500
GUITAR	42	MARTIN	**D-45** SERIAL #80014-83107	156,800	**120,400**	106,400	93,800
GUITAR	68	MARTIN	**D-45** BRAZILIAN ROSEWOOD, 12-STRING, SERIAL #230096-241925	29,120	**22,360**	19,760	17,420
GUITAR	69	MARTIN	**D-45** BRAZILIAN ROSEWOOD, SERIAL #241926-256003	29,120	**22,360**	19,760	17,420
GUITAR	70	MARTIN	**D-45** INDIAN ROSEWOOD, SERIAL #256004-271633	7,168	**5,504**	4,864	4,288
GUITAR	71	MARTIN	**D-45** SERIAL #271634-294270	7,168	**5,504**	4,864	4,288
GUITAR	75	MARTIN	**D-45** SERIAL #353388-371828	6,720	**5,160**	4,560	4,020
GUITAR	83	MARTIN	**D-45 150th ANNIVERSARY** CUSTOM, MARK LEAF CASE	19,885	**15,269**	13,493	11,895
GUITAR	69	MARTIN	**D-45S** BRAZILIAN ROSEWOOD	25,307	**19,432**	17,172	15,139
GUITAR	76	MARTIN	**D-76 BICENTENNIAL EDITION** SERIAL #371829-388800	3,136	**2,408**	2,128	1,876
GUITAR	21	MARTIN	**DITSON STYLE 2** MAHOGANY BACK/SIDES, SERIAL #15849-16758	1,537	**1,180**	1,043	919
GUITAR	40	MARTIN	**F-1** ARCHTOP, SERIAL #74062-76734	2,240	**1,720**	1,520	1,340

TYPE	YR	MFG	PRICES--BASED ON 100% ORIGINAL MODEL	SELL EXC	SELL AVG	BUY EXC	BUY AVG
GUITAR	41	MARTIN	F-1 ARCHTOP, SERIAL #76735-80013	2,240	**1,720**	1,520	1,340
GUITAR	41	MARTIN	F-2 ARCHTOP, SERIAL #76735-80013	2,912	**2,236**	1,976	1,742
GUITAR	42	MARTIN	F-2 ARCHTOP, SERIAL #80014-83107	2,912	**2,236**	1,976	1,742
GUITAR	35	MARTIN	F-7 ARCHTOP SERIAL #58680-61947	7,280	**5,590**	4,940	4,355
GUITAR	36	MARTIN	F-7 ARCHTOP SERIAL #61948-65176	7,280	**5,590**	4,940	4,355
GUITAR	37	MARTIN	F-7 ARCHTOP SERIAL #65177-68865,RSWD B/S,SPRUCE TOP,GROVER TUNERS	7,280	**5,590**	4,940	4,355
GUITAR	38	MARTIN	F-7 ARCHTOP SERIAL #68866-71866	7,280	**5,590**	4,940	4,355
GUITAR	35	MARTIN	F-7 FLATTOP BRAZILIAN ROSEWOOD	17,092	**13,124**	11,598	10,224
GUITAR	35	MARTIN	F-9 ARCHTOP SERIAL #58680-61947	13,440	**10,320**	9,120	8,040
GUITAR	15	MARTIN	FODEN SPECIAL STYLE D	12,451	**9,560**	8,448	7,448
GUITAR	75	MARTIN	HD-28 INDIAN ROSEWOOD	1,680	**1,290**	1,140	1,005
GUITAR	86	MARTIN	HD-28 CUSTOM	7,154	**5,493**	4,854	4,279
GUITAR	79	MARTIN	HD-28L LEFT-HANDED	2,340	**1,797**	1,588	1,400
GUITAR	79	MARTIN	HD-38	1,574	**1,209**	1,068	942
GUITAR	88	MARTIN	J-40MC THINLINE PU, SERIAL #483825-	2,244	**1,723**	1,523	1,342
GUITAR	77	MARTIN	M-38 SERIAL #388801-399625	2,240	**1,720**	1,520	1,340
GUITAR	78	MARTIN	M-38 SERIAL #399626-407800	2,240	**1,720**	1,520	1,340
GUITAR	79	MARTIN	M-38 INDIAN ROSEWOOD	2,240	**1,720**	1,520	1,340
GUITAR	68	MARTIN	N-10 CLASSICAL SERIAL #230096-241925	1,680	**1,290**	1,140	1,005
GUITAR	69	MARTIN	N-10 CLASSICAL SERIAL #241926-256003	1,680	**1,290**	1,140	1,005
GUITAR	70	MARTIN	N-10 CLASSICAL SERIAL #256004-271633	1,456	**1,118**	988	871
GUITAR	69	MARTIN	N-20 CLASSICAL SERIAL #241926-256004	3,279	**2,518**	2,225	1,961
GUITAR	71	MARTIN	N-20 CLASSICAL	1,644	**1,262**	1,115	983
GUITAR	72	MARTIN	N-20 CLASSICAL SERIAL #294271-313302	1,585	**1,217**	1,076	948
GUITAR	76	MARTIN	N-20 CLASSICAL	1,674	**1,285**	1,136	1,001
GUITAR	35	MARTIN	O-15 2 MADE, MAPLE/BIRCH,ALL MAHOG,RSWD FNGRBRD,14 FRET	3,006	**2,308**	2,039	1,798
GUITAR	40	MARTIN	O-15 SERIAL #74062-76734	1,676	**1,287**	1,137	1,002
GUITAR	41	MARTIN	O-15 SERIAL #76735-80013	1,673	**1,284**	1,135	1,000
GUITAR	42	MARTIN	O-15 SERIAL #80014-83107	1,669	**1,282**	1,133	998
GUITAR	43	MARTIN	O-15 SERIAL #83108-86724	1,660	**1,275**	1,127	993
GUITAR	48	MARTIN	O-15 SERIAL #103469-108269	1,654	**1,270**	1,122	989
GUITAR	49	MARTIN	O-15 ALL MAHOG,RSWD FNGRBRD,SOLID PEGHEAD,14 FRET	1,644	**1,262**	1,115	983
GUITAR	50	MARTIN	O-15 SERIAL #112962-117961	1,648	**1,265**	1,118	986
GUITAR	51	MARTIN	O-15 ALL MAHOG,RSWD FNGRBRD,14,FRET,SOLID PEGHEAD	1,291	**991**	876	772
GUITAR	52	MARTIN	O-15 ALL MAHOG,RSWD FNGRBRD,SOLID PEGHEAD,14 FRET	1,289	**989**	874	771
GUITAR	53	MARTIN	O-15 SERIAL #128437-134501	1,350	**1,037**	916	808
GUITAR	54	MARTIN	O-15 ALL MAHOG,RSWD FNGRBRD,SOLID PEGHEAD,14 FRET	1,289	**989**	874	771
GUITAR	55	MARTIN	O-15 SERIAL #141346-147328	1,756	**1,348**	1,191	1,050
GUITAR	56	MARTIN	O-15 SERIAL #147329-152775	1,747	**1,341**	1,185	1,045
GUITAR	57	MARTIN	O-15 SERIAL #152776-159061	1,739	**1,335**	1,180	1,040
GUITAR	58	MARTIN	O-15 ALL MAHOG,RSWD FNGRBRD,SOLID PEGHEAD,14 FRET	1,286	**988**	873	769
GUITAR	59	MARTIN	O-15 MAHOGANY	1,336	**1,025**	906	799
GUITAR	60	MARTIN	O-15 SERIAL #171048-175689	1,654	**1,270**	1,122	989
GUITAR	61	MARTIN	O-15 SERIAL #175690-181297	1,646	**1,264**	1,117	984

TYPE	YR	MFG	PRICES--BASED ON 100% ORIGINAL MODEL	SELL EXC	SELL AVG	BUY EXC	BUY AVG
GUITAR	40	MARTIN	O-15H HAWAIIAN SERIAL #74062-76734	854	656	579	511
GUITAR	60	MARTIN	O-15T TENOR SERIAL #171048-175689	854	656	579	511
GUITAR	61	MARTIN	O-15T TENOR NATURAL MAHOGANY, STYLE 15 APPOINTMENTS	843	647	572	504
GUITAR	62	MARTIN	O-15T TENOR NATURAL MAHOGANY, STYLE 15 APPOINTMENTS	841	645	570	503
GUITAR	63	MARTIN	O-15T TENOR NATURAL MAHOGANY, STYLE 15 APPOINTMENTS	840	645	570	502
GUITAR	61	MARTIN	O-16 SIX MADE	1,879	1,443	1,275	1,124
GUITAR	61	MARTIN	O-16NY	1,576	1,210	1,070	943
GUITAR	62	MARTIN	O-16NY	1,576	1,210	1,070	943
GUITAR	63	MARTIN	O-16NY SERIAL #187385-193327	1,571	1,206	1,066	940
GUITAR	64	MARTIN	O-16NY SERIAL #193328-199626	1,560	1,197	1,058	933
GUITAR	65	MARTIN	O-16NY LEFT-HANDED	1,377	1,041	918	761
GUITAR	66	MARTIN	O-16NY 12-FRET NECK, SERIAL #207031-217215	1,531	1,175	1,038	915
GUITAR	67	MARTIN	O-16NY SERIAL #217216-230095	1,396	1,072	947	835
GUITAR	68	MARTIN	O-16NY SERIAL #230096-241925	1,385	1,063	940	828
GUITAR	69	MARTIN	O-16NY	1,380	1,060	937	826
GUITAR	70	MARTIN	O-16NY SERIAL #256004-271633	1,263	970	857	755
GUITAR	71	MARTIN	O-16NY SERIAL #271634-294270	1,317	1,011	893	787
GUITAR	72	MARTIN	O-16NY MAHOG BACK/SIDES, 12 FRET, EXTRA WIDE RSWD FNGRBRD	1,301	999	883	778
GUITAR	73	MARTIN	O-16NY MAHOG BACK/SIDES,12 FRET,EXTRA WIDE RSWD FNGRBRD	1,289	989	874	771
GUITAR	74	MARTIN	O-16NY 12-FRET NECK, SERIAL #25340-25679	1,304	1,001	885	780
GUITAR	75	MARTIN	O-16NY SERIAL #353388-371828	1,237	950	839	740
GUITAR	76	MARTIN	O-16NY MAHOG BACK/SIDES, 12 FRET, EXTRA WIDE RSWD FNGRBRD	1,301	999	883	778
GUITAR	77	MARTIN	O-16NY MAHOG BACK/SIDES, 12 FRET, EXTRA WIDE RSWD FNGRBRD	1,291	991	876	772
GUITAR	78	MARTIN	O-16NY MAHOG BACK/SIDES, 12 FRET, EXTRA WIDE RSWD FNGRBRD	1,279	982	867	765
GUITAR	79	MARTIN	O-16NY MAHOG BACK/SIDES, 12 FRET, EXTRA WIDE RSWD FNGRBRD	1,267	973	860	758
GUITAR	06	MARTIN	O-17 GUT,MAHOG B/S,RSWD BOUND, 12 FRETS,SLOTTED PEGHEAD	1,761	1,352	1,195	1,053
GUITAR	07	MARTIN	O-17 GUT,MAHOG B/S,RSWD BOUND, 12 FRETS,SLOTTED PEGHEAD	1,761	1,352	1,195	1,053
GUITAR	08	MARTIN	O-17 GUT,MAHOG B/S,RSWD BOUND, 12 FRETS,SLOTTED PEGHEAD	1,761	1,352	1,195	1,053
GUITAR	09	MARTIN	O-17 GUT,MAHOG B/S,RSWD BOUND, 12 FRETS,SLOTTED PEGHEAD	1,761	1,352	1,195	1,053
GUITAR	10	MARTIN	O-17 SERIAL #11019-11203	1,761	1,352	1,195	1,053
GUITAR	11	MARTIN	O-17 GUT,MAHOG B/S,RSWD BOUND, 12 FRETS,SLOTTED PEGHEAD	1,761	1,352	1,195	1,053
GUITAR	12	MARTIN	O-17 GUT,MAHOG B/S,RSWD BOUND, 12 FRETS,SLOTTED PEGHEAD	1,761	1,352	1,195	1,053
GUITAR	13	MARTIN	O-17 GUT,MAHOG B/S,RSWD BOUND, 12 FRETS,SLOTTED PEGHEAD	1,761	1,352	1,195	1,053
GUITAR	14	MARTIN	O-17 GUT,MAHOG B/S,RSWD BOUND, 12 FRETS,SLOTTED PEGHEAD	1,761	1,352	1,195	1,053
GUITAR	15	MARTIN	O-17 GUT,MAHOG B/S,RSWD BOUND, 12 FRETS,SLOTTED PEGHEAD	1,761	1,352	1,195	1,053
GUITAR	16	MARTIN	O-17 GUT,MAHOG B/S,RSWD BOUND, 12 FRETS,SLOTTED PEGHEAD	1,761	1,352	1,195	1,053
GUITAR	17	MARTIN	O-17 GUT,MAHOG B/S,RSWD BOUND, 12 FRETS,SLOTTED PEGHEAD	1,761	1,352	1,195	1,053
GUITAR	28	MARTIN	O-17 SERIAL #34436-37568	1,584	1,216	1,075	948
GUITAR	29	MARTIN	O-17 ALL MAHOG, SLOTTED PEGHEAD, 12 BAR FRETS	1,879	1,443	1,275	1,124
GUITAR	30	MARTIN	O-17 ALL MAHOG, SLOTTED PEGHEAD, 12 BAR FRETS	1,879	1,443	1,275	1,124
GUITAR	31	MARTIN	O-17 ALL MAHOG, SLOTTED PEGHEAD, 12 BAR FRETS	1,879	1,443	1,275	1,124
GUITAR	32	MARTIN	O-17 ALL MAHOG, SLOTTED PEGHEAD, 12 BAR FRETS	1,879	1,443	1,275	1,124
GUITAR	33	MARTIN	O-17 SERIAL #52591-55084	1,879	1,443	1,275	1,124

TYPE	YR	MFG	PRICES--BASED ON 100% ORIGINAL MODEL	SELL EXC	SELL AVG	BUY EXC	BUY AVG
GUITAR	34	MARTIN	O-17 ALL MAHOG, 12 BAR FRETS, SLOTTED PEGHEAD	1,879	1,443	1,275	1,124
GUITAR	34	MARTIN	O-17 ALL MAHOG, 14 T-FRETS, SOLID PEGHEAD	2,113	1,622	1,434	1,264
GUITAR	35	MARTIN	O-17 SERIAL #58680-61947	2,113	1,622	1,434	1,264
GUITAR	36	MARTIN	O-17 SERIAL #61948-65176	2,113	1,622	1,434	1,264
GUITAR	37	MARTIN	O-17 SERIAL #65177-68865	2,113	1,622	1,434	1,264
GUITAR	38	MARTIN	O-17 ALL MAHOG, SOLID PEGHEAD, 14 FRETS	2,113	1,622	1,434	1,264
GUITAR	39	MARTIN	O-17 ALL MAHOG, SOLID PEGHEAD, 14 FRET	2,113	1,622	1,434	1,264
GUITAR	40	MARTIN	O-17 ALL MAHOG, SOLID PEGHEAD, 14 FRET	1,761	1,352	1,195	1,053
GUITAR	41	MARTIN	O-17 ALL MAHOG, SOLID PEGHEAD, 14 FRET	1,761	1,352	1,195	1,053
GUITAR	42	MARTIN	O-17 SERIAL#80014-83107	1,761	1,352	1,195	1,053
GUITAR	43	MARTIN	O-17 SERIAL #83108-86724	1,761	1,352	1,195	1,053
GUITAR	44	MARTIN	O-17 SERIAL #86725-90149	1,761	1,352	1,195	1,053
GUITAR	45	MARTIN	O-17 ALL MAHOG, SOLID PEGHEAD, 14 FRET	1,761	1,352	1,195	1,053
GUITAR	46	MARTIN	O-17 ALL MAHOG, SOLID PEGHEAD, 14 FRET	1,702	1,307	1,155	1,018
GUITAR	47	MARTIN	O-17 SERIAL #98159-103468	1,702	1,307	1,155	1,018
GUITAR	48	MARTIN	O-17 ALL MAHOG, SOLID PEGHEAD, 14 FRET	1,702	1,307	1,155	1,018
GUITAR	66	MARTIN	O-17 ONE MADE, ALL MAHOG, 14 FRETS	1,526	1,172	1,035	913
GUITAR	68	MARTIN	O-17 SIX MADE, ALL MAHOG, 14 FRETS	1,408	1,081	956	842
GUITAR	30	MARTIN	O-17H HAWAIIAN 60 MADE, MAHOG BACK/SIDES, 12 FRETS, NATURAL	1,761	1,352	1,195	1,053
GUITAR	35	MARTIN	O-17H HAWAIIAN MAHOG BACK/SIDES, 12 FRETS, NATURAL	1,702	1,307	1,155	1,018
GUITAR	36	MARTIN	O-17H HAWAIIAN SERIAL #61948-65176	1,341	1,030	910	802
GUITAR	37	MARTIN	O-17H HAWAIIAN SERIAL #67033	1,376	1,056	934	823
GUITAR	38	MARTIN	O-17H HAWAIIAN SERIAL #68866-71866	1,323	1,016	898	791
GUITAR	39	MARTIN	O-17H HAWAIIAN MAHOG BACK/SIDES, 12 FRETS, NATURAL	1,702	1,307	1,155	1,018
GUITAR	40	MARTIN	O-17H HAWAIIAN MAHOG BACK/SIDES, 12 FRETS, NATURAL	1,691	1,298	1,147	1,011
GUITAR	41	MARTIN	O-17H HAWAIIAN MAHOG BACK/SIDES, 12 FRETS, NATURAL	1,691	1,298	1,147	1,011
GUITAR	32	MARTIN	O-17T TENOR MAHOG BACK/SIDES, NATURAL	1,053	809	715	630
GUITAR	33	MARTIN	O-17T TENOR SERIAL #52591-55084, MAHOG BACK/SIDES, NATURAL	1,053	809	715	630
GUITAR	34	MARTIN	O-17T TENOR MAHOG BACK/SIDES, NATURAL	1,053	809	715	630
GUITAR	35	MARTIN	O-17T TENOR MAHOG BACK/SIDES, NATURAL	1,053	809	715	630
GUITAR	36	MARTIN	O-17T TENOR MAHOG BACK/SIDES, NATURAL	1,053	809	715	630
GUITAR	37	MARTIN	O-17T TENOR MAHOG BACK/SIDES, NATURAL	1,053	809	715	630
GUITAR	38	MARTIN	O-17T TENOR MAHOG BACK/SIDES, NATURAL	1,053	809	715	630
GUITAR	39	MARTIN	O-17T TENOR MAHOG BACK/SIDES, NATURAL	1,053	809	715	630
GUITAR	40	MARTIN	O-17T TENOR MAHOG BACK/SIDES, NATURAL	1,053	809	715	630
GUITAR	41	MARTIN	O-17T TENOR MAHOG BACK/SIDES, NATURAL	1,053	809	715	630
GUITAR	42	MARTIN	O-17T TENOR MAHOG BACK/SIDES, NATURAL	1,053	809	715	630
GUITAR	43	MARTIN	O-17T TENOR MAHOG BACK/SIDES, NATURAL	1,053	809	715	630
GUITAR	44	MARTIN	O-17T TENOR MAHOG BACK/SIDES, NATURAL	1,053	809	715	630
GUITAR	45	MARTIN	O-17T TENOR MAHOG BACK/SIDES, NATURAL	1,053	809	715	630
GUITAR	46	MARTIN	O-17T TENOR MAHOG BACK/SIDES, NATURAL	1,053	809	715	630
GUITAR	47	MARTIN	O-17T TENOR MAHOG BACK/SIDES, NATURAL	1,053	809	715	630

TYPE	YR	MFG	PRICES--BASED ON 100% ORIGINAL MODEL	SELL EXC	SELL AVG	BUY EXC	BUY AVG
GUITAR	48	MARTIN	O-17T TENOR SERIAL #103469-108269, MAHOG BACK/SIDES, NATURAL	1,053	**809**	715	630
GUITAR	49	MARTIN	O-17T TENOR MAHOG BACK/SIDES, NATURAL	1,053	**809**	715	630
GUITAR	50	MARTIN	O-17T TENOR MAHOG, NATURAL	948	**728**	643	567
GUITAR	51	MARTIN	O-17T TENOR MAHOG, NATURAL	948	**728**	643	567
GUITAR	52	MARTIN	O-17T TENOR SERIAL #122800-128436, MAHOG, NATURAL	948	**728**	643	567
GUITAR	53	MARTIN	O-17T TENOR SERIAL #128437-134501, MAHOG, NATURAL	948	**728**	643	567
GUITAR	54	MARTIN	O-17T TENOR MAHOG, NATURAL	948	**728**	643	567
GUITAR	55	MARTIN	O-17T TENOR MAHOG, NATURAL	948	**728**	643	567
GUITAR	56	MARTIN	O-17T TENOR MAHOG, NATURAL	948	**728**	643	567
GUITAR	57	MARTIN	O-17T TENOR MAHOG, NATURAL	948	**728**	643	567
GUITAR	58	MARTIN	O-17T TENOR MAHOG, NATURAL	948	**728**	643	567
GUITAR	59	MARTIN	O-17T TENOR SERIAL #165577-171047, MAHOG, NATURAL	948	**728**	643	567
GUITAR	60	MARTIN	O-17T TENOR MAHOG, NATURAL	948	**728**	643	567
GUITAR	98	MARTIN	O-18 1898, GUT STRING BRACING,RSWD B/S,SPRUCE TOP,12 FRETS	3,279	**2,518**	2,225	1,961
GUITAR	n/a	MARTIN	O-18 1899, GUT STRING BRACING,RSWD B/S,SPRUCE TOP,12 FRETS	3,279	**2,518**	2,225	1,961
GUITAR	00	MARTIN	O-18 1900, GUT STRING BRACING,RSWD B/S,SPRUCE TOP,12 FRETS	3,279	**2,518**	2,225	1,961
GUITAR	01	MARTIN	O-18 GUT STRING BRACING,RSWD B/S,SPRUCE TOP,12 FRETS	3,279	**2,518**	2,225	1,961
GUITAR	02	MARTIN	O-18 GUT STRING BRACING,RSWD B/S,SPRUCE TOP,12 FRETS	3,279	**2,518**	2,225	1,961
GUITAR	03	MARTIN	O-18 GUT STRING BRACING,RSWD B/S,SPRUCE TOP,12 FRETS	3,279	**2,518**	2,225	1,961
GUITAR	04	MARTIN	O-18 GUT STRING BRACING,RSWD B/S,SPRUCE TOP,12 FRETS	3,279	**2,518**	2,225	1,961
GUITAR	05	MARTIN	O-18 GUT STRING BRACING,RSWD B/S,SPRUCE TOP,12 FRETS	3,279	**2,518**	2,225	1,961
GUITAR	06	MARTIN	O-18 GUT STRING BRACING,RSWD B/S,SPRUCE TOP,12 FRETS	3,279	**2,518**	2,225	1,961
GUITAR	07	MARTIN	O-18 GUT STRING BRACING,RSWD B/S,SPRUCE TOP,12 FRETS	3,279	**2,518**	2,225	1,961
GUITAR	08	MARTIN	O-18 GUT STRING BRACING,RSWD B/S,SPRUCE TOP,12 FRETS	3,279	**2,518**	2,225	1,961
GUITAR	09	MARTIN	O-18 GUT STRING BRACING,RSWD B/S,SPRUCE TOP,12 FRETS	3,279	**2,518**	2,225	1,961
GUITAR	10	MARTIN	O-18 GUT STRING BRACING,RSWD B/S,SPRUCE TOP,12 FRETS	3,279	**2,518**	2,225	1,961
GUITAR	11	MARTIN	O-18 GUT STRING BRACING,RSWD B/S,SPRUCE TOP,12 FRETS	3,279	**2,518**	2,225	1,961
GUITAR	12	MARTIN	O-18 GUT STRING BRACING,RSWD B/S,SPRUCE TOP,12 FRETS	3,279	**2,518**	2,225	1,961
GUITAR	13	MARTIN	O-18 GUT STRING BRACING,RSWD B/S,SPRUCE TOP,12 FRETS	3,279	**2,518**	2,225	1,961
GUITAR	14	MARTIN	O-18 GUT STRING BRACING,RSWD B/S,SPRUCE TOP,12 FRETS	3,279	**2,518**	2,225	1,961
GUITAR	15	MARTIN	O-18 GUT STRING BRACING,RSWD B/S,SPRUCE TOP,12 FRETS	3,279	**2,518**	2,225	1,961
GUITAR	16	MARTIN	O-18 GUT STRING BRACING,RSWD B/S,SPRUCE TOP,12 FRETS	3,279	**2,518**	2,225	1,961
GUITAR	17	MARTIN	O-18 GUT STRING BRACING,RSWD B/S,SPRUCE TOP,12 FRETS	3,279	**2,518**	2,225	1,961
GUITAR	18	MARTIN	O-18 SERIAL #12989-13450,MAHOG B/S,SPRUCE TOP,12 FRETS	3,279	**2,518**	2,225	1,961
GUITAR	19	MARTIN	O-18 MAHOG B/S, SPRUCE TOP,SLOTTED PEGHEAD,12 FRETS	3,279	**2,518**	2,225	1,961
GUITAR	20	MARTIN	O-18 SERIAL #14513-15848,MAHOG B/S,SPRUCE TOP,12 FRETS	3,279	**2,518**	2,225	1,961
GUITAR	21	MARTIN	O-18 MAHOG B/S, SPRUCE TOP, SLOTTED PEGHEAD, 12 FRETS	3,279	**2,518**	2,225	1,961
GUITAR	22	MARTIN	O-18 MAHOG B/S, SPRUCE TOP, SLOTTED PEGHEAD, 12 FRETS	3,279	**2,518**	2,225	1,961
GUITAR	23	MARTIN	O-18 MAHOG B/S, SPRUCE TOP, SLOTTED PEGHEAD, 12 FRETS	3,279	**2,518**	2,225	1,961
GUITAR	23	MARTIN	O-18 BRACED FOR STEE.MAHOG B/S,SPRUCE TOP,SLOTTED PEGHEAD	3,431	**2,635**	2,328	2,052
GUITAR	25	MARTIN	O-18 SERIAL #22009-24116	3,679	**2,825**	2,496	2,200
GUITAR	26	MARTIN	O-18 SERIAL #24117-28689	3,274	**2,514**	2,222	1,959

TYPE	YR	MFG	PRICES--BASED ON 100% ORIGINAL MODEL	SELL EXC	SELL AVG	BUY EXC	BUY AVG
GUITAR	27	MARTIN	O-18 SERIAL #28690-34435	3,309	2,541	2,245	1,979
GUITAR	28	MARTIN	O-18 SERIAL #34436-37568	3,299	2,533	2,238	1,973
GUITAR	29	MARTIN	O-18 SERIAL #37569-40843	3,287	2,524	2,230	1,966
GUITAR	32	MARTIN	O-18 SERIAL #49590-52590	3,263	2,506	2,214	1,952
GUITAR	33	MARTIN	O-18 SERIAL #52591-55084	2,934	2,253	1,991	1,755
GUITAR	34	MARTIN	O-18 SHADED TOP, SERIAL #52324	4,948	3,799	3,357	2,960
GUITAR	34	MARTIN	O-18 SUNBURST	5,252	4,033	3,564	3,142
GUITAR	35	MARTIN	O-18 SERIAL #58680-61947	2,936	2,254	1,992	1,756
GUITAR	36	MARTIN	O-18 SERIAL #61948-65176	2,926	2,247	1,985	1,750
GUITAR	37	MARTIN	O-18 SERIAL #65177-68865	2,924	2,245	1,984	1,749
GUITAR	38	MARTIN	O-18 SERIAL #68866-71866	2,915	2,238	1,978	1,744
GUITAR	39	MARTIN	O-18 SERIAL #71867-74061	2,906	2,231	1,972	1,738
GUITAR	40	MARTIN	O-18 SERIAL #74062-76734	2,104	1,615	1,428	1,258
GUITAR	42	MARTIN	O-18 SERIAL #80014-83107	2,101	1,613	1,425	1,256
GUITAR	43	MARTIN	O-18 SERIAL #83108-86724	2,116	1,625	1,436	1,266
GUITAR	44	MARTIN	O-18	2,306	1,770	1,564	1,379
GUITAR	45	MARTIN	O-18 SERIAL #90150-93623	2,094	1,608	1,421	1,252
GUITAR	46	MARTIN	O-18 SERIAL #93624-98158	2,086	1,602	1,415	1,248
GUITAR	47	MARTIN	O-18 SERIAL #98159-103468	2,085	1,601	1,415	1,247
GUITAR	48	MARTIN	O-18 SERIAL #103469-108269	2,078	1,596	1,410	1,243
GUITAR	49	MARTIN	O-18 SERIAL #108270-112961	2,073	1,591	1,406	1,240
GUITAR	50	MARTIN	O-18 LEFT-HANDED, SERIAL #112962-117961	2,156	1,655	1,463	1,289
GUITAR	51	MARTIN	O-18 SERIAL #117962-122799	1,836	1,410	1,246	1,098
GUITAR	52	MARTIN	O-18 SERIAL #122800-128436	1,803	1,384	1,223	1,078
GUITAR	53	MARTIN	O-18 SERIAL #128437-134501	1,792	1,376	1,216	1,072
GUITAR	54	MARTIN	O-18 SERIAL #134502-141345	1,879	1,443	1,275	1,124
GUITAR	55	MARTIN	O-18 SERIAL #141346-147328	1,867	1,433	1,266	1,116
GUITAR	56	MARTIN	O-18 SERIAL #147329-152775	1,872	1,437	1,270	1,120
GUITAR	57	MARTIN	O-18 SERIAL # 156856	1,579	1,212	1,071	944
GUITAR	58	MARTIN	O-18 SERIAL #159062-165576	1,854	1,424	1,258	1,109
GUITAR	59	MARTIN	O-18 SERIAL #165577-171047	1,850	1,420	1,255	1,106
GUITAR	60	MARTIN	O-18 SERIAL #171048-175689	1,844	1,416	1,251	1,103
GUITAR	61	MARTIN	O-18 SERIAL #175690-181297	1,837	1,411	1,247	1,099
GUITAR	62	MARTIN	O-18 SERIAL #181298-187384	1,839	1,412	1,247	1,100
GUITAR	63	MARTIN	O-18 SERIAL #187385-193327	1,832	1,406	1,243	1,096
GUITAR	64	MARTIN	O-18 SERIAL #193328-199626	1,828	1,404	1,241	1,094
GUITAR	65	MARTIN	O-18 SERIAL #199627-207030	1,824	1,400	1,238	1,091
GUITAR	66	MARTIN	O-18 SERIAL #207031-217215	1,818	1,396	1,234	1,088
GUITAR	67	MARTIN	O-18 SERIAL #217216-230095	1,569	1,204	1,064	938
GUITAR	68	MARTIN	O-18 SERIAL #960224T2-106	1,468	1,127	996	878
GUITAR	69	MARTIN	O-18 SERIAL #241926-256003	1,948	1,496	1,322	1,165
GUITAR	70	MARTIN	O-18 SERIAL #256004-271633	1,333	1,024	905	797

TYPE	YR	MFG	PRICES--BASED ON 100% ORIGINAL MODEL	SELL EXC	SELL AVG	BUY EXC	BUY AVG
GUITAR	71	MARTIN	O-18 SERIAL #271634-294270	1,266	**972**	859	757
GUITAR	72	MARTIN	O-18 SERIAL #294271-313302	1,228	**943**	833	734
GUITAR	73	MARTIN	O-18 SERIAL #313303-333873	1,221	**938**	829	730
GUITAR	75	MARTIN	O-18	1,215	**933**	824	726
GUITAR	20	MARTIN	O-18K HAWAIIAN KOA WOOD, SERIAL #14513-15848	2,800	**2,150**	1,900	1,675
GUITAR	21	MARTIN	O-18K HAWAIIAN KOA WOOD, SERIAL #15849-16758	2,800	**2,150**	1,900	1,675
GUITAR	24	MARTIN	O-18K HAWAIIAN KOA WOOD, SERIAL #19892-22008	3,024	**2,322**	2,052	1,809
GUITAR	26	MARTIN	O-18K HAWAIIAN KOA WOOD, SERIAL #24117-28689	3,024	**2,322**	2,052	1,809
GUITAR	27	MARTIN	O-18K HAWAIIAN KOA WOOD, SERIAL #28690-34435	3,024	**2,322**	2,052	1,809
GUITAR	28	MARTIN	O-18K HAWAIIAN KOA WOOD, SERIAL #34436-37568	3,024	**2,322**	2,052	1,809
GUITAR	29	MARTIN	O-18K HAWAIIAN KOA WOOD, SERIAL #37569-40843	3,136	**2,408**	2,128	1,876
GUITAR	30	MARTIN	O-18K HAWAIIAN KOA WOOD, SERIAL 340844-45317	3,136	**2,408**	2,128	1,876
GUITAR	30	MARTIN	O-18K HAWAIIAN KOA WOOD, SERIAL #40844-45317	3,136	**2,408**	2,128	1,876
GUITAR	31	MARTIN	O-18K HAWAIIAN KOA WOOD, SERIAL #45318-49589	3,136	**2,408**	2,128	1,876
GUITAR	34	MARTIN	O-18K HAWAIIAN KOA WOOD, SERIAL #55085-58679	3,136	**2,408**	2,128	1,876
GUITAR	35	MARTIN	O-18K HAWAIIAN KOA WOOD	3,136	**2,408**	2,128	1,876
GUITAR	29	MARTIN	O-18T TENOR	2,151	**1,652**	1,459	1,287
GUITAR	30	MARTIN	O-18T TENOR, SERIAL #40844-45317	2,294	**1,762**	1,557	1,372
GUITAR	36	MARTIN	O-18T TENOR	1,554	**1,193**	1,054	929
GUITAR	40	MARTIN	O-18T TENOR, SERIAL #74062-76734	1,411	**1,083**	957	844
GUITAR	42	MARTIN	O-18T TENOR, SERIAL #80014-83107	1,331	**1,022**	903	796
GUITAR	44	MARTIN	O-18T TENOR, SERIAL #86725-90149	1,329	**1,020**	902	795
GUITAR	49	MARTIN	O-18T TENOR, SERIAL #108270-112961	1,324	**1,017**	899	792
GUITAR	52	MARTIN	O-18T TENOR, SERIAL #122800-128436	1,324	**1,017**	899	792
GUITAR	64	MARTIN	O-18T TENOR, SERIAL #198923	1,266	**972**	859	757
GUITAR	68	MARTIN	O-18T TENOR, SERIAL #199627-207030	1,229	**944**	834	735
GUITAR	n/a	MARTIN	O-21 1899	3,875	**2,975**	2,629	2,318
GUITAR	11	MARTIN	O-21 SERIAL #11204-11413	3,788	**2,909**	2,571	2,266
GUITAR	18	MARTIN	O-21 SERIAL #12989-13450	3,736	**2,868**	2,535	2,235
GUITAR	19	MARTIN	O-21 SERIAL #13451-14512	3,729	**2,863**	2,530	2,231
GUITAR	21	MARTIN	O-21	3,438	**2,640**	2,333	2,056
GUITAR	23	MARTIN	O-21 SERIAL #17840-19891	3,758	**2,886**	2,550	2,248
GUITAR	24	MARTIN	O-21 SERIAL #19892-22008	3,754	**2,882**	2,547	2,245
GUITAR	25	MARTIN	O-21 SERIAL #22009-24116	3,749	**2,879**	2,544	2,243
GUITAR	26	MARTIN	O-21 SERIAL #24117-28689	3,739	**2,871**	2,537	2,237
GUITAR	27	MARTIN	O-21 SERIAL #28690-34435	3,729	**2,863**	2,530	2,231
GUITAR	28	MARTIN	O-21 SERIAL #34436-37568	5,088	**3,906**	3,452	3,043
GUITAR	29	MARTIN	O-21 SERIAL #37569-40843	5,080	**3,900**	3,447	3,039
GUITAR	30	MARTIN	O-21 SERIAL #40844-45317	5,443	**4,179**	3,693	3,256
GUITAR	31	MARTIN	O-21	4,878	**3,746**	3,310	2,918
GUITAR	37	MARTIN	O-21 SERIAL #65177-68865	5,434	**4,172**	3,687	3,250
GUITAR	40	MARTIN	O-21 SERIAL #74062-76734	5,163	**3,964**	3,503	3,088
GUITAR	46	MARTIN	O-21 SERIAL #94526	5,139	**3,946**	3,487	3,074

TYPE	YR	MFG	PRICES--BASED ON 100% ORIGINAL MODEL	SELL EXC	SELL AVG	BUY EXC	BUY AVG
GUITAR	47	MARTIN	O-21 SERIAL #98159-103468	5,134	3,942	3,483	3,071
GUITAR	01	MARTIN	O-28 1901, SERIAL #9129-9310	5,470	4,200	3,711	3,272
GUITAR	13	MARTIN	O-28	5,444	4,180	3,694	3,256
GUITAR	26	MARTIN	O-28 SERIAL #24117-28689	7,256	5,571	4,924	4,340
GUITAR	27	MARTIN	O-28 SERIAL #28690-34435	7,248	5,565	4,918	4,336
GUITAR	30	MARTIN	O-28 SERIAL #40844-45317	7,982	6,129	5,416	4,775
GUITAR	31	MARTIN	O-28 SERIAL #45318-49589	8,344	6,407	5,662	4,991
GUITAR	82	MARTIN	O-28 HERRINGBONE 1882	5,489	4,214	3,724	3,283
GUITAR	89	MARTIN	O-28 HERRINGBONE 1889, SERIAL #8350-8716	5,482	4,209	3,720	3,279
GUITAR	90	MARTIN	O-28 HERRINGBONE 1890	3,654	2,806	2,479	2,186
GUITAR	91	MARTIN	O-28 HERRINGBONE 1891	5,470	4,200	3,711	3,272
GUITAR	93	MARTIN	O-28 HERRINGBONE 1893	5,465	4,196	3,708	3,269
GUITAR	94	MARTIN	O-28 HERRINGBONE 1894	5,461	4,193	3,705	3,266
GUITAR	98	MARTIN	O-28 HERRINGBONE 1898	5,447	4,183	3,696	3,258
GUITAR	n/a	MARTIN	O-28 HERRINGBONE 1899	5,444	4,180	3,694	3,256
GUITAR	04	MARTIN	O-28 HERRINGBONE 1904, SERIAL #9811-9988	5,454	4,188	3,701	3,262
GUITAR	13	MARTIN	O-28 HERRINGBONE SERIAL #11566-11821	5,445	4,181	3,695	3,257
GUITAR	18	MARTIN	O-28 HERRINGBONE	5,434	4,172	3,687	3,250
GUITAR	20	MARTIN	O-28 HERRINGBONE SERIAL #14513-15848	5,421	4,163	3,679	3,243
GUITAR	25	MARTIN	O-28 HERRINGBONE SERIAL #22009-24116	9,487	7,285	6,437	5,675
GUITAR	20	MARTIN	O-28K HAWAIIAN KOA WOOD	6,883	5,285	4,670	4,117
GUITAR	21	MARTIN	O-28K HAWAIIAN KOA WOOD, SERIAL #15849-16758	5,577	4,282	3,784	3,336
GUITAR	26	MARTIN	O-28K HAWAIIAN KOA WOOD, SERIAL #24117-28689	6,784	5,209	4,604	4,058
GUITAR	29	MARTIN	O-28K HAWAIIAN KOA WOOD, SERIAL #37569-40843	6,880	5,282	4,668	4,115
GUITAR	31	MARTIN	O-28K HAWAIIAN KOA WOOD	5,544	4,257	3,762	3,316
GUITAR	39	MARTIN	O-28K HAWAIIAN KOA WOOD, SERIAL #71867-74061	3,726	2,861	2,528	2,229
GUITAR	31	MARTIN	O-28T TENOR, SERIAL #45318-49589	3,267	2,508	2,216	1,954
GUITAR	17	MARTIN	O-30	5,576	4,281	3,784	3,335
GUITAR	86	MARTIN	O-42 1886	11,295	8,673	7,664	6,756
GUITAR	96	MARTIN	O-42 1896	10,852	8,333	7,364	6,492
GUITAR	04	MARTIN	O-42 1904, SERIAL #9811-9988	7,452	5,722	5,057	4,458
GUITAR	19	MARTIN	O-42 SERIAL #13451-14512	7,385	5,670	5,011	4,417
GUITAR	24	MARTIN	O-42 SERIAL #19892-22008	14,230	10,927	9,656	8,513
GUITAR	26	MARTIN	O-42 SERIAL #24117-28689	10,898	8,368	7,395	6,519
GUITAR	28	MARTIN	O-42 SERIAL #34436-37568	10,886	8,359	7,387	6,512
GUITAR	30	MARTIN	O-42 SERIAL #40844-45317	10,872	8,348	7,378	6,504
GUITAR	35	MARTIN	O-42 SERIAL #58680-61947	14,230	10,927	9,656	8,513
GUITAR	41	MARTIN	O-42 SERIAL #76735-80013	13,479	10,350	9,146	8,063
GUITAR	42	MARTIN	O-42 SERIAL #80014-83107	13,474	10,346	9,143	8,060
GUITAR	44	MARTIN	O-42 SERIAL #86725-90149	13,466	10,340	9,138	8,056
GUITAR	43	MARTIN	O-44 SOLOIST SERIAL #83108-86724	5,936	4,558	4,028	3,551
GUITAR	06	MARTIN	O-45 1906	31,118	23,894	21,115	18,615
GUITAR	26	MARTIN	O-45 SERIAL #24117-28689	17,416	13,373	11,818	10,418

TYPE	YR	MFG	PRICES--BASED ON 100% ORIGINAL MODEL	SELL EXC	SELL AVG	BUY EXC	BUY AVG
GUITAR	26	MARTIN	O-45 SERIAL #29856	31,896	**24,491**	21,644	19,080
GUITAR	27	MARTIN	O-45	17,569	**13,490**	11,922	10,510
GUITAR	29	MARTIN	O-45 SERIAL #37569-40843	17,407	**13,366**	11,811	10,413
GUITAR	38	MARTIN	O-45 SERIAL #68866-71866	17,398	**13,359**	11,805	10,407
GUITAR	40	MARTIN	O-45 SERIAL #74062-76734	16,652	**12,786**	11,299	9,961
GUITAR	34	MARTIN	OM-000-18 TRANSITIONAL SERIAL #55083-58679	7,769	**5,965**	5,272	4,647
GUITAR	30	MARTIN	OM-18 SERIAL #40844-45317	13,138	**10,088**	8,915	7,859
GUITAR	31	MARTIN	OM-18 SERIAL #45318-49589	13,107	**10,064**	8,894	7,841
GUITAR	32	MARTIN	OM-18 SERIAL #49590-52590	13,088	**10,049**	8,881	7,829
GUITAR	33	MARTIN	OM-18 SERIAL #52591-55084	15,640	**12,009**	10,613	9,356
GUITAR	34	MARTIN	OM-18	6,804	**5,224**	4,617	4,070
GUITAR	31	MARTIN	OM-18P PLECTRUM, SERIAL #45318-49589	6,329	**4,859**	4,294	3,786
GUITAR	41	MARTIN	OM-18P PLECTRUM, SERIAL #76735-80013	6,666	**5,118**	4,523	3,987
GUITAR	29	MARTIN	OM-28 SERIAL #37569-40843	35,660	**27,382**	24,198	21,332
GUITAR	30	MARTIN	OM-28 SERIAL #40844-45317	35,598	**27,334**	24,155	21,295
GUITAR	31	MARTIN	OM-28 SERIAL #45318-49589	29,120	**22,360**	19,760	17,420
GUITAR	32	MARTIN	OM-28 SERIAL #49590-52590	29,120	**22,360**	19,760	17,420
GUITAR	33	MARTIN	OM-28 SERIAL #52591-55084	29,120	**22,360**	19,760	17,420
GUITAR	31	MARTIN	OM-45 SERIAL #45318-49589	92,960	**71,380**	63,080	55,610
GUITAR	32	MARTIN	OM-45 SERIAL #49590-52590	92,960	**71,380**	63,080	55,610
GUITAR	77	MARTIN	OM-45 SERIAL #388801-399625	9,387	**7,208**	6,370	5,615
GUITAR	30	MARTIN	OM-45 DLX SERIAL #40844-45317	120,960	**92,880**	82,080	72,360
GUITAR	62	MARTIN	OO-16C CLASSICAL SERIAL #181298-187384	1,232	**946**	836	737
GUITAR	65	MARTIN	OO-16C CLASSICAL	1,232	**946**	836	737
GUITAR	66	MARTIN	OO-16C CLASSICAL SERIAL #207031-217215	1,232	**946**	836	737
GUITAR	67	MARTIN	OO-16C CLASSICAL	1,344	**1,032**	912	804
GUITAR	68	MARTIN	OO-16C CLASSICAL SERIAL #230096-241925	1,232	**946**	836	737
GUITAR	71	MARTIN	OO-16C CLASSICAL SERIAL #271634-294270	950	**730**	645	568
GUITAR	15	MARTIN	OO-17 SERIAL #12048-12209	2,382	**1,829**	1,616	1,425
GUITAR	31	MARTIN	OO-17 SERIAL #45318-49589	2,301	**1,767**	1,561	1,376
GUITAR	41	MARTIN	OO-17 SERIAL #76735-80013	2,383	**1,830**	1,617	1,425
GUITAR	45	MARTIN	OO-17 SERIAL #90150-93623	1,942	**1,491**	1,317	1,161
GUITAR	46	MARTIN	OO-17 SERIAL #93624-98158	1,862	**1,430**	1,263	1,114
GUITAR	47	MARTIN	OO-17 SERIAL #98159-103468	1,688	**1,296**	1,146	1,010
GUITAR	49	MARTIN	OO-17 SERIAL #108270-112961	1,649	**1,266**	1,119	986
GUITAR	50	MARTIN	OO-17 SERIAL #112962-117961	1,641	**1,260**	1,114	982
GUITAR	52	MARTIN	OO-17 SERIAL #122800-128436	1,528	**1,173**	1,037	914
GUITAR	53	MARTIN	OO-17 SERIAL #128437-134501	1,527	**1,173**	1,036	913
GUITAR	55	MARTIN	OO-17 SERIAL #141346-147328	1,450	**1,113**	984	867
GUITAR	56	MARTIN	OO-17	1,660	**1,275**	1,127	993
GUITAR	57	MARTIN	OO-17 SERIAL #157809	1,408	**1,081**	956	842
GUITAR	58	MARTIN	OO-17 SERIAL #159062-165576	1,378	**1,058**	935	824
GUITAR	22	MARTIN	OO-18 SERIAL #16759-17839	4,704	**3,612**	3,192	2,814
GUITAR	24	MARTIN	OO-18	5,152	**3,956**	3,496	3,082

TYPE	YR	MFG	PRICES--BASED ON 100% ORIGINAL MODEL	SELL EXC	SELL AVG	BUY EXC	BUY AVG
GUITAR	26	MARTIN	OO-18 SERIAL #24117-28689	5,152	**3,956**	3,496	3,082
GUITAR	27	MARTIN	OO-18 SERIAL #28690-34435	5,152	**3,956**	3,496	3,082
GUITAR	29	MARTIN	OO-18 SERIAL #37569-40843	5,152	**3,956**	3,496	3,082
GUITAR	30	MARTIN	OO-18	5,152	**3,956**	3,496	3,082
GUITAR	34	MARTIN	OO-18 SERIAL #55085-58679	5,712	**4,386**	3,876	3,417
GUITAR	35	MARTIN	OO-18 SERIAL #58680-61947	5,712	**4,386**	3,876	3,417
GUITAR	36	MARTIN	OO-18 SERIAL #61948-65176	5,712	**4,386**	3,876	3,417
GUITAR	37	MARTIN	OO-18 SERIAL #65177-68865 SUNBURST	5,712	**4,386**	3,876	3,417
GUITAR	38	MARTIN	OO-18	5,712	**4,386**	3,876	3,417
GUITAR	39	MARTIN	OO-18 SERIAL #71867-74061	5,712	**4,386**	3,876	3,417
GUITAR	42	MARTIN	OO-18	3,405	**2,615**	2,311	2,037
GUITAR	43	MARTIN	OO-18 SERIAL #83108-86724	4,480	**3,440**	3,040	2,680
GUITAR	44	MARTIN	OO-18 SERIAL #86725-90149	4,480	**3,440**	3,040	2,680
GUITAR	46	MARTIN	OO-18 SERIAL #93624-98158	3,435	**2,637**	2,330	2,054
GUITAR	47	MARTIN	OO-18 SERIAL #98159-103468	3,318	**2,548**	2,251	1,985
GUITAR	48	MARTIN	OO-18	3,318	**2,548**	2,251	1,985
GUITAR	49	MARTIN	OO-18 SERIAL #108270-112961	3,349	**2,572**	2,273	2,003
GUITAR	52	MARTIN	OO-18	3,063	**2,352**	2,078	1,832
GUITAR	53	MARTIN	OO-18 SERIAL #128437-134501	2,912	**2,236**	1,976	1,742
GUITAR	54	MARTIN	OO-18 SERIAL #134502-141345	2,912	**2,236**	1,976	1,742
GUITAR	55	MARTIN	OO-18 SERIAL #141346-147328	2,912	**2,236**	1,976	1,742
GUITAR	56	MARTIN	OO-18 SERIAL #147329-152775	2,912	**2,236**	1,976	1,742
GUITAR	57	MARTIN	OO-18 SERIAL #152776-159061	2,912	**2,236**	1,976	1,742
GUITAR	58	MARTIN	OO-18 SERIAL #159062-165576	2,912	**2,236**	1,976	1,742
GUITAR	59	MARTIN	OO-18 SERIAL #165577-171047	2,912	**2,236**	1,976	1,742
GUITAR	60	MARTIN	OO-18 SERIAL #175537	2,107	**1,618**	1,430	1,260
GUITAR	61	MARTIN	OO-18 SERIAL #175690-181297	2,800	**2,150**	1,900	1,675
GUITAR	62	MARTIN	OO-18 SERIAL #181298-187384	2,800	**2,150**	1,900	1,675
GUITAR	64	MARTIN	OO-18 SERIAL #193328-199626	2,223	**1,707**	1,508	1,329
GUITAR	65	MARTIN	OO-18 SERIAL #199627-207030	2,157	**1,656**	1,463	1,290
GUITAR	66	MARTIN	OO-18 SERIAL #207031-217215	2,151	**1,652**	1,459	1,287
GUITAR	67	MARTIN	OO-18 SERIAL #217216-230095	2,141	**1,644**	1,453	1,281
GUITAR	68	MARTIN	OO-18 SERIAL #230096-241925	1,901	**1,460**	1,290	1,137
GUITAR	69	MARTIN	OO-18 SERIAL #241926-256003	1,674	**1,285**	1,136	1,001
GUITAR	70	MARTIN	OO-18 SERIAL #256004-271633	1,232	**946**	836	737
GUITAR	71	MARTIN	OO-18 SERIAL #271634-294270	1,232	**946**	836	737
GUITAR	72	MARTIN	OO-18 SERIAL #294271-313302	1,232	**946**	836	737
GUITAR	74	MARTIN	OO-18	1,232	**946**	836	737
GUITAR	75	MARTIN	OO-18 SERIAL #353388-371828	1,232	**946**	836	737
GUITAR	63	MARTIN	OO-18C CLASSICAL SERIAL #187385-193327	1,680	**1,290**	1,140	1,005
GUITAR	64	MARTIN	OO-18C CLASSICAL SERIAL #193328-199626	1,680	**1,290**	1,140	1,005
GUITAR	67	MARTIN	OO-18C CLASSICAL SERIAL #217216-230095	1,680	**1,290**	1,140	1,005
GUITAR	68	MARTIN	OO-18C CLASSICAL SERIAL #230096-241925	1,680	**1,290**	1,140	1,005
GUITAR	69	MARTIN	OO-18C CLASSICAL SERIAL #241926-256003	1,680	**1,290**	1,140	1,005

TYPE	YR	MFG	MODEL	SELL EXC	SELL AVG	BUY EXC	BUY AVG
GUITAR	70	MARTIN	OO-18C CLASSICAL SERIAL #256004-271633	1,456	1,118	988	871
GUITAR	72	MARTIN	OO-18C CLASSICAL SERIAL #294271-313302	1,456	1,118	988	871
GUITAR	59	MARTIN	OO-18E FLATTOP, 1 PU, SERIAL #165577-171047	2,800	2,150	1,900	1,675
GUITAR	64	MARTIN	OO-18E FLATTOP, 1 PU, SERIAL #193328-199626	2,800	2,150	1,900	1,675
GUITAR	38	MARTIN	OO-18G CLASSICAL	1,904	1,462	1,292	1,139
GUITAR	39	MARTIN	OO-18G CLASSICAL SERIAL #71867-74061	1,904	1,462	1,292	1,139
GUITAR	40	MARTIN	OO-18G CLASSICAL SERIAL #74062-76734	1,792	1,376	1,216	1,072
GUITAR	54	MARTIN	OO-18G CLASSICAL SERIAL #134502-141345	1,568	1,204	1,064	938
GUITAR	55	MARTIN	OO-18G CLASSICAL	1,568	1,204	1,064	938
GUITAR	56	MARTIN	OO-18G CLASSICAL	1,568	1,204	1,064	938
GUITAR	57	MARTIN	OO-18G CLASSICAL SERIAL #152776-159061	1,556	1,195	1,056	931
GUITAR	58	MARTIN	OO-18G CLASSICAL SERIAL #159062-165576	1,568	1,204	1,064	938
GUITAR	60	MARTIN	OO-18G CLASSICAL SERIAL #171048-175689	1,568	1,204	1,064	938
GUITAR	61	MARTIN	OO-18G CLASSICAL SERIAL #175690-181297	1,568	1,204	1,064	938
GUITAR	24	MARTIN	OO-18H HAWAIIAN SERIAL #19892-22008	3,025	2,322	2,052	1,809
GUITAR	34	MARTIN	OO-18H HAWAIIAN SERIAL #55085-58679	3,018	2,317	2,048	1,805
GUITAR	37	MARTIN	OO-18H HAWAIIAN SERIAL #65177-68865	4,032	3,096	2,736	2,412
GUITAR	41	MARTIN	OO-18H HAWAIIAN	4,032	3,096	2,736	2,412
GUITAR	26	MARTIN	OO-21 SERIAL #24117-28689	5,936	4,558	4,028	3,551
GUITAR	27	MARTIN	OO-21 SERIAL #28690-34435	8,512	6,536	5,776	5,092
GUITAR	29	MARTIN	OO-21 SERIAL #37569-40843	8,512	6,536	5,776	5,092
GUITAR	30	MARTIN	OO-21 SERIAL #40844-45317	8,512	6,536	5,776	5,092
GUITAR	31	MARTIN	OO-21 SERIAL #45318-49589	8,512	6,536	5,776	5,092
GUITAR	32	MARTIN	OO-21	8,064	6,192	5,472	4,824
GUITAR	34	MARTIN	OO-21 SERIAL #55085-58679	8,064	6,192	5,472	4,824
GUITAR	37	MARTIN	OO-21 SERIAL #65177-68865	8,064	6,192	5,472	4,824
GUITAR	40	MARTIN	OO-21 SERIAL #74062-76734	7,392	5,676	5,016	4,422
GUITAR	50	MARTIN	OO-21	2,992	2,297	2,030	1,790
GUITAR	53	MARTIN	OO-21 SERIAL #128437-134501	4,592	3,526	3,116	2,747
GUITAR	60	MARTIN	OO-21C	4,032	3,096	2,736	2,412
GUITAR	63	MARTIN	OO-21 SERIAL #187385-193327	4,032	3,096	2,736	2,412
GUITAR	65	MARTIN	OO-21 SERIAL #199627-207030	4,032	3,096	2,736	2,412
GUITAR	66	MARTIN	OO-21 BRAZILIAN ROSEWOOD	3,808	2,924	2,584	2,278
GUITAR	67	MARTIN	OO-21 SERIAL #217216-230095	3,808	2,924	2,584	2,278
GUITAR	69	MARTIN	OO-21 SERIAL #241926-256003	3,808	2,924	2,584	2,278
GUITAR	71	MARTIN	OO-21	1,680	1,290	1,140	1,005
GUITAR	72	MARTIN	OO-21 SERIAL # 297575	1,792	1,376	1,216	1,072
GUITAR	73	MARTIN	OO-21 SERIAL #313303-333873	1,792	1,376	1,216	1,072
GUITAR	75	MARTIN	OO-21	1,629	1,251	1,105	974
GUITAR	63	MARTIN	OO-21NY SERIAL #187385-193327	3,763	2,889	2,553	2,251
GUITAR	64	MARTIN	OO-21NY SERIAL #193328-199626	3,757	2,885	2,549	2,247
GUITAR	n/a	MARTIN	OO-28 1899	5,924	4,549	4,020	3,544
GUITAR	12	MARTIN	OO-28 SERIAL #11414-11565	10,080	7,740	6,840	6,030
GUITAR	13	MARTIN	OO-28	5,924	4,549	4,020	3,544
GUITAR	20	MARTIN	OO-28 SERIAL #14513-15848	10,080	7,740	6,840	6,030
GUITAR	24	MARTIN	OO-28 SERIAL #21260	11,200	8,600	7,600	6,700

TYPE	YR	MFG	PRICES--BASED ON 100% ORIGINAL MODEL	SELL EXC	SELL AVG	BUY EXC	BUY AVG
GUITAR	27	MARTIN	OO-28 SERIAL #28690-34435	11,200	8,600	7,600	6,700
GUITAR	31	MARTIN	OO-28 SERIAL #45318-49589	13,440	10,320	9,120	8,040
GUITAR	32	MARTIN	OO-28 SERIAL #49590-52590	11,851	9,100	8,042	7,089
GUITAR	39	MARTIN	OO-28 SERIAL #71867-74061	10,080	7,740	6,840	6,030
GUITAR	40	MARTIN	OO-28 SERIAL #74062-76734	10,080	7,740	6,840	6,030
GUITAR	44	MARTIN	OO-28 SERIAL #86725-90149	6,879	5,282	4,667	4,115
GUITAR	47	MARTIN	OO-28 SERIAL #98159-103468	5,443	4,179	3,693	3,256
GUITAR	51	MARTIN	OO-28	5,040	3,870	3,420	3,015
GUITAR	59	MARTIN	OO-28	2,231	1,713	1,513	1,334
GUITAR	77	MARTIN	OO-28	1,653	1,269	1,121	988
GUITAR	51	MARTIN	OO-28C NATURAL BRAZILIAN	3,589	2,756	2,435	2,147
GUITAR	66	MARTIN	OO-28C CLASSICAL SERIAL #207031-217215	3,696	2,838	2,508	2,211
GUITAR	68	MARTIN	OO-28C CLASSICAL SERIAL #230096-241925	3,696	2,838	2,508	2,211
GUITAR	69	MARTIN	OO-28C CLASSICAL SERIAL #241926-256003	3,696	2,838	2,508	2,211
GUITAR	71	MARTIN	OO-28C CLASSICAL SERIAL #271634-294270	1,680	1,290	1,140	1,005
GUITAR	38	MARTIN	OO-28G CLASSICAL SERIAL #68866-71866	6,384	4,902	4,332	3,819
GUITAR	40	MARTIN	OO-28G CLASSICAL SERIAL #74062-76734	5,936	4,558	4,028	3,551
GUITAR	42	MARTIN	OO-28G CLASSICAL SERIAL #81588	5,936	4,558	4,028	3,551
GUITAR	45	MARTIN	OO-28G CLASSICAL	5,936	4,558	4,028	3,551
GUITAR	46	MARTIN	OO-28G CLASSICAL SERIAL #93624-98158	5,936	4,558	4,028	3,551
GUITAR	47	MARTIN	OO-28G CLASSICAL SERIAL #98159-103468	5,936	4,558	4,028	3,551
GUITAR	49	MARTIN	OO-28G CLASSICAL SERIAL #108270-112961	5,936	4,558	4,028	3,551
GUITAR	50	MARTIN	OO-28G CLASSICAL SERIAL #112962-117961	5,600	4,300	3,800	3,350
GUITAR	51	MARTIN	OO-28G CLASSICAL	4,592	3,526	3,116	2,747
GUITAR	55	MARTIN	OO-28G CLASSICAL	4,592	3,526	3,116	2,747
GUITAR	56	MARTIN	OO-28G CLASSICAL SERIAL #147329-152775	4,592	3,526	3,116	2,747
GUITAR	59	MARTIN	OO-28G CLASSICAL BRAZILIAN ROSEWOOD	3,376	2,592	2,291	2,020
GUITAR	60	MARTIN	OO-28G CLASSICAL SERIAL #171048-175689	4,592	3,526	3,116	2,747
GUITAR	62	MARTIN	OO-28G CLASSICAL SERIAL #181934	4,592	3,526	3,116	2,747
GUITAR	07	MARTIN	OO-30 1907, SERIAL #10330-10727	1,938	1,488	1,315	1,159
GUITAR	29	MARTIN	OO-40H HAWAIIAN SERIAL #37569-40843	11,200	8,600	7,600	6,700
GUITAR	30	MARTIN	OO-40H HAWAIIAN SERIAL #40844-45317	11,200	8,600	7,600	6,700
GUITAR	32	MARTIN	OO-40H HAWAIIAN SERIAL #49590-52590	11,200	8,600	7,600	6,700
GUITAR	34	MARTIN	OO-40H HAWAIIAN SERIAL #55085-58679	11,200	8,600	7,600	6,700
GUITAR	35	MARTIN	OO-40H HAWAIIAN SERIAL #58680-61947	11,200	8,600	7,600	6,700
GUITAR	37	MARTIN	OO-40H HAWAIIAN	11,200	8,600	7,600	6,700
GUITAR	32	MARTIN	OO-40H HAWAIIAN CUSTOM	18,571	14,260	12,602	11,109
GUITAR	30	MARTIN	OO-40K FLAMED KOA TOP/BACK/SIDES,ABALONE INLAY,EBONY FRTBRD	23,822	18,292	16,165	14,250
GUITAR	00	MARTIN	OO-42 1900	16,800	12,900	11,400	10,050
GUITAR	04	MARTIN	OO-42 1904, SERIAL #9811-9988	14,364	11,029	9,747	8,592
GUITAR	23	MARTIN	OO-42 SERIAL #17840-19891	15,680	12,040	10,640	9,380
GUITAR	29	MARTIN	OO-42 SERIAL #37569-40843	22,171	17,024	15,044	13,263
GUITAR	30	MARTIN	OO-42	18,499	14,204	12,552	11,066
GUITAR	36	MARTIN	OO-42 SERIAL #61948-65176	23,520	18,060	15,960	14,070
GUITAR	37	MARTIN	OO-42 SERIAL #65177-68865	23,520	18,060	15,960	14,070
GUITAR	38	MARTIN	OO-42 SERIAL #68866-71866	23,520	18,060	15,960	14,070

TYPE	YR	MFG	PRICES--BASED ON 100% ORIGINAL MODEL	SELL EXC	SELL AVG	BUY EXC	BUY AVG
GUITAR	43	MARTIN	OO-42 SERIAL #83108-86724	22,951	**17,623**	15,573	13,729
GUITAR	22	MARTIN	**OO-42 (WURLITZER MODEL)**	17,786	**13,657**	12,069	10,640
GUITAR	05	MARTIN	OO-45 1905, SERIAL #9989-10120	36,143	**27,753**	24,525	21,621
GUITAR	11	MARTIN	OO-45 SERIAL #11204-11413	36,133	**27,745**	24,519	21,615
GUITAR	19	MARTIN	OO-45 SERIAL #13451-14512	36,134	**27,746**	24,519	21,616
GUITAR	20	MARTIN	OO-45 SERIAL #14513-15848	36,127	**27,741**	24,515	21,612
GUITAR	24	MARTIN	OO-45 SERIAL #19892-22008	36,113	**27,729**	24,505	21,603
GUITAR	25	MARTIN	OO-45 SERIAL #22009-24116	37,067	**28,462**	25,152	22,174
GUITAR	29	MARTIN	OO-45 SERIAL #37569-40843	46,623	**35,800**	31,637	27,890
GUITAR	38	MARTIN	OO-45 SERIAL #68866-71866	51,188	**39,305**	34,735	30,621
GUITAR	26	MARTIN	OOO-18 SERIAL #24117-28689	8,960	**6,880**	6,080	5,360
GUITAR	27	MARTIN	OOO-18 SERIAL #28690-34435	8,960	**6,880**	6,080	5,360
GUITAR	29	MARTIN	OOO-18 SERIAL #37569-40843	8,960	**6,880**	6,080	5,360
GUITAR	31	MARTIN	OOO-18 SERIAL #45318-49589	8,960	**6,880**	6,080	5,360
GUITAR	34	MARTIN	OOO-18 SERIAL #55085-58679	12,320	**9,460**	8,360	7,370
GUITAR	35	MARTIN	OOO-18 SERIAL #58680-61947	12,320	**9,460**	8,360	7,370
GUITAR	36	MARTIN	OOO-18 SERIAL #61948-65176	12,320	**9,460**	8,360	7,370
GUITAR	37	MARTIN	OOO-18 SERIAL #65177-68865	12,320	**9,460**	8,360	7,370
GUITAR	39	MARTIN	OOO-18 SUNBURST	6,969	**5,351**	4,729	4,169
GUITAR	40	MARTIN	OOO-18	10,080	**7,740**	6,840	6,030
GUITAR	41	MARTIN	OOO-18 SERIAL #76735-80013	10,080	**7,740**	6,840	6,030
GUITAR	42	MARTIN	OOO-18 SERIAL #80014-83107	7,840	**6,020**	5,320	4,690
GUITAR	43	MARTIN	OOO-18 SERIAL #83108-86724	8,960	**6,880**	6,080	5,360
GUITAR	44	MARTIN	OOO-18 SERIAL #86725-90149	5,578	**4,283**	3,785	3,337
GUITAR	45	MARTIN	OOO-18 SERIAL #90150-93623	5,577	**4,282**	3,784	3,336
GUITAR	46	MARTIN	OOO-18 SERIAL #93624-98158	5,575	**4,281**	3,783	3,335
GUITAR	47	MARTIN	OOO-18 SERIAL #98159-103468	5,569	**4,276**	3,779	3,331
GUITAR	48	MARTIN	OOO-18 SERIAL #103469-108269	5,712	**4,386**	3,876	3,417
GUITAR	49	MARTIN	OOO-18 SERIAL #108270-112961	5,560	**4,269**	3,773	3,326
GUITAR	50	MARTIN	OOO-18 SERIAL #112962-117961	4,256	**3,268**	2,888	2,546
GUITAR	51	MARTIN	OOO-18 SERIAL #117962-122799	4,256	**3,268**	2,888	2,546
GUITAR	52	MARTIN	OOO-18 SERIAL #122800-128436	4,256	**3,268**	2,888	2,546
GUITAR	54	MARTIN	OOO-18 SERIAL #134502-141345	3,696	**2,838**	2,508	2,211
GUITAR	55	MARTIN	OOO-18 SERIAL #141346-147328	3,696	**2,838**	2,508	2,211
GUITAR	56	MARTIN	OOO-18 SERIAL #147329-152775	3,696	**2,838**	2,508	2,211
GUITAR	57	MARTIN	OOO-18 SERIAL #152776-159061	3,696	**2,838**	2,508	2,211
GUITAR	58	MARTIN	OOO-18 SERIAL #159062-165576	3,696	**2,838**	2,508	2,211
GUITAR	59	MARTIN	OOO-18 SERIAL #165577-171047	3,808	**2,924**	2,584	2,278
GUITAR	61	MARTIN	OOO-18 SERIAL #175690-181297	3,696	**2,838**	2,508	2,211
GUITAR	62	MARTIN	OOO-18 SERIAL #181298-187384	3,696	**2,838**	2,508	2,211
GUITAR	63	MARTIN	OOO-18 SERIAL #187385-193327	3,024	**2,322**	2,052	1,809
GUITAR	64	MARTIN	OOO-18	3,024	**2,322**	2,052	1,809
GUITAR	65	MARTIN	OOO-18 SERIAL #199627-207030	3,024	**2,322**	2,052	1,809

TYPE	YR	MFG	PRICES--BASED ON 100% ORIGINAL MODEL	SELL EXC	SELL AVG	BUY EXC	BUY AVG
GUITAR	66	MARTIN	OOO-18 SERIAL #207031-217215	2,800	2,150	1,900	1,675
GUITAR	67	MARTIN	OOO-18 SERIAL #217216-230095	2,576	1,978	1,748	1,541
GUITAR	68	MARTIN	OOO-18 SERIAL #230096-241925	2,128	1,634	1,444	1,273
GUITAR	69	MARTIN	OOO-18	1,792	1,376	1,216	1,072
GUITAR	70	MARTIN	OOO-18	1,400	1,075	950	837
GUITAR	71	MARTIN	OOO-18	1,400	1,075	950	837
GUITAR	72	MARTIN	OOO-18 SERIAL #294271-313302	1,400	1,075	950	837
GUITAR	74	MARTIN	OOO-18	1,400	1,075	950	837
GUITAR	30	MARTIN	OOO-18P SERIAL #40844-45317 PLECTRUM	1,547	1,188	1,050	925
GUITAR	38	MARTIN	OOO-18T TENOR, SERIAL #68866-71866	1,543	1,185	1,047	923
GUITAR	68	MARTIN	OOO-18T TENOR	1,228	943	833	734
GUITAR	38	MARTIN	OOO-21 SERIAL #68866-71866	16,800	12,900	11,400	10,050
GUITAR	39	MARTIN	OOO-21 SERIAL #71867-74061	16,800	12,900	11,400	10,050
GUITAR	40	MARTIN	OOO-21 SERIAL #74062-76734	16,800	12,900	11,400	10,050
GUITAR	43	MARTIN	OOO-21 SERIAL #83108-86724	15,680	12,040	10,640	9,380
GUITAR	44	MARTIN	OOO-21 SERIAL #86725-90149	10,640	8,170	7,220	6,365
GUITAR	45	MARTIN	OOO-21 NON-SCALLOPED	10,640	8,170	7,220	6,365
GUITAR	46	MARTIN	OOO-21 SERIAL #93624-98158	10,640	8,170	7,220	6,365
GUITAR	47	MARTIN	OOO-21 SERIAL #98159-103468	6,248	4,797	4,240	3,737
GUITAR	48	MARTIN	OOO-21 SERIAL #103469-108269	6,272	4,816	4,256	3,752
GUITAR	49	MARTIN	OOO-21 SERIAL #108270-112961	6,272	4,816	4,256	3,752
GUITAR	50	MARTIN	OOO-21 SERIAL #112962-117961	6,160	4,730	4,180	3,685
GUITAR	54	MARTIN	OOO-21 SERIAL #134502-141345	6,160	4,730	4,180	3,685
GUITAR	58	MARTIN	OOO-21 SERIAL #159062-165576	6,160	4,730	4,180	3,685
GUITAR	59	MARTIN	OOO-21 SERIAL #165577-171047	6,160	4,730	4,180	3,685
GUITAR	66	MARTIN	OOO-21C NATURAL	3,535	2,715	2,399	2,115
GUITAR	26	MARTIN	OOO-28 SERIAL #24117-28689	26,880	20,640	18,240	16,080
GUITAR	28	MARTIN	OOO-28 SERIAL #34436-37568	33,600	25,800	22,800	20,100
GUITAR	29	MARTIN	OOO-28	33,600	25,800	22,800	20,100
GUITAR	32	MARTIN	OOO-28 14 FRETS	33,600	25,800	22,800	20,100
GUITAR	34	MARTIN	OOO-28 SERIAL #55085-58679	25,760	19,780	17,480	15,410
GUITAR	35	MARTIN	OOO-28 SERIAL #58680-61947	25,760	19,780	17,480	15,410
GUITAR	37	MARTIN	OOO-28 SERIAL #66437	24,281	18,644	16,476	14,525
GUITAR	37	MARTIN	OOO-28 SERIAL #68449-68865	25,613	19,667	17,380	15,322
GUITAR	38	MARTIN	OOO-28 SERIAL #68866-71866	25,613	19,667	17,380	15,322
GUITAR	40	MARTIN	OOO-28 SERIAL #74062-76734	24,640	18,920	16,720	14,740
GUITAR	41	MARTIN	OOO-28 SERIAL #76735-80013	24,640	18,920	16,720	14,740
GUITAR	42	MARTIN	OOO-28 SERIAL #80014-83107	22,400	17,200	15,200	13,400
GUITAR	43	MARTIN	OOO-28 SERIAL #84460	22,400	17,200	15,200	13,400
GUITAR	44	MARTIN	OOO-28 SCALLOPED BRACES, SERIAL #86725-90149	22,400	17,200	15,200	13,400
GUITAR	45	MARTIN	OOO-28 SERIAL #90150-93623, NON-SCALLOPED	14,560	11,180	9,880	8,710
GUITAR	46	MARTIN	OOO-28 SERIAL #93624-98158, NON-SCALLOPED	16,352	12,556	11,096	9,782
GUITAR	47	MARTIN	OOO-28 SERIAL #98159-103468	8,861	6,804	6,013	5,301
GUITAR	48	MARTIN	OOO-28 SERIAL #103469-108269	8,825	6,776	5,988	5,279

TYPE	YR	MFG	PRICES--BASED ON 100% ORIGINAL MODEL	SELL EXC	SELL AVG	BUY EXC	BUY AVG
GUITAR	49	MARTIN	OOO-28 SERIAL #108270-112961	8,813	6,767	5,980	5,272
GUITAR	50	MARTIN	OOO-28 SERIAL #112962-117961	8,204	6,299	5,567	4,907
GUITAR	51	MARTIN	OOO-28 SERIAL #117962-122799	8,197	6,294	5,562	4,903
GUITAR	52	MARTIN	OOO-28 SERIAL #122800-128436	8,192	6,290	5,559	4,901
GUITAR	53	MARTIN	OOO-28 SERIAL #128437-134501	7,056	5,418	4,788	4,221
GUITAR	54	MARTIN	OOO-28	7,056	5,418	4,788	4,221
GUITAR	55	MARTIN	OOO-28 SERIAL #142772	7,056	5,418	4,788	4,221
GUITAR	56	MARTIN	OOO-28 SERIAL #147329-152775	7,056	5,418	4,788	4,221
GUITAR	57	MARTIN	OOO-28 SERIAL #152776-159061	7,056	5,418	4,788	4,221
GUITAR	58	MARTIN	OOO-28	6,720	5,160	4,560	4,020
GUITAR	60	MARTIN	OOO-28	5,824	4,472	3,952	3,484
GUITAR	65	MARTIN	OOO-28 BRAZILIAN ROSEWOOD	5,424	4,164	3,680	3,244
GUITAR	66	MARTIN	OOO-28 SERIAL #207031-217215	4,816	3,698	3,268	2,881
GUITAR	67	MARTIN	OOO-28 SERIAL #217216-230095	4,480	3,440	3,040	2,680
GUITAR	68	MARTIN	OOO-28	4,256	3,268	2,888	2,546
GUITAR	70	MARTIN	OOO-28 INDIAN ROSEWOOD, SERIAL #256004-271633	1,680	1,290	1,140	1,005
GUITAR	73	MARTIN	OOO-28 SERIAL #313303-333873	1,680	1,290	1,140	1,005
GUITAR	74	MARTIN	OOO-28 SERIAL #333874-353387	1,828	1,404	1,241	1,094
GUITAR	62	MARTIN	OOO-28C CLASSICAL SERIAL #181298-187384	3,696	2,838	2,508	2,211
GUITAR	63	MARTIN	OOO-28C CLASSICAL SERIAL #187385-193327	3,808	2,924	2,584	2,278
GUITAR	21	MARTIN	OOO-42 SERIAL #15849-16758	38,080	29,240	25,840	22,780
GUITAR	38	MARTIN	OOO-42	42,560	32,680	28,880	25,460
GUITAR	39	MARTIN	OOO-42 SERIAL #71867-74061	42,560	32,680	28,880	25,460
GUITAR	40	MARTIN	OOO-42	42,560	32,680	28,880	25,460
GUITAR	41	MARTIN	OOO-42 SERIAL #76735-80013	42,560	32,680	28,880	25,460
GUITAR	42	MARTIN	OOO-42	42,560	32,680	28,880	25,460
GUITAR	11	MARTIN	OOO-45 12-FRET SLOTHEAD	39,469	30,307	26,783	23,611
GUITAR	13	MARTIN	OOO-45 SERIAL #11566-11821	20,391	15,658	13,837	12,198
GUITAR	23	MARTIN	OOO-45 SERIAL #17840-19891	56,000	43,000	38,000	33,500
GUITAR	24	MARTIN	OOO-45 SERIAL #19892-22008	56,000	43,000	38,000	33,500
GUITAR	27	MARTIN	OOO-45 SERIAL #28690-34435	58,240	44,720	39,520	34,840
GUITAR	28	MARTIN	OOO-45	67,200	51,600	45,600	40,200
GUITAR	30	MARTIN	OOO-45 SERIAL #40844-45317	78,400	60,200	53,200	46,900
GUITAR	34	MARTIN	OOO-45 SERIAL #55085-58679	89,600	68,800	60,800	53,600
GUITAR	35	MARTIN	OOO-45 SERIAL #58680-61947	89,600	68,800	60,800	53,600
GUITAR	36	MARTIN	OOO-45 SERIAL #61948-65176	89,600	68,800	60,800	53,600
GUITAR	37	MARTIN	OOO-45 14-FRET NECK, SERIAL #65177-68865	88,480	67,940	60,040	52,930
GUITAR	38	MARTIN	OOO-45 SERIAL #6866-71866	88,480	67,940	60,040	52,930
GUITAR	39	MARTIN	OOO-45 SERIAL #71867-74061	88,480	67,940	60,040	52,930
GUITAR	40	MARTIN	OOO-45 SERIAL #74062-76734	84,000	64,500	57,000	50,250
GUITAR	41	MARTIN	OOO-45 BRAZILIAN ROSEWOOD, ADIRONDACK TOP, PREWAR	59,599	45,764	40,442	35,653
GUITAR	70	MARTIN	OOO-45 INDIAN ROSEWOOD, SERIAL #256004-271633	9,681	7,433	6,569	5,791
GUITAR	35	MARTIN	R-17 MAHOGANY, ARCHTOP, SERIAL #58680-61947	1,008	774	684	603
GUITAR	37	MARTIN	R-17 MAHOGANY, ARCHTOP, SERIAL #65177-68865	1,008	774	684	603
GUITAR	38	MARTIN	R-17 NATURAL, ALL MAHOGANY	2,151	1,652	1,459	1,287

TYPE	YR	MFG	PRICES--BASED ON 100% ORIGINAL MODEL	SELL EXC	SELL AVG	BUY EXC	BUY AVG
GUITAR	40	MARTIN	R-17 MAHOGANY, ARCHTOP, SERIAL #74062-76734	1,008	**774**	684	603
GUITAR	32	MARTIN	R-18 ARCHTOP	1,792	**1,376**	1,216	1,072
GUITAR	33	MARTIN	R-18 ARCHTOP, SERIAL #52591-55084	1,792	**1,376**	1,216	1,072
GUITAR	34	MARTIN	R-18 ARCHTOP, SERIAL #55085-58679	1,792	**1,376**	1,216	1,072
GUITAR	35	MARTIN	R-18 ARCHTOP, SERIAL #58680-61947	1,792	**1,376**	1,216	1,072
GUITAR	37	MARTIN	R-18 ARCHTOP	1,792	**1,376**	1,216	1,072
GUITAR	38	MARTIN	R-18 ARCHTOP, SERIAL #68866-71866	1,792	**1,376**	1,216	1,072
GUITAR	37	MARTIN	R-18T TENOR, ARCHTOP, SERIAL #65177-68865	1,535	**1,179**	1,041	918
GUITAR	40	MARTIN	R-18T TENOR, ARCHTOP, SERIAL #74062-76734	1,444	**1,109**	980	864
GUITAR	46	MARTIN	S-18 MARTY ROBBINS HALF SIZE,MAHOG BODY/NECK,SPRUCE TOP,RSWD FNGRBRD/BRDG	3,254	**2,499**	2,208	1,947
GUITAR	70	MARTIN	SO-18 T8	1,352	**1,038**	918	809
GUITAR	77	MARTIN	SOM-45 SERIAL #388801-399625	5,906	**4,535**	4,008	3,533
GUITAR	33	MARTIN	STAUFFER STYLE (1830's)	32,500	**24,955**	22,053	19,442
GUITAR	80	MARTIN	STYLE 1-21 1880's, BRAZILIAN ROSEWOOD BACK/SIDES	2,959	**2,272**	2,007	1,770
MANDOLIN	12	MARTIN	00 BOWL BACK, SERIAL #3431-3847	772	**593**	524	462
MANDOL	14	MARTIN	00 BRAZILIAN ROSEWOOD RIBS, BOWL BACK	764	**587**	519	457
MANDOL	17	MARTIN	00 BOWL BACK	757	**581**	513	452
MANDOL	18	MARTIN	00 BOWL BACK, SERIAL# 5753-6370	772	**593**	524	462
MANDOL	14	MARTIN	000 MAHOGANY BOWL	789	**606**	535	472
MANDOL	27	MARTIN	1 SERIAL #28690-34435	1,313	**1,008**	891	785
MANDOL	14	MARTIN	2 BOWL BACK	785	**602**	532	469
MANDOL	20	MARTIN	2 BOWL BACK	772	**593**	524	462
MANDOL	40	MARTIN	2-15 SUNBURST, CARVED TOP/BACK	1,708	**1,311**	1,159	1,021
MANDOL	46	MARTIN	2-15	1,052	**808**	714	629
MANDOL	48	MARTIN	2-15 CARVED TOP/BACK, SERIAL #18304-19078	1,544	**1,185**	1,048	923
MANDOL	49	MARTIN	2-15 CARVED TOP/BACK	1,487	**1,142**	1,009	889
MANDOL	51	MARTIN	2-15 CARVED TOP/BACK, SERIAL #20066-20496	1,478	**1,135**	1,003	884
MANDOL	53	MARTIN	2-15 CARVED TOP/BACK	1,198	**920**	813	716
MANDOL	55	MARTIN	2-15 SUNBURST	1,517	**1,165**	1,029	907
MANDOL	63	MARTIN	2-15 CARVED TOP/BACK	1,232	**946**	836	737
MANDOL	64	MARTIN	2-15 CARVED TOP/BACK	1,202	**923**	816	719
MANDOL	64	MARTIN	2-15	1,216	**933**	825	727
MANDOL	65	MARTIN	2-15 CARVED TOP/BACK, SERIAL #24340-24439	976	**749**	662	584
MANDOL	29	MARTIN	2-20 ARCHED TOP/BACK	3,199	**2,457**	2,171	1,914
MANDOL	36	MARTIN	2-20 CARVED TOP/BACK	3,520	**2,702**	2,388	2,105
MANDOL	37	MARTIN	2-20 CARVED TOP/BACK	2,966	**2,278**	2,013	1,774
MANDOL	40	MARTIN	2-20 CARVED TOP/BACK, SERIAL #16748-16957	3,588	**2,755**	2,435	2,146
MANDOL	38	MARTIN	2-30 CARVED TOP/BACK, SERIAL #16438-16580	3,349	**2,572**	2,273	2,003
MANDOL	42	MARTIN	2-30 CARVED TOP/BACK, SERIAL #17264-17405	3,198	**2,456**	2,170	1,913
MANDOL	98	MARTIN	3 1898, BOWL BACK, SERIAL #156-359	1,336	**1,025**	906	799
MANDOL	17	MARTIN	3 BOWL BACK, SERIAL #5008-5752	804	**617**	545	481
MANDOL	19	MARTIN	3 BOWL BACK, SERIAL #6371-7237	1,318	**1,012**	894	788
MANDOL	01	MARTIN	4 1901, BOWL BACK, SERIAL #801-881	1,734	**1,332**	1,177	1,037
MANDOL	08	MARTIN	4 1908, BOWL BACK, SERIAL #2358-2510	1,655	**1,271**	1,123	990

TYPE	YR	MFG	PRICES--BASED ON 100% ORIGINAL MODEL	SELL EXC	SELL AVG	BUY EXC	BUY AVG
MANDOL	05	MARTIN	**5** 1905, BOWL BACK	3,896	**2,991**	2,644	2,330
MANDOL	09	MARTIN	**5** 1906, BOWL BACK	3,859	**2,963**	2,618	2,308
MANDOL	19	MARTIN	**6** SNOWFLAKE INLAY	4,021	**3,088**	2,729	2,405
MANDOL	19	MARTIN	**6A** BOWL BACK	4,016	**3,083**	2,725	2,402
MANDOL	10	MARTIN	**7** BOWL BACK	4,314	**3,312**	2,927	2,580
MANDOL	20	MARTIN	**A**	878	**674**	595	525
MANDOL	22	MARTIN	**A** SERIAL #9628-10196	973	**747**	660	582
MANDOL	23	MARTIN	**A** SERIAL #10197-11020	915	**702**	620	547
MANDOL	26	MARTIN	**A** SERIAL #12521-13359	910	**699**	617	544
MANDOL	28	MARTIN	**A**	939	**721**	637	562
MANDOL	30	MARTIN	**A** SERIAL #14631-14892	930	**714**	631	556
MANDOL	34	MARTIN	**A** SERIAL #15529-15729	1,932	**1,483**	1,311	1,155
MANDOL	37	MARTIN	**A** SERIAL #16157-16437	925	**710**	627	553
MANDOL	38	MARTIN	**A**	920	**706**	624	550
MANDOL	39	MARTIN	**A** SERIAL #16581-16747	888	**681**	602	531
MANDOL	47	MARTIN	**A** SERIAL #17642-18303	896	**688**	608	536
MANDOL	50	MARTIN	**A**	827	**635**	561	495
MANDOL	51	MARTIN	**A** SERIAL #20066-20496	804	**617**	545	481
MANDOL	54	MARTIN	**A** SERIAL #21453-21952	810	**622**	550	485
MANDOL	55	MARTIN	**A** SERIAL #21953-22254	805	**618**	546	481
MANDOL	57	MARTIN	**A** SERIAL #22630-22985	810	**622**	550	485
MANDOL	60	MARTIN	**A**	779	**598**	528	466
MANDOL	61	MARTIN	**A**	769	**590**	522	460
MANDOL	66	MARTIN	**A** SERIAL #24440-24564	764	**587**	519	457
MANDOL	67	MARTIN	**A** SERIAL #25465-24639	764	**587**	519	457
MANDOL	72	MARTIN	**A**	726	**558**	493	434
MANDOL	73	MARTIN	**A**	722	**554**	490	432
MANDOL	74	MARTIN	**A** SERIAL #12589	759	**583**	515	454
MANDOL	75	MARTIN	**A** SERIAL #25680-25895	672	**516**	456	402
MANDOL	76	MARTIN	**A** SERIAL #25896-26045,259996-260020	749	**575**	508	448
MANDOL	77	MARTIN	**A** SERIAL #26046-26101	745	**572**	506	446
MANDOL	23	MARTIN	**A-K** KOA WOOD, SERIAL #10197-11020	1,279	**982**	867	765
MANDOL	25	MARTIN	**A-K** KOA WOOD, SERIAL #11810-12520	1,024	**786**	695	613
MANDOL	26	MARTIN	**A-K** KOA WOOD, SERIAL #12521-13359	967	**743**	656	578
MANDOL	27	MARTIN	**A-K** KOA WOOD, SERIAL #13360-13833	955	**733**	648	571
MANDOL	31	MARTIN	**A-K** KOA WOOD, SERIAL #14893-15290	845	**649**	573	505
MANDOL	19	MARTIN	**B** BRAZILIAN ROSEWOOD	871	**669**	591	521
MANDOL	20	MARTIN	**B** HERRINGBONE TRIM, SERIAL #7238-8761	846	**650**	574	506
MANDOL	22	MARTIN	**B** BRAZILIAN ROSEWOOD	1,006	**773**	683	602
MANDOL	23	MARTIN	**B** HERRINGBONE TRIM	1,284	**986**	871	768
MANDOL	25	MARTIN	**B** HERRINGBONE TRIM	878	**674**	595	525
MANDOL	31	MARTIN	**B** HERRINGBONE TRIM, SERIAL #14893-15290	846	**650**	574	506
MANDOL	41	MARTIN	**B** HERRINGBONE TRIM, SERIAL #16958-17263	804	**617**	545	481
MANDOL	20	MARTIN	**BB** BRAZILIAN ROSEWOOD	1,423	**1,093**	965	851
MANDOL	15	MARTIN	**C** ABALONE SOUNDHOLE RING, SERIAL #4463-4767	2,111	**1,621**	1,432	1,262
MANDOL	19	MARTIN	**C**	2,157	**1,656**	1,463	1,290

TYPE	YR	MFG	PRICES--BASED ON 100% ORIGINAL MODEL	SELL EXC	SELL AVG	BUY EXC	BUY AVG
MANDOL	20	MARTIN	C PEARL BIND TOP/SOUNDBOARD	1,927	1,480	1,307	1,153
MANDOL	17	MARTIN	E ROSEWOOD	4,006	3,076	2,718	2,396
MANDOL	20	MARTIN	E	8,816	6,769	5,982	5,274
MANDOL	25	MARTIN	T-18 ORGINAL CANVAS CASE, SERIAL #26437	1,961	1,505	1,330	1,173
MANDOL	26	MARTIN	T-18 TIPLE	1,979	1,519	1,342	1,183
MANDOL	68	MARTIN	T-18 BRAZILIAN ROSEWOOD, SERIAL #239362	1,618	1,242	1,098	968
MANDOL	68	MARTIN	T-28 TIPLE, BRAZILIAN ROSEWOOD	2,349	1,804	1,594	1,405
UKULELE							
UKE	20	MARTIN	0	764	587	519	457
UKE	27	MARTIN	0 FRICTION PEGS, SERIAL #28690-34435	1,030	791	699	616
UKE	30	MARTIN	0 SERIAL #40844-45317	703	540	477	420
UKE	35	MARTIN	0 MAHOGANY, TANG FRETS	633	486	430	379
UKE	40	MARTIN	0	701	538	475	419
UKE	50	MARTIN	0 SERIAL #112962-117961	703	540	477	420
UKE	53	MARTIN	0	739	567	501	442
UKE	55	MARTIN	0 SERIAL #141346-147328	538	413	365	322
UKE	56	MARTIN	0	688	528	467	412
UKE	57	MARTIN	0	682	523	462	408
UKE	64	MARTIN	0	590	453	400	353
UKE	65	MARTIN	0	688	528	467	412
UKE	66	MARTIN	0	564	433	383	337
UKE	25	MARTIN	1 SOPRANO, SERIAL #22009-24116	1,276	980	866	763
UKE	26	MARTIN	1 SOPRANO, SERIAL #24117-28689	922	708	626	552
UKE	27	MARTIN	1 SOPRANO	917	704	622	548
UKE	30	MARTIN	1 SOPRANO, SERIAL #40844-45317	906	695	614	542
UKE	40	MARTIN	1 SOPRANO, SERIAL #74062-76734	677	520	459	405
UKE	50	MARTIN	1 SOPRANO, SERIAL #112962-117961	743	571	504	444
UKE	54	MARTIN	1 SOPRANO	773	594	525	462
UKE	30	MARTIN	1C CONCERT MAHOGANY, SERIAL #40844-45317	1,024	786	695	613
UKE	35	MARTIN	1C CONCERT MAHOGANY	817	627	554	489
UKE	25	MARTIN	1K KOA WOOD	834	640	566	499
UKE	30	MARTIN	1K KOA WOOD	787	604	534	471
UKE	35	MARTIN	1K KOA WOOD	794	609	538	475
UKE	40	MARTIN	1K KOA WOOD, SERIAL #74062-76734	789	606	535	472
UKE	50	MARTIN	1K KOA WOOD, SERIAL #112962-117961	1,214	932	823	726
UKE	29	MARTIN	1T TENOR, SERIAL #37569-40843	1,295	995	879	775
UKE	33	MARTIN	1T TENOR, SERIAL #52591-55084	1,024	786	695	613
UKE	40	MARTIN	1T TENOR, SERIAL #74062-76734	846	650	574	506
UKE	50	MARTIN	1T TENOR, SERIAL #112962-117961	805	618	546	481
UKE	55	MARTIN	1T TENOR	792	608	538	474
UKE	60	MARTIN	1T TENOR, SERIAL #171048-175689	781	600	530	467
UKE	62	MARTIN	1T TENOR	748	574	507	447
UKE	58	MARTIN	1T BARITONE	682	523	462	408
UKE	28	MARTIN	2 SERIAL #34436-37568	1,582	1,215	1,073	946
UKE	35	MARTIN	2 MAHOGANY, BOUND	789	606	535	472
UKE	50	MARTIN	2 MAHOGANY	962	738	652	575
UKE	55	MARTIN	2 SERIAL #141346-147328	803	616	544	480

TYPE	YR	MFG	PRICES--BASED ON 100% ORIGINAL MODEL	SELL EXC	SELL AVG	BUY EXC	BUY AVG
UKE	27	MARTIN	**2K** SOPRANO, KOA WOOD	954	**732**	647	570
UKE	30	MARTIN	**2K** KOA WOOD, SERIAL #40844-45317	845	**649**	573	505
UKE	27	MARTIN	**2M** SERIAL #28690-34435	843	**647**	572	504
UKE	20	MARTIN	**3** MAHOGANY, HEADSTOCK INLAY	1,284	**986**	871	768
UKE	50	MARTIN	**3** MAHOGANY	1,202	**923**	816	719
UKE	21	MARTIN	**3K** KOA WOOD	3,312	**2,543**	2,248	1,981
UKE	25	MARTIN	**3K** KOA WOOD, SERIAL #22009-24116	1,643	**1,261**	1,114	982
UKE	33	MARTIN	**3K** KOA WOOD	2,377	**1,825**	1,613	1,422
UKE	30	MARTIN	**3M** SERIAL #40844-45317	1,248	**958**	847	747
UKE	55	MARTIN	**3M** SOPRANO, DOT NECK INLAY	937	**719**	636	560
UKE	25	MARTIN	**5** KOA, PEARL TRIM	5,860	**4,500**	3,977	3,506
UKE	41	MARTIN	**5** SERIAL #40844-45317	5,350	**4,108**	3,630	3,200
UKE	30	MARTIN	**5K** SOPRANO, KOA WOOD, SERIAL #40844-45317	5,708	**4,383**	3,873	3,414
UKE	30	MARTIN	**5K** HAWAIIAN KOA, FIGURED	7,357	**5,649**	4,992	4,401
UKE	32	MARTIN	**5K** SOPRANO, KOA WOOD	5,210	**4,000**	3,535	3,116
UKE	35	MARTIN	**5K** SOPRANO, KOA WOOD	3,693	**2,792**	2,462	2,042
UKE	51	MARTIN	**51** BARITONE, SERIAL #117962-122799	945	**725**	641	565
UKE	52	MARTIN	**51** BARITONE	1,204	**924**	817	720
UKE	60	MARTIN	**51** BARITONE, SERIAL #171048-175689	926	**711**	628	554
UKE	61	MARTIN	**51** BARITONE	976	**749**	662	584
UKE	62	MARTIN	**51** BARITONE	1,216	**933**	825	727
UKE	63	MARTIN	**51** BARITONE	1,033	**793**	701	618
UKE	64	MARTIN	**51** BARITONE	1,023	**786**	694	612
UKE	70	MARTIN	**51** BARITONE	950	**730**	645	568
UKE	70	MARTIN	**BARITONE** MAHOGANY	1,385	**1,063**	940	828
UKE	18	MARTIN	**STYLE 1 TAROPATCH** 8-STRING	2,989	**2,295**	2,028	1,788
UKE	20	MARTIN	**STYLE 1 TAROPATCH** MAHOGANY, 8-STRING,RSWD FRTBRD,CONCERT SIZE BODY	2,074	**1,592**	1,407	1,240
UKE	20	MARTIN	**STYLE 1K TAROPATCH** KOA WOOD, RSWD FRTBRD, 8-STRING, SERIAL #14513-15848	3,177	**2,439**	2,156	1,900
UKE	18	MARTIN	**STYLE 2 TAROPATCH** 8-STRING	2,989	**2,295**	2,028	1,788
UKE	18	MARTIN	**STYLE 3 TAROPATCH** 8-STRING	3,064	**2,352**	2,079	1,833
UKE	50	MARTIN	**T-15 TIPLE** MAHOGANY	758	**582**	514	453
UKE	17	MARTIN	**T-17 TIPLE**	1,254	**963**	851	750
UKE	28	MARTIN	**T-17 TIPLE**	982	**754**	666	587
UKE	31	MARTIN	**T-17 TIPLE**	878	**674**	595	525
UKE	40	MARTIN	**T-17 TIPLE**	962	**738**	652	575
UKE	23	MARTIN	**T-18 TIPLE** SERIAL #17840-19891	1,809	**1,389**	1,228	1,082
UKE	26	MARTIN	**T-18 TIPLE** SERIAL #24117-28689	805	**618**	546	481
UKE	27	MARTIN	**T-18 TIPLE**	781	**600**	530	467
UKE	35	MARTIN	**T-18 TIPLE**	724	**556**	491	433
UKE	55	MARTIN	**T-18 TIPLE** SPRUCE & MAHOGANY	735	**565**	499	440
UKE	27	MARTIN	**T-28 TIPLE** HERRINGBONE TRIM, SERIAL #28690-34435	1,608	**1,234**	1,091	962
UKE	50	MARTIN	**T-28 TIPLE** INDIAN ROSEWOOD, SPRUCE TOP	1,553	**1,192**	1,054	929
UKE	68	MARTIN	**T-28 TIPLE** BRAZILIAN ROSEWOOD, 10-STRING	1,486	**1,141**	1,008	889
UKE	71	MARTIN	**T-28 TIPLE** INDIAN ROSEWOOD	1,062	**816**	721	635

TYPE	YR	MFG	PRICES--BASED ON 100% ORIGINAL MODEL	SELL EXC	SELL AVG	BUY EXC	BUY AVG
UKE	74	MARTIN	T-28 TIPLE INDIAN ROSEWOOD	972	746	659	581

McINTOSH LABS

TYPE	YR	MFG	MODEL	SELL EXC	SELL AVG	BUY EXC	BUY AVG
PRE	02	MCINTOSH	AE-2 VACUUM MONO TUBE	227	174	154	136
PRE	50	MCINTOSH	C- 4 VACUUM MONO TUBE	221	170	150	132
PRE	54	MCINTOSH	C- 4P MONO TUBE POWER SUPPLY	239	184	162	143
PRE	55- 59	MCINTOSH	C- 8 VACUUM MONO TUBE	477	366	323	285
PRE	55- 59	MCINTOSH	C- 8P MONO TUBE POWER SUPPLY	400	307	272	239
PRE	58- 60	MCINTOSH	C- 8S VACUUM STEREO TUBE	560	430	380	335
PRE	61- 63	MCINTOSH	C- 11 VACUUM STEREO TUBE	987	758	670	590
PRE	59- 63	MCINTOSH	C- 20 STEREO TUBE	1,021	784	693	611
PRE	63- 68	MCINTOSH	C- 22 VACUUM STEREO TUBE	2,237	1,718	1,518	1,338
PRE	64	MCINTOSH	C- 24 SOLID STATE	291	223	197	174
PRE	52- 55	MCINTOSH	C-104 VACUUM MONO TUBE	295	227	200	176
PRE	53- 55	MCINTOSH	C-108 VACUUM MONO TUBE	225	172	152	134
PRE	62	MCINTOSH	MX-110 TUBE PREAMP/TUNER	675	518	458	404
PRE	71	MCINTOSH	MX-115 SOLID STATE PREAMP/TUNER	762	585	517	456
PWR	49	MCINTOSH	15W-1 VACUUM MONO TUBE	308	236	209	184
PWR	51	MCINTOSH	20W-2 MONO TUBE 20 WATTS	422	324	286	252
PWR	49	MCINTOSH	50W-1 VACUUM MONO TUBE	516	396	350	308
PWR	51	MCINTOSH	50W-2 MONO TUBE 50 WATTS	604	464	410	361
PWR	53- 55	MCINTOSH	A-116 MONO TUBE 30 WATTS	483	371	328	289
PWR	54- 62	MCINTOSH	MC- 30 VACUUM MONO TUBE 30 WATTS	993	762	674	594
PWR	59	MCINTOSH	MC- 30A MONO TUBE	717	551	487	429
PWR	62- 69	MCINTOSH	MC- 40 VACUUM MONO TUBE 40 WATTS	909	698	617	544
PWR	69- 70	MCINTOSH	MC- 50 SOLID STATE MONO	468	359	317	280
PWR	55- 61	MCINTOSH	MC- 60 VACUUM MONO TUBE 60 WATTS	1,462	1,123	992	875
PWR	59	MCINTOSH	MC- 60A MONO TUBE	1,531	1,175	1,038	915
PWR	61- 70	MCINTOSH	MC- 75 VACUUM MONO TUBE	1,438	1,104	975	860
PWR	70	MCINTOSH	MC- 100 SOLID STATE MONO	595	457	404	356
PWR	61- 70	MCINTOSH	MC- 225 VACUUM STEREO TUBE 25 WATTS	1,021	784	693	611
PWR	60- 69	MCINTOSH	MC- 240 VACUUM STEREO TUBE 40 WATTS	1,677	1,288	1,138	1,003
PWR	67	MCINTOSH	MC- 250 SOLID STATE STEREO 75 WATTS	806	619	547	482
PWR	67	MCINTOSH	MC- 250 TRANSISTOR 50 WATTS	596	458	405	357
PWR	67	MCINTOSH	MC- 250E TRANSISTOR 50 WATTS	700	537	475	418
PWR	61- 70	MCINTOSH	MC- 275 VACUUM STEREO TUBE 75 WATTS	3,477	2,670	2,359	2,080
PWR	67	MCINTOSH	MC-2105 SOLID STATE 105 WATTS	910	699	617	544
PWR	67	MCINTOSH	MC-2505 50Wpc METERED	651	500	442	389
PWR	67	MCINTOSH	MC-2505 SOLID STATE 50 WATTS	1,349	1,036	915	807
PWR	68	MCINTOSH	MC-3500 MONO TUBE	3,769	2,894	2,558	2,255
PWR	60	MCINTOSH	MK-30 KIT MONO TUBE 30 WATTS	435	334	295	260
SPKR	75	MCINTOSH	ST 1 8 OHMS, 10" WOOFER, 2" TWEETER	1,406	1,080	954	841
SPKR	75	MCINTOSH	ST 2 8 OHMS, 10" WOOFER, 5" MIDRANGE, 1.75" TWEETER	1,406	1,080	954	841
SPKR	75	MCINTOSH	ST 3 8 OHMS, 12" WOOFER, 5" MIDRANGE, 1.75" TWEETER	1,406	1,080	954	841
SPKR	75	MCINTOSH	ST 4 8 8 OHMS, 12" WOOFER, 5" MIDRANGE, 1-5/8" TWEETER	1,406	1,080	954	841
TEST	64	MCINTOSH	MI-3 STEREO OSCILLOSCOPE	412	316	279	246
TEST	73	MCINTOSH	MPI-4 DUAL TRACE OSCILLOSCOPE	883	678	599	528
TUNER	57	MCINTOSH	MR- 55 TUBE	288	221	196	172
TUNER	59	MCINTOSH	MR- 55A AM/FM MONO TUBE	268	206	182	160
TUNER	60- 62	MCINTOSH	MR- 65 VACUUM MONO TUBE	442	339	300	264
TUNER	62- 64	MCINTOSH	MR- 65B VACUUM MONO TUBE	554	425	376	331
TUNER	60	MCINTOSH	MR- 66 AM/FM TUBE	234	179	158	140
TUNER	63- 68	MCINTOSH	MR- 67 VACUUM STEREO TUBE	694	533	471	415
TUNER	63- 69	MCINTOSH	MR- 71 VACUUM TUBE	959	737	651	574
TUNER	69	MCINTOSH	MR- 73 AM/FM SOLID STATE	672	516	456	402
TUNER	70- 78	MCINTOSH	MR- 77 FM STEREO SOLID STATE	695	534	471	416
TUNER	62	MCINTOSH	MX-110 FM TUBE TUNER/PREAMP	703	540	477	420
TUNER	71	MCINTOSH	MX-113 AM/FM STEREO TUNER/PREAMP	624	479	424	373

	TYPE	YR	MFG	PRICES--BASED ON 100% ORIGINAL MODEL	SELL EXC	SELL AVG	BUY EXC	BUY AVG
	TUNER	69	MCINTOSH	**MX-114 AM/FM SS TUNER/PREAMP**	510	**392**	346	305
XOVER		55	MCINTOSH	**3 MONO TUBE**	3,328	**2,555**	2,258	1,991

MELLOTRON

	TYPE	YR	MFG	MODEL	SELL EXC	SELL AVG	BUY EXC	BUY AVG
SYNTHESIZER		64	MELLOTRON	**MELLOTRON MARK II**	4,763	**3,657**	3,232	2,849
	SYNTH	68	MELLOTRON	**MELLOTRON MODEL 300**	5,274	**4,049**	3,578	3,155
	SYNTH	70	MELLOTRON	**MELLOTRON MODEL 400**	1,009	**774**	684	603

MESSANGER by MUSIC CRAFT

	TYPE	YR	MFG	MODEL	SELL EXC	SELL AVG	BUY EXC	BUY AVG
ELEC. GUITAR & BASS		67	MESSANGER	**HOLLOW BODY** ALUMINUM BODY/NECK	3,604	**2,767**	2,445	2,156
	ELGUIT	68	MESSANGER	**SOLID BODY** NATURAL ON FLAME MAPLE	5,483	**4,210**	3,720	3,280

MICROFRET

	TYPE	YR	MFG	MODEL	SELL EXC	SELL AVG	BUY EXC	BUY AVG
ELEC. GUITAR & BASS		71	MICROFRET	**BARITONE SIGNATURE** DOUBLE CUTAWAY	628	**482**	426	375
	ELGUIT	72	MICROFRET	**BARITONE STAGE II** DOUBLE CUTAWAY, 2 PU's	580	**445**	393	347
	ELGUIT	69	MICROFRET	**CALIBRA** BROWN	617	**473**	418	369
	ELGUIT	70	MICROFRET	**CALIBRA** BROWN	658	**505**	446	393
	ELGUIT	69	MICROFRET	**CALIBRA I**	645	**495**	437	385
	ELGUIT	70	MICROFRET	**CALIBRA I** RED	651	**500**	442	389
	ELGUIT	72	MICROFRET	**CALIBRA I** RED	598	**459**	405	357
	ELGUIT	72	MICROFRET	**COVINGTON**	910	**699**	617	544
	ELGUIT	68	MICROFRET	**GOLDEN COMET**	722	**554**	490	432
	ELGUIT	69	MICROFRET	**GOLDEN COMET**	617	**473**	418	369
	ELGUIT	71	MICROFRET	**GOLDEN MELODY** SUNBURST	695	**534**	471	416
	ELGUIT	69	MICROFRET	**HUNTINGTON**	677	**520**	459	405
	ELGUIT	74	MICROFRET	**HUNTINGTON**	670	**515**	455	401
	ELGUIT	70	MICROFRET	**HUSKY BASS** RED	459	**352**	311	274
	ELGUIT	68	MICROFRET	**ORBITER** TRIPLE CUTAWAY	749	**575**	508	448
	ELGUIT	67	MICROFRET	**PLAINSMAN** TOBACCO SUNBURST	761	**584**	516	455
	ELGUIT	70	MICROFRET	**RENDEZVOUS BASS** ORANGE SUNBURST, 1 PU	607	**466**	411	363
	ELGUIT	79	MICROFRET	**SABRE BASS** NATURAL	1,276	**980**	866	763
	ELGUIT	69	MICROFRET	**SIGNATURE** DOUBLE CUTAWAY, 2 PU's	668	**513**	453	399
	ELGUIT	69	MICROFRET	**SIGNATURE BASS** NATURAL	673	**516**	456	402
	ELGUIT	71	MICROFRET	**SIGNATURE BASS** SUNBURST	661	**508**	449	395
	ELGUIT	72	MICROFRET	**SIGNATURE BASS** BARITONE, SUNBURST	636	**488**	431	380
	ELGUIT	69	MICROFRET	**SPACETONE** DOUBLE CUTAWAY, 2 PU's	673	**516**	456	402
	ELGUIT	69	MICROFRET	**SPACETONE**	749	**575**	508	448
	ELGUIT	68	MICROFRET	**STAGE II BASS**	673	**516**	456	402
	ELGUIT	70	MICROFRET	**STAGE II BASS** BROWN	660	**507**	448	395
	ELGUIT	71	MICROFRET	**STAGE II BASS**	645	**495**	437	385
	ELGUIT	73	MICROFRET	**STAGE II BASS**	658	**505**	446	393
	ELGUIT	70	MICROFRET	**STAGE VII BASS** SUNBURST	617	**473**	418	369
	ELGUIT	71	MICROFRET	**SWINGER**	668	**513**	453	399
	ELGUIT	70	MICROFRET	**THUNDERMASTER BASS** SUNBURST	588	**451**	399	351
	ELGUIT	70	MICROFRET	**WANDERER**	648	**497**	440	387

MONTERREY

	TYPE	YR	MFG	MODEL	SELL EXC	SELL AVG	BUY EXC	BUY AVG
GUITAR (ACOUSTIC)		36	MONTERREY	**12-STRING**	2,878	**2,210**	1,953	1,721
	GUITAR	39	MONTERREY	**12-STRING**	2,238	**1,719**	1,519	1,339
	GUITAR	39	MONTERREY	**CUSTOM** 12-STRING	3,523	**2,705**	2,390	2,107
	GUITAR	47	MONTERREY	**DELUXE** ARCHTOP	3,083	**2,367**	2,092	1,844
	GUITAR	48	MONTERREY	**DELUXE** ARCHTOP	2,854	**2,192**	1,937	1,707
	GUITAR	47	MONTERREY	**F-70 FLATTOP**	3,984	**3,059**	2,704	2,383

MOOG MUSICAL INSTRUMENTS

	TYPE	YR	MFG	MODEL	SELL EXC	SELL AVG	BUY EXC	BUY AVG
EQUAL		78	MOOG	**SPGE-1 SIG** GRAPHIC	692	**531**	469	414
	EQUAL	78	MOOG	**SPPE-1 PARA**	1,033	**793**	701	618

TYPE	YR	MFG	PRICES--BASED ON 100% ORIGINAL MODEL	SELL EXC	SELL AVG	BUY EXC	BUY AVG
GUITAR AMP	63	MOOG	MR-71 VACUUM STEREO TUBE	800	614	543	479
SIGNAL PROCESSOR	79	MOOG	SPVP-1 12 STAGE PHASER	627	481	425	375
SYNTHESIZER	70	MOOG	MINIMOOG ANALOG	1,461	1,122	991	874
SYNTH	75	MOOG	POLYMOOG ANALOG	695	534	471	416
SYNTH	77	MOOG	POLYSYNTH POLYPEDAL	1,448	1,111	982	866
SYNTH	81	MOOG	ROGUE ANALOG	759	583	515	454
SYNTH	74	MOOG	SATELLITE	275	211	186	164
SYNTH	74	MOOG	SONIC-SIX	805	618	546	481

MOONSTONE

TYPE	YR	MFG	MODEL	SELL EXC	SELL AVG	BUY EXC	BUY AVG
ELEC. GUITAR & BASS	78	MOON	ECLIPSE DELUXE	1,321	1,014	896	790
ELGUIT	78	MOON	ECLIPSE STANDARD	1,044	802	709	625
ELGUIT	81	MOON	EXPLODER	1,293	993	877	773
ELGUIT	81	MOON	FLAMING V	1,443	1,108	979	863
ELGUIT	78	MOON	M-80	2,143	1,646	1,454	1,282
ELGUIT	82	MOON	M-80 GRAPHITE	3,607	2,770	2,447	2,158
ELGUIT	81	MOON	TREMOLO V	1,277	981	867	764
ELGUIT	78	MOON	VULCAN DELUXE	1,514	1,162	1,027	905
ELGUIT	78	MOON	VULCAN STANDARD	1,252	961	849	749

MOSRITE

TYPE	YR	MFG	MODEL	SELL EXC	SELL AVG	BUY EXC	BUY AVG
BANJO	65	MOSRITE	DOBRO ELECTRIC, 12-STRING	803	616	544	480
BANJO	67	MOSRITE	DOBRO NATURAL, STYLE C RESONATOR	776	595	526	464
BANJO	68	MOSRITE	DOBRO NATURAL, MAHOGANY, 12-STRING	714	548	484	427
BANJO	68	MOSRITE	DOBRO BROWN, RESONATOR	894	687	607	535
ELEC. GUITAR & BASS	69	MOSRITE	BASS SUNBURST, VENTURES BODY STYLE	819	629	556	490
ELGUIT	70	MOSRITE	BASS SUNBURST, VENTURES BODY STYLE, 2 PU's	808	620	548	483
ELGUIT	70	MOSRITE	BASS BLUE METALLIC, VENTURES BODY STYLE, 2 PU's	808	620	548	483
ELGUIT	70	MOSRITE	BASS SOLID MAHOGANY, 1 PU	1,003	770	680	600
ELGUIT	76	MOSRITE	BRASS RAIL BLACK	1,542	1,184	1,046	922
ELGUIT	76	MOSRITE	BRASS RAIL	1,569	1,204	1,064	938
ELGUIT	77	MOSRITE	BRASS RAIL BLACK	1,388	1,066	942	830
ELGUIT	77	MOSRITE	BRASS RAIL	1,508	1,158	1,023	902
ELGUIT	69	MOSRITE	CALIFORNIAN MAROON, DOUBLE CUTAWAY, 2 PU's	1,116	844	744	617
ELGUIT	65	MOSRITE	CELEBRITY SUNBURST, TRAPEZE TAIL PIECE	875	672	594	523
ELGUIT	67	MOSRITE	CELEBRITY SUNBURST	816	626	554	488
ELGUIT	68	MOSRITE	CELEBRITY SUNBURST, DOUBLE CUTAWAY, 2 PU's	777	596	527	464
ELGUIT	70	MOSRITE	CELEBRITY RED, VIBRATO, 2 PU's	652	501	443	390
ELGUIT	70	MOSRITE	CELEBRITY SUNBURST	669	514	454	400
ELGUIT	70	MOSRITE	CELEBRITY RED & BLACK SUNBURST, 12-STRING	754	579	512	451
ELGUIT	70	MOSRITE	CELEBRITY GREEN, 12-STRING	756	580	513	452
ELGUIT	72	MOSRITE	CELEBRITY RED & BLACK SUNBURST, 12-STRING	677	520	459	405
ELGUIT	72	MOSRITE	CELEBRITY RED, VIBROLA	712	546	483	426
ELGUIT	74	MOSRITE	CELEBRITY AMBER SUNBURST	706	542	479	422
ELGUIT	70	MOSRITE	CELEBRITY BASS RED & BLACK SUNBURST	764	587	519	457
ELGUIT	68	MOSRITE	CELEBRITY 3 SUNBURST, 2 PU's	761	584	516	455
ELGUIT	70	MOSRITE	CELEBRITY 3 SUNBURST, 12-STRING	756	580	513	452
ELGUIT	67	MOSRITE	CELEBRITY 3 BASS	866	665	588	518
ELGUIT	68	MOSRITE	CELEBRITY 3 BASS	770	591	522	460
ELGUIT	70	MOSRITE	CELEBRITY 3 BASS CHERRY RED	756	580	513	452
ELGUIT	70	MOSRITE	CELEBRITY 3 BASS TRANSLUCENT BLUE, SERIAL #Z0477	756	580	513	452
ELGUIT	69	MOSRITE	CELEBRITY I ORANGE SUNBURST, MOSLEY TREMOLO, DUAL HB's	855	657	580	511

TYPE	YR	MFG	PRICES--BASED ON 100% ORIGINAL MODEL	SELL EXC	SELL AVG	BUY EXC	BUY AVG
ELGUIT	68	MOSRITE	**COMBO** SUNBURST, 12-STRING	672	**516**	456	402
ELGUIT	68	MOSRITE	**COMBO** RED, TREMOLO	915	**702**	620	547
ELGUIT	66	MOSRITE	**COMBO MARK I** CHERRY SUNBURST	855	**657**	580	511
ELGUIT	56	MOSRITE	**CUSTOM** SUNBURST, LEFT-HANDED, CARVED SOLID MAHOGANY	4,415	**3,390**	2,995	2,641
ELGUIT	66	MOSRITE	**D-100 CALIFORNIAN** CANDY APPLE RED, ELECTRONIC RESONATOR, 2 PU's	953	**731**	646	570
ELGUIT	64	MOSRITE	**MAPHIS** DOUBLE NECK	3,697	**2,838**	2,508	2,211
ELGUIT	67	MOSRITE	**MAPHIS** SUNBURST, DOUBLE NECK	2,098	**1,611**	1,424	1,255
ELGUIT	67	MOSRITE	**MAPHIS** CANDY APPLE RED, DOUBLE NECK	2,428	**1,864**	1,647	1,452
ELGUIT	68	MOSRITE	**MAPHIS** SUNBURST, DOUBLE NECK	2,992	**2,297**	2,030	1,790
ELGUIT	65	MOSRITE	**MAPHIS MARK I**	1,329	**1,020**	902	795
ELGUIT	66	MOSRITE	**MAPHIS MARK I**	1,279	**982**	867	765
ELGUIT	67	MOSRITE	**MAPHIS MARK I**	1,329	**1,020**	902	795
ELGUIT	68	MOSRITE	**MAPHIS MARK I**	1,295	**995**	879	775
ELGUIT	67	MOSRITE	**MAPHIS MARK X**	810	**622**	550	485
ELGUIT	68	MOSRITE	**MAPHIS MARK XII**	871	**669**	591	521
ELGUIT	67	MOSRITE	**MAPHIS MARK XVIII** LAKE PLACID BLUE	3,427	**2,631**	2,325	2,050
ELGUIT	70	MOSRITE	**RAMBO PREMIER** BLOND, DOUBLE CUTAWAY	666	**511**	452	398
ELGUIT	73	MOSRITE	**V-11** SUNBURST	672	**516**	456	402
ELGUIT	63	MOSRITE	**VENTURES** SUNBURST	3,969	**3,047**	2,693	2,374
ELGUIT	64	MOSRITE	**VENTURES** SUNBURST	3,703	**2,844**	2,513	2,215
ELGUIT	64	MOSRITE	**VENTURES** VIBRAMUTE	4,326	**3,322**	2,935	2,588
ELGUIT	64	MOSRITE	**VENTURES** PEARL WHITE	5,078	**3,899**	3,445	3,037
ELGUIT	65	MOSRITE	**VENTURES** SUNBURST, 12-STRING, VIBRATO	1,700	**1,305**	1,153	1,017
ELGUIT	65	MOSRITE	**VENTURES** LPB BLUE, ALL ORIGINAL TRUSSROD	2,990	**2,296**	2,029	1,788
ELGUIT	65	MOSRITE	**VENTURES** SUNBURST	3,573	**2,744**	2,425	2,137
ELGUIT	66	MOSRITE	**VENTURES** SUNBURST, 12-STRING	2,643	**2,029**	1,793	1,581
ELGUIT	66	MOSRITE	**VENTURES** CANDY APPLE RED	3,384	**2,598**	2,296	2,024
ELGUIT	66	MOSRITE	**VENTURES** FIESTA RED	4,855	**3,728**	3,294	2,904
ELGUIT	67	MOSRITE	**VENTURES** SUNBURST, 12-STRING	1,695	**1,302**	1,150	1,014
ELGUIT	67	MOSRITE	**VENTURES** WHITE, 12-STRING	1,697	**1,303**	1,152	1,015
ELGUIT	67	MOSRITE	**VENTURES** SUNBURST	3,447	**2,647**	2,339	2,062
ELGUIT	67	MOSRITE	**VENTURES** METALLIC BLUE	4,800	**3,685**	3,257	2,871
ELGUIT	68	MOSRITE	**VENTURES** CANDY APPLE RED	3,233	**2,482**	2,194	1,934
ELGUIT	60	MOSRITE	**VENTURES BASS** RED	2,141	**1,644**	1,453	1,281
ELGUIT	66	MOSRITE	**VENTURES BASS** METALLIC BLUE	1,673	**1,284**	1,135	1,000
ELGUIT	68	MOSRITE	**VENTURES BASS** METALLIC BLUE	1,285	**987**	872	769
ELGUIT	68	MOSRITE	**VENTURES BASS** SUNBURST	1,400	**1,075**	950	837
ELGUIT	67	MOSRITE	**VENTURES II** SUNBURST, MOSE VIBRATO	1,219	**936**	827	729
ELGUIT	74	MOSRITE	**VENTURES II**	819	**629**	556	490
ELGUIT	66	MOSRITE	**VENTURES MARK I**	1,764	**1,354**	1,197	1,055
ELGUIT	67	MOSRITE	**VENTURES MARK I** SUNBURST	1,713	**1,315**	1,162	1,025
ELGUIT	65	MOSRITE	**VENTURES MARK V** SUNBURST, MOSELEY TREM, TRUSS ROD ADJUST AT BODY END OF NECK	1,439	**1,105**	976	860
ELGUIT	66	MOSRITE	**VENTURES MARK V** BLUE	1,443	**1,108**	979	863
ELGUIT	66	MOSRITE	**VENTURES MARK V** MAHOGANY	1,445	**1,110**	981	864
ELGUIT	68	MOSRITE	**VENTURES MARK V** SUNBURST	1,337	**1,026**	907	799
ELGUIT	64	MOSRITE	**VENTURES MARK X BASS**	692	**531**	469	414

TYPE	YR	MFG	PRICES--BASED ON 100% ORIGINAL MODEL	SELL EXC	SELL AVG	BUY EXC	BUY AVG
ELGUIT	65	MOSRITE	**VENTURES MARK XII** SUNBURST	2,990	**2,296**	2,029	1,788
ELGUIT	66	MOSRITE	**VENTURES MARK XVIII** SUNBURST	3,099	**2,379**	2,102	1,853
ELGUIT	65	MOSRITE	**VENTURES XII** LPB BLUE	3,865	**2,967**	2,622	2,312
GUITAR (ACOUSTIC)	66	MOSRITE	**CELEBRITY MARK I** ARCHTOP	630	**484**	427	377
GUITAR	67	MOSRITE	**CELEBRITY MARK I-T** ARCHTOP	551	**423**	373	329
GUITAR	67	MOSRITE	**CELEBRITY MARK XII** ARCHTOP	638	**490**	433	381
GUITAR	67	MOSRITE	**D- 3 3/4-SIDE** BLOND TOP	771	**592**	523	461
GUITAR	65	MOSRITE	**D- 8**	888	**681**	602	531
GUITAR	66	MOSRITE	**D- 8**	797	**612**	541	477
GUITAR	66	MOSRITE	**D- 12** ALL MAHOGANY, 12-STRING	763	**586**	518	456
GUITAR	65	MOSRITE	**D- 40** SUNBURST	714	**548**	484	427
GUITAR	66	MOSRITE	**D- 40** SUNBURST	969	**744**	658	580
GUITAR	64	MOSRITE	**D- 40S** SUNBURST	922	**708**	626	552
GUITAR	64	MOSRITE	**D- 50** MAHOGANY	728	**559**	494	435
GUITAR	66	MOSRITE	**D- 50S** SQUARE NECK	987	**758**	670	590
GUITAR	67	MOSRITE	**D- 65** MAPLE TOP, MAHOGANY BODY	852	**654**	578	509
GUITAR	68	MOSRITE	**D- 65**	941	**723**	639	563
GUITAR	68	MOSRITE	**D- 65E**	719	**552**	487	430
GUITAR	60	MOSRITE	**D-100** SUNBURST, DOUBLE CUTAWAY, RESONATOR	1,268	**974**	861	759
GUITAR	67	MOSRITE	**D-100** DOUBLE CUTAWAY, THIN BODY	909	**698**	617	544
GUITAR	68	MOSRITE	**D-100**	665	**510**	451	397

MOSSMAN

TYPE	YR	MFG	MODEL	SELL EXC	SELL AVG	BUY EXC	BUY AVG
ELEC. GUITAR & BASS	77	MOSSMAN	**STINGRAY II** NATURAL	617	**473**	418	369
GUITAR (ACOUSTIC)	73	MOSSMAN	**D** ROSEWOOD BACK/SIDES	1,382	**1,061**	937	826
GUITAR	73	MOSSMAN	**DAVID CHRISTIANSON** ROSEWOOD	1,453	**1,116**	986	869
GUITAR	74	MOSSMAN	**FLINT HILLS**	1,449	**1,112**	983	866
GUITAR	75	MOSSMAN	**FLINT HILLS**	1,274	**978**	864	762
GUITAR	76	MOSSMAN	**FLINT HILLS** ROSWOOD BACK/SIDES	1,209	**928**	820	723
GUITAR	73	MOSSMAN	**GREAT PLAINS** BRAZILIAN ROSEWOOD	1,834	**1,408**	1,244	1,097
GUITAR	76	MOSSMAN	**GREAT PLAINS**	1,868	**1,434**	1,267	1,117
GUITAR	77	MOSSMAN	**GREAT PLAINS**	1,531	**1,175**	1,038	915
GUITAR	75	MOSSMAN	**SOUTHWIND** ABALONE TRIM TOP	1,591	**1,222**	1,079	952
GUITAR	75	MOSSMAN	**TENNESSEE** 12-STRING	887	**681**	601	530
GUITAR	76	MOSSMAN	**WINTER WHEAT** 12-STRING	1,584	**1,216**	1,075	948
GUITAR	76	MOSSMAN	**WINTER WHEAT** ABALONE TOP	1,956	**1,502**	1,327	1,170

MUSIC MAN/ERNIE BALL

TYPE	YR	MFG	MODEL	SELL EXC	SELL AVG	BUY EXC	BUY AVG
ELEC. GUITAR & BASS	80	MUSICMAN	**CUTLASS I BASS** NATURAL, ASH GRAPHITE, STRING-THRU	1,018	**781**	690	609
ELGUIT	91	MUSICMAN	**EDDIE VAN HALEN** TREMOLO	3,972	**3,050**	2,695	2,376
ELGUIT	78	MUSICMAN	**SABRE BASS** BROWN	641	**492**	435	383
ELGUIT	78	MUSICMAN	**SABRE BASS** NATURAL	641	**492**	435	383
ELGUIT	78	MUSICMAN	**SABRE I** SUNBURST	661	**508**	449	395
ELGUIT	76	MUSICMAN	**STINGRAY BASS** SUNBURST, STRING-THRU	855	**657**	580	511
ELGUIT	76	MUSICMAN	**STINGRAY BASS** WHITE	6,378	**4,897**	4,328	3,815
ELGUIT	77	MUSICMAN	**STINGRAY BASS** BLACK, 9/10	1,898	**1,457**	1,288	1,135
ELGUIT	78	MUSICMAN	**STINGRAY BASS** SUNBURST	632	**485**	429	378
ELGUIT	73	MUSICMAN	**STINGRAY I** 6-STRING	887	**681**	601	530

TYPE	YR	MFG	PRICES--BASED ON 100% ORIGINAL MODEL	SELL EXC	SELL AVG	BUY EXC	BUY AVG
ELGUIT	76	MUSICMAN	STINGRAY I NATURAL	673	516	456	402
ELGUIT	77	MUSICMAN	STINGRAY I NATURAL	670	515	455	401
ELGUIT	78	MUSICMAN	STINGRAY I SUNBURST	636	488	431	380
ELGUIT	76	MUSICMAN	STINGRAY II	665	510	451	397
ELGUIT	65	MUSICMAN	VENTURES BASS SUNBURST, 1 PU	2,464	1,892	1,672	1,474
ELGUIT	66	MUSICMAN	VENTURES BASS SUNBURST 1 PU	2,458	1,887	1,668	1,470
ELGUIT	66	MUSICMAN	VENTURES BASS SUNBURST, 2 PU	2,464	1,892	1,672	1,474
GUITAR AMP	74	MUSICMAN	410 65 AMP	554	425	376	331
GTAMP	75	MUSICMAN	HD-212 130 AMP	610	468	414	365
GTAMP	75	MUSICMAN	RD- 50 HEAD 50 WATT, TUBE	446	343	303	267
GTAMP	79	MUSICMAN	Z 2x12" SPEAKERS	499	383	338	298

MUTRON

TYPE	YR	MFG	MODEL	SELL EXC	SELL AVG	BUY EXC	BUY AVG
SIGNAL PROCESSOR	81	MUT	MU-TRON III	278	214	189	166

MXR

TYPE	YR	MFG	MODEL	SELL EXC	SELL AVG	BUY EXC	BUY AVG
SIGNAL PROCESSOR	80	MXR	MINI/LIMITER	530	407	360	317

NADY

TYPE	YR	MFG	MODEL	SELL EXC	SELL AVG	BUY EXC	BUY AVG
MIC	02	NADY	SP-9 VOCAL/INSTRUMENT	66	50	44	39

NATIONAL RESO-PHONIC GUITARS, INC

TYPE	YR	MFG	MODEL	SELL EXC	SELL AVG	BUY EXC	BUY AVG
ELEC. GUITAR & BASS	64	NATIONAL	AIRLINE BLACK-RED SUNBURST, 2 PU's	390	300	265	233
ELGUIT	61	NATIONAL	BASS 85 RESOGLASS	658	505	446	393
ELGUIT	55	NATIONAL	BEL-AIRE	778	597	528	465
ELGUIT	56	NATIONAL	BEL-AIRE SUNBURST, ARCHTOP, SINGLE CUTAWAY	548	421	372	328
ELGUIT	57	NATIONAL	BEL-AIRE SUNBURST, ARCHTOP, CUTAWAY	711	546	482	425
ELGUIT	57	NATIONAL	BOLERO SUNBURST	711	546	482	425
ELGUIT	45	NATIONAL	BOSTONIAN RED SUNBURST, CUTAWAY	712	546	483	426
ELGUIT	59	NATIONAL	DEBONAIR SUNBURST, SINGLE PU, CUTAWAY, ARCHTOP	864	663	586	517
ELGUIT	56	NATIONAL	DUAL TONE SUNBURST, BOUND TOP	619	475	420	370
ELGUIT	38	NATIONAL	ERIC JOHNSON LAP VIBRATO	742	570	503	444
ELGUIT	65	NATIONAL	GLENWOOD 95 RED RESOGLASS	1,963	1,507	1,332	1,174
ELGUIT	62	NATIONAL	GLENWOOD 98 BLACK, SEMI-HOLLOW	2,091	1,605	1,418	1,250
ELGUIT	50	NATIONAL	L- 7 SUNBURST, SINGLE CUTAWAY, 2 PU's	353	271	240	211
ELGUIT	64	NATIONAL	NATIONAL 85 RED	854	656	579	511
ELGUIT	38- 40	NATIONAL	NEW YORKER SUNBURST, NO F HOLES	1,023	786	694	612
ELGUIT	64	NATIONAL	RESOPHONIC BLACK, 1 PU	757	581	513	452
ELGUIT	64	NATIONAL	STEREO-MATIC SUNBURST	355	272	240	212
ELGUIT	64	NATIONAL	STUDENT 1033	392	296	261	216
ELGUIT	59	NATIONAL	STUDENT 1133	626	480	424	374
ELGUIT	64	NATIONAL	STUDIO 66 BLACK, RESOGLASS	392	301	266	234
ELGUIT	65	NATIONAL	STUDIO 66 BLACK, RESOGLASS	366	281	248	219
ELGUIT	60	NATIONAL	VAL PRO 82 RED, MAP SHAPED	1,368	1,050	928	818
ELGUIT	62	NATIONAL	VAL PRO 82 RED, MAP SHAPED	1,345	1,032	912	804
ELGUIT	62	NATIONAL	VAL PRO 84 WHITE, MAP SHAPED	1,542	1,184	1,046	922
ELGUIT	61	NATIONAL	VAL PRO 85 BASS WHITE, RESOGLASS	712	546	483	426
ELGUIT	63	NATIONAL	VAL PRO 85 BASS WHITE, RESOGLASS	683	524	463	408
ELGUIT	62	NATIONAL	VAL PRO 88	1,609	1,235	1,092	962
ELGUIT	63	NATIONAL	VAL PRO 88 BLACK, RESOGLASS	1,843	1,415	1,250	1,102

TYPE	YR	MFG	PRICES--BASED ON 100% ORIGINAL MODEL	SELL EXC	SELL AVG	BUY EXC	BUY AVG
ELGUIT	60	NATIONAL	**VAL TROL** CREAM, 1 HB PU, SERIAL #T27573	584	**448**	396	349
ELGUIT	62	NATIONAL	**WESTWOOD 72**	1,364	**1,047**	925	816
ELGUIT	63	NATIONAL	**WESTWOOD 72**	1,218	**935**	826	728
ELGUIT	65	NATIONAL	**WESTWOOD 72**	804	**617**	545	481
ELGUIT	62	NATIONAL	**WESTWOOD 75** WHITE BLOCK INLAYS	723	**555**	490	432
ELGUIT	63	NATIONAL	**WESTWOOD 75**	661	**508**	449	395
ELGUIT	64	NATIONAL	**WESTWOOD 75**	670	**515**	455	401
ELGUIT	63	NATIONAL	**WESTWOOD 77**	1,776	**1,363**	1,205	1,062
ELGUIT	64	NATIONAL	**WESTWOOD 77** CHERRY RED	1,609	**1,235**	1,092	962
ELGUIT	65	NATIONAL	**WESTWOOD 77**	1,260	**967**	855	753
GUITAR AMP	48	NATIONAL	**1200** TAN, 12" SPEAKERS, 6 TUBES	560	**430**	380	335
GTAMP	62	NATIONAL	**1260 VAL-VERB** 20 WATT, 2x10"	557	**428**	378	333
GTAMP	40	NATIONAL	**B** BLACK, 20 WATT, 12" SPEAKER	562	**431**	381	336
GTAMP	40	NATIONAL	**NEW YORKER**	740	**568**	502	442
GTAMP	56	NATIONAL	**TREMOTONE** YELLOW TWEED	257	**197**	174	154
GUITAR (ACOUSTIC)	59	NATIONAL	**1155** NATURAL, ROSEWOOD BRIDGE	1,571	**1,206**	1,066	940
GUITAR	41	NATIONAL	**ARISTOCRAT**	1,579	**1,212**	1,071	944
GUITAR	53	NATIONAL	**ARISTOCRAT**	955	**733**	648	571
GUITAR	54	NATIONAL	**ARISTOCRAT**	832	**638**	564	497
GUITAR	57	NATIONAL	**BEL-AIRE**	1,303	**1,001**	884	779
GUITAR	64	NATIONAL	**BLUEGRASS 35** WHITE, RESOGLASS	975	**749**	661	583
GUITAR	65	NATIONAL	**BLUEGRASS 35** RESOGLASS	947	**727**	642	566
GUITAR	51	NATIONAL	**CALIFORNIA** NATURAL, ARCHTOP	924	**709**	627	552
GUITAR	52	NATIONAL	**CALIFORNIA**	852	**644**	568	471
GUITAR	53	NATIONAL	**CLUB COMBO**	1,229	**944**	834	735
GUITAR	42	NATIONAL	**COLLEGIAN** YELLOW, MAPLE, ROUND NECK	3,993	**3,066**	2,710	2,389
GUITAR	52	NATIONAL	**COSMOPOLITAN**	642	**493**	436	384
GUITAR	31	NATIONAL	**DON #1**	6,272	**4,816**	4,256	3,752
GUITAR	35	NATIONAL	**DON #2** GEOMETRIC ENGRAVINGS	10,609	**8,146**	7,199	6,346
GUITAR	36	NATIONAL	**DON #3**	8,363	**6,421**	5,674	5,002
GUITAR	30	NATIONAL	**DUOLIAN**	2,296	**1,763**	1,558	1,373
GUITAR	30	NATIONAL	**DUOLIAN** GRAY, ROUND NECK, RESONATOR	3,533	**2,713**	2,397	2,113
GUITAR	30	NATIONAL	**DUOLIAN** 12-FRET, RESONATOR	3,895	**2,991**	2,643	2,330
GUITAR	31	NATIONAL	**DUOLIAN** 12-FRET, ROUND NECK	3,588	**2,755**	2,435	2,146
GUITAR	32	NATIONAL	**DUOLIAN** GRAY CRYSTAL	2,382	**1,829**	1,616	1,425
GUITAR	34	NATIONAL	**DUOLIAN** 14-FRET	2,306	**1,770**	1,564	1,379
GUITAR	35	NATIONAL	**DUOLIAN** GRAY, ROUND NECK, 14-FRET	3,353	**2,574**	2,275	2,005
GUITAR	37	NATIONAL	**DUOLIAN** GRAY, ROUND NECK, 14-FRET	2,061	**1,583**	1,399	1,233
GUITAR	38	NATIONAL	**DUOLIAN** BROWN, 14-FRET	2,124	**1,631**	1,441	1,270
GUITAR	35	NATIONAL	**DUOLIAN HAWAIIAN** SQUARE NECK	2,108	**1,619**	1,431	1,261
GUITAR	36	NATIONAL	**DUOLIAN HAWAIIAN** SQUARE NECK	2,061	**1,583**	1,399	1,233
GUITAR	37	NATIONAL	**DUOLIAN HAWAIIAN** SQUARE NECK	2,055	**1,578**	1,394	1,229
GUITAR	30	NATIONAL	**DUOLIAN SPANISH**	3,454	**2,652**	2,343	2,066
GUITAR	31	NATIONAL	**DUOLIAN SPANISH**	3,504	**2,690**	2,378	2,096
GUITAR	32	NATIONAL	**DUOLIAN SPANISH**	2,891	**2,220**	1,962	1,729
GUITAR	34	NATIONAL	**DUOLIAN SPANISH**	3,178	**2,440**	2,156	1,901
GUITAR	35	NATIONAL	**DUOLIAN SPANISH**	2,447	**1,879**	1,660	1,463
GUITAR	40	NATIONAL	**DUOLIAN SPANISH**	2,306	**1,770**	1,564	1,379
GUITAR	54	NATIONAL	**DYNAMIC 1125** SUNBURST, F-HOLES	590	**446**	393	326
GUITAR	30	NATIONAL	**ESTRELITA**	1,361	**1,045**	924	814
GUITAR	58	NATIONAL	**GLENWOOD** RESOGLASS	2,196	**1,686**	1,490	1,313
GUITAR	63	NATIONAL	**GLENWOOD 95** RESOGLASS	2,097	**1,610**	1,423	1,254
GUITAR	64	NATIONAL	**GLENWOOD 98** RESOGLASS	3,365	**2,584**	2,283	2,013

TYPE	YR	MFG	PRICES--BASED ON 100% ORIGINAL MODEL	SELL EXC	SELL AVG	BUY EXC	BUY AVG
GUITAR	64	NATIONAL	**GLENWOOD 99** SURF GREEN, MAP SHAPE	2,201	**1,690**	1,494	1,317
GUITAR	64	NATIONAL	**GLENWOOD 99** RESOGLASS	3,609	**2,771**	2,449	2,159
GUITAR	59	NATIONAL	**GLENWOOD DELUXE**	1,303	**1,001**	884	779
GUITAR	40	NATIONAL	**HAVANA** NATURAL, SPRUCE TOP	1,587	**1,218**	1,076	949
GUITAR	41	NATIONAL	**HAVANA** SUNBURST, SPRUCE TOP	1,303	**1,001**	884	779
GUITAR	54	NATIONAL	**JUMBO** SUNBURST, FLATTOP	772	**584**	514	427
GUITAR	67	NATIONAL	**N-720 DREADNOUGHT** NATURAL	741	**569**	503	443
GUITAR	68	NATIONAL	**N-720 DREADNOUGHT** SPRUCE TOP, MAHOGANY BACK/SIDES	731	**561**	496	437
GUITAR	68	NATIONAL	**N-730** SUNBURST, NATURAL, SPRUCE BACK/SIDES	731	**561**	496	437
GUITAR	64	NATIONAL	**NEWPORT 82** RED, MAP SHAPE, 1 PU	1,206	**926**	818	721
GUITAR	65	NATIONAL	**NEWPORT 82** RESOGLASS	984	**755**	668	588
GUITAR	64	NATIONAL	**NEWPORT 84** SEAFOAM GREEN	1,370	**1,052**	930	820
GUITAR	66	NATIONAL	**NEWPORT 84** RESOGLASS	984	**755**	668	588
GUITAR	64	NATIONAL	**NEWPORT 88** RESOGLASS	1,571	**1,206**	1,066	940
GUITAR	61	NATIONAL	**RESONATOR TOWN & COUNTY** BLACK, RESOGLASS	1,314	**1,009**	892	786
GUITAR	50	NATIONAL	**RESOPHONIC** GRAY, PEARLOID BODY	827	**635**	561	495
GUITAR	56	NATIONAL	**RESOPHONIC** BLACK	1,000	**767**	678	598
GUITAR	58	NATIONAL	**RESOPHONIC** RESONATOR	1,303	**1,001**	884	779
GUITAR	59	NATIONAL	**RESOPHONIC** GRAY	1,379	**1,059**	936	825
GUITAR	60	NATIONAL	**RESOPHONIC** GRAY, PEARLOID, RESONATOR	1,356	**1,041**	920	811
GUITAR	61	NATIONAL	**RESOPHONIC** WHITE PEARLOID	1,356	**1,041**	920	811
GUITAR	66	NATIONAL	**RESOPHONIC** WHITE PEARLOID	1,319	**1,013**	895	789
GUITAR	56	NATIONAL	**RESOPHONIC 3/4** GREEN-WHITE	1,426	**1,095**	968	853
GUITAR	30	NATIONAL	**ROSITA** SUNBURST	1,216	**933**	825	727
GUITAR	35	NATIONAL	**ROSITA**	1,333	**1,024**	905	797
GUITAR	30	NATIONAL	**STYLE 0** 12-FRET, SQUARE NECK	2,097	**1,610**	1,423	1,254
GUITAR	30	NATIONAL	**STYLE 0** BRASS	4,287	**3,292**	2,909	2,564
GUITAR	30	NATIONAL	**STYLE 0** EBONY, 14-FRET, ROUND NECK	4,401	**3,379**	2,986	2,633
GUITAR	30	NATIONAL	**STYLE 0** 12-FRET, CHROME-PLATED STEEL BODY, ETCHED HAWAIIAN SCENES	4,421	**3,395**	3,000	2,645
GUITAR	32	NATIONAL	**STYLE 0** TENOR	1,919	**1,474**	1,302	1,148
GUITAR	32	NATIONAL	**STYLE 0** 12-FRET, ROUND NECK	3,588	**2,755**	2,435	2,146
GUITAR	32	NATIONAL	**STYLE 0**	5,306	**4,074**	3,600	3,174
GUITAR	33	NATIONAL	**STYLE 0** HAWAIIAN SCENES ON BODY	3,800	**2,917**	2,578	2,273
GUITAR	34	NATIONAL	**STYLE 0** 12-FRET, SQUARE NECK	3,198	**2,456**	2,170	1,913
GUITAR	34	NATIONAL	**STYLE 0** 14-FRET, ROUND NECK	3,875	**2,975**	2,629	2,318
GUITAR	35	NATIONAL	**STYLE 0** ROUND NECK	3,646	**2,800**	2,474	2,181
GUITAR	35	NATIONAL	**STYLE 0** 14-FRET, SQUARE NECK	3,719	**2,856**	2,523	2,225
GUITAR	35	NATIONAL	**STYLE 0** 14-FRET, ROUND NECK	4,415	**3,390**	2,995	2,641
GUITAR	36	NATIONAL	**STYLE 0** METAL BODY, SQUARE NECK	3,180	**2,442**	2,158	1,902
GUITAR	37	NATIONAL	**STYLE 0** TENOR	1,912	**1,468**	1,298	1,144
GUITAR	37	NATIONAL	**STYLE 0** CHROME-PLATED BODY	4,978	**3,822**	3,378	2,978
GUITAR	38	NATIONAL	**STYLE 0** 14-FRET, ROUND NECK	3,997	**3,069**	2,712	2,391
GUITAR	40	NATIONAL	**STYLE 0** SQUARE NECK	3,366	**2,585**	2,284	2,014

TYPE	YR	MFG	PRICES--BASED ON 100% ORIGINAL MODEL	SELL EXC	SELL AVG	BUY EXC	BUY AVG
GUITAR	40	NATIONAL	**STYLE 0** 14-FRET, ROUND NECK	3,433	**2,636**	2,330	2,054
GUITAR	31	NATIONAL	**STYLE 0 CUSTOM** CHROME-PLTD BDY,STYLE #3 LILY OF THE VLLY ENGRVNG ON BODY	8,363	**6,421**	5,674	5,002
GUITAR	38	NATIONAL	**STYLE 0 HAWAIIAN** SQUARE NECK	2,293	**1,761**	1,556	1,372
GUITAR	43	NATIONAL	**STYLE 0 HAWAIIAN** 14-FRET, ROUND NECK	4,939	**3,792**	3,351	2,954
GUITAR	32	NATIONAL	**STYLE 0 SPANISH** 12-FRET, SLOT HEAD, ROUND NECK	3,944	**3,028**	2,676	2,359
GUITAR	35	NATIONAL	**STYLE 0 SPANISH**	3,896	**2,991**	2,644	2,330
GUITAR	36	NATIONAL	**STYLE 0 SPANISH**	3,997	**3,069**	2,712	2,391
GUITAR	39	NATIONAL	**STYLE 0 SPANISH**	3,827	**2,938**	2,596	2,289
GUITAR	30	NATIONAL	**STYLE 2** ROUND NECK	10,740	**8,247**	7,288	6,425
GUITAR	36	NATIONAL	**STYLE 3** PLECTRUM	2,428	**1,864**	1,647	1,452
GUITAR	38	NATIONAL	**STYLE 3** TENOR	2,378	**1,826**	1,614	1,423
GUITAR	28	NATIONAL	**STYLE 0** ROUND NECK, ROSE PATTERN	14,221	**10,920**	9,650	8,507
GUITAR	32	NATIONAL	**STYLE N** NICKEL	3,557	**2,731**	2,413	2,127
GUITAR	27	NATIONAL	**TRICONE STYLE 1** SQUARE NECK	3,999	**3,071**	2,713	2,392
GUITAR	28	NATIONAL	**TRICONE STYLE 1** TENOR	3,132	**2,405**	2,125	1,873
GUITAR	28	NATIONAL	**TRICONE STYLE 1** SQUARE NECK	4,428	**3,400**	3,005	2,649
GUITAR	28	NATIONAL	**TRICONE STYLE 1** ROUND NECK	7,152	**5,491**	4,853	4,278
GUITAR	29	NATIONAL	**TRICONE STYLE 1** SQUARE NECK	4,036	**3,099**	2,739	2,414
GUITAR	30	NATIONAL	**TRICONE STYLE 1** TENOR	1,915	**1,470**	1,299	1,145
GUITAR	30	NATIONAL	**TRICONE STYLE 1** SQUARE NECK	4,006	**3,076**	2,718	2,396
GUITAR	30	NATIONAL	**TRICONE STYLE 1** ROUND NECK	7,109	**5,459**	4,824	4,253
GUITAR	32	NATIONAL	**TRICONE STYLE 1** TENOR	2,065	**1,585**	1,401	1,235
GUITAR	32	NATIONAL	**TRICONE STYLE 1** ROUND NECK	6,969	**5,351**	4,729	4,169
GUITAR	40	NATIONAL	**TRICONE STYLE 1** SQUARE NECK	3,405	**2,615**	2,311	2,037
GUITAR	31	NATIONAL	**TRICONE STYLE 1 HAWAIIAN**	3,992	**3,065**	2,709	2,388
GUITAR	29	NATIONAL	**TRICONE STYLE 1 SPANISH**	7,264	**5,577**	4,929	4,345
GUITAR	27	NATIONAL	**TRICONE STYLE 2** ROUND NECK	11,872	**9,116**	8,056	7,102
GUITAR	28	NATIONAL	**TRICONE STYLE 2** ROUND NECK	6,272	**4,816**	4,256	3,752
GUITAR	28	NATIONAL	**TRICONE STYLE 2** SQUARE NECK	6,287	**4,828**	4,266	3,761
GUITAR	29	NATIONAL	**TRICONE STYLE 2** SQUARE NECK	7,666	**5,886**	5,202	4,586
GUITAR	30	NATIONAL	**TRICONE STYLE 2** SQUARE NECK	6,272	**4,816**	4,256	3,752
GUITAR	30	NATIONAL	**TRICONE STYLE 2** ROUND NECK	7,666	**5,886**	5,202	4,586
GUITAR	31	NATIONAL	**TRICONE STYLE 2** SQUARE NECK	4,841	**3,717**	3,285	2,896
GUITAR	32	NATIONAL	**TRICONE STYLE 2** ROSE PATTERN ENGRAVING	10,365	**7,959**	7,033	6,200
GUITAR	30	NATIONAL	**TRICONE STYLE 2 HAWAIIAN**	4,314	**3,312**	2,927	2,580
GUITAR	30	NATIONAL	**TRICONE STYLE 2 SPANISH**	10,167	**7,807**	6,899	6,082
GUITAR	28	NATIONAL	**TRICONE STYLE 2.5** SQUARE NECK	5,057	**3,883**	3,432	3,025
GUITAR	27	NATIONAL	**TRICONE STYLE 3**	28,455	**21,850**	19,309	17,022
GUITAR	28	NATIONAL	**TRICONE STYLE 3** PLECTRUM	3,693	**2,836**	2,506	2,209
GUITAR	28	NATIONAL	**TRICONE STYLE 3**	38,897	**29,867**	26,394	23,269
GUITAR	29	NATIONAL	**TRICONE STYLE 3** ROUND NECK	13,977	**10,732**	9,484	8,361
GUITAR	30	NATIONAL	**TRICONE STYLE 3** SQUARE NECK	8,712	**6,689**	5,912	5,211
GUITAR	30	NATIONAL	**TRICONE STYLE 3** ROUND NECK	14,471	**11,112**	9,819	8,657
GUITAR	31	NATIONAL	**TRICONE STYLE 3** ROUND NECK	14,702	**11,289**	9,976	8,795
GUITAR	31	NATIONAL	**TRICONE STYLE 3 HAWAIIAN** SQUARE NECK	8,758	**6,725**	5,943	5,239
GUITAR	29	NATIONAL	**TRICONE STYLE 3 SPANISH**	14,138	**10,856**	9,594	8,458

TYPE	YR	MFG	PRICES--BASED ON 100% ORIGINAL MODEL	SELL EXC	SELL AVG	BUY EXC	BUY AVG
GUITAR	29	NATIONAL	**TRICONE STYLE 4** SQUARE NECK	10,603	**8,141**	7,194	6,342
GUITAR	30	NATIONAL	**TRICONE STYLE 4** SQUARE NECK	10,457	**8,029**	7,096	6,255
GUITAR	33	NATIONAL	**TRICONE STYLE 4** ROUND NECK	31,118	**23,894**	21,115	18,615
GUITAR	39	NATIONAL	**TRICONE STYLE 4** SQUARE NECK	9,011	**6,919**	6,114	5,390
GUITAR	35	NATIONAL	**TRICONE STYLE 4 HAWAIIAN**	10,717	**8,229**	7,272	6,411
GUITAR	37	NATIONAL	**TRICONE STYLE 4 SPANISH**	20,380	**15,649**	13,829	12,191
GUITAR	39	NATIONAL	**TRICONE STYLE 35 HAWAIIAN**	3,002	**2,305**	2,037	1,796
GUITAR	38	NATIONAL	**TRICONE STYLE 35 SPANISH**	4,421	**3,395**	3,000	2,645
GUITAR	37	NATIONAL	**TRICONE STYLE 92 SPANISH**	3,441	**2,642**	2,335	2,058
GUITAR	38	NATIONAL	**TRICONE STYLE 97 HAWAIIAN**	5,389	**4,138**	3,657	3,224
GUITAR	28	NATIONAL	**TRIOLIAN** BROWN SUNBURST, ARCHTOP	2,406	**1,848**	1,633	1,439
GUITAR	28	NATIONAL	**TRIOLIAN**	2,976	**2,285**	2,020	1,780
GUITAR	28	NATIONAL	**TRIOLIAN** YELLOW, RESONATOR	3,398	**2,609**	2,305	2,032
GUITAR	29	NATIONAL	**TRIOLIAN** TENOR	1,762	**1,353**	1,196	1,054
GUITAR	29	NATIONAL	**TRIOLIAN** BROWN SUNBURST, 12-FRET, SLOT HEAD, ROUND NECK	3,091	**2,373**	2,097	1,849
GUITAR	29	NATIONAL	**TRIOLIAN** YELLOW	3,373	**2,590**	2,289	2,018
GUITAR	30	NATIONAL	**TRIOLIAN** PLECTRUM, SUNBURST	1,302	**1,000**	883	779
GUITAR	30	NATIONAL	**TRIOLIAN** TENOR, YELLOW	1,721	**1,321**	1,168	1,029
GUITAR	30	NATIONAL	**TRIOLIAN** RESONATOR	3,113	**2,390**	2,112	1,862
GUITAR	30	NATIONAL	**TRIOLIAN** BROWN SUNBURST, YELLOW, 12-FRET	3,307	**2,539**	2,244	1,978
GUITAR	30	NATIONAL	**TRIOLIAN** YELLOW	3,346	**2,569**	2,270	2,001
GUITAR	31	NATIONAL	**TRIOLIAN** BROWN SUNBURST	2,969	**2,279**	2,014	1,776
GUITAR	31	NATIONAL	**TRIOLIAN** YELLOW	3,991	**3,065**	2,708	2,387
GUITAR	32	NATIONAL	**TRIOLIAN** TENOR, SUNBURST, RESONATOR	1,618	**1,242**	1,098	968
GUITAR	32	NATIONAL	**TRIOLIAN** TENOR, YELLOW	1,727	**1,326**	1,171	1,033
GUITAR	32	NATIONAL	**TRIOLIAN** SUNBURST, ROUND NECK	1,995	**1,532**	1,354	1,193
GUITAR	32	NATIONAL	**TRIOLIAN** BROWN SUNBURST, METAL BODY	2,340	**1,797**	1,588	1,400
GUITAR	32	NATIONAL	**TRIOLIAN** SUNBURST, ROUND NECK	2,462	**1,891**	1,671	1,473
GUITAR	33	NATIONAL	**TRIOLIAN** TENOR	1,512	**1,161**	1,026	904
GUITAR	33	NATIONAL	**TRIOLIAN** BROWN SUNBURST, 12-FRET	3,575	**2,745**	2,425	2,138
GUITAR	34	NATIONAL	**TRIOLIAN** BROWN SUNBURST	3,046	**2,339**	2,067	1,822
GUITAR	35	NATIONAL	**TRIOLIAN** BROWN SUNBURST, METAL BODY	2,298	**1,764**	1,559	1,374
GUITAR	35	NATIONAL	**TRIOLIAN** BROWN SUNBURST, YELLOW	2,411	**1,851**	1,636	1,442
GUITAR	35	NATIONAL	**TRIOLIAN** SUNBURST, 14-FRET	3,519	**2,702**	2,387	2,105
GUITAR	36	NATIONAL	**TRIOLIAN** TENOR, CRYSTAL FINISH	999	**767**	677	597
GUITAR	36	NATIONAL	**TRIOLIAN** METAL BODY, 14-FRET, ROUND NECK	2,260	**1,735**	1,533	1,352
GUITAR	36	NATIONAL	**TRIOLIAN** ROSEWOOD, METAL BODY	2,269	**1,742**	1,539	1,357
GUITAR	36	NATIONAL	**TRIOLIAN**	3,971	**3,049**	2,694	2,375
GUITAR	37	NATIONAL	**TRIOLIAN** 14-FRET, SQUARE NECK	1,787	**1,372**	1,212	1,069
GUITAR	37	NATIONAL	**TRIOLIAN** WOOD GRAIN, METAL BODY	2,072	**1,591**	1,406	1,239
GUITAR	37	NATIONAL	**TRIOLIAN** BROWN SUNBURST, 14-FRET	2,264	**1,738**	1,536	1,354
GUITAR	30	NATIONAL	**TRIOLIAN HAWAIIAN**	2,948	**2,264**	2,001	1,764
GUITAR	29	NATIONAL	**TRIOLIAN HAWAIIAN GIRL** YELLOW	4,027	**3,092**	2,732	2,409
GUITAR	30	NATIONAL	**TRIOLIAN SPANISH**	2,107	**1,618**	1,430	1,260
GUITAR	35	NATIONAL	**TRIOLIAN SPANISH**	2,108	**1,619**	1,431	1,261
GUITAR	30	NATIONAL	**TRIOLIAN UKE** BROWN SUNBURST, METAL BODY	2,335	**1,793**	1,584	1,396
GUITAR	28	NATIONAL	**TRIPLATE STYLE 2** TENOR, 4-STRING	2,468	**1,895**	1,675	1,476

TYPE	YR	MFG	PRICES--BASED ON 100% ORIGINAL MODEL	SELL EXC	SELL AVG	BUY EXC	BUY AVG
GUITAR	30	NATIONAL	**TRIPLATE STYLE 2** SQUARE NECK	3,992	**3,065**	2,709	2,388
GUITAR	30	NATIONAL	**TRIPLATE STYLE 3** ROUND NECK	13,189	**10,127**	8,949	7,889
GUITAR	30	NATIONAL	**TRIPLATE STYLE 4** SQUARE NECK	9,938	**7,631**	6,744	5,945
GUITAR	30	NATIONAL	**TRIPLATE STYLE 4** ROUND NECK	16,544	**12,703**	11,226	9,897
GUITAR	30	NATIONAL	**TROJAN** WOOD BODY. 14-FRET, SQUARE NECK, RESONATOR	1,329	**1,020**	902	795
GUITAR	30	NATIONAL	**TROJAN** WOOD BODY, 14-FRET, ROUND NECK	1,889	**1,450**	1,282	1,130
GUITAR	33	NATIONAL	**TROJAN** WOOD BODY	1,974	**1,516**	1,339	1,181
GUITAR	35	NATIONAL	**TROJAN** SUNBURST, WOOD BODY	1,747	**1,341**	1,185	1,045
GUITAR	38	NATIONAL	**TROJAN** WOOD BODY	1,743	**1,339**	1,183	1,043
GUITAR	45	NATIONAL	**TROJAN** SUNBURST, ROUND NECK w/BINDING	863	**663**	585	516
GUITAR	34	NATIONAL	**TROJAN HAWAIIAN** WOOD BODY	1,033	**793**	701	618
GUITAR	29	NATIONAL	**TROJAN SPANISH** WOOD BODY	1,653	**1,269**	1,121	988
GUITAR	36	NATIONAL	**TROJAN SPANISH** WOOD BODY	988	**747**	659	546
GUITAR	62	NATIONAL	**WESTWOOD 75** MAP SHAPED	792	**608**	538	474
GUITAR	65	NATIONAL	**WESTWOOD 77** CHERRY	797	**612**	541	477
MANDOLIN	51	NATIONAL	**1135** ICE TEA SUNBURST,GIBSON L-7 BODY,SPLIT HALF CIRCLE INLAY	959	**737**	651	574
MANDOL	39	NATIONAL	**SILVO** CHROME-PLATED METAL BODY	1,662	**1,276**	1,127	994
MANDOL	30	NATIONAL	**STYLE 0**	2,989	**2,295**	2,028	1,788
MANDOL	29	NATIONAL	**STYLE 1** SHINY FINISH	2,377	**1,825**	1,613	1,422
MANDOL	30	NATIONAL	**STYLE 2**	2,989	**2,295**	2,028	1,788
MANDOL	29	NATIONAL	**TRIOLIAN** SUNBURST	2,270	**1,743**	1,540	1,358
MANDOL	30	NATIONAL	**TRIOLIAN** SUNBURST	1,863	**1,431**	1,264	1,114
STEEL GUITAR	40	NATIONAL	**6-STRING LAP STEEL** BROWN	604	**464**	410	361
STGUIT	40	NATIONAL	**CHICAGO LAP STEEL** MAHOGANY SUNBURST	613	**471**	416	367
STGUIT	48	NATIONAL	**CHICAGO LAP STEEL** GRAY PEARLOID, 1 PU	472	**362**	320	282
STGUIT	53	NATIONAL	**CHICAGO LAP STEEL**	430	**330**	291	257
STGUIT	60	NATIONAL	**CHICAGO LAP STEEL** GRAY	451	**346**	306	270
STGUIT	39	NATIONAL	**CONSOLE** BLACK & WHITE, 2 8-STRING NECKS	753	**578**	511	450
STGUIT	51	NATIONAL	**DOUBLE-8 LAP STEEL** WHITE	973	**747**	660	582
STGUIT	48	NATIONAL	**DYNAMIC LAP STEEL**	517	**397**	351	309
STGUIT	52	NATIONAL	**DYNAMIC LAP STEEL** BLACK & WHITE ART DECO	538	**413**	365	322
STGUIT	62	NATIONAL	**DYNAMIC LAP STEEL** RED, WHITE & BLACK, 6-STRING. 3 LEGS	580	**445**	393	347
STGUIT	42	NATIONAL	**DYNAMIC NEW YORK STYLE** BLACK & WHITE	632	**485**	429	378
STGUIT	48	NATIONAL	**GRAND CONSOLE** COPPER. 2 8-STRING NECKS	677	**520**	459	405
STGUIT	49	NATIONAL	**GRAND CONSOLE** COPPER, 2 8-STRING NECKS	756	**580**	513	452
STGUIT	50	NATIONAL	**GRAND CONSOLE** COPPER, 2 8-STRING NECKS	750	**576**	509	448
STGUIT	36	NATIONAL	**NEW YORKER** BLACK & WHITE ART DECO	701	**538**	475	419
STGUIT	38	NATIONAL	**NEW YORKER** BLACK & WHITE ART DECO	663	**509**	449	396
STGUIT	39	NATIONAL	**NEW YORKER**	682	**523**	462	408
STGUIT	40	NATIONAL	**NEW YORKER** NATURAL	632	**485**	429	378
STGUIT	41	NATIONAL	**NEW YORKER** NATURAL	605	**465**	411	362
STGUIT	42	NATIONAL	**NEW YORKER** BLACK & WHITE ART DECO	589	**452**	399	352
STGUIT	42	NATIONAL	**NEW YORKER** NATURAL, SPANISH SPRUCE TOP	992	**761**	673	593
STGUIT	47	NATIONAL	**NEW YORKER** BLACK & WHITE ART DECO	555	**426**	376	332

TYPE	YR	MFG	MODEL	SELL EXC	SELL AVG	BUY EXC	BUY AVG
STGUIT	49	NATIONAL	**NEW YORKER** BLACK/WHITE	605	**465**	411	362
STGUIT	54	NATIONAL	**NEW YORKER** NATURAL	621	**477**	421	371
STGUIT	55	NATIONAL	**NEW YORKER** NATURAL	612	**470**	415	366
STGUIT	48	NATIONAL	**PRINCESS STEEL** WHITE PEARLOID	605	**465**	411	362
STGUIT	33	NATIONAL	**PROFESSIONAL HAWAIIAN LAP STEEL**	789	**606**	535	472
STGUIT	58	NATIONAL	**ROCKET ONE** BLACK, 10-STRING	724	**556**	491	433
STGUIT	58	NATIONAL	**ROCKET ONE TEN** BLACK & WHITE	708	**544**	481	424
STGUIT	64	NATIONAL	**ROCKET ONE TEN** WHITE, ROCKET SHAPE	554	**425**	376	331
STGUIT	50	NATIONAL	**TRAILBLAZER** CREAM	472	**362**	320	282
STGUIT	50	NATIONAL	**TRIPLEX 1088** NATURAL, MAPLE	603	**463**	409	361
STGUIT	50	NATIONAL	**TRIPLEX CHORD CHANGER LAP STEEL**	570	**437**	386	341
UKULELE	33	NATIONAL	**STYLE 1**	4,019	**3,086**	2,727	2,404

NEUMANN

TYPE	YR	MFG	MODEL	SELL EXC	SELL AVG	BUY EXC	BUY AVG
MIC	28	NEUMANN	**CMV-3 "NEUMANN BOTTLE"** TUBE	5,210	**4,000**	3,535	3,116
MIC	49	NEUMANN	**CMV-5B** CONDENSER, M7 CAPSULE	3,578	**2,747**	2,428	2,140
MIC	53	NEUMANN	**KM-53i**	2,400	**1,842**	1,628	1,435
MIC	53	NEUMANN	**KM-54iA** BLACK, CONDENSER	1,880	**1,443**	1,276	1,124
MIC	54	NEUMANN	**KM-54iA** SILVER, CONDENSER	1,880	**1,443**	1,276	1,124
MIC	55	NEUMANN	**KM-56i**	3,500	**2,687**	2,375	2,093
MIC	64-71	NEUMANN	**KM-64i** TUBE	1,296	**995**	880	775
MIC	66	NEUMANN	**KM-83i** OMNI FET	1,024	**786**	695	613
MIC	66	NEUMANN	**KM-84i** XLR CARDIOID FET-80	1,024	**786**	695	613
MIC	66	NEUMANN	**KM-85i** XLR CARDIOID LOW FREQUENCY	1,018	**781**	690	609
MIC	98	NEUMANN	**KM-100** OUTPUT STAGE MODULE	583	**448**	395	349
MIC	63	NEUMANN	**KM-254i** LARGE DIAPHRAGM TUBE	1,815	**1,394**	1,231	1,086
MIC	66	NEUMANN	**KM-264i**	1,454	**1,117**	987	870
MIC	51	NEUMANN	**M-49** LARGE DIAPHRAGM TUBE	9,979	**7,662**	6,771	5,969
MIC	54	NEUMANN	**M-49B**	10,227	**7,853**	6,940	6,118
MIC	55	NEUMANN	**M-49C** MONO, TUBE CONDENSER	9,979	**7,662**	6,771	5,969
MIC	51	NEUMANN	**M-50** OMNIDIRECTIONAL TUBE	11,333	**8,702**	7,690	6,779
MIC	60	NEUMANN	**M-249** LARGE DIAPHRAGM TUBE	10,609	**8,146**	7,199	6,346
MIC	62	NEUMANN	**M-269** LARGE DIAPHRAGM TUBE	10,728	**8,237**	7,280	6,417
MIC	74	NEUMANN	**QM-69** QUAD	7,231	**5,553**	4,907	4,326
MIC	57	NEUMANN	**SM-2**	3,454	**2,652**	2,343	2,066
MIC	57	NEUMANN	**SM-2** STEREO	3,841	**2,949**	2,606	2,298
MIC	61	NEUMANN	**SM-23**	3,722	**2,858**	2,526	2,227
MIC	64	NEUMANN	**SM-69** STEREO TUBE, LARGE DIAPHRAGM, FET	5,234	**4,019**	3,552	3,131
MIC	65	NEUMANN	**SM-69** STEREO TUBE	4,896	**3,759**	3,322	2,929
MIC	49	NEUMANN	**U-47** VF-14 TUBE	8,607	**6,609**	5,840	5,148
MIC	49	NEUMANN	**U-47** LONG, CHROME	9,356	**7,184**	6,349	5,597
MIC	69	NEUMANN	**U-47 fet** CARDIOID FET-80	2,367	**1,818**	1,606	1,416
MIC	57	NEUMANN	**U-48** LARGE DIAPHRAGM TUBE	8,731	**6,704**	5,924	5,223
MIC	60	NEUMANN	**U-67** 3 PATTERN LARGE DIAPHRAGM TUBE w/POWER SUPPLY	5,244	**4,027**	3,559	3,137
MIC	67	NEUMANN	**U-87i** 3 PATTERN FET-80	3,579	**2,748**	2,428	2,141

OAHU

TYPE	YR	MFG	MODEL	SELL EXC	SELL AVG	BUY EXC	BUY AVG
ELEC. GUITAR & BASS	49	OAHU	**OAHU** SUPRO STYLE PU	415	**319**	281	248

TYPE	YR	MFG	PRICES--BASED ON 100% ORIGINAL MODEL	SELL EXC	SELL AVG	BUY EXC	BUY AVG
ELGUIT	51	OAHU	**OAHU** 2-6-STRING NECKS	412	**316**	279	246
GUITAR AMP	49	OAHU	**TUNEMASTER**	548	**421**	372	328
GTAMP	50	OAHU	**TUNEMASTER**	430	**330**	291	257
STEEL GUITAR	30	OAHU	**HAWAIIAN LAP STEEL** SUNBURST, SQUARE NECK	539	**414**	366	322
STGUIT	50	OAHU	**LOLANA DUAL** 6-STRING, GOLD HARDWARE	724	**556**	491	433
STGUIT	52	OAHU	**LOLANA DUAL 6 LAP STEEL**	762	**585**	517	456

OLDKRAFT

TYPE	YR	MFG	MODEL	SELL EXC	SELL AVG	BUY EXC	BUY AVG
ELEC. GUITAR & BASS	58	OLDKRAFT	**THIN TWIN JIMMY REED**	663	**509**	449	396
ELGUIT	60	OLDKRAFT	**THIN TWIN JIMMY REED**	661	**508**	449	395
GUITAR (ACOUSTIC)	36	OLDKRAFT	**16" WIDE** SUNBURST, CURLY MAPLE	1,361	**1,045**	924	814
GUITAR	38	OLDKRAFT	**OLD KRAFTSMAN** METAL BODY	1,533	**1,177**	1,040	917

ORANGE

TYPE	YR	MFG	MODEL	SELL EXC	SELL AVG	BUY EXC	BUY AVG
GUITAR AMP	75	ORANGE	**BASS 113** CABINET, 2x15", 120 WATT	1,263	**970**	857	755
GTAMP	74	ORANGE	**BASS 114** 1x15", 60 WATT, CABINET	759	**583**	515	454
GTAMP	76	ORANGE	**COMBO 5** 2x12", 120 WATT	1,424	**1,093**	966	852
GTAMP	78	ORANGE	**GRAPHIC 112** OVERDRIVE HEAD	745	**572**	506	446
GTAMP	76	ORANGE	**GRAPHIC 120**	1,033	**793**	701	618

OVATION INSTRUMENTS

TYPE	YR	MFG	MODEL	SELL EXC	SELL AVG	BUY EXC	BUY AVG
ELEC. GUITAR & BASS	75	OVATION	**BREADWINNER** BLACK, 2 PU's	468	**359**	317	280
ELGUIT	84	OVATION	**CLASSIC** DEEP BOWL, GOLD-PLATED TUNERS	476	**365**	323	284
ELGUIT	74	OVATION	**CLASSICAL ELECTRIC FLATTOP**	656	**503**	445	392
ELGUIT	70	OVATION	**DEACON** 12-STRING	557	**428**	378	333
ELGUIT	70	OVATION	**H 218** BLACK, DOUBLE CUTAWAY, THIN BODY	636	**488**	431	380
ELGUIT	67	OVATION	**HURRICANE** SUNBURST, 12-STRING	1,002	**769**	680	599
ELGUIT	68	OVATION	**HURRICANE** SUNBURST, 12-STRING	1,002	**769**	680	599
ELGUIT	78	OVATION	**MAGNUM BASS I 1261** VINTAGE CHERRY, SOLID BODY	612	**470**	415	366
ELGUIT	68	OVATION	**MONSOON** BURGUNDY, CHERRY, DOUBLE CUTAWAY, 2 PU's	611	**469**	414	365
ELGUIT	68	OVATION	**MONSOON 1272** BURGUNDY, CHERRY, DOUBLE CUTAWAY, 2 PU's	640	**491**	434	383
ELGUIT	70	OVATION	**PREACHER**	553	**424**	375	330
ELGUIT	72	OVATION	**PREACHER** SERIAL #7000	543	**417**	368	324
ELGUIT	74	OVATION	**PREACHER** RED MAHOGANY	669	**514**	454	400
ELGUIT	78	OVATION	**PREACHER 1281** SOLID BODY	633	**486**	430	379
ELGUIT	76	OVATION	**PREACHER DELUXE** SERIAL #67000-86000	567	**436**	385	339
ELGUIT	68	OVATION	**TORNADO** BURGUNDY, DOUBLE CUTAWAY, 2 PU's	636	**488**	431	380
ELGUIT	70	OVATION	**TORNADO 1260**	573	**440**	389	343
ELGUIT	70	OVATION	**TYPHOON BASS** RED	327	**251**	221	195
ELGUIT	77	OVATION	**UK-II** SUNBURST	705	**541**	478	422
ELGUIT	78	OVATION	**UK-II** GRAY SUNBURST, ABALONE INLAY, SERIAL #114001-157000	616	**473**	418	368
ELGUIT	80	OVATION	**UK-II** BLACK,K ABALONE INLAY	577	**443**	392	345
ELGUIT	74	OVATION	**VIPER**	535	**411**	363	320
ELGUIT	77	OVATION	**VIPER** SERIAL #86000-114000	603	**463**	409	361
GUITAR AMP	78	OVATION	**MAGNUM II BASS** PREAMP, EQUALIZER	533	**409**	361	318
GUITAR (ACOUSTIC)	75	OVATION	**1112-1** SUNBURST, DIAMOND INLAYS	747	**573**	506	446
GUITAR	66	OVATION	**1115** BLACK, 12-STRING	822	**631**	557	491
GUITAR	74	OVATION	**1115-1** SUNBURST, 12-STRING	717	**551**	487	429
GUITAR	66	OVATION	**1115-4** BLACK	846	**650**	574	506
GUITAR	78	OVATION	**1612-4** NATURAL	700	**537**	475	418

TYPE	YR	MFG	PRICES--BASED ON 100% ORIGINAL MODEL	SELL EXC	SELL AVG	BUY EXC	BUY AVG
GUITAR	75	OVATION	1617 ACOUSTIC/ELECTRIC SUNBURST	660	507	448	395
GUITAR	75	OVATION	1617 BALLADEER RED TOP	695	534	471	416
GUITAR	77	OVATION	ADAMAS GRAY-BEIGE	1,319	1,013	895	789
GUITAR	78	OVATION	ADAMAS BLUE	846	650	574	506
GUITAR	78	OVATION	ADAMAS YELLOW AND BLUE SUNBURST	846	650	574	506
GUITAR	70	OVATION	ADAMAS II BROWN	1,352	1,038	918	809
GUITAR	61	OVATION	BALLADEER 1861, SUNBURST	1,736	1,333	1,178	1,038
GUITAR	67	OVATION	BALLADEER IVORY	1,678	1,289	1,139	1,004
GUITAR	68	OVATION	BALLADEER IVORY	1,330	1,021	902	795
GUITAR	69	OVATION	BALLADEER IVORY	1,008	774	684	603
GUITAR	72	OVATION	BALLADEER NATURAL	922	708	626	552
GUITAR	77	OVATION	BALLADEER IVORY	954	732	647	570
GUITAR	78	OVATION	BALLADEER IVORY	911	700	618	545
GUITAR	68	OVATION	BALLADEER DELUXE NATURAL	660	507	448	395
GUITAR	77	OVATION	BALLADEER DELUXE SUNBURST	857	658	582	513
GUITAR	74	OVATION	COUNTRY ARTIST NYLON STRING	769	590	522	460
GUITAR	76	OVATION	CUSTOM LEGEND	1,324	1,017	899	792
GUITAR	68	OVATION	ELITE NATURAL, SINGLE CUTAWAY, SHALLOW BOWL	1,342	1,031	911	803
GUITAR	69	OVATION	GLEN CAMPBELL	1,470	1,129	997	879
GUITAR	71	OVATION	GLEN CAMPBELL	1,357	1,042	921	812
GUITAR	72	OVATION	GLEN CAMPBELL	1,317	1,011	893	787
GUITAR	75	OVATION	GLEN CAMPBELL SIGNATURE 12-STRING	1,712	1,314	1,162	1,024
GUITAR	68	OVATION	JOSH WHITE	686	527	465	410
GUITAR	36	OVATION	M-2 SUNBURST, L-50 SIZE	857	658	582	513
GUITAR	40	OVATION	M-2 SUNBURST	734	564	498	439
GUITAR	70	OVATION	THUNDERHEAD SEMI-HOLLOW	623	479	423	373

PARAMOUNT

TYPE	YR	MFG	MODEL	SELL EXC	SELL AVG	BUY EXC	BUY AVG
BANJO	28	PARAMOUNT	ARISTOCRAT TENOR	2,219	1,704	1,506	1,327
BANJO	30	PARAMOUNT	ARTIST SUPREME PLECTRUM	9,867	7,576	6,695	5,902
BANJO	33	PARAMOUNT	ARTIST SUPREME PLECTRUM	8,688	6,671	5,896	5,197
BANJO	28	PARAMOUNT	BANNER BLUE TENOR, WALNUT, RESONATOR	797	612	541	477
BANJO	25	PARAMOUNT	LEADER TENOR, ROSEWOOD NECK/RESONATOR	1,563	1,200	1,060	935
BANJO	27	PARAMOUNT	LEADER TENOR, 19-FRET	1,328	1,019	901	794
BANJO	25	PARAMOUNT	LEADER POT ROSEWOOD NECK, 5-STRING	2,232	1,713	1,514	1,335
BANJO	28	PARAMOUNT	LEADER SPECIAL TENOR, BRAZILIAN ROSEWOOD	3,778	2,901	2,564	2,260
BANJO	25	PARAMOUNT	PAL TENOR	926	711	628	554
BANJO	25	PARAMOUNT	STYLE 1 TENOR	1,990	1,528	1,350	1,190
BANJO	22	PARAMOUNT	STYLE A PLECTRUM	2,119	1,627	1,437	1,267
BANJO	24	PARAMOUNT	STYLE A TENOR	1,758	1,350	1,193	1,051
BANJO	25	PARAMOUNT	STYLE A TENOR	1,361	1,045	924	814
BANJO	25	PARAMOUNT	STYLE A PLECTRUM	2,160	1,658	1,466	1,292
BANJO	27	PARAMOUNT	STYLE A TENOR	1,283	985	870	767
BANJO	28	PARAMOUNT	STYLE A TENOR	1,290	990	875	771
BANJO	28	PARAMOUNT	STYLE A PLECTRUM	1,356	1,041	920	811

TYPE	YR	MFG	PRICES--BASED ON 100% ORIGINAL MODEL	SELL EXC	SELL AVG	BUY EXC	BUY AVG
BANJO	22	PARAMOUNT	STYLE B TENOR, NATURAL	1,905	1,462	1,292	1,139
BANJO	23	PARAMOUNT	STYLE B TENOR	1,808	1,388	1,227	1,082
BANJO	25	PARAMOUNT	STYLE B TENOR	1,986	1,525	1,348	1,188
BANJO	26	PARAMOUNT	STYLE B TENOR	1,298	996	880	776
BANJO	20	PARAMOUNT	STYLE C TENOR	2,384	1,830	1,618	1,426
BANJO	25	PARAMOUNT	STYLE C TENOR, 19-FRET, SERIAL #2781	1,949	1,497	1,323	1,166
BANJO	26	PARAMOUNT	STYLE C TENOR	1,636	1,256	1,110	978
BANJO	27	PARAMOUNT	STYLE C TENOR	1,932	1,483	1,311	1,155
BANJO	29	PARAMOUNT	STYLE C TENOR	1,518	1,166	1,030	908
BANJO	25	PARAMOUNT	STYLE D PLECTRUM	3,643	2,797	2,472	2,179
BANJO	28	PARAMOUNT	STYLE D TENOR	3,355	2,576	2,276	2,007
BANJO	26	PARAMOUNT	STYLE E TENOR, HOLLY NECK/RESONATOR	3,071	2,358	2,083	1,837
BANJO	22	PARAMOUNT	STYLE F TENOR	5,968	4,582	4,050	3,570
BANJO	25	PARAMOUNT	STYLE F TENOR	4,840	3,716	3,284	2,895
BANJO	27	PARAMOUNT	STYLE F TENOR, GOLD-PLATED, ENGRAVED	6,451	4,953	4,377	3,859
BANJO	28	PARAMOUNT	STYLE F TENOR	4,008	3,077	2,720	2,397
BANJO	29	PARAMOUNT	STYLE F TENOR	5,059	3,884	3,432	3,026
BANJO	31	PARAMOUNT	STYLE X 5-STRING	2,142	1,645	1,453	1,281
BANJO	30	PARAMOUNT	SUPER PARAMOUNT PROFESSIONAL TENOR	6,163	4,732	4,182	3,687
BANJO	33	PARAMOUNT	SUPER PARAMOUNT PROFESSIONAL TENOR	4,237	3,203	2,824	2,342

PARK

TYPE	YR	MFG	MODEL	SELL EXC	SELL AVG	BUY EXC	BUY AVG
GUITAR AMP	68	PARK	MODEL 75 AMP HEAD 2xKT88, SMALL BOX PLEXI	1,599	1,228	1,085	956

PEAVEY

TYPE	YR	MFG	MODEL	SELL EXC	SELL AVG	BUY EXC	BUY AVG
BASS AMP	83	PEAVEY	MAX BASS FC @ 4 OHM AMP HEAD, FLIGHT CASE	579	444	392	346
ELEC. GUITAR & BASS	83-88	PEAVEY	T-15 AMP IN CASE	200	153	136	119
ELGUIT	83-88	PEAVEY	T-15 NATURAL, MAPLE, GRAFT CASE ONLY	217	166	147	129
ELGUIT	79	PEAVEY	T-25 SUNBURST, SYNTHETIC BODY, 2 PU's	163	125	110	97
ELGUIT	79	PEAVEY	T-27 LTD	277	213	188	166
ELGUIT	78	PEAVEY	T-60 ASH BODY, DOUBLE CUTAWAY, 2 HB PU's	537	412	364	321
GUITAR AMP	75	PEAVEY	ARTIST VI 1x12", 120 WATT, 3-BAND EQ	238	183	161	142
GTAMP	77	PEAVEY	BACKSTAGE	140	107	95	83
GTAMP	74	PEAVEY	CLASSIC BLACK, 2x12", TUBE, REVERB	358	275	243	214
GTAMP	80	PEAVEY	DEUCE 2-12" SPEAKERS, 120 WATT	274	210	186	164
GTAMP	78	PEAVEY	HERITAGE PHASE SHIFT	446	343	303	267
GTAMP	75	PEAVEY	LTD	206	158	139	123
GTAMP	84-88	PEAVEY	RENOWN 2x12" SPEAKERS, 160 WATT	379	291	257	227
GTAMP	79	PEAVEY	STANDARD HEAD	358	275	243	214

PHILLIPS

TYPE	YR	MFG	MODEL	SELL EXC	SELL AVG	BUY EXC	BUY AVG
MIC	38	PHILLIPS	TORPEDO AUSTRALIAN	295	227	200	176

PIMENTEL

TYPE	YR	MFG	MODEL	SELL EXC	SELL AVG	BUY EXC	BUY AVG
GUITAR (ACOUSTIC)	76	PIMENTEL	001-A MAHOGANY BACK/SIDES	1,228	943	833	734

POLLMAN

TYPE	YR	MFG	MODEL	SELL EXC	SELL AVG	BUY EXC	BUY AVG
UPRIG	73	POLLMAN	4-STRING LION'S HEAD	15,973	12,265	10,839	9,555
UPRIGHT	73	POLLMAN	5-STRING BASS HIGHLY FLAMED	16,256	12,482	11,031	9,725

TYPE	YR	MFG	PRICES--BASED ON 100% ORIGINAL MODEL	SELL EXC	SELL AVG	BUY EXC	BUY AVG
			POLYTONE				
GUITAR AMP	77	POLYTONE	MINIBRITE III	633	**486**	430	379
			PPG				
SYNTHESIZER	80	PPG	PPG 2.2	785	**602**	532	469
SYNTH	80	PPG	PPG 2.2 MIDI	1,062	**816**	721	635
SYNTH	80	PPG	PPG 2.3	1,047	**804**	710	626
			PREMIER				
GUITAR AMP	65	PREMIER	B-160 CLUB BASS 6V6 TUBES	478	**367**	324	286
GTAMP	69	PREMIER	B-160 CLUB BASS	478	**367**	324	286
GTAMP	57	PREMIER	MODEL 50 1x10" SPEAKER, COMBO	327	**251**	221	195
GTAMP	65	PREMIER	MODEL 90 REVERB	470	**361**	319	281
GTAMP	66	PREMIER	TWIN 8 2x8" COMBO	478	**367**	324	286
GUITAR (ACOUSTIC)	68	PREMIER	A-300 DREADNOUGHT SUNBURST	598	**459**	405	357
GUITAR	65	PREMIER	E-781 SCROLL BODY, 2 PU's	695	**534**	471	416
			PRESCOTT				
UPRIG	60	PRESCOTT	4-STRING BASS 1860, BIRD'S EYE MAPLE	52,344	**40,192**	35,519	31,313
UPRIGHT	20	PRESCOTT	BIRD'S EYE MAPLE 1820, SPRUCE TOP, VIOLIN CORNERS	23,935	**18,379**	16,241	14,318
			PRS/PAUL REED SMITH GUITARS				
ELEC. GUITAR & BASS	91	PRS	ARTIST SERIES I	5,837	**4,482**	3,961	3,492
ELGUIT	86	PRS	BASS-4	1,820	**1,397**	1,235	1,088
ELGUIT	86	PRS	BASS-5	1,303	**1,001**	884	779
ELGUIT	86	PRS	CURLY BASS-4	1,594	**1,224**	1,082	954
ELGUIT	86	PRS	CURLY BASS-5	2,001	**1,536**	1,358	1,197
ELGUIT	85	PRS	CUSTOM BIRD INLAY	7,530	**5,782**	5,110	4,505
ELGUIT	85	PRS	CUSTOM 24 CARVED MAPLE TOP,MAHOG BACK,24-FRET,ABALONE INLAYS,CASE	5,042	**3,871**	3,421	3,016
ELGUIT	95	PRS	LIMITED EDITION 10TH ANNIVERSARY MAHOGANY BODY,GOLD PU'S,GOLD HRDWARE,DLX INLAYS	7,537	**5,787**	5,114	4,509
ELGUIT	88	PRS	SIGNATURE	5,658	**4,344**	3,839	3,384
ELGUIT	85	PRS	STANDARD 24 CARVED MAHOG BODY/NECK, 24 FRET, PEARL INLAY, CASE	4,686	**3,598**	3,179	2,803
			QUAD U.S.A.				
PRE	62	QUAD	22 STEREO TUBE	431	**331**	292	257
PWR	73	QUAD	II MONO TUBE 15 WATT	680	**522**	462	407
TUNER	73	QUAD	FM 2 STEREO HYBRID	336	**258**	228	201
			RAMIREZ GUITARS, DIST by DAVID PERRY GUITAR IMPORTS				
GUITAR (ACOUSTIC)	66	RAMIREZ	1a CLASSICAL BRAZILIAN ROSEWOOD BACK/SIDES	3,633	**2,789**	2,465	2,173
GUITAR	69	RAMIREZ	1a CLASSICAL FLAMINGO CYPRESS BACK/SIDES	4,814	**3,697**	3,267	2,880
GUITAR	70	RAMIREZ	1a CLASSICAL FLAMINGO CYPRESS BACK/SIDES	4,159	**3,194**	2,822	2,488
GUITAR	72	RAMIREZ	1a CLASSICAL INDIAN ROSEWOOD BACK/SIDES	2,886	**2,216**	1,958	1,726
GUITAR	72	RAMIREZ	1a CLASSICAL BRAZILIAN ROSEWOOD BACK/SIDES	3,752	**2,881**	2,546	2,244
GUITAR	73	RAMIREZ	1a CLASSICAL BRAZILIAN ROSEWOOD BACK/SIDES	3,830	**2,941**	2,599	2,291
GUITAR	76	RAMIREZ	1a CLASSICAL INDIAN ROSEWOOD BACK/SIDES	3,374	**2,591**	2,289	2,018
GUITAR	76	RAMIREZ	1a CLASSICAL BRAZILIAN ROSEWOOD BACK/SIDES	3,752	**2,881**	2,546	2,244
GUITAR	78	RAMIREZ	1a CLASSICAL INDIAN ROSEWOOD BACK/SIDES	3,355	**2,576**	2,276	2,007
GUITAR	72	RAMIREZ	2 CLASSICAL INDIAN ROSEWOOD BACK/SIDES	1,318	**1,012**	894	788
GUITAR	70	RAMIREZ	2a CLASSICAL FLAMINGO CYPRESS BACK/SIDES	1,239	**952**	841	741
GUITAR	71	RAMIREZ	2a CLASSICAL FLAMINGO CYPRESS BACK/SIDES	1,562	**1,199**	1,060	934
GUITAR	75	RAMIREZ	SEGOVIA MODEL INDIAN ROSEWOOD BACK/SIDES	2,886	**2,216**	1,958	1,726
GUITAR	65	RAMIREZ	STYLE A CLASSICAL BRAZILIAN ROSEWOOD	3,841	**2,949**	2,606	2,298

TYPE	YR	MFG	PRICES--BASED ON 100% ORIGINAL MODEL	SELL EXC	SELL AVG	BUY EXC	BUY AVG
			RCA				
MIC	34	RCA	**30A** LAPEL RIBBON	554	**425**	376	331
MIC	31	RCA	**44A** BI DIRECTIONAL RIBBON, DIAMOND SHAPED	3,944	**3,028**	2,676	2,359
MIC	32	RCA	**44A**	2,430	**1,866**	1,649	1,453
MIC	48	RCA	**44B** BI DIRECTIONAL, DIAMOND SHAPED	2,458	**1,887**	1,668	1,470
MIC	32	RCA	**44BX** BI DIRECTIONAL, DIAMOND SHAPED	3,288	**2,524**	2,231	1,967
MIC	49	RCA	**44BX** STRIPES ALL AROUND	788	**605**	535	471
MIC	36	RCA	**74B** JUNIOR DIAMOND SHAPED	1,927	**1,480**	1,307	1,153
MIC	36	RCA	**77** UNIDIRECTIONAL, RIBBON	4,228	**3,246**	2,869	2,529
MIC	32	RCA	**77A** LARGE, ORIGINAL	4,314	**3,312**	2,927	2,580
MIC	37	RCA	**77B** UNIDIRECTIONAL, DOUBLE RIBBON	4,020	**3,087**	2,728	2,405
MIC	36	RCA	**77B1** UNIDIRECTIONAL,	3,681	**2,783**	2,454	2,035
MIC	38	RCA	**77C** 3 PATTERN EXTERNAL SWITCH, DOUBLE RIBBON	4,021	**3,088**	2,729	2,405
MIC	38	RCA	**77C1** 3 PATTERN INTERNAL SWITCH, DOUBLE RIBBON	4,021	**3,088**	2,729	2,405
MIC	40	RCA	**77D** POLYDIRECTIONAL, ROUND PATTERN SELECTOR PLATE	3,007	**2,309**	2,040	1,798
MIC	47	RCA	**77D**	3,343	**2,567**	2,268	1,999
MIC	47	RCA	**77DX** POLYDIRECTIONAL, DIAMOND PATTERN SELECTOR PLATE	3,561	**2,734**	2,416	2,130
MIC	70	RCA	**BK- 5** UNIAXIAL RIBBON	1,323	**1,016**	898	791
MIC	70	RCA	**BK- 5B** UNIAXIAL RIBBON	1,245	**956**	845	745
MIC	70	RCA	**BK- 6** LAVALIER MIC's, NON DIRECTIONAL	1,233	**946**	836	737
MIC	56	RCA	**BK- 6B** LAVALIER MIC's, NON DIRECTIONAL	1,471	**1,112**	980	813
MIC	52	RCA	**BK- 7A**	1,339	**1,028**	908	801
MIC	53	RCA	**BK-11** BIDIRECTIONAL, RIBBON	1,967	**1,511**	1,335	1,177
MIC	63	RCA	**BK-11A**	1,023	**786**	694	612
MIC	49	RCA	**KU-3A** UNIDIRECTIONAL RIBBON	3,577	**2,746**	2,427	2,139
MIC	70	RCA	**KU-3A** UNIDIRECTIONAL	3,700	**2,841**	2,511	2,213
MIC	70	RCA	**MI-10001** UNIDIRECTIONAL	3,694	**2,837**	2,507	2,210
MIC	47	RCA	**MI-11001** UNIDIRECTIONAL RIBBON	592	**454**	402	354
MIC	56	RCA	**SK45B**	962	**738**	652	575
MIC	55	RCA	**SK46**	517	**397**	351	309
PWR	49	RCA	**AP-952 TUBE**	218	**167**	148	130
			RECORDING KING by GIBSON GUITAR CORP				
GUITAR (ACOUSTIC)	36	RECORDKIN	**ARCHTOP** TENOR, ROSEWOOD, PEARL INLAYS	837	**643**	568	501
GUITAR	35	RECORDKIN	**CARSON ROBINSON** SUNBURST	1,631	**1,253**	1,107	976
GUITAR	36	RECORDKIN	**CARSON ROBINSON** SUNBURST, SERIAL #93500	1,619	**1,243**	1,098	968
GUITAR	40	RECORDKIN	**CARSON ROBINSON** SUNBURST	1,540	**1,182**	1,045	921
GUITAR	36	RECORDKIN	**M-2** SUNBURST	840	**645**	570	502
GUITAR	40	RECORDKIN	**M-2** SUNBURST	734	**564**	498	439
GUITAR	35	RECORDKIN	**M-3** SUNBURST	1,283	**985**	870	767
GUITAR	36	RECORDKIN	**M-3** SUNBURST	1,359	**1,044**	922	813
GUITAR	39	RECORDKIN	**M-3** SUNBURST	1,202	**923**	816	719
GUITAR	40	RECORDKIN	**M-3** SUNBURST	1,047	**804**	710	626
GUITAR	36	RECORDKIN	**M-5** SUNBURST	2,126	**1,633**	1,443	1,272
GUITAR	37	RECORDKIN	**M-5** SUNBURST	1,999	**1,535**	1,356	1,195
GUITAR	38	RECORDKIN	**M-5** SUNBURST	1,869	**1,435**	1,268	1,118

TYPE	YR	MFG	PRICES--BASED ON 100% ORIGINAL MODEL	SELL EXC	SELL AVG	BUY EXC	BUY AVG
GUITAR	39	RECORDKIN	**M-5** SUNBURST	1,669	1,282	1,133	998
GUITAR	35	RECORDKIN	**ROY SMECK** SUNBURST	1,438	1,104	975	860
GUITAR	36	RECORDKIN	**WARD** SUNBURST, ARCHTOP, SERIAL #93500	715	549	485	428
STEEL GUITAR	40	RECORDKIN	**MODEL D LAP STEEL** BROWN	716	550	486	428
STGUIT	38	RECORDKIN	**ROY SMECK LAP STEEL** SUNBURST	778	597	528	465
STGUIT	39	RECORDKIN	**ROY SMECK LAP STEEL** SUNBURST	741	569	503	443
STGUIT	43	RECORDKIN	**ROY SMECK LAP STEEL** SUNBURST	605	465	411	362

REGAL by DOBRO

TYPE	YR	MFG	MODEL	SELL EXC	SELL AVG	BUY EXC	BUY AVG
BANJO	35	REGAL	**27** SUNBURST, SCREEN HOLES	1,658	1,273	1,125	992
BANJO	35	REGAL	**27** SUNBURST, RESONATOR, SQUARE NECK	2,061	1,583	1,399	1,233
BANJO	30	REGAL	**45** SQUARE NECK	1,961	1,505	1,330	1,173
BANJO	35	REGAL	**45** NATURAL, SPRUCE TOP, F-HOLES	1,561	1,198	1,059	933
BANJO	30	REGAL	**BANJO-UKE** WALNUT NECK/RESONATOR	542	416	367	324
BANJO	30	REGAL	**COLLEGIATE** TENOR, RESONATOR	796	611	540	476
BANJO	75	REGAL	**NASHVILLE** SUNBURST, MAHOGANY, SQUARE NECK	922	708	626	552
BANJO	30	REGAL	**TENOR** 17-FRET, OPEN BACK	766	588	519	458
BANJO	30	REGAL	**TENOR** RESONATOR	779	598	528	466
BANJO	30	REGAL	**TENOR** 19-FRET, MAPLE RESONATOR	797	612	541	477
BANJO	25	REGAL	**UB-1 BANJO-UKE** FLAT RESONATOR	551	423	373	329
GUITAR (ACOUSTIC)	35	REGAL	**00** ROSEWOOD, EBONY FINGERBOARD, FLATTOP, SERIAL # 5700-7600	801	615	544	479
GUITAR	41	REGAL	**00** SUNBURST TOP, ROSEWOOD, FLATTOP	734	564	498	439
GUITAR	38	REGAL	**14 M** NICKEL PLATED, BRASS BODY	2,072	1,591	1,406	1,239
GUITAR	25	REGAL	**B&J SERENADER** BLACK, 2-POINT BODY	791	608	537	473
GUITAR	40	REGAL	**BASSO**	772	584	514	427
GUITAR	76	REGAL	**BICENTENNIAL DREADNOUGHT** RED, WHITE AND BLUE	703	540	477	420
GUITAR	36	REGAL	**BOBCAT** SERIAL # 5700-7600	805	618	546	481
GUITAR	36	REGAL	**BOLERO** PIN BRIDGE, FLATTOP, SERIAL # 5700-7600	674	517	457	403
GUITAR	36	REGAL	**BROMAN ACE** SUNBURST, (EQUIVALENT TO DOBRO MODEL 37), SERIAL # 5700-7600	1,721	1,321	1,168	1,029
GUITAR	30	REGAL	**DOBRO** MAHOGANY, SERIAL a# 3000-	1,990	1,528	1,350	1,190
GUITAR	32	REGAL	**DOBRO** BROWN, SUNBURST BACK, ROUND NECK	1,966	1,510	1,334	1,176
GUITAR	33	REGAL	**DOBRO** SPRUCE TOP, MAHOGANY BACK/SIDES, BOUND	1,800	1,382	1,222	1,077
GUITAR	38	REGAL	**DOBRO** 12-FRET, SQUARE NECK, SOLID PEGHEAD, SCREEN HOLES	2,200	1,689	1,493	1,316
GUITAR	35	REGAL	**DOBRO HAWAIIAN** SUNBURST, 12-FRET, ROUND NECK, POINSETTIA PATTERN COVER PLATE	1,622	1,246	1,101	970
GUITAR	33	REGAL	**DOBRO STYLE 37**	1,361	1,045	924	814
GUITAR	34	REGAL	**DOBRO STYLE 37**	1,512	1,161	1,026	904
GUITAR	30	REGAL	**DOBRO STYLE 45** SPRUCE TOP, SQUARE NECK, RESONATOR	1,995	1,532	1,354	1,193
GUITAR	40	REGAL	**DOBRO STYLE 47**	1,544	1,185	1,048	923
GUITAR	17	REGAL	**HARP GUITAR** MAHOGANY, DOUBLE NECK	2,430	1,866	1,649	1,453
GUITAR	34	REGAL	**HAWAIIAN** PLECTRUM, DARK, BOUND FNGRBOARD, 12-FRET, SLOT HEAD, ROUND NECK	1,262	969	856	755
GUITAR	34	REGAL	**LE DOMINO BIG BOY** SUNBURST	801	615	544	479
GUITAR	40	REGAL	**M-19**	788	605	535	471
GUITAR	25	REGAL	**MARTELLE** SUNBURST, 2-POINT BODY	789	606	535	472
GUITAR	35	REGAL	**OLD KRAFTSMAN** SUNBURST, ARCHTOP	788	605	535	471
GUITAR	37	REGAL	**R-6 HAWAIIAN** RESONATOR	1,283	985	870	767

TYPE	YR	MFG	PRICES--BASED ON 100% ORIGINAL MODEL	SELL EXC	SELL AVG	BUY EXC	BUY AVG
GUITAR	36	REGAL	**R-25** RESONATOR	832	**638**	564	497
GUITAR	37	REGAL	**R-25** TENOR, RESONATOR	1,039	**798**	705	621
GUITAR	39	REGAL	**R-25 HAWAIIAN** RESONATOR	992	**761**	673	593
GUITAR	38	REGAL	**R-27 HAWAIIAN** RESONATOR	1,355	**1,040**	919	810
GUITAR	37	REGAL	**R-32**	1,610	**1,236**	1,092	963
GUITAR	38	REGAL	**R-32 HAWAIIAN**	1,064	**817**	722	636
GUITAR	35	REGAL	**R-37** RESONATOR	1,328	**1,019**	901	794
GUITAR	36	REGAL	**R-45** RESONATOR	2,042	**1,568**	1,386	1,222
GUITAR	37	REGAL	**R-45** RESONATOR	1,889	**1,450**	1,282	1,130
GUITAR	38	REGAL	**R-45** RESONATOR	1,769	**1,358**	1,200	1,058
GUITAR	39	REGAL	**R-45** RESONATOR	1,542	**1,184**	1,046	922
GUITAR	39	REGAL	**R-46**	1,531	**1,175**	1,038	915
GUITAR	36	REGAL	**R-55** RESONATOR	1,757	**1,349**	1,192	1,051
GUITAR	35	REGAL	**R-60** RESONATOR	2,442	**1,875**	1,657	1,461
GUITAR	37	REGAL	**R-62** NICKEL-PLATED	3,151	**2,420**	2,138	1,885
GUITAR	38	REGAL	**R-62 HAWAIIAN** NICKEL-PLATED	1,450	**1,096**	966	801
GUITAR	36	REGAL	**R-65** RESONATOR	3,355	**2,576**	2,276	2,007
GUITAR	38	REGAL	**R-75** WALNUT	2,073	**1,591**	1,406	1,240
GUITAR	39	REGAL	**R-75 HAWAIIAN** WALNUT	1,468	**1,127**	996	878
GUITAR	37	REGAL	**RADIO TONE**	649	**491**	432	359
GUITAR	35	REGAL	**REGAL PRINCE**	1,033	**793**	701	618
GUITAR	70	REGAL	**T-242 DREADNOUGHT** 12-STRING, FLATTOP	612	**470**	415	366
GUITAR	76	REGAL	**T-376 BICENTENNIAL** RED, WHITE AND BLUE	598	**459**	405	357
GUITAR	76	REGAL	**T-476 BICENTENNIAL DREADNOUGHT** RED, WHITE AND BLUE	613	**471**	416	367
GUITAR	30	REGAL	**TENOR** SUNBURST, SERIAL # 3000-	474	**364**	322	284
MANDOLIN	28	REGAL	**MANDOLA** BLACK	743	**571**	504	444
MANDOL	30	REGAL	**MB-1 MANDOLIN-BANJO** MAPLE, RESONATOR	690	**521**	460	381
MANDOL	30	REGAL	**OCTOFONE** TEARDROP SHAPED OCTAVE	649	**498**	440	388
MANDOL	35	REGAL	**STYLE A** MAHOGANY	357	**274**	242	213
STEEL GUITAR	40	REGAL	**DOUBLENECK** BROWN, 2 8-STRING NECKS	740	**568**	502	442
STGUIT	70	REGAL	**LAP STEEL**	399	**307**	271	239
UKULELE	30	REGAL	**TIPLE**	448	**344**	304	268
UKE	50	REGAL	**TIPLE**	343	**264**	233	205
UKE	30	REGAL	**UKE** MAHOGANY BOUND	225	**172**	152	134

RENKUS

RAW	81	RENKUS	**SSD 1800-8** 1" HF DRIVER, 8 OHMS	473	**363**	321	283

B. C. RICH INTERNATIONAL, INC

ELEC. GUITAR & BASS	79	RICH	**DOUBLE EAGLE BASS** MAHOGANY	863	**663**	585	516
ELGUIT	77	RICH	**EAGLE ACTIVE** FLAMED KOA	1,305	**1,002**	886	781
ELGUIT	77	RICH	**EAGLE BASS** KOA BODY, VARI-TONE	1,043	**801**	708	624
ELGUIT	77	RICH	**EAGLE SUPREME**	1,311	**1,007**	889	784
ELGUIT	76	RICH	**GULL** WHITE, SOLID BODY, 2 PU's	810	**622**	550	485
ELGUIT	96	RICH	**INNOVATOR BASS 4-STRING** BOLT-ON	769	**590**	522	460
ELGUIT	96	RICH	**INNOVATOR BASS 5-STRING** BOLT-ON	759	**583**	515	454
ELGUIT	76	RICH	**MOCKINGBIRD** MAPLE BODY	1,311	**1,007**	889	784
ELGUIT	76	RICH	**MOCKINGBIRD** KOA BODY	1,562	**1,199**	1,060	934

TYPE	YR	MFG	PRICES--BASED ON 100% ORIGINAL MODEL	SELL EXC	SELL AVG	BUY EXC	BUY AVG
ELGUIT	77	RICH	**MOCKINGBIRD** PURPLE, SOLID BODY	1,486	**1,141**	1,008	889
ELGUIT	77	RICH	**MOCKINGBIRD** KOA BODY	1,553	**1,192**	1,054	929
ELGUIT	78	RICH	**MOCKINGBIRD** KOA BODY	1,383	**1,062**	938	827
ELGUIT	80	RICH	**MOCKINGBIRD** BLACK, SOLID BODY	1,359	**1,044**	922	813
ELGUIT	82	RICH	**MOCKINGBIRD** KOA BODY	1,249	**959**	848	747
ELGUIT	83	RICH	**MOCKINGBIRD** MAPLE BODY	968	**743**	657	579
ELGUIT	83	RICH	**MOCKINGBIRD** KOA BODY	1,018	**781**	690	609
ELGUIT	84	RICH	**MOCKINGBIRD** MAPLE BODY	960	**737**	652	574
ELGUIT	85	RICH	**MOCKINGBIRD** MAPLE BODY	866	**665**	588	518
ELGUIT	87	RICH	**MOCKINGBIRD** MAPLE BODY	891	**684**	604	533
ELGUIT	60	RICH	**MOCKINGBIRD BASS** RED, BOLT ON NECK	1,046	**803**	709	625
ELGUIT	84	RICH	**MOCKINGBIRD BASS** NECK-THRU, PREAMP	902	**693**	612	540
ELGUIT	76	RICH	**MOCKINGBIRD SPECIAL** NATURAL	1,472	**1,130**	999	881
ELGUIT	77	RICH	**MOCKINGBIRD SUPREME** RED	1,562	**1,199**	1,060	934
ELGUIT	80	RICH	**NIGHTHAWK** BOLT-ON NECK	764	**587**	519	457
ELGUIT	79	RICH	**PHOENIX** MAHOGANY, 2 PU's	612	**470**	415	366
ELGUIT	80	RICH	**PHOENIX** BOLT-ON NECK	641	**492**	435	383
ELGUIT	75	RICH	**SEAGULL** WHITE, SINGLE CUTAWAY, SOLIDBODY,NECK-THRU,2 HB	1,069	**821**	725	639
ELGUIT	78	RICH	**SEAGULL** CHERRY RED	1,005	**772**	682	601
ELGUIT	76	RICH	**SEAGULL II** DOUBLE CUTAWAY, SOLIDBODY, NECK-THRU, 2 HB	910	**699**	617	544
ELGUIT	82	RICH	**WARLOCK**	816	**626**	554	488
ELGUIT	80	RICH	**WARLOCK BASS**	938	**720**	636	561
GUITAR (ACOUSTIC)	71	RICH	**B-28** ROSEWOOD BACK/SIDES, HERRINGBONE	1,373	**1,054**	931	821
GUITAR	72	RICH	**B-28** ROSEWOOD BACK/SIDES, HERRINGBONE TRIM	1,205	**925**	817	720
GUITAR	73	RICH	**B-28** ROSEWOOD BACK/SIDES, HERRINGBONE TRIM	1,008	**774**	684	603
GUITAR	67	RICH	**B-30** NATURAL, MAPLE BACK/SIDES, HERRINGBONE TRIM	1,453	**1,116**	986	869
GUITAR	70	RICH	**B-30** NATURAL, MAPLE BACK/SIDES, HERRINGBONE TRIM	1,261	**968**	855	754
GUITAR	75	RICH	**B-38** FIGURED BACK/SIDES, HERRINGBONE	1,361	**1,045**	924	814
GUITAR	76	RICH	**B-38** FIGURED BACK/SIDES, HERRINGBONE TRIM	1,319	**1,013**	895	789
GUITAR	79	RICH	**B-38** FIGURED BACK/SIDES, HERRINGBONE	1,237	**950**	839	740

RICKENBACKER INTERNATIONAL CORP.

TYPE	YR	MFG	MODEL	SELL EXC	SELL AVG	BUY EXC	BUY AVG
BANJO	69	RICKENBAC	**BANJOLINE**	1,388	**1,066**	942	830
BANJO	67	RICKENBAC	**BANTAR**	1,800	**1,382**	1,222	1,077
BANJO	67	RICKENBAC	**BANTAR DELUXE** NATURAL	2,250	**1,727**	1,526	1,346
BANJO	69	RICKENBAC	**ELECTRIC** PLECTRUM, FIREGLO	1,646	**1,264**	1,117	984
ELEC. GUITAR & BASS	66	RICKENBAC	**310** MAPLEGLO, 3/4 SCALE, 2 PU's	975	**749**	661	583
ELGUIT	67	RICKENBAC	**315** FIREGLO, 3/4 SCALE, VIBRTO, 2 PU's	1,690	**1,297**	1,146	1,011
ELGUIT	58	RICKENBAC	**320** SHORT SCALE HOLLOW BODY, 3 PU	12,387	**9,511**	8,405	7,410
ELGUIT	59	RICKENBAC	**320** SHORT SCALE HOLLOW BODY, 3 PU	12,387	**9,511**	8,405	7,410
ELGUIT	60	RICKENBAC	**320** SHORT SCALE HOLLOW BODY, 3 PU	12,387	**9,511**	8,405	7,410
ELGUIT	61	RICKENBAC	**320** SHORT SCALE HOLLOW BODY, 3 PU	12,387	**9,511**	8,405	7,410
ELGUIT	62	RICKENBAC	**320** SHORT SCALE HOLLOW BODY, 3 PU	12,387	**9,511**	8,405	7,410
ELGUIT	63	RICKENBAC	**320** SHORT SCALE HOLLOW BODY, 3 PU	12,387	**9,511**	8,405	7,410
ELGUIT	64	RICKENBAC	**320** SHORT SCALE HOLLOW BODY, 3 PU	12,387	**9,511**	8,405	7,410

TYPE	YR	MFG	PRICES--BASED ON 100% ORIGINAL MODEL	SELL EXC	SELL AVG	BUY EXC	BUY AVG
ELGUIT	65	RICKENBAC	320 SHORT SCALE HOLLOW BODY, 3 PU	12,387	9,511	8,405	7,410
ELGUIT	66	RICKENBAC	320 SHORT SCALE HOLLOW BODY, 3 PU	12,387	9,511	8,405	7,410
ELGUIT	67	RICKENBAC	320 SHORT SCALE HOLLOW BODY, 3 PU	12,387	9,511	8,405	7,410
ELGUIT	68	RICKENBAC	320 SHORT SCALE HOLLOW BODY, 3 PU	12,387	9,511	8,405	7,410
ELGUIT	75	RICKENBAC	320 FIREGLO, 3/4 SCALE, 3 PU's	807	620	547	483
ELGUIT	77	RICKENBAC	320	963	739	653	576
ELGUIT	58	RICKENBAC	325	5,883	4,517	3,992	3,519
ELGUIT	59	RICKENBAC	325	5,883	4,517	3,992	3,519
ELGUIT	60	RICKENBAC	325	5,883	4,517	3,992	3,519
ELGUIT	64	RICKENBAC	325 1996 ROSE MORRIS	1,753	1,346	1,190	1,049
ELGUIT	89	RICKENBAC	325JL JOHN LENNON LIMITED EDITION 3 VIN RIC PU, VIN VIB, MAPLE BODY, 3/4 SIZE RSWD NECK	2,231	1,713	1,513	1,334
ELGUIT	90	RICKENBAC	325JL JOHN LENNON LIMITED EDITION 3 VIN RIC PU, VIN VIB, MAPLE BODY, 3/4 SIZE RSWD NECK	2,231	1,713	1,513	1,334
ELGUIT	63	RICKENBAC	330 MAPLE, STANDARD, FULL SCALE, 2 PU's	2,876	2,208	1,951	1,720
ELGUIT	65	RICKENBAC	330	1,486	1,141	1,008	889
ELGUIT	67	RICKENBAC	330 FIREGLO	1,321	1,014	896	790
ELGUIT	67	RICKENBAC	330 SUNBURST, 2 PU's	2,396	1,840	1,626	1,433
ELGUIT	66	RICKENBAC	330-12 FIREGLO, 12-STRING, 2 PU's	2,636	2,024	1,789	1,577
ELGUIT	67	RICKENBAC	330-12	1,486	1,141	1,008	889
ELGUIT	64	RICKENBAC	330-12 1993 ROSE MORRIS BLACK	3,678	2,824	2,495	2,200
ELGUIT	70	RICKENBAC	331 LIGHT SHOW TYPE 1, FIRST EDITION	7,231	5,553	4,907	4,326
ELGUIT	71	RICKENBAC	331 LIGHT SHOW TYPE 1, FIRST EDITION	7,231	5,553	4,907	4,326
ELGUIT	72	RICKENBAC	331 LIGHT SHOW TYPE 2, SECOND EDITION	8,947	6,870	6,071	5,352
ELGUIT	73	RICKENBAC	331 LIGHT SHOW TYPE 2, SECOND EDITION	8,947	6,870	6,071	5,352
ELGUIT	74	RICKENBAC	331 LIGHT SHOW TYPE 2, SECOND EDITION	8,947	6,870	6,071	5,352
ELGUIT	75	RICKENBAC	331 LIGHT SHOW TYPE 2, SECOND EDITION	8,947	6,870	6,071	5,352
ELGUIT	67	RICKENBAC	335 MAPLEGLO, VIBRATO, 2 PU's	2,396	1,840	1,626	1,433
ELGUIT	64	RICKENBAC	335 1997 ROSE MORRIS	1,863	1,408	1,242	1,030
ELGUIT	66	RICKENBAC	335 1997 ROSE MORRIS FIREGLO, 2 PU's	1,779	1,345	1,186	983
ELGUIT	58	RICKENBAC	335 CAPRI FIREGLO, VIBRATO, 2 PU's	4,838	3,715	3,283	2,894
ELGUIT	58	RICKENBAC	335 CAPRI NATURAL, VIBRATO, 2 PU's	4,838	3,715	3,283	2,894
ELGUIT	59	RICKENBAC	335 CAPRI FIREGLO, VIBRATO, 2 PU's	4,838	3,715	3,283	2,894
ELGUIT	59	RICKENBAC	335 CAPRI NATURAL, VIBRATO, 2 PU's	4,838	3,715	3,283	2,894
ELGUIT	60	RICKENBAC	335 CAPRI FIREGLO, VIBRATO, 2 PU's	5,376	4,128	3,648	3,216
ELGUIT	67	RICKENBAC	336-12 FIREGLO, 12-STRING, 2 PU's	3,274	2,514	2,222	1,959
ELGUIT	58	RICKENBAC	340 1 MADE,2 SINGLE COIL PU,THIN SEMI HOLLOW BODY	3,554	2,729	2,412	2,126
ELGUIT	62	RICKENBAC	340 1 MADE,2 SINGLE COIL PU,THIN SEMI HOLLOW BODY	3,554	2,729	2,412	2,126
ELGUIT	63	RICKENBAC	340 1 MADE,2 SINGLE COIL PU,THIN SEMI HOLLOW BODY	3,554	2,729	2,412	2,126
ELGUIT	64	RICKENBAC	340 2 MADE,2 SINGLE COIL PU,THIN SEMI HOLLOW BODY	3,554	2,729	2,412	2,126
ELGUIT	65	RICKENBAC	340 4 MADE,2 SINGLE COIL PU,THIN SEMI HOLLOW BODY	3,554	2,729	2,412	2,126
ELGUIT	66	RICKENBAC	340 43 MADE,2 SINGLE COIL PU,THIN SEMI HOLLOW BODY	2,396	1,840	1,626	1,433
ELGUIT	68	RICKENBAC	340 BLACK, 12-STRING, 3 PU's	2,396	1,840	1,626	1,433
ELGUIT	64	RICKENBAC	345 1998 ROSE MORRIS	1,684	1,293	1,143	1,007
ELGUIT	58	RICKENBAC	345 CAPRI THINLINE, 3 PU, VIBRATO TAILPIECE	4,045	3,106	2,745	2,420
ELGUIT	59	RICKENBAC	345 CAPRI THINLINE, 3 PU, VIBRATO TAILPIECE	4,045	3,106	2,745	2,420
ELGUIT	60	RICKENBAC	345 CAPRI THINLINE, 3 PU, VIBRATO TAILPIECE	4,045	3,106	2,745	2,420
ELGUIT	63	RICKENBAC	360 MAPLEGLO	3,763	2,889	2,553	2,251

TYPE	YR	MFG	MODEL	SELL EXC	SELL AVG	BUY EXC	BUY AVG
ELGUIT	64	RICKENBAC	360 FIREGLO	2,968	2,279	2,014	1,775
ELGUIT	65	RICKENBAC	360 FIREGLO	3,595	2,760	2,439	2,150
ELGUIT	65	RICKENBAC	360 MAPLEGLO	3,655	2,807	2,480	2,186
ELGUIT	66	RICKENBAC	360 MAPLEGLO	3,440	2,641	2,334	2,058
ELGUIT	66	RICKENBAC	360 FIREGLO	3,595	2,760	2,439	2,150
ELGUIT	67	RICKENBAC	360 FIREGLO	3,595	2,760	2,439	2,150
ELGUIT	67	RICKENBAC	360 MAPLEGLO	3,595	2,760	2,439	2,150
ELGUIT	68	RICKENBAC	360 JETGLO, LEFT-HANDED	3,115	2,392	2,114	1,863
ELGUIT	68	RICKENBAC	360 FIREGLO	3,296	2,530	2,236	1,971
ELGUIT	69	RICKENBAC	360 BURGUNDYGLO	2,996	2,300	2,033	1,792
ELGUIT	70	RICKENBAC	360 FIREGLO	2,636	2,024	1,789	1,577
ELGUIT	72	RICKENBAC	360 FIREGLO	2,396	1,840	1,626	1,433
ELGUIT	76	RICKENBAC	360 BURGUNDYGLO	2,157	1,656	1,463	1,290
ELGUIT	79	RICKENBAC	360	1,018	781	690	609
ELGUIT	57	RICKENBAC	360 CAPRI FULL SIZE DELUXE	4,365	3,352	2,962	2,611
ELGUIT	59	RICKENBAC	360 CAPRI FIREGLO	4,838	3,715	3,283	2,894
ELGUIT	59	RICKENBAC	360 CAPRI SUNBURST	4,838	3,715	3,283	2,894
ELGUIT	60	RICKENBAC	360 CAPRI FIREGLO	4,838	3,715	3,283	2,894
ELGUIT	65	RICKENBAC	360-12 FIREGLO, 12-STRING	3,595	2,760	2,439	2,150
ELGUIT	66	RICKENBAC	360-12 FIREGLO, 12-STRING	3,595	2,760	2,439	2,150
ELGUIT	66	RICKENBAC	360-12 MAPLEGLO, 12-STRING	3,595	2,760	2,439	2,150
ELGUIT	67	RICKENBAC	360-12 FIREGLO, 12-STRING	3,595	2,760	2,439	2,150
ELGUIT	67	RICKENBAC	360-12 JETGLO, 12-STRING	3,595	2,760	2,439	2,150
ELGUIT	67	RICKENBAC	360-12 MAPLEGLO, 12-STRING	3,595	2,760	2,439	2,150
ELGUIT	68	RICKENBAC	360-12 MAPLEGLO, 12-STRING	3,355	2,576	2,276	2,007
ELGUIT	71	RICKENBAC	360-12	1,789	1,374	1,214	1,070
ELGUIT	74	RICKENBAC	360-12 JETGLO, 12-STRING	2,157	1,656	1,463	1,290
ELGUIT	74	RICKENBAC	360-12 MAPLEGLO, 12-STRING	2,157	1,656	1,463	1,290
ELGUIT	75	RICKENBAC	360-12 FIREGLO, 12-STRING	2,037	1,564	1,382	1,218
ELGUIT	76	RICKENBAC	360-12 MAPLEGLO, 12-STRING	1,917	1,472	1,301	1,147
ELGUIT	65	RICKENBAC	360-12 1993 ROSE MORRIS	3,336	2,561	2,264	1,995
ELGUIT	59	RICKENBAC	360-F MAPLEGLO, CAPRI SINGLE CUT	5,913	4,540	4,012	3,537
ELGUIT	59	RICKENBAC	365 FIREGLO, VIBRATO	4,300	3,302	2,918	2,572
ELGUIT	61	RICKENBAC	365 FIREGLO, VIBRATO	4,085	3,137	2,772	2,444
ELGUIT	65	RICKENBAC	365 FIREGLO, VIBRATO	3,356	2,577	2,277	2,007
ELGUIT	65	RICKENBAC	365 MAPLEGLO, VIBRATO	3,440	2,641	2,334	2,058
ELGUIT	66	RICKENBAC	365 MAPLEGLO, VIBRATO	3,440	2,641	2,334	2,058
ELGUIT	66	RICKENBAC	365 FIREGLO, VIBRATO	3,763	2,889	2,553	2,251
ELGUIT	67	RICKENBAC	365 FIREGLO, VIBRATO	3,655	2,807	2,480	2,186
ELGUIT	68	RICKENBAC	365 FIREGLO, VIBRATO	3,548	2,724	2,407	2,122
ELGUIT	68	RICKENBAC	365 JETGLO, VIBRATO	3,595	2,760	2,439	2,150
ELGUIT	68	RICKENBAC	365 MAPLEGLO, VIBRATO	3,595	2,760	2,439	2,150
ELGUIT	67	RICKENBAC	366-12 FIREGLO, 12-STRING	2,998	2,302	2,034	1,793

TYPE	YR	MFG	PRICES--BASED ON 100% ORIGINAL MODEL	SELL EXC	SELL AVG	BUY EXC	BUY AVG
ELGUIT	66	RICKENBAC	**366-12 CONVERTIBLE** 7 MADE, 12-STRING, 2 PU	3,142	**2,413**	2,132	1,880
ELGUIT	68	RICKENBAC	**366-12 CONVERTIBLE** 125 MADE, 2 PU, 12-STRING	3,142	**2,413**	2,132	1,880
ELGUIT	58	RICKENBAC	**370** BROWN SUNBURST, 3 PU's	3,763	**2,889**	2,553	2,251
ELGUIT	59	RICKENBAC	**370** 4 MADE	4,658	**3,576**	3,160	2,786
ELGUIT	67	RICKENBAC	**370** MAPLEGLO, 3 PU's	3,082	**2,366**	2,091	1,843
ELGUIT	68	RICKENBAC	**370** MAPLEGLO, 3 PU's	2,274	**1,746**	1,543	1,360
ELGUIT	68	RICKENBAC	**370** FIREGLO, 3 PU's	3,355	**2,576**	2,276	2,007
ELGUIT	73	RICKENBAC	**370** FIREGLO, 3 PU's	1,592	**1,222**	1,080	952
ELGUIT	69	RICKENBAC	**370-12** FIREGLO, 12-STRING, 3 PU's	3,595	**2,760**	2,439	2,150
ELGUIT	73	RICKENBAC	**370-12** MAPLEGLO, 12-STRING	2,996	**2,300**	2,033	1,792
ELGUIT	88	RICKENBAC	**370-12 ROGER MGUINN LTD EDITION** CHECKED BINDING,3 VINTAGE PU's,CUSTOM ACTIVE ELECTRONICS	4,300	**3,302**	2,918	2,572
ELGUIT	58	RICKENBAC	**375** BROWN SUNBURST, VIBRATO, 3 PU's	4,300	**3,302**	2,918	2,572
ELGUIT	61	RICKENBAC	**375** MAPLEGLO, VIBRATO, 3 PU's	2,400	**1,842**	1,628	1,435
ELGUIT	65	RICKENBAC	**375** FIREGLO, VIBRATO, 3 PU's	2,097	**1,610**	1,423	1,254
ELGUIT	67	RICKENBAC	**375** MAPLEGLO, VIBRATO, 3 PU's	2,044	**1,569**	1,387	1,222
ELGUIT	67	RICKENBAC	**375** JETGLO, VIBRATO, 3 PU's	2,220	**1,705**	1,507	1,328
ELGUIT	69	RICKENBAC	**381** SUNBURST, 2 PU's	2,278	**1,749**	1,545	1,362
ELGUIT	70	RICKENBAC	**381** JETGLO, RICKO-SOUND, 2 PU's	3,485	**2,676**	2,365	2,085
ELGUIT	63	RICKENBAC	**425** FIREGLO	1,345	**1,032**	912	804
ELGUIT	73	RICKENBAC	**425**	803	**616**	544	480
ELGUIT	60	RICKENBAC	**450-12** FIREGLO, 12-STRING	2,086	**1,602**	1,415	1,248
ELGUIT	65	RICKENBAC	**450-12** MAPLEGLO, 12-STRING	1,571	**1,206**	1,066	940
ELGUIT	66	RICKENBAC	**450-12** FIREGLO, 12-STRING	1,877	**1,441**	1,273	1,122
ELGUIT	66	RICKENBAC	**450-12** BLACK, 12-STRING	2,033	**1,561**	1,380	1,216
ELGUIT	66	RICKENBAC	**450-12** MAPLEGLO, 12-STRING	2,085	**1,601**	1,415	1,247
ELGUIT	67	RICKENBAC	**450-12** FIREGLO, 12-STRING	1,637	**1,257**	1,111	979
ELGUIT	67	RICKENBAC	**450-12** MAPLEGLO, 12-STRING	1,710	**1,313**	1,160	1,023
ELGUIT	74	RICKENBAC	**450-12** BLACK, 12-STRING	1,051	**807**	713	629
ELGUIT	67	RICKENBAC	**456-12** 12-STRING	1,861	**1,429**	1,263	1,113
ELGUIT	68	RICKENBAC	**456-12** 12-STRING	1,674	**1,285**	1,136	1,001
ELGUIT	64	RICKENBAC	**460**	1,264	**970**	858	756
ELGUIT	73	RICKENBAC	**480** PURPLE, 2 PU's	945	**725**	641	565
ELGUIT	73	RICKENBAC	**480** NATURAL, 2 PU's	954	**732**	647	570
ELGUIT	73	RICKENBAC	**480** BLUE, 2 PU's	991	**761**	672	592
ELGUIT	76	RICKENBAC	**480** WALNUT, 2 PU's	939	**721**	637	562
ELGUIT	76	RICKENBAC	**481** BLACK, 2 HB PU's	900	**691**	611	538
ELGUIT	77	RICKENBAC	**481** RED, 2 HB PU's	882	**677**	598	527
ELGUIT	64	RICKENBAC	**615**	1,264	**970**	858	756
ELGUIT	75	RICKENBAC	**620** RED, 2 PU's	803	**616**	544	480
ELGUIT	77	RICKENBAC	**620**	910	**699**	617	544
ELGUIT	63	RICKENBAC	**625** VIBRATO, 2 PU's	2,033	**1,561**	1,380	1,216
ELGUIT	68	RICKENBAC	**625** MAPLEGLO, VIBRATO, 2 PU's	1,340	**1,029**	909	801
ELGUIT	76	RICKENBAC	**625** MAPLEGLO, VIBRATO, 2 PU's	1,243	**954**	843	743
ELGUIT	63	RICKENBAC	**900** BABY BLUE, 1 PU	870	**668**	590	520

TYPE	YR	MFG	PRICES--BASED ON 100% ORIGINAL MODEL	SELL EXC	SELL AVG	BUY EXC	BUY AVG
ELGUIT	67	RICKENBAC	**1997 PETE TOWNSEND EXPORT** SUNBURST	3,214	**2,468**	2,181	1,922
ELGUIT	73	RICKENBAC	**2001 BASS** BLACK	805	**618**	546	481
ELGUIT	76	RICKENBAC	**3000 BASS** BROWN SUNBURST, 1 PU	749	**575**	508	448
ELGUIT	76	RICKENBAC	**3000 BASS** NATURAL	930	**714**	631	556
ELGUIT	76	RICKENBAC	**3001** MAROON, 1 PU	944	**724**	640	564
ELGUIT	76	RICKENBAC	**3001** ROSEWOOD, DOT NECK, 1 PU	944	**724**	640	564
ELGUIT	76	RICKENBAC	**3001 BASS** WINE RED	749	**575**	508	448
ELGUIT	66	RICKENBAC	**330** MAPLE GLO	3,865	**2,967**	2,622	2,312
ELGUIT	66	RICKENBAC	**335** JET GLO	3,110	**2,388**	2,110	1,860
ELGUIT	68	RICKENBAC	**360** BURGANDY GLO	3,865	**2,967**	2,622	2,312
ELGUIT	66	RICKENBAC	**360 XII** FIRE GLO	4,940	**3,793**	3,352	2,955
ELGUIT	66	RICKENBAC	**365** JET GLO	3,865	**2,967**	2,622	2,312
ELGUIT	67	RICKENBAC	**375** FIRE GLO	3,865	**2,967**	2,622	2,312
ELGUIT	57	RICKENBAC	**4000 BASS** HORSESHOE MAGNET	5,376	**4,128**	3,648	3,216
ELGUIT	58	RICKENBAC	**4000 BASS**	5,376	**4,128**	3,648	3,216
ELGUIT	59	RICKENBAC	**4000 BASS** AUTUMNGLO	5,376	**4,128**	3,648	3,216
ELGUIT	59	RICKENBAC	**4000 BASS** MAPLEGLO, GOLD GUARDS	5,376	**4,128**	3,648	3,216
ELGUIT	60	RICKENBAC	**4000 BASS** FIREGLO, GOLD GUARDS	4,151	**3,188**	2,817	2,483
ELGUIT	63	RICKENBAC	**4000 BASS** BLACK	4,300	**3,302**	2,918	2,572
ELGUIT	65	RICKENBAC	**4000 BASS** FIREGLO, LONG HEAD	4,382	**3,365**	2,973	2,621
ELGUIT	67	RICKENBAC	**4000 BASS** FIREGLO, 1 PU	2,283	**1,753**	1,549	1,366
ELGUIT	70	RICKENBAC	**4000 BASS** AUTUMNGLO	1,877	**1,441**	1,273	1,122
ELGUIT	70	RICKENBAC	**4000 BASS** 1 PU	3,595	**2,760**	2,439	2,150
ELGUIT	72	RICKENBAC	**4000 BASS** FIREGLO, 1 PU, CHECKERBOARD BINDING	2,428	**1,864**	1,647	1,452
ELGUIT	74	RICKENBAC	**4000 BASS** MAPLEGLO	5,376	**4,128**	3,648	3,216
ELGUIT	61	RICKENBAC	**4001 BASS** FIREGLO	4,300	**3,302**	2,918	2,572
ELGUIT	63	RICKENBAC	**4001 BASS** FIREGLO	4,300	**3,302**	2,918	2,572
ELGUIT	64	RICKENBAC	**4001 BASS** FIREGLO	4,300	**3,302**	2,918	2,572
ELGUIT	67	RICKENBAC	**4001 BASS** FIREGLO	3,487	**2,678**	2,366	2,086
ELGUIT	68	RICKENBAC	**4001 BASS** MAPLEGLO	2,968	**2,279**	2,014	1,775
ELGUIT	68	RICKENBAC	**4001 BASS** FIREGLO	3,763	**2,889**	2,553	2,251
ELGUIT	69	RICKENBAC	**4001 BASS** FIREGLO	2,964	**2,276**	2,011	1,773
ELGUIT	70	RICKENBAC	**4001 BASS** MAPLEGLO	2,296	**1,763**	1,558	1,373
ELGUIT	70	RICKENBAC	**4001 BASS** LEFT-HANDED	2,309	**1,773**	1,567	1,381
ELGUIT	71	RICKENBAC	**4001 BASS** SUNBURST	2,232	**1,713**	1,514	1,335
ELGUIT	71	RICKENBAC	**4001 BASS** BLACK	2,996	**2,300**	2,033	1,792
ELGUIT	72	RICKENBAC	**4001 BASS** BLACK	1,852	**1,422**	1,257	1,108
ELGUIT	72	RICKENBAC	**4001 BASS** NATURAL	1,854	**1,424**	1,258	1,109
ELGUIT	72	RICKENBAC	**4001 BASS** FIREGLO	1,858	**1,426**	1,260	1,111
ELGUIT	72	RICKENBAC	**4001 BASS** MAPLEGLO	1,858	**1,426**	1,260	1,111
ELGUIT	72	RICKENBAC	**4001 BASS** BURGANDY, WHITE PICKGUARD, RSWD FRTBRD, 2 SINGLE COIL PU	1,858	**1,426**	1,260	1,111
ELGUIT	72	RICKENBAC	**4001 BASS** NATURAL, CHECKERBOARD, LEFT-HANDED	1,888	**1,449**	1,281	1,129

TYPE	YR	MFG	PRICES--BASED ON 100% ORIGINAL MODEL	SELL EXC	SELL AVG	BUY EXC	BUY AVG
ELGUIT	73	RICKENBAC	**4001 BASS** MAPLEGLO	1,852	**1,422**	1,257	1,108
ELGUIT	73	RICKENBAC	**4001 BASS** WINE RED	1,853	**1,423**	1,257	1,108
ELGUIT	73	RICKENBAC	**4001 BASS** BROWN	1,854	**1,424**	1,258	1,109
ELGUIT	73	RICKENBAC	**4001 BASS** BLUE	1,858	**1,426**	1,260	1,111
ELGUIT	73	RICKENBAC	**4001 BASS** FIREGLO, LEFT-HANDED	1,883	**1,446**	1,278	1,126
ELGUIT	73	RICKENBAC	**4001 BASS** BLACK	2,157	**1,656**	1,463	1,290
ELGUIT	74	RICKENBAC	**4001 BASS** WHITE	948	**728**	643	567
ELGUIT	74	RICKENBAC	**4001 BASS** BLACK	955	**733**	648	571
ELGUIT	74	RICKENBAC	**4001 BASS** WHITE, LEFT-HANDED	960	**737**	652	574
ELGUIT	75	RICKENBAC	**4001 BASS** BLACK	948	**728**	643	567
ELGUIT	75	RICKENBAC	**4001 BASS** FIREGLO, FRETLESS	954	**732**	647	570
ELGUIT	75	RICKENBAC	**4001 BASS** WHITE, LEFT-HANDED	1,917	**1,472**	1,301	1,147
ELGUIT	76	RICKENBAC	**4001 BASS** NATURAL	947	**727**	642	566
ELGUIT	76	RICKENBAC	**4001 BASS** BLACK	948	**728**	643	567
ELGUIT	76	RICKENBAC	**4001 BASS** BLUE	948	**728**	643	567
ELGUIT	76	RICKENBAC	**4001 BASS** WHITE	948	**728**	643	567
ELGUIT	76	RICKENBAC	**4001 BASS** WINE RED	948	**728**	643	567
ELGUIT	76	RICKENBAC	**4001 BASS** BLACK, FRETLESS	950	**730**	645	568
ELGUIT	76	RICKENBAC	**4001 BASS** MAPLEGLO	950	**730**	645	568
ELGUIT	76	RICKENBAC	**4001 BASS** WHITE, LEFT-HANDED	959	**737**	651	574
ELGUIT	77	RICKENBAC	**4001 BASS** CREAM	948	**728**	643	567
ELGUIT	77	RICKENBAC	**4001 BASS** NATURAL	948	**728**	643	567
ELGUIT	77	RICKENBAC	**4001 BASS** WHITE	949	**729**	644	568
ELGUIT	77	RICKENBAC	**4001 BASS** AUTUMNGLO	953	**731**	646	570
ELGUIT	78	RICKENBAC	**4001 BASS** BLACK	948	**728**	643	567
ELGUIT	78	RICKENBAC	**4001 BASS** CLEAR DEEP RED	948	**728**	643	567
ELGUIT	78	RICKENBAC	**4001 BASS** CREAM	950	**730**	645	568
ELGUIT	78	RICKENBAC	**4001 BASS** WHITE	950	**730**	645	568
ELGUIT	78	RICKENBAC	**4001 BASS** BLUE	953	**731**	646	570
ELGUIT	78	RICKENBAC	**4001 BASS** MAPLEGLO,WHITE PICKIGUARD,RSWD FNGRBRD,2 HIGH GAIN PU's	953	**731**	646	570
ELGUIT	78	RICKENBAC	**4001 BASS** AUTUMNGLO	954	**732**	647	570
ELGUIT	79	RICKENBAC	**4001 BASS** NATURAL	948	**728**	643	567
ELGUIT	79	RICKENBAC	**4001 BASS** WHITE	948	**728**	643	567
ELGUIT	79	RICKENBAC	**4001 BASS** BLACK	949	**729**	644	568
ELGUIT	79	RICKENBAC	**4001 BASS** BLOND	949	**729**	644	568
ELGUIT	79	RICKENBAC	**4001 BASS** MAPLEGLO	950	**730**	645	568
ELGUIT	79	RICKENBAC	**4001 BASS** AUTUMNGLO	953	**731**	646	570
ELGUIT	79	RICKENBAC	**4001 BASS** BLACK, LEFT-HANDED, FRETLESS	957	**735**	649	572
ELGUIT	81	RICKENBAC	**4001 BASS**	889	**682**	603	531
ELGUIT	86	RICKENBAC	**4001 BASS** FIREGLO	885	**680**	601	529
ELGUIT	80	RICKENBAC	**4001S BASS** JETGLO	1,031	**792**	699	617
ELGUIT	65	RICKENBAC	**4005 BASS** HOLLOW BODY	1,813	**1,392**	1,230	1,084

TYPE	YR	MFG	PRICES--BASED ON 100% ORIGINAL MODEL	SELL EXC	SELL AVG	BUY EXC	BUY AVG
ELGUIT	65	RICKENBAC	**4005 BASS** MAPLEGLO	3,552	**2,727**	2,410	2,125
ELGUIT	67	RICKENBAC	**4005 BASS** NATURAL, 2 PU's	3,615	**2,776**	2,453	2,162
ELGUIT	67	RICKENBAC	**4005 BASS** CRUSHED PEARL, DOUBLE BOUND	3,616	**2,776**	2,454	2,163
ELGUIT	67	RICKENBAC	**4005 BASS** FIREGLO, 2 PU's	3,635	**2,791**	2,466	2,174
ELGUIT	68	RICKENBAC	**4005 BASS** BLACK, 2 PU's	3,366	**2,585**	2,284	2,014
ELGUIT	68	RICKENBAC	**4005 BASS** FIREGLO, 2 PU's	4,202	**3,226**	2,851	2,513
ELGUIT	76	RICKENBAC	**4005 BASS** FIREGLO	2,016	**1,548**	1,368	1,206
ELGUIT	78	RICKENBAC	**4005 BASS** BLACK, 2 PU's	3,204	**2,460**	2,174	1,916
ELGUIT	79	RICKENBAC	**4005 BASS** FIREGLO, 2 PU's	1,881	**1,444**	1,276	1,125
ELGUIT	80	RICKENBAC	**4005 BASS** HOLLOW BODY	1,725	**1,325**	1,171	1,032
ELGUIT	66	RICKENBAC	**4005-6 BASS** MAPLEGLO, DOUBLE BOUND	3,604	**2,767**	2,445	2,156
ELGUIT	67	RICKENBAC	**4005-8 BASS** FIREGLO, 8-STRING	2,947	**2,263**	2,000	1,763
ELGUIT	67	RICKENBAC	**4005WB BASS** BLACK, 2 PU's	2,909	**2,234**	1,974	1,740
ELGUIT	67	RICKENBAC	**4005WB BASS** MAPLEGLO, DOUBLE BOUND	2,927	**2,248**	1,986	1,751
ELGUIT	78	RICKENBAC	**4080 BASS** MAPLEGLO, DOUBLE NECK	2,366	**1,817**	1,605	1,415
ELGUIT	74	RICKENBAC	**480** FIRE GLO	1,552	**1,191**	1,053	928
ELGUIT	37	RICKENBAC	**B-6** BLACK & CHROME, BAKELITE NECK & BODY, ORIGINAL KAUFFMAN VIB	1,038	**797**	704	621
ELGUIT	38	RICKENBAC	**B-6** BLACK & WHITE	1,028	**789**	697	615
ELGUIT	48	RICKENBAC	**B-6** BLACK & WHITE	948	**728**	643	567
ELGUIT	50	RICKENBAC	**B-6** BLACK & WHITE	832	**638**	564	497
ELGUIT	56	RICKENBAC	**COMBO 400** BLUE TURQUOISE, DBL CUT TULIP BODY, GOLD ANODIZED PICKGUARD	1,644	**1,262**	1,115	983
ELGUIT	56	RICKENBAC	**COMBO 400** BLACK, DBL CUT TULIP BODY,GOLD ANODIZED PICKGUARD	1,700	**1,305**	1,153	1,017
ELGUIT	56	RICKENBAC	**COMBO 400** CLOVERFIELD GREEN,DBL CUT TULIP BODY,GOLD ANODIZE PICKGUARD	2,881	**2,212**	1,955	1,723
ELGUIT	57	RICKENBAC	**COMBO 400** BLACK, DBL CUT TULIP BODY, GOLD ANODIZED PICKGUARD	1,646	**1,264**	1,117	984
ELGUIT	57	RICKENBAC	**COMBO 400** BLUE TURQUOISE, DBL CUT TULIP BODY, GOLD ANODIZED PICKGUARD	1,646	**1,264**	1,117	984
ELGUIT	57	RICKENBAC	**COMBO 400** CLOVERFIELD GREEN,DBL CUT TULIP BODY,GOLD ANODIZE PICKGUARD	2,881	**2,212**	1,955	1,723
ELGUIT	58	RICKENBAC	**COMBO 400** BLACK, DBL CUT TULIP BODY, GOLD ANODIZED PICKGUARD	1,053	**809**	715	630
ELGUIT	58	RICKENBAC	**COMBO 400** BLUE TURQUOISE, DBL CUT TULIP BODY, GOLD ANODIZED PICKGUARD	1,644	**1,262**	1,115	983
ELGUIT	58	RICKENBAC	**COMBO 400** CLOVERFIELD GREEN,DBL CUT TULIP BODY,GOLD ANODIZE PICKGUARD	2,881	**2,212**	1,955	1,723
ELGUIT	62	RICKENBAC	**COMBO 420** FIREGLO	687	**528**	466	411
ELGUIT	66	RICKENBAC	**COMBO 420** FIREGLO	645	**495**	437	385
ELGUIT	72	RICKENBAC	**COMBO 420** MAPLEGLO	607	**466**	411	363
ELGUIT	63	RICKENBAC	**COMBO 425** FIREGLO	909	**698**	617	544
ELGUIT	64	RICKENBAC	**COMBO 425**	978	**751**	664	585
ELGUIT	58	RICKENBAC	**COMBO 450** SUNBURST	2,192	**1,683**	1,488	1,311
ELGUIT	59	RICKENBAC	**COMBO 450**	1,310	**1,006**	889	783
ELGUIT	60	RICKENBAC	**COMBO 450**	1,441	**1,106**	978	862
ELGUIT	61	RICKENBAC	**COMBO 450**	1,438	**1,104**	975	860
ELGUIT	65	RICKENBAC	**COMBO 450**	1,274	**978**	864	762
ELGUIT	66	RICKENBAC	**COMBO 450** MAPLEGLO	1,069	**821**	725	639
ELGUIT	67	RICKENBAC	**COMBO 450** FIREGLO	1,296	**995**	880	775
ELGUIT	74	RICKENBAC	**COMBO 450** BURGUNDY	800	**614**	543	479
ELGUIT	78	RICKENBAC	**COMBO 450** BLACK	720	**552**	488	430
ELGUIT	63	RICKENBAC	**COMBO 460**	1,277	**981**	867	764
ELGUIT	64	RICKENBAC	**COMBO 460**	973	**747**	660	582

TYPE	YR	MFG	PRICES--BASED ON 100% ORIGINAL MODEL	SELL EXC	SELL AVG	BUY EXC	BUY AVG
ELGUIT	66	RICKENBAC	COMBO 460	910	699	617	544
ELGUIT	67	RICKENBAC	COMBO 460 FIREGLO	910	699	617	544
ELGUIT	56	RICKENBAC	COMBO 600	982	743	655	543
ELGUIT	64	RICKENBAC	COMBO 615	1,046	803	709	625
ELGUIT	65	RICKENBAC	COMBO 615	669	514	454	400
ELGUIT	63	RICKENBAC	COMBO 625	854	656	579	511
ELGUIT	57	RICKENBAC	COMBO 650	917	693	611	507
ELGUIT	56	RICKENBAC	COMBO 800 BLOND	1,828	1,404	1,241	1,094
ELGUIT	57	RICKENBAC	COMBO 800	1,681	1,290	1,140	1,005
ELGUIT	57	RICKENBAC	COMBO 850	2,261	1,736	1,534	1,352
ELGUIT	58	RICKENBAC	COMBO 850	1,844	1,416	1,251	1,103
ELGUIT	57	RICKENBAC	COMBO 900	3,041	2,335	2,064	1,819
ELGUIT	66	RICKENBAC	COMBO 950	2,430	1,866	1,649	1,453
ELGUIT	60	RICKENBAC	COMBO 1000	2,916	2,239	1,979	1,744
ELGUIT	64	RICKENBAC	COMBO 1000 FIREGLO	3,072	2,358	2,084	1,837
ELGUIT	67	RICKENBAC	COMBO 1000	2,431	1,867	1,649	1,454
ELGUIT	71	RICKENBAC	CONVERTIBLE NATURAL, 12-STRING	1,587	1,218	1,076	949
ELGUIT	63	RICKENBAC	CW-6 NATURAL WALNUT, 6-STRING	537	412	364	321
ELGUIT	50	RICKENBAC	D-16 METAL w/2 8-STRING NECKS	698	536	474	418
ELGUIT	50	RICKENBAC	DC-12 METAL w/2 6-STRING NECKS	807	620	547	483
ELGUIT	50	RICKENBAC	DC-16 METAL & BRONZE w/2 8-STRING NECKS	860	660	583	514
ELGUIT	57	RICKENBAC	DW DOUBLE NECK STEEL w/2 6-STRING NECKS	714	548	484	427
ELGUIT	38	RICKENBAC	ELECTRO	1,729	1,327	1,173	1,034
ELGUIT	65	RICKENBAC	ELECTRO 6-STRING	673	516	456	402
ELGUIT	67	RICKENBAC	ELECTRO 6-STRING	1,302	1,000	883	779
ELGUIT	65	RICKENBAC	ELECTRO 3/4 1 PU, SERIAL #2230-	673	516	456	402
ELGUIT	62	RICKENBAC	ELECTRO 102 RED	675	518	458	404
ELGUIT	63	RICKENBAC	ELECTRO BASS FIREGLO, 1 PU	555	426	376	332
ELGUIT	65	RICKENBAC	ELECTRO BASS SOLID, 1 PU, SERIAL #2601-	649	498	440	388
ELGUIT	64	RICKENBAC	ELECTRO ES-16	666	511	452	398
ELGUIT	65	RICKENBAC	ELECTRO ES-17 FIREGLO	673	516	456	402
ELGUIT	46	RICKENBAC	ELECTRO ITALIAN	739	567	501	442
ELGUIT	47	RICKENBAC	ELECTRO ITALIAN	745	572	506	446
ELGUIT	48	RICKENBAC	ELECTRO NS METAL & GREY	711	546	482	425
ELGUIT	35	RICKENBAC	ELECTRO SPANISH HOLLOW BAKELITE BODY, FIVE CHROME PLATES	4,780	3,670	3,243	2,859
ELGUIT	36	RICKENBAC	ELECTRO SPANISH HOLLOW BAKELITE BODY, FIVE CHROME PLATES	4,780	3,670	3,243	2,859
ELGUIT	38	RICKENBAC	ELECTRO SPANISH HOLLOW BAKELITE BODY, FIVE CHROME PLATES	4,412	3,388	2,994	2,639
ELGUIT	39	RICKENBAC	ELECTRO SPANISH HOLLOW BAKELITE BODY, FIVE CHROME PLATES	4,412	3,388	2,994	2,639
ELGUIT	40	RICKENBAC	ELECTRO SPANISH MODEL B, HOLLOW BAKELITE BODY, FIVE CHROME PLATES	4,167	3,200	2,827	2,493
ELGUIT	41	RICKENBAC	ELECTRO SPANISH MODEL B, HOLLOW BAKELITE BODY, FIVE CHROME PLATES	4,167	3,200	2,827	2,493
ELGUIT	42	RICKENBAC	ELECTRO SPANISH MODEL B, HOLLOW BAKELITE BODY, FIVE CHROME PLATES	4,167	3,200	2,827	2,493
ELGUIT	43	RICKENBAC	ELECTRO SPANISH MODEL B, HOLLOW BAKELITE BODY, FIVE CHROME PLATES	4,167	3,200	2,827	2,493
ELGUIT	33	RICKENBAC	FRYING PAN A-25 ELECTRIC STEEL	4,219	3,239	2,862	2,523
ELGUIT	35	RICKENBAC	FRYING PAN A-25 ELECTRIC STEEL	4,206	3,230	2,854	2,516
ELGUIT	50	RICKENBAC	SD METAL & COPPER	711	546	482	425
ELGUIT	37	RICKENBAC	SILVER HAWAIIAN CHROME-PLATED BODY	607	466	411	363
GUITAR AMP	55	RICKENBAC	8ME GRAY, 8" SPEAKER	430	330	291	257
GTAMP	40	RICKENBAC	ELECTRO 1x12", 10 WATT	603	463	409	361
GTAMP	55	RICKENBAC	M-88 GRAY TOLEX	568	429	378	314
GTAMP	78	RICKENBAC	TR-75G 2x12" SPEAKERS, 75 WATT	380	292	258	227

TYPE	YR	MFG	MODEL	SELL EXC	SELL AVG	BUY EXC	BUY AVG
			PRICES--BASED ON 100% ORIGINAL				
GTAMP	78	RICKENBAC	**TR- 75SG** 1x10" AND 1x15" SPEAKERS	357	**274**	242	213
GTAMP	78	RICKENBAC	**TR-100G** 4x12" SPEAKERS, 100 WATT	577	**443**	392	345
GTAMP	68	RICKENBAC	**TRANSONIC** 2x12" REV	512	**393**	348	306
GTAMP	68	RICKENBAC	**TRANSONIC BASS** 1x18"	602	**462**	408	360
GUITAR (ACOUSTIC)	60	RICKENBAC	**310** THIN HOLLOW BODY	1,455	**1,100**	970	804
GUITAR	64	RICKENBAC	**315** THIN HOLLOW BODY	1,067	**819**	724	638
GUITAR	67	RICKENBAC	**320** THIN HOLLOW BODY	2,437	**1,871**	1,653	1,457
GUITAR	58	RICKENBAC	**325** THIN HOLLOW BODY	5,037	**3,868**	3,418	3,013
GUITAR	64	RICKENBAC	**325** THIN HOLLOW BODY	3,745	**2,875**	2,541	2,240
GUITAR	66	RICKENBAC	**325** THIN HOLLOW BODY	2,998	**2,302**	2,034	1,793
GUITAR	70	RICKENBAC	**325** BLACK, 3 PU's, THIN HOLLOW BODY	1,700	**1,305**	1,153	1,017
GUITAR	60	RICKENBAC	**330F** THIN HOLLOW BODY	1,609	**1,235**	1,092	962
GUITAR	61	RICKENBAC	**330F** THIN HOLLOW BODY	2,362	**1,813**	1,602	1,413
GUITAR	66	RICKENBAC	**330F** FIREGLO, THIN HOLLOW BODY	2,169	**1,665**	1,472	1,297
GUITAR	68	RICKENBAC	**330F** THIN HOLLOW BODY	1,844	**1,416**	1,251	1,103
GUITAR	72	RICKENBAC	**331** LIGHT SHOW	5,270	**4,047**	3,576	3,153
GUITAR	60	RICKENBAC	**335F** THIN HOLLOW BODY	1,732	**1,330**	1,175	1,036
GUITAR	66	RICKENBAC	**335F** THIN HOLLOW BODY	1,252	**961**	849	749
GUITAR	68	RICKENBAC	**336-12** FIREGLO, THIN HOLLOW BODY	1,354	**1,039**	918	810
GUITAR	66	RICKENBAC	**340F** THIN HOLLOW BODY	1,358	**1,043**	921	812
GUITAR	61	RICKENBAC	**345F** THIN FULL BODY	1,609	**1,235**	1,092	962
GUITAR	66	RICKENBAC	**345F** THIN HOLLOW BODY	1,925	**1,478**	1,306	1,151
GUITAR	59	RICKENBAC	**360** AUTUMNGLO	3,851	**2,957**	2,613	2,304
GUITAR	67	RICKENBAC	**360** MAPLEGLO	1,603	**1,231**	1,088	959
GUITAR	71	RICKENBAC	**360** NATURAL	1,834	**1,408**	1,244	1,097
GUITAR	65	RICKENBAC	**360-12** MAPLEGLO	3,008	**2,309**	2,041	1,799
GUITAR	66	RICKENBAC	**360-12** MAPLEGLO	1,775	**1,363**	1,204	1,061
GUITAR	67	RICKENBAC	**360-12** FIREGLO, SERIAL #GC1417	2,261	**1,736**	1,534	1,352
GUITAR	72	RICKENBAC	**360-12** FIREGLO	1,428	**1,096**	969	854
GUITAR	66	RICKENBAC	**360-12F** THIN FULL BODY	2,141	**1,644**	1,453	1,281
GUITAR	65	RICKENBAC	**360-12WB** FIREGLO, SERIAL #EJ967	2,957	**2,271**	2,007	1,769
GUITAR	59	RICKENBAC	**360F** THIN FULL BODY	4,337	**3,330**	2,943	2,594
GUITAR	60	RICKENBAC	**360F** THIN FULL BODY	3,857	**2,961**	2,617	2,307
GUITAR	68	RICKENBAC	**360F** THIN FULL BODY	2,346	**1,801**	1,592	1,403
GUITAR	59	RICKENBAC	**365** NATURAL	2,924	**2,245**	1,984	1,749
GUITAR	60	RICKENBAC	**365** FIREGLO	2,201	**1,690**	1,494	1,317
GUITAR	66	RICKENBAC	**365** FIREGLO	1,288	**989**	874	770
GUITAR	60	RICKENBAC	**365F** NATURAL	6,494	**4,910**	4,329	3,590
GUITAR	68	RICKENBAC	**365WB** FIREGLO	5,904	**4,464**	3,936	3,264
GUITAR	64	RICKENBAC	**366** CONVERTIBLE 6 & 12-STRING	3,277	**2,516**	2,223	1,960
GUITAR	68	RICKENBAC	**366-12** BURGUNDY	2,200	**1,689**	1,493	1,316
GUITAR	69	RICKENBAC	**366-12** BLACK	2,904	**2,229**	1,970	1,737

TYPE	YR	MFG	MODEL (PRICES--BASED ON 100% ORIGINAL)	SELL EXC	SELL AVG	BUY EXC	BUY AVG
GUITAR	66	RICKENBAC	**370-12** MAPLEGLO	2,954	**2,268**	2,004	1,767
GUITAR	68	RICKENBAC	**370F** THIN FULL BODY	1,868	**1,434**	1,267	1,117
GUITAR	68	RICKENBAC	**370WB** FIREGLO	2,387	**1,805**	1,591	1,319
GUITAR	59	RICKENBAC	**375** CAPRI	3,351	**2,573**	2,273	2,004
GUITAR	61	RICKENBAC	**375** CAPRI	3,689	**2,832**	2,503	2,206
GUITAR	67	RICKENBAC	**375** CAPRI	2,145	**1,647**	1,456	1,283
GUITAR	60	RICKENBAC	**375F** THIN FULL BODY	4,052	**3,111**	2,749	2,424
GUITAR	59	RICKENBAC	**381** THICK BODY	4,838	**3,715**	3,283	2,894
GUITAR	69	RICKENBAC	**381** FIREGLO, THICK BODY	2,344	**1,799**	1,590	1,402
GUITAR	70	RICKENBAC	**381** THICK BODY	2,924	**2,245**	1,984	1,749
GUITAR	58	RICKENBAC	**385** THICK BODY, FLATTOP	4,038	**3,101**	2,740	2,416
GUITAR	67	RICKENBAC	**385** D SHAPE, THICK BODY	1,868	**1,434**	1,267	1,117
GUITAR	68	RICKENBAC	**385S** JUMBO FLATTOP, THICK BODY	2,075	**1,593**	1,408	1,241
GUITAR	63	RICKENBAC	**390** THICK BODY	3,643	**2,797**	2,472	2,179
GUITAR	76	RICKENBAC	**360MG** MAPLE GLO	1,313	**1,008**	891	785
GUITAR	40	RICKENBAC	**PATRICIAN** ARCHTOP	1,340	**1,029**	909	801
STEEL GUITAR	56	RICKENBAC	**100** BROWN, 6-STRING	603	**463**	409	361
STGUIT	32	RICKENBAC	**A-22** 22 1/2" SCALE	1,671	**1,283**	1,133	999
STGUIT	46	RICKENBAC	**ACADEMY** BAKELITE, STUDENT MODEL	682	**523**	462	408
STGUIT	47	RICKENBAC	**ACADEMY** BAKELITE, STUDENT MODEL	658	**505**	446	393
STGUIT	48	RICKENBAC	**ACADEMY** BAKELITE, STUDENT MODEL	560	**430**	380	335
STGUIT	50	RICKENBAC	**BD** BLACK, 6-STRING	723	**555**	490	432
STGUIT	53	RICKENBAC	**BD** BLACK, 6-STRING	601	**461**	408	359
STGUIT	50	RICKENBAC	**BRONSON** BROWN, MODEL 52	724	**556**	491	433
STGUIT	60	RICKENBAC	**CW-6** WALNUT, 6-STRING, 3 LEGS	723	**555**	490	432
STGUIT	60	RICKENBAC	**CW-6** WALNUT, 6-STRING	817	**627**	554	489
STGUIT	40	RICKENBAC	**ELECTRO** LAP STEEL, DOUBLE NECK	1,286	**988**	873	769
STGUIT	42	RICKENBAC	**ELECTRO** 2 8-STRING NECKS, DOUBLE NECK	922	**708**	626	552
STGUIT	43	RICKENBAC	**ELECTRO** 2 8-STRING NECKS, DOUBLE NECK	893	**686**	606	534
STGUIT	45	RICKENBAC	**ELECTRO** 2 8-STRING NECKS, DOUBLE NECK	816	**626**	554	488
STGUIT	34	RICKENBAC	**ELECTRO B** BAKELITE, 6-STRING	1,767	**1,357**	1,199	1,057
STGUIT	36	RICKENBAC	**ELECTRO B** 6-STRING	1,556	**1,195**	1,056	931
STGUIT	37	RICKENBAC	**ELECTRO B** 6-STRING	1,542	**1,184**	1,046	922
STGUIT	38	RICKENBAC	**ELECTRO B** 6-STRING	1,523	**1,169**	1,033	911
STGUIT	38	RICKENBAC	**ELECTRO B** 8-STRING	1,927	**1,480**	1,307	1,153
STGUIT	39	RICKENBAC	**ELECTRO B** 6-STRING	1,384	**1,062**	939	828
STGUIT	40	RICKENBAC	**ELECTRO B** 6-STRING	1,341	**1,030**	910	802
STGUIT	40	RICKENBAC	**ELECTRO B** 8-STRING	1,723	**1,323**	1,169	1,031
STGUIT	41	RICKENBAC	**ELECTRO B** 8-STRING	1,621	**1,225**	1,080	896
STGUIT	46	RICKENBAC	**ELECTRO B** 8-STRING	732	**562**	497	438
STGUIT	49	RICKENBAC	**ELECTRO B** 6-STRING	762	**585**	517	456
STGUIT	48	RICKENBAC	**ELECTRO DOUBLE NECK**	781	**600**	530	467

TYPE	YR	MFG	MODEL	SELL EXC	SELL AVG	BUY EXC	BUY AVG
			PRICES--BASED ON 100% ORIGINAL				
STGUIT	48	RICKENBAC	**ELECTRO NS** GRAY, 6-STRING	605	**465**	411	362
STGUIT	49	RICKENBAC	**ELECTRO NS** GRAY, 6-STRING	588	**451**	399	351
STGUIT	52	RICKENBAC	**ELECTRO SD** TAN 2-TONE, 6-STRING	570	**437**	386	341
STGUIT	53	RICKENBAC	**ELECTRO SD** TAN, 6-STRING	751	**577**	509	449
STGUIT	54	RICKENBAC	**G DELUXE HAWAIIAN STEEL**	781	**600**	530	467
STGUIT	64	RICKENBAC	**LAP STEEL** FIREGLO, WOOD BODY	586	**450**	398	351
STGUIT	46	RICKENBAC	**MODEL S** GRAY SPARKLE, 6-STRING, PU	682	**523**	462	408
STGUIT	48	RICKENBAC	**MODEL S** GRAY SUNBURST, METAL BODY	728	**559**	494	435
STGUIT	49	RICKENBAC	**MODEL S** GRAY, 6-STRING, METAL BODY	605	**465**	411	362
STGUIT	49	RICKENBAC	**MODEL SD** COPPER FINISH, 6-STRING	645	**495**	437	385

RIDGELAND

TYPE	YR	MFG	MODEL	SELL EXC	SELL AVG	BUY EXC	BUY AVG
BANJO	81	RIDGE	**B-200 5-STRING** 16-BRACKET	95	**73**	64	56
BANJO	81	RIDGE	**B-200R 5-STRING** 16-BRACKET	96	**73**	65	57
BANJO	81	RIDGE	**B-200WR 5-STRING** 16-BRACKET	96	**73**	65	57
BANJO	81	RIDGE	**B-230 5-STRING** 30-BRACKET	98	**75**	66	58
BANJO	81	RIDGE	**B-230R 5-STRING** 30-BRACKET	96	**73**	65	57
BANJO	81	RIDGE	**B-230RC 5-STRING** 30-BRACKET	98	**75**	66	58
BANJO	81	RIDGE	**BK-160 5-STRING** 16-BRACKET	89	**68**	60	53
BANJO	81	RIDGE	**BK-160R** TENOR, 16-BRACKET	96	**73**	65	57
BANJO	81	RIDGE	**BK-160R 5-STRING** 16-BRACKET	95	**73**	64	56
BANJO	81	RIDGE	**BT-200** TENOR, 16-BRACKET	96	**73**	65	57
BANJO	81	RIDGE	**BT-200R** TENOR	98	**75**	66	58
BANJO	81	RIDGE	**BT-230R** TENOR, 30-BRACKET	95	**73**	64	56

ROAD

TYPE	YR	MFG	MODEL	SELL EXC	SELL AVG	BUY EXC	BUY AVG
MIC	97	ROAD	**TLM-103**	856	**657**	581	512

ROLAND CORPORATION

TYPE	YR	MFG	MODEL	SELL EXC	SELL AVG	BUY EXC	BUY AVG
EFFECTS	74	ROLAND	**AF- 60 BEE GEE FUZZ**	204	**157**	139	122
EFFECTS	75	ROLAND	**AF-100 BEE BAA FUZZ TREBLE BASS**	378	**290**	256	226
GUITAR AMP	78	ROLAND	**CUBE- 20** ORANGE	266	**204**	180	159
GTAMP	78	ROLAND	**CUBE- 40**	342	**263**	232	205
GTAMP	82	ROLAND	**CUBE- 40** ORANGE	446	**343**	303	267
GTAMP	79	ROLAND	**CUBE- 60** ORANGE, 1 SPEAKER	456	**350**	310	273
GTAMP	78	ROLAND	**CUBE- 60B BASS** 1 SPEAKER	380	**292**	258	227
GTAMP	79	ROLAND	**CUBE- 60B BASS**	364	**279**	247	217
SIGNAL PROCESSOR	70	ROLAND	**MI-11001**	3,543	**2,721**	2,404	2,119
SGNPRO	79	ROLAND	**SDD-320 DIMENSION D**	1,051	**807**	713	629
SGNPRO	79	ROLAND	**SRE-556 CHORUS ECHO**	1,697	**1,303**	1,152	1,015
SGNPRO	79	ROLAND	**SVC-350 VOCODER**	1,697	**1,303**	1,152	1,015
SYNTHESIZER	75	ROLAND	**GR-500 GUITAR/MODULE** 3 PU's	703	**540**	477	420
SYNTH	78	ROLAND	**RS-09** ORGAN, STRING	342	**263**	232	205
SYNTH	78	ROLAND	**SH 7** ANALOG	670	**515**	455	401
SYNTH	81- 82	ROLAND	**SH-01 MINIANALOT SYNTH**	371	**285**	252	222

OSCAR SCHMIDT, DIVISION of US MUSIC CORP

TYPE	YR	MFG	MODEL	SELL EXC	SELL AVG	BUY EXC	BUY AVG
MANDOLA	91	SCHMIDT	**OM-10 "A" STYLE** TOBACCO SUNBURST, SELECT SPRUCE TOP, MAHOG BACK/SIDES	311	**239**	211	186

SCOTT

TYPE	YR	MFG	MODEL	SELL EXC	SELL AVG	BUY EXC	BUY AVG
BANJO	65	SCOTT	**232 TUBE**	150	**115**	101	89
BANJO	56	SCOTT	**240 TUBE**	176	**135**	120	105
BANJO	61	SCOTT	**4100 TUBE**	651	**500**	442	389
BANJO	66	SCOTT	**LK-150 KIT TUBE**	443	**340**	300	265

TYPE	YR	MFG	PRICES--BASED ON 100% ORIGINAL MODEL	SELL EXC	SELL AVG	BUY EXC	BUY AVG
TUNER	53	SCOTT	311A	135	104	91	81

SELMER CO, INC - Now CONN-SELMER

TYPE	YR	MFG	MODEL	SELL EXC	SELL AVG	BUY EXC	BUY AVG
GUITAR AMP	67	SELMER	**BASSMASTER HEAD**	1,061	815	720	635
GTAMP	65	SELMER	**CONSTELLATION 20**	1,599	1,228	1,085	956
GTAMP	64	SELMER	**EXTENSION CAB 2x12"**	1,196	918	811	715
GTAMP	64	SELMER	**THUNDERBIRD** 50 WATT	976	749	662	584
GTAMP	62	SELMER	**TRUE VOICE BASS** 50 WATT	663	509	449	396
GTAMP	63	SELMER	**TRUE VOICE LEAD** 30 WATT	495	380	335	296
GTAMP	65	SELMER	**ZODIAC** 100 WATT HEAD	673	516	456	402
GTAMP	66	SELMER	**ZODIAC** 50 WATT	950	730	645	568
SAXOPHONE	79	SELMER	**55 BARITONE**	2,382	1,829	1,616	1,425
SAX	79	SELMER	**55A BARITONE** LOW A	3,892	2,988	2,641	2,328
SAX	74	SELMER	**MARK 6**	3,529	2,709	2,394	2,111

SENNHEISER ELECTRONICS CORPORATION

TYPE	YR	MFG	MODEL	SELL EXC	SELL AVG	BUY EXC	BUY AVG
MIC	85	SENN	**MD- 21N DYNAMIC**	430	330	291	257
MIC	65	SENN	**MD-211 DYNAMIC**	673	516	456	402

SEQUENTIAL CIRCUITS

TYPE	YR	MFG	MODEL	SELL EXC	SELL AVG	BUY EXC	BUY AVG
SYNTHESIZER	81	SEQU	**100 PRO-ONE** MONO ANALOG	1,048	804	711	627
SYNTH	78	SEQU	**1000 PROPHET- 5** REV. 1 or 2	624	479	424	373
SYNTH	79	SEQU	**1000 PROPHET- 5** REV. 3, MIDI	1,031	792	699	617
SYNTH	80	SEQU	**1010 PROPHET-10** MIDI	1,324	1,017	899	792

SHURE BROTHERS, INC.

TYPE	YR	MFG	MODEL	SELL EXC	SELL AVG	BUY EXC	BUY AVG
MIC	39	SHURE	**55B "ELVIS"**	388	298	263	232
MIC	68	SHURE	**55SW**	54	42	37	32
MIC	58	SHURE	**55s** OLD STYLE, ROUND SIDES	131	100	88	78
MIC	75	SHURE	**330 UNI RIBOON**	645	495	437	385
MIC	38	SHURE	**555B DYNAMIC**	448	344	304	268
MIC	46	SHURE	**556S UNIDYNE**	336	258	228	201
MIC	67	SHURE	**BROWN BULLET**	155	119	105	93
MIC	67	SHURE	**GREEN BULLET**	551	423	373	329
MIC	69	SHURE	**PE 53V SPHERE-O-DYNE**	239	184	162	143
MIC	57	SHURE	**PE 566 UNISPHERE I** GOLD-PLATED	216	165	146	129
MIC	81	SHURE	**SM 33 UNI RIBBON**	658	505	446	393
MIC	78	SHURE	**SM 76 OMNI DYNAMIC**	604	464	410	361
TEST	73	SHURE	**II-QUAD CLASSIC MONO TUBE**	314	241	213	188
TEST	62	SHURE	**S-3000 II**	248	190	168	148

SILVERTONE by DANELECTRO

TYPE	YR	MFG	MODEL	SELL EXC	SELL AVG	BUY EXC	BUY AVG
ELEC. GUITAR & BASS	58	SILVERTON	**BASS** BROWN, WHITE SIDES, SINGLE CUTAWAY, 1 PU	627	481	425	375
ELGUIT	59	SILVERTON	**BASS** BROWN, WHITE SIDES, SINGLE CUTAWAY, 1 PU	488	374	331	292
ELGUIT	60	SILVERTON	**BASS** SUNBURST, SINGLE CUTAWAY, 1 PU	458	351	310	274
ELGUIT	63	SILVERTON	**BASS** RED SUNBURST, 2 PU's	441	338	299	263
ELGUIT	64	SILVERTON	**BASS** BLACK, SINGLE CUTAWAY, 1 PU	409	314	278	245
ELGUIT	64	SILVERTON	**BASS** RED SPARKLE, 2 PU's	620	476	421	371
ELGUIT	60	SILVERTON	**BASS IV** 1 LIPSTICK PU	632	485	429	378
ELGUIT	58	SILVERTON	**DAN ELECTRO** WHITE, SINGLE CUTAWAY, 1 PU	365	280	247	218
ELGUIT	58	SILVERTON	**DAN ELECTRO** BROWN, SINGLE CUTAWAY, 1 PU	495	380	335	296
ELGUIT	64	SILVERTON	**DAN ELECTRO** RED SPARKLE, 2 PU's	323	248	219	193
ELGUIT	63	SILVERTON	**ESPANADA** BLACK, 2 PU's	555	426	376	332
ELGUIT	64	SILVERTON	**ESPANADA**	594	456	403	355
ELGUIT	55	SILVERTON	**JIMMY REED MODEL** SUNBURST	893	686	606	534
ELGUIT	55	SILVERTON	**METEOR** SUNBURST, SINGLE CUTAWAY, 1 PU	329	252	223	196
ELGUIT	64	SILVERTON	**STANDARD** BRONZE, SINGLE CUTAWAY, 1 PU	364	279	247	217

TYPE	YR	MFG	PRICES--BASED ON 100% ORIGINAL MODEL	SELL EXC	SELL AVG	BUY EXC	BUY AVG
GUITAR AMP	65	SILVERTON	1 x 12" TREMOLO	243	186	164	145
GTAMP	40	SILVERTON	1304 RED	603	463	409	361
GTAMP	55	SILVERTON	1331	430	330	291	257
GTAMP	59	SILVERTON	1459 BLACK, 2x12" TUBES	390	300	265	233
GTAMP	61	SILVERTON	1472 TREMOLO, 12" JENSEN	226	173	153	135
GTAMP	63	SILVERTON	1472	328	251	222	196
GTAMP	63	SILVERTON	1481	229	176	155	137
GTAMP	64	SILVERTON	1481 1x6" SPEAKER	171	131	116	102
GTAMP	67	SILVERTON	1481 GRAY, 1x8", TUBE	155	119	105	93
GTAMP	60	SILVERTON	1482 1x12" SPEAKER	209	160	142	125
GTAMP	61	SILVERTON	1482 TREMOLO, 6V6GT TUBES	201	154	136	120
GTAMP	62	SILVERTON	1482 1x12" SPEAKER	162	124	110	97
GTAMP	63	SILVERTON	1482 TREMOLO, 12" JENSEN	171	131	116	102
GTAMP	64	SILVERTON	1483 50 WATT	178	136	120	106
GTAMP	64	SILVERTON	1484 2x12" JENSENS	328	251	222	196
GTAMP	66	SILVERTON	1484 2X12" SPEAKER	448	344	304	268
GTAMP	65	SILVERTON	1485 6x12" JENSENS	560	430	380	335
GTAMP	64	SILVERTON	TWIN 12	456	350	310	273
GUITAR (ACOUSTIC)	60	SILVERTON	1448 BLACK SPARKLE, FORMICA TOP	260	200	177	156
GUITAR	58	SILVERTON	JUMBO BLOND, SPRUCE TOP, FLATTOP	547	420	371	327
GUITAR	58	SILVERTON	K-11 BLOND, SPRUCE TOP, MAPLE BACK/SIDES	562	431	381	336
MANDOLIN	59	SILVERTON	1417L COPPER FINISH, LIPSTICK PU, DOLPHIN HEADSTOCK	574	441	389	343
MANDOL	64	SILVERTON	1457L RED SPARKLE,2 PU's,CONCENTRIC CONTROLS,AMP,CASE	579	444	392	346
STEEL GUITAR	50	SILVERTON	6-STRING LAP STEEL	163	125	110	97

SLINGERLAND

TYPE	YR	MFG	MODEL	SELL EXC	SELL AVG	BUY EXC	BUY AVG
BANJO	24	SLINGER	BANJO-UKE	481	369	326	288
BANJO	20	SLINGER	MANDOLIN-BANJO	472	362	320	282
BANJO	25	SLINGER	MAYBELL PLECTRUM, WALNUT, RESONATOR	797	612	541	477
BANJO	30	SLINGER	MAYBELL PLECTRUM, WALNUT, RESONATOR	787	604	534	471
BANJO	23	SLINGER	MAYBELL BANJO-UKE	735	565	499	440
BANJO	30	SLINGER	MAYBELL QUEEN TENOR	785	602	532	469
BANJO	28	SLINGER	MAYBELL RECORDING SONGSTER TENOR	813	624	551	486
BANJO	30	SLINGER	MAYBELL RECORDING SONGSTER TENOR	797	612	541	477
BANJO	28	SLINGER	MAYBELL TENOR 17-FRET	812	623	551	485
BANJO	27	SLINGER	PRO-TONE MODEL 20 BANJO-UKE	647	497	439	387
BANJO	28	SLINGER	TROUBADOUR TENOR, BRAZILIAN ROSEWOOD	747	573	506	446
GUITAR (ACOUSTIC)	37	SLINGER	GOLDEN HAWAIIAN SUNBURST, BIRCH BODY	571	438	387	341
GUITAR	30	SLINGER	MAYBELL TENOR, NATURAL, MAHOGANY BACK/SIDES	789	606	535	472
GUITAR	33	SLINGER	MAYBELL SUNBURST, MAHOGANY BACK/SIDES, VIOLIN CRAFT	840	645	570	502
GUITAR	35	SLINGER	MAYBELL SUNBURST, ARCHTOP, MAHOGANY BACK/SIDES	822	631	557	491
GUITAR	35	SLINGER	MAYBELL SUNBURST, ARCHTOP, F-HOLES	824	632	559	493
GUITAR	37	SLINGER	MAYBELL SUNBURST, ARCHTOP	837	643	568	501
GUITAR	38	SLINGER	NIGHTHAWK SUNBURST, ARCHTOP, MAPLE BACK/SIDES	789	606	535	472
GUITAR	38	SLINGER	SILVERHAWK SUNBURST, ARCHTOP, MAPLE BACK/SIDES	797	612	541	477
GUITAR	37	SLINGER	SONGSTER SUNBURST, DOT INLAYS	819	629	556	490

TYPE		YR	MFG	PRICES--BASED ON 100% ORIGINAL MODEL	SELL EXC	SELL AVG	BUY EXC	BUY AVG
				SOLANO				
UPRIG		80	SOLANO	**PANORMO** FLAT BLACK	27,108	**20,815**	18,395	16,216
	UPRIGHT	80	SOLANO	**PRESCOTT CARVED BASS**	32,652	**25,072**	22,157	19,533
				SONANCE				
SPKR		92	SONANCE	**DB4** SPEAKER DISTRIBUTION SYSTEM	144	**110**	98	86
				SONY PRO AUDIO				
MIC		73	SONYP	**C -77 SHOTGUN FET CONDENSER**	2,057	**1,579**	1,396	1,230
	MIC	59	SONYP	**C- 37A TUBE**	3,232	**2,481**	2,193	1,933
	MIC	71	SONYP	**C- 37P FIXED CARDIOD OMNI**	1,290	**990**	875	771
	MIC	78	SONYP	**C- 38B FIXED**	1,234	**947**	837	738
	MIC	71	SONYP	**C-500 S/B OMNI-DIRECTIONAL ECM**	2,058	**1,580**	1,396	1,231
	MIC	89	SONYP	**ECM-77 S/B OMNIDIRECTIONAL ECM**	2,219	**1,704**	1,506	1,327
				SOUNDCITY				
GUITAR AMP		74	SOUNDCITY	**CONCORD COMBO**	696	**526**	464	384
	GTAMP	72	SOUNDCITY	**TUBE GUITAR HEAD** 100 WATT	706	**533**	470	390
				STEINBERGER SOUND by GIBSON MUSICAL INST				
ELEC. GUITAR & BASS		n/a	STEINBERG	**SPIRIT GU DELUXE** DBL CUTAWAY MAPLE, HEADLESS MAPLE NECK, HSH EMG SELECT PU's	413	**317**	280	247
				STEINER SYNTHESIZERS				
SYNTHESIZER		79	STEINER	**BASIC STUDIO SYNTHACON ANALOG**	1,961	**1,505**	1,330	1,173
	SYNTH	79	STEINER	**KEYBOARDLESS SYNTHACON ANALOG**	1,305	**1,002**	886	781
	SYNTH	79	STEINER	**MULTIPHONIC SYNTHACON ANALOG**	2,177	**1,671**	1,477	1,302
	SYNTH	79	STEINER	**SYNTHACON ANALOG**	1,524	**1,170**	1,034	911
	SYNTH	79	STEINER	**SYNTHACON II ANALOG**	1,961	**1,505**	1,330	1,173
	SYNTH	79	STEINER	**SYNTHACON SYSTEM ANALOG**	3,291	**2,527**	2,233	1,969
				STELLA				
BANJO		65	STELLA	**TENOR**	354	**267**	236	195
GUITAR (ACOUSTIC)		31	STELLA	**6-STRING AUDITORIUM SIZE**	688	**528**	467	412
	GUITAR	26	STELLA	**12-STRING** LEAD BELLY MODEL	1,359	**1,044**	922	813
	GUITAR	27	STELLA	**12-STRING** LEAD BELLY MODEL	7,303	**5,608**	4,955	4,369
	GUITAR	30	STELLA	**12-STRING** LEAD BELLY MODEL	6,969	**5,351**	4,729	4,169
	GUITAR	32	STELLA	**12-STRING** LEAD BELLY MODEL	6,620	**5,083**	4,492	3,960
	GUITAR	33	STELLA	**12-STRING** LEAD BELLY MODEL	6,558	**5,036**	4,450	3,923
	GUITAR	55	STELLA	**12-STRING**	1,273	**977**	864	761
	GUITAR	30	STELLA	**TENOR** WALNUT, BIRCH BODY	426	**327**	289	255
	GUITAR	50	STELLA	**TENOR** SUNBURST, 4-STRING	488	**374**	331	292
UKULELE		20	STELLA	**UKE** BIRCH	224	**172**	152	134
				S. S. STEWART				
BANJO		25	STEWART	**OPEN BACK** CURVED NECK	612	**470**	415	366
	BANJO	89	STEWART	**SPECIAL** 1889, IVORY TUNERS, DECORATIVE	1,624	**1,247**	1,102	971
	BANJO	89	STEWART	**SPECIAL THOROUGHBRED** 1889, OPEN BACK, 5-STRING	1,544	**1,185**	1,048	923
				STROMBERG				
BANJO		20	STROMBERG	**BOSTON TENOR** OPEN BACK	1,552	**1,191**	1,053	928
	BANJO	51	STROMBERG	**G-3 CUTAWAY SUNBURST** SS #602,BIG LEAF MAPLE B/S/NECK,SPRUCE TOP,EBONY FRET	77,583	**59,573**	52,645	46,411
	BANJO	30	STROMBERG	**MARIMBA TENOR**	2,084	**1,600**	1,414	1,246
	BANJO	54	STROMBERG	**MASTER 400 CUTAWAY** SS #629,BLOND,BIG LEAF MAPLE B/S,SPRUCE TOP,EBONY FRET	297,160	**228,176**	201,644	177,765
	BANJO	48	STROMBERG	**MASTER 400 SUNBURST REFIN** SS #556,MAPLE B/S/NECK,SPRUCE TOP,EBONY FRET,INLAYS	65,540	**50,325**	44,473	39,207
GUITAR (ACOUSTIC)		51	STROMBERG	**APPRENTICE 100** SUNBURST, FULL BODY	30,346	**23,301**	20,592	18,153
	GUITAR	48	STROMBERG	**APPRENTICE 200** BLOND, FULL BODY	37,796	**29,022**	25,647	22,610
	GUITAR	35	STROMBERG	**DELUXE** SUNBURST, ARCHTOP	28,446	**21,843**	19,303	17,017
	GUITAR	47	STROMBERG	**DELUXE** SUNBURST, 17" FULL BODY	21,238	**16,308**	14,411	12,705

TYPE	YR	MFG	PRICES--BASED ON 100% ORIGINAL MODEL	SELL EXC	SELL AVG	BUY EXC	BUY AVG
GUITAR	50	STROMBERG	**DELUXE** SUNBURST, CUTAWAY	27,235	**20,912**	18,480	16,292
GUITAR	40	STROMBERG	**G-1**	8,957	**6,878**	6,078	5,358
GUITAR	48	STROMBERG	**G-1** ARCHTOP	5,524	**4,242**	3,749	3,305
GUITAR	37	STROMBERG	**G-3** SUNBURST, 17" SPLIT F-HOLES	6,566	**5,042**	4,455	3,928
GUITAR	48	STROMBERG	**MASTER 300** BLOND, FULL BODY	42,267	**32,455**	28,681	25,285
GUITAR	50	STROMBERG	**MASTER 300** SUNBURST, CUTAWAY	37,500	**28,795**	25,447	22,433
GUITAR	51	STROMBERG	**MASTER 300** SUNBURST, FULL BODY	36,305	**27,877**	24,636	21,718
GUITAR	50	STROMBERG	**MASTER 400** SUNBURST	62,408	**47,920**	42,348	37,333
GUITAR	52	STROMBERG	**MASTER 400** NATURAL, ARCHTOP	114,008	**87,541**	77,362	68,201
GUITAR	54	STROMBERG	**MASTER 400** BLOND, CUTAWAY	195,923	**150,441**	132,948	117,204

SUPERTONE

TYPE	YR	MFG	MODEL	SELL EXC	SELL AVG	BUY EXC	BUY AVG
BANJO	25	SUPER	**ORPHEUM #2 TENOR** WALNUT NECK, RESONATOR	1,006	**773**	683	602
ELEC. GUITAR & BASS	37	SUPER	**S-39 TREBLE CLEF DESIGN V-NECK**	387	**297**	262	231
GUITAR (ACOUSTIC)	35	SUPER	**BRADLEY KINKAID HOUND DOG** MAHOGANY BACK/SIDES	380	**292**	258	227
GUITAR	40	SUPER	**BRADLEY KINKAID HOUND DOG**	426	**327**	289	255
GUITAR	32	SUPER	**GENE AUTRY** STENCILED COWBOY SCENE	431	**331**	292	257
GUITAR	37	SUPER	**S-39** TREBLE CLEF DESIGN, V-NECK	426	**327**	289	255
GUITAR	35	SUPER	**SUPERTONE GENE AUTRY by REGAL** TRIPLE BINDING AROUND EDGE OF TOP AND SOUND HOLE	521	**394**	347	288
UKULELE	27	SUPER	**UKE** KOA	268	**206**	182	160

SUPRO by NATIONAL

TYPE	YR	MFG	MODEL	SELL EXC	SELL AVG	BUY EXC	BUY AVG
ELEC. GUITAR & BASS	50	SUPRO	**BELMONT** RED	730	**560**	495	436
ELGUIT	63	SUPRO	**BELMONT** RED RESOGLASS, 1 PU	398	**306**	270	238
ELGUIT	60	SUPRO	**CORONADO** BLACK RESOGLASS	571	**438**	387	341
ELGUIT	65	SUPRO	**CORONADO S482**	281	**215**	190	168
ELGUIT	56	SUPRO	**DEBONAIRE** CREAM, ARCHTOP	693	**532**	470	414
ELGUIT	50	SUPRO	**DUAL-TONE** 2 PU's	665	**510**	451	397
ELGUIT	55	SUPRO	**DUAL-TONE** WHITE, 2 PU's	652	**501**	443	390
ELGUIT	56	SUPRO	**DUAL-TONE** WHITE, 2 PU's	682	**523**	462	408
ELGUIT	57	SUPRO	**DUAL-TONE** WHITE, SINGLE CUTAWAY	683	**524**	463	408
ELGUIT	58	SUPRO	**DUAL-TONE** WHITE, 3 PU's	686	**527**	465	410
ELGUIT	60	SUPRO	**DUAL-TONE** WHITE RESOGLASS, 2 PU's	468	**359**	317	280
ELGUIT	63	SUPRO	**DUAL-TONE**	430	**330**	291	257
ELGUIT	53	SUPRO	**EL CAPITAN** SUNBURST	581	**446**	394	347
ELGUIT	58	SUPRO	**GAUCHO** BLUE, FLOATING PU	468	**359**	317	280
ELGUIT	63	SUPRO	**HOLIDAY** WHITE, 1 PU	417	**320**	283	249
ELGUIT	63	SUPRO	**KINGSTON** SAND BUFF RESOGLASS, 1 PU	432	**331**	293	258
ELGUIT	59	SUPRO	**KORD KING** 2 PU's	978	**751**	664	585
ELGUIT	65	SUPRO	**MARTINIQUE** ERMINE WHITE RESOGLASS	590	**453**	400	353
ELGUIT	66	SUPRO	**MARTINIQUE**	466	**352**	310	257
ELGUIT	52	SUPRO	**OZARK** NON-CUTAWAY	487	**374**	330	291
ELGUIT	65	SUPRO	**OZARK**	203	**156**	138	121
ELGUIT	60	SUPRO	**POCKET BASS** BLACK, 2 PU's	682	**523**	462	408
ELGUIT	64	SUPRO	**POCKET BASS** BLACK, 2 PU's	696	**534**	472	416
ELGUIT	66	SUPRO	**POCKET BASS** BLACK, 2 PU's	651	**500**	442	389
ELGUIT	55	SUPRO	**RANCHERO** SUNBURST, FLOATING PU	456	**350**	310	273

TYPE	YR	MFG	PRICES--BASED ON 100% ORIGINAL MODEL	SELL EXC	SELL AVG	BUY EXC	BUY AVG
ELGUIT	66	SUPRO	S-535 SHADED	421	323	285	251
ELGUIT	64	SUPRO	SAHARA 70 BLUE RESOGLASS	590	453	400	353
ELGUIT	66	SUPRO	SAHARA 70	484	372	329	290
ELGUIT	59	SUPRO	SUPER TWIN IVORY-BLACK SUNBURST	749	575	508	448
ELGUIT	63	SUPRO	SUPERSONIC RED, 1 PU	258	198	175	154
ELGUIT	65	SUPRO	SUPERSONIC 30	206	158	139	123
ELGUIT	67	SUPRO	SUPRO SUNBURST, 12-STRING, SOLID, 2 PU's	275	211	186	164
ELGUIT	58	SUPRO	TONEMASTER GOLD HARDWARE	682	523	462	408
ELGUIT	62	SUPRO	TONEMASTER BLACK, DUAL TONE BODY	470	361	319	281
ELGUIT	63	SUPRO	TONEMASTER 2 PU's	511	393	347	306
ELGUIT	63	SUPRO	TREMO-LECTRIC BLUE RESOGLASS, 2 PU's	635	487	430	379
ELGUIT	64	SUPRO	TREMO-LECTRIC BLUE RESOGLASS	607	466	411	363
GUITAR AMP	59	SUPRO	1616T GRAY 2-TONE, 6x9" SPEAKER, VIB	166	128	113	99
GTAMP	64	SUPRO	BANTAM RED TOLEX, TUBE, 6" SPEAKER	128	98	87	77
GTAMP	64	SUPRO	BANTAM RED AND GOLD 8" JENSEN	134	103	91	80
GTAMP	60	SUPRO	SUPER	455	350	309	272
GTAMP	52	SUPRO	SUPREME 10" SPEAKER	170	130	115	101
GTAMP	52	SUPRO	TB SUPREME 10" SPEAKER	170	130	115	101
GTAMP	60	SUPRO	THUNDERBOLT 1x15" SPEAKER	304	233	206	182
GTAMP	64	SUPRO	THUNDERBOLT GRAY, 1x15" SPEAKER	292	224	198	174
GTAMP	65	SUPRO	THUNDERBOLT LIGHTNING BOLT LOGO	409	314	278	245
GTAMP	66	SUPRO	VIBROVERB 2X12" JENSENS	339	260	230	203
GUITAR (ACOUSTIC)	38	SUPRO	ARCADIA WOOD BODY, RESONATOR	715	549	485	428
GUITAR	58	SUPRO	FOLKSTAR	980	752	665	586
GUITAR	60	SUPRO	FOLKSTAR RED RESOGLASS, RESONATOR	741	569	503	443
GUITAR	62	SUPRO	FOLKSTAR RED RESOGLASS, RESONATOR	695	534	471	416
GUITAR	64	SUPRO	FOLKSTAR RED RESOGLASS, RESONATOR	781	600	530	467
GUITAR	67	SUPRO	FOLKSTAR RED RESOGLASS, RESONATOR	725	557	492	434
GUITAR	64	SUPRO	HOLIDAY WHITE	338	255	225	187
STEEL GUITAR	40	SUPRO	6-STRING LAP STEEL IVORY	608	466	412	363
STGUIT	41	SUPRO	6-STRING LAP STEEL CREAM	615	465	410	340
STGUIT	50	SUPRO	6-STRING LAP STEEL GREY	555	426	376	332
STGUIT	54	SUPRO	6-STRING LAP STEEL PEARLOID	610	468	414	365
STGUIT	61	SUPRO	6-STRING LAP STEEL CREAM	592	454	402	354
STGUIT	57	SUPRO	60 ROSEWOOD NECK, 1 PU	548	421	372	328
STGUIT	58	SUPRO	60 WHITE, 1 PU	607	466	411	363
STGUIT	43	SUPRO	CLIPPER LAP STEEL	430	330	291	257
STGUIT	60	SUPRO	COMET PEARLOID	502	386	341	300
STGUIT	58	SUPRO	CONSOLE BLACK & WHITE, 8-STRING	603	463	409	361
STGUIT	36	SUPRO	ELECTRIC HAWAIIAN CAST ALUMINUM	712	546	483	426
STGUIT	62	SUPRO	JET AIRLINER 8-STRING	574	441	389	343
STGUIT	63	SUPRO	JET AIRLINER 8-STRING	509	391	345	304
STGUIT	64	SUPRO	JET AIRLINER	412	316	279	246
STGUIT	50	SUPRO	PROFESSIONAL LAP STEEL	527	405	357	315
STGUIT	51	SUPRO	SPECTATOR	517	397	351	309
STGUIT	52	SUPRO	STUDENT DELUXE LAP STEEL	498	382	338	298

TYPE	YR	MFG	PRICES--BASED ON 100% ORIGINAL MODEL	SELL EXC	SELL AVG	BUY EXC	BUY AVG
STGUIT	50	SUPRO	**TWIN LAP STEEL** DOUBLE NECK	655	**503**	444	391

TANNOY

TYPE	YR	MFG	MODEL	SELL EXC	SELL AVG	BUY EXC	BUY AVG
RAW	73	TANNOY	**10" MONITOR GOLD**	610	**468**	414	365
RAW	47	TANNOY	**12" MONITOR BLACK**	201	**154**	136	120
RAW	73	TANNOY	**12" MONITOR GOLD**	641	**492**	435	383
RAW	58	TANNOY	**12" MONITOR RED**	576	**442**	391	345
RAW	51	TANNOY	**12" MONITOR SILVER**	274	**210**	186	164
RAW	47	TANNOY	**15" MONITOR BLACK**	257	**197**	174	154
RAW	73	TANNOY	**15" MONITOR GOLD**	624	**479**	424	373
RAW	58	TANNOY	**15" MONITOR RED**	1,350	**1,037**	916	808
RAW	51	TANNOY	**15" MONITOR SILVER**	362	**278**	246	217
SIGNAL PROCESSOR	80	TANNOY	**1176-LN LIMITING AMP** SILVER FRONT	1,034	**794**	702	619
SPKR	73	TANNOY	**AUTOGRAPH PRO**	2,881	**2,212**	1,955	1,723
SPKR	74	TANNOY	**AUTOGRAPH TUDOR**	1,812	**1,391**	1,229	1,084
SPKR	64	TANNOY	**BELVEDERE 10"**	562	**431**	381	336
SPKR	64	TANNOY	**BELVEDERE 12"**	900	**691**	611	538
SPKR	64	TANNOY	**BELVEDERE 15"**	900	**691**	611	538
SPKR	64	TANNOY	**CADET 10"**	878	**674**	595	525
SPKR	68	TANNOY	**CHATSWORTH 12"**	677	**520**	459	405
SPKR	68	TANNOY	**LANCASTER 12"**	980	**752**	665	586
SPKR	69	TANNOY	**MALLORCAN**	664	**509**	450	397
SPKR	74	TANNOY	**TUDOR AUTOGRAPH**	1,655	**1,271**	1,123	990
SPKR	68	TANNOY	**WINDSOR GRF**	3,034	**2,329**	2,058	1,815

TATAY

TYPE	YR	MFG	MODEL	SELL EXC	SELL AVG	BUY EXC	BUY AVG
GUITAR (ACOUSTIC)	70	TATAY	**7R**	6,662	**5,116**	4,521	3,985
GUITAR	47	TATAY	**VINCENTE** SPRUCE, MAHOGANY BACK/SIDES	3,614	**2,733**	2,409	1,998
STEEL GUITAR	70	TATAY	**7R CLASSICAL** ROSEWOOD, SPRUCE	7,264	**5,577**	4,929	4,345

TC

TYPE	YR	MFG	MODEL	SELL EXC	SELL AVG	BUY EXC	BUY AVG
SIGNAL PROCESSOR	04	TC	**TC-BLD** BOOSTER/LINE DRIVER & DISTORT	256	**196**	174	153

TEISCO DEL RAY

TYPE	YR	MFG	MODEL	SELL EXC	SELL AVG	BUY EXC	BUY AVG
ELEC. GUITAR & BASS	60	TEISCO	**EG-27** SUNBURST, 2 PU's	318	**244**	215	190
ELGUIT	66	TEISCO	**EP-200B BASS** SEMI-HOLLOW	253	**194**	171	151
ELGUIT	64	TEISCO	**KL-4**	291	**223**	197	174
ELGUIT	67	TEISCO	**SPECTRUM II** 2 PU's	424	**325**	288	253
ELGUIT	66	TEISCO	**SPECTRUM V** CANDY APPLE RED	458	**351**	310	274
ELGUIT	67	TEISCO	**SPECTRUM V** METALLIC BLUE	442	**339**	300	264

TELEFUNKEN BY NEUMANN

TYPE	YR	MFG	MODEL	SELL EXC	SELL AVG	BUY EXC	BUY AVG
MIC	65	TELE	**ELAM 250** TUBE BY AKG	18,120	**13,913**	12,296	10,839

TRAVIS BEAN

TYPE	YR	MFG	MODEL	SELL EXC	SELL AVG	BUY EXC	BUY AVG
ELEC. GUITAR & BASS	78	TRAVIS	**TB- 500** BLACK	816	**626**	554	488
ELGUIT	74	TRAVIS	**TB-1000** NATURAL, KOA BODY, 2 PU's	1,311	**1,007**	889	784
ELGUIT	78	TRAVIS	**TB-1000S** WHITE, 2 PU's	1,330	**1,021**	902	795
ELGUIT	77	TRAVIS	**TB-2000 BASS** NATURAL, ALUMINUM NECK	990	**760**	671	592
ELGUIT	77	TRAVIS	**TB-3000 WEDGE** PEARL RED	1,508	**1,158**	1,023	902
ELGUIT	76	TRAVIS	**TB-4000 WEDGE BASS** PEARL RED	1,451	**1,114**	984	868
ELGUIT	78	TRAVIS	**WEDGE BASS** WHITE, 2 PU's	3,187	**2,447**	2,162	1,906

J. TRIGGS

TYPE	YR	MFG	MODEL	SELL EXC	SELL AVG	BUY EXC	BUY AVG
ELEC. GUITAR & BASS	92	TRIGGS	**FAERIE TALES** SS #69300024,CHERRY SUNBURST,SPRUCE TOP,QUILT MAPLE B/S	43,376	**33,306**	29,434	25,948

UNIVOX

TYPE	YR	MFG	MODEL	SELL EXC	SELL AVG	BUY EXC	BUY AVG
ELEC. GUITAR & BASS	68	UNIVOX	**MOSRITE COPY**	268	**206**	182	160
ELGUIT	74	UNIVOX	**STATOCASTER COPY** WHITE, 3 HB PU's	229	**176**	155	137
GUITAR AMP	76	UNIVOX	**U-130B BASS**	126	**97**	85	75
GTAMP	76	UNIVOX	**U-130L LEAD**	155	**119**	105	93
GTAMP	65	UNIVOX	**U-305R** SINGLE JENSEN	196	**150**	133	117

TYPE	YR	MFG	PRICES--BASED ON 100% ORIGINAL MODEL	SELL EXC	SELL AVG	BUY EXC	BUY AVG
			UREI				
SIGNAL PROCESSOR	79	UREI	LA-2A LEVEL AMP-TUBES	2,469	1,896	1,675	1,477
SGNPRO	80	UREI	LA-3A AUDIO LEVELER	963	739	653	576
			VALCO				
ELEC. GUITAR & BASS	60	VALCO	AIRLINE SUNBURST, 2 PU's, F-HOLE	551	423	373	329
ELGUIT	60	VALCO	AIRLINE BLACK, 6-STRING	612	470	415	366
ELGUIT	61	VALCO	AIRLINE CANDY APPLE RED, WOOD BODY	492	378	334	294
ELGUIT	61	VALCO	AIRLINE SUNBURST, DOUBLE CUTAWAY, 1 PU	577	443	392	345
ELGUIT	62	VALCO	AIRLINE SUNBURST, 1 PU	577	443	392	345
ELGUIT	62	VALCO	AIRLINE BLACK RESOGLASS, RESONATOR	669	514	454	400
ELGUIT	62	VALCO	AIRLINE RED RESOGLASS, 2 PU's, VIBRATO	688	528	467	412
ELGUIT	63	VALCO	AIRLINE RED & BLACK SUNBURST, 2 PU's	670	515	455	401
ELGUIT	64	VALCO	AIRLINE CHERRY RED, 3 PU's	677	520	459	405
ELGUIT	64	VALCO	AIRLINE BLACK RES-O-GLA, 2 SOUNDHOLES	683	524	463	408
ELGUIT	65	VALCO	AIRLINE RESOGLASS, SINGLE CUTAWAY, 2 PU's	695	534	471	416
ELGUIT	66	VALCO	AIRLINE RED RESOGLASS, 2 PU's	669	514	454	400
ELGUIT	60	VALCO	CUSTOM KRAFT RED, 1 PU	388	298	263	232
ELGUIT	57	VALCO	DUAL-TONE WHITE	652	501	443	390
ELGUIT	64	VALCO	SUPRO GOLD 2 PU's	380	292	258	227
ELGUIT	55	VALCO	TONEMASTER YELLOW, ENGLISH ELECTRIC	495	380	335	296
ELGUIT	62	VALCO	TONEMASTER BLACK RESOGLASS	361	277	245	216
GUITAR AMP	59	VALCO	AIRLINE 67 2 CHANNEL, 12" JENSEN	517	397	351	309
GTAMP	48	VALCO	FULL-TONE TWEED, TUBE 6x6"	560	430	380	335
GTAMP	40	VALCO	SUPRO GREY CABINET	404	310	274	241
GTAMP	66	VALCO	SUPRO 1606 GREY, 8" JENSEN	358	275	243	214
GTAMP	63	VALCO	VALCO TWEED, 1x10", 6 WATT	328	251	222	196
GUITAR (ACOUSTIC)	65	VALCO	AIRLINE AUTO HARP by OSCAR SCHMIDT	338	259	229	202
GUITAR	66	VALCO	AIRLINE AUTO HARP by OSCAR SCHMIDT	321	246	218	192
GUITAR	67	VALCO	AIRLINE AUTO HARP by OSCAR SCHMIDT	296	227	201	177
STEEL GUITAR	50	VALCO	AIRLINE STUDENT 6-STRING	343	264	233	205
STGUIT	64	VALCO	ROCKET 6-STRING	652	501	443	390
			VEGA				
BANJO	26	VEGA	ARTIST TENOR	2,061	1,583	1,399	1,233
BANJO	27	VEGA	ARTIST TENOR	2,026	1,555	1,374	1,212
BANJO	27	VEGA	ARTIST PLECTRUM, INDIVIDUAL FLANGES	3,307	2,539	2,244	1,978
BANJO	29	VEGA	ARTIST TENOR, INDIVIDUAL FLANGES	1,825	1,401	1,238	1,092
BANJO	14	VEGA	CUSTOM 9 ABALONE INLAY	8,215	6,308	5,574	4,914
BANJO	24	VEGA	DELUXE PLECTRUM	7,371	5,660	5,002	4,409
BANJO	26	VEGA	DELUXE TENOR, CURLY MAPLE, RESONATOR	5,136	3,943	3,485	3,072
BANJO	30	VEGA	DELUXE PLECTRUM	4,008	3,077	2,720	2,397
BANJO	32	VEGA	DELUXE PLECTRUM	3,494	2,683	2,371	2,090
BANJO	24	VEGA	DELUXE TUBAPHONE PLECTRUM	5,274	4,049	3,578	3,155
BANJO	65	VEGA	EARL SCRUGGS MODEL	3,650	2,802	2,476	2,183
BANJO	36	VEGA	ELECTRIC TENOR, BLACK, HUMBUCKING HORSESHOE PU	3,136	2,408	2,128	1,876

TYPE	YR	MFG	PRICES--BASED ON 100% ORIGINAL MODEL	SELL EXC	SELL AVG	BUY EXC	BUY AVG
BANJO	17	VEGA	FAIRBANKS 2 SPECIAL	1,968	1,511	1,336	1,177
BANJO	14	VEGA	FAIRBANKS 2 TUBAPHONE 5-STRING, OPEN BACK	2,364	1,815	1,604	1,414
BANJO	10	VEGA	FAIRBANKS 3 TUBAPHONE FLOWERPOT	3,878	2,978	2,631	2,320
BANJO	24	VEGA	FAIRBANKS 3 TUBAPHONE 5-STRING	2,329	1,788	1,580	1,393
BANJO	30	VEGA	FAIRBANKS 3 TUBAPHONE	2,026	1,555	1,374	1,212
BANJO	22	VEGA	FAIRBANKS 9 TUBAPHONE 5-STRING, ELABORATE ENGRVD INLAY, CARVED HEEL,11.5"HEAD	6,444	4,948	4,373	3,855
BANJO	23	VEGA	FAIRBANKS 9 TUBAPHONE CARVED HEEL	6,065	4,657	4,116	3,628
BANJO	09	VEGA	FAIRBANKS ELEC "O" POT 1909, 5-STRING	1,693	1,300	1,149	1,013
BANJO	14	VEGA	FAIRBANKS IMPERIAL ELECTRIC	2,094	1,608	1,421	1,252
BANJO	20	VEGA	FAIRBANKS LITTLE WONDER BANJO/MANDOLIN, OPEN BACK	555	426	376	332
BANJO	03	VEGA	FAIRBANKS REGENT 1903	1,658	1,273	1,125	992
BANJO	14	VEGA	FAIRBANKS REGENT	1,628	1,250	1,105	974
BANJO	15	VEGA	FAIRBANKS REGENT	1,392	1,068	944	832
BANJO	19	VEGA	FAIRBANKS REGENT	1,003	770	680	600
BANJO	11	VEGA	FAIRBANKS SENATOR	1,341	1,030	910	802
BANJO	27	VEGA	FAIRBANKS SENATOR	1,002	769	680	599
BANJO	29	VEGA	FAIRBANKS SENATOR	963	739	653	576
BANJO	31	VEGA	FAIRBANKS SENATOR	1,404	1,078	953	840
BANJO	09	VEGA	FAIRBANKS SENATOR 1 1909	972	746	659	581
BANJO	22	VEGA	FAIRBANKS STYLE X 9 CRVD HEEL,11 13/16"HD,17-FRET CLEAR OF RIM,4-FRET EXTENSION	2,085	1,601	1,415	1,247
BANJO	23	VEGA	FAIRBANKS STYLE X 9	2,072	1,591	1,406	1,239
BANJO	19	VEGA	FAIRBANKS TUBAPHONE STYLE M	1,968	1,511	1,336	1,177
BANJO	22	VEGA	FAIRBANKS TUBAPHONE STYLE M TENOR	1,983	1,523	1,345	1,186
BANJO	65	VEGA	FOLK RANGER OPEN BACK	641	492	435	383
BANJO	68	VEGA	FOLK RANGER OPEN BACK	703	540	477	420
BANJO	62	VEGA	FOLK RANGER FR-5 OPEN BACK	747	573	506	446
BANJO	63	VEGA	FOLK WONDER FW-5	650	491	433	359
BANJO	65	VEGA	FOLKLORE SUNBURST, 5-STRING, LONG NECK	777	596	527	464
BANJO	67	VEGA	FOLKLORE SS-5	834	640	566	499
BANJO	22	VEGA	IMPERIAL ELECTRIC	1,658	1,273	1,125	992
BANJO	24	VEGA	IMPERIAL ELECTRIC 5-STRING, OPEN BACK	1,453	1,116	986	869
BANJO	14	VEGA	LITTLE WONDER TENOR	732	562	497	438
BANJO	19	VEGA	LITTLE WONDER TENOR	796	611	540	476
BANJO	21	VEGA	LITTLE WONDER TENOR, OPEN BACK	816	626	554	488
BANJO	22	VEGA	LITTLE WONDER TENOR	677	520	459	405
BANJO	23	VEGA	LITTLE WONDER TENOR, OPEN BACK, 11 13/16" HEAD	668	513	453	399
BANJO	24	VEGA	LITTLE WONDER TENOR	686	527	465	410
BANJO	25	VEGA	LITTLE WONDER TENOR	810	622	550	485
BANJO	26	VEGA	LITTLE WONDER TENOR, 17-FRET	769	590	522	460
BANJO	30	VEGA	LITTLE WONDER TENOR	762	585	517	456
BANJO	31	VEGA	LITTLE WONDER TENOR	753	578	511	450
BANJO	50	VEGA	LITTLE WONDER TENOR, SUNBURST	588	451	399	351
BANJO	58	VEGA	LITTLE WONDER TENOR	548	421	372	328
BANJO	65	VEGA	LITTLE WONDER TENOR	556	427	377	332
BANJO	27	VEGA	LITTLE WONDER BANJO-GUITAR TENOR	3,280	2,518	2,226	1,962
BANJO	19	VEGA	LITTLE WONDER BANJO-MANDOLIN TENOR	694	533	471	415
BANJO	23	VEGA	LITTLE WONDER BANJO-MANDOLIN TENOR	672	516	456	402
BANJO	32	VEGA	MODERNE TENOR	2,364	1,815	1,604	1,414

TYPE	YR	MFG	PRICES--BASED ON 100% ORIGINAL MODEL	SELL EXC	SELL AVG	BUY EXC	BUY AVG
BANJO	63	VEGA	**PETE SEEGER** 5-STRING, LONG NECK	4,128	**3,169**	2,801	2,469
BANJO	64	VEGA	**PETE SEEGER** 5-STRING	3,652	**2,804**	2,478	2,184
BANJO	65	VEGA	**PETE SEEGER** 5-STRING, LONG NECK	3,311	**2,543**	2,247	1,981
BANJO	66	VEGA	**PETE SEEGER** 5-STRING, LONG NECK	4,035	**3,098**	2,738	2,414
BANJO	69	VEGA	**PETE SEEGER** 5-STRING, LONG NECK	2,196	**1,686**	1,490	1,313
BANJO	67	VEGA	**PRO II** PLECTRUM	835	**641**	566	499
BANJO	69	VEGA	**PRO II**	889	**682**	603	531
BANJO	25	VEGA	**PROFESSIONAL** TENOR	972	**746**	659	581
BANJO	26	VEGA	**PROFESSIONAL** TENOR	934	**717**	633	558
BANJO	28	VEGA	**PROFESSIONAL** TENOR	907	**696**	615	542
BANJO	29	VEGA	**PROFESSIONAL** PLECTRUM	1,658	**1,273**	1,125	992
BANJO	30	VEGA	**PROFESSIONAL** PLECTRUM	1,591	**1,222**	1,079	952
BANJO	31	VEGA	**PROFESSIONAL** TENOR	916	**703**	621	548
BANJO	09	VEGA	**REGENT** 1909, 5-STRING, OPEN BACK	3,233	**2,482**	2,194	1,934
BANJO	12	VEGA	**REGENT** 5-STRING, OPEN BACK	3,101	**2,381**	2,104	1,855
BANJO	16	VEGA	**REGENT** 5-STRING, OPEN BACK	2,982	**2,290**	2,023	1,784
BANJO	25	VEGA	**REGENT** 5-STRING, OPEN BACK	3,332	**2,558**	2,261	1,993
BANJO	27	VEGA	**REGENT** 5-STRING, OPEN BACK	2,219	**1,704**	1,506	1,327
BANJO	28	VEGA	**SOLOIST** TENOR	1,731	**1,329**	1,174	1,035
BANJO	29	VEGA	**SOLOIST** TENOR, RESONATOR	2,066	**1,586**	1,402	1,236
BANJO	30	VEGA	**SOLOIST** TENOR, GOLD, 15/16" HEAD, 19 FRETS	1,411	**1,083**	957	844
BANJO	21	VEGA	**STYLE 2 SPECIAL** OPEN BACK	1,010	**775**	685	604
BANJO	21	VEGA	**STYLE 3 TUBAPHONE** PLECTRUM	2,591	**1,959**	1,727	1,432
BANJO	26	VEGA	**STYLE 3 TUBAPHONE** PLECTRUM	1,884	**1,447**	1,279	1,127
BANJO	28	VEGA	**STYLE 3 TUBAPHONE** PLECTRUM	1,457	**1,118**	988	871
BANJO	30	VEGA	**STYLE 3 TUBAPHONE** PLECTRUM	1,352	**1,038**	918	809
BANJO	23	VEGA	**STYLE 9 TUBAPHONE** PLECTRUM	5,566	**4,274**	3,777	3,329
BANJO	12	VEGA	**STYLE 40** TENOR	779	**598**	528	466
BANJO	23	VEGA	**STYLE F** TENOR	1,001	**768**	679	598
BANJO	26	VEGA	**STYLE F** TENOR	990	**760**	671	592
BANJO	30	VEGA	**STYLE F** TENOR, RESONATOR	964	**740**	654	576
BANJO	31	VEGA	**STYLE F** TENOR	938	**720**	636	561
BANJO	19	VEGA	**STYLE K MANDOLIN-BANJO**	1,226	**941**	832	733
BANJO	22	VEGA	**STYLE K MANDOLIN-BANJO**	918	**705**	623	549
BANJO	24	VEGA	**STYLE K MANDOLIN-BANJO**	972	**746**	659	581
BANJO	30	VEGA	**STYLE K MANDOLIN-BANJO**	953	**731**	646	570
BANJO	17	VEGA	**STYLE L MANDOLIN-BANJO**	1,888	**1,449**	1,281	1,129
BANJO	20	VEGA	**STYLE M** TENOR	1,062	**816**	721	635
BANJO	26	VEGA	**STYLE M** TENOR	808	**611**	538	446
BANJO	26	VEGA	**STYLE M** 5-STRING	972	**746**	659	581
BANJO	28	VEGA	**STYLE M** 5-STRING	1,458	**1,119**	989	872
BANJO	13	VEGA	**STYLE N** TENOR	792	**608**	538	474
BANJO	14	VEGA	**STYLE N** TENOR	816	**626**	554	488
BANJO	22	VEGA	**STYLE N** TENOR	913	**701**	620	546

TYPE	YR	MFG	PRICES--BASED ON 100% ORIGINAL MODEL	SELL EXC	SELL AVG	BUY EXC	BUY AVG
BANJO	23	VEGA	**STYLE N** TENOR	907	**696**	615	542
BANJO	24	VEGA	**STYLE N** TENOR	901	**692**	611	539
BANJO	27	VEGA	**STYLE N** TENOR	719	**552**	487	430
BANJO	28	VEGA	**STYLE N** TENOR	764	**587**	519	457
BANJO	21	VEGA	**STYLE R** TENOR	1,258	**966**	854	753
BANJO	24	VEGA	**STYLE R** TENOR	1,067	**819**	724	638
BANJO	22	VEGA	**STYLE X 9** TENOR	2,020	**1,551**	1,371	1,208
BANJO	23	VEGA	**STYLE X 9** TENOR	1,880	**1,443**	1,276	1,124
BANJO	26	VEGA	**STYLE X 9** TENOR	1,674	**1,285**	1,136	1,001
BANJO	30	VEGA	**STYLE X 9** TENOR	1,533	**1,177**	1,040	917
BANJO	31	VEGA	**SUPER PARAMOUNT ARTIST** TENOR, PROFESSIONAL	6,163	**4,732**	4,182	3,687
BANJO	27	VEGA	**TUBAPHONE** 4-STRING	1,555	**1,194**	1,055	930
BANJO	10	VEGA	**TUBAPHONE 3**	4,952	**3,802**	3,360	2,962
BANJO	16	VEGA	**TUBAPHONE 3**	5,193	**3,987**	3,524	3,106
BANJO	21	VEGA	**TUBAPHONE 3**	5,043	**3,872**	3,422	3,017
BANJO	23	VEGA	**TUBAPHONE 3**	4,962	**3,810**	3,367	2,968
BANJO	25	VEGA	**TUBAPHONE 3**	4,794	**3,681**	3,253	2,868
BANJO	26	VEGA	**TUBAPHONE 3**	4,012	**3,081**	2,723	2,400
BANJO	30	VEGA	**TUBAPHONE 3** 5-STRING	3,498	**2,686**	2,374	2,093
BANJO	23	VEGA	**TUBAPHONE 9**	4,794	**3,681**	3,253	2,868
BANJO	25	VEGA	**TUBAPHONE 9** PLECTRUM, OPEN BACK, SERIAL #65708	4,216	**3,237**	2,861	2,522
BANJO	26	VEGA	**TUBAPHONE 9** CARVED HEEL	8,215	**6,308**	5,574	4,914
BANJO	11	VEGA	**TUBAPHONE BANJARINE** 21" SCALE	3,047	**2,340**	2,067	1,823
BANJO	29	VEGA	**TUBAPHONE GUITAR-BANJO**	1,324	**1,017**	899	792
BANJO	12	VEGA	**TUBAPHONE MANDOLIN-BANJO**	3,036	**2,331**	2,060	1,816
BANJO	10	VEGA	**TUBAPHONE STYLE M** TENOR	2,374	**1,823**	1,611	1,420
BANJO	17	VEGA	**TUBAPHONE STYLE M** TENOR	2,187	**1,679**	1,484	1,308
BANJO	19	VEGA	**TUBAPHONE STYLE M**	1,291	**991**	876	772
BANJO	21	VEGA	**TUBAPHONE STYLE M** TENOR, NATURAL	1,594	**1,224**	1,082	954
BANJO	23	VEGA	**TUBAPHONE STYLE M** 11-3/4" HEAD	1,557	**1,196**	1,057	931
BANJO	24	VEGA	**TUBAPHONE STYLE M** TENOR	1,560	**1,197**	1,058	933
BANJO	27	VEGA	**VEGAPHONE** TENOR	1,356	**1,041**	920	811
BANJO	30	VEGA	**VEGAPHONE** TENOR	1,251	**960**	848	748
BANJO	30	VEGA	**VEGAPHONE DELUXE** TENOR, 4-PC FLNGE,STAR INLD BK RESONATOR/ENGRVD IVRY SIDES	6,078	**4,667**	4,124	3,636
BANJO	29	VEGA	**VEGAPHONE PROFESSIONAL** TENOR, RESONATOR	954	**732**	647	570
BANJO	30	VEGA	**VEGAPHONE PROFESSIONAL** PLECTRUM	909	**698**	617	544
BANJO	29	VEGA	**VEGAVOX** TENOR	1,557	**1,196**	1,057	931
BANJO	30	VEGA	**VEGAVOX I** TENOR	3,809	**2,924**	2,584	2,278
BANJO	31	VEGA	**VEGAVOX I** PLECTRUM	3,384	**2,598**	2,296	2,024
BANJO	36	VEGA	**VEGAVOX I** TENOR	5,834	**4,479**	3,958	3,490
BANJO	56	VEGA	**VEGAVOX I** PLECTRUM	2,279	**1,750**	1,546	1,363
BANJO	62	VEGA	**VEGAVOX I** PLECTRUM	1,520	**1,167**	1,032	909
BANJO	65	VEGA	**VEGAVOX I** TENOR	1,389	**1,067**	943	831
BANJO	67	VEGA	**VEGAVOX I** TENOR	1,376	**1,056**	934	823
BANJO	68	VEGA	**VEGAVOX I** TENOR	1,368	**1,050**	928	818
BANJO	31	VEGA	**VEGAVOX II** TENOR	1,756	**1,348**	1,191	1,050

TYPE	YR	MFG	PRICES--BASED ON 100% ORIGINAL MODEL	SELL EXC	SELL AVG	BUY EXC	BUY AVG
BANJO	59	VEGA	**VEGAVOX III** TENOR	1,948	**1,496**	1,322	1,165
BANJO	70	VEGA	**VEGAVOX III** TENOR	1,416	**1,087**	961	847
BANJO	31	VEGA	**VEGAVOX IV** PLECTRUM	5,959	**4,576**	4,043	3,565
BANJO	64	VEGA	**VEGAVOX IV** TENOR	2,359	**1,812**	1,601	1,411
BANJO	65	VEGA	**VEGAVOX IV** TENOR	2,888	**2,217**	1,960	1,727
BANJO	64	VEGA	**VEGAVOX IV DELUXE** TENOR	3,870	**2,972**	2,626	2,315
BANJO	01	VEGA	**WHYTE LAYDIE** 1901, 5-STRING	6,436	**4,942**	4,367	3,850
BANJO	09	VEGA	**WHYTE LAYDIE** 1909, 26" SCALE, SERIAL #25443	3,179	**2,441**	2,157	1,902
BANJO	19	VEGA	**WHYTE LAYDIE** 5-STRING	3,418	**2,624**	2,319	2,044
BANJO	20	VEGA	**WHYTE LAYDIE**	2,290	**1,758**	1,554	1,370
BANJO	31	VEGA	**WHYTE LAYDIE** 5-STRING	1,346	**1,033**	913	805
BANJO	03	VEGA	**WHYTE LAYDIE 2** 1903	4,018	**3,085**	2,726	2,403
BANJO	06	VEGA	**WHYTE LAYDIE 2** 1906	3,487	**2,678**	2,366	2,086
BANJO	08	VEGA	**WHYTE LAYDIE 2** 1908	3,984	**3,059**	2,704	2,383
BANJO	10	VEGA	**WHYTE LAYDIE 2** 5-STRING	3,271	**2,512**	2,219	1,957
BANJO	11	VEGA	**WHYTE LAYDIE 2** OPEN BACK	2,348	**1,803**	1,593	1,404
BANJO	11	VEGA	**WHYTE LAYDIE 2** OPEN BACK	2,907	**2,232**	1,972	1,739
BANJO	21	VEGA	**WHYTE LAYDIE 2** 5-STRING	3,682	**2,827**	2,498	2,202
BANJO	22	VEGA	**WHYTE LAYDIE 2** PLECTRUM, 5-STRING, SERIAL #48215	3,112	**2,389**	2,112	1,861
BANJO	23	VEGA	**WHYTE LAYDIE 2** 5-STRING	3,520	**2,702**	2,388	2,105
BANJO	24	VEGA	**WHYTE LAYDIE 2** PLECTRUM	2,385	**1,831**	1,618	1,427
BANJO	24	VEGA	**WHYTE LAYDIE 2** 5-STRING	3,448	**2,647**	2,340	2,062
BANJO	26	VEGA	**WHYTE LAYDIE 2** 5-STRING	3,306	**2,538**	2,243	1,977
BANJO	26	VEGA	**WHYTE LAYDIE 2** FIBERSKYN HEAD, SERIAL #68755	5,054	**3,881**	3,429	3,023
BANJO	28	VEGA	**WHYTE LAYDIE 2** 5-STRING	3,228	**2,479**	2,191	1,931
BANJO	39	VEGA	**WHYTE LAYDIE 2** 5-STRING	3,062	**2,351**	2,077	1,831
BANJO	09	VEGA	**WHYTE LAYDIE 7** 1909	11,184	**8,587**	7,589	6,690
BANJO	21	VEGA	**WHYTE LAYDIE 7** CARVED HEEL	9,685	**7,437**	6,572	5,794
BANJO	22	VEGA	**WHYTE LAYDIE 7**	9,586	**7,360**	6,504	5,734
BANJO	24	VEGA	**WHYTE LAYDIE 7** 5-STRING	10,271	**7,887**	6,969	6,144
BANJO	25	VEGA	**WHYTE LAYDIE 7** 5-STRING, 27" SCALE	9,423	**7,236**	6,394	5,637
BANJO	26	VEGA	**WHYTE LAYDIE 7** 5-STRING, OPEN BACK	9,168	**7,039**	6,221	5,484
BANJO	27	VEGA	**WHYTE LAYDIE 7** 5-STRING, OPEN BACK	9,010	**6,918**	6,114	5,390
BANJO	21	VEGA	**WHYTE LAYDIE GUITAR-BANJO**	1,715	**1,317**	1,164	1,026
BANJO	16	VEGA	**WHYTE LAYDIE STYLE R** 5-STRING	2,881	**2,212**	1,955	1,723
BANJO	18	VEGA	**WHYTE LAYDIE STYLE R** 5-STRING	2,140	**1,643**	1,452	1,280
BANJO	22	VEGA	**WHYTE LAYDIE STYLE R** TENOR	779	**598**	528	466
BANJO	23	VEGA	**WHYTE LAYDIE STYLE R** TENOR	1,069	**821**	725	639
BANJO	26	VEGA	**WHYTE LAYDIE STYLE R** TENOR	919	**706**	623	550
BANJO	30	VEGA	**WHYTE LAYDIE STYLE R** TENOR	969	**744**	658	580
ELEC. GUITAR & BASS	45	VEGA	**COMMANDER** BLACK & WHITE, 6-STRING	409	**314**	278	245
GUITAR (ACOUSTIC)	40	VEGA	**C-26**	714	**548**	484	427
GUITAR	38	VEGA	**C-56** SUNBURST, F HOLES	1,350	**1,037**	916	808
GUITAR	40	VEGA	**C-56** SUNBURST	1,303	**1,001**	884	779

TYPE	YR	MFG	MODEL	SELL EXC	SELL AVG	BUY EXC	BUY AVG
GUITAR	35	VEGA	C-60	728	559	494	435
GUITAR	37	VEGA	C-66	571	438	387	341
GUITAR	39	VEGA	C-66 BLOND, ARCHTOP	530	407	360	317
GUITAR	38	VEGA	C-70 FANCY PEGHEAD AND INLAY	902	693	612	540
GUITAR	40	VEGA	C-80	954	732	647	570
GUITAR	50	VEGA	DUO-TRON SUNBURST, FULL BODY, 1 PU	547	420	371	327
GUITAR	64	VEGA	FT-J MAHOGANY BACK/SIDES	1,263	970	857	755
GUITAR	20	VEGA	LUTE TENOR, 2 POINT BODY SHAPE	762	585	517	456
GUITAR	53	VEGA	R-26 SUNBURST, NON-CUTAWAY	955	733	648	571
GUITAR	20	VEGA	VEGA 12-F BRAZILIAN ROSEWOOD BACK/SIDES, WHITE TRIM, 13 5/8" WIDE	2,430	1,866	1,649	1,453
MANDOLA	10	VEGA	STYLE 302 LUTE MANDOLA SPRUCE TOP, MAHOG SIDES, CYLINDER BACK, PEARL DOT INLAY	878	674	595	525
MANDOLIN	00	VEGA	BOWL BACK 1900, ABALONE SOUNDHOLE	1,513	1,161	1,026	905
MANDOL	31	VEGA	PROFESSIONAL MANDOLIN-BANJO FLAME	1,294	994	878	774
MANDOL	16	VEGA	STYLE K MANDOLIN-BANJO	757	581	513	452
MANDOL	22	VEGA	STYLE K MANDOLIN-BANJO	789	606	535	472
MANDOL	26	VEGA	STYLE K MANDOLIN-BANJO	627	481	425	375
MANDOL	30	VEGA	STYLE K MANDOLIN-BANJO	554	425	376	331
MANDOL	21	VEGA	STYLE L MANDOLIN-BANJO	724	556	491	433
MANDOL	24	VEGA	STYLE L MANDOLIN-BANJO	757	581	513	452
MANDOL	13	VEGA	STYLE X TUBAPHONE MANDOLIN-BANJO	1,068	820	725	639
STEEL GUITAR	48	VEGA	DOUBLE 8 STEEL NATURAL, MAHOGANY	794	609	538	475
STGUIT	30	VEGA	LAP STEEL	448	344	304	268
STGUIT	49	VEGA	LAP STEEL	388	298	263	232
UKULELE	50	VEGA	ARTHUR GODFREY BARITONE	472	362	320	282
UKE	55	VEGA	ARTHUR GODFREY BARITONE	539	414	366	322
UKE	60	VEGA	ARTHUR GODFREY BARITONE	404	310	274	241

VEILLETTE-CITRON

ELEC. GUITAR & BASS	77	VEILL	ELECTRIC 12-STRING BLUE-BLACK	2,444	1,877	1,659	1,462
ELGUIT	78	VEILL	ELECTRIC BASS TIGER STRIPED MAPLE, GOLD HARDWARE, TRIPLE IMPEDENCE PU's	2,139	1,642	1,451	1,279
ELGUIT	78	VEILL	STANDARD BASS TIGER-STRIPED MAPLE	1,596	1,225	1,083	954

VILLER & NELSON

ELEC. GUITAR & BASS	55	VILLER	EXCEL MAPLE BACK/SIDES, 16", 1 PU	1,441	1,106	978	862

VIVI-TONE

ELEC. GUITAR & BASS	35	VIVI-TONE	ELECTRIC SOLID	1,974	1,516	1,339	1,181
GUITAR (ACOUSTIC)	35	VIVI-TONE	ACOUSTIC (LOAR)	3,940	2,979	2,627	2,178
GUITAR	34	VIVI-TONE	LOAR ARCHTOP SIGNED LABEL	11,384	8,741	7,725	6,810
GUITAR	35	VIVI-TONE	PARLOR SIZE B. JOSEPH SIGNED LABEL	2,959	2,272	2,007	1,770

VOX AMPLIFICATION

EFFECTS	67	VOX	CLYCE MCCOY WAH-WAH PEDAL, NON PICTURE FACE	661	508	449	395
EFFECTS	65	VOX	CLYDE MCCOY WAH-WAH PEDAL	787	604	534	471
EFFECTS	67	VOX	ECHO REVERB UNIT SOLID STATE	594	456	403	355
EFFECTS	67	VOX	V-807 ECHO-REVERB	708	544	481	424
EFFECTS	66	VOX	V-828 TONE BENDER GREY, FUZZ	421	323	285	251
EFFECTS	67	VOX	V-837 ECHO DELUXE TAPE ECHO	378	290	256	226
EFFECTS	68	VOX	V-846 WAH	588	451	399	351
EFFECTS	63	VOX	VOLUME PEDAL	193	148	131	115
GUITAR AMP	68	VOX	1x18" BASS CABINET	593	455	402	355
GTAMP	63	VOX	1x18" FOUNDATION CABINET	821	621	547	454
GTAMP	63	VOX	2x12" EXTENSION CABINET	1,216	933	825	727
GTAMP	69	VOX	75 WATT PLEXI	1,245	956	845	745
GTAMP	70	VOX	75 WATT STEEL FRONT	3,218	2,471	2,184	1,925
GTAMP	68	VOX	6120 100 WATTS, REVERB, HEAD, HYBRED	1,714	1,316	1,163	1,025

TYPE	YR	MFG	PRICES--BASED ON 100% ORIGINAL MODEL	SELL EXC	SELL AVG	BUY EXC	BUY AVG
GTAMP	68	VOX	**7120 BASS** 100 WATTS, HEAD, HYBRED	1,701	**1,306**	1,154	1,017
GTAMP	68	VOX	**9120 BASS** 200 WATTS, HEAD, HYBRED	1,744	**1,339**	1,184	1,043
GTAMP	62	VOX	**AC- 4**	554	**425**	376	331
GTAMP	63	VOX	**AC- 4**	516	**396**	350	308
GTAMP	64	VOX	**AC- 4** BLACK, 1x8"	495	**380**	335	296
GTAMP	62	VOX	**AC- 4 COMBO** SMOOTH GREY VINYL	546	**419**	370	326
GTAMP	61	VOX	**AC- 10** TAN	1,280	**982**	868	765
GTAMP	66	VOX	**AC- 10**	1,061	**815**	720	635
GTAMP	64	VOX	**AC- 10 HEAD** 2x10" CABINET	2,116	**1,625**	1,436	1,266
GTAMP	59	VOX	**AC- 10 TWIN** WHITE TV, 2x10"	1,450	**1,113**	984	867
GTAMP	64	VOX	**AC- 10 TWIN**	1,216	**933**	825	727
GTAMP	65	VOX	**AC- 10VG**	929	**713**	630	556
GTAMP	58	VOX	**AC- 15** WHITE, BLACK PANEL, TV FRONT	3,877	**2,977**	2,631	2,319
GTAMP	62	VOX	**AC- 15** RED PANEL, 2x10", SERIAL #2820	1,216	**933**	825	727
GTAMP	63	VOX	**AC- 15** BROWN GRILL, GRAY TOLEX, 1x12"	1,910	**1,467**	1,296	1,143
GTAMP	64	VOX	**AC- 15** BLACK, 1x12"	926	**711**	628	554
GTAMP	64	VOX	**AC- 15 BASS** BLACK, GRAY PANEL, 1x15"	1,016	**780**	690	608
GTAMP	62	VOX	**AC- 15 COMBO** BEIGE, RED PANEL	1,296	**995**	880	775
GTAMP	64	VOX	**AC- 15 TWIN** BLACK STAND, 2x12"	1,317	**1,011**	893	787
GTAMP	66	VOX	**AC- 15 TWIN** 12x12"	1,256	**964**	852	751
GTAMP	67	VOX	**AC- 15 TWIN COMBO** 2x12"	2,973	**2,283**	2,017	1,778
GTAMP	60	VOX	**AC- 30**	3,508	**2,694**	2,381	2,099
GTAMP	62	VOX	**AC- 30** RED PANEL, 2x12", SERIAL #4261	2,246	**1,725**	1,524	1,344
GTAMP	62	VOX	**AC- 30** GRAY PANEL, 2x12", SERIAL #4077	2,878	**2,210**	1,953	1,721
GTAMP	62	VOX	**AC- 30** FAWN	4,864	**3,734**	3,300	2,909
GTAMP	63	VOX	**AC- 30** BLACK, 2x12" SPEAKERS	1,441	**1,106**	978	862
GTAMP	63	VOX	**AC- 30** GRAY TOLEX	1,939	**1,489**	1,316	1,160
GTAMP	64	VOX	**AC- 30**	2,413	**1,853**	1,637	1,443
GTAMP	65	VOX	**AC- 30** GRAY PANEL, TOP BOOST	3,321	**2,550**	2,254	1,987
GTAMP	66	VOX	**AC- 30** TOP BOOST	2,976	**2,285**	2,020	1,780
GTAMP	67	VOX	**AC- 30** SILVER, TOP BOOST	2,287	**1,756**	1,551	1,368
GTAMP	68	VOX	**AC- 30**	2,116	**1,625**	1,436	1,266
GTAMP	60	VOX	**AC- 30 COMBO** RED PANEL, SERIAL #0001-4561	1,659	**1,274**	1,126	992
GTAMP	61	VOX	**AC- 30 COMBO** BEIGE, RED PANEL, 2x12"	3,642	**2,796**	2,471	2,178
GTAMP	62	VOX	**AC- 30 COMBO** RED PANEL, SERIAL #0001-4561	1,659	**1,274**	1,126	992
GTAMP	62	VOX	**AC- 30 COMBO** BEIGE, TOP BOOST	3,317	**2,547**	2,251	1,984
GTAMP	63	VOX	**AC- 30 COMBO** BLACK, TOP BOOST, FACTORY, SERIAL #4406-4600	2,078	**1,596**	1,410	1,243
GTAMP	64	VOX	**AC- 30 COMBO** BLACK, BLACK PANEL, 2x12"	1,708	**1,311**	1,159	1,021
GTAMP	64	VOX	**AC- 30 COMBO** TOP BOOST, BULLDOG SPEAKERS, SERIAL #46000	1,870	**1,436**	1,269	1,118
GTAMP	65	VOX	**AC- 30 COMBO** BROWN GRILL	1,826	**1,402**	1,239	1,092
GTAMP	65	VOX	**AC- 30 COMBO** BLACK, TOP BOOST, FACTORY, 2x12", SERIAL #15770-16	1,830	**1,405**	1,241	1,094
GTAMP	67	VOX	**AC- 30 COMBO** SILVER	1,349	**1,036**	915	807
GTAMP	79	VOX	**AC- 30 COMBO** 2x12"	1,310	**1,006**	889	783
GTAMP	62	VOX	**AC- 30 HEAD**	1,430	**1,098**	970	855
GTAMP	63	VOX	**AC- 30 HEAD** BLACK TOLEX	1,408	**1,081**	956	842
GTAMP	64	VOX	**AC- 30 HEAD** BROWN GRILL, 2x12" CABINET	3,414	**2,622**	2,317	2,042

TYPE	YR	MFG	PRICES--BASED ON 100% ORIGINAL MODEL	SELL EXC	SELL AVG	BUY EXC	BUY AVG
GTAMP	64	VOX	**AC- 30 HEAD** COPPER	3,679	**2,825**	2,496	2,200
GTAMP	65	VOX	**AC- 30 HEAD** GRAY, SQUARE BOX, JMI	1,615	**1,240**	1,095	966
GTAMP	63	VOX	**AC- 30 TWIN** BLACK, TOP BOOST, REVERB	2,078	**1,596**	1,410	1,243
GTAMP	64	VOX	**AC- 30 TWIN** TOP BOOST. SERIAL #46000	2,120	**1,627**	1,438	1,268
GTAMP	65	VOX	**AC- 30 TWIN** BLACK, TOP BOOST, 2x12"	1,946	**1,494**	1,320	1,164
GTAMP	66	VOX	**AC- 30 TWIN**	2,172	**1,668**	1,474	1,299
GTAMP	63	VOX	**AC- 30HF** BLACK, GRAY PANEL, 2x12" CELESTION	2,204	**1,692**	1,495	1,318
GTAMP	63	VOX	**AC- 30HG** BLACK, RED PANEL, 2x12"	2,245	**1,724**	1,523	1,343
GTAMP	64	VOX	**AC- 50** BLACK, SERIAL #56001	1,449	**1,112**	983	866
GTAMP	65	VOX	**AC- 50** BLACK, REVERB	1,402	**1,076**	951	838
GTAMP	65	VOX	**AC- 50** BLACK, TOP BOOST	1,402	**1,076**	951	838
GTAMP	65	VOX	**AC- 50** GRAY PANEL	1,714	**1,316**	1,163	1,025
GTAMP	60	VOX	**AC- 50 HEAD** JMI MODEL	1,284	**986**	871	768
GTAMP	64	VOX	**AC- 50 HEAD**	1,216	**933**	825	727
GTAMP	66	VOX	**AC- 50 HEAD**	1,048	**804**	711	627
GTAMP	70	VOX	**AC- 50 HEAD** VSL MODEL	414	**318**	281	247
GTAMP	63	VOX	**AC- 50 TWIN** BLACK, GRAY PANEL	1,674	**1,285**	1,136	1,001
GTAMP	64	VOX	**AC- 50 TWIN** BLACK, TOP BOOST, REV	1,384	**1,062**	939	828
GTAMP	65	VOX	**AC- 50 TWIN** BLACK, GRAY PANEL, 2x12"	2,204	**1,692**	1,495	1,318
GTAMP	63	VOX	**AC-100** GRAY PANEL, 4x12", SERIAL #48574	1,626	**1,248**	1,103	972
GTAMP	64	VOX	**AC-100** BLACK, BLACK PANEL, HEAD ONLY	1,408	**1,081**	956	842
GTAMP	64	VOX	**AC-100** BLACK, REV, 4x12"	1,646	**1,264**	1,117	984
GTAMP	65	VOX	**AC-100** BLACK, 4x12"	1,738	**1,334**	1,179	1,039
GTAMP	64	VOX	**AC-100 TWIN** REVERB, 4x12"	2,139	**1,642**	1,451	1,279
GTAMP	65	VOX	**AC-100 TWIN** BLACK, BLACK PANEL, 4x15"	1,714	**1,316**	1,163	1,025
GTAMP	66	VOX	**CAMBRIDGE REVERB** V102 TUBE, 18 WATT, 1x18"	722	**554**	490	432
GTAMP	67	VOX	**CAMBRIDGE REVERB** TRANSISTOR, 30 WATT, 2 CHANNEL	599	**460**	406	358
GTAMP	68	VOX	**CAMBRIDGE REVERB**	670	**515**	455	401
GTAMP	67	VOX	**CONQUEROR HEAD**	838	**644**	569	501
GTAMP	66	VOX	**CONQUEROR TWIN** 30 WATT, SOLID STATE, 2x12"	679	**522**	461	406
GTAMP	67	VOX	**DEFIANT** 50 WATT, SOLID STATE, 1 HORN, 2x12"	1,006	**773**	683	602
GTAMP	67	VOX	**DEFIANT HEAD**	564	**433**	383	337
GTAMP	66	VOX	**DEFIANT TWIN** 50 WATT, SOLID STATE, 2x12"	399	**307**	271	239
GTAMP	65	VOX	**DOMINO** GRAY/BLUE	977	**750**	663	584
GTAMP	66	VOX	**DYNAMIC BASS** 50 WATT, SOLID STATE, 1x15"	703	**540**	477	420
GTAMP	63	VOX	**FOUNDATION BASS** COVER, 1x18"	834	**640**	566	499
GTAMP	64	VOX	**FOUNDATION BASS** BLACK COVER, 1x18"	778	**597**	528	465
GTAMP	64	VOX	**FOUNDATION BASS** 2x15"	947	**727**	642	566
GTAMP	65	VOX	**FOUNDATION BASS** BLACK COVER, 1x18"	549	**422**	373	328
GTAMP	67	VOX	**FOUNDATION CABINET**	599	**460**	406	358
GTAMP	68	VOX	**FOUNDATION HEAD**	645	**495**	437	385
GTAMP	62	VOX	**REVERB TANK** BEIGE	1,764	**1,354**	1,197	1,055
GTAMP	64	VOX	**REVERB UNIT** RICHARD MODEL	332	**255**	225	198
GTAMP	65	VOX	**REVERB UNIT** BLACK, ALL TUBE	1,486	**1,141**	1,008	889
GTAMP	67	VOX	**SCORPION V116** 60 WATT, SOLID STATE, REV, 4x10"	542	**416**	367	324

TYPE	YR	MFG	PRICES--BASED ON 100% ORIGINAL MODEL	SELL EXC	SELL AVG	BUY EXC	BUY AVG
GTAMP	67	VOX	**SOVEREIGN BASS V117 TWIN** 60 WATT, 4x12"	647	**497**	439	387
GTAMP	64	VOX	**STUDENT** BLACK, 1x6" BULLDOG	369	**283**	250	221
GTAMP	64	VOX	**STUDENT** GRAY TOLEX, 1x6" BULLDOG	619	**475**	420	370
GTAMP	66	VOX	**SUPREME** 100 WATT, SOLID STATE, 4x12"	703	**540**	477	420
GTAMP	67	VOX	**SUPREME HEAD**	838	**644**	569	501
GTAMP	63	VOX	**T- 60** RED PANEL, STAND, SERIAL #1450	1,619	**1,243**	1,098	968
GTAMP	62	VOX	**T- 60 BASS** BLACK, RED PANEL, 2x12"	1,430	**1,098**	970	855
GTAMP	62	VOX	**T- 60 BASS** BEIGE, RED PANEL, STAND, SERIAL #00100-00500	1,584	**1,216**	1,075	948
GTAMP	63	VOX	**T- 60 BASS** BLACK, STAND, SERIAL #45265	1,501	**1,153**	1,019	898
GTAMP	64	VOX	**T- 60 BASS** BLACK	1,385	**1,063**	940	828
GTAMP	64	VOX	**T- 60 BASS** BLACK, GRAY PANEL, STAND	1,389	**1,067**	943	831
GTAMP	65	VOX	**T- 60 BASS** BLACK, BLACK PANEL, 1x12"	1,336	**1,025**	906	799
GTAMP	70	VOX	**TONE BENDER** BLACK	319	**245**	216	190
GTAMP	66	VOX	**TRAVELER** 20 WATT, SOLID STATE	564	**433**	383	337
GTAMP	68	VOX	**TREBLE-BASS** BOOSTER	281	**215**	190	168
GTAMP	70	VOX	**V-15 VSL** TUBE BOOST, COMBO, 2x10"	632	**485**	429	378

VOX/JMI, LTD

TYPE	YR	MFG	MODEL	SELL EXC	SELL AVG	BUY EXC	BUY AVG
ELEC. GUITAR & BASS	61	VOX/JMI	**ACE** RED, SOLID BODY, 2 PU's	516	**396**	350	308
ELGUIT	67	VOX/JMI	**ASTRO IV** SUNBURST, HOLLOW BODY	723	**555**	490	432
ELGUIT	61	VOX/JMI	**BASSMASTER** WHITE, SOLID BODY, 2 PU's, SERIAL #1B-000/1B-320	652	**501**	443	390
ELGUIT	63	VOX/JMI	**BOUZOUKI** SOLID BODY, 12-STRING, 3 PU's, TREM	1,337	**1,026**	907	799
ELGUIT	62	VOX/JMI	**CLUBMAN** RED, 2 PU's	554	**425**	376	331
ELGUIT	62	VOX/JMI	**CLUBMAN BASS** RED, 1 PU	593	**455**	402	355
ELGUIT	66	VOX/JMI	**CLUBMAN BASS** RED	540	**415**	367	323
ELGUIT	63	VOX/JMI	**CLUBMAN DELUXE** RED, 3 PU's	603	**463**	409	361
ELGUIT	62	VOX/JMI	**CONSORT** WHITE, SOLID BODY, 3 PU's	516	**396**	350	308
ELGUIT	66	VOX/JMI	**COUGAR 335** SUNBURST, 2 PU's	695	**534**	471	416
ELGUIT	60	VOX/JMI	**DELTA IV BASS**	607	**466**	411	363
ELGUIT	62	VOX/JMI	**FOLK 12** FLATTOP	556	**427**	377	332
ELGUIT	60	VOX/JMI	**HARLEM**	357	**274**	242	213
ELGUIT	70	VOX/JMI	**HAWK IV** CREAM	451	**346**	306	270
ELGUIT	70	VOX/JMI	**HAWK IV BASS** CREAM	635	**487**	430	379
ELGUIT	67	VOX/JMI	**INVADER** BUILT-IN EFFECTS	855	**657**	580	511
ELGUIT	60	VOX/JMI	**MANDO**	603	**463**	409	361
ELGUIT	60	VOX/JMI	**MARK IV BASS**	679	**522**	461	406
ELGUIT	63	VOX/JMI	**MARK IV BASS**	705	**541**	478	422
ELGUIT	60	VOX/JMI	**MARK IX**	1,216	**933**	825	727
ELGUIT	62	VOX/JMI	**MARK IX**	1,033	**793**	701	618
ELGUIT	65	VOX/JMI	**MARK IX** BLACK, TEARDROP	916	**703**	621	548
ELGUIT	63	VOX/JMI	**MARK VI** TEARDROP	820	**630**	557	491
ELGUIT	64	VOX/JMI	**MARK VI** TEARDROP	909	**698**	617	544
ELGUIT	63	VOX/JMI	**MARK XII** TEARDROP, 12-STRING	1,055	**810**	715	631
ELGUIT	66	VOX/JMI	**MARK XII** TEARDROP, 12-STRING	1,271	**976**	862	760
ELGUIT	67	VOX/JMI	**MARK XII** TEARDROP, 12-STRING	841	**645**	570	503
ELGUIT	60	VOX/JMI	**METEOR**	552	**423**	374	330
ELGUIT	60	VOX/JMI	**NEW ORLEANS** HOLLOW BODY	561	**430**	380	335

TYPE	YR	MFG	PRICES--BASED ON 100% ORIGINAL MODEL	SELL EXC	SELL AVG	BUY EXC	BUY AVG
ELGUIT	62	VOX/JMI	PANTHER BASS 1 PU	640	491	434	383
ELGUIT	65	VOX/JMI	PANTHER BASS	651	500	442	389
ELGUIT	68	VOX/JMI	PANTHER BASS SUNBURST	642	493	436	384
ELGUIT	68	VOX/JMI	PHANTOM GEMINI BASS WHITE	1,200	921	814	718
ELGUIT	65	VOX/JMI	PHANTOM IV BASS	1,218	935	826	728
ELGUIT	67	VOX/JMI	PHANTOM IV BASS	884	679	600	529
ELGUIT	62	VOX/JMI	PHANTOM VI	1,280	982	868	765
ELGUIT	65	VOX/JMI	PHANTOM VI WHITE	1,202	923	816	719
ELGUIT	63	VOX/JMI	PHANTOM XII	1,431	1,099	971	856
ELGUIT	65	VOX/JMI	PHANTOM XII BLACK, 12-STRING	900	691	611	538
ELGUIT	67	VOX/JMI	PHANTOM XII BLACK, 12-STRING	956	734	649	572
ELGUIT	68	VOX/JMI	PHANTOM XII WHITE, 12-STRING	962	738	652	575
ELGUIT	69	VOX/JMI	PHANTOM XII 12-STRING, SOLID BODY	889	682	603	531
ELGUIT	67	VOX/JMI	SATURN IV BASS SUNBURST, SINGLE CUTAWAY, 1 PU	664	509	450	397
ELGUIT	68	VOX/JMI	SATURN IV BASS 3-TONE SUNBURST, SINGLE CUTAWAY	660	507	448	395
ELGUIT	61	VOX/JMI	SHADOW BLACK, SOLID BODY, TREMOLO, 2 PU's	435	334	295	260
ELGUIT	60	VOX/JMI	SIDEWINDER IV BASS	771	592	523	461
ELGUIT	65	VOX/JMI	SIDEWINDER IV BASS	695	534	471	416
ELGUIT	67	VOX/JMI	SIDEWINDER IV BASS	803	616	544	480
ELGUIT	68	VOX/JMI	SIDEWINDER IV BASS SUNBURST, 2 PU's	668	513	453	399
ELGUIT	61	VOX/JMI	SOUNDCASTER RED, SOLID BODY, 3 PU's, TREM	574	441	389	343
ELGUIT	62	VOX/JMI	SPITFIRE	570	437	386	341
ELGUIT	68	VOX/JMI	SPITFIRE SUNBURST	562	431	381	336
ELGUIT	69	VOX/JMI	SPITFIRE SUNBURST	553	424	375	330
ELGUIT	61	VOX/JMI	STROLLER WHITE, SOLID BODY, 1 PU, SERIAL #1-250/1-500	435	334	295	260
ELGUIT	60	VOX/JMI	STUDENT PRINCE HOLLOW BODY	477	366	323	285
ELGUIT	61	VOX/JMI	SUPER ACE WHITE, 3 PU's	604	464	410	361
ELGUIT	62	VOX/JMI	SUPER ACE RED, 3 PU's	564	433	383	337
ELGUIT	63	VOX/JMI	SUPER LYNX DELUXE	683	524	463	408
ELGUIT	68	VOX/JMI	SUPER LYNX DELUXE	647	497	439	387
ELGUIT	66	VOX/JMI	SUPER LYNX V-243 2 SC PU's	617	473	418	369
ELGUIT	60	VOX/JMI	SUPER METEOR	673	516	456	402
ELGUIT	68	VOX/JMI	SUPER METEOR	616	473	418	368
ELGUIT	60	VOX/JMI	TORNADO SEMI-HOLLOW BODY	678	521	460	406
ELGUIT	67	VOX/JMI	TORNADO SUNBURST	425	326	288	254
ELGUIT	60	VOX/JMI	TYPHOON HOLLOW BODY	686	527	465	410
ELGUIT	68	VOX/JMI	TYPHOON HOLLOW BODY	460	353	312	275
ELGUIT	67	VOX/JMI	TYPHOON JAZZ RED, SEMI-HOLLOW BODY	665	510	451	397
ELGUIT	62	VOX/JMI	VICTO HOLLOW BODY, DOUBLE CUTAWAY, 2 PU's	660	507	448	395
ELGUIT	68	VOX/JMI	VIOLIN BASS SUNBURST, HOLLOW BODY 2 PU's	695	534	471	416
ELGUIT	66	VOX/JMI	WYMAN BASS SUNBURST	1,331	1,022	903	796

VOX/THOMAS

TYPE	YR	MFG	MODEL	SELL EXC	SELL AVG	BUY EXC	BUY AVG
GUITAR AMP	64	VOX/THOM	BEATLE 4x12"	1,380	1,060	937	826
GTAMP	68	VOX/THOM	BEATLE 4x12"	1,687	1,296	1,145	1,009
GTAMP	65	VOX/THOM	BERKLEY 2x10", SOLID STATE	565	434	383	338
GTAMP	69	VOX/THOM	BERKLEY II	615	465	410	340
GTAMP	67	VOX/THOM	BERKLEY III 2x10", 32 WATT, SOLID STATE	639	491	433	382
GTAMP	68	VOX/THOM	BERKLEY III 2x10", BOTTOM	703	540	477	420

TYPE	YR	MFG	PRICES--BASED ON 100% ORIGINAL MODEL	SELL EXC	SELL AVG	BUY EXC	BUY AVG
GTAMP	65	VOX/THOM	**BERKLEY SUPER REVERB** 2x10", TUBE	980	**752**	665	586
GTAMP	64	VOX/THOM	**BUCKINGHAM**	719	**552**	487	430
GTAMP	68	VOX/THOM	**ECHO UNIT CO 3**	673	**516**	456	402
GTAMP	70	VOX/THOM	**ESCORT** PORTABLE	283	**217**	192	169
GTAMP	65	VOX/THOM	**ESSEX BASS** STAND	589	**452**	399	352
GTAMP	66	VOX/THOM	**ESSEX BASS**	398	**306**	270	238
GTAMP	64	VOX/THOM	**KENSINGTON BASS** 1x12"	563	**432**	382	337
GTAMP	68	VOX/THOM	**KENSINGTON BASS** TOLEX	645	**495**	437	385
GTAMP	67	VOX/THOM	**KENSINGTON BASS V** 22 WATT, SOLID STATE	700	**537**	475	418
GTAMP	60	VOX/THOM	**PACEMAKER** TUBE	695	**534**	471	416
GTAMP	64	VOX/THOM	**PACEMAKER**	706	**542**	479	422
GTAMP	65	VOX/THOM	**PACEMAKER** TUBE	599	**460**	406	358
GTAMP	68	VOX/THOM	**PACEMAKER** 10" SPEAKER, SINGLE CHANNEL	574	**441**	389	343
GTAMP	66	VOX/THOM	**PACEMAKER V102** TUBE, 18 WATT, 1x10"	639	**491**	433	382
GTAMP	65	VOX/THOM	**PATHFINDER** TUBE	399	**307**	271	239
GTAMP	66	VOX/THOM	**PATHFINDER** V101 TUBE, 1x8"	478	**367**	324	286
GTAMP	64	VOX/THOM	**ROYAL GUARDSMAN** 4x12"	723	**555**	490	432
GTAMP	67	VOX/THOM	**ROYAL GUARDSMAN** 2x12" CABINET	640	**491**	434	383
GTAMP	71	VOX/THOM	**ROYAL GUARDSMAN** SOLID STATE	555	**426**	376	332
GTAMP	68	VOX/THOM	**SUPER BEATLE 1141**	788	**605**	535	471
GTAMP	72	VOX/THOM	**SUPER BEATLE 1143** HEAD ONLY	673	**516**	456	402
GTAMP	64	VOX/THOM	**SUPER BEATLE 1144** 4x12"	1,314	**1,009**	892	786
GTAMP	67	VOX/THOM	**VISCOUNT V1154** 2x12", 35 WATT, SOLID STATE	399	**307**	271	239
GTAMP	64	VOX/THOM	**WESTMINSTER** 1x18"	537	**412**	364	321
GTAMP	65	VOX/THOM	**WESTMINSTER BASS** 2x15"	688	**528**	467	412
GTAMP	67	VOX/THOM	**WESTMINSTER BASS V1182 TWIN** 120 WATT, SOLID STATE	700	**537**	475	418
GUITAR (ACOUSTIC)	60	VOX/THOM	**COUNTRY WESTERN** FLATTOP, DREADNOUGHT	618	**474**	419	369
GUITAR	65	VOX/THOM	**COUNTRY WESTERN** FLATTOP, DREADNOUGHT	703	**540**	477	420
GUITAR	60	VOX/THOM	**FOLK 12** FLATTOP, DREADNOUGHT	621	**477**	421	371
MANDOLIN	67	VOX/THOM	**MANDO GUITAR** 12-STRING	1,372	**1,053**	931	820

VOX/THOMAS by EKO

TYPE	YR	MFG	MODEL	SELL EXC	SELL AVG	BUY EXC	BUY AVG
ELEC. GUITAR & BASS	64	VOX/THOME	**BOBCAT** HOLLOW BODY	677	**520**	459	405
ELGUIT	66	VOX/THOME	**BOBCAT** TREMOLO, 3 SC PU's	607	**466**	411	363
ELGUIT	60	VOX/THOME	**BULLDOG** SUNBURST	1,249	**959**	848	747
ELGUIT	63	VOX/THOME	**BULLDOG** SUNBURST	1,242	**953**	842	743
ELGUIT	68	VOX/THOME	**BULLDOG** SUNBURST	1,027	**788**	696	614
ELGUIT	63	VOX/THOME	**COUGAR BASS**	573	**440**	389	343
ELGUIT	63	VOX/THOME	**GUITORGAN** w/TRANSFORMER ONLY	1,342	**1,031**	911	803
ELGUIT	63	VOX/THOME	**HURRICANE** VIBRATO, 2 PU's	449	**344**	304	268
ELGUIT	68	VOX/THOME	**HURRICANE** SUNBURST	543	**417**	368	324
ELGUIT	68	VOX/THOME	**LYNX** SUNBURST, 2 PU's	500	**384**	339	299
ELGUIT	63	VOX/THOME	**SERENADER** FLATTOP	347	**266**	235	207
ELGUIT	67	VOX/THOME	**STEREO PHANTOM 12** BOOK BOUND, EBONY FINGERBOARD	855	**657**	580	511
ELGUIT	68	VOX/THOME	**STINGER IV BASS** SUNBURST, 2 PU's	645	**495**	437	385
ELGUIT	64	VOX/THOME	**TEMPEST XII**	452	**347**	307	270

TYPE	YR	MFG	PRICES--BASED ON 100% ORIGINAL MODEL	SELL EXC	SELL AVG	BUY EXC	BUY AVG
ELGUIT	68	VOX/THOME	**TEMPEST XII** SUNBURST, 12-STRING	399	**307**	271	239
ELGUIT	64	VOX/THOME	**V-250 BASS** SUNBURST, VIOLIN SHAPE	551	**423**	373	329
ELGUIT	67	VOX/THOME	**V-250 BASS** SUNBURST, VIOLIN SHAPE	645	**495**	437	385
ELGUIT	63	VOX/THOME	**VIOLIN BASS** SUNBURST	1,228	**943**	833	734
ELGUIT	67	VOX/THOME	**VIOLIN BASS** SUNBURST, VIOLIN BODY	1,010	**775**	685	604
ELGUIT	68	VOX/THOME	**VIOLIN BASS** SUNBURST, SEMI-HOLLOW BODY	1,293	**993**	877	773
ELGUIT	64	VOX/THOME	**WYMAN BASS**	1,265	**971**	858	757

WASHBURN INTERNATIONAL, INC.

TYPE	YR	MFG	MODEL	SELL EXC	SELL AVG	BUY EXC	BUY AVG
BANJO	00	WASHBURN	**BANJO 25.5"SCLE 11"HD OPEN BK** 1900, MTAL CLAD RIM,AFRICAN TURBO SNL INLAY,/ENGRVD FNGRBRD	1,319	**1,013**	895	789
BANJO	20	WASHBURN	**MANDOLIN-BANJO** OPEN BACK	370	**284**	251	221
BANJO	20	WASHBURN	**PLECTRUM** MAHOGANY, RESONATOR	655	**503**	444	391
BANJO	20	WASHBURN	**STYLE C** TENOR	572	**439**	388	342
BANJO	23	WASHBURN	**STYLE C** TENOR	546	**419**	370	326
BANJO	10	WASHBURN	**STYLE D** OPEN BACK	819	**629**	556	490
BANJO	10	WASHBURN	**WASHBURN** TENOR, OPEN BACK	651	**500**	442	389
BANJO	20	WASHBURN	**WASHBURN PARLOR**	644	**494**	437	385
ELEC. GUITAR & BASS	97	WASHBURN	**SIGNATURE NUNO BETTENCOURT N1** HH PU, FULCRUM TREM BRIDGE, RSWD FINGRBRD	338	**259**	229	202
ELGUIT	74	WASHBURN	**TB-2000 BASS** NATURAL, ALUMINUM NECK	1,069	**821**	725	639
GUITAR (ACOUSTIC)	98	WASHBURN	**1898** 1898, BRAZILIAN ROSEWOOD BACK/SIDES, 13" WIDE	1,064	**817**	722	636
GUITAR	91	WASHBURN	**C-80S CLASSIC** SOLID SPRUCE TOP, QUILTED ASH BACK/SIDES	469	**360**	318	280
GUITAR	35	WASHBURN	**COLLEGIAN**	819	**629**	556	490
GUITAR	78	WASHBURN	**D-50S** ROSEWOOD INLAYS	677	**520**	459	405
GUITAR	38	WASHBURN	**INSPIRATION**	591	**454**	401	353
GUITAR	37	WASHBURN	**JUNIOR**	791	**608**	537	473
GUITAR	96	WASHBURN	**PARLOR GUITAR** 1896	1,714	**1,316**	1,163	1,025
GUITAR	35	WASHBURN	**SOLO**	579	**438**	386	320
GUITAR	38	WASHBURN	**SOLO DELUXE**	632	**485**	429	378
GUITAR	00	WASHBURN	**STYLE 217** 1900, ROSEWOOD BACK/SIDES	817	**627**	554	489
GUITAR	15	WASHBURN	**STYLE E** BRAZILIAN ROSEWOOD	857	**658**	582	513
GUITAR	37	WASHBURN	**SUPERB** SUNBURST, PEARL STRIPE INLAY	1,284	**986**	871	768
GUITAR	10	WASHBURN	**WASHBURN # 80** BRAZILIAN ROSEWOOD	2,073	**1,591**	1,406	1,240
GUITAR	01	WASHBURN	**WASHBURN # 101** 1901, ROSEWOOD BACK/SIDES	1,321	**1,014**	896	790
GUITAR	00	WASHBURN	**WASHBURN # 111** 1900	719	**544**	479	397
GUITAR	05	WASHBURN	**WASHBURN # 112** 1905	840	**645**	570	502
GUITAR	01	WASHBURN	**WASHBURN # 115** 1901, BRAZILIAN ROSEWOOD BACK/SIDES	937	**719**	636	560
GUITAR	01	WASHBURN	**WASHBURN # 211** 1901	837	**643**	568	501
GUITAR	00	WASHBURN	**WASHBURN # 225** 1900	2,140	**1,643**	1,452	1,280
GUITAR	11	WASHBURN	**WASHBURN # 312**	822	**631**	557	491
GUITAR	14	WASHBURN	**WASHBURN # 345**	837	**643**	568	501
GUITAR	24	WASHBURN	**WASHBURN # 350** ARTIST SPECIAL	756	**580**	513	452
GUITAR	10	WASHBURN	**WASHBURN # 388**	805	**618**	546	481
GUITAR	12	WASHBURN	**WASHBURN # 399**	913	**690**	609	505
GUITAR	14	WASHBURN	**WASHBURN # 423**	591	**454**	401	353
GUITAR	26	WASHBURN	**WASHBURN # 425** INLAID G. HART & SON	865	**664**	587	517
GUITAR	20	WASHBURN	**WASHBURN #1118** ROSEWOOD, "0" SIZE	765	**578**	510	422
GUITAR	30	WASHBURN	**WASHBURN #5237** ROSEWOOD BACK/SIDES, 12-FRET	1,068	**820**	725	639
GUITAR	30	WASHBURN	**WASHBURN #5238** HERRINGBONE TRIM, GOLD FLORAL	3,588	**2,755**	2,435	2,146

	TYPE	YR	MFG	PRICES--BASED ON 100% ORIGINAL MODEL	SELL EXC	SELL AVG	BUY EXC	BUY AVG
	GUITAR	35	WASHBURN	**WASHBURN #5250** MAHOGANY BACK/SIDES, ARCHTOP	818	**628**	555	489
MANDOLIN		35	WASHBURN	**0-18** SPRUCE TOP	632	**485**	429	378
	MANDOL	30	WASHBURN	**00-28** BRAZILIAN ROSEWOOD, HERRINGBONE	1,671	**1,283**	1,133	999
	MANDOL	00	WASHBURN	**BOWL BACK** 1900, ROSEWOOD	724	**556**	491	433
	MANDOL	92	WASHBURN	**STYLE 80** 1892	1,542	**1,184**	1,046	922
	MANDOL	00	WASHBURN	**STYLE 115** 1900, BRAZILIAN ROSEWOOD, BOWL BACK	959	**737**	651	574
	MANDOL	01	WASHBURN	**STYLE 115** 1901, ROSEWOOD BACK, BOWL BACK, 9 RIBS	764	**587**	519	457
	MANDOL	90	WASHBURN	**STYLE 122** 1890, BOWL BACK	768	**589**	521	459
	MANDOL	97	WASHBURN	**STYLE 175** 1897, SPRUCE, ABALONE	1,671	**1,283**	1,133	999
	MANDOL	20	WASHBURN	**STYLE A** BRAZILIAN ROSEWOOD	757	**581**	513	452
	MANDOL	15	WASHBURN	**STYLE E** BRAZILIAN ROSEWOOD	785	**602**	532	469
	MANDOL	23	WASHBURN	**STYLE E** BRAZILIAN ROSEWOOD	627	**481**	425	375
	MANDOL	20	WASHBURN	**WASHBURN PROF A-SERIES** MAPLE BACK/SIDES	1,962	**1,506**	1,331	1,173
STEEL GUITAR		26	WASHBURN	**TONK BROTHERS 00-28** ROSEWOOD, HERRINGBONE	3,452	**2,651**	2,343	2,065
UKULELE		30	WASHBURN	**MODEL 701** ROSEWOOD, MAHOGANY	594	**456**	403	355

WEBSTER

	TYPE	YR	MFG	MODEL	SELL EXC	SELL AVG	BUY EXC	BUY AVG
MIC		42	WEBSTER	**W-1248 L RIBBON BAKELITE BODY**	2,337	**1,794**	1,586	1,398

WEISSENBORN

	TYPE	YR	MFG	MODEL	SELL EXC	SELL AVG	BUY EXC	BUY AVG
GUITAR (ACOUSTIC)		25	WEISSENBO	**STYLE 1 HAWAIIAN**	3,536	**2,715**	2,400	2,115
	GUITAR	26	WEISSENBO	**STYLE 1 HAWAIIAN**	3,307	**2,539**	2,244	1,978
	GUITAR	28	WEISSENBO	**STYLE 1 HAWAIIAN**	2,957	**2,271**	2,007	1,769
	GUITAR	32	WEISSENBO	**STYLE 1 HAWAIIAN**	2,259	**1,734**	1,532	1,351
	GUITAR	34	WEISSENBO	**STYLE 1 HAWAIIAN**	2,388	**1,834**	1,621	1,429
	GUITAR	35	WEISSENBO	**STYLE 1 HAWAIIAN**	2,247	**1,726**	1,525	1,344
	GUITAR	20	WEISSENBO	**STYLE 2 HAWAIIAN**	2,061	**1,583**	1,399	1,233
	GUITAR	25	WEISSENBO	**STYLE 2 HAWAIIAN**	2,362	**1,813**	1,602	1,413
	GUITAR	33	WEISSENBO	**STYLE 2 HAWAIIAN**	2,170	**1,666**	1,472	1,298
	GUITAR	20	WEISSENBO	**STYLE 3 HAWAIIAN** FLATTOP	2,914	**2,237**	1,977	1,743
	GUITAR	25	WEISSENBO	**STYLE 3 HAWAIIAN**	3,298	**2,532**	2,238	1,973
	GUITAR	35	WEISSENBO	**STYLE 3 HAWAIIAN**	2,291	**1,759**	1,554	1,370
	GUITAR	20	WEISSENBO	**STYLE 4 HAWAIIAN**	5,576	**4,281**	3,784	3,335
	GUITAR	25	WEISSENBO	**STYLE 4 HAWAIIAN**	4,231	**3,249**	2,871	2,531
	GUITAR	27	WEISSENBO	**STYLE 4 HAWAIIAN**	3,964	**3,044**	2,690	2,371
	GUITAR	35	WEISSENBO	**STYLE 4 HAWAIIAN**	3,703	**2,844**	2,513	2,215
	GUITAR	32	WEISSENBO	**STYLE A SPANISH NECK**	3,300	**2,534**	2,239	1,974
UKULELE		20	WEISSENBO	**SOPRANO** KOAWOOD BODY	358	**275**	243	214
	UKE	30	WEISSENBO	**UKE** ROPE BINDING	476	**365**	323	284
	UKE	60	WEISSENBO	**UKE #2**	495	**380**	335	296

WEYMANN

	TYPE	YR	MFG	MODEL	SELL EXC	SELL AVG	BUY EXC	BUY AVG
BANJO		10	WEYMANN	**KEYSTONE STATE** TENOR	555	**426**	376	332
	BANJO	24	WEYMANN	**KEYSTONE STATE** TENOR	484	**372**	329	290
	BANJO	25	WEYMANN	**STYLE 1** TENOR	2,102	**1,614**	1,426	1,257
	BANJO	26	WEYMANN	**STYLE 1** TENOR	2,026	**1,555**	1,374	1,212
	BANJO	27	WEYMANN	**STYLE 1** TENOR	1,984	**1,523**	1,346	1,187
	BANJO	28	WEYMANN	**STYLE 1** TENOR	1,895	**1,455**	1,285	1,133
	BANJO	20	WEYMANN	**STYLE 2** TENOR, CURLY MAPLE	1,276	**980**	866	763
	BANJO	25	WEYMANN	**STYLE 2** TENOR, MAPLE NECK	1,228	**943**	833	734
	BANJO	28	WEYMANN	**STYLE 2** TENOR, RESONATOR, FLANGE	1,295	**995**	879	775
	BANJO	28	WEYMANN	**STYLE 2** PLECTRUM, CURLY MAPLE	1,324	**1,017**	899	792
	BANJO	25	WEYMANN	**STYLE 30** TENOR	788	**605**	535	471

TYPE	YR	MFG	PRICES--BASED ON 100% ORIGINAL MODEL	SELL EXC	SELL AVG	BUY EXC	BUY AVG
BANJO	30	WEYMANN	STYLE 30 TENOR, MAHOGANY, RESONATOR	796	611	540	476
BANJO	28	WEYMANN	STYLE 85 TENOR	786	603	533	470
BANJO	25	WEYMANN	STYLE 180 TENOR	919	706	623	550
BANJO	23	WEYMANN	STYLE 1500 TENOR, 19-FRET	1,291	991	876	772
BANJO	25	WEYMANN	STYLE A TENOR, MAHOGANY, RESONATOR	797	612	541	477
MANDOLIN	10	WEYMANN	BOWL ROSEWOOD AND BIRDSEYE MAPLE BACK	498	382	338	298
MANDOL	12	WEYMANN	MANDOCELLO ARCHED SPRUCE TOP	1,068	808	712	590
MANDOL	22	WEYMANN	MANDOLUTE NATURAL, MAPLE BACK/SIDES	586	450	398	351
MANDOL	30	WEYMANN	MANDOLUTE MAPLE, FLAME, EBONY BOARD	361	277	245	216
MANDOL	20	WEYMANN	MANDOLUTE 30 CURLY MAPLE BACK/SIDES	728	559	494	435
MANDOL	00	WEYMANN	PRESENTAION 1900, SPRUCE, ENGRAVED BORDER	1,637	1,257	1,111	979
MANDOL	20	WEYMANN	STYLE 40 CURLY MAPLE BACK/SIDES/NECK	663	509	449	396
UKULELE	25	WEYMANN	SOPRANO MAHOGANY BODY	377	289	256	225
UKE	31	WEYMANN	SOPRANO KOAWOOD BODY, PEARL INLAY	1,294	994	878	774

YAMAHA CORPORATION OF AMERICA

TYPE	YR	MFG	MODEL	SELL EXC	SELL AVG	BUY EXC	BUY AVG
ELEC. GUITAR & BASS	80	YAMAHA	B-800 BURGUNDY	302	232	205	180
ELGUIT	80	YAMAHA	BB-350F BASS FRETLESS BOLT-ON NECK	302	232	205	180
ELGUIT	80	YAMAHA	SA-2000 TOBACCO SUNBURST, 2 PU's	645	495	437	385
ELGUIT	72	YAMAHA	SBG-2100	554	425	376	331
ELGUIT	67	YAMAHA	SG-2 JAZZMASTER 1 SINGLE COIL, 1 HUMBUCKER	434	333	294	259
ELGUIT	68	YAMAHA	SG-3 BASS BLUE	254	195	172	152
ELGUIT	66	YAMAHA	SG-5 SUNBURST, SOLID BODY, MAPLE, 3 PU's	291	223	197	174
GUITAR AMP	80	YAMAHA	JX-20A BASS 30 WATT	301	231	204	180
GTAMP	80	YAMAHA	JX-30B BASS 30 WATT	301	231	204	180
GUITAR (ACOUSTIC)	81	YAMAHA	CJ-818SB FOLK CJ JUMBO 6-STRING	323	248	219	193
GUITAR	78	YAMAHA	ETERNA	470	361	319	281
GUITAR	72	YAMAHA	FG- 75	162	124	110	97
GUITAR	75	YAMAHA	FG- 160 DREADNOUGHT	187	143	126	111
GUITAR	79	YAMAHA	FG- 336 SUNBURST	229	176	155	137
GUITAR	73	YAMAHA	FG-1500 BRAZILIAN ROSEWOOD	608	466	412	363
GUITAR	77	YAMAHA	G-255-S CLASSICAL INDIAN ROSEWOOD	446	343	303	267
GUITAR	85	YAMAHA	LL-35 JUMBO HANDCRAFTED SOLID WHITE SPRUCE TOP, SOLID JACARANDA B/S, GOLD HDWR	2,449	1,880	1,662	1,465
RCV	74	YAMAHA	CS- 70R	452	347	307	270
SYNTHESIZER	77	YAMAHA	CS- 80 ANALOG	2,128	1,634	1,444	1,273

ZORKO

TYPE	YR	MFG	MODEL	SELL EXC	SELL AVG	BUY EXC	BUY AVG
UPRIG	48	ZORKO	ELECTRIC UPRIGHT	3,629	2,787	2,463	2,171
UPRIGHT	48	ZORKO	ELECTRIC UPRIGHT	3,629	2,787	2,463	2,171

2006 Orion Blue Book Survey Form

Orion Research Corporation

14555 N. Scottsdale Rd. suite #330
Scottsdale, AZ 85254
voice: 480.951.1114
fax: 800.375.1315
email: sales@orionbluebook.com

You can receive a **$20 coupon** toward your next purchase of an Orion Blue Book. Simply return this form completely filled out (45 items in section 1 and 5 items each in sections 2 and 3). Mail or fax completed surveys to the address above. Please mark which book this survey is for:

☐ AUDIO   ☐ CAMERA   ☐ CAR STEREO

☐ COMPUTER   ☐ COPIER   ☐ GUN

☐ GUITARS & MUSICAL INSTRUMENTS   ☐ KEYBOARD   ☐ POWER TOOL

☐ PROFESSIONAL SOUND   ☐ VIDEO & TELEVISION   ☐ VINTAGE GUITARS & COLLECTIBLES

Name: _____   **Company:** _____

Address: _____   **Phone:** _____

City: _____   **State:** _____   **Zip:** _____

1. List 45 Products you have taken into your inventory of used equipment:

Product type	Mfg.	Model	Amount Given	Selling Price	Days to sell
1.					
2.					
3.					
4.					
5.					
6.					
7.					
8.					
9.					
10.					
11.					
12.					
13.					
14.					
15.					
16.					
17.					
18.					
19.					
20.					
21.					
22.					
23.					
24.					
25.					
26.					

1. Continued:

Product type	Mfg.	Model	Amount Given	Selling Price	Days to sell
27.					
28.					
29.					
30.					
31.					
32.					
33.					
34.					
35.					
36.					
37.					
38.					
39.					
40.					
41.					
42.					
43.					
44.					
45.					

2. List 5 products that have gone up in value over the last year:

Product type	Mfg.	Model	Amount Given	Selling Price	Days to sell
1.					
2.					
3.					
4.					
5.					

3. List 5 products that have dramatically decreased in value over the last year:

Product type	Mfg.	Model	Amount Given	Selling Price	Days to sell
1.					
2.					
3.					
4.					
5.					

2006 Orion Blue Book Survey Form

Orion Research Corporation

14555 N. Scottsdale Rd. suite #330
Scottsdale, AZ 85254
voice: 480.951.1114
fax: 800.375.1315
email: sales@orionbluebook.com

You can receive a **$20 coupon** toward your next purchase of an Orion Blue Book. Simply return this form completely filled out (45 items in section 1 and 5 items each in sections 2 and 3). Mail or fax completed surveys to the address above. Please mark which book this survey is for:

☐ AUDIO   ☐ CAMERA   ☐ CAR STEREO

☐ COMPUTER   ☐ COPIER   ☐ GUN

☐ GUITARS & MUSICAL   ☐ KEYBOARD   ☐ POWER TOOL
    INSTRUMENTS

☐ PROFESSIONAL SOUND   ☐ VIDEO & TELEVISION   ☐ VINTAGE GUITARS
                                                                                                        & COLLECTIBLES

Name: _____   **Company:** _____

Address: _____   **Phone:** _____

City: _____   **State:** _____   **Zip:** _____

1. List 45 Products you have taken into your inventory of used equipment:

Product type	Mfg.	Model	Amount Given	Selling Price	Days to sell
1.					
2.					
3.					
4.					
5.					
6.					
7.					
8.					
9.					
10.					
11.					
12.					
13.					
14.					
15.					
16.					
17.					
18.					
19.					
20.					
21.					
22.					
23.					
24.					
25.					
26.					

Orion Research reserves the right to refuse any survey
because of incomplete information

1. Continued:

Product type	Mfg.	Model	Amount Given	Selling Price	Days to sell
27.					
28.					
29.					
30.					
31.					
32.					
33.					
34.					
35.					
36.					
37.					
38.					
39.					
40.					
41.					
42.					
43.					
44.					
45.					

2. List 5 products that have gone up in value over the last year:

Product type	Mfg.	Model	Amount Given	Selling Price	Days to sell
1.					
2.					
3.					
4.					
5.					

3. List 5 products that have dramatically decreased in value over the last year:

Product type	Mfg.	Model	Amount Given	Selling Price	Days to sell
1.					
2.					
3.					
4.					
5.					

Orion Research Corporation
voice: 480.951.1114   fax: 800.375.1315